Dictionary of Literary Biography

71 *American Literary Critics and Scholars, 1880–1900*, edited by John W. Rathbun and Monica M. Grecu (1988)

72 *French Novelists, 1930–1960*, edited by Catharine Savage Brosman (1988)

73 *American Magazine Journalists, 1741–1850*, edited by Sam G. Riley (1988)

74 *American Short-Story Writers Before 1880*, edited by Bobby Ellen Kimbel, with the assistance of William E. Grant (1988)

75 *Contemporary German Fiction Writers, Second Series*, edited by Wolfgang D. Elfe and James Hardin (1988)

76 *Afro-American Writers, 1940–1955*, edited by Trudier Harris (1988)

77 *British Mystery Writers, 1920–1939*, edited by Bernard Benstock and Thomas F. Staley (1988)

78 *American Short-Story Writers, 1880–1910*, edited by Bobby Ellen Kimbel, with the assistance of William E. Grant (1988)

79 *American Magazine Journalists, 1850–1900*, edited by Sam G. Riley (1988)

80 *Restoration and Eighteenth-Century Dramatists, First Series*, edited by Paula R. Backscheider (1989)

81 *Austrian Fiction Writers, 1875–1913*, edited by James Hardin and Donald G. Daviau (1989)

82 *Chicano Writers, First Series*, edited by Francisco A. Lomelí and Carl R. Shirley (1989)

83 *French Novelists Since 1960*, edited by Catharine Savage Brosman (1989)

84 *Restoration and Eighteenth-Century Dramatists, Second Series*, edited by Paula R. Backscheider (1989)

85 *Austrian Fiction Writers After 1914*, edited by James Hardin and Donald G. Daviau (1989)

86 *American Short-Story Writers, 1910–1945, First Series*, edited by Bobby Ellen Kimbel (1989)

87 *British Mystery and Thriller Writers Since 1940, First Series*, edited by Bernard Benstock and Thomas F. Staley (1989)

88 *Canadian Writers, 1920–1959, Second Series*, edited by W. H. New (1989)

89 *Restoration and Eighteenth-Century Dramatists, Third Series*, edited by Paula R. Backscheider (1989)

90 *German Writers in the Age of Goethe, 1789–1832*, edited by James Hardin and Christoph E. Schweitzer (1989)

91 *American Magazine Journalists, 1900–1960, First Series*, edited by Sam G. Riley (1990)

92 *Canadian Writers, 1890–1920*, edited by W. H. New (1990)

93 *British Romantic Poets, 1789–1832, First Series*, edited by John R. Greenfield (1990)

94 *German Writers in the Age of Goethe: Sturm und Drang to Classicism*, edited by James Hardin and Christoph E. Schweitzer (1990)

95 *Eighteenth-Century British Poets, First Series*, edited by John Sitter (1990)

96 *British Romantic Poets, 1789–1832, Second Series*, edited by John R. Greenfield (1990)

97 *German Writers from the Enlightenment to Sturm und Drang, 1720–1764*, edited by James Hardin and Christoph E. Schweitzer (1990)

98 *Modern British Essayists, First Series*, edited by Robert Beum (1990)

99 *Canadian Writers Before 1890*, edited by W. H. New (1990)

100 *Modern British Essayists, Second Series*, edited by Robert Beum (1990)

101 *British Prose Writers, 1660–1800, First Series*, edited by Donald T. Siebert (1991)

102 *American Short-Story Writers, 1910–1945, Second Series*, edited by Bobby Ellen Kimbel (1991)

103 *American Literary Biographers, First Series*, edited by Steven Serafin (1991)

104 *British Prose Writers, 1660–1800, Second Series*, edited by Donald T. Siebert (1991)

105 *American Poets Since World War II, Second Series*, edited by R. S. Gwynn (1991)

106 *British Literary Publishing Houses, 1820–1880*, edited by Patricia J. Anderson and Jonathan Rose (1991)

107 *British Romantic Prose Writers, 1789–1832, First Series*, edited by John R. Greenfield (1991)

108 *Twentieth-Century Spanish Poets, First Series*, edited by Michael L. Perna (1991)

109 *Eighteenth-Century British Poets, Second Series*, edited by John Sitter (1991)

110 *British Romantic Prose Writers, 1789–1832, Second Series*, edited by John R. Greenfield (1991)

111 *American Literary Biographers, Second Series*, edited by Steven Serafin (1991)

112 *British Literary Publishing Houses, 1881–1965*, edited by Jonathan Rose and Patricia J. Anderson (1991)

113 *Modern Latin-American Fiction Writers, First Series*, edited by William Luis (1992)

114 *Twentieth-Century Italian Poets, First Series*, edited by Giovanna Wedel De Stasio, Glauco Cambon, and Antonio Illiano (1992)

115 *Medieval Philosophers*, edited by Jeremiah Hackett (1992)

116 *British Romantic Novelists, 1789–1832*, edited by Bradford K. Mudge (1992)

117 *Twentieth-Century Caribbean and Black African Writers, First Series*, edited by Bernth Lindfors and Reinhard Sander (1992)

118 *Twentieth-Century German Dramatists, 1889–1918*, edited by Wolfgang D. Elfe and James Hardin (1992)

119 *Nineteenth-Century French Fiction Writers: Romanticism and Realism, 1800–1860*, edited by Catharine Savage Brosman (1992)

120 *American Poets Since World War II, Third Series*, edited by R. S. Gwynn (1992)

121 *Seventeenth-Century British Nondramatic Poets, First Series*, edited by M. Thomas Hester (1992)

122 *Chicano Writers, Second Series*, edited by Francisco A. Lomelí and Carl R. Shirley (1992)

123 *Nineteenth-Century French Fiction Writers: Naturalism and Beyond, 1860–1900*, edited by Catharine Savage Brosman (1992)

124 *Twentieth-Century German Dramatists, 1919–1992*, edited by Wolfgang D. Elfe and James Hardin (1992)

125 *Twentieth-Century Caribbean and Black African Writers, Second Series*, edited by Bernth Lindfors and Reinhard Sander (1993)

126 *Seventeenth-Century British Nondramatic Poets, Second Series*, edited by M. Thomas Hester (1993)

127 *American Newspaper Publishers, 1950–1990*, edited by Perry J. Ashley (1993)

128 *Twentieth-Century Italian Poets, Second Series*, edited by Giovanna Wedel De Stasio, Glauco Cambon, and Antonio Illiano (1993)

129 *Nineteenth-Century German Writers, 1841–1900*, edited by James Hardin and Siegfried Mews (1993)

130 *American Short-Story Writers Since World War II*, edited by Patrick Meanor (1993)

131 *Seventeenth-Century British Nondramatic Poets, Third Series*, edited by M. Thomas Hester (1993)

132 *Sixteenth-Century British Nondramatic Writers, First Series*, edited by David A. Richardson (1993)

133 *Nineteenth-Century German Writers to 1840*, edited by James Hardin and Siegfried Mews (1993)

134 *Twentieth-Century Spanish Poets, Second Series*, edited by Jerry Phillips Winfield (1994)

135 *British Short-Fiction Writers, 1880–1914: The Realist Tradition*, edited by William B. Thesing (1994)

136 *Sixteenth-Century British Nondramatic Writers, Second Series*, edited by David A. Richardson (1994)

137 *American Magazine Journalists, 1900–1960, Second Series*, edited by Sam G. Riley (1994)

138 *German Writers and Works of the High Middle Ages: 1170–1280*, edited by James Hardin and Will Hasty (1994)

139 *British Short-Fiction Writers, 1945–1980*, edited by Dean Baldwin (1994)

Dictionary of Literary Biography Documentary Series

11 *American Proletarian Culture: The Twenties and The Thirties,* edited by Jon Christian Suggs (1993)

12 *Southern Women Writers: Flannery O'Connor, Katherine Anne Porter, Eudora Welty,* edited by Mary Ann Wimsatt and Karen L. Rood (1994)

13 *The House of Scribner, 1846–1904,* edited by John Delaney (1996)

14 *Four Women Writers for Children, 1868–1918,* edited by Caroline C. Hunt (1996)

15 *American Expatriate Writers: Paris in the Twenties,* edited by Matthew J. Bruccoli and Robert W. Trogdon (1997)

16 *The House of Scribner, 1905–1930,* edited by John Delaney (1997)

17 *The House of Scribner, 1931–1984,* edited by John Delaney (1998)

18 *British Poets of The Great War: Sassoon, Graves, Owen,* edited by Patrick Quinn (1999)

19 *James Dickey,* edited by Judith S. Baughman (1999)

See also DLB 210, 216, 219, 222, 224, 229, 237, 247, 253, 254, 263, 269, 273, 274, 280, 284, 288, 291, 294, 298, 301, 304, 308, 309, 315, 316, 320, 324, 338

Dictionary of Literary Biography Yearbooks

1980 edited by Karen L. Rood, Jean W. Ross, and Richard Ziegfeld (1981)

1981 edited by Karen L. Rood, Jean W. Ross, and Richard Ziegfeld (1982)

1982 edited by Richard Ziegfeld; associate editors: Jean W. Ross and Lynne C. Zeigler (1983)

1983 edited by Mary Bruccoli and Jean W. Ross; associate editor Richard Ziegfeld (1984)

1984 edited by Jean W. Ross (1985)

1985 edited by Jean W. Ross (1986)

1986 edited by J. M. Brook (1987)

1987 edited by J. M. Brook (1988)

1988 edited by J. M. Brook (1989)

1989 edited by J. M. Brook (1990)

1990 edited by James W. Hipp (1991)

1991 edited by James W. Hipp (1992)

1992 edited by James W. Hipp (1993)

1993 edited by James W. Hipp, contributing editor George Garrett (1994)

1994 edited by James W. Hipp, contributing editor George Garrett (1995)

1995 edited by James W. Hipp, contributing editor George Garrett (1996)

1996 edited by Samuel W. Bruce and L. Kay Webster, contributing editor George Garrett (1997)

1997 edited by Matthew J. Bruccoli and George Garrett, with the assistance of L. Kay Webster (1998)

1998 edited by Matthew J. Bruccoli, contributing editor George Garrett, with the assistance of D. W. Thomas (1999)

1999 edited by Matthew J. Bruccoli, contributing editor George Garrett, with the assistance of D. W. Thomas (2000)

2000 edited by Matthew J. Bruccoli, contributing editor George Garrett, with the assistance of George Parker Anderson (2001)

2001 edited by Matthew J. Bruccoli, contributing editor George Garrett, with the assistance of George Parker Anderson (2002)

2002 edited by Matthew J. Bruccoli and George Garrett; George Parker Anderson, Assistant Editor (2003)

Concise Series

Concise Dictionary of American Literary Biography, 7 volumes (1988–1999): *The New Consciousness, 1941–1968; Colonization to the American Renaissance, 1640–1865; Realism, Naturalism, and Local Color, 1865–1917; The Twenties, 1917–1929; The Age of Maturity, 1929–1941; Broadening Views, 1968–1988; Supplement: Modern Writers, 1900–1998.*

Concise Dictionary of British Literary Biography, 8 volumes (1991–1992): *Writers of the Middle Ages and Renaissance Before 1660; Writers of the Restoration and Eighteenth Century, 1660–1789; Writers of the Romantic Period, 1789–1832; Victorian Writers, 1832–1890; Late-Victorian and Edwardian Writers, 1890–1914; Modern Writers, 1914–1945; Writers After World War II, 1945–1960; Contemporary Writers, 1960 to Present.*

Concise Dictionary of World Literary Biography, 4 volumes (1999–2000): *Ancient Greek and Roman Writers; German Writers; African, Caribbean, and Latin American Writers; South Slavic and Eastern European Writers.*

Dictionary of Literary Biography® • Volume Three Hundred Thirty-Eight

Thomas Carlyle:
A Documentary Volume

Dictionary of Literary Biography® • Volume Three Hundred Thirty-Eight

Thomas Carlyle:
A Documentary Volume

Frances Frame
The Citadel

A Bruccoli Clark Layman Book

THOMSON
GALE

Detroit • New York • San Francisco • New Haven, Conn. • Waterville, Maine • London • Munich

Dictionary of Literary Biography
Volume 338: Thomas Carlyle:
A Documentary Volume
Frances Frame

Advisory Board
John Baker
William Cagle
Patrick O'Connor
George Garrett
Trudier Harris
Alvin Kernan

Editorial Directors
Matthew J. Bruccoli and Richard Layman

LIBRARY OF CONGRESS CATALOGING-IN-PUBLICATION DATA

Thomas Carlyle : a documentary volume / edited by E. Frances Frame.
   p. cm. — (Dictionary of literary biography ; v. 338)
"A Bruccoli Clark Layman Book."
Includes bibliographical references and index.
ISBN-13: 978–0–7876–8156–2
ISBN-10: 0–7876–8156–3
1. Carlyle, Thomas, 1795–1881. 2. Authors, Scottish—19th century—Biography.
I. Frame, E. Frances.
PR4433.T46 2007
824'.8—dc22
[B]
           2007017966

Printed in the United States of America
10 9 8 7 6 5 4 3 2 1

To my parents,
Bill and Janet Frame,
whose continual love and support
enabled me to complete this project.

Contents

Contents

Contents

Plan of the Series

. . . Almost the most prodigious asset of a country, and perhaps its most precious possession, is its native literary product—when that product is fine and noble and enduring.

Mark Twain*

The advisory board, the editors, and the publisher of the *Dictionary of Literary Biography* are joined in endorsing Mark Twain's declaration. The literature of a nation provides an inexhaustible resource of permanent worth. Our purpose is to make literature and its creators better understood and more accessible to students and the reading public, while satisfying the needs of teachers and researchers.

To meet these requirements, *literary biography* has been construed in terms of the author's achievement. The most important thing about a writer is his writing. Accordingly, the entries in *DLB* are career biographies, tracing the development of the author's canon and the evolution of his reputation.

The purpose of *DLB* is not only to provide reliable information in a usable format but also to place the figures in the larger perspective of literary history and to offer appraisals of their accomplishments by qualified scholars.

The publication plan for *DLB* resulted from two years of preparation. The project was proposed to Bruccoli Clark by Frederick G. Ruffner, president of the Gale Research Company, in November 1975. After specimen entries were prepared and typeset, an advisory board was formed to refine the entry format and develop the series rationale. In meetings held during 1976, the publisher, series editors, and advisory board approved the scheme for a comprehensive biographical dictionary of persons who contributed to literature. Editorial work on the first volume began in January 1977, and it was published in 1978. In order to make *DLB* more than a dictionary and to compile volumes that individually have claim to status as literary history, it was decided to organize volumes by topic, period, or genre. Each of these freestanding volumes provides a

From an unpublished section of Mark Twain's autobiography, copyright by the Mark Twain Company

biographical-bibliographical guide and overview for a particular area of literature. We are convinced that this organization—as opposed to a single alphabet method—constitutes a valuable innovation in the presentation of reference material. The volume plan necessarily requires many decisions for the placement and treatment of authors. Certain figures will be included in separate volumes, but with different entries emphasizing the aspect of his career appropriate to each volume. Ernest Hemingway, for example, is represented in *American Writers in Paris, 1920–1939* by an entry focusing on his expatriate apprenticeship; he is also in *American Novelists, 1910–1945* with an entry surveying his entire career, as well as in *American Short-Story Writers, 1910–1945, Second Series* with an entry concentrating on his short fiction. Each volume includes a cumulative index of the subject authors and articles.

Between 1981 and 2002 the series was augmented and updated by the *DLB Yearbooks*. There have also been nineteen *DLB Documentary Series* volumes, which provide illustrations, facsimiles, and biographical and critical source materials for figures, works, or groups judged to have particular interest for students. In 1999 the *Documentary Series* was incorporated into the *DLB* volume numbering system beginning with *DLB 210: Ernest Hemingway.*

We define literature as the *intellectual commerce of a nation:* not merely as belles lettres but as that ample and complex process by which ideas are generated, shaped, and transmitted. *DLB* entries are not limited to "creative writers" but extend to other figures who in their time and in their way influenced the mind of a people. Thus the series encompasses historians, journalists, publishers, book collectors, and screenwriters. By this means readers of *DLB* may be aided to perceive literature not as cult scripture in the keeping of intellectual high priests but firmly positioned at the center of a nation's life.

DLB includes the major writers appropriate to each volume and those standing in the ranks behind them. Scholarly and critical counsel has been sought in deciding which minor figures to include and how full their entries should be. Wherever possible, useful references are made to figures who do not warrant separate entries.

Each *DLB* volume has an expert volume editor responsible for planning the volume, selecting the figures for inclusion, and assigning the entries. Volume editors are also responsible for preparing, where appropriate, appendices surveying the major periodicals and literary and intellectual movements for their volumes, as well as lists of further readings. Work on the series as a whole is coordinated at the Bruccoli Clark Layman editorial center in Columbia, South Carolina, where the editorial staff is responsible for accuracy and utility of the published volumes.

One feature that distinguishes *DLB* is the illustration policy–its concern with the iconography of literature. Just as an author is influenced by his surroundings, so is the reader's understanding of the author enhanced by a knowledge of his environment. Therefore *DLB* volumes include not only drawings, paintings, and photographs of authors, often depicting them at various stages in their careers, but also illustrations of their families and places where they lived. Title pages are regularly reproduced in facsimile along with dust jackets for modern authors. The dust jackets are a special feature of *DLB* because they often document better than anything else the way in which an author's work was perceived in its own time. Specimens of the writers' manuscripts and letters are included when feasible.

Samuel Johnson rightly decreed that "The chief glory of every people arises from its authors." The purpose of the *Dictionary of Literary Biography* is to compile literary history in the surest way available to us–by accurate and comprehensive treatment of the lives and work of those who contributed to it.

The *DLB* Advisory Board

Introduction

In 1838, in response to a request by German writer Johann H. Kunzel, Thomas Carlyle offered a brief description of his life:

> Born 4th December 1795 in the village of Ecclefechan, Dumfriesshire, Scotland; of peasant parents in tolerable circumstances, and distinguished, both of them, for faculty and worth. Educated at Edinburgh University, with a view first to the church, but quitted that; then to the Law, but quitted that also; quitted several things; came at last to Literature. Had learned German (a very rare language in England then) about 1820, from a comrade who had been to Gottingen. Published &c &c. Thanks Goethe and certain other Germans always for much. Has nearly quitted all study of German these seven years, and altogether quitted all Verbreitung [dissemination] of it, or speech about it,—seeing tha[t] go on fast enough without him. Has written two Books: *Sartor Resartus;* and *The French Revolution;*—which two let any one that wants to know him see (*The Collected Letters of Thomas and Jane Welsh Carlyle,* v. 10, p. 93).

The account is significant, not for the well-known facts it states, but for what it reveals about Carlyle's understanding of himself and about how he wished to be perceived.

Carlyle not only mentions the date and place of his birth, he also calls particular attention to his parents' social and economic circumstances, their "faculty," and their moral merit, implying that these factors were the most important in shaping the life of their eldest son. Indeed, Carlyle's deep ambition to achieve financial independence might be traced to James Carlyle's financial self-sufficiency and example of hard work. Further, while his humble origins sensitized Carlyle to the abuse of aristocratic power and privilege, his father's example of dignity in low rank and respectful conduct toward those in authority, however undeserving, account for Carlyle's superficially paradoxical opposition to both those who locate dignity in social position and those who advocate leveling all social distinction. Carlyle attributed his scholarly ability and ambition to his father's intellectual curiosity and linguistic "faculty" as well as to the value his father placed upon education. Further, Carlyle's lifelong insistence on writing only what he sincerely believed his countrymen needed to hear, rather than what he believed would be popular, echoes the honest craftsmanship practiced by James Carlyle. Margaret Carlyle, Thomas' mother, also profoundly influenced the moral dimension of Carlyle's life. She possessed a strong religious faith, which her son struggled to emulate. While neither Carlyle's Victorian contemporaries nor modern scholars have formulated with certainty a coherent statement of Carlyle's religious beliefs, the spiritual focus of much of Carlyle's work attests the fundamental and continuing influence of his mother.

In his account for Kunzel, Carlyle also chronicles his difficulty finding a suitable career, using the word "quitted" three times in a single sentence. The term also appears twice later in the note, for a total of five uses. Carlyle's repeated use of this word to describe his life points to an idea that is quite important for understanding it: perseverance. Perseverance, the exertion of the will until all obstacles are overcome or all enemies are defeated, is a recurrent, even dominant, theme in Carlyle's life. By 1838 Carlyle knew for a fact that he was no quitter. The manuscript of the first volume of *The French Revolution* (1837) had been lost, and, in a tremendous act of will and determination, Carlyle had rewritten it. His use of the "quitted" in his note for Kunzel is ironic. The "quittings" which characterized his early years were, he knew, merely garments that cloaked an unswerving fidelity to his underlying goal, meaningful work—a goal he did reach and never relinquished. Carlyle's work also embodies, even glorifies, the perseverance his life demonstrates. In *On Heroes and Hero-worship, & The Heroic in History* (1841), the two-volume *Oliver Cromwell's Letters and Speeches* (1845), and the six-volume work *History of Friedrich II. of Prussia, called Frederick the Great* (1858–1865), he lauds his heroes for persisting until they successfully shape reality according to their wills.

Carlyle's account for Kunzel also mentions the German phase of Carlyle's career. Carlyle played an important role in introducing German literature to England. In addition to making German writing available to English readers by doing translations, in the 1820s Carlyle wrote essays on German authors. These essays, which usually began as reviews of German works, called attention to German literature and spread German Idealism among British men of letters. Carlyle's work on German materials was important not only to the British reading public, however. It was also profoundly significant to the author himself. As Chris R. Vanden Bossche explains in *Carlyle and the Search for Authority* (1991), Carlyle's early career represents a search for the confidence to express his own ideas. As a translator and reviewer of others' work, Carlyle was able to promote ideas he cared about indirectly. Carlyle found translation to be comfortable, enjoyable work as compared to writing in his own voice, which stressed Carlyle to the point that he often became physically ill. His eventual "quitting" of translation signals, again, not a surrender but a conquest, an attainment of the confidence to articulate his own message.

A key player in the drama by which Carlyle achieved the confidence to preach his own sermons is the only German he mentions by name in his paragraph for Kunzel, poet and novelist Johann Wolfgang von Goethe. While Carlyle's father provided him with an intellectual thirst, a university education, and the work ethic necessary to succeed, the young writer lacked a mentor–a thinker who could help him work through his spiritual doubts, a man of letters after whom he could model his own life. In Goethe, Carlyle found such a second father.

Once he found his own voice, Carlyle was eager to write his own, original compositions. The adamant assertion in his paragraph for Kunzel that he has "nearly quitted all study of German these seven years, and altogether quitted all Verbreitung of it, or speech about it" attests to his desire to break the link in the public mind that his work as a translator had fashioned between his name and German literature. In the 1830s, Carlyle wrote two of his greatest works, one of which, *Sartor Resartus* (1836), is certainly his most original. The reviews included in *DLB 338: Thomas Carlyle: A Documentary Volume* demonstrate the difficulty Carlyle experienced in gaining acceptance for *Sartor Resartus* in England and the warm welcome he received in America, especially among the New England Transcendentalists, led by Ralph Waldo Emerson. With *The French Revolution*, written in a more reader-friendly style in response to Emerson's advice, Carlyle was finally recognized in England as a great writer in his own right, not merely a popularizer of German authors, and attained long-sought financial security.

At the close of his note for Kunzel, Carlyle instructs those who would know him to read his works. The advice is both sincere and facetious, and it points to the simultaneous revealing and concealing that goes on in Carlyle's work and the need to look beyond it to know the man. Carlyle's work does express who he is; into it he poured his wisest insights, his strongest feelings, his greatest hopes, and his most intense labor. Many of his works, even his biographies, are highly autobiographical because he not infrequently projects his own personality onto his subjects. However, to read his personal letters is to meet a Carlyle different from the Carlyle of the works, and even his correspondence conceals the particulars of certain aspects of his life–his religious beliefs and his relations with his wife, Jane, for example–from his closest friends and family. While Carlyle's statement, that one who wishes to know him should read his works, is sincere, his implication– that one who reads his works will know him–is an exaggeration. *DLB 338* offers evidence from Carlyle's letters and from the papers of those who knew him that provides a corrective, or at least a complementary, context for his public self-presentation.

Finally, Carlyle's note to Kunzel is significant for what it omits. Carlyle provides more information about his parents than one might expect him to supply for Kunzel's purpose, an encyclopedia article, but he does not mention Jane or his marriage at all. The omission suggests the difficulty Carlyle experienced in integrating professional and personal aspects of his life. His courtship of Jane took place against the wishes of Jane's mother and was conducted almost exclusively through a correspondence over the course of more than four years. After their marriage, the two lived in the same house, but Carlyle's need for complete silence and freedom from distraction while he worked kept Jane at a distance throughout their marriage, especially in the late 1850s and early 1860s, when he closeted himself in his "soundproof" garret study to write his history of Frederick the Great. Carlyle scholars have debated whether the marriage, which produced no children, was ever consummated. *DLB 338* includes correspondence documenting the Carlyles' relationship, with special emphasis on their courtship, Jane's experience as the wife of an author, and tension in the marriage over Carlyle's attraction to Lady Harriet Ashburton.

Carlyle's note to Kunzel, of course, provides no thoughts on his life after 1838, but the theme of "quitting" he sounds repeatedly in the note provides ironic comment not only upon his life to that point but also upon his career until his death in 1881. Carlyle persevered in at least two important ways. First, he persevered despite struggles with his materials. To edit and write *Cromwell's Letters and Speeches* and *Frederick the Great* he tackled mountains of primary and secondary materials that often nearly overwhelmed him. He won his battle with the Cromwell papers by electing to produce an edition of the revolutionary's letters instead of a biography. With *Frederick the Great* he doggedly completed the six volumes he came to see as necessary instead of the four he initially projected. Carlyle also persevered despite growing public criticism of his work, especially *Latter-Day Pamphlets* (1850). His former supporters reacted badly to what they viewed as Carlyle's desertion from the cause of radical reform. The voice of revolution in *Sartor Resartus* and *The French Revolution* had, in their view, given way to a "might makes right" philosophy. The documents included in *DLB 338* show Carlyle's struggles with both his materials and his readers.

In 1868 an anonymous review titled "Matthew Arnold Versus Thomas Carlyle" appeared in *The Spectator*. The piece elucidates the place Carlyle had made for himself in the public consciousness by the close of his career and complements nicely Carlyle's own comments in the paragraph he wrote for Kunzel. The reviewer quotes a letter by Carlyle to a young man, in which Carlyle suggests that humanity's purpose is action, not thought. The reviewer observes that perhaps it would have been better had Carlyle's correspondent done a bit more thinking before he acted, given that he is currently on trial for forgery, and notes that Arnold, whose *Culture and Anarchy* (1869) was then appearing periodically in *The Cornhill Magazine,* would surely have advised the man to do more thinking before he acted. The reviewer, equally dissatisfied with Arnold's practice of making any action contingent upon virtually perfect knowledge, sums up his comparison of these two literary giants as follows: "If Mr. Carlyle makes an idol of action apart from knowledge, Mr. Arnold makes an idol of knowledge apart from action; and both seem to us to miss the vital relation between the two" (*The Spectator,* 4 July 1868, p. 790). Here, in a nutshell, is the way many of Carlyle's contemporaries came to view him by the autumn of his career—as an exponent of "Hebraism," a narrow obsession with morality, earnestness, and will at the expense of broadened intellectual horizons, progressive ideas, and social reform. The qualities that had enabled Carlyle to overcome all the internal and external obstacles to bringing his thoughts before his readers became the ground of their attack upon him.

Despite the reaction against Carlyle late in his life, at his death all acknowledged his profound influence. Carlyle was an innovator. When *Sartor Resartus* burst on the scene, few knew how to classify it. Was it an autobiography? a novel? a sermon? It certainly does not fit easily into either of the two most popular Victorian

courses taught to undergraduate students—the Victorian novel and Victorian poetry—and often, unfortunately, as a consequence it is not frequently taught. Carlyle also consciously set out to redefine biography and history. The popularity of his "Mirabeau" and *The Life of Friedrich Schiller* (1825) argues his success in recasting the English idea of biography, while his readers' practice of invoking *The French Revolution* as a standard by which to judge his *Frederick the Great* suggests the influence of his idea, exemplified in the earlier work, that true history is an "epic poem."

In his diary, published after his death as *William Allingham: A Diary* (1907), the poet recorded the following commentary by Carlyle on the topic of his own biography:

> In answer to a remark of mine one day Carlyle blazed up—"Write my autobiography? I would as soon think of cutting my throat with my pen-knife when I get back home! The Biographers too! If those gentlemen would let me alone I should be much obliged to them. I would say, as Shakespeare would say to Peter Cunningham, 'Sweet Friend, for Jesus' sake forbear'" (p. 196).

By including certain documents and illustrations and excluding others, and by presenting those pieces it includes in a certain arrangement, *DLB 338: Thomas Carlyle* undeniably constructs a "story of Thomas Carlyle," interpreting both the man and his career. In doing this it stands convicted of violating its subject's wishes as recorded by Allingham. Nonetheless, there is consolation both in the fact that Carlyle himself succumbed to the biographical impulse many times—to write about Friedrich Schiller, Robert Burns, Sir Walter Scott, and Frederick the Great, to name only his best-known subjects—and in his choice to edit primary materials, Oliver Cromwell's letters and speeches, as a useful way of providing insight into a man's life.

It is worth keeping Carlyle in our consciousness in the twenty-first century. His declaration of the reality of the spiritual realm will remain germane as long as the existence of this sphere is contested. Also, his struggle to integrate action and passion, authorship and relationship, is relevant to anyone who wishes both to work and to love. Finally, his life and work address a fundamental tension, between asserting the individual will and accepting its limits, that is universal in human experience.

—Frances Frame

Acknowledgments

This book was produced by Bruccoli Clark Layman, Inc. George Parker Anderson was the in-house editor.

Production manager is Philip B. Dematteis.

Administrative support was provided by Carol A. Cheschi.

Accountant is Ann-Marie Holland.

Copyediting supervisor is Sally R. Evans. The copyediting staff includes Phyllis A. Avant, Caryl Brown, and Rebecca Mayo. Freelance copyeditors are Brenda L. Cabra, Jennifer E. Cooper, and David C. King.

Pipeline manager is James F. Tidd Jr.

Editorial associates are Elizabeth Leverton and Dickson Monk.

Permissions editor is Amber L. Coker.

Office manager is Kathy Lawler Merlette.

Photography editor is Kourtnay King.

Digital photographic copy work was performed by Kourtnay King.

Systems manager is James Sellers.

Typesetting supervisor is Kathleen M. Flanagan. The typesetting staff includes Patricia M. Flanagan.

Library research was facilitated by the following librarians at the Thomas Cooper Library of the University of South Carolina: Elizabeth Sudduth and the rare-book department; Jo Cottingham, interlibrary loan department; circulation department head Tucker Taylor; reference department head Virginia W. Weathers; reference department staff Marilee Birchfield, Karen Brown, Mary Bull, Gerri Corson, Joshua Garris, Beki Gettys, Laura Ladwig, Tom Marcil, Anthony Diana McKissick, Bob Skinder, and Sharon Verba; interlibrary loan department head Marna Hostetler; and interlibrary loan staff Robert Amerson and Timothy Simmons.

The editor thanks Patrick Scott and Elizabeth Sudduth of Rare Books and Special Collections, Thomas Cooper Library, the University of South Carolina, for their guidance and assistance over several summers of research. Linda Skippings and Josephine Eaton also provided invaluable help at the Carlyle House Museum in Chelsea. I am indebted to William B. Thesing, who initially interested me in Carlyle and in this project. Finally, I am grateful to Ian Campbell for meeting with me in Edinburgh and for making several useful suggestions about the project.

Permissions

Thomas Carlyle:
A Documentary Volume

Dictionary of Literary Biography

Works by Thomas Carlyle

BOOKS: *The Life of Friedrich Schiller. Comprehending an Examination of His Works* (London: Printed for Taylor and Hessey, 1825; Boston: Carter, Hendee, 1833).

German Romance: Specimens of Its Chief Authors; with Biographical and Critical Notices (4 volumes, Edinburgh: William Tait / London: Charles Tait, 1827; 2 volumes, Boston: Munroe, 1841).

Sartor Resartus (Boston: Munroe, 1836; London: Saunders & Otley, 1838).

The French Revolution: A History (3 volumes, London: Fraser, 1837; 2 volumes, Boston: Little & Brown, 1838).

Critical and Miscellaneous Essays, 4 volumes (Boston: Munroe, 1838; London: Fraser, 1839).

Chartism (London: Fraser, 1840 [i.e. 1839]; Boston: Little & Brown, 1840).

On Heroes, Hero-Worship & the Heroic in History (London: Fraser, 1841; New York: Appleton, 1841).

Past and Present (London: Chapman & Hall, 1843; Boston: Little & Brown, 1843).

Oliver Cromwell's Letters and Speeches: with Elucidations, 2 volumes (London: Chapman & Hall, 1845; New York: Wiley & Putnam) 1845; revised and enlarged, 3 volumes (London: Chapman & Hall, 1846); revised and enlarged, 4 volumes (London: Chapman & Hall, 1850).

Latter-Day Pamphlets (London: Chapman & Hall, 1850; Boston: Phillips, Sampson, 1850).

The Life of John Sterling (London: Chapman & Hall, 1851; Boston: Phillips, Sampson, 1851).

Occasional Discourse on the Nigger Question (London: Bosworth, 1853).

History of Friedrich II. of Prussia, called Frederick the Great, 6 volumes (London: Chapman & Hall, 1858–1865; New York: Harper, 1858–1866).

Inaugural Address at Edinburgh, April 2, 1866 (Edinburgh: Edmonston & Douglas / London: Chapman & Hall, 1866); enlarged as *On the Choice of Books* (London: Hotten, 1869; Boston: Osgood, 1877).

Shooting Niagara: and After? (London: Chapman & Hall, 1867).

The Early Kings of Norway: Also An Essay on the Portraits of John Knox (London: Chapman & Hall, 1875; New York: Harper, 1875).

Reminiscences by Thomas Carlyle, edited by James Anthony Froude (2 volumes, London: Longmans, Green, 1881; 1 volume, New York: Scribners, 1881).

Reminiscences of my Irish Journey in 1849 (London: Low, Marston, Searle & Rivington, 1882; New York: Harper, 1882).

Last Words of Thomas Carlyle, on Trades-Unions, Promoterism and The Signs of the Times (Edinburgh: William Paterson, 1882).

Reminiscences, 2 volumes, edited by Charles Eliot Norton (London & New York: Macmillan, 1887).

Last Words of Thomas Carlyle (London: Longmans, Green, 1892; New York: Appleton, 1892).

Wotton Reinfred, A Posthumous Novel (New York: Waverly, 1892).

Carlyle's Unpublished Lectures: Lectures on the History of Literature or the Successive Periods of European Culture, Delivered in 1838, edited by R. P. Karkaria (London & Bombay: Kurwen, Kane, 1892); also published as *Lectures on the History of Literature, Delivered by Thomas Carlyle, April to July 1838,* edited by J. Reay Greene (London: Ellis & Elvey, 1892).

Montaigne and Other Essays, Chiefly Biographical (London: Gowans, 1897; Philadelphia: Lippincott, 1897).

Historical Sketches of Notable Persons and Events in the Reigns of James I. and Charles I., edited by Alexander Carlyle (London: Chapman & Hall / New York: Scribners, 1898).

Two Note Books of Thomas Carlyle from 23rd March 1822 to 16th May 1832, edited by Norton (New York: Grolier Club, 1898).

Collectanea. Thomas Carlyle, 1821–1855, edited by Samuel Arthur Jones (Canton, Pa.: Kirgate Press, 1903).

Collection: *The Works of Thomas Carlyle,* Centenary Edition, 30 volumes, edited by H. D. Traill (London: Chapman & Hall, 1896–1899; New York: Scribners, 1896–1901).

OTHER: *Letters and Memorials of Jane Welsh Carlyle,* prepared for publication by Carlyle, edited by James Anthony Froude (3 volumes, London: Longmans, Green, 1883; 2 volumes, New York: Scribners, 1883).

New Letters and Memorials of Jane Welsh Carlyle, 2 volumes, annotated by Carlyle, edited by Alexander Carlyle (London & New York: John Lane/Bodley Head, 1903).

TRANSLATIONS: A. M. Legendre, *Elements of Geometry and Trigonometry; with Notes,* translated, with an essay by Carlyle, edited by David Brewster (Edinburgh: Oliver & Boyd, 1822); revised edition, edited by Charles Davis (New York: Ryan, 1828).

Johann Wolfgang von Goethe, *Wilhelm Meister's Apprenticeship. A Novel,* 3 volumes (Edinburgh: Oliver & Boyd / London: Whittaker, 1824; Boston: Wells & Lilly, 1828); revised and enlarged as *William Meister's Apprenticeship and Travels* (London: Fraser, 1839; Philadelphia: Lea & Blanchard, 1840).

LETTERS: *The Correspondence of Thomas Carlyle and Ralph Waldo Emerson, 1834–1872,* 2 volumes (Boston: Osgood, 1883; London: Chatto & Windus, 1883); enlarged edition (Boston: Ticknor, 1886).

Early Letters of Thomas Carlyle, 2 volumes, edited by Charles Eliot Norton (London & New York: Macmillan, 1886).

Correspondence between Goethe and Carlyle, edited by Norton (London & New York: Macmillan, 1887).

Letters of Thomas Carlyle, 1826–1836, 2 volumes, edited by Norton (London & New York: Macmillan, 1888).

Letters of Thomas Carlyle to His Youngest Sister, edited by Charles Townsend Copeland (Boston & New York: Houghton, Mifflin, 1899; London: Chapman & Hall, 1899).

New Letters of Thomas Carlyle, 2 volumes, edited by Alexander Carlyle (London & New York: John Lane/Bodley Head, 1904).

The Love Letters of Thomas Carlyle and Jane Welsh, 2 volumes, edited by Alexander Carlyle (London & New York: John Lane/Bodley Head, 1909).

Letters of Thomas Carlyle to John Stuart Mill, John Sterling and Robert Browning, edited by Alexander Carlyle (London: Unwin, 1923; New York: Stokes, 1923).

Letters of Thomas Carlyle to William Graham, edited by John Graham (Princeton: Princeton University Press, 1950).

Thomas Carlyle: Letters to His Wife, edited by Trudy Bliss (London: Gollancz, 1953; Cambridge, Mass.: Harvard University Press, 1953).

The Correspondence of Emerson and Carlyle, edited by Joseph Slater (New York & London: Columbia University Press, 1964).

The Letters of Thomas Carlyle to His Brother Alexander, edited by Edwin W. Marrs Jr. (Cambridge: Harvard University Press, 1968).

The Collected Letters of Thomas and Jane Welsh Carlyle, volumes 1–   , edited by Charles Richard Sanders, K. J. Fielding, Clyde de L. Ryals, and others (Durham, N.C.: Duke University Press, 1970–   ).

Thomas and Jane: Selected Letters from the Edinburgh University Library Collection, edited by Ian Campbell (Edinburgh: Friends of Edinburgh University Library, 1980).

The Correspondence of Thomas Carlyle and John Ruskin, edited by George Alan Cate (Stanford, Cal.: Stanford University Press, 1982).

Chronology

1795

4 December   Birth of Thomas Carlyle at Arched House, Ecclefechan, first child of James and Margaret Aitken Carlyle.

1801

4 July   Birth of Jane Baillie Welsh at Haddington, a small town near Edinburgh, the only child of Dr. John and Grace Welsh.

1806

Attends Annan Academy.

1809

November   Enters Edinburgh University.

1814

Enters Divinity Hall at Edinburgh University.

1816

November   Begins teaching at Kirkcaldy with Edward Irving.

1817

Abandons plans for the ministry.

1818

September   Becomes romantically interested in Margaret Gordon.
October   Resigns from teaching school and moves to Edinburgh.

1819

Studies German.

1820

Winter   Writes articles for David Brewster's *Edinburgh Encyclopedia*.
March   Romance with Margaret Gordon ends.

1821

Late May   Meets Jane Welsh through Irving at Haddington.

1822

Spring   Serves as a tutor to Charles and Andrew Buller, a position he held until July 1824.
April   Publication of first article on German literature, a review of a translation of Johann Wolfgang von Goethe's *Faust* in the *New Edinburgh Review*.

| August | Publication of *Elements of Geometry*, Carlyle's first book, a translation of Adrien Legendre's text. Experiences spiritual transformation in Leith Walk, Edinburgh. |

1823

| October | Publication of first installment of "Life of Schiller" in *London Magazine;* serialization runs through five installments until September 1824. |

1824

| May | Publication of *Wilhelm Meister's Apprenticeship*. |
| September–October | Visits London and Paris. |

1825

| March | Publication of *The Life of Friedrich Schiller*. |
| May | Begins translating works for *German Romance*. |

1826

| 17 October | Marries Jane Baillie Welsh at Templand and settles with her at Comely Bank house in Edinburgh. |

1827

January	Publication of *German Romance*.
February	Meets Francis Jeffrey, editor of *The Edinburgh Review*.
Spring	Works on autobiographical novel *Wotten Reinfred*, which is published unfinished in 1892.
June	Publication of "Jean Paul Friedrich Richter" in *The Edinburgh Review*.
October	Publication of "State of German Literature" in *The Edinburgh Review*.

1828

January	Publication of "Life and Writings of Werner" in *Foreign Review*.
April	Publication of "Goethe's *Helena*" in *Foreign Review*.
May	Moves with Jane to Craigenputtoch.
July	Publication of "Goethe" in *Foreign Review*.
October	Jeffrey visits the Carlyles at Craigenputtoch. Publication of "The Life of Heyne" in *Foreign Review*.
December	Publication of "Burns" in *The Edinburgh Review*.

1829

January	Publication of "German Playwrights" in *Foreign Review*.
April	Publication of "Voltaire" in *Foreign Review*.
June	Publication of "Signs of the Times" in *The Edinburgh Review*.
July	Publication of "Novalis" in *Foreign Review*.
Winter	Carlyle works on "History of German Literature," a work he later abandons.

1830

| January | Publication of "Jean Paul Friedrich Richter, Again" in *Foreign Review*. |
| February/May | Publication of "Jean Paul Friedrich Richter's Review of Madame De Staël's 'Allemagne'" in *Fraser's Magazine*. |

October	Writes draft of essay that becomes *Sartor Resartus*.
November	Publication of "Thoughts on History" in *Fraser's Magazine*.

1831

March	Publication of "Schiller" in *Fraser's Magazine* and "Taylor's Historic Survey of German Poetry" in *The Edinburgh Review*.
July	Publication of "Nibelungen Lied" in *The Westminster Review*. Finishes *Sartor Resartus*.
2 September	Meets John Stuart Mill.
October	Publication of "German Literature of the Fourteenth and Fifteenth Centuries" in *Foreign Quarterly Review*.
December	Publication of "Characteristics" in *The Edinburgh Review*.

1832

22 January	Death of James Carlyle; spends week writing reminiscences of father.
March	Publication of "Schiller, Goethe, and Madame de Staël" and "The Baron von Goethe" in *Fraser's Magazine*.
April	Publication of "Biography" in *Fraser's Magazine*.
May	Publication of "Boswell's Life of Johnson" in *Fraser's Magazine*.
June	Publication of "Death of Goethe" in *New Monthly Magazine*.
July	Publication of "Corn-Law Rhymes" in *The Edinburgh Review*.
August	Publication of "Goethe's *Works*" in *Foreign Quarterly Review*.

1833

April	Publication of "Diderot" in *Foreign Quarterly Review*.
May	Publication of "Quae Cogitavit" in *Fraser's Magazine*.
July–August	Publication of "Count Cagliostro" in *Fraser's Magazine*.
25–26 August	Ralph Waldo Emerson visits Craigenputtoch.
November	Publication of *Sartor Resartus* begins in *Fraser's Magazine;* it appears in eight installments until August 1834.

1834

10 June	Moves to 5 Cheyne Row in Chelsea area of London, his home for the rest of his life.
September	Begins writing *The French Revolution*.

1835

January	Publication of "Death of the Rev. Edward Irving" in *Fraser's Magazine*.
February	Meets John Sterling.
6 March	Mill reports to Carlyle that manuscript of volume I of *The French Revolution* has accidentally been destroyed by fire.
April–August	Rewrites volume I of *The French Revolution*.
December	Resumes work on *The French Revolution*.

1836

April	Meets Robert Browning at Leigh Hunt's. Finishes volume II of *The French Revolution*.
9 April	Publication of the American edition of *Sartor Resartus*.
July	Begins volume III of *The French Revolution*.

1837

January   Finishes writing *The French Revolution*.
                  Publication of "Memoirs of Mirabeau" in *London and Westminster Review*.

January–February Publication of "The Diamond Necklace" in *Fraser's Magazine*.

April   Publication of "Parliamentary History of the French Revolution" in *London and Westminster Review*.

May   Delivers first series of lectures, "On German Literature."
                  Publication of *The French Revolution*.

1838

January   Publication of "Memoirs of the Life of Scott" in *London and Westminster Review*.

May–June   Delivers second lecture series, "On the History of Literature."

July   Publication of first English trade edition of *Sartor Resartus*.
                  Publication of volumes I and II of *Critical and Miscellaneous Essays* in America.

December   Publication of "Varnhagen von Ense's Memoirs" in *London and Westminster Review*.

1839

27 January   Writes to *The Examiner* about new London Library.

7 April   Publication of petition on international copyright in *The Examiner*.

May   Delivers lectures on modern European revolutions.

June   Publication of volumes III and IV of *Critical and Miscellaneous Essays* in America; publication in England follows in September.

July   Publication of "On the Sinking of the Vengeur" in *Fraser's Magazine*.

August–November   Writes *Chartism*.

28 December   Publication of *Chartism*.

1840

March   Meets Charles Dickens.

May   Delivers lectures, "On Heroes."

June–September   Revises lectures for publication.

26 June   Speaks to a meeting of London Library supporters at Freemason's Tavern.

September   Publication of "Heintze's Translation of Burns" in *The Examiner*.
                  Begins research about Oliver Cromwell and his period.

1841

March   Publication of *On Heroes, Hero-Worship, & the Heroic in History*.

1842

January   Publication of "Baillie, the Covenanter" in *The Westminster Review*.

28 February   Death of Grace Welsh; Jane collapses at the news.

26 March   Writes to Dickens in support of copyright.

October   Borrows Jocelin of Brakeland's *Chronicle* about Abbot Sampson of Bury St. Edmunds from London Library.

1843

April   Publication of *Past and Present*.

May	Jane meets Harriet Baring, Lady Ashburton; over the next fourteen years tensions in the Carlyles' marriage develop because of Carlyle's attentions to Lady Ashburton.
July	Publication of "Dr. Francia" in *Foreign Quarterly Review.*
5 December	Decides to focus on collecting Cromwell's letters and speeches instead of a biography.

1844

18 September	John Sterling dies, leaving Carlyle and Julius Hare as executors.
October	Publication of "An Election to the Long Parliament" in *Fraser's Magazine.*

1845

April	Charles Gavan Duffy and members of Young Ireland movement visit the Carlyles.
November	Publication of *Oliver Cromwell's Letters and Speeches.*

1846

September	Tours Ireland with Duffy.
December	Begins reading about Frederick the Great.

1847

February	Using Edward Fitzgerald as his agent, begins inquiries into William Squire's claims to possess Cromwell manuscripts.
25–29 October	Emerson stays with Carlyles at Cheyne Row.
December	Publication of "Thirty-Five Unpublished Letters of Oliver Cromwell" in *Fraser's Magazine* provokes controversy.

1848

March	Publication of "Louis-Philippe" in *The Examiner.*
April	Publication of "Repeal of the Union" in *The Examiner.*
May	Publication of "Legislation for Ireland" and "Ireland and the British Chief Governor" in *The Examiner* and "Irish Regiments (of the New Æra)" in *The Spectator.*
July	Visits Stonehenge with Emerson.
December	Publication of "Death of the Right Hon. Charles Buller" in *The Examiner.*

1849

23 January	William Squire meets Carlyle at Cheyne Row.
April	Publication of "Ireland and Sir Robert Peel" in *The Spectator.*
May	Publication of "Indian Meal" in *Fraser's Magazine.*
July–August	Visits Ireland with Duffy.
October	Writes reminiscence of Irish tour, which is published posthumously as *Reminiscences of My Irish Journey in 1849* in 1881.
December	Publication of "Trees of Liberty" in *Nation.*
	Publication of "Occasional Discourse on the Negro Question" in *Fraser's Magazine.*

1850

February	Publication of first *Latter-Day Pamphlet,* "The Present Time."
March	Publication of second *Latter-Day Pamphlet,* "Model Prisons."
April	Publication of third *Latter-Day Pamphlet,* "Downing Street."

15 April	Publication of fourth *Latter-Day Pamphlet*, "New Downing Street."
May	Publication of fifth *Latter-Day Pamphlet*, "Stump-Orator."
June	Publication of sixth *Latter-Day Pamphlet*, "Parliaments."
July	Publication of seventh *Latter-Day Pamphlet*, "Hudson's Statue."
August	Publication of eighth *Latter-Day Pamphlet*, "Jesuitism."
	Publication of *Latter-Day Pamphlets* in book form.

1851

February–March	Writes *Life of John Sterling*.
September	Visits Paris with Robert and Elizabeth Barrett Browning.
October	Publication of *Life of John Sterling*.

1852

February–June	Collects German books and maps.
September	Travels in Germany with Joseph Neuberg.

1853

June	Indexes notes on Frederick the Great.
	Publication of *Occasional Discourse on the Nigger Question*.
25 December	Death of Margaret Aitken Carlyle.

1854

March	Completion of a "sound-proof" attic study at Cheyne Row.
August	Publication of *Hard Times*, which Dickens dedicates to Carlyle.

1855

January	Publication of "The Prinzenraub; A Glimpse of Saxon History" in *The Westminster Review*.

1857

May	Death of Lady Harriet Ashburton.

1858

September	Travels in Germany with Neuberg again.
	Publication of volumes I and II of *History of Friedrich II. Of Prussia, called Frederick the Great*.

1863

April	Publication of volume III of *Frederick the Great*.
September	Jane badly injured in a fall.

1864

February	Publication of volume IV of *Frederick the Great*.
July–October	Jane is ill, resides with friends who nurse her.

1865

	Publication of volumes V and VI of *Frederick the Great*.

1866

2 April	Installed as Rector of Edinburgh University.

21 April	Death of Jane Welsh Carlyle.
25 May–28 July	Writes reminiscence of Jane.
September	Carlyle supports Governor John Eyre in speeches to Eyre Defence Fund.

1867

January	Writes reminiscences of Edward Irving and Francis Jeffrey.
February	Writes reminiscence of Robert Southey.
March	Writes reminiscence of William Wordsworth.
August	Publication of "Shooting Niagara: and After?" in *Macmillan's Magazine*.

1868

Begins preparing *Letters and Memorials of Jane Welsh Carlyle,* which he works on until 1873. Carlyle's niece Mary Aitken moves to Cheyne Row to care for her uncle.

1869

| March | Audience with Queen Victoria. |

1873

Receives Prussian Order of Merit.

1874

Declines Grand Cross of Bath.

1875

January–March	Publication of "Early Kings of Norway" in *Fraser's Magazine*.
April	Publication of "The Portraits of John Knox" in *Fraser's Magazine*.
4 December	Eightieth birthday is celebrated; receives a medal and address from 119 friends as well as a letter from German chancellor Otto von Bismark.

1879

| August | Marriage of Mary Aitken and Alexander Carlyle, who comes to live with her at Cheyne Row. |

1881

| 5 February | Death of Thomas Carlyle. |

Birth to Marriage: 1795–1826

On 4 December 1795, Thomas Carlyle was born in remote Ecclefechan in Dumfriesshire, Scotland. Thomas, named for his paternal grandfather, was the oldest of nine children, four boys and five girls, born to Margaret Aitken Carlyle, James Carlyle's second wife. All but one of the children lived to adulthood. In an otherwise happy childhood, Thomas remembered his little sister being measured for her coffin.

James and Margaret Carlyle were sober, frugal, God-fearing members of the Scottish Burgher Seceder sect. Earnest and strict in its Calvinistic beliefs, the church subscribed wholeheartedly to the doctrines of the depravity of man and the efficacy of divine grace but was more tolerant than other dissenting congregations in the region, valuing classical education and liberal culture. Carlyle's father, respected in the community as an honest, conscientious stonemason, shaped the life of his family around the precepts of his faith. From age five to age eleven, Thomas Carlyle attended services at the meetinghouse. He never lost respect for the church of his youth; its influence is evident in his enduring belief in the spiritual realm, his condemnation of worldly vanities, and his devotion to discerning and spreading truth.

"Boundless Hopes"

Despite his wife's initial opposition, James Carlyle insisted that his son receive an education, funding his attendance at a private school in Ecclefechan and then at Annan Academy, which prepared boys for entry into the university at Edinburgh. In Reminiscences (1887) Carlyle recalls leaving home on 26 May 1806 for Annan Academy, six miles away: "It was a bright morning, and to me full of moment; of fluttering boundless Hopes, saddened by parting with Mother, with Home; and which afterward were cruelly disappointed." Carlyle lived with pedantic schoolmasters and bullying schoolmates, making him long for the weekends he spent at home. He was still thirteen—a typical age for students in the Scottish system—when he began his studies at Edinburgh University in November 1809. He enrolled as a divinity student in November 1813, and continued in this program until the spring of 1817, when he declared himself unfit to pursue a career in the church because of his religious doubts.

In January 1832, shortly after the death of James Carlyle, Carlyle composed a memoir of his father from which the following text is excerpted. He refers to the German philosopher

Thomas Carlyle, circa 1832. This illustration is the earliest known image of Carlyle (drawing by Daniel Maclise; from The Love Letters of Thomas Carlyle and Jane Welsh, Special Collections, Thomas Cooper Library, University of South Carolina).

Johann Gotlieb Fichte and his friend Francis Jeffrey, a critic and jurist.

Remembering James Carlyle
Thomas Carlyle

In several respects, I consider my Father as one of the most interesting men I have known. He was a man of perhaps *the* very largest natural endowment of any it had been my lot to converse with: none of us will ever forget that bold glowing style of his, flowing free from the untutored Soul; full of metaphors (though he knew not what a metaphor was), with all manner of potent words (which he appropriated and applied with *surprising* accuracy, you often could not guess whence); brief, energetic; and which I should say conveyed the most perfect picture, definite, clear not in ambitious *colours* but in full *white* sunlight, of all the dialects I have ever listened to. Nothing did I ever hear him undertake to render visible, which did not become almost ocularly so. Never shall we again hear such speech as that was: the whole district knew of it; and laughed joyfully over it, not knowing how otherwise to express the feeling it gave them. Emphatic I have heard him beyond all men. In anger he had no need of oaths; his words were like sharp arrows that smote into the very heart. The fault was that he exaggerated (which tendency I also inherit); yet only in description and for the sake chiefly of *humorous* effect: he was a man of rigid, even scrupulous veracity; I have often heard him turn back, when he thought his strong words were misleading, and correct them into mensurative accuracy. *Ach, und dies alles ist hin!*

I call him a natural man; singularly free from all manner of affectation: he was among the last of the true men, which Scotland (on the old system) produced, or can produce; a man healthy in body and in mind; fearing God, and diligently working in God's Earth with contentment hope and unwearied resolution. *He* was never visited with Doubt; the old Theorem of the Universe was sufficient for him, and

Thomas Carlyle's mother, Margaret Aitken Carlyle (painting by Maxwell of Dumfries, circa 1842, Carlyle House; from Carlyle's Birthplace: The Arched House, Ecclefechan, *Special Collections, Thomas Cooper Library, University of South Carolina)*

he worked well in it, and in all senses *successfully* and wisely as few now can do; so quick is the motion of Transition becoming: the new generation almost to a man must make "their Belly their God," and alas even find *that* an empty one. Thus curiously enough, and blessedly, *he* stood a true man on the verge of the Old; while his son stands here lovingly surveying him on the verge of the New, and sees the possibility of also being true there. God make the possibility, blessed possibility, into a reality!

. . . .

. . . Another virtue, the example of which has passed strongly into me, was his settled placid indifference to the clamours or the murmurs of Public Opinion. For the judgment of those that had no right or power to judge him, he seemed simply to care nothing at all. He very rarely *spoke* of despising such things, he contented himself with altogether disregarding them. Hollow babble it was; for him a thing as Fichte said "that did not exist," *das gar nicht existirte.* There was something truly great in this; the very

---

"Second Volume"

. . . I can see my dear Father's Life in some measure as the sunk pillar on which mine was to rise and be built; the waters of Time have now swelled up round his (as they will round mine); I can *see* it (all transfigured) though I *touch* it no longer. I might almost say his spirit seems to have entered into me (so clearly do I discern and love him); I seem to myself only the continuation, and *second volume* of my Father.

—Reminiscences, v. 1, p. 52

Arched House, which was built by Carlyle's father and uncle. The room in which Carlyle was born is marked by
him with an asterisk (from The Love Letters of Thomas Carlyle and Jane Welsh,
Thomas Cooper Library, University of South Carolina).

Carlyle's cradle (from Shirley Hoover Biggers, British Author House Museums and Other Memorials,
Thomas Cooper Library, University of South Carolina)

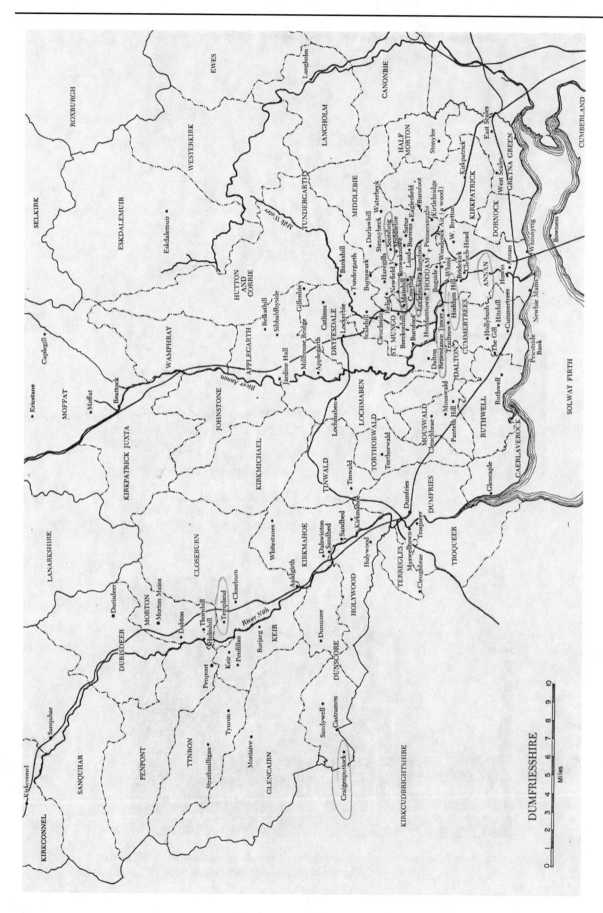

Map of Dumfriesshire in southwest Scotland. Carlyle lived most of his first forty years in this region (from The Letters of Thomas Carlyle to His Brother Alexander, Thomas Cooper Library, University of South Carolina).

Burgher Seceder Meeting House in Ecclefechan (from John M. Sloan, The Carlyle Country, *Special Collections, Thomas Cooper Library, University of South Carolina)*

perfection of it hid from you the extent of the attainment.

Or rather let me call it a new phasis of the *health* which in mind as in body was conspicuous in him. Like a healthy man, he wanted *only* to get along with his Task: whatsoever could not forward him in this (and how could Public Opinion and much else of the like sort do it?) was of no moment to him, was not there for him.

This great maxim of Philosophy he had gathered by the teaching of nature alone: That man was created to work, not to speculate, or feel, or dream. Accordingly he set his whole heart thitherwards: he did work wisely and unweariedly *(ohne Hast aber ohne Rast),* and perhaps *performed* more (with the tools he had) than any man I now know. It should have made me sadder than it did to hear the young ones sometimes complaining of his slow punctuality and thoroughness; he would leave nothing till it was *done.* Alas! the age of Substance and

Solidity is gone (for the time); that of Show and hollow Superficiality (in all senses) is in full course—

And yet he was a man of open sense; wonderfully so. I could have entertained him for days talking of *any* matter interesting to man. He delighted to hear of *all* things that were worth talking of; the mode of living men had, the mode of working, their opinions, virtues, whole spiritual and temporal environment. It is some two years ago (in summer) since I entertained him highly (he was hoeing turnips and perhaps I helped him) with an account of the character and manner of existence of Francis Jeffrey. Another evening he enjoyed (probably it was on that very visit) with the heartiest relish my description of the people (I think) of Turkey. The Chinese had astonished him much: in some Magazine (from Little's of Cressfield) he had got a sketch of *Macartney's Embassy,* the memory of which never left him. Adam Smith's *Wealth of Nations,* greatly as it lay out of his course, he had also fallen in with; and admired, and

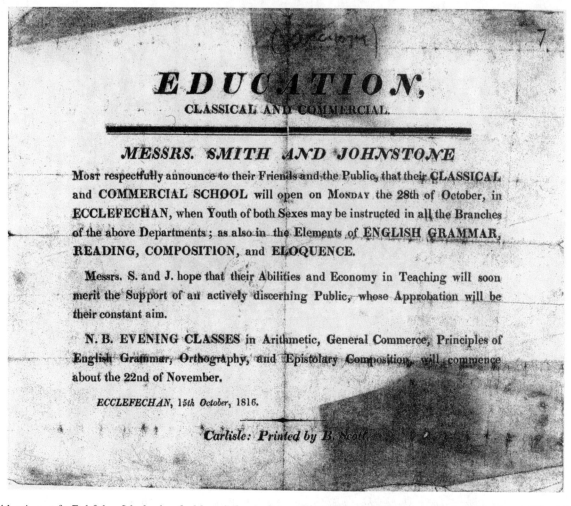

*Advertisement for Ecclefechan School, where Carlyle studied under Reverend John Johnstone before going on to Annan Academy in May 1806
(The Trustees of National Library of Scotland, MS 2883)*

"The Misery of Non-Understanding"

In his autobiography, John Ruskin recalls what Carlyle told him of his first experience in school.

His own first teacher in Latin, an old clergyman. He had indeed been sent first to a schoolmaster in his own village, "the joyfullest little mortal, he believed, on earth," learning his declensions out of an eighteen-penny book! giving his whole might and heart to understand. And the master could teach him nothing, merely involved him day by day in misery of non-understanding, the boy getting crushed and sick, till (his mother?) saw it, and then he was sent to this clergyman, "a perfect sage, on the humblest scale."

–Praeterita, p. 461

*Annan Academy, where Carlyle attended school from 1806 till 1809.
In* Reminiscences *he called it a "doleful and hateful" place (from
John M. Sloan,* The Carlyle Country, *Special Collections,
Thomas Cooper Library, University of South Carolina).*

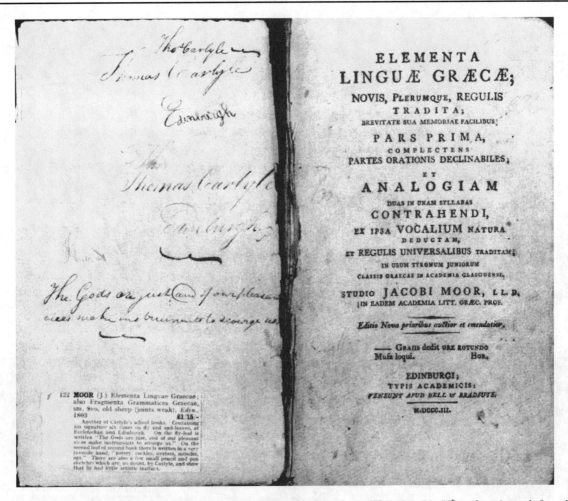

Carlyle's Greek grammar textbook. The inscription in Carlyle's handwriting is from King Lear, *III.iii.171–172: "The gods are just and of our pleasant vices make instruments to scourge us" (Norman and Charlotte Strouse Collection of the University Library, University of California, Santa Cruz; from Carlisle Moore, Rodger Tarr, and Chris Vanden Bossche,* Lectures on Carlyle & His Era, *Thomas Cooper Library, University of South Carolina).*

understood and remembered,–so far as he had any business with it.–I once wrote him about my being in Smithfield Market (seven years ago); of my seeing St. Paul's: both things interested him heartily, and dwelt with him. I had hoped to tell him much, much of what I saw in this second visit; and that many a long cheerful talk would have given us both some sunny hours: but *es konnte nimmer seyn!*–Patience! Hope!

At the same time he had the most entire and open contempt for all idle tattle, what he called "clatter." *Any* talk that had meaning in it he could listen to: what had *no* meaning in it, above all, what seemed false, he absolutely could and would not hear; but abruptly turned aside from it, or if that might not suit, with the besom of destruction swept it far away from him. Long may we remember his "I don't believe thee;" his tongue-paralysing, cold, indifferent "Hah!"– I should say of him, as I did of our Sister whom we lost, that he seldom or never spoke except actually to

convey an idea. Measured by quantity of words, he was a talker of fully average copiousness; by extent of meaning communicated, he was the most copious I have listened to. How, in few sentences, he would sketch you off an entire Biography, an entire Object or Transaction: keen, clear, rugged, genuine, completely rounded in! His words came direct from the heart, by the inspiration of the moment: "It is no idle tale," said he to some laughing rustics, while stating in his strong way some complaint against them; and their laughter died into silence. Dear good Father! There looked *honesty* through those clear earnest eyes; a sincerity that compelled belief and regard. "Moffat!" said he one day to an incorrigible reaper, "thou has every feature of a bad shearer: high, and rough, and little on't. Thou maun *alter* thy figure or slant the bog"–pointing to the man's road homewards.–

–*Reminiscences*, v. 1, pp. 5–9

Eulefa 24th June 181[?]

Dear Murray,

I return you my sincerest thanks for the kind letter you favoured me with & for the punctual manner in which you executed my requests. In fact I don't know how to write to you, for shame at not writing you long ago. I can assure you however, that every day, since I came home, I have intended to write you, and every day some thing has prevented me from putting my intention in execution. —

Brunton, I hear, has got the Hebrew chair notwithstanding the good Dr's recommendation of Scott, aye 'aye! "Kissing goes by favour" true yet, I see.

Johnston is a-teaching at present, that same school of which he wrote, you know, has £26. per an. and meat; in my opinion he has exchanged a bad for a worse.

What in the name of wonder is Clint

First page of Carlyle's earliest extant letter, written from Ecclefechan when he was seventeen and home from school on summer vacation. His correspondent, Thomas Murray, was a friend he made at the University of Edinburgh (The Trustees of National Library of Scotland, MS 8992).

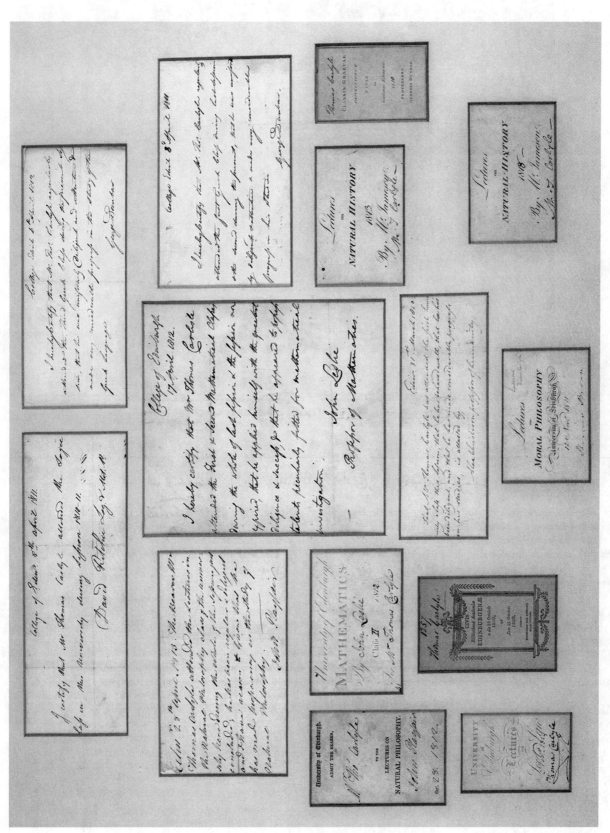

Carlyle's class cards, certificates, and library card. Cards were issued for admission to individual courses, and certificates were awarded for completion of the courses (Edinburgh University Library PC12).

One of Carlyle's college notebooks (Carlyle's House Museum, London)

Peter Nimmo

The following excerpt is the first section from Carlyle's "Peter Nimmo: A Rhapsody," a satiric poem in five sections that was originally published in the February 1831 issue of Fraser's Magazine. *Peter Nimmo was an eccentric and legendary student who enrolled in courses at Edinburgh University for decades. "His Essence," Carlyle writes in his concluding lines, "Like yours and mine, was VANITY."*

Thrice-loved Nimmo! art thou still, in spite of Fate,
    Footing those cold pavements, void of meal and mutton;
To and from that everlasting College-gate,
    With thy blue hook-nose, and ink-horn hung on button?

Always have I noted that long simple nose of thine,
    How it droops most meekly over shallowest chin,
Ever-smiling lips with scarcely-squinting eyes does join:
    Fittest bush for the "mild penny-wheep" is sold within!

Soot brown coat, I know, is button'd, and thy motion
    To all class-rooms is a short half-hurried trudge:
Peter! is there, was there any fact or notion
    In that porous head of thine one night will lodge?

No one! Simplest Peter, wilt thou never know
    That thy brain is made of substance adipose?
Whilst thou bear'st and heat'st it, all to oil does go:
    Cease, fond struggling man, what bootless toils are those!

Canst thou τιμή yet decline, or know the gender
    (On thy oath) of Neuter from a Feminine?
Peter, no! Thou know'st it not, thou vain pretender:
    Met the Sun's eye ever so strange a case as thine?

For 'tis twenty years and five since thou art seen
    In all Class-rooms, Lectures, thou unwearied biped,
Listening, prying, jolting, with an eye so mildly keen;
    And what boots it? Vain were even the Delphic Tripod.

Danaus's daughters had a water-sieve to fill;
    Fate like thine, poor Nimmo, yet in other guise:
Thee no Fear doth urge, but Hope and readiest will,
    Hope that springs eternal, Hope of being wise!

—Memoirs of the Life and Writings of Thomas Carlyle,
v. 1, pp. 365–366

Mainhill House, where Carlyle vacationed and visited his parents from 1815 to 1825 (photograph by J. Patrick, from The Love Letters of
Thomas Carlyle and Jane Welsh, *Special Collections, Thomas Cooper Library, University of South Carolina)*

. . . When I remember how he admired Intellectual Force, how much he had of it himself, and yet how
unconsciously and contentedly he gave others credit for
superiority, I again see the *healthy* spirit, the genuine
man. Nothing could please him better than a
well-ordered Discourse of Reason; the clear Solution
and Exposition of any object: and he knew well, in such
cases, when the nail had been hit; and contemptuously
enough recognised where it had been missed. He has
said of a bad Preacher: "He was like a fly wading
among Tar." Clearness, emphatic Clearness, was his
highest category of man's thinking power: he delighted
always to hear good "Argument;" he would often say, "I
would like to hear thee argue with him:" he said this of
Jeffrey and me,–with an air of such simple earnestness
(not two years ago); and it was his true feeling. I have
often pleased him much by arguing with men (as many
years ago I was prone to do) in his presence: he rejoiced
greatly in my success, at all events in my dexterity and
manifested force. Others of us he admired for our

"activity," our practical valour and skill; all of us (generally speaking) for our decent demeanour in the world.
It is now one of my greatest blessings (for which I
would thank Heaven from the heart) that he lived to see
me, through various obstructions, attain some look of
doing well. He had "educated" me against much
advice, I believe, and chiefly, if not solely, from his own
noble faith: James Bell (one of our wise men) had told
him: "Educate a boy, and he grows up to despise his
ignorant parents." My Father once told me this; and
added: "Thou hast not done so. God be thanked for
it!" I have reason to think my Father was proud of me
(not vain, for he never, except provoked, openly
bragged of us); that here too he lived to "see the pleasure of the Lord prosper in his hands." Oh, was it not a
happiness for me! The fame of all this Planet were not
henceforth so precious.–

–*Reminiscences*, v. 1, pp. 18–19

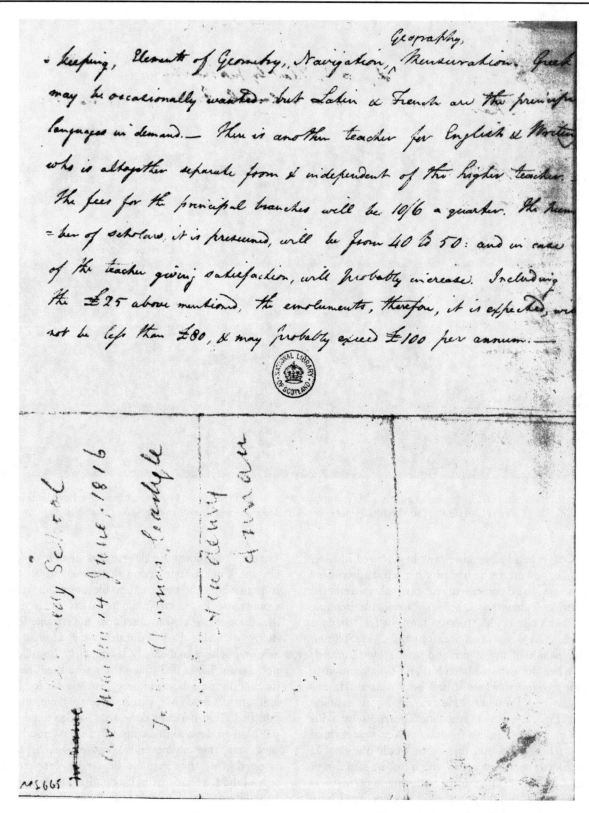

-keeping, Elements of Geometry, Navigation, Mensuration. Greek Geography, may be occasionally wanted—but Latin & French are the principal languages in demand.— There is another teacher for English & Writing who is altogether separate from & independent of the higher teacher. The fees for the principal branches will be 10/6 a quarter. The number of scholars, it is presumed, will be from 40 to 50: and in case of the teacher giving satisfaction, will probably increase. Including the £25 above mentioned, the emoluments, therefore, it is expected, will not be less than £80, & may probably exceed £100 per annum.—

Reverend John Martin's letter to Carlyle describing the teaching position available at Kirkaldy.
Carlyle taught at the school from November 1816 to November 1818
(The Trustees of National Library of Scotland, MS 665).

Kirkcaldy, a Letter by Mr Martin

Rev. Martin to Thomas Carlyle, Annan, 14 June 1816.

What is at present wanted for the school of Kirkcaldy is not, properly speaking, a _parochial teacher_, but an assistant to the person who now fills that office.

The school, under the present teacher, has fallen into disrepute & inefficiency. The scholars have not exceeded 10 for a year past. Every one is satisfied that this is owing to the personal character of the teacher; who, tho' perfectly correct in morals, is deficient in energy. As the place suffers by this circumstance, various plans have been devised to supply the want; and the master himself has offered to resign, on condition of being permitted to retain the salary, or of having an equivalent annuity for life. There are no funds from which the annuity demanded can be paid. & it is presumed to be illegal to separate the salary from the office. — In these circumstances, it has appeared to be the only step left for adoption, to elect an assistant to the present teacher, under the understood arrangement, that the latter shall have nothing to do with the management of the school, & that while he retains the salary, the assistant shall be entitled to the whole fees. As a farther encouragement to the assistant, some gentlemen have agreed to pay, for three years, a sum not less than £25 annually, as a salary to him. — Any engagement with an assistant therefore cannot be made certain for more than three years as the continuance of this salary, beyond that term, depends on the will of the subscribers, who do not, at present, bind themselves for more. — No other functions or duties but those of teaching the higher department of the parochial school, will fall to the assistant. This comprehends Latin, French, Arithmetic, Book-keeping

"Expositor and Enforcer"

To support himself as he prepared for the ministry, Carlyle taught school at Kirkaldy for two years. While he enjoyed the friendship of fellow teacher and Annan native Edward Irving, Carlyle deplored teaching and came to regard it as incompatible with true intellectual achievement.

. . . As to my Schoolmaster function it was never said I *misdid* it much ("a clear and correct" expositor and enforcer): but from the first, especially with such adjuncts, I disliked it, and by swift degrees grew to hate it more and more. Some four years, in all, I had of it, two in Annan, two in Kirkcaldy (under much improved *social* accompaniments);–and at the end, my solitary desperate conclusion was fixed, That I, for my own part, would prefer to perish in the ditch, if necessary, rather than continue living by such a trade:–and peremptorily gave it up accordingly.

–Reminiscences, v. 2, p.19

House at Kirkaldy where Carlyle lived from 1816 till 1818 (from G. K. Chesterton and J. E. Hodder Williams, Thomas Carlyle, *Special Collections, Thomas Cooper Library, University of South Carolina)*

Margaret Gordon, whom Carlyle courted from late 1818 until early 1820 (miniature, circa 1824, from David Alec Wilson, Life of Carlyle, *Special Collections, Thomas Cooper Library, University of South Carolina)*

Edward Irving, who became Carlyle's close friend when the two men were teaching in Kirkaldy and introduced him to Jane Welsh. In the late 1820s Irving became the charismatic leader of a group of religious enthusiasts who split off from the National Church of Scotland. Carlyle's disapproval of his friend's flamboyant religious rhetoric contributed to their estrangement (drawing by A. Robertson; from Andrew Landale Drummond, Edward Irving and His Circle, *Special Collections, Thomas Cooper Library, University of South Carolina).*

Jane Welsh

Jane Baillie Welsh, circa 1826 (from David Alec Wilson, Life of Carlyle; *Special Collections, Thomas Cooper Library, University of South Carolina)*

The most important influence on the adult Carlyle was the woman who became his wife, Jane Welsh. Born in 1801, Jane Baillie Welsh was the daughter of John and Grace Welsh. Dr. Welsh, a successful physician, provided a comfortable life for his family at Haddington, just east of Edinburgh, and supplied his intelligent, independent, and imaginative daughter with tutors— one of whom was Carlyle's friend Edward Irving—to instruct her well beyond the scope of conventional female education. John Welsh's death in 1819 robbed Jane of a crucial champion for her intellectual ambition. The following excerpts provide a glimpse of Jane Welsh before she met Carlyle.

Carlyle included Geraldine Jewsbury's tribute to his wife in his Reminiscences. *Jewsbury was twenty-eight in spring 1840 when she first wrote to Carlyle in response to his writings, asking guidance in her own spiritual struggles. She visited the Carlyles at their home March 1841 and became a close friend to Jane. This excerpt, from an essay written upon Jane's death in 1866 and published as "In Memoriam Jane Welsh Carlyle," presents scenes from her youth.*

John and Grace Welsh, the parents of Carlyle's wife (from Jane Welsh Carlyle, Jane Welsh Carlyle: Letters to Her Family, 1839–1863, *Special Collections, Thomas Cooper Library, University of South Carolina)*

Jane Welsh's Childhood
Geraldine Jewsbury

She told me that once, when she was a very little girl, there was going to be a dinner-party at home, and she was left alone with some tempting custards, ranged in their glasses upon the stand. She stood looking at them, and the thought came into her mind 'What *would* be the consequence if I should eat one of them?' A whimsical sense of the dismay it would cause took hold of her; she thought of it again, and scarcely knowing what she was about, she put forth her hand, and—took a little from the top of each! She was discovered; the sentence upon her was, to eat *all* the remaining custards, and to hear the company told the reason why there were none for them! The poor child hated custards for a long time afterwards.

THE BUBBLY JOCK.

On her road to school, when a very small child, she had to pass a gate where a horrid turkey-cock was generally standing. He always ran up to her, gobbling and looking very hideous and alarming. It frightened her at first a good deal; and she dreaded having to pass the place; but after a little time she hated the thought of living in fear. The next time she passed the gate several labourers and boys were near, who seemed to enjoy the thought of the turkey running at her. She gathered herself together and made up her mind. The turkey ran at her as usual, gobbling and swelling; she suddenly darted at him and seized him by the throat and swung him round! The men clapped their hands, and shouted 'Well done, little Jeannie Welsh!' and the Bubbly Jock never molested her again.

LEARNING LATIN.

She was very anxious to learn lessons like a Boy; and, when a very little thing, she asked her father to let her 'learn Latin like a boy.' Her mother did not wish her to learn so much; her father always tried to push her forwards; there was a division of opinion on the subject. Jeannie went to one of the town scholars in Haddington and made him teach her a noun of the first declension ('*Penna,* a pen,' I think it was). Armed with this, she watched her opportunity; instead of going to bed, she crept under the table, and was concealed by the cover. In a pause of conversation, a little voice was heard, *Penna,* a pen; *pennæ,* of a pen;' etc., and as there was a pause of surprise, she crept out, and went up to her father saying, 'I want to learn Latin; please let me be a boy.' Of course she had her own way in the matter.

SCHOOL AT HADDINGTON.

Boys and girls went to the same school; they were in separate rooms, except for Arithmetic and Algebra. Jeannie was the best of the girls at Algebra. Of course she had many devoted slaves among the boys; one of them especially taught her, and helped her all he knew; but he was quite a poor boy, whilst Jeannie was one of the gentry of the place; but she felt no difficulty, and they were great friends. She was fond of doing everything difficult that boys did. There was one particularly dangerous feat, to which the boys dared each other; it was to walk on a *very* narrow ledge on the outside of the bridge overhanging the water; the ledge went in an arch, and the height was considerable. One fine morning Jeannie got up early and went to the Nungate Bridge; she lay down on her face and crawled from one end of the bridge to the other, to the imminent risk of either breaking her neck or drowning.

One day in the boys' school-room, one of the boys said something to displease her. She lifted her hand, doubled it, and hit him hard; his nose began to bleed, and in the midst of the scuffle the master came in. He saw the traces of the fray, and said in an angry voice, 'You boys, you know, I have forbidden you to fight in school, and have promised that I would flog the next. Who has been fighting this time?' Nobody spoke; and the master grew angry, and threatened *tawse* all round unless the culprit were given up. Of course no boy would tell of a girl, so there was a pause; in the midst of it, Jeannie looked up and said, 'Please, I gave that black eye' *[sic]*. The master tried to look grave, and pursed up his mouth; but the boy was big, and Jeannie was little; so, instead of the *tawse* he burst out laughing and told her she was 'a little deevil,' and had no business there, and to go her way back to the girls.

Her friendship with her schoolfellow-teacher came to an untimely end. An aunt who came on a visit saw her standing by a stile with him, and a book between them. She was scolded, and desired not to keep his company. This made her very sorry, for she knew how good he was to her; but she never had a notion of disobedience in any matter small or great. She did not know how to tell him or to explain; she thought it shame to tell him he was not thought good enough, so she determined he should imagine it a fit of caprice, and from that day she never spoke a word to him or took the least notice; she thought a sudden cessation would pain him less than a gradual coldness. Years and years afterwards, going back on a visit to Haddington, when she was a middle-aged woman, and he was a man married and doing well in the world, she saw him again, and then, for the first time, told him the explanation.

She was always anxious to work hard, and would sit up half the night over her lessons. One day she had been greatly perplexed by a problem in Euclid; she *could not* solve it. At last she went to bed; and in a dream got up and did it, and went to bed again. In the morning she had no con-

The Welsh house at Haddington, where Jane Welsh was born (from
The Love Letters of Thomas Carlyle and Jane Welsh, *Special Collections, Thomas Cooper Library, University of South Carolina)*

sciousness of her dream; but on looking at her slate, there was the problem solved.

She was afraid of sleeping too much, and used to tie a weight to one of her ankles that she might awake. Her mother discovered it; and her father forbade her to rise before five o'clock. She was a most healthy little thing then; only she did her best to ruin her health, not knowing what she did. She always would push everything to its extreme to find out if possible the ultimate consequence. One day her mother was ill, and a bag of ice had to be applied to her head. Jeannie wanted to know the sensation, and took an opportunity when no one saw to get hold of the bag, and put it on her own head, and kept it on till she was found lying on the ground insensible.

She made great progress in Latin, and was in Virgil when nine years old. She always loved her doll; but when she got into Virgil she thought it shame to care for a doll. On her tenth birthday she built a funeral pile of lead pencils and sticks of cinnamon, and poured some sort of perfume over all, to represent a funeral pile. She then recited the speech of Dido, stabbed her doll and let out all the sawdust; after which she consumed her to ashes, and then burst into a passion of tears.

HER APPEARANCE IN GIRLHOOD.

As a child she was remarkable for her large black eyes with their curved lashes. As a girl she was extremely pretty,–a graceful and beautifully formed figure, upright and supple,–a delicate complexion of creamy white with a pale rose tint in the cheeks, lovely eyes full of fire and softness, and with great depths of meaning. Her head was finely formed, with a noble arch, and a broad forehead. Her other features were not regular; but they did not prevent her conveying all the impression of being beautiful. Her voice was clear, and full of subtle intonations and capable of

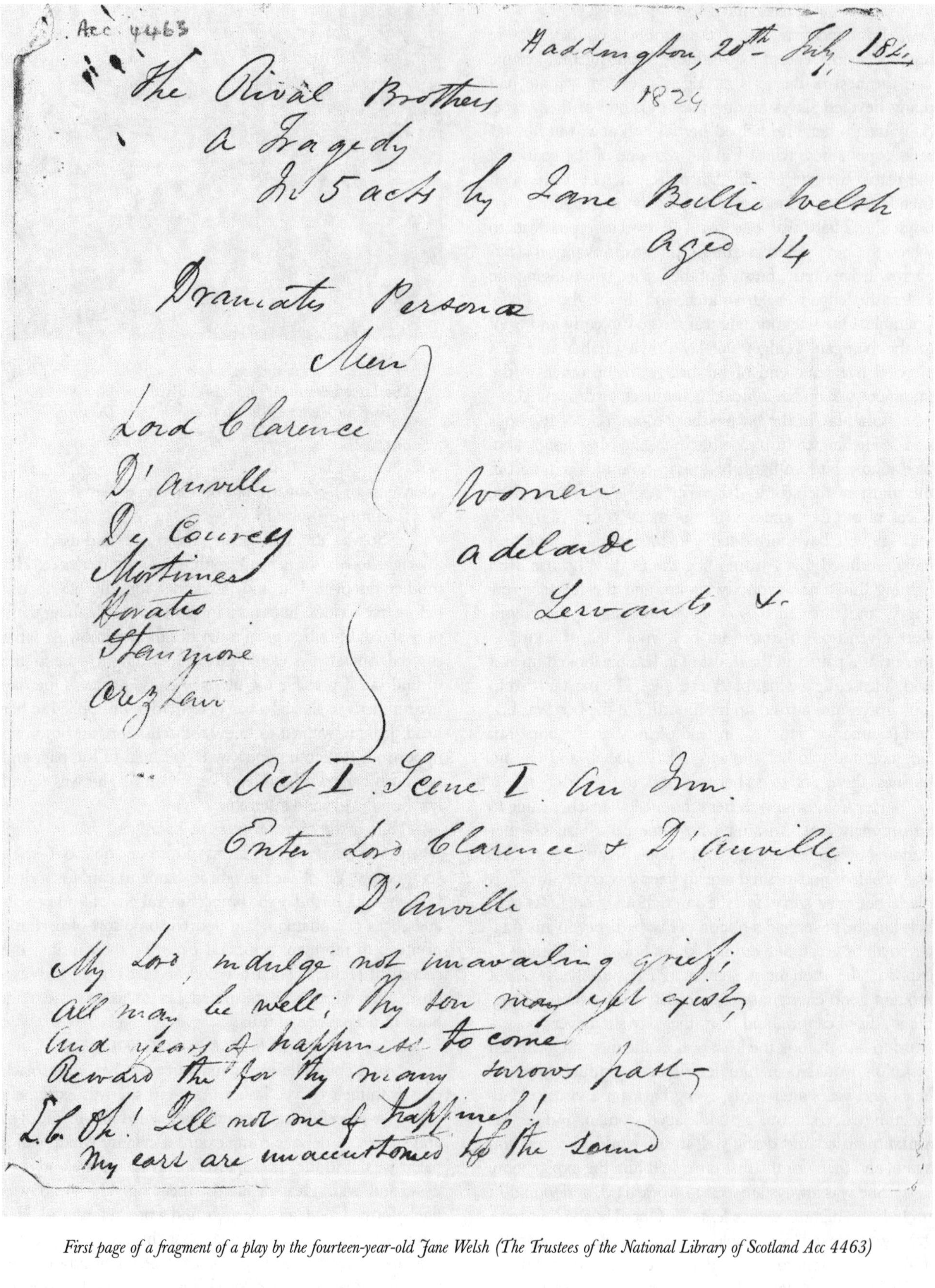

Acc. 4463

Haddington, 20th July, 182—
1824

The Rival Brothers
A Tragedy
In 5 acts by Jane Baillie Welsh
Aged 14

Dramatis Personæ

Men

Lord Clarence
D'Anville
De Courcy
Mortimer
Horatio
Stanmore
Crezlaw

Women

Adelaide

Servants &.

Act I. Scene I. An Inn.

Enter Lord Clarence & D'Anville.

D'Anville

My Lord, indulge not unavailing grief;
All may be well; thy son may yet exist,
And years of happiness to come
Reward thee for thy many sorrows past,

L.C. Oh! tell not me of happiness!
My ears are unaccustomed to the sound

First page of a fragment of a play by the fourteen-year-old Jane Welsh (The Trustees of the National Library of Scotland Acc 4463)

great variety of expression. She had it under full control. She danced with much grace; and she was a good musician. She was ingenious in all works that required dexterity of hand; she could draw and paint, and she was a good carpenter. She could do anything well to which she chose to give herself. She was fond of logic,–too much so; and she had a keen clear incisive faculty of seeing through things, and hating all that was make-believe or pretentious. She had good sense that amounted to genius. She loved to learn, and she cultivated all her faculties to the utmost of her power. She was always witty, with a gift for narration;–in a word she was fascinating and everybody fell in love with her. A relative of hers told me that every man who spoke to her for five minutes felt impelled to make her an offer of marriage! From which it resulted that a great many men were made unhappy. She seemed born 'for the destruction of mankind.' Another person told me that she was 'the most beautiful starry-looking creature that could be imagined,' with a peculiar grace of manner and motion that was more charming than beauty. She had a great quantity of very fine silky black hair, and she always had a natural taste for dress. The first thing I ever heard about her was that she dressed well,–an excellent gift for a woman.

–*Reminiscences*, v. 2, pp. 54–59

* * *

Jane Carlyle was a remarkable writer, especially of letters. This excerpt is from an essay she is believed to have written around 1852 in response to Carlyle's opinion that love takes up little space in a man's life–"Mr C's computation of 'a very few years,–a quite insignificant fraction of Man's Life.'"

"My First Love Resembled My Last"
Jane Welsh Carlyle

Before beginning what she called "The simple Story of my own first Love," Jane recalled that she had first been disappointed in love when she was six and a companion of her brother, after calling her his "Little Wife," had abandoned her and married another.

Well, then: I was somewhat more advanced in Life than the Child in the foresaid breach-of-promise case, when I fell in love for the first time. In fact I had completed my ninth year, or, as I phrased it, was "going ten." One night, at a Dancing-school-Ball, a Stranger-Boy put a slight on me which I resented to my very finger-ends, and out of that tumult of hurt vanity sprang my first love to life, like Venus out of the froth of the Sea!!–So my first love resembled my last in this at least, that it began in *quasi* hatred. Curious! that recalling so many particulars of this old story, as vividly as if I had it under an Opera-glass: I should have nevertheless quite forgot the Boy's first name! His surname, or as the Parson of

St Marks would say, his "name by nature" was Scholey,–a name which, whether bestowed by nature or art, I have never fallen in with since; but the Charles, or Arthur, or whatever it was that preceded it; couldn't have left less trace of itself had it been written in the "*New Permanent Marking Ink*"! He was only child, this Boy, of an Artillery Officer at the Barracks, and was seen by me then for the first time; a Boy of twelve, or perhaps thirteen, tall for his years, and very slight,–with sunshiny hair, and dark blue eyes,–a dark blue ribbon about his neck, and grey jacket with silver buttons. Such the Image that "stamped itself on my soul forever"!–And I have gone and forgot his first name!

Nor were *his* the only details which impressed me at that Ball: If you would like to know my own Ball-dress, I can tell you every item of it; a white Indian muslin frock open behind, & trimmed with twelve rows of satin ribbon, a broad white satin sash reaching to my heels, little white kid shoes, and embroidered silk stockings,–which last are in a box up stairs, 'along with the cap I was christened in,'–my poor Mother having reserved both in lavender up to the day of her death.

Thus elegantly attired, and with my "magnificent eyelashes" (I never know what became of those eyelashes!) and my dancing "unsurpassed in "private life" (so our dancing-Master described it),–with all that and much more to make me "one and somewhat" in my own eyes; what did I not feel of astonishment, rage, desire of vengeance, when this Boy, whom all were remarking the beauty of, told by his Mama (I heard her with my own ears) to ask little Miss W-h for a quadrille, declined *kurt und gut* [short and good], and led up another Girl!–a Girl that I was "worth a million of,"–if you'll believe me,–a fair, fat, sheep-looking Thing, with next to no sense,–and her dancing!–you should have seen it! Our dancing-Master was always shaking his head at her and saying; "heavy! heavy!–" But her wax-doll face took the fancy of Boys at that period, as afterwards, it was *the rage* with men; till her *head,* unsteady from the first discovery of her, got fairly turned with admiration, and she ended in a Madhouse, that Girl! Ah! Had I seen, by *second sight,* at the Ball there, the ghastly doom ahead of her,–only some dozen years ahead!–could I have had the heart to grudge her one triumph over me, or any Partner she could get? But no foreshadow of the future Madhouse rested on her and me that glancing evening; tho' one of us–and I don't mean *her* was feeling rather *mad.* No! never had I been so outraged in my short life! never so enraged at a Boy! I would have given a guinea, if I had had one, that he would yet ask *me* to dance, that I might have said him *such* a 'No'! But he didn't ask me; neither that night–nor any other night; indeed, to tell the plain truth, if my "magnificent eyelashes," my dancing

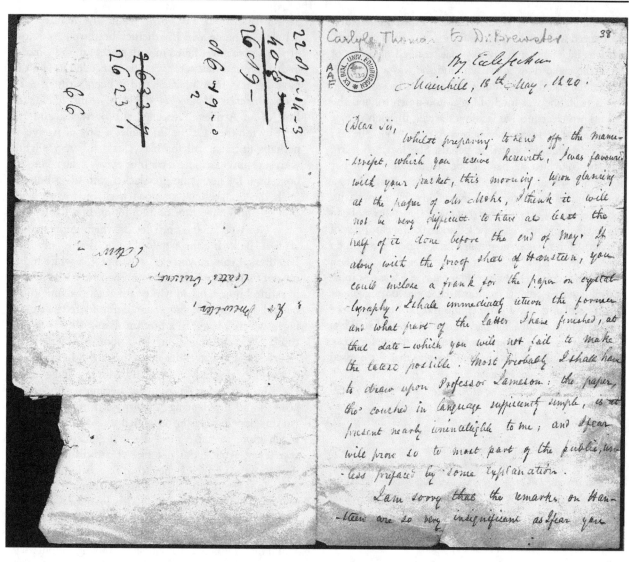

A letter to Professor David Brewster in which Carlyle comments on his writing assignments for the Edinburgh Encyclopedia *(Edinburgh University Library, Special Collections AAF Carlyle 38)*

"unsurpassed in private life," my manifold fascinations, personal and spiritual, were ever so much as noticed by that Boy, he remained from the first to last impracticable to them!

–"*The Simple Story* of My Own First Love," pp. 15–16

Literature and Love

Determined by 1819 to pursue a career as an author, Carlyle earned money by writing for Professor David Brewster's Edinburgh Encyclopedia. *While he wrote, taught, and tutored to earn money, his main projects—a biography of Friedrich Schiller and his translation of Johann Wolfgang von Goethe's novel* Wilhelm Meisters Lehrjahre: Ein Roman *(1795–1796) as* Wilhelm Meister's Apprenticeship—*were the result of his ever-increasing interest in German literature.*

When Jane Welsh's former tutor Edward Irving brought his friend Thomas Carlyle with him on a visit in 1821, Carlyle offered himself to the young woman as a guide to German studies and other topics of interest to both parties. Although Carlyle soon became romantically attached to Jane, Grace Welsh disapproved of him as a suitor because of his uncertain economic prospects and unpolished manners. Jane, secretly enamored of Irving, refused to regard Carlyle as anything more than a friend. However, Irving was bound by late 1820 to marry Isabella Martin, whom he had courted for years and could not abandon without scandal, despite returning Jane's interest. Thomas and Jane corre-

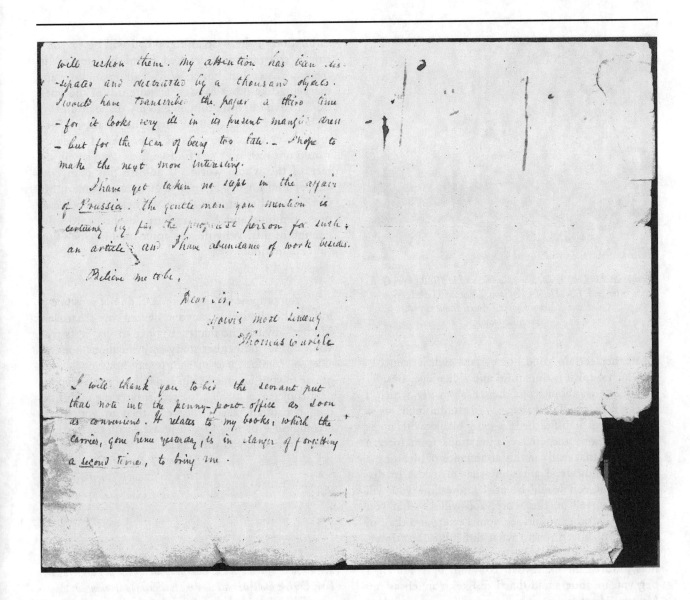

sponded for more than five years, at times negotiating their difficult relationship with brutal honesty. Jane at last consented to marry Carlyle, and the two were wed 17 October 1826 at the Welsh home.

These excerpts from an early letter in the Carlyle-Welsh correspondence show Welsh's reluctance to take Carlyle seriously as a suitor. Welsh wrote from her home in Haddington to Carlyle in Leith Walk, Edinburgh.

Jane Welsh to Carlyle, 17 January 1822

. . . I have moreover read your Letter. For *it* I do *not* thank you. It afforded me neither pleasure nor amusement. Indeed, my Friend, this Letter of yours has, to my mind, more than one fault. I do not allude

to its being egotistical. To speak of oneself is, they say, a privilege of Friendship; . . . But there is about it an air of levity which I dislike; which seems to me to form an unnatural union with the other qualities of your head and heart, and to be ill-timed in treating of a subject to you the most important of all subjects–your own *Destiny*. In a statesman venturing the hopes of his ambition on one decisive stroke; in a soldier rushing to the Battle to conquer or die,–I might admire the spirit of gay daring with which you seem to have been animated. But in a man sitting quietly in his chamber, contemplating years of labour, unattended with any danger (for I do not see that it is incumbent on you to "perish" because you fail in writing a good Novel, good Tragedy, or good anything else),–years of labour the result of which may

Moray Street in Leith Walk, where Carlyle lived in 1820 (from G. K. Chesterton and J. E. Hodder Williams, Thomas Carlyle, *Special Collections, Thomas Cooper Library, University of South Carolina)*

be neither certain good nor certain evil, it seems to me, such a spirit is unnatural and ridiculous. Besides this there is about your Letter a *mystery* which I detest. It is so full of *meaning* words underlined; *meaning* sentences half-finished; *meaning* blanks with notes of admiration; and *meaning* quotations from foreign languages, that really in this abundance of meaning it seems to indicate, I am somewhat at a loss to discover what you would be at. I know how you will excuse yourself on this score: You will say that you knew my Mother would see your Letter; and that, of course, you cared not to what difficulties I as Interpreter might be subjected, so that you got your feelings towards me expressed. Now Sir, once for all, I beg you to understand that I dislike as much as my Mother disapproves your somewhat too ardent expressions of Friendship towards me; and that if you cannot write to me as to a man who feels a deep interest in your welfare, who admires your talents, respects your virtues, and for the sake of these has often,–perhaps too often, overlooked your faults;–if you cannot write to me as if–as if you were married, you need never waste ink or paper on me more.

"Alles für Ruhm und Ihr"!! [All for Glory and Her] On my word, most gay and gallantly said! One would almost believe the man fancies I have fallen in love with him, and entertain the splendid project of rewarding his literary labours with my self. Really, Sir, I do not design for you a recompense so worthless. If you render yourself an honoured member of society (and it seems to me that the pursuit of literary fame is, from the talents you possess, an easy, and, from the manner of life you have adopted, the *only* way of raising yourself from obscurity into the

estimation of the wise and good), I will be to you a true, a constant, and devoted *Friend*–but not a Mistress, a Sister but not a Wife. Falling in love and marrying like other Misses, is quite out of the question. I have too little romance in my disposition ever to be in love with you or any other man; and too much ever to marry without love. Were I a man, I would not wait till *others* find your *worth* to say in the face of the whole world, "I admire this man, and choose him for my Friend." But I am a woman, Mr. Carlyle, and what is worse a young woman. Weakness, timidity and bondage are in the word.–But enough of this. Why do you force me into such horrid explanations?

. . . .

You propose coming here. As I do not presume to forbid this house to anyone whom my "excellent Mother" invites, the matter, I grieve to say, rests with yourself. As you neither study *my* inclinations nor consider *my* comfort, it is in vain to say how much I am averse to your intended visit, and to how many impertinent conjectures it will at present subject me in this tattling ill-natured place. I leave it then to yourself to accomplish it or not, as you please,–with the warning that if you come you will repent it.

–*The Love Letters of Thomas Carlyle and Jane Welsh*, v. 1, pp. 20–23

* * *

Carlyle declined a position as a secretary in order to devote himself to literature. In this excerpt to an apothecary at York Asylum, Carlyle compares his literary endeavor to working in the silver mines of Potosi, which supplied the aristocracy of Spain with riches for some three centuries. The Bolivian city—one of the largest cities in the world in the seventeenth century—became a byword for splendor, but work in the surrounding mines was brutal, resulting in the deaths of millions.

Carlyle to Matthew Allen, 22 January 1822

. . . You asked me lately if I 'would really take your secretary's place?' And tho' I felt all the kindness implied in this question; and tho' my prospects here are not the most brilliant, my situation not the most comfortable; I should not have experienced *very* much hesitation in answering No. Literature is like money, the appetite increases by gratification: the mines of literature too are unwholesome and dreary as the mines of Potosi; yet from either there is no return–and tho' little confident of finding contentment–happiness is too proud a term–I must work, I believe, in those damp

With the Bramah's Pen.

If pens could feel like men, few men I ween
    Were glad as thou – poor pen of Bramah!
To think what must be and what might have been
    The tenor of their life's small drama.

How oft a pen all clear as thou has graced
    The choppy fist of Scotch compiler;
The lies of Faction or Chicane has traced
    With Lawyer pens or hired Reviler;

In rustic Manse in parson's ink has pin'd,
    Seen nought but sermons, punch, backgammon;
With dandy clerk or bloated cit confined,
    Like him been ever drudge to Mammon!

Now mark the fate I give thee Lucky steel,
    Prefer'd how far to all thy brothers!
The pressure of my Jane's soft hand to feel,
    Still hers to be and ne'er anothers.

No cold ignoble thought is thine to write,
    No word from crooked purpose flowing;
But dictates of a lofty spirit pure and bright
    For Good and Great with fervour glowing.

And thine it may be, if thy Mistress will,
    To mark some high and hallow'd pages,
Which stamped with genius, shrined on Fame's steep hill,
    Shall live with men thro' unborn ages

So fair a fate, thy fears and perils past
    Hast thou; if Jane her favour grant thee;
And happy I if holding thee, she cast
    One thought on him the Friend that sent thee.

A poem Carlyle sent to Jane Welsh on 9 August 1822 (Beinecke Rare Book and Manuscript Library, Yale University)

caverns—till once the whole mind is recast or the lamp of life has ceased to burn within it.

> —*The Collected Letters of Thomas and Jane Welsh Carlyle*, v. 1, p. 310–311

* * *

In January 1822, Carlyle became a private tutor to Charles and Arthur Buller, accompanying the Buller family in the spring of 1823 to their country retreat north of Edinburgh, where he lived in a small cottage near the main house. In this excerpt from his unpublished journal, dated May 1833, Carlyle describes his living conditions and work while he was with the Buller family.

Schiller *and* Meister

I lodged and slept in the *old* mansion, a queer, old-fashioned, snug enough, entirely secluded edifice, sunk among trees, about a gunshot from the new big House; hither I came to smoke about twice or thrice in the daytime; had a good oak-wood fire at night, and sat in a seclusion, in a silence not to be surpassed above ground. I was writing *Schiller,* translating *Meister;* my health, in spite of my diligent riding, grew worse and worse; thoughts all wrapt in gloom, in weak dispiritment and discontent, wandering mournfully to my loved ones far away; letters to and from, it may well be supposed, were my most genial solacement. At times, too, there was something of noble in my sorrows, in the great solitude among the rocking winds; but not often.

> —*Early Letters of Thomas Carlyle*, p. 275

* * *

These excerpts are from Carlyle's reply to Jane's letter of 24 March 1823. Throughout the year 1823, Carlyle wrote at times as a brother and at times as a suitor.

Carlyle to Jane Welsh, 26 March 1823

. . . It seems to me as if our destiny were yet long to be intermingled, as if we were yet to walk side by side thro' many bright scenes, to assist each other in many a noble purpose; and Oh! what a pitiful conclusion to all this would a vulgar wedding make! It is true they manage it otherwise in the common world: there the great object of a young woman's existence is to get a rich Husband, and a fine house, and give dinners; just as it is the great object of ravens to find carrion, or of pawn brokers to amass a *plum;* and the sooner they attain their

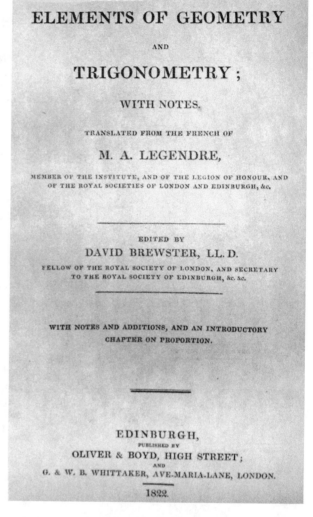

ELEMENTS OF GEOMETRY

AND

TRIGONOMETRY ;

WITH NOTES.

TRANSLATED FROM THE FRENCH OF

M. A. LEGENDRE,

MEMBER OF THE INSTITUTE, AND OF THE LEGION OF HONOUR, AND OF THE ROYAL SOCIETIES OF LONDON AND EDINBURGH, &c.

EDITED BY

DAVID BREWSTER, LL. D.

FELLOW OF THE ROYAL SOCIETY OF LONDON, AND SECRETARY TO THE ROYAL SOCIETY OF EDINBURGH, &c. &c.

WITH NOTES AND ADDITIONS, AND AN INTRODUCTORY CHAPTER ON PROPORTION.

EDINBURGH,

PUBLISHED BY

OLIVER & BOYD, HIGH STREET;

AND

G. & W. B. WHITTAKER, AVE-MARIA-LANE, LONDON.

1822.

Title page for Carlyle's first book, a translation of Adrien Legendre's 1794 text. Offered the job by Dr. David Brewster, Carlyle collaborated on the translation with his brother John and added an original essay on proportion (Special Collections, Thomas Cooper Library, University of South Carolina).

respective destinations it is surely the better. But if each creature ought to follow the good its nature aims at, then *you* are right to take another path—right to press forward towards the golden summit of mental eminence, and to shrink at no sacrifice which you believe that elevation will repay you for. The time *will* come indeed, when you must "fall in love" and be wedded as others have been; it is the general law, and must be fulfilled: but I fear not that I shall ever have the pain of seeing your happiness entrusted to one unworthy however desirous of the charge, or the high ambitions of your youth given up for anything less sacred than the feelings of the heart, if these unhappily should come to oppose them. I say *unhappily;* for the love of knowledge is a passion which, once in possession of the mind, can hardly ever be extinguished; it is noble in its nature too, and like other noble passions elevates itself into a kindred with all the virtues of the character: if stinted, and still more if checked, in its gratification, it leaves a painful hankering behind it, which is inconsistent with true peace of mind, and often, I imagine, with the free exercise of the moral faculties. In the mean time, therefore, you must just continue on your way. If I had my will you should not be married till—not till a considerable period after this. Literary women have many things to suffer, but they have likewise something to enjoy. I confess it appears to me more enviable to be a sister of Madame de Staël's for half a year, than "to suckle fools and chronicle small beer" for half a century.

....

I am also glad that you like my thrice illustrious Goethe, and can *not* understand him. What expounding and reading and chit-chatting we shall have together when you come! I beg only that you do not disappoint me again. At first I was rather disconcerted at this postponement: I had calculated on your arrival as a perfect certainty; nay it was only on Monday, that I got into the most wonderful flurry at what I conceived to be the actual sight of you! The small divine who was with me on Princes Street might as well have spoken to the winds, I could answer his prosing statements but by monosyllables which I daresay had no connection oftener than once with the "subject matter of his discourse": the lady before us seemed to have your very dress and form and gait, and I heard not what he said.—Alas! we overtook this beatific vision and she had a nose about the length of a moderate *dibble!* So abrupt is often the transition from the height of poetry to the depth of prose.

On second thoughts, however, I am satisfied. By the time you arrive, I shall have finished Schiller; I shall see more of you, and be more at leisure to see you. It will be absolutely cruel, if you do not come about the very beginning of the month. We could be so happy, I often think, wandering at large beneath these clear Spring skies, talking over all our plans and hopes, arguing or discussing—or doing nothing at all beside each other! You *must* come in less than a fortnight. You will write to me just once before that time, and the next message will be that "Miss Welsh condescends to allow the dyspeptical Philosopher to behold the light of her countenance tomorrow-morning about ten." Said Philosopher will be punctual to the hour, and promises to conduct himself with great submissiveness and propriety. If you have any heart—which I sometimes

do believe is the case, in spite of all your sinful indifference and manifold railleries—you will think of this and do it. I look forward to April as to a *white month.*

— *The Love Letters of Thomas Carlyle and Jane Welsh,*
v. 1, pp. 185–188

* * *

In this excerpt Carlyle refers to the first part of his work on Schiller. His reference to a "Love-and-cottage theory" is to a romanticized vision of married life in poverty. His allusion to his years of "incessant torture" is to his time spent teaching, tutoring, translating, reviewing, writing biography—doing everything other than the original writing he desired to commence.

Carlyle to Jane Welsh, 17 April 1823

It is but half an instant since I finished this wretched bundle of papers, at the sight of which you are turned so *pall:* "they will yet make you *paller*"— count on that. You must read them all over with the eye not of a friend, but of a *critic:* I must have your voice and decision and advice about twenty things before they go away. Besides I want to secure at least *three* readers—you, myself, and the Printer's devil: more I can do without. The thing is absolutely execrable: I have written as if I had been steeped in Lethe to the chin. "My soul is black as the middle of night Lady"—or rather gray and heavy as the middle of a Liddesdale mist. But never mind: tear the ugly thing to pieces, and give me your *severe and solid criticism* and counsel, when you arrive.

— *The Love Letters of Thomas Carlyle and Jane Welsh,*
v. 1, pp. 204–205

* * *

This excerpt was sent from Carlyle at Kinnard House—a mansion in the Tay Valley where he was serving as tutor to the Buller family—to Jane at the Welsh home at Templand.

Carlyle to Jane Welsh, 31 August 1823

. . . What a frank and true and noble spirit is my Jane's! No artifice, no vulgar management; her sentiments come warm and fearless from her heart, because they are pure and honest as herself, and the friend whom she trusts, she trusts without reserve. I often ask myself: "Is not all this a dream? Is it true that the most enchanting creature I have ever seen does actually love me? No! thank God it is not a dream: Jane loves me!

she loves me! and I swear by the Immortal Powers that she shall yet be mine, as I am hers, thro' life and death and all the dark vicissitudes that await us here or hereafter." In more reasonable moments, I perceive that I am very selfish and almost mad. Alas! my fate is dreary and obscure and perilous: is it fit that you, whom I honour as among the fairest of God's works, whom I love more dearly than my own soul, should partake in it? No, my own best of Maidens, I will not deceive you. Think of me as of one that will live and die to do you service; whose good will if his good deeds cannot, may perhaps deserve some gratitude; but whom it is dangerous and useless to love. If I were intellectual sovereign of all the world, if I were—But it is vain to speculate: I know that I am nothing, I know not that I shall not always be so. The only thing I know is that you are the most delightful, enthusiastic, contemptuous, affectionate, sarcastic, capricious, warm-hearted, lofty-minded, half-devil, half-angel of a woman that ever ruled over the heart of a man; that I will love you, must love you, whatever may betide, till the last moment of my existence; and that if we both act rightly our lot *may* be the happiest of a thousand mortal lots. So let us cling to one another (if you dare when thus forewarned)—forever and forever! Let us put faith in one another, and live in hope that prospects so glorious and heavenly will not end in darkness and despair. If your happiness be shipwrecked by my means, then woe, woe is to me without end! But it will not: no, you will yet be blessed yourself in making me more blessed than man has right to look for being upon earth. God bless you my heart's darling; and grant that our honest purposes may prosper in our hands!

All these incoherent inconsistent things you have often heard already: but you bear with me in uttering them yet again. For me no subject connected with our correspondence and affection for each other needs the charm of novelty to make it interesting. If it were repeated to me fifty times a day that you loved me, I should still desire to hear it oftener. For the present, however, I must let you go.

—The Love Letters of Thomas Carlyle
and Jane Welsh, v. 1,
pp. 269–271

* * *

Jane sent this response to Carlyle's 31 August letter from Haddington. In the last paragraph, Jane refers to Johann Karl August Musäus's Volksmärchen der Deutschen, *which Carlyle had sent to her in July to translate. Carlyle himself eventually translated three stories by Musäus and included them in* German Romance *(1827).*

Jane Welsh to Carlyle, 16 September 1823

My Dear Friend,—Your Letter only reached me this morning,—I having sojourned at Templand more than ten days, "expecting an opportunity." Charming as it is, I could almost wish it had not cast up at all, for it has troubled me more than I can tell. I feel there is need I should answer it without delay. And what can I say to you? It is so hard to explain oneself in such a situation! But I must, and in plain terms; for any reserve at present were criminal and might be very fatal in its consequences to [us] both.

You misunderstand me. You regard me no longer as a Friend, a Sister, but as one who at some future period may be more to you than both. Is it not so? Is it not true that you believe me, like the bulk of my silly sex, incapable of entertaining a strong affection for a man of my own age without having for its ultimate object our union for life? "Useless and dangerous to love you"! "My happiness wrecked by you"! I cannot have misinterpreted your meaning! And, my God! what have I said or done to mislead you into an error so destructive to the confidence that subsists betwixt us, so dangerous to the peace of both? In my treatment of you, I have indeed disregarded all maxims of womanly prudence; have shaken myself free from the shackles of etiquette; I have loved and admired you for your noble qualities, and for the extraordinary affection you have shown me; and I have told you so without reserve or disguise; but not till our repeated quarrels had produced an explanation betwixt us, which I foolishly believed would guarantee my future conduct from all possibility of misconstruction. I have been to blame. I might have foreseen that such implicit confidence might mislead you as to the nature of my sentiments, and should have expressed my friendship for you with a more prudent reserve. But it is of no use talking of what I might or should have done in the time past. I have only to repair the mischief in as far as I can, now that my eyes are opened to it, now that I am startled to find our relation actually assuming the aspect of an engagement for life.

My Friend, I love you. I repeat it, tho' I find the expression a rash one. All the best feelings of my nature are concerned in loving you. But were you my Brother I would love you the same; were I married to another I would love you the same. And is this sentiment so calm, so delightful, but so unimpassioned, enough to recompense the freedom of my heart, enough to reconcile me to the existence of a married woman, the hopes and wishes and ambitions of which are all so different from mine, the cares and occupations of which are my disgust! Oh no! Your Friend I will be, your truest most devoted Friend, while I breathe the breath of life; but your Wife! Never, never! not though you were as rich as Crœsus, as honoured and as renowned as you yet shall be.

indeed disregarded all maxims of womanly prudence,
have shaken myself free from the shackles of etiquette—
I have loved and admired you for your noble qualities,
and for the extraordinary affection you have shewn me,
and I have told you so without reserve or disguise—
but not till our repeated quarrels had produced an
explanation betwixt us, which I foolishly believed would
guarantee my future conduct from all possibility
of misconstruction — I have been to blame — I might
have foreseen that such implicit confidence might
mislead you
as to the nature of my sentiments, and should have
expressed my friendship for you with a more prudent
reserve — but it is of no use talking ▬▬ of what I
might or should have done in the time past — I have
only to repair the mischief in as far as I can, now
that my eyes are opened to it   now that I am startled
to find our relation actually assuming the aspect of
our engagement for life.

My friend I love you — I repeat it tho' I find the
expression a rash one — all the best feelings of my
nature are concerned in loving you — But were you my
Brother I would love you the same, were I married
to another I would love you the same. — and is this
sentiment so calm, so delightful — but so unimpassioned

*The second page of Jane Welsh's 16 September 1823 letter to Carlyle in which she explains her regard for him as a friend, not a suitor
(The Trustees of the National Library of Scotland, MS 529)*

You may think I am viewing the matter by much too seriously; taking fright when there is nothing to fear. It is well if it be so! But suffering as I am at this very moment from the horrid pain of seeing a true and affectionate heart near breaking for my sake, it is not to be wondered at tho' I be overanxious for your peace on which my own depends in a still greater degree. Write to me and reassure me, for God's sake if you can! Your friendship at this time is almost necessary to my existence. Yet I will resign it cost what it may,—will, will resign it, if it can only be enjoyed at the risk of your future peace.

I had many things to say to you,—about *Musäus* and all that; but I must wait till another opportunity. At present I scarcely know what I am about.

Ever affectionately yours,
Jane B. Welsh.
—*The Love Letters of Thomas Carlyle
and Jane Welsh*, v. 1,
pp. 275–277

* * *

Of his three younger brothers, Alexander ("Alick"), John Aitken ("Jack"), and James, Carlyle was closest to Jack, to whom he reports on his progress on Wilhelm Meister's Apprenticeship *in this excerpt.*

Carlyle to John A. Carlyle, 17 September 1823

Meanwhile I make a point of going on with Goethe. Ten pages I find more than I can almost ever execute; for it is very hard; and I scarcely ever get fairly into the spirit of it till I must leave it off. If I take tea at night I am lively for three or four hours; but I sleep none, and next day I could *eat the wind*. If I take porridge which I almost always do, the chances are that I shall succeed in sleeping, "to a certain extent"; but it gives me headache, and makes [me] stupid as a fatted pig. Besides it is six o'clock at night before ever I get begun. So that I seldom exceed seven or eight pages. One day, when left altogether to myself, I scarcely exceeded eighteen. *Nevertheless* I *gar mysel* [make myself: underscored twice] (as our Father would do) go on with this thing: and accordingly my keep-lesson *is* travelling slowly but surely thro' poetry and prose to the end of the volume. I am now more than half thro' the first: it will all be ready long ere spring. *You and I* could do it in four weeks, if we had quiet quarters, and the fiend would give me any respite.

—*The Collected Letters of Thomas
and Jane Welsh Carlyle*,
v. 2, p. 430

* * *

These excerpts show Carlyle concerned with both love and literature.

Carlyle to Jane Welsh, 18 September 1823

My dear Jane,—If I were not a fool of some standing, I should not have vexed you on this occasion, or given you this fresh opportunity of testifying how true is the affection which you bear me. Your letter has set me a-thinking about matters which, with my accustomed heedlessness, I was letting take their course without accurate investigation, tho' conscious that a right understanding of them was of vital consequence to both of us. I honour your wisdom and decision: you have put our concerns *on the very footing where I wished them to stand.* So be of good cheer, for no harm is done.

When I placed the management of our intercourse and whatever mutual interests we had or might have, entirely at your own disposal, making you sole queen and arbitress of the "commonweal," I stipulated for myself as much freedom of speech as you could conveniently grant, leaving to you an unbounded power of acting, then and in all time coming. It is to the terms of this *compact* that I still adhere in their widest acceptation. I know very well you will never be my wife. Never! Never!—I never believed it above five minutes at a time all my days. "'T is all one as I should love a bright particular star, and think to wed it." My fancy can form scenes, indeed, which with you to share them were worthy of a place in the heaven above; but there are items wanting, without which all these blessings were a curse, and which not your consent (if that were ever to be dreamed of) nor any influence of man can assure me of realizing. Such illusions do in truth haunt me, nor am I very sedulous to banish them. The harsh hand of Time will do it speedily enough without help of mine, and leave no truth behind that will ever give me half the pleasure. I grant it is absurd, and might be more than absurd, to utter them so freely: but what then? They give a momentary pleasure to myself, and do harm to no one. Strip life of all its baseless hopes and beautiful chimeras; it seems to me there would be little left worth having.

Thus then it stands: You love me as a sister, and will not wed: I love you in all possible senses of the word, and will not wed, any more than you. Does this reassure you? If so, let us return to our old position: let me continue writing what comes into my head, and do you continue acting now or forever after just as you judge best. I seek no engagement, I will make none. By God's blessing, I will love you with all my heart and all my soul, while the blood continues warm within me; I will reverence you as the fairest living emblem of all that is most exalted and engaging in my conceptions of human nature; I will help you according to my slender power, and stand by you closer than a

1823.]   *Schiller's Life and Writings.*   381

SCHILLER'S LIFE AND WRITINGS.

PART I.

HIS YOUTH (1759—1784).

AMONG the writers of the concluding part of the last century, there is none more deserving of our notice than Friedrich Schiller. Distinguished alike for the splendour of his intellectual faculties, and the elevation of his tastes and feelings, he has left behind him in his works a noble emblem of these great qualities: and the reputation which he thus enjoys, and has merited, excites our attention the more on considering the circumstances under which it was acquired. Schiller had peculiar difficulties to strive with, and his success has likewise been peculiar. Much of his life was deformed by inquietude and disease, and it terminated at middle age; he composed in a language then scarcely settled into form, or admitted to a rank among the cultivated languages of Europe: yet his writings are remarkable for their extent and variety as well as their intrinsic excellence; and his own countrymen are not his only, or, perhaps, his principal admirers. It is difficult to collect or interpret the general voice; but the world, no less than Germany, seems already to have dignified him with the reputation of a classic,—to have enrolled him among that select number whose works belong not wholly to any age or nation, but who, having instructed their own contemporaries, are claimed as instructors by the great family of mankind, and set apart for many centuries from the common oblivion which soon overtakes the mass of authors, as it does the mass of other men.

Such has been the high destiny of Schiller. His history and character deserve our study for more than one reason. A natural and harmless feeling attracts us towards such a subject; we are anxious to know how so great a man passed through the world, how he lived, and moved, and had his being; and the question, if properly investigated, might yield advantage as well as pleasure. It would be interesting to discover by what gifts and what employment of

Oct. 1823.

them he reached the eminence on which we now see him; to follow the steps of his intellectual and moral culture; to gather from his life and works some picture of himself. It is worth inquiring, whether he, who could represent noble actions so well, did himself act nobly; how those powers of intellect, which in philosophy and art achieved so much, applied themselves to the every-day emergencies of life; how the generous ardour, which delights us in his poetry, displayed itself in the common intercourse between man and man. It would at once instruct and gratify us if we could understand him thoroughly, could transport ourselves into his circumstances outward and inward, could see as he saw, and feel as he felt.

But if the various utility of such a task is palpable enough, its difficulties are not less so. We should not lightly think of comprehending the very simplest character, in all its bearings; and it might argue vanity to boast of even a common acquaintance with one like Schiller's. Such men as he are misunderstood by their daily companions; much more by the distant observer, who gleans his information from scanty records, and casual notices of characteristic events, which biographers are often too indolent or injudicious to collect, and which the peaceful life of a man of letters usually supplies in little abundance. The published details of Schiller's history are meagre and insufficient; and his writings, like those of every author, can afford but a dubious copy of his mind. Nor is it easy to decipher even this, with moderate accuracy. The haze of a foreign language, of foreign manners, and modes of thinking, strange to us, confuses and obscures the light, often magnifying what is trivial, softening what is rude, and sometimes hiding or distorting what is beautiful. To take the dimensions of Schiller's mind were a hard enterprize, in any case; harder still with these impediments.

Accordingly we do not, in this

2 C

The initial page of the first installment for the serialization in The London Magazine *of Carlyle's biography later published as* The Life of Friedrich Schiller *(Thomas Cooper Library, University of South Carolina)*

brother: but these feelings are entertained for myself alone; let them be their own reward, or go unrewarded–that is *my* concern. So long as you have charity to hear me talk about affections that must end in nothingness, and plans which seem destined to be all abortive, I will speak and listen; when you tire of this, when you marry, or cast me off in any of the thousand ways that fortune is ever offering, I shall of course cease to correspond with you, I shall cease to love Mrs. –, but not Jane Welsh; the image she will have left in my mind I shall always love, for even this tho' the original is gone forever, will still have more reality than mere fantasies that would replace it.

. . . .

Meanwhile I go on with Goethe's *Wilhelm Meister;* a book which I love not, which I am sure will never sell, but which I am determined to print and finish. There are touches of the very highest and most ethereal genius in it; but diluted with floods of insipidity, which even *I* would not have written for the world. I sit down to it every night at six, with the ferocity of a hyæna; and in spite of all obstructions my keep-lesson is more than half thro' the first volume, and travelling over poetry and prose, slowly but surely to the end. Some of the poetry is very bad, some of it rather good.

–*The Love Letters of Thomas Carlyle and*
Jane Welsh, v. 1, pp. 277–279, 281

* * *

In this excerpt Jane responds to Carlyle's letter of 18 September.

Jane Welsh to Carlyle, 3 October 1823

. . . Oh I do love you my own Brother! I even wish that Fate had designed me for your Wife; for I feel that such a destiny would have been happier than mine is like to be–But Fate is every whit as capricious as Fortune; if it is not the selfsame Deity, and rarely unites those whom nature meant to be united–And so you will cease to correspond with me when I marry! and you think I will ever marry at such a cost? Where is the Lover on the face of this earth that could console me for the loss of my Friend? We *shall not* cease to correspond! never never as far as it depends on me–If "M*rs* –" is to be estranged from your affections I am Jane Welsh for life–

–*The Collected Letters of Thomas*
and Jane Welsh Carlyle, v. 2,
pp. 442–443

* * *

Carlyle's 1823 sketch for the design of a seal that he used for his correspondence. The Latin phrase "Terar dum prosim" means "Let me be burnt away (or wasted), so that I be of use." Beside the sketch Carlyle wrote in Latin, "What if I do not make myself useful? Why then, I will waste away still, so that I cannot help it!" (from The Story of a Flitting, a Hundred Years Ago, *Special Collections, Thomas Cooper Library, University of South Carolina*).

Carlyle's intense anxiety to achieve something useful as an author may have contributed to the chronic intestinal upset from which he suffered throughout his life.

Notebook, 31 December 1823

The year is closing; this time eight and twenty years I was a child of three weeks old lying sleeping in my mother's bosom.

Oh little did my mither think
   That day she cradled me,
The lands that I should travel in
   The death I was to die.

Another hour and 1823 is with the years beyond the flood. What have I done to mark the course of it? Suffered the pangs of Tophet almost daily, grown sicker and sicker, alienated by my misery certain of my friends, and worn out from my own mind a few remaining capabilities of enjoyment, reduced my world a *little* nearer the condition of a bare haggard desart, where peace and rest for me is none. Hopeful youth Mr. C.! Another year or two and it will do; another year or two and thou

Nasty Gingerbread or Eye Strain?

Carlyle had recurrent bouts of ill heath—dyspepsia, consti-pation, sleeplessness, depression—which plagued him from his early twenties into his sixties. His problems may well have been psychosomatic, brought on by a growing spiritual crisis and tension. No definitive physical cause for his malady can be certainly credited, despite the assertion in the British Medical Journal *by Sir Richard Quain, Carlyle's physician during his last years, that his patient's dyspepsia "was fully accounted for by the fact that he was particularly fond of a very nasty gingerbread." In the following assessment, George M. Gould proposes that Carlyle over taxed himself with reading and research when he was in the throes of a project.*

On the whole it is clear both from the profound reality of suffering and from the impossibility of localizing it in any organ, that there was never any organic disease whatever. "Gastrodynia" there was, if one has any satisfaction in such tautologic and meaningless words, and many other *dynias,* and *dys's,* but not "gastric ulcer" or any other morbid tissue changes or lesions. Such pathologic conditions do not disappear suddenly at 60 years of age, and leave one free for 25 more. The mystery of his affliction had struck the attention of Carlyle (as under similar circumstances it had done with De Quincey), and he said, "What the cause is would puzzle me to explain." Looking at the symptomatology more closely we find that the daily rhythm of the rise depends exactly upon the amount of reading and writing, and of the fall upon the amount of disuse of the eyes. Then there is the enormously heightened intensities clustering about the execution of the more important works. After each, except at Craigenput-tock, there is a terrible revulsion. After the comple-tion of Meister at 29, things were so bad as to warrant the sadly ludicrous Badams incident. Wide and miscellaneous reading brings a great increase of the bitter complaints at the age of 31.

–George M. Gould, *Biographic Clinics,*
v. 1, p. 68

wilt *wholly* be the *caput mortuum* of thy former self, a creature ignorant, stupid, peevish, disappointed, broken-hearted; the veriest wretch upon the surface of the globe. My curse seems deeper and blacker than that of any man: to be immured in a rotten car-cass, every avenue of which is changed into an inlet of pain; till my intellect is obscured and weakened, and my head and heart are alike desolate and dark. How have I deserved this? Or is it merely a dead inexorable Fate that orders these things, caring no jot for merit or demerit, crushing our poor mortal interests among its ponderous machinery, and grinding us and them to dust relentlessly? I know not; shall I ever know? "Then why don't you kill yourself Sir? Is there not arsenic? Is there not rats-bane of various kinds, and hemp and steel?" Most true, Sathanas, all these things *are:* but it will be time enough to use them when I have *lost* the game, which I am as yet but losing. You observe Sir I have still a glimmering of hope; and while my friends (my *friends,* my Mother, Father, brothers and sisters) live, the duty of *not* breaking their hearts would still remain to be performed when hope had utterly fled. For which reasons, even if there were no other (which however I believe there are), the benevolent Sathanas will excuse me. I do not design to be a *sui-cide:* God in Heaven forbid! That way I was never tempted.

But where is the use of going on with this? I am not writing like a reasonable man: if I am miser-able, the more reason there is to gather my faculties together, and see what can be done to help myself. I want health, health, health. On this subject I am becoming quite furious: my torments are greater than I am able to bear. If I do not soon recover I am miserable for ever and ever. They talk of the benefit of ill-health in a moral point of view. I declare sol-emnly without exaggeration that I impute nine tenths of my present wretchedness, and rather more than nine tenths of all my faults to this infernal dis-order in the stomach. If it were once away I think I could snap my fingers in the face of all the world. The *only* good of it is the *friends* it tries for us and endears to us! Oh! there is a charm in the true affec-tion that suffering cannot weary, that abides by us in the day of fretfulness and dark calamity—a charm which almost makes amends for misery. Love to my friends—Alas! I may almost say relations!—is now almost the sole religion of my mind.

In a month we quit this place; they with a view to amusement, I in the hope of getting *Meister* printed. I have better hopes of *Meister* than I had; tho' still they are very faint. *Schiller* P. III. I began just three nights ago. I absolutely could not sooner. These drugs leave me scarcely the consciousness of existence. They take away all ambition, all wish for

They chide thee, fair and fervid one!
     At glory's goal for aiming:
Does not Love's bird, its flight begun,
Soar up against the beaming sun,
     Undazed, in splendour flaming?

Young brilliant creature, even so
     A lofty instinct draws thee:
Heaven's fires within thy bosom glow,
Could Earth's vain fading vulgar shew
     One hour's contentment cause thee?

The gay saloon thine were to tread,
     Its stateliest scenes adorning;
Thine be by nobler wishes led,
With bays to crown thy lofty head
     All meaner homage scorning.

Bright maid! thy generous destiny I read,
     Unutter'd thoughts come o'er me;
Enroll'd 'mong Earth's elected few,
Lovely as morning, pure as dew,
     Thy image stands before me.

O! that on fame's far-shining peak,
     With great and mighty number'd,
Unfading laurels I could seek;
This longing spirit then might speak
     The thoughts within that slumber'd.

A poem Carlyle wrote and sent to Jane in December 1823 (Beinecke Rare Book and Manuscript Library, Yale University)

O! in the battle's wildest swell
   By hero's deeds to win thee!
To meet the charge, the stormy yell,
Th' artill'ry's flash, its thund'ring knell
   And thine the light within me!

What man, in Fate's dark day of pow'r,
   While thoughts of thee upbore him,
Would shrink at danger's blackest lour,
Or faint in life's last ebbing hour,
   If tears of thine fell o'er him?

But oh! if war's grim sweeping blast
   In vict'ry's radiance ended,
What Heav'n to find my — at last,
Within my arms to fold her fast,
   Our souls forever blended!

Two Books

In 1824 Carlyle negotiated the publication of Wilhelm Meister's Apprenticeship *by Oliver & Boyd and* The Life of Friedrich Schiller *by Taylor & Hessey. He wrote to Oliver & Boyd on 10 March 1824.*

Gentlemen,

I beg leave to offer you the Publishing of my Translation of Goethe's *Wilhelm Meister* (which you are now engaged in Printing) on the following terms–

1*st* That this first Edition of 1000 Copies shall be entirely yours, in return for the sum of £180 to be paid me on the day of Publication, by your Bill at three months after date–

2*d* That I shall not have liberty to print a second Edition till the first is altogether sold–Nor till I have made you the offer specified in the next article, and which you are entitled to demand of me at any time–

3*d* That for the second Edition, I shall consider myself bound to offer it to you, at the rate of £250 per 1000 Copies; the number to be fixed by you, and the money to be paid as in the present instance–

4*th* That after this, the Copy-right of the work shall be mine–

If you agree to these terms be so good as tell me so in writing, & the bargain will be settled–

Wilhelm Meister's Apprenticeship *was published in May 1824, while "Schiller's Life and Writings" was appearing in installments in* The London Magazine *(October 1823–September 1824). Carlyle wrote to Taylor & Hessey on 6 August 1824.*

Gentlemen

Being desirious of publishing, in a separate form with various alterations and enlargements, the Essay on Schiller's Life and Writings; several parts of which have already appeared in your Magazine, I beg leave to offer it to you on the following terms

1*st* It being understood that as matters actually stand I am entitled to a remuneration at the rate of 7½ guineas per sheet for the Article as it now appears or is to appear in the London Magazine, you shall for an additional Sum of £50 have liberty to print 1000 copies of the new and enlarged work, as a separate book

2*d* The extent of my enlargements shall be such as would make the book occupy at least Six Sheets of the Magazine

3*d* The fifty Pounds above mentioned, together with the preceding remuneration at the rate of 7½ guineas per sheet shall be paid me on the day of publication

4*th* That I shall have 25 Author's Copies

5*th* That after the sale of this first edition, the Copy right of the Work shall be mine

Should these terms meet with your acceptance be so good as [to] tell me so in writing and the bargain will be concluded. I remain Gentlemen. Your obedient Serv*t*

–The Collected Letters of Thomas
and Jane Welsh Carlyle,
v. 3, pp. 45, 119–120

Taylor and Hessey published the biographical work in book form as The Life of Friedrich Schiller *on 15 March 1825.*

---

aught beyond deep sleep if that might by any means be made to fall upon me. I am scribbling not writing Schiller: my mind *will* not catch hold of it; I skim it, do as I will, and I am anxious as possible to get it off my hands. It will *not* do for publishing separately: it is not in my natural vein. I wrote a very little of it tonight, and then went and talked ineptitudes at the house. Also there is mercurial powder in me, and a gnawing pain over all the organs of digestion–especially in the pit and left side of the stomach. Let this excuse the wild absurdity above.

Half past eleven! The silly Denovan is coming down (at least so I interpreted his threat) with punch or wishes; which curtails the few reflections this mercury might still leave it in my power to make. To make none at all will perhaps be as well. It exhibits not an interesting but a true picture of my present mood–stupid, unhappy, by fits wretched, but also dull, dull and very weak.

Now fare thee well old twenty-three!
No power, no art can thee retain

–Two Note Books of Thomas Carlyle, 55–59

* * *

In this excerpt Carlyle responds to Jane's lack of enthusiasm for Goethe's work.

Carlyle to Jane Welsh, 15 April 1824

So you laugh at my venerated Goethe and my *Herzenskind* [heart's child] poor little wood-eating Mignon! O! The hardness of man's and still more of woman's heart! If you were not lost to all true feeling, now, your eyes would be as a fountain of tears in the perusing of *Meister*. Have you really no pity for the Hero, or the Count, or the Frau Melina, or Philine, or the Manager? Well! it cannot be helped. I must not quarrel with you, do what you like; but taken on the whole, a more provoking young woman is not to be met with, I am sure, between Cape Wrath and Kirk-Maiden. Will you not cry in the least? Not a jot! Not a jot!–Seriously you are right about this book, it is worth next to nothing as a novel; except *Mignon* who *will* touch you yet perhaps, there is no person in it one has any care about. But for its wisdom, its eloquence, its wit; and even for its folly, and its dullness, it interests me much; far more the second time than it did the first. I have not got as many ideas from any book for six years. You will like Goethe better ten years hence than you do at present. It is pity the man were not known among us. The English have begun to speak about him of late years; but no light has yet been thrown upon him, "no light but only darkness visible." The syllables *Goethe* excite an idea as vague and monstrous as the word *Gorgon* or *Chimaera.*–It would do you good to see with what regularity I progress in translating. Clockwork is scarcely steadier. Nothing do I allow to interfere with me; my movements might be almost calculated like the moon's. It is not unpleasant work, nor is it pleasant. Original composition is ten times as laborious. It is an agitating, fiery, consuming business when your heart is in it: I can easily conceive a man writing the soul out of him; writing till it evaporate "like the snuff of a farthing candle," when the matter interests him properly. I always recoil from again engaging with it. But this present business is cool and quiet; one feels over it, as a shoemaker does when he sees the leather gathering into a shoe; as any mortal does when he sees the activity of his mind expressing itself in some external material shape. You are facetious [about] my mine of gold: it has often struck me as the most accursed item in men's lot that they had to toil for filthy lucre; but I am not sure now that it is not the *ill-best* way it could have been arranged. Me it would make happy, at least for half a year, if I saw the certain prospect before me of making £500 per annum: a pampered Lord (e.g. Byron) would turn with loathing from a pyramid of ingots. I *may* be blessed in this way: he never. Let us be content! When I get that weary *Cottage* erected, and all things put in order, who knows but it may be well with me, after all? Will *you* go? Will you? "Not a hairs breadth!" Well, it is very cruel of you.

–*The Collected Letters of Thomas and Jane Welsh Carlyle*, v. 3, pp. 59–60

Johann Wolfgang von Goethe, in whose writing Carlyle believed he found "true wisdom" (from Froude's Life of Carlyle, *Thomas Cooper Library, University of South Carolina)*

Wilhelm Meister's Apprenticeship

Carlyle sent a copy of his translation of Goethe's bildungsroman to the author after its publication in May. He inscribed the work: "To Goethe / With the most respectful Compliments of his Admirer & devoted Servant, / – The Translator–."

Carlyle to Johann Wolfgang von Goethe, 24 June 1824

Permit me, Sir, in soliciting your acceptance of this Translation to return you my sincere thanks for the profit which, in common with many millions, I have derived from the Original.

That you will honour this imperfect copy of your work with a perusal I do not hope: but the thought that some portion of my existence has been connected with that of the Man whose intellect and mind I most admire, is pleasing to my imagination; nor will I neglect the present opportunity of communing with you even in this slight and transitory manner. Four years ago, when I read your *Faust* among the mountains of my native Scotland, I could not but fancy I might one day see you, and pour out before you, as before a Father, the woes and wanderings of a heart whose mysteries you seemed so thoroughly to comprehend, and could so beautifully represent. The hope of meeting you is still among my dreams. Many saints have been expunged from my literary Calendar since I first knew you; but your name still stands there, in characters more bright than ever. That your life may be long, long spared, for the solace and instruction of this and future generations, is the earnest prayer of, Sir, your most devoted servant,

Thomas Carlyle.

P.S.—As the conveyance is uncertain, a line signifying that you have received this packet would be peculiarly acceptable.

—*Correspondence between Goethe and Carlyle,* 1–2

* * *

Wilhelm Meister's Apprenticeship *received mainly positive reviews. This excerpt is from the "Literary Notices" section of* The Examiner.

"A Great Favour"
Review of *Wilhelm Meister's Apprenticeship*

The translator of this extraordinary work, who evidently possesses in a high degree the leading requisites for his very difficult task, has conferred a great favour on the more intellectual English reader, by his able version of a production so impregnated with spirit and originality as the *Meister of Goethe*. Altogether of his opinion, that German mind is not sufficiently known to us, we rejoice at the prospect of similar obligations to the present, from the same pen, especially as there is reason to hope that the indifference complained of is beginning to subside. A few more labourers in the vineyard of German literature, as competent as himself, would entirely dispel it; and we are perfectly satisfied that *Meister,* in his English dress, will effectively lead the way. Not that we expect this book will attract the great mob of novel-readers,—few creations of superlative genius do;—but the stamp of a profound and vigorous mind is so deeply impressed on its pages, the flashes of an intelligence as vivid and excursive as the lightning it resembles, so abound, it is impossible, in the present day, that it can fail of correspondent effect. The translator is less sanguine in this respect, and ingenuously enumerates various impediments to popularity. We think, however, that he over-rates them, especially when he adverts to the absence of a romance interest and of generally amusing adventure. So far from deeming *Meister* barren in these attractions, we expressly trust to them for a due reception of certain remote and therefore we fear occasionally obscure perceptions, and of the elevated ratiocination, which, by themselves, would scarcely gain attention.

—*The Examiner,* no. 858 (11 July 1824): 451

* * *

The most negative review of Carlyle's translation was written by Thomas De Quincey (1785–1859) and appeared in The London Magazine, *the literary magazine where De Quincey's* Confessions of an English Opium-Eater *had first been published in 1821. In his long review article De Quincey first attacked the work of Goethe—maintaining it presented "a case not merely of infatuation, but of infatuation degrading to literature, beyond anything which is on record in the history of human levity"—and then turned to Carlyle's translation.*

"Coarseness of Diction"
Goethe's *Wilhelm Meister's Apprenticeship*
Thomas De Quincey

. . . And first, before we speak of the book itself (which is our thesis), a word or two on the Translation. . . . [I]t is necessary to declare our opinion very frankly that this translation does not do justice to the original work—which, however worthless in other respects, is not objectionable in the way in which the translation is so. For the "style" of Goethe, in the true meaning of that word, we profess no respect: but, according to the common use of the expression as implying no more than a proper choice of words, and a proper arrangement of them (pure diction in a collocation agreeable to the idiom in the language), we know of nothing to object to it. Living in a court, and familiar with most of his distinguished contemporaries in Germany since the French revolution, Goethe of necessity speaks and therefore writes his own language as it is commonly written and spoken in the best circles, by which circles we mean, in a question of this nature, the upper circles. He is no great master, nor was ever reputed a master, of the idiomatic wealth of his own language; but he does not offend by provincialisms, vulgarisms, or barbarisms of any sort: with all which the translation is overrun.

First, for *provincialisms:*—these are in this case chiefly perhaps altogether, *Scotticisms.* . . . For instance the Scotticism of "open *up*" is perfectly insufferable. We have lived a little, for these last ten years, in the Scotch capital; and *there* at least we never heard of such an expression in any well-bred society. Yet in the work before us hardly a page but is infested with this strange phrase, which many a Scotch gentleman will stare at as much as the English of every class. No man in these volumes opens a book; he opens it *"up:"* no man open a door; he opens it "up": no man opens a letter; he opens it "up." . . . However, Scotch provincialisms, though grievous blots in regular composition, are too little familiar to have the effect of vulgarisms upon southern ears: they are in general simply uncouth or unintelligible . . . . From these however, which are but semi-vulgarisms to an English ear, because but doubtfully intelligible,—we pass to such as are downright, full, and absolute vulgarisms. . . . [T]he most shocking is the word *thrash* as used in the following

WILHELM MEISTER'S

APPRENTICESHIP.

A NOVEL.

FROM THE GERMAN OF

GOETHE.

IN THREE VOLUMES.

VOL. I.

EDINBURGH;
PUBLISHED BY
OLIVER & BOYD, TWEEDDALE-COURT;
AND
G. & W. B. WHITTAKER, LONDON.

1824.

Title page for Carlyle's first book (Special Collections, Thomas Cooper Library, University of South Carolina)

passage, vol. Ii. P. 111. "His father was convinced that the minds of children could be kept awake and stedfast by no other means than blows: hence, in the studying of any part, he used to *thrash* him at stated periods." In whatever way men will allow themselves to talk amongst men, where intimate acquaintance relaxes the restraints of decorum, every gentleman abjures any coarse language which he may have learned at school or elsewhere under two circumstances—in the presence of strangers—and in the presence of women; or whenever, in short, he is recalled to any scrupulous anxiety about his own honour and reputation for gentlemanly feeling. Now an author, with some special

exceptions, is to be presumed always in the presence of both; and ought to allow himself no expressions but such as he would judge consistent with his own self-respect in a miscellaneous company of good breeding and of both sexes. This granted, we put it to the translator's candour—whether the word "thrash" (except in its literal and grave meaning) be endurable in "dress" composition? For our own parts, we never heard a gentleman of polished habits utter the word—except under the circumstances pointed out above, where people allow themselves a sort of "undress" manners. Besides, the word is not even used accurately: "to thrash" is never applied to the act of beating without provocation, but to a retaliatory beating: and the brutal father, who should adopt the treatment of an unoffending child which Goethe here describes, would not call a beating inflicted under the devilish maximum supposed, "a thrashing." These instances are sufficient to illustrate the coarseness of diction which disfigures the English translation, and which must have arisen from want of sufficient intercourse with society. One winter's residence in the metropolis either of England or Scotland,—or the revisal of a judicious friend, would enable the translator to weed his book of these deformities, which must be peculiarly offensive in two quarters which naturally he must wish to conciliate; first to his readers, secondly to Mr. Goethe—who, besides that he is Mr. *Von* Goethe and naturally therefore anxious to appear before foreigners in a dress suitable to his pretensions as a man of quality, happens to be unusually jealous on this point; and would be more shocked, than perhaps a "philosopher" ought to be, if he were told that his Wilhelm Meister spoke an English any ways underbred or below the tone of what is technically understood in English by the phrase "good company" or company *"comme il faut."* . . . [W]e shall pass on to complain of his archaisms or revivals of obsolete English phrases, which however may also be provincialisms; many old English expressions still being current in the remote provinces, which have long been dismissed from our literature. Be that as it may, these are the peculiarities which are at least licentious; for the phrases are in themselves often beautiful. . . . Again, the word *want* used in the antique sense exposes the writer to be thoroughly misunderstood. "I cannot want them," said Charles I, speaking of some alleged prerogatives of his crown; and his meaning was he could not do without them, that they were indispensable to him. But in modern English he, who says "I cannot want them," gives his hearer to understand that no possible occasion can arise to make them of any use to him. This archaic use of the word "want" survives however, we believe, as the current use in some parts of Scotland.

—The London Magazine, 10 (August 1824): 192–195

* * *

Carlyle remarked on De Quincey's review in this excerpt from a letter to his brother.

Carlyle to John A. Carlyle, 22 January 1825

. . . There was a luckless wight of an *opium-eater* [underscored twice] here, one Dequincey, for instance, who wrote a very vulgar and brutish Review of "Meister" in the *London Magazine:* I read three pages of it one *sick* day at Birmingham; and said: "Here is a man who writes of things which he does not rightly understand; I see clean over the top of *him,* and his vulgar spite, and his common-place philosophy; and I will away and have a ride on (Badams') Taffy, and leave *him* to cry in the ears of the simple." So I went out, and had my ride accordingly; and if Dequincey, poor little fellow, *made* any thing by his review, he can put it in his waistcoat pocket, and thank the god Mercurius. A *counter-*criticism of *Meister* (or something like one) is to appear in the February number. I believe: to this also I hope I shall present the same tolerant spirit. The "reviews" of that book *Meister* must not go without their effect on me: I know it and believe it and feel it to be a book containing traces of a higher, far higher, spirit, altogether more *genius* than any book published in my day: and yet to see the Cockney animalcules rendering an account of it! praising it, or blaming it! sitting in judgement on Goethe with the light tolerance of a country Justice towards a suspected Poacher! As the child says: "It was *grend!*"

–Early Letters of Thomas Carlyle, v. 1, pp. 323–324

"No Ordinary Master"

Two years before he met Carlyle, Francis Jeffrey, the editor of The Edinburgh Review, *one of the most influential literary journals in Britain, commended his translation of Goethe's novel. He professed no enthusiasm for the novel itself, which he found,"after the most deliberate consideration, to be eminently absurd, puerile, incongruous, vulgar, and affected."*

. . . We have perused it, indeed, only in the translation of which we have prefixed the title: But it is a translation by a professed admirer, and by one who is proved by his Preface to be a person of talents, and by every part of the work to be no ordinary master, at least of one of the languages with which he has to deal.

–The Edinburgh Review,
42 (August 1825):
409–449

Courtship and Marriage

By summer 1824, Carlyle and Jane Welsh had reached a tacit understanding about their mutual affection, but the pretense of a platonic friendship continued, if only to placate Jane's mother. This excerpted letter–sent from London where Carlyle had moved to see his biography of Schiller through the press at Taylor and Hessey–indicates that their relationship was taking a serious turn. The Nithsdale Farm that Carlyle refers to is better known as Craigenputtoch, a 1,200-acre farm, which had been willed to Jane by her father.

Carlyle to Jane Welsh, 9 January 1825

My Dearest,–I trust that the same cheerful spirit of affection which breathes in every line of your last charming Letter, still animates you, and disposes you kindly towards me. I have somewhat to propose to you; which it may require all your love of me to make you look upon with favour. If you are not the best woman in this world, it may prove a sorry business for both of us.

You bid me tell you how I have decided; what I mean to do. My Dearest! it is you that must decide: I will endeavour to explain to you what I wish; it must rest with you to say whether it can ever be attained. You tell me, "*You* have land which needs improvement; why not work on that?" In one word then: Will you go with me, will you be my own forever; and I embrace the project with my whole heart? Say, Yes! And I send my Brother Alick over to rent that Nithsdale Farm for me without delay; I proceed to it, the moment I am freed from my engagements here; I labour in arranging it, and fitting everything for your reception; and the instant it is ready, I take you home to my hearth, and my bosom, never more to part from me whatever fate betide us!

I fear you think this scheme a baseless vision: and yet it is the sober best among the many I have meditated; the best for me, and I think also as far as I can judge of it, for yourself. If it take effect and be well conducted, I look upon the recovery of my health and equanimity, and with these, of regular profitable and natural habits of activity, as things which are no longer doubtful. I have lost them by departing from Nature. I must find them by returning to her. A stern experience has taught me this; and I am a fool if I do not profit by the lesson. Depend on it, Jane, this literature, which both of us are so bent on pursuing, will *not* constitute the sole nourishment of any true human spirit. No truth has been forced upon me, after more resistance, or with more invincible impressiveness, than this. I feel it in myself, I see it daily in others. Literature is the *wine* of life; it will not, cannot be its *food.* What is it that makes Blue-stockings of women, Magazine-hacks of men? They neglect household and social duties, they have no

Kitty Kirkpatrick, whom Carlyle met in 1824 through Irving, inspired the jealousy of Jane Welsh (from David Alec Wilson, Life of Carlyle; *Thomas Cooper Library, University of South Carolina).*

household and social enjoyments. Life is no longer with them a verdant field, but a *hortus siccus* [parched garden]; they exist pent up in noisome streets, amid feverish excitements; they despise or overlook the common blessedness which Providence has laid out for *all* his creatures, and try to substitute for it a distilled quintessence prepared in the alembic of Painters and Rhymers and sweet Singers. What is the result? This *ardent spirit* parches up their nature; they become discontented and despicable, or wretched and dangerous. Byron and all strong souls go the latter way; Campbell and all weak souls the former. *"Hinaus!"* as the Devil says to Faust, *"Hinaus ins frey Feld!"* [Out into the free field!]. There is no soul in these vapid "articles" of yours: away! Be men, before attempting to be *writers!*

You, too, my Darling, are unhappy; and I see the reason. You have a deep, earnest, vehement spirit, and no earnest task has ever been assigned it. You despise and ridicule the meanness of the things about you: to the things you honour you can only pay a fervent adoration, which issues in no practical effect. O that I saw you the mistress of a house; diffusing over human souls that loved you those clear faculties of order, judgement,

elegance, which you are now reduced to spend on pictures and portfolios; blessing living hearts with that enthusiastic love which you must now direct to the distant and dimly seen! All this is in you, Jane! You have a heart and an intellect and a resolute decision, which might make you the model of wives, however widely your thoughts and your experience have hitherto wandered from that highest destination of even the noblest woman. I too, have wandered wide and far! Let us return, my Dearest! Let us return *together!* Let us learn thro' one another what it is to live; let us become citizens of this world; let us set our minds and habitudes in order, and grow under the peaceful sunshine of Nature, that whatever fruit or flowers have been implanted in our spirits may ripen wholesomely and be distributed in due season!

. . . .

Two laws I have laid down to myself: That I must and will recover health, without which to think or even to live is burdensome or unprofitable; and that I will *not* degenerate into the wretched thing which calls itself an Author in our Capitals, and scribbles for the sake of filthy lucre in the periodicals of the day. Thank Heaven! there are other means of living: if there were not, I for one should beg to be excused! My projects I will give you in detail *when we meet.* That Translation of *Schiller* I think will *not* take effect; that of the *Lives* has brightened up in me again, and I think *will.* Perhaps it is better for me: I ought to thank the timorousness of Booksellers for driving me back on it. Failing both, there are other schemes, schemes unconnected with writing altogether. But here is not an inch of space for speaking of them.

On the whole I begin to entertain a certain degree of contempt for the Destiny, which has so long persecuted me. I will be a man in spite of it! Yet it lies with you, my Dearest, whether I shall be a *right* man, or only a hard bitter Stoic. What say you, Jane? Decide for yourself and me! Consent, if you dare trust me! Consent, and come to my faithful breast, and let us live and die together! Yet fear not to deny me, if your judgement so determine. It will be a sharp pang that tears away from me forever the hope, which now for years has been the solace of my existence: but better to endure it and all its consequences, than to witness and to cause the forfeit of your happiness. At times, I confess, when I hear you speak of your gay Cousins, and contrast with their brilliant equipments my own simple exterior, and scanty prospects, and humble but to me most dear and honourable-minded kinsmen, whom I were the veriest dog if I ever ceased to love and venerate and cherish for their true affection, and the rugged sterling [worth] of their characters; when I think of all this, I could almost counsel you to cast me utterly away, and connect yourself with one whose friends and station were more analogous to your own. But anon in some moment of self-love, I say proudly, There is a spirit in *me*, which is worthy of this noble maiden, which shall be worthy of her! I will take her to my heart, care-laden but ever true to her; I will teach her, I will guide her, I will make her happy! Together we will share the joys and sorrows of existence; I will bear her in my arms thro' all its vicissitudes, and Fate itself shall not divide us.

Speak, then, my Angel! How say you? Will you be mine, mine? Or am I a fool for having hoped it? Think well; of me, of yourself, of our circumstances; and determine. Or have you not already thought? You love me do you not? Dare you trust me; dare you trust your fate with me, as I trust mine with you? Say Yes! and I see you in February, and take "sweet counsel" with you about all our hopes and plans and future life, thenceforward to be one and indivisible. Say No! and— But you will not say no, if you can help it; for you *do* love me, deny it as you will; and your spirit longs to be mingled with mine, as mine with yours, that we may be *one* in the sight of God and man forever and ever!

Now judge if I wait your answer with impatience! I know you will not keep me waiting.—Of course it will be necessary to explain all things to your Mother, and take her serious advice respecting them. For your other "friends" it is not worth consulting one of them. I know not that there is one among them that would give you as disinterested an advice as even I, judging in my own cause. May God bless you, and direct you, my Dearest! Decide as you will, I am yours forever,

T. Carlyle.

–*The Love Letters of Thomas Carlyle and Jane Welsh*, v. 2, pp. 62–68

* * *

Jane responds to Carlyle's letter of 9 January. Despite Jane's dread of a hard, isolated life at Craigenputtoch–when she misbehaved as a child she had been threatened with banishment there–the couple would move to the farm after their marriage and live there for six years.

Jane Welsh to Carlyle, 13 January 1825

My Dearest Friend,–I little thought that my joke about your farming Craigenputtock was to be made the basis of such a serious and extraordinary project. If you had foreseen the state of perplexity which your Letter has thrown me into, you would have practised *any* self-denial (I am sure) rather than have written it. But there is no use in talking of what is *done–"Cosa latta ha capo!"* [The thing done has an end!] The thing to be considered now is what to do.

You have sometimes asked me, did I ever think. For once in my life at least, I have thought myself into a vertigo, and without coming to any positive conclusion. However, my mind (such as it is) on the matter you have thus precipitately forced on my consideration, I will explain to you frankly and explicitly as the happiness of us both requires.

I love you, I have told you so a hundred times; and I should be the most ungrateful and injudicious of mortals if I did not; but I am not *in love* with you; that is to say, my love for you is not a passion which overclouds my judgment, and absorbs all my regard for myself and others. It is a simple, honest, serene affection made up of admiration and sympathy and better perhaps, to found domestic enjoyment on than any other. In short, it is a love which *influences,* does not *make* the destiny of a life.

Such temperate sentiments lend no false colouring, no *"rosy light"* to your project. I see it such as it is, with all the arguments for and against it; I see that my consent under existing circumstances would indeed secure to *me* the only fellowship and support I have found in the world; and perhaps, too, shed some sunshine of joy on *your* existence which has hitherto been sullen and cheerless; but, on the other hand, that it would involve you and myself in numberless cares and difficulties; and expose *me* to petty tribulations, which I want fortitude to despise, and which, not despised, would imbitter the peace of us both.

I do not wish for fortune more than is sufficient for my wants; my natural wants, and the artificial ones which habit has rendered nearly as importunate as the other; but I will not marry on less, because in that case every inconvenience I was subjected to, would remind me of what I had quitted; and the idea of a sacrifice should have no place in a voluntary union. Neither have I any wish for grandeur. The glittering baits of titles and honours are only for children and fools. But I conceive it a duty which everyone owes to society, not to throw up that station in it which Providence has assigned him; and having this conviction I could not marry into a station inferior to my own with the approval of my judgement, *which* alone could enable me to brave the censures of my acquaintance.

And now let me ask you, have you any *certain* livelihood to maintain me in the manner I have been used to live in? Any *fixed* place in the rank of society I have [been] born and bred in? No! You have projects for attaining both, capabilities for attaining both, and much more! But as yet you have *not* attained them. Use the noble gifts which God has given you! You have prudence (tho' by the way this last proceeding is no great proof of it), devise then how you may gain yourself a modest but *settled* income; think of some more promising plan than farming the most barren spot in the county of Dumfriesshire. What a thing that would be to

The Welsh house at Templand, where Thomas Carlyle and Jane Welsh were married on 17 October 1826 (from The Love Letters of
Thomas Carlyle and Jane Welsh; *Special Collections, Thomas Cooper Library, University of South Carolina)*

be sure! You and I keeping house at Craigenputtock! I would just as soon think of building myself a nest on the Bass Rock. Nothing but your ignorance of the place saves you from the imputation of insanity for admitting such a thought. Depend upon it you could not *exist* there a twelve-month. For my part, I would not spend a month at it with an Angel. Think of something else then, apply your industry to carry it into effect, your talents to gild over the inequality of our births; and then—we will talk of marrying. If all this were realised, I *think* I should have good sense enough to abate something of my romantic ideal, and to content myself with stopping short on this side idolatry,–at all events I will marry no one else. This is all the promise I can or will make. A positive engagement to marry a certain person at a certain time, at all haps and hazards, I have always considered the most ridiculous thing on earth: it is either altogether useless or altogether miserable; if the parties continue faithfully attached to each other, it is a mere ceremony; if otherwise, it becomes a galling fetter riveting them to wretchedness and only to be broken with disgrace.

Such is the result of my deliberations on this very serious subject. You may approve of it or not; but you cannot either persuade me or convince me out of it. My decisions when I *do* decide are unalterable as the Laws of the Medes and Persians. Write instantly and tell me that you are content to leave the event to time and destiny, and in the meanwhile to continue my Friend and Guardian which you have so long and so faithfully been,–and *nothing more.*

It would be more agreeable to etiquette and perhaps also to prudence, that I should adopt no middle course in an affair such as this; that I should not for another instant encourage an affection I *may* never reward, and a hope I *may* never fulfil; but cast your heart away from me at once, since I cannot embrace the resolution which would give me the right to it forever. This I would assuredly do if *you* were like the generality of lovers, or if it were still in my power to be happy independent of your affection; but as it [is] neither etiquette nor prudence can obtain this of me. If there is any change to be made in the terms on which we have so long lived with one another, it must be made by *you* not *me,* I *cannot* make any.

All this I have written with my Mother's sanction; if my decision had been more favourable to you, she might have *disapproved* it, but would not have *opposed* it. And this I think is more than you could expect, considering how little she knows you.–I shall not be comfortable till I hear from you again; so I beg you will not keep me waiting. God bless you!

Ever affectionately yours,

Jane Welsh.

*–The Love Letters of Thomas Carlyle
and Jane Welsh,* v. 2,
pp. 68–72

* * *

In this excerpt, Carlyle addresses Jane's concerns about marriage.

In this excerpt, Carlyle addresses Jane's concerns about marriage.

Carlyle to Jane Welsh, 20 January 1825

. . . Now in exploring the chaotic structure of my fortunes, I find my affection for you intertwined with every part of it, connected with whatever is holiest in my feelings or most imperative in my duties. It is necessary for me to understand completely how this matter stands; to investigate my own wishes and powers in regard to it, to know of you both what you will do and what you will not do. These things once clearly settled, our line of conduct will be clear also. It was in such a spirit that I made this proposal; not, as you suppose, grounded on a casual jest of yours, or taken up in a moment of insane selfishness; but deliberated with such knowledge as I had of it, for months; and calmly decided on as with all its strangeness absolutely the best for both of us. There was nothing in it of the Love-and-cottage theory; which none but very young novel-writers now employ their thoughts about. Had you accepted it, I should not by any means have thought the battle won: I should have hailed your assent, and the disposition of mind it bespoke, with a deep but serious joy, with a solemn hope, as indicating the distinct possibility that two true hearts might be united and made happy thro' each other, might by their joint unwearied efforts be transplanted from the parched wilderness where both seemed out of place, into scenes of pure and wholesome activity such as Nature fitted both of them to enjoy and adorn. You have rejected it; I think, wisely. With your actual purposes and views, we should both have been doubly wretched, had you acted otherwise. Your love of me is completely under the control of judgment, and subordinate to other principle of duty or expediency, your happiness is not by any means irretrievably connected with mine. Believe me, I am not hurt or angry: I merely wished to know. It was only in brief moments of enthusiasm that I ever looked for a different result. My plan was no wise one, if it did not include the chance of your denial as well as that of your assent.

* * *

In your opinion about sacrifices, felt to be such, I entirely agree: but at the same time, need I remind your warm and generous heart that the love which will *not* make sacrifices to its object is no proper love? Grounded in admiration and the feeling of enjoyment,

it is fit love for a picture, a statue or a poem; but for a living soul it is not fit. Alas, my Dearest, without deep sacrifices on *both* sides the possibility of our union is an empty dream. It remains for us both to determine what extent of sacrifices it is worth. To me, I confess, the union with a spirit such as yours might be, is beyond all price; worth every sacrifice, but the sacrifice of those very principles which would enable me to deserve it and enjoy it.

Then why not make an effort, attain rank and wealth, and confidently ask what is or might be so precious to me? Now, my best friend, are you sure that you have ever formed to yourself a true picture of me and my circumstances; of a man who has spent seven long years in *incessant* torture, till his heart and head are alike darkened and blasted, and who sees *no* outlet from this state, but in a total alteration of the purposes and exertions which brought it on? I speak not these things in the vain spirit of complaint, which is unworthy of me; but simply to show you how they stand. I must not and cannot continue this sort of life: my patience with it is utterly gone; it were better for me, on the soberest calculation, to be dead than to continue it much longer.

—The Love Letters of Thomas Carlyle
and Jane Welsh, v. 2,
pp. 74–76

* * *

The letter from which these excerpts are taken begins, "Well, Dearest, you have criticised my Letter; it is now my turn to criticise yours." Jane goes on to compare her critique to that of Thomas De Quincey, who had attacked Carlyle's translation of Wilhelm Meister's Apprenticeship: *"Be patient, then, and good, I beg; for you shall find me a severer critic than the Opium eater." From this point forward in their correspondence, Jane Welsh felt herself to be committed to Carlyle.*

Jane Welsh to Carlyle, 29 January 1825

The maxims I proceed by (you tell me) are those of common and acknowledged prudence; and you do *not say* it is unwise in me to walk by them exclusively. The maxims I proceed by are the convictions of my own judgement; and being so, it would be unwise in me were I *not* to proceed by them, whether they are *right* or *wrong*. Yet I am prudent, I fear, only because I am not strongly tempted to be otherwise. My heart is capable (I feel it is) of a love to which *no* deprivation would be a sacrifice—a love which would overleap that reverence for opinion with which education and weakness have begirt my sex, would bear down all the restraints which *duty* and *expediency* might throw in the way, and carry every thought and feeling of my being impetuously along with it. But the all-perfect mortal who could inspire me with a love so extravagant, is nowhere to be found, exists nowhere but in the romance of my own imagination!

. . . .

. . . in requiring you to better your fortune, I had some view to an improvement in my sentiments towards you in the meantime. I am not sure that they are proper sentiments for a Husband; they are proper for a Brother, a Father, a Guardian-spirit; but a Husband, it seems to me, should be dearer still. This, then, independently of prudential considerations, would make me withhold my immediate assent to your proposal. At the same time, from the change which my sentiments towards you have already undergone during the period of our acquaintance, I have little doubt but that in time I shall be perfectly satisfied with them. One loves you (as Madame de Staël said of Necker) in proportion to the ideas and sentiments which are in oneself; according as my mind enlarges and my heart improves, I become capable of comprehending the goodness and greatness which are in you, and my affection for you increases. Not many months ago, I would have said it was impossible that I should ever be your Wife; at present, I consider this the most probable destiny for me. And in a year or so perhaps, I shall consider it the only one. *Die Zeit ist noch nicht da* [The time is not yet here]!

– *The Love Letters of Thomas Carlyle*
and Jane Welsh, v. 2,
pp. 80–87

* * *

In her letter of 29 January, Jane had urged to Carlyle to "write immediately." This excerpt is taken from a letter Carlyle begins with the declaration, "My own Jane! You are a noble girl; and your true and generous heart shall not be oppressed another instant under any weight that I can take from it."

Carlyle to Jane Welsh, 31 January 1825

. . . This Letter is, I think, the best you ever sent me; there is more of the true woman, of the essence of *my* Jane's honourable nature in it, than I ever saw before. Such calm quiet good-sense, and such confiding, simple, true affection! I were myself a pitiable man, if it did not move me. Had my last solemn Letter been directed to a common "accomplished Heiress," mercy! what a fume it would have put her into! Tears and hysterics; followed by all the

abusive epithets in the romance vocabulary; objurgations and recriminations; till the whole concern went off like a rocket, leaving nothing but smoke and darkness behind it. In place of all which, you see in that very grave epistle nothing but the sincere attempt, however awkward, of a man that loves you faithfully, and longs with all his heart to find out the proper path for himself and you to walk in; and you come frankly forward with your own meek and clear and kind sentiments to help him in that arduous undertaking. Let us proceed in this spirit, my Dearest; and I feel confident the result will be blest to us both. It is not our circumstances alone, as you observe, but ourselves that require change: Fortune, niggard as she is, will not deny us the means of making one another happy, if we know how to use and deserve them. Shall I confess it, dear as you are to my heart, I feel that I do not love you with a tithe of that affection which you might merit and obtain from me. It seems as if I *dared* not love you! That nobleness of nature, that generous tho' aimless striving for perfection attracts me towards you as with the force of fascination: but my understanding seems to call upon me to beware, seems to tell me that situated and intentioned as we are, it can be for good to neither of us. A thousand times have I denounced the artificial misdirection and delusions that defaced the pure celestial ardour of your soul; a thousand times have I wished that you had been some humble maiden with no possession no accomplishment but the ethereal spirit, the true fervent heart, which Nature gave you; that you might have joined with me, mind and hand, in the great and only right pursuit of life the *real* not *seeming* perfection of our characters, the proper guidance and contentment of the faculties that Providence has committed to our charge. Alas! Jane, we are both far astray! But we shall return, we shall; and be good and happy after all our errors. Is there not a fund of honesty in both of us? Have we not hearts to reverence true excellence, and judgements which must at length perceive it? I have been sharply taught; and you too seem to be finding out the truth. There is in that very Letter a spirit of genuine womanhood which gives me the most precious hopes. O my own Darling, *were* you but the being which your endowments indicate, with what entireness could I give up my whole soul to you, and love and reverence you the fairest work of God, and *be* one heart and mind and life with you to the latest moment of my existence! This is Elysian, and I swear it shall not all fail and pass away in vain. Is it not worth striving for! To be enshrined in one another's hearts forever; united by the bonds of Truth; blest in each other beyond the power of Fate

THE LIFE

OF

FRIEDRICH SCHILLER.

COMPREHENDING

AN

EXAMINATION OF HIS WORKS.

Quique pii vates et Phœbo digna locuti.—VIRGIL.

LONDON:

PRINTED FOR TAYLOR AND HESSEY,

13, WATERLOO PLACE, PALL MALL,
AND 93, FLEET STREET.

1825.

Title page for Carlyle's second book (Special Collections, Thomas Cooper Library, University of South Carolina).

to ruin us utterly! O that I could banish from myself and you the pitiful impediments and deceptions that distort our nature! The rest were *all* within our reach. Think, then, study, strive along with me, my own brave Jane! Let our love for each other be the Divinity that guides our steps to genuine felicity and worth; and we shall bless forever the hour that first brought us together.

One sovereign aid in our progress I take to be *sincerity;* and this I propose that we should practise more and more towards one another. For *us,* for our affection, there *is* no basis but Truth; let us know one another as we are and shape our conduct and principles by our united judgement. I blush to think how often other motives than real love for your permanent advantage have mingled in what I said to you; how often I have turned my words to the interest of

the passing hour, and repressed the honest tho' discordant voice of truth that was speaking at the bottom of my heart, and might have chased the smile from your eye but would have profited you notwithstanding. It was wrong, and we have strength enough to take another course. It is the common fault of the thing called love: but now that we have the hope, the glorious probability before us of passing our existence together, it is fit that we discard such errors as much as is in our power. Let us learn to speak truth to one another! It is a bitter morsel, that same truth, bitter nauseous morsel; but it is the grand specific of the soul. The man that dares to meet it in all its forms is happy, become of him what may. Depend upon it then, my Dearest, we must gradually introduce the custom of lecturing one another on our faults, and showing to each other aspects of our own minds that are far from pleasant! As yet, it seems to me, I am but in contact with you on some small corner of my being; but you shall yet see me and know me altogether. I hope you will not hate me; ultimately, I know you will not; but at any rate you shall not be deceived. You abhor cant as deeply, and have as quick an eye for it, as myself or any one: it is our duty to help each other to get rid of it and destroy it utterly.

—The Love Letters of Thomas Carlyle and Jane Welsh, v. 2, pp. 87–91

* * *

This excerpt is from a letter that Jane wrote after learning that Carlyle was leaving London and returning to Scotland.

Jane Welsh to Carlyle, 14 February 1825

. . . I know not how your spirit has gained such a mastery over mine in spite of my pride and stubbornness; but so it is. Tho' self-willed as a mule with others, I am tractable and submissive towards *you; I* hearken to your voice as to the dictates of a second conscience, hardly less awful to me than that which nature has implanted in my breast. How comes it you have this power over me? For it is not the effect of your genius and virtue merely. Sometimes in my serious moods, I believe it is a *charm* with which my Good Angel has fortified my heart against evil. Be that as it may, your influence has brought me nothing but good.

When will you be here? Be sure you write beforehand; for I hate *surprises,* however agreeable. I am longing to see you again; to hear your travels' history since we parted; and to talk with you over all

56

our concerns. But how *am* I to meet you *now?* Do you know I think it is more than probable that I will take to my own room, when you come, and not go out of it as long as you are in the house. Upon my word, Mr. Thomas Carlyle, I can hardly forgive you for bringing me into this very shocking predicament. Here am I blushing like an idiot whenever your name is mentioned, so that any body who looks at me, may read the whole matter in my face; and then to be *half-engaged!* I who have such a natural horror at engagements! It gives me asthma every time I think of it. And yet, such is the inconsistency of human nature, or of my particular nature, that I *would* not if I *might,* be free: "*Ce que j'ai fait, je le ferois encore*" [what I have done I would do again].

— *The Love Letters of Thomas Carlyle
and Jane Welsh,* v. 2,
pp. 95–96

* * *

The following exchange of letters concerns Jane's earlier attachment to Edward Irving, which she confesses here. In the letter Jane mentions enclosing, her friend Mrs. Anna Montagu advised her that "the past as well as the present must be laid open; there must be no Bluebeard's closet in which the skeleton may one day be discovered. You have received a new and a dear guest to occupy your heart, not as tenant at will, but as tenant for life; and if, with a noble show of friendship, you have still only a show of it, what conclusion will that 'soul of fire' arrive at?"

Jane Welsh to Carlyle, 24 July 1825

My Dearest,—I thought to write to you from this place with joy; I write with shame and tears. The enclosed Letter, which I found lying for me, has distracted my thoughts from the prospect of our meeting, the brightest in my mind for many months, and forced them on a part of my own conduct which makes me unworthy ever to see you again, or to be clasped to your true heart again. I cannot come to you, cannot be

---

The Prospects of *Friedrich Schiller*

This excerpt is from Carlyle's 28 February 1825 letter to Jane Welsh, a response to her letter of 14 February. He had been delayed in London, in part because of problems in the publishing of The Life of Friedrich Schiller.

My projected movements, you perceive, have been altogether overturned; far from the danger of surprising you by my presence, i am yeat week from Annandale, and perhaps three weeks from you. The poor Book was ready on my part at the time predicted; but just two days before the appointed time of publication, our Engraver discovered that the plate was incomplete, and could not be *properly* rectified in less than a fortnight! As I had myself recommended this man to the job, on the faith of Irving's testimony that he was an indigent *genius,* I had nothing for it but to digest my spleen in silence, and to tell the *feckless speldring* of a creature, that as his future reputation depended on the work, he was at liberty to do his best, and take what time he needed for so doing. I settled with Hessey for my labour; had ten copies done up in their actual state for distribution in London; and so washed my hands of the concern, after exacting a solemn promise that they would lose *no* time in forwarding the rest to Edinburgh. The fortnight is already past and another fortnight to keep it company; yet I left Bull still picking and scraping at his copper, still "three days" from the end of his labour! So much for the patronage of genius! Yet I suffer willingly; for my purpose was good, and this poor Cockney has actually a meritorious heart; and a meagre, patient tho' dejected wife depends upon the scanty

proceeds of his burin. In two weeks from the present date, I calculate that you *will* see *Schiller;* sooner I dare not promise. It will do little, I conjecture, to justify your impatience; yet as the first fruit of a mind that is one with yours forever, I know that it will meet a kind reception from you; and with your approbation and my own, the chief part of my wishes in the way of *fame* are satisfied. I have not put my name to it; for I desire no place among "the mob of gentlemen that write with ease;" and if mere selfish ambition *were* my motive, I had rather not be named at all, than named among that slender crew, as the author of a lank octavo with so few pretensions. I seem to see the secret of these things. Let a man be *true* in his intentions and his efforts to fulfil them; and the point is gained, whether he succeed or not! I smile when I hear of people dying of Reviews. What is a reviewer sitting in his critical majesty, but *one* man, with the usual modicum of brain, who thinks ill of us or well of us, and tells the Earth that *he* thinks so, at the rate of fifteen guineas a sheet? The vain pretender, who lives on the breath of others, he may hurt; but to the honest workman who understands the worth and worthlessness of his own performance, he tells nothing that was not far better understood already, or else he tells weak *lies;* in both of which cases his intelligence is one of the simplest things in Nature.

— *The Love Letters of Thomas Carlyle
and Jane Welsh,* v. 2,
pp. 100–102

at peace with myself, till I have made the confession which Mrs. Montagu so impressively shows me the need of.

Let me tell it then out at once. I have deceived you—*I* whose truth and frankness you have so often praised, have deceived my bosom friend! I told you that I did not care for Edward Irving; took pains to make you believe this. It was false: I loved him—must I say it—*once* passionately loved him. Would to Heaven that this were all! it might not perhaps lower me much in your opinion; for he is no unworthy man. And if I showed weakness in loving one whom I knew to be engaged to another, I made amends in persuading him to marry that other and preserve his honour from reproach. But I have concealed and disguised the truth; and for this I have no excuse; none, at least, that would bear a moment's scrutiny. Woe to me then, if your reason be my judge and not your love! I cannot even plead the merit of a *voluntary* disclosure as a claim to your forgiveness. I make it because I *must,* because this extraordinary woman has moved me to honesty whether I would or no. Read her letter, and judge if it was possible for me to resist it.

Write, I beseech you, instantly and let me know my fate. This suspense is worse to endure than any certainty. Say, if you *can,* that I may come to you, that you will take me to your heart after all as your own, your trusted Jane, and I will arrange it as soon as ever I am able; say no, that you no longer wish to see me, that my image is defaced in your soul, and I will think you *not unjust.* Oh that I had your answer! Never were you so dear as at this moment when I am in danger of losing your affection, or what is still more precious to me, your respect

> Jane B Welsh.
> —*The Love Letters of Thomas Carlyle
> and Jane Welsh,* v. 2,
> pp. 146–148

* * *

Although Carlyle in a much later hand dismissed the enclosed letter with the written comment "Some of Mrs. Montagu's nonsense (Pff!)," the excerpt from this letter shows that he took his future wife's scruples seriously.

Carlyle to Jane Welsh, 29 July 1825

My Dearest,—Your Letter reached me but a few hours ago: I was doubly shocked on reading it a second time to find it dated *Sunday.* What a week you must have had! It were inhuman to keep you another moment in uncertainty.

You exaggerate this matter greatly: it is an evil, but it may be borne; we must bear it *together;* what else can we do? Much of the annoyance it occasions to me proceeds from selfish sources, of a poor enough description; this is unworthy of our notice. Let it go to strengthen the schoolings of experience, let it be another chastisement to Vanity: perhaps she needs it; and if not, who is *She* that I should take thought of her?

Nor is the other, more serious part of the mischief half so heinous in my eyes as it seems to be in yours. There was a want of firmness in withholding an avowal which you thought might give me pain, there must have been much suffering in the concealments and reservations it imposed on you: but there is a heroism in your present frankness, a fund of truth and probity, which ought to cancel all that went before. You say it was not voluntary: so much the more difficult; I honour it the more. You ask me to *forgive* you, you stand humbled and weeping before me. No more of this, for God's sake! Forgiveness! Where is the living man that dare look steadfastly into his "painted sepulchre" of a heart, and say: "I have lived one year without committing fifty faults of a deeper dye than this?" My Dear Jane! My best Jane! Your soul is of a more ethereal temper than befits this very despicable world. You love truth and nobleness, you are forced to love them; and you know not how they may be reached. O God! What a heartless slave were I, if I discouraged you, for any paltry momentary interests of my own, in the sacred object you are aiming at! Believe me, my Dearest, this struggling of a pure soul to escape from the contaminations that encircle it, is but the more touching to me that its success is incomplete. It is human nature in the loveliest aspect our poor Earth admits of; flesh and spirit, the clay of the ground made living by the breath of the Almighty.

> —*The Love Letters of Thomas Carlyle
> and Jane Welsh,* v. 2,
> pp. 150–155

* * *

These excerpts are from a letter that Carlyle believed would "vex" Jane but that he hoped would "not fail to produce some peaceable fruit."

Carlyle to Jane Welsh, 26 February 1826

O Jane, Jane! Your half-jesting enumeration of your wooers does anything but make me laugh. A thousand and a thousand times have I thought the same thing in deepest earnest. That you have the power making many good matches is no secret to me, nay it would

Chaining Spiritual Dragons

Beginning in May 1825 Carlyle was working on translations of German works, which were published as German Romance *in 1827. In this personal note, Carlyle comments on the work of translation as well as the sense of spiritual peace he achieved in 1826.*

My *Translation* work went steadily on;–the *pleasantest* kind of labour I ever had; c*d* be done by *task,* in what*r* hum*r* or condit*n* one was in: and was, day by day (ten pages a-day, I think) punctually and comfortably so performed. *Internally,* too, there were far higher things going on; a grand and *ever*-joyful victory getting itself achieved at last! The final chaining down, and trampling home, "for good," home into their caves forever, of all my *Spiritual Dragons,* wh*h* had wrought me such woe and, for a decade past, had made my life black and bitter: this year 1826 saw the end of all that. With such a feeling on my part as may be fancied. I found it to be, essentially, what Methodist people call their "Conversion," the deliverance of their soul from the Devil and the Pit; precisely enough that, in my new form;–and there burnt, accordingly, a sacred flame of joy in me, silent in my inmost being, as of one henceforth superior to Fate, able to look down on *its* stupid injuries with pardon and contempt, almost with a kind of thanks and pity. This "holy joy," of wh*h* I kept silence, lasted sensibly in me for several years, in blessed counterpoise to sufferings and discourage*ts* enough; nor has it proved what I can call fallacious at any time since: my "spirit*l* dragons" (thank Heaven) do still remain strictly in their caves, forgotten and dead;–wh*h* is indeed a conquest, and the beginning of conquests.–I rode ab*t,* a great deal, in all kinds of weather, that winter & summer; generally quite alone; & did not want for medita*tns,* no longer of defiantly hopeless, or quite *un*pious nature–

–The Collected Letters of Thomas and Jane Welsh Carlyle, v. 4, p.142

wounded in the house of your friends. Can you believe it with the good nature which I declare it deserves? . . . You tell me that you often weep when you think what is to become of us. It is unwise in you to weep: if you are reconciled to be my Wife (not the Wife of an ideal *me,* but the simple actual prosaic *me*), there is nothing frightful in the future. I look into it with more and more confidence and composure. Alas! Jane, you do not know me: it is not the poor, unknown, rejected Thomas Carlyle that you know, but the prospective rich, known and admired. . . .

. . . .

These are hard sayings, my beloved Child; but I cannot spare them; and I hope, tho' bitter at first, they may not remain without wholesome influence. Do not get angry with me! Do not! I swear I deserve it not! Consider this as a true glimpse into my heart which it is good that you contemplate with the gentleness and tolerance you have often shown me. I do not love you? If you judge it fit, I will clasp you to my bosom and my heart, as my wedded Wife, this very week: if you judge it fit, I will this very week forswear you forever. More I cannot do, but all this, when I compare myself with you, it is my duty to do.–Now think if I long for your answer! Yet not in my time, but in yours. I have lived as a widower from you these two days, I must live so till I hear from you again. Till I hear from you? Good God! Perhaps, first rightly, when I hear from you!–Adieu, my heart's Darling! God Bless you and have you always in His keeping! I am yours, at your own disposal, forever and ever,

T. Carlyle.

–The Love Letters of Thomas Carlyle and Jane Welsh, v. 2, pp. 241–243

* * *

This excerpt is from a letter that Jane began "You were right in supposing that your Letter would give me pain; but as for the 'peaceable fruit' *(if any) it is yet to come."*

Jane Welsh to Carlyle, 4 March 1826

One thing more and I am done. Look cross at me, reproach me, even whip me, if you have the heart; your next kiss will make amends for all. But if you love me, cease, I beseech you, to make me offers of freedom; for this is an outrage which I find it not easy to forgive. If made with any idea that it is in the nature of things I should take you at your word, they do a wrong to my love, my truth, my modesty, that is, to my whole character as a woman; if not, they are a mocking better

be a piece of news for me to learn that I am not the very *worst* you ever thought of. And you add with the same tearful smile: "Alas! we are married already." Let me now cut off this interjection, and say simply what is true that we are *not* married already; and do you hereby receive further my distinct and deliberate declaration that it depends on yourself, and shall always depend on yourself whether we ever be married or not. God knows I do not say this in a vulgar spirit of defiance; which in our present relation were coarse and cruel, but I say it in the spirit of disinterested affection for you, and of fear for the reproaches of my own conscience should your fair destiny be marred by me, and you

Jane Welsh, as painted in 1826 (miniature by Kenneth Macleay; from Elizabeth A. Drew, Jane Welsh and Jane Carlyle, *Special Collections, Thomas Cooper Library, University of South Carolina)*

spared, since you know my answer must be still: "Permit me, O Shindarig, to wear out my days in prison, for its walls are to me more pleasing than the most splendid Palace!"–*But Ohe jam satis!*–Farewell, my Beloved. I am still yours,

Jane Baillie Welsh.
–*The Love Letters of Thomas Carlyle
and Jane Welsh,* v. 2,
pp. 247–248

* * *

This letter was posted eight days before the marriage ceremony.

Carlyle to Jane Welsh, 9 October 1826

"The Last Speech and *marrying* words of that unfortunate young woman Jane Baillie *Welsh,*" I received on Friday-morning; and truly a most delightful and swan-like melody was in them; a tenderness and warm devoted trust, worthy of such a maiden bidding farewell to the (unmarried) Earth, of which she was the fairest ornament. Dear little Child! How is it that I have deserved thee; deserved a purer and nobler heart than falls to the lot of millions? I swear I will love thee with my whole heart, and think my life well spent if it can make thine happy.

In fine these preliminaries are in the way towards adjustment. After some vain galloping and consultation, I have at length got that certificate which the Closeburn Session in their sapience deem necessary; I have ordered the Proclaiming of Banns in this parish of Middlebie, and written out a note giving order for it in your parish of Closeburn. Pity, by the way, that there is no man in the Closeburn Church possessed of any little fraction of vulgar earthly logic! It might have saved me a ride to Hoddam Manse this morning (the good Yorstoun, my native parson, was away), and a most absurd application to the "glass Minister" my neighbour. One would think that after fair *crying* three times through the organs of Archibald Blacklock, this certificate of celibacy would be like gilding refined gold, or adding a perfume to the violet: for would not my existing wife, in case I had one, forthwith, at the first hum from Archibald's windpipe, start up in her place, and state aloud that *she* had "objections"?–But I will not quarrel with these Reverend men; *laissez les faire,* they will buckle us fast enough at length, and for the *How* I care not.

Your own day, Tuesday, as was fitting, I have made mine. Jack and I will surely call on Monday evening at Templand, most likely *after* tea; but I think it will be more commodious for all parties that we sleep at the Inn. You will not see me on Monday-night? I bet two to one you will! At all events I hope you will on Tuesday; so as Jack says, "it is much the same."

All hands are sorting, packing, rummaging and rioting here. To Jane I read her part of your Letter; she will accompany us in our Edinburgh sojourn with all the pleasure in the world. Jack will bring her out, when we want her: she may try the household for awhile; if it suit she will have cause to love her Sister for her life long.

Your mother will take down this note to the Minister and appoint the hour? I think it should be an early one, for we have far to go. Perhaps also she might do something towards engaging post-horses at the Inn; but I suppose there is little fear of failure in that point.

Do you know aught of wedding-gloves? I must leave all that to you; for except a vague tradition of some such thing I am profoundly ignorant concerning the whole matter. Or will you give *any? Ach du guter Gott!* Would we were off and away, three months before all these observances of the Ceremonial Law!

The house at Comely Bank where the Carlyles lived from 1826 to 1828 (from The Homes and Haunts of Thomas Carlyle, *Special Collections, Thomas Cooper Library, University of South Carolina)*

Yet fear not, Darling; for it must and will be all accomplished, and I admitted to thy bosom and thy heart, and we two made one life in the sight of God and man! O my own Jane! I could say much; and what were words to the sea of thoughts that rolls thro' my heart, when I feel that thou art mine, that I am thine, that henceforth we live not for ourselves but for each other! Let us pray to God that our holy purposes be not frustrated; let us trust in Him and in each other, and fear no evil that can befall us. My last blessing as a Lover is with you; this is my last letter to Jane Welsh: my first blessing as a Husband, my first kiss to Jane Carlyle is at hand! O my Darling! I will always love thee.

Good night, then, for the last time we have to part! In a week I see you, in a week you are my own! Adieu *Meine Eigene!*

In haste, I am forever yours,
T. Carlyle.
–*The Love Letters of Thomas Carlyle and Jane Welsh,* v. 2, pp. 335–337

* * *

These excerpts are from a letter Carlyle wrote two days after his marriage.

Carlyle to Margaret A. Carlyle, 19 October 1826

My Dear Mother,

Had it not been that I engaged to let you hear of me on Saturday, I should not have been tempted to "put pen to paper this night"; for I am still dreadfully confused, still far from being at home in my new situation, inviting and hopeful as in all points it appears. But I know your motherly anxieties, I felt in my heart the suppressed tears that you did not shed before my departure, and I write at present to tell you that you are not to shed any more.

Jane has run upstairs for a few minutes to unpack the last remnants of our household luggage: I have but a few minutes to spare, and must give you matters in the lump.

Jack would tell you of our being wedded after the most doleful ride (on his and my part) thither; and then rolled off in the Coach towards Edinr on Tuesday morning. Poor Jack! I daresay he did *greet* [weep] that

Early Years

In his Reminiscences, *Carlyle included Geraldine Jewsbury's comments on Jane.*

I do not know in what year she married, nor anything connected with her marriage. I believe that she brought no money or very little at her marriage. Her father had left everything to her, but she made it over to her mother, and only had what her mother gave her. Of course people thought she was making a dreadfully bad match; they only saw the *outside* of the thing; but she had faith in her own insight. Long afterwards, when the world began to admire her husband, at the time he delivered the Lectures on 'Hero Worship,' she gave a little half-scornful laugh, and said 'they tell me things as if they were new that I found out years ago.' She knew the power of help and sympathy that lay in her; and she knew she had strength to stand the struggle and pause before he was recognised. She told me that she resolved that he should never write for money, only when he wished it, when he had a message in his heart to deliver, she determined that she would make whatever money he gave her answer for all needful purposes; and she was ever faithful to this resolve. She bent her faculties to economical problems, and she managed so well that comfort was never absent from her house, and no one looking on could have guessed whether they were rich or poor. Until she married, she had never minded household things; but she took them up when necessary, and accomplished them as she accomplished everything else she undertook, well and gracefully. Whatever she had to do she did it with a peculiar personal grace that gave a charm to the most prosaic details. No one who in later years saw her lying on the sofa in broken health, and languor, would guess the amount of energetic hard work she had done in her life. She could do everything and anything, from mending the Venetian blinds to making picture-frames or trimming a dress. Her judgment in all literary matters was thoroughly good; she could get to the very core of a thing, and her insight was like witchcraft.

. . . .

At first on their marriage they lived in a small pretty house in Edinburgh called Cromlech Bank [*sic*]. Whilst there her first experience of the difficulties of housekeeping began. She had never been accustomed to anything of the kind; but Mr. Carlyle was obliged to be very careful in diet. She learned to make bread partly from recollecting how she had seen an old servant set to work; and she used to say that the *first* time she attempted brown bread, it was with awe. She mixed the dough and saw it rise; and then she put it into the oven, and sat down to watch the oven-door with feelings like Benvenuto Cellini's when he watched his Perseus put into the furnace. She did not feel too sure what it would come out! But it came out a beautiful crusty loaf, very light and sweet; and proud of it she was. The first time she tried a pudding, she went into the kitchen and locked the door on herself, having got the servant out of the road. It was to be a suet pudding–not just a common suet pudding but something special–and it was good, being made with care by weight and measure with exactness.

–Reminiscences, v. 2, pp. 62–63

---

morning when alone; he looked so very *wae,* and scarcely knew more than myself what to make of it. Our journey passed without incident, and we arrived here in safety about nine o'clock, where a blazing fire and covered table stood ready waiting to receive us.

On the whole I have reason to say that I have been mercifully dealt with; and if an outward man worn with continual harassments and spirits wasted with so many agitations would let me see it, that when once re[c]overed into my usual tone of health, I may fairly calculate on being far happier than I have ever been. The house is a perfect model of a house, furnished with every accommodation that heart could desire; and for my wife I may say in my heart that she is far better than any other wife, and loves me with a devotedness, which it is a mystery to me how I have ever deserved. She is gay and happy as a lark, and looks with such soft cheerfulness into my gloomy countenance that new hope passes over into me every time I meet her eye. You yourself (and that is saying much) could not have nursed and watched over me with kinder affection, wrecked as I am, by my movements and counter-movements; all my despondency cannot make her despond, she seems happy enough if she can but see me, and minister to me.

For in truth I was very sullen yesterday, sick with sleeplessness, quite nervous, *billus,* splenetic and all the rest of it. Good Jane! I feel that she will be all to me that heart could wish; for she loves me in her soul, one of the warmest and truest souls that ever animated any human being. Last night I got a good sleep; and tho' several sleeps will be necessary to give me back my old train of acting, I am already far better today, and all that was so dark yesterday is now becoming *grey,* and promising ere long to be quite sunshiny and bright.

I must huddle things together, for if I had a whole day I could not put them in order. You will ask about sleep: fear not for that, my good Mother; I shall sleep better than ever, Scotsbrig or the Hill were not quieter than this, and our bed is, I should think, about *seven feet wide!* Besides she herself (the good soul!) has ordered another bed to be made for me in the adjoining room, to which I may retire whenever I shall see good. On this score therefore all is well. Yesterday and today we have spent in sorting and arranging our household goods, and projecting our household economy. She calculates at the moderate scale of £2 per week: I am to give her two pound notes every Saturday morning, and with this she undertakes to meet all charges. At this rate, which astonishes myself far more than her, there can be no fear. She seems Thrift itself as well as Goodness.

· · · · · · · · · ·

Jane would not look at this letter, for I told her you so wished it. She sends her warmest love to you all. Is not mine still with you? I have told her all that you said and looked that morning I went away, and she loves you all along with me, and sorrows with me for your absence. My prayers and affection are with you all from little Jenny upwards to the head of the house. Remember me to my Brothers, my trusty Alick (Jack must write) and all the rest. Mag and her sisters are not forgotten either. I will write again, when *I have recovered my senses.* Good-night, my dear Mother; I *have* "told you the worst" which is that I am half as *billus* as might have been expected; overshadowed with confusion, therefore, but with hope on all sides looking thro' it. Jane will write to you soon, so will I; you shall not want for letters; or for love while there is life in me. Again I say I will write when I have recovered my bewilderment. Tell Jack to write us in the mean while; and fear nothing: I am, forever your

affectionate son, / T. Carlyle

–The Collected Letters of Thomas and Jane Welsh Carlyle, v. 4, pp. 151–154

Not Without Honor: 1827–1837

Living with Jane at Comely Bank, a rented house outside of Edinburgh, from their marriage until June 1828, Carlyle translated German works and wrote biographical sketches of German authors for a four-volume anthology of German literature. The couple then moved to an isolated Scottish farm called Craigenputtoch, where they lived for six years. Carlyle solidified his reputation as a scholar during this period as he published essays in periodicals and also wrote a major original work, Sartor Resartus, *which was first published as a book in the United States (1836). In 1834 the Carlyles moved to London, settling into the house they lived in the rest of their lives.* The French Revolution: A History *(1837) established Carlyle as a major literary figure.*

German Romance and Early Essays

German Romance *was published by James Munroe in 1827. The book represented yet another significant step toward educating his British audience about German literary achievement.*

This letter was accompanied by German Romance, *the fourth volume of which included* Wilhelm Meister's Travels; or, The Renunciants, *Carlyle's translation of Goethe's* Wilhelm Meisters Wanderjahre oder Die Entsagenden *(1821), as well as his biography* The Life of Friedrich Schiller, *which Goethe later translated.*

Carlyle to Johann Wolfgang von Goethe, 15 April 1827

Respected Sir—It is now above two years since Lord Bentinck's Servant delivered me at London the packet from Weimar, containing your kind Letter and Present; of both which, to say that they were heartily gratifying to me, would be saying little; for I received them and keep them with a regard which can belong to nothing else. To me they are memorials of one whom I never saw, yet whose voice came to me from afar, with counsel and help, in my utmost need. For if I have been delivered from darkness into any measure of light, if I know aught of myself and my duties and destination, it is to the study of your writings more than to any other circumstance that I

Carlyle in the 1830s (sketch by Samuel Lawrence; from David Alec Wilson, Life of Carlyle, *Thomas Cooper Library, University of South Carolina)*

owe this; it is you more than any other man that I should always thank and reverence with the feeling of a Disciple to his Master, nay of a Son to his spiritual Father. This is no idle compliment, but a heartfelt truth; and humble as it is I feel that the knowledge of such truths must be more pleasing to you than all other glory.

The Books, which I here take the liberty to offer you, are the poor product of endeavours, obstructed by sickness and many other causes; and in themselves little worthy of your acceptance: but perhaps they may find some favour for my sake, and interest you likewise as evidences of the progress of German Literature in England. Hitherto it has not been injustice but ignorance that has blinded us in

GERMAN ROMANCE:

SPECIMENS

OF

ITS CHIEF AUTHORS;

WITH

BIOGRAPHICAL AND CRITICAL

NOTICES.

BY THE TRANSLATOR OF WILHELM MEISTER, AND
AUTHOR OF THE LIFE OF SCHILLER.

IN FOUR VOLUMES.

VOL. I.

CONTAINING

MUSÆUS AND LA MOTTE FOUQUÉ.

EDINBURGH:

WILLIAM TAIT, PRINCE'S STREET;
AND CHARLES TAIT, FLEET STREET, LONDON.
MDCCCXXVII.

*Title page for Carlyle's collection of eighteen translations
(Special Collections, Thomas Cooper Library,
University of South Carolina)*

this matter: at all events a different state of things seems approaching; with respect to yourself, it is at hand, or rather has already come. This *Wanderjahre,* which I reckon somewhat better translated than its forerunner, I in many quarters hear deeply, if not loudly, praised; and even the character with which I have prefaced it, appears to excite not objection but partial compliance, or at worst, hesitation and inquiry.

Of the *Lehrjahre [Wilhelm Meister's Apprenticeship]* also I am happy to give a much more flattering account than I could have anticipated at first. Above a thousand copies of the Book are already in the hands of the public; loved also, with more or less insight, by all persons of any culture; and, what it has many times interested me to observe, with a degree of estimation determined not less by the intellectual

force than by the moral earnestness of the reader. One of its warmest admirers known to me is a lady of rank, and intensely religious.

I may mention further that, some weeks ago, a stranger London bookseller applied to me to translate your *Dichtung und Wahrheit;* a proposal which I have perhaps only postponed, not rejected.

All this warrants me to believe that your name and doctrines will ere long be English as well as German; and certainly there are few things which I have more satisfaction in contemplating than the fact that to this result my own efforts have contributed; that I have assisted in conquering for you a new province of mental empire; and for my countrymen a new treasure of wisdom which I myself have found so precious. One day, it may be, if there is any gift in me, I shall send you some Work of my own; and along with it, you will deserve far deeper thanks than those of Hilaria to her friendly Artist.

About six months ago I was married: my young wife, who sympathises with me in most things; agrees also in my admiration of you; and would have me, in her name, beg of you to accept this purse, the work, as I can testify, of dainty fingers and true love; that so something, which she had handled and which had been hers, might be in your hands and be yours. In this little point I have engaged that you would gratify her. She knows you in your own language; and her first criticism was the following, expressed with some surprise: "This Goethe is a greater genius than Schiller, though he does not make me cry!" A better judgment than many which have been pronounced with more formality.

May I hope to hear, by Post, that this packet has arrived safely, and that health and blessings are still continued to you? *Frey ist das Herz, doch ist der Fuss gebunden.* My wishes are joined with those of the world that you may be long spared to see good, and do good.–I am ever, Respected Sir, your humble servant and thankful Scholar,

Thomas Carlyle.

If you stand in any relation with Mr. Tieck, it would give me pleasure to assure him of my esteem. Except him and Richter, who has left us, there is no other of these Novelists, whom I ought not to beg your pardon for placing you beside, even as their King.

–*Correspondence between Goethe
and Carlyle,* pp. 6–11

***

ART. II.—1. *Die Poesie und Beredsamkeit der Deutschen, von Luthers Zeit bis zur Gegenwart. Dargestellt von Franz Horn.* (The Poetry and Oratory of the Germans, from Luther's Time to the Present. Exhibited by FRANZ HORN). Berlin, 1822—23—24. 3 vols. 8vo.

2. *Umrisse zur Geschichte und Kritik der schönen Litteratur Deutschlands während der Jahre 1790—1818.* (Outlines for the History and Criticism of Polite Literature in Germany, during the Years 1790—1818). By FRANZ HORN. Berlin, 1819. 8vo.

THESE two books, notwithstanding their diversity of title, are properly parts of one and the same; the 'Outlines,' though of prior date in regard to publication, having now assumed the character of sequel and conclusion to the larger work,—of fourth volume to the other three. It is designed, of course, for the home market; yet the foreign student also will find in it a safe and valuable help, and, in spite of its imperfections, should receive it with thankfulness and good-will. Doubtless we might have wished for a keener discriminative and descriptive talent, and perhaps for a somewhat more Catholic spirit, in the writer of such a history; but in their absence we have still much to praise. Horn's literary creed would, on the whole, we believe, be acknowledged by his countrymen as the true one; and this, though it is chiefly from one immovable station that he can survey his subject, he seems heartily anxious to apply with candour and tolerance. Another improvement might have been a deeper principle of arrangement, a firmer grouping into periods and schools; for, as it stands, the work is more a critical sketch of German Poets, than a history of German Poetry.

Let us not quarrel, however, with our author: his merits as a literary historian are plain, and by no means inconsiderable. Without rivalling the almost frightful laboriousness of Bouterwek or Eichhorn, he gives creditable proofs of research and general information, and possesses a lightness in composition, to which neither of these erudite persons can well pretend. Undoubtedly he has a flowing pen, and is at home in this province; not only a speaker of the word, indeed, but a doer of the work; having written, besides his great variety of tracts and treatises biographical, philosophical, and critical, several very deserving works of a poetic sort. He is not, it must be owned, a very strong man, but he is nimble and orderly, and goes through his work with a certain gaiety of heart; nay, at times, with a frolicsome alacrity which might even require to be pardoned. His

First page of Carlyle's article in the October 1827 issue of The Edinburgh Review
(Thomas Cooper Library, University of South Carolina)

As was his habit throughout his life, Carlyle dismissed negative criticism of his work. In this excerpt he comments on a review of his anthology that appeared in the June 1827 issue of the Monthly Review.

Carlyle to John A. Carlyle, 4 June 1827

This day, I was in the Advocates' Library seeking German Books, and I found (directed by Dr. Irving) the first Article in the *Monthly Review* devoted to our "German Romance." The man is little better than an ass; but a well-disposed one; and never dreams that his ears are long. He calls me pointblank by the name of the city *Carlisle,* without apology or introduction; says my lives are much the best thing in the Book, indeed sticks fast by them; and advises me to cultivate the field of Biography as my great concern. Goethe is very pretty, indeed they are all "goody-good." Only the words *Herr, Rittmeister* &c have been used here and there; and I write, tho' with *spunk* and ornately, yet in a devilish–*careless* style. In short, the man is an *entire* blockhead: seems to have read some few pages of German, perhaps only of a German Grammar; but other[wise] rests in the pro[fo]undest ignorance, of what he talks about. However I am [not vexed at] him (Heaven mend all our stupidities!); for he means well to me: but I will not cu[ltivate] Biography for all that.

—*The Collected Letters of Thomas and Jane Welsh Carlyle,* v. 4, pp. 229–230

* * *

In February 1827 Carlyle formed an acquaintance with Francis Jeffrey, lawyer and editor of The Edinburgh Review, *an influential literary periodical through which Jeffrey advocated a conservative Whig political agenda. For the June issue of Jeffrey's magazine, Carlyle wrote a brief essay on the German writer Jean Paul Richter—one of the models for the hero of* Sartor Resartus, *Diogenes Teufelsdröckh—and, for the October issue, a more expansive article, "The State of German Literature." These and other articles on German topics earned Carlyle recognition at home and abroad.*

In this excerpt Carlyle's reference to "the Stot" is to John M'Diarmid, who was called "The Galway Stot."

Carlyle to John A. Carlyle, 29 November 1827

The Edin*r* Review is out some time ago; and the "State of German Literature" has been received with considerable surprise and approbation by the Universe. Thus for instance, De Quinc[e]y praises it in his Saturday Post; Sir W. Hamilton tells me that it is *"cap'tal";* and Wilson informs John Gordon that it has "done me a *deal* o' good." May a bountiful Heaven be praised for its mercies! I suppose I shall by and by rise into a pitch of literary glory, which may all but equal me with the Stot himself. In the meanwhile I have written another long paper on *Zacharias Werner,* and sent it off the other day to Frazer, who seems very anxious to have it.

—*The Collected Letters of Thomas and Jane Welsh Carlyle,* v. 4, p. 290

* * *

Foreign Review published Carlyle's "Life and Writings of Werner" in January 1828, which occasioned Carlyle's comment in this excerpt. The review published Carlyle's essay "Goethe's Helena" in April 1828.

Carlyle to John A. Carlyle, 7 March 1828

It, appears, however, that I am become a sort of newspaper *Literatus* in London; on the strength of these *Articles* (bless them!), and that certain persons wonder what manner of man I am. A critic in the Courier (apparently the worst in nature–from the one sentence I read of him) says that I am the supremest German Scholar in the British Empire!– *Das hole der Teufel* [Let the devil take it]!–However I was rather amused at the *naiveté* with which Crabbe Robinson talks to me on this subject. He characterizes the Papers as a *splendid* instance of literary *ratting* on the part of the Editor, and says it has some eloquence, and tho' it cuts its own throat (to speak in a figure) will do good.–I know not whether you have seen the *Foreign Review;* it is not worth going far to see. A stupid Book, but pays well, and edited by a very civil and well-meaning man: I design from time to time to correspond with it. They gave me £47 for my trash on *Werner:* I have sent them a far better paper on Goethe's *Helena* [underscored twice], for which I shall not get so much. The man Frazer expresses a real anxiety to hear from [me] on *any* subject.

—*The Collected Letters of Thomas and Jane Welsh Carlyle,* v. 4, pp. 335–336

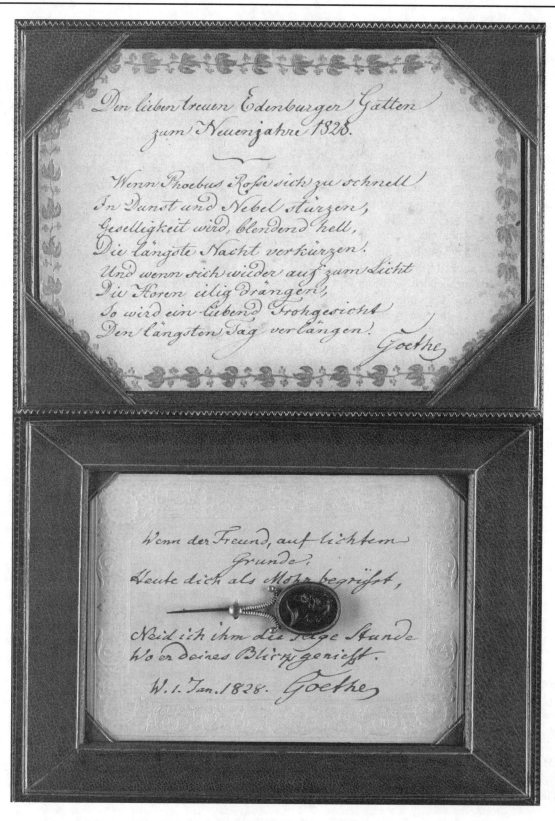

Pin, with Goethe's image, that the German author sent to the Carlyles on 1 January 1828
(Beinecke Rare Book and Manuscript Library, Yale University)

The Scholar at Craigenputtoch

Despite his growing success in Edinburgh, Carlyle decided to leave the city for Craigenputtoch, an isolated farm owned by the Welsh family. His refined, social wife was reluctant to live in such rustic circumstances; however, she complied with her husband's wishes.

Despite its privations, Craigenputtoch proved a boon for Carlyle's work. He wrote additional essays on German subjects and biographical sketches of Scottish poet Robert Burns, the French writer Voltaire, and the English man of letters Samuel Johnson. He also ventured into social criticism with "Signs of the Times" in June 1829 and "Characteristics" in December 1831, both of which appeared in Jeffrey's Edinburgh Review. In the early 1830s, Carlyle formed friendships with other people of letters, including the social and political philosopher John Stuart Mill and the American writer Ralph Waldo Emerson. Most important, Carlyle's sojourn at Craigenputtoch allowed him to write the work that was later published as Sartor Resartus.

In this excerpt Carlyle provides an early positive description of their circumstances.

Carlyle to Goethe, 25 September 1828

You inquire with such affection touching our present abode and employments, that I must say some words on that subject, while I have still space. Dumfries is a pretty town, of some 15,000 inhabitants; the Commercial and Judicial Metropolis of a considerable district on the Scottish border. Our dwelling place is not in it, but fifteen miles (two hours' riding) to the north-west of it, among the Granite Mountains and black moors which stretch west-

Farm at Craigenputtoch, the Carlyles' home from 1828 to 1834 (photograph by J. Patrick; from Joan M. Sloan, The Carlyle Country, *Special Collections, Thomas Cooper Library, University of South Carolina)*

"The Stillness was Almost Awful"

In his Reminiscences, *Carlyle included Geraldine Jewsbury's account of the Carlyles' life at Craigenputtoch as Jane had reported it to her in later years. Carlyle criticized Jewsbury's accuracy. "Few or none of these Narratives are correct in the details," he wrote, and "Each consists of two or three, in confused, exaggerated state, rolled with new confusion into one, and given wholly to her, when perhaps they were mainly some maid-servant's in whom she was concerned" (*Reminiscences, *v. 2, pp. 68, 80). Nonetheless, Carlyle admits that her "recognition of the character is generally true and faithful" (*Reminiscences, *v. 2, p. 68).*

. . . She used to say that the stillness was almost awful, and that when she walked out she could hear the sheep nibbling the grass, and they used to look at her with innocent wonder. The letters came in once a week, which was as often as they sent into Dumfries. All she needed had to be sent for there or done without. One day she had desired the farm-servant to bring her a bottle of yeast. The weather was very hot. The man came back looking scared; and without the yeast. He said doggedly that he would do anything lawful for her; but he begged she would never ask him to fetch such an uncanny thing again, for it had just worked and worked till it flew away with the bottle! When asked where it was, he replied, 'it had a'just gane into the ditch, and he had left it there!'

—*Reminiscences,* v. 2, pp. 63–64

---

ward through Galloway almost to the Irish Sea. This is, as it were, a green oasis in that desert of health and rock; a piece of ploughed and partially sheltered and ornamented ground, where corn ripens and trees yield umbrage, though encircled on all hands by moorfowl and only the hardiest breeds of sheep. Here, by dint of great endeavour we have pargetted and garnished for ourselves a clean substantial dwelling; and settled down in defect of any Professional or other Official appointment, to cultivate Literature, on our own resources, by way of occupation, and roses and garden shrubs, and if possible health and a peaceable temper of mind to forward it. The roses are indeed still mostly to plant; but they already blossom in Hope; and we have two swift horses, which, with the mountain air, are better than all physicians for sick nerves. That exercise, which I am very fond of, is almost my sole amusement; for this is one of the most solitary spots in Britain, being six miles from *any* individual of the formally visiting class. It might have suited Rousseau almost as well as his Island of St. Pierre; indeed I find that most of my city friends impute to me a motive similar to his in coming hither, and predict no good from it. But I came hither purely for this one reason: that I might not have to write

Francis Jeffrey, one of the founders of The Edinburgh Review, *whom Carlyle knew by reputation as a critic before they became friends (from David Alec Wilson,* Life of Carlyle, *Thomas Cooper Library, University of South Carolina)*

for bread, might not be tempted to tell lies for money. This space of Earth is our own, and we can live in it and write and think as seems best to us, though Zoilus himself should become king of letters. And as to its solitude, a mail-coach will any day transport us to Edinburgh, which is our British Weimar. Nay, even at this time. I have a whole horse-load of French, German, American, English Reviews and Journals, were they of any worth, encumbering the tables of my little library. Moreover, from any of our heights I can discern a Hill, a day's journey to the eastward, where Agricola with his Romans has left a camp; at the foot of which I was born, where my Father and Mother are still living to love me. Time, therefore, must be left to try: but if I sink into folly, myself and not my situation will be to blame. Nevertheless I have many doubts about my future literary activity; on all which, how gladly would I take *your* counsel! Surely, you will write to me again, and ere long; that I may still feel myself united to you. Our best prayers for all good to you and yours are ever with you!

—*Correspondence between Goethe and Carlyle,*
pp. 124–126

* * *

Francis Jeffrey visited the Carlyles at Craigenputtoch in October 1828. In this excerpt Carlyle comments on Jeffrey's editing of his essay on Burns, which was published in December in The Edinburgh Review.

Carlyle to John A. Carlyle, 10 October 1828

The Paper on *Burns* is finished; and I suppose will appear in December; being too late for this present Number. The Proof-sheets of it are even now in the house, and corrected. Jeffrey had clipt the first portion of it all into shreds (partly by my permission), simply because it was 'too long.' My first feeling was of indignation, and to demand the whole back again, that it might lie in my drawer and worm-eat, rather than come before the world in that horrid souterkin shape; the body of a quadruped with the head of a bird; a man *shortened* by cutting out his thighs, and fixing the knee-pans on the hips! However, I determined to *do nothing for three days;* and now by replacing and readjusting many parts of the first sixteen pages (there are three sheets in all; and the last two were not meddled with) I have once more put the thing into a kind of publishable state; and mean to send it back, with a private persuasion that probably I shall not soon write another for that quarter. Nevertheless, I will keep friends with the man; for he really has extraordinary worth, and likes me, at least heartily wishes me well.

—*Letters of Thomas Carlyle, 1826–1836,* pp. 123–124

* * *

Jane and 'Harry'

Geraldine Jewsbury gives this account of Jane preparing for a visit of Lord Jeffrey.

During their residence at Craigenputtock, she had a good little horse, called 'Harry,' on which she sometimes rode long distances. She was an excellent and fearless horsewoman, and went about like the women used to do before carriages were invented. One day she received news that Lord Jeffrey and his family, with some visitors, were coming. The letter only arrived the day they were expected (for letters only came in one day in the week). She mounted 'Harry' and galloped off to Dumfries to get what was needed and galloped back, and was all ready and dressed to receive her visitors with no trace of her thirty-mile ride except the charming history she made of it. She said that 'Harry' understood all was needed of him.

—*Reminiscences,* v. 2, p. 66

My own Four Walls.

The storm and night is on the waste,
Wild thro' the wind the herdsman calls,
As fast, on willing Nag, I haste,
          Home to my own four walls.

                    tossing
Black, stormwatost clouds, with scarce a glimmer,
Even Envelope Earth, like sevenfold palls:
But wifekin watches, coffee-pot doth simmer,
                    Home in my own four walls!

At home and wife I two have got,
A hearth to blaze whate'er befals!
What needs a man that I have not
                    Within my own four walls?

King George has palaces of pride,
And armed grooms must ward their halls: Their orig.ly chang-
With one stout bolt, I safe abide   ed to their &c
                    Within my own four walls.   ?
                                        A.C.

Not all his men may sever this,
It yields to friends, not monarch's calls,
My whinstone house my Castle is,
                    I have my own four walls.

                         do   a
When fools or knaves make any rout,
With gigman dinners, balls, cabals,
I turn my back, and shut them out;
                    There are my own four walls.

The moorland house, tho' moor it be
May stand the brunt, when prouder falls;
Twill screen my wife, my Books and me,
                    All in my own four walls.

About 1830
A.C.
                         16:

Poem written by Carlyle, circa 1828–1830. In his letters to Jane, Carlyle often wrote of his desire to have his "own four walls"
(Beinecke Rare Book and Manuscript Library, Yale University).

An entry in Carlyle's notebook in 1829 attests to his early interest in Martin Luther. He again considered writing about Luther in the early 1840s but chose to write about Oliver Cromwell instead.

An Interest in Luther

Luther's character appears to me the most worth discussing of all modern men's. He is, to say it in a word, a great man in *every* sense; has the soul at once of a Conqueror and a Poet. His attachment to Music is to me a very interesting circumstance: it was the channel for many of his finest emotions; for which words, even words of prayer, were but an ineffectual exponent. Is it true that he *did* leave Wittenberg for Worms 'with nothing but his Bible and his Flute'? There is no scene in European History so splendid and significant.–I have long had a sort of notion to write some life or characteristic of Luther. A picture of the public Thought in those days, and of this strong lofty mind over-turning and new-moulding it, would be a fine affair in many senses. It would require immense research.–Alas! Alas!–When are we to have another Luther? Such men are needed from century to century: there seldom has been more need of one than now.

–*Two Note Books of Thomas Carlyle*, 139–140

* * *

This excerpt is a translation of Goethe's German original.

Goethe to Carlyle, 6 June 1830

[Y]ou will find in the little box the last sheets of the translation of your *Life of Schiller*. The publication has been delayed, and I wished to make the little work especially pretty, for the sake of the publisher as well as for its own. I have certainly pleased the public; I only hope you will excuse it.

The frontispiece represents your house from a near point of view, the vignette on the title page, the same from a distance,–I hope, so engraved from the drawings which you sent, that they cannot fail to please in England also.

–*Correspondence between Goethe and Carlyle*, 200–207

* * *

Carlyle's essay "Signs of the Times" was embraced by the Saint-Simonians, a group of Christian socialists in France that had evolved from the teachings of Claude-Henri de Rouvroy Saint-Simon. This excerpt is from a letter in which Car-

Title page for Goethe's German translation of Carlyle's biography of Schiller (engraving by George Moir; Special Collections, Thomas Cooper Library, University of South Carolina)

lyle acknowledged that he had received a gift of books from the Saint-Simonian Society, which had been addressed "A l'Auteur de l'Article intitulé Caractère de notre Epoque." Gustave D'Eichthal was a prominent Saint-Simonian. Although he rejected the group's religious belief in Saint-Simon as an incarnation of God, Carlyle was interested enough in the Saint-Simonians' thoughts on society to translate Saint-Simon's Nouveau Christianisme *into English. Evidence of Saint-Simonian ideas in John Stuart Mill's essays on "The Spirit of the Age" prompted Carlyle to track down Mill in London in 1831, and it was through Mill that Carlyle met D'Eichthal and presented him with his translation.*

Carlyle to Gustave D'Eichthal, 9 August 1830

Allow me to express, to yourself and the *Saint-Simonian Society*, my friendly acknowledgments for the interest you take in my inquiries; my true satisfaction

The foregoing Works, with many others of less moment, were sent to me at Craigenputtock, in 1830 and
subsequently. The Saint-Simonian Sect, after attracting
considerable notice for a space of two years, began to
split in pieces, underwent a Sentence of Law (apparently
on false charges) in 1832, and soon dissolved and dis-
-appeared. The little Truth that lay among their crudi-
-ties has not disappeared, or even properly _appeared_,
but yet waits its time. As a constituted Sect these
men are not without significance; not undeserving
some slight remembrance.

T. C.

6th May, 1834 —

Carlyle's note on the flyleaf of his copy of a Saint-Simonian pamphlet (The Trustees of the National Library of Scotland MS 2275)

Carlyle's Abandoned "History of German Literature"

As this excerpt from his 23 May 1830 letter to Goethe indicates, Carlyle had begun working on an ambitious history of German literature. He worked on his planned multivolume history for some two years.

Since you are friendly enough to offer me help and countenance in my endeavours that way, let me lose no time in profiting thereby. In regard to that *History of German Literature,* I need not say, for it is plain by itself, that no word of yours can be other than valuable. Doubtless it were a high favour, could you impart to me any summary of that great subject, in the structure and historical sequence and coherence it has with you: your views, whether from my point of vision or not, whether contradictory of mine, or confirmatory, could not fail to be instructive.

—Correspondence between Goethe and Carlyle, p. 187

Growing weary of his large project, Carlyle made the following observation about himself on 28 April 1832.

N. B. Be very cautious how you *take up* anything. I have a strange reluctance to renounce the road I have entered on, how stony soever, how roundabout soever. You do not like to turn back: On then!

—Two Note Books of Thomas Carlyle, p. 266

Carlyle did eventually abandon his "History of German Literature" after his publisher withdrew the contract, but the truth of his observation about himself is evident in his later refusal to let go of two other massive projects, editing Oliver Cromwell's letters and writing a biography of Frederick the Great.

that these views of mine find some acceptance with you. Here too, in favour of that same Material and Mechanical Disposition of our age, against which so much is objected, be it thankfully admitted and considered that, by means of it and of its physical triumphs, the thought of a solitary man, which he casts forth silently into the stream of things, can travel onward over seas to distant Capitals; and in due time, bring him back, to his remote Scottish granite-mountains, a brotherly response.

—"Letters from Thomas Carlyle to the Socialists of 1830," New Quarterly, 2 (April 1909): 279–280

* * *

Carlyle's reputation as a translator and as a writer was growing in America, as is suggested by this excerpt. Nathaniel P. Willis was the founding editor of the American Monthly Magazine.

"A Great Mind Truly Noted and Estimated" Review of *German Romance*
Nathaniel P. Willis

Open before us lies an odd volume of translation from German Romance, with biographical notices of the authors. This particular volume contains a part of one of the novels of Goethe, preceded by a sketch of that great man and poet, written by the able translator of Wilhelm Meister. We have never seen a mind so nobly and worthily measured. It is the finest specimen of prose that we have read for years, and we sit down and mark it for your perusal now, with a glow of pleasure that it will be shared and admired by you, which would scarce be warmer in our heart if it had been our own. We love to see a great mind truly noted and estimated. . . . We loved Goethe before. His Autobiography is more fascinating than a romance. But as we see him here—magnificently drawn by the graphic pencil of the translator, though the features are the same we have studied and admired, and though it is only naming our own and everybody's thoughts of the great German, we love him, since another has spoken of him, better and more. The shadow of an affection has been called out by name from our fancy and become substantial. A master spirit, equal almost to his theme, could alone have done it.

—American Monthly Magazine, 2 (September 1830): 430

* * *

This excerpt indicates the appreciation of Carlyle in Germany.

Julius Edward Hitzig to Goethe, 24 September 1830

As to Mr. Thomas Carlyle, who enjoys the inestimable good fortune of having his literary labours guided by your advice, furthered by your co-operation, and quickened and elevated by your friendship, and who so well deserves this favour of fate, we have unanimously chosen him a Foreign Member of our Society, believing that thereby we could best prove our high esteem for him and our desire for a closer relation with him. Since your Excellency has brought about this connection, nay more, has, through the adoption of his Work conse-

History of German Literature.

Chapter II.

Introduction Of Literature, and its Influences.—_Literary Histories_: De
-sign of the present.

(Let the Printer be careful to put _Capitals_ where he finds them
in the Ms.

It has often been remarked that Institutions and Establishments em-
-brace but a small portion of human affairs; that many of our deepest pub-
-lic interests, and best public endeavours are still unrecognised by the State. They
have sprung up and prospered without extraneous interference, often in direct op-
-position to such. It is but a short way that legislative forethought can look; a
still shorter sometimes that it is disposed to look: neither when the commonwealth
is already to the people covered with old Interests, is it easy for a new one to ob-
-tain a legal settlement there. Nevertheless increased culture, mere change it-
-self, brings new complexities and new wants; the old Institutions are found inad-
-equate, new Activities and from time to time new Activities, dimly and by slow
degrees, body themselves forth from the general mass; and with or without a legal Constitution, come to
discharge for us the most vital functions. Thus, in material things, the seven
or ten old Corporate Trades nowise, in these days, occupy the whole field of industry,
but some of our most essential conveniences are now furnished by miscellaneous
craftsmen of no guild-privilege whatever; so likewise is it in things spiritual: the
ancient guildhall is no longer, in either case, represents the collective handicrafts
but often only a small and half-obsolete part thereof of them.

Q^d: There is a Church of long standing in most countries; but no Tithes
are anywhere levied, or Convocations held, for behoof of the Newspaper Press: the
artists who make Laws for us are an old, wealthy, well-known Corporation,
while again our Song-makers are poor and without charter, who nevertheless, as
we have heard on good authority, are the more important Clan of the two

_Page from the manuscript of Carlyle's unfinished "History of German Literature" (Beinecke Rare Book and
Manuscript Library, Yale University)_

crated to our immortal Schiller, as it were, already made him one of us, we trust he will comply with our invitation to join us in the promotion of our high aim, and we beg of you to permit this, our sincere desire, to reach him through your kind mediation.

We conclude with the wish, which in every noble-minded German becomes a prayer, that Heaven will spare your life to our country for many years to come,—a life whose every moment is a fruitful seed of ennoblement and elevation for the present time and future ages.

Done at Berlin at the Meeting on the 24th of September 1830.

For the Society for Foreign Literature,
Hitzig.

—*Correspondence between Goethe and Carlyle*, p. 227

* * *

This excerpt is from a letter in which Carlyle thanked Goethe for his efforts on his behalf with the Society for Foreign Literature.

Carlyle to Goethe, 15 November 1830

Concerning the Box and its Books, I must first mention that wonderful *Life of Schiller*, with its proud Introduction, fitter to have stood at the head of some Epic Poem of my writing than there. That I should see myself, before all the world, set forth as the Friend of Goethe, is an honour of which, some few years ago, I could not, in my wildest flights, have dreamed; of which I should still desire no better happiness than to feel myself worthy. For the rest the book is nearly the most beautiful I have ever seen; the Preface graceful and pertinent, as well as highly flattering: these House-pictures themselves seem more appropriate than I could have fancied. On the whole, as one of our rhymers says: "'Tis distance lends enchantment to the view"; had this Craigenputtock mansion stood among the Harz Mountains or the Vosges, this authentic image of it

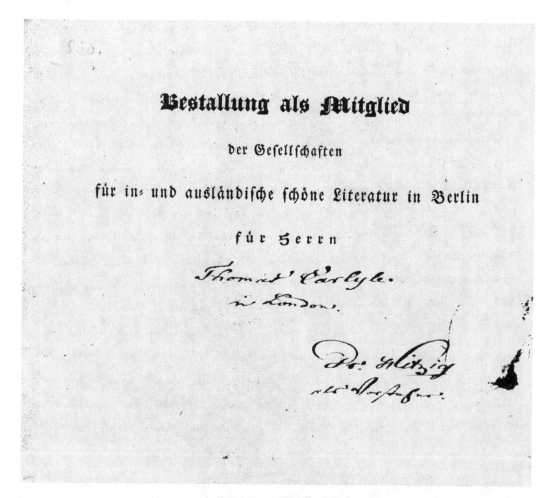

Certificate of Membership in the Society for Foreign Literature of Berlin, awarded to Carlyle in recognition of his furtherance of German literature abroad (The Trustees of the National Library of Scotland CH 880)

John Stuart Mill (from Simon Heffer, Moral Desperado: A Life
of Thomas Carlyle, *Thomas Cooper Library, University
of South Carolina)*

John Stuart Mill Meets Carlyle

*In this excerpt from an October 1831 letter to his friend
John Sterling, John Stuart Mill provides his first impressions
of Carlyle, who was then in London trying to arrange the publication of* Sartor Resartus *and who had sought Mill out
after reading the essays in his "The Spirit of the Age" series.
Although Mill presumes that his correspondent is acquainted
with Carlyle, Sterling at the time would only have known Carlyle through his writings. Carlyle and Sterling met and became
close friends in 1835.*

Another acquaintance which I have recently made is
that of Mr. Carlyle, whom I believe you are also
acquainted with. I have long had a very keen relish for
his articles in the Edinburgh & Foreign Reviews, which I
formerly thought to be such consummate nonsense; and
I think he improves upon a nearer acquaintance. He
does not seem to me so entirely the reflexion or shadow
of the great German writers as I was inclined to consider
him; although undoubtedly his mind has derived from
their inspiration whatever breath of life is in it. He seems
to me as a man who has had his eyes unsealed, and who
now looks round him & sees the aspects of things with
his own eyes, but by the light supplied by others; not the

pure light of day, but another light compounded of the
same simple rays but in different proportions. He has by
far the largest & widest liberality & tolerance (not in the
sense which Coleridge justly disavows, but in the good
sense) that I have met with in any one; & he differs from
most men who see as much as he does into the defects
of the age, by a circumstance greatly to his advantage in
my estimation, that he looks for a safe landing *before* and
not *behind:* he sees that if we could replace things as they
once were, we should only retard the final issue, as we
should in all human probability go on just as we then
did, & arrive again at the very place where we now
stand. . . . He is a great hunter-out of acquaintances; he
hunted me out, or rather hunted out the author of certain papers in the Examiner (the first as he said, which
he had ever seen in a newspaper, hinting that the age
was not the best of all possible ages): & his acquaintance
is the only substantial good I have yet derived from writing those papers, & a much greater one than I expected
when I wrote them.

*–The Earlier Letters of John Stuart Mill,
1812–1848, v. 2, pp. 85–86*

would have interested me as well as another. But that our remote Scottish Home should stand here, faithfully represented by a German burin under *your* auspices, this is a fact which we shall never get to understand. The King's Palace of Holy-Rood was not dealt with so royally; and that our rough-cast Dwelling, with its humble Sycamores, and unfrequented hills, should have such preferment! We repeat often: a House, like a Prophet, save in its own country, is not without Honour.

–*Correspondence between Goethe and Carlyle*, pp. 237–239

* * *

This excerpt is from a letter to the man who succeeded Jeffrey as editor of The Edinburgh Review.

Carlyle to Macvey Napier, 17 December 1831

My Dear Sir, I have, barely within my time, finished that paper ["Characteristics"], to which you are now heartily welcome, if you have room for it. The doctrines here set forth have mostly long been familiar convictions with me; yet it is perhaps only within the last twelvemonth that the public utterance of some of them could have seemed a duty. I have striven to express myself with what guardedness was possible: and, as there will now be no time for correcting Proofs, I must leave it wholly in your Editorial hands. Please to keep the Ms. for me; and *three Copies* of the printed paper.

Nay, should it on due consideration appear to you in your place (for I see that matter dimly, and nothing is clear but my own mind and the general condition of the world) unadviseable to print the Paper at all, then pray understand, my dear Sir, now and always, that I am no unreasonable man: but if dogmatic enough (as Jeffrey used to call it) in my own beliefs, also truly desirous to be just towards those of others. I shall, in all sincerity, beg of you to do, without fear of offence (for in *no* point of view [indeed] will there be any), what you yourself see good.

A mighty work lies before the writers of this time: I have a great faith and a great hope that the *Edinburgh Review* will not be wanting on its part, but stand forth in the van, where it has some right to be.

–*Memoirs of the Life and Writings of Thomas Carlyle*, pp. 118–119

* * *

Carlyle's friend records Carlyle's enthusiasm for Goethe in his diary of 12 February 1832.

Goethe as Carlyle's Prophet
Henry Crabb Robinson

Carlyle breakfasted with me, and I had an interesting morning with him. He is a deep-thinking German scholar, a character, and a singular compound. His voice and manner, and even the style of his conversation, are those of a religious zealot, and he keeps up that character in his declamations against the anti-religious. And yet, if not the god of his idolatry, at least he has a priest and prophet of his church in Goethe, of whose profound wisdom he speaks like an enthusiast. But for him Carlyle says, he should not now be alive. He owes everything to him!

–*Diary, Reminiscences, and Correspondence of Henry Crabb Robinson*, v. 3, p. 2

* * *

In this excerpt Mill refers to Carlyle's review of Boswell's Life of Johnson, *which was published in two parts in the April and May issues of* Fraser's Magazine: *"Biography" and "Boswell's Life of Johnson."*

Mill to Carlyle, 29 May 1832

Your parting gift, the paper on Biography and on Johnson, has been more precious to me than I well know how to state. I have read it over and over till I could almost repeat it by heart; and have derived from it more edification and more comfort, than from all else that I have read for years past. I have moreover lent it to various persons, whom I thought likely to reap the same benefit from it, and have in no instance been disappointed. . . .

–*The Earlier Letters of John Stuart Mill*, v. 1, p. 104

* * *

Mill to Carlyle, 17 July 1832

You also call me one of your teachers; but if I am this, it is as yet only in the sense in which a schoolmaster might speak of his teachers, meaning those who teach under him. I certainly could not now write, and perhaps shall never be able to write, any thing from which any person can derive so much edification as I, and several others, have derived in particular from your paper on Johnson. My vocation, as far as I yet see, lies in a humbler sphere; I am rather fitted to be a logical expounder than an artist. You I look upon as an artist, and perhaps the only genuine one now living in this country: the highest destiny of all, lies in that direction; for it is the artist alone in whose hands Truth becomes impressive, and a living principle of action.

–*The Earlier Letters of John Stuart Mill*, v. 1, p. 113

* * *

(507)

DEATH OF GOETHE.

In the Obituary of these days stands one article of quite peculiar import; the time, and place, and particulars of which will have to be often repeated, and re-written, and continue in remembrance for many centuries: this, namely, that Johann Wolfgang von Goethe died at Weimar, on the 22nd of March 1832. It was about eleven in the morning: "he expired," says the record, "without any apparent suffering, having, a few minutes previously, called for paper for the purpose of writing, and expressed his delight at the arrival of spring." A beautiful death: like that of a soldier found faithful at his post, and in the cold hand his arms still grasped! The Poet's last words are a greeting of the new-awakened Earth; his last movement is to work at his appointed task. Beautiful: what we might call a Classic sacred-death; if it were not rather an Elijah-translation,—in a chariot, not of fire and terror, but of hope and soft vernal sunbeams! It was at Frankfort on the Mayn, on the 28th of August 1749, that this man entered the world; and now, gently welcoming the very birthday of his eighty-second spring, he closes his eyes, and takes farewell.

So, then, our Greatest has departed. That melody of life, with its cunning tones, which took captive ear and heart, has gone silent; the heavenly force that dwelt here, victorious over so much, is here no longer: thus far, not farther, by speech and by act, shall the wise man utter himself forth. The End! What solemn meaning lies in that word, as it peals mournfully through the soul, when a living Friend has passed away! All now is closed, irrevocable: the changeful life-picture, growing daily into new coherence, under new touches and hues, has suddenly become completed and unchangeable: there as it lay, it is dipped, from this moment, in the æther of the Heavens, and shines transfigured, to endure even so—for ever. Time, and Time's empire; stern, wide-devouring, yet not without their grandeur! The week-day man, who was as one of us, has put on the garment of Eternity, and become radiant and triumphant: the Present is all at once the Past; Hope is suddenly cut away, and only the backward vistas of Memory remain, shone on by a light that proceeds not from this earthly sun.

The death of Goethe, even for the many hearts that personally loved him, is not a thing to be lamented over; is to be viewed, in his own spirit, as a thing full of greatness and sacredness. "For all men it is appointed once to die." To this man the full measure of a man's life had been granted, and a course and task such as to only a few in the whole generations of the world: what else could we hope or require but that now he should be called hence, and have leave to depart, "having finished the work that was given him to do?" If his course, as we may say of him more justly than of any other, was like the Sun's, so also was his going down. For, indeed, as the material Sun is the eye and revealer of all things, so is Poetry, so is the World-Poet, in a spiritual sense: Goethe's life, too, if we examine it, is well represented in that emblem of a solar Day. Beautifully rose our summer sun, gorgeous in the red fervid East, scattering the spectres and sickly damps (of both of which there were enough to scatter);—strong, benignant in his noon-day clearness, walking triumphant

First page of Carlyle's article in the June 1832 issue of New Monthly Magazine. *Goethe died 22 March 1832 (Thomas Cooper Library, University of South Carolina).*

My dear Carlyle

This note will be given to you by Mr R. W. Emerson of Boston (United States) who having been long a reader of your writings, is desirous to take the first opportunity of making your acquaintance. Mr. Emerson met with our friend Gustave D'Eichthal at Rome, and was by him referred to me as one who could give him the introduction to you which he wished for – I have great pleasure in doing so –

Yours faithfully

J. S. Mill.

Mill's letter of introduction for Ralph Waldo Emerson in which he mentions the American's acquaintainceship with Gustave D'Eichthal (The Trustees of the National Library of Scotland MS 618.f.26)

Ralph Waldo Emerson, who became one of Carlyle's most ardent
supporters and his correspondent for some thirty-eight years (from
The Correspondence of Thomas Carlyle and
Ralph Waldo Emerson, *Thomas Cooper*
Library, University of South Carolina)

Early in his career Carlyle came to the attention of
New England writer Ralph Waldo Emerson, who traveled to
Craigenputtoch to meet the Scot in 1833. Emerson, a leader
in the Transcendentalist movement, later worked on Carlyle's
behalf, facilitating the publication of Sartor Resartus *in*
book form in America.

In this excerpt Emerson describes meeting Carlyle.
Alexander Ireland, an Edinburgh journalist, served as Emer-
son's tour guide when he visited the city in 1833, and the
men formed a friendship. When Emerson died in 1882, Ire-
land published a biography of him, Ralph Waldo Emerson: His Life, Genius, and Writings.

Ralph Waldo Emerson to Alexander Ireland, 30 August 1833

Mr C. lives among some desolate hills in the
parish of Dunscore 15 or 16 miles from Dumfries.
He had heard of my purpose from his friend who
gave me my letter & insisted on dismissing my gig
which went back to Dumfries to return for me the
next day in time to secure my seat in the evening
coach for the south. So I spent near 24 hours with
him. He lives with his wife, a most agreeable accomplished woman, in perfect solitude. There is not a
person to speak to within 7 miles. He is the most
simple frank amiable person–I became acquainted
with him at once, we walked over several miles of
hills & talked upon all the great questions that interest us most. The comfort of meeting a man of genius
is that he speaks sincerely that he feels himself to be
so rich that he is above the meanness of pretending
to knowledge which he h[as] not & Carlyle does not
pretend to have solved the great problems but rather
to be an observer of their solution as it goes forward
in the world. I asked him at what religious development the concluding passage in his piece in the Edin.
Review upon German Literature (say 5 years ago) &
some passages in the piece called Characteristics,
pointed? he replied, that he was not competent to
state it even to himself–he waited rather to see.–My
own feeling was that I had met with men of far less
power who had yet greater insight into religious
truth.–He is as you might guess from his papers the
most catholic of philosophers–he forgives & loves
everybody & wishes each to struggle on in his own
place & arrive at his own ends, but his respect for
eminent men or rather his scale of eminence is
almost the reverse of the popular scale; Scott, Mack-
intosh,–Jeffrey;–Gibbon;–even Bacon are no heroes
of his; stranger yet he hardly admires Socrates, the
glory of the Greek world–but Burns & Samuel
Johnson; Mirabeau he said, interested him, & I suppose whoever [els]e has given himself with all his
heart to a leading instinct & has not *calculated* too
much. But I cannot think of sketching even his opinions or repeating his conversation here. I will cheerfully do it when you visit me in America. He talks
finely, seems to love the broad Scotch, & I loved him
very much, at once. I am afraid he finds his entire
solitude tedious, but I could not help congratulating
him upon his treasure in his wife & I hope they will
not leave the moors. tis so much better for a man of
letters to nurse himself in seclusion than to be filed
down to the common level by the compliances & imitations of city society.

–*The Letters of Ralph Waldo Emerson,*
v. 1, pp. 394–395

* * *

Emerson Remembers Carlyle at Craigenputtoch

In an essay written more than twenty years after the fact, Emerson gave this account of meeting Carlyle.

. . . He was tall and gaunt, with a cliff-like brow, self-possessed, and holding his extraordinary powers of conversation in easy command; clinging to his northern accent with evident relish; full of lively anecdote, and with a streaming humor, which floated every thing he looked upon. His talk playfully exalting the familiar objects, put the companion at once into an acquaintance with his Lars and Lemurs, and it was very pleasant to learn what was predestined to be a pretty mythology. Few were the objects and lonely the man, "not a person to speak to within sixteen miles except the minister of Dunscore;" so that books inevitably made his topics.

He had names of his own for all the matters familiar to his discourse. "Blackwood's" was the "sand magazine;" "Fraser's" nearer approach to possibility of life was the "mud magazine;" a piece of road near by that marked some failed enterprise was the "grave of the last sixpence." When too much praise of any genius annoyed him, he professed hugely to admire the talent shown by his pig. He had spent much time and contrivance in confining the poor beast to one enclosure in his pen, but pig, by great strokes of judgment, had found out how to let a board down, and had foiled him. . . .

We talked of books. Plato he does not read, and he disparaged Socrates; and, when pressed, persisted in making Mirabeau a hero. Gibbon he called the splendid bridge from the old world to the new. His own reading had been multifarious. Tristram Shandy was one of his first books after Robinson Crusoe, and Robertson's America an early favorite. Rousseau's Confessions had discovered to him that he was not a dunce; and it was now ten years since he had learned German, by the advice of a man who told him he would find in that language what he wanted.

. . . .

We went out to walk over long hills, and looked at Criffel, then without his cap, and down into Wordsworth's country. There we sat down, and talked of the immortality of the soul. It was not Carlyle's fault that we talked on that topic, for he had the natural disinclination of every nimble spirit to bruise itself against walls, and did not like to place himself where no step can be taken. But he was honest and true, and cognizant of the subtile links that bind ages together, and saw how every event affects all the future. 'Christ died 'on the tree: that built Dunscore kirk yonder: that 'brought you and me together. Time has only a 'relative existence.'

He was already turning his eyes towards London with a scholar's appreciation. London is the heart of the world, he said, wonderful only from the mass of human beings. He liked the huge machine. Each keeps its own round. The baker's boy brings muffins to the window at a fixed hour every day, and that is all the Londoner knows or wishes to know on the subject. But it turned out good men.

—Ralph Waldo Emerson, *English Traits*, pp. 21–24

An American edition of Carlyle's The Life of Friedrich Schiller *was prepared and published in 1833 to favorable reviews, a reception that prefigured the welcome Carlyle's* Sartor Resartus *later received in the United States.*

This excerpt is from an unsigned review.

"The Heart of an Universal Scholar"
Review of *The Life of Friedrich Schiller*

This life of Schiller has been selected by the proprietor, Mr. Park Benjamin, as the first volume of a series of works of a high literary character. The plan is to present from time to time to the public a book, similar in size and appearance to the present volume, which shall be either an original work, a translation, or a republication. This life of Schiller is in some respects of a very high order. It was written in England, and is edited by Mr. Follen, the German professor of Harvard. It is a finished specimen of mechanical execution. The paper, engraving, printing, and binding, are all in excellent taste. The biography and remarks on Schiller's writings are discriminating, philosophical, and interesting in a remarkable degree. The English writer is not an Englishman or a German, but a citizen of the world. He has the heart of an universal scholar.

—*American Quarterly Observer*, 2 (January 1834): 172–174

* * *

These excerpts are from a twenty-seven-page review by a minister and friend of Ralph Waldo Emerson, who sent the article to Carlyle in November 1835.

"No Ordinary Merit"
Review of *The Life of Friedrich Schiller*
Frederick Henry Hedge

He who is called to be a prophet in his generation,—whose office it is to unfold new forms of truth and beauty,—enjoys, among other prerogatives peculiar to his calling, the privilege of a two-fold life. He is at once a dweller in the dust, and a denizen of that land where all truth and beauty spring. . . . Oftentimes, however, the mortal and the spiritual, the earthly calling and the high calling, the prophet and the man, are so interwoven, that it becomes almost impossible to distinguish the one from the other. Hence the biography of such an one, when conceived in the spirit of this double nature, is a task of peculiar difficulty. The biographer must not only exhibit each part of his subject in its individual distinctness and fullness, but he must also explain the relation between them; he must show how the intellectual life has sprung from the earthly condition, and how the earthly condition has in turn been modified by the intellectual life. Now it is evident, that none but an *auto*-biography can fully satisfy the conditions of such a problem, inasmuch as the whole mystery of the connexion between the moral and the spiritual, can be known only to individual consciousness. But as far as it is possible for one mind to interpret another,—so far as it is possible for the disciple of one nation or literature to comprehend and exhibit the intellectual offspring of a different nation and literature, so far this object has been accomplished in the work before us. The "Biography of Schiller" is a production of no ordinary merit, from whatever point of view we regard it; to us, it is chiefly remarkable as one of the very few instances in which full justice has been rendered by an English mind, to the character and claims of a foreign writer.

. . . .

The "Life of Schiller" is distinguished by its clear and happy method, its luminous critiques, its just appreciation of the characteristic excellences and deficiencies of the poet whom it portrays. From scanty materials the author has constructed a work full of instruction, and pregnant with more than romantic interest. A life usually barren of vicissitude is made to appear eventful in the strong light which is thrown upon the revolutions of a master mind. In short, this biography is what the biography of a poet should always be,—the history of the mind rather than the history of the person, a record of thoughts and feelings rather than events, a faithful exposition of the struggles

and vicissitudes, the trials and triumphs, which have befallen a human intellect in the service of truth.

The literary faults, which an impartial critic might discover, have arisen almost entirely from the want of a sufficient acquaintance with the German idiom. The author's translations are for the most part excellent; occasionally, however, a misapprehension of some word or phrase has betrayed him into errors, which sometimes distort, but oftener weaken the original. The most important of these errors have been pointed out and judiciously corrected by the American editor; the few that remain are, comparatively, trifling. In some instances they seem to be wilful deviations from, rather than misapprehensions of the poet's meaning.

Not to dwell, however, on these *literary* imperfections, there is one portion of this work;—we rejoice to say *only* one,—of which we feel ourselves constrained to express a decided disapprobation. We allude to the manner in which our author mentions Schiller's use of stimulants. This practice, he seems to regard, as not only innocent, but praiseworthy; the evils, which sprung from it,—the enfeebling of the bodily frame and the shortening of life, are represented as noble sacrifices the cause of the letters. . . . We believe that much mischief is done by such representation, or, indeed, by any exposure of similar practices on the part of distinguished men. Young aspirants after literary eminence are led, by the hearing of such things, to believe that there is some essential connection between the faults and fame of the great, and that the one will necessarily lead to the other. . . . The biographer is bound by no obligation that we can understand, to reveal these secrets of the fleshly prison-house; if he must reveal them, let it not be in the spirit of commendation, but with the rebuke which the error deserves.

—*Christian Examiner*, 16 (July 1834): 365–392

* * *

Horseshoe with screw cogs invented by Carlyle in 1834 (Carlyle's House Museum, London)

The Carlyles' years at Craigenputtoch affected them as a couple, and each looked back on their time there as a defining period in their lives. This excerpt is from an interview Ellen Twistleton recorded in 1855.

"The Dreariest Place"
Jane Welsh Carlyle Remembers Craigenputtoch

I asked Mrs. Carlyle if the description of "Craigenputtoch" in this Memoir was like;—she said, "Yes, for it was the dreariest place on the face of the earth—I lived there five years, & the only wonder is I didn't go mad; the only women that had ever been there before me, were four farmer's wives,—& of that *kind* of woman, with all their own rough work about them which they used to occupy themselves with doing, three went mad, & the fourth took to drinking!"

"But what made you go there, or what made you stay there," I said; "did you like the idea of it *before* you went?"

"Oh no I *never* liked the idea of it—oh, there's no way of making ye understand what kind of a wretched place it was,—I had seen it only once in my life, when my *grandfather* took me there, when I was quite a little child, & had always remembered it as the most dreadful, lonesome, barren of places,—and all thro' my childhood I used to be *frightened* with it,—it used to be the *threat* if ye understand, "if ye behave so badly, ye shall go to Craigenputtoch;"–& I remember once, when I must have been fourteen years old, & was self-willed about something, my Mother's telling me that I "deserved to be sent to Craiggen-puttoch to live on a hundred a year."–and to think that I *did* live there *five* years, with not much more than a hundred a year. . . . Mr. Carlyle's brother came, & he was to manage the farm, & to pay rent to my Mother. But nothing cld. turn out worse than that, for he was a man of the most outrageous, coarse, violent temper,–(he's gone to Canada, since, & done very well there, I believe,) & nobody can imagine what I went through with that man,—and it had to be all alone,—for I could never say a word to Carlyle,—that would be to drive him perfectly crazy, & "my dear, what *can* I possibly know, or do, about all this!" So his brother was always getting into difficulties with his workmen, & everybody on the place, & all were brought to me, to "the mistress," as they called me, to settle; –(they called him "the Master," & me "the Mistress," & Carlyle "the Laird"–) . . . . In those days, no bargain was ever concluded in Scotland without the parties *drinking* together, they always must sit down together over their whisky, or gin, or whatever it was,—so, of course, every time he went into Dumfries on his

business, he came back as drunk as a man could be– and at that time he did all the errands of the household, & got me all the things I needed from Dumfries–so ye may imagine the state they used to come in, the keg of gin broken into the bag of flour–& the powdered sugar mixed up with the *sugar-of-lead* I was goin' to say, & so forth. I had to learn to do & undo everything, & down to doctoring horses.

. . . .

"And that man lived with us for four years; after he was gone, I could manage to live better. But one of my miseries was about the rent–for he seemed to think because he was Carlyle's brother, it was no matter to be accurate about that, when he paid it, or almost whether he paid it at all,–& and there was my Mother, I knew, wanting her money & waiting for it–& she that had had every luxury all her life, not knowing where to turn for ten pounds,–as I knew, tho' she never told me so–and I not able to get her rent paid her! I remember one time, it had not been paid for four months beyond the time, & Carlyle got some money from London, for something he'd written, in a cheque upon the Dumfries bank; I seized the cheque, got on my pony, & rode, all alone no servant with me, into the town, to the bank, got my money, & off another sixteen miles to my Mother's (for it was in a kind of *triangle* we were, 16 miles one way from her, & the other way from the town, –) and gave her the money, & then another 16 miles home again."

. . . .

. . . Finally I had a sister of Carlyle's come, & she was with me 18 months, & those were the worst of the whole–she was a coarse, rude girl and had such a temper, & such a tre-MENDOUS will as I never met with in any other woman but herself,–a will just like Carlyle's, without anything besides to induce ye to put up with it.–She assumed authority over the servants, & made constant quarrels with them *in* the house, as his brother did out,–& I had no authority over her, for if I found fault with her, she went to Carlyle, & "Jane" was doing this & that to her; & that couldn't be done, you know. So she came to breakfast with her hair in curl-papers, which I never could put up with, & other things of the sort. I used to go out & sit down in the middle of the moor, on a stone, & *wonder* if this were I, & how the same persons could live such a life, that had lived the one I'd been used to before,–so petted generally, (though I got whipping enough, to be sure, at times;) but, being an only child, even if I was *punished,* I always felt myself an object of importance, at any rate.

"He Left Her to Her Own Resources": A Hard Time at Craigenputtoch

The Carlyles' family friend Geraldine Jewsbury provides this account of Jane Carlyle during a difficult period.

One hard winter her servant, Grace, asked leave to go home to see her parents; there was some sort of a fair held in her village. She went and was to return at night. The weather was bad, and she did not return. The next morning there was nothing for it but for her to get up to light the fires and prepare breakfast. The house had beautiful and rather elaborate steel grates; it seemed a pity to let them rust, so she cleaned them carefully, and then looked round for wood to kindle the fire. There was none in the house; it all lay in a little outhouse across the yard. On trying to open the door, she found it was frozen beyond her power to open it, so Mr. Carlyle had to be roused; it took all his strength, and when opened a drift of snow six feet high fell into the hall! Mr. Carlyle had to make a path to the wood-house, and bring over a supply of wood and coal; after which he left her to her own resources.

The fire at length made, the breakfast had to be prepared; but it had to be raised from the foundation. The bread had to be made, the butter to be churned, and the coffee ground. All was at last accomplished, and the breakfast was successful! After breakfast she went about the work of the house, as there was no chance of the servant being able to return. The work fell into its natural routine. Mr. Carlyle always kept a supply of wood ready; he cut it, and piled it ready for her use inside the house; and he fetched the water, and did things she had not the strength to do. The poor cow was her greatest perplexity. She could continue to get hay down to feed it, but she had never in her life milked a cow. The first day the servant of the farmer's wife, who lived at the end of the yard, milked it for her willingly, but the next day Mrs. Carlyle heard the poor cow making an uncom-

fortable noise; it had not been milked. She went herself to the byre, and took the pail and sat down on the milking stool and began to try to milk the cow. It was not at first easy; but at last she had the delight of hearing the milk trickle into the can. She said she felt quite proud of her success; and talked to the cow like a human creature. The snow continued to lie thick and heavy on the ground, and it was impossible for her maid to return. Mrs. Carlyle got on easily with all the house-work, and kept the whole place bright and clean except the large kitchen or house place, which grew to need scouring very much. At length she took courage to attack it. Filling up two large pans of hot water, she knelt down and began to scrub; having made a clean space round the large arm-chair by the fireside, she called Mr. Carlyle and installed him with his pipe to watch her progress. He regarded her beneficently, and gave her from time to time words of encouragement. Half the large floor had been successfully cleansed, and she felt anxious of making a good ending, when she heard a gurgling sound. For a moment or two she took no notice, but it increased and there was a sound of something falling upon the fire, and instantly a great black thick stream came down the chimney, pouring like a flood along the floor, taking precisely the lately cleaned portion first in its course, and extinguishing the fire. It was too much; she burst into tears. The large fire, made up to heat the water, had melted the snow on the top of the chimney, it came down mingling with the soot, and worked destruction to the kitchen floor. All that could be done was to dry up the flood. She had no heart to recommence her task. She rekindled the fire and got tea ready. That same night her maid came back, having done the impossible to get home. She clasped Mrs. Carlyle in her arms, crying and laughing, saying 'Oh, my dear mistress, my dear mistress, I dreamed ye were deed!'

–Reminiscences, v. 2, pp. 65–66

Living at Craigenputtock, it wasn't as if I saw anything of Carlyle;–he went to his own room directly after breakfast, & worked there till 2 hours before dinner, & always rode those two hours. And he rode *alone,* because he only galloped or walked, and it fretted him to have my horse cantering along by the of his side, so he rode alone & I rode alone, then he came to dinner very much *worked-up,* as bilious people always are by a ride, & he was "dangerous," you know, & there was no freedom of communication during dinner; then he went to walk for an hour, which wasn't very wholesome, I always tho't, right after eating, & to his room till tea; & afterward to his room, until about ten o'clock, & then he'd come in, quite tired out with his work, & say, "Jane,

will ye play me a few of those Scotch tunes"–& so I would sit down & play Scotch tunes till he went to bed,–oftenest with the tears running down my face the while I played."–

"And was there nobody you cared for in the *town,*–had you no friends that ever came to see you from Dumfries?" "No, nobody:–sometimes, when I couldn't bear it any longer, I'd go over to my Mother & spend the night with her;–but I had to be back in the morning, for it couldn't go on without me,–we'd no servants that could be trusted."

–The Collected Letters of Thomas and Jane Welsh Carlyle, v. 30, pp. 267–274

* * *

The kitchen at Craigenputtoch (photograph by J. Patrick; from Joan M. Sloan, The Carlyle Country, *Special Collections, Thomas Cooper Library, University of South Carolina)*

"Not Without an Intrinsic Dignity" Carlyle on Craigenputtoch

Of our History at Craigenputtock there might a great deal be written which might amuse the curious: for it was in fact a very singular scene and arena for such a pair as my Darling and me, with such a Life ahead; and bears some analogy to the settlement of Robinson Crusoe in his desert Isle, surrounded mostly by wild populations, not wholly helpful or even harmless; and requiring, for its equipment into habitability and convenience, infinite contrivance, patient adjustment, and natural ingenuity in the head of Robinson himself. . . . It looks to me now like a kind of humble russet-coated *epic,* that seven years' settlement at Craigenputtock; very poor in this world's goods, but not without an intrinsic dignity greater and more important than then appeared. Thanks very mainly to Her, and her faculties and magnanimities; without whom it had not been possible! I incline to think it the poor-*best* place that could have been selected for the ripening into fixity and composure, of anything useful which there may have been in me, against the years that were coming. And it is certain that for living in, and thinking in, I have never since found in the world a place so favourable.

—*Reminiscences,* v. 2, pp. 243–244

The Travails of Teufelsdreck

As he struggled with his "History of German Literature," Carlyle felt a desire to compose an original work, a project that both exhilarated and intimidated him. By October 1830 he had begun the work that became Sartor Resartus. *Initially, Carlyle offered his work as a long article titled "Thoughts on Clothes" to James Fraser, editor of* Fraser's Magazine, *for periodical publication, but in January 1831 he changed his mind and set about revising the manuscript into a book.*

By the end of July 1831 Carlyle finished expanding and revising the manuscript he sometimes called "poor Teufelsdreck" after his protagonist, and from August through October 1831 he sought a publisher in London. This foray into the world of book publication was emotionally trying and unsuccessful, in part because of the unusual nature of the manuscript but also because of Carlyle's inexperience and his volatile temperament. He began his search with John Murray, publisher of Byron, but Murray delayed in reviewing the manuscript, prompting the impatient author to show it to other London publishers. Jeffrey intervened with Murray on Carlyle's behalf on 28 August 1831, and the publisher offered a contract, which he withdrew after learning of Carlyle's earlier circulation of the manuscript. Receiving his returned manuscript along with nonplussed comments from Murray's reader, Carlyle relegated his work to the drawer, awaiting a more favorable climate for publication.

"Something Strange May Come"

In this excerpt from his 31 August 1830 letter to Goethe, Carlyle confides his decision to put aside his "History of German Literature" for a new project.

. . . The present undertaking once fairly put to a side, as it now nearly is, I must forthwith betake me to something more congenial and original: except writing from the heart and if possible to the heart, Life has no other business for me, no other pleasure. When I look at the wonderful Chaos within me, full of natural Supernaturalism, and all manner of Antideluvian *[sic]* fragments; and how the Universe is daily growing more mysterious as well as more august, and the influences from without more heterogeneous and perplexing; I see not well what is to come of it all, and only conjecture from the violence of the fermentation that something strange may come.

—Correspondence between Goethe and Carlyle, pp. 210–211

This excerpt is from Carlyle's 18 September 1830 letter to his brother John A. Carlyle.

I am going to *write something of my own;* I have sworn it.

—The Collected Letters of Thomas and Jane Welsh Carlyle, v. 5, p.164

Carlyle made the following notations in his notebook.

September 1830

I am going to write—Nonsense. It is on "Clothes." Heaven be my comforter —

October 1830

Written a strange piece "On clothes": know not what will come of it.

—Two Note Books of Thomas Carlyle, pp. 176, 177

In May 1833 Carlyle offered Sartor Resartus *to James Fraser for periodical publication, and the work appeared anonymously in* Fraser's Magazine *in eight installments from November 1833 to August 1834. In 1834 fifty-eight copies of the work in book form were published for distribution among Carlyle's friends.*

In January 1830, at Carlyle's request, his brother retrieved the manuscript of "Thoughts on Clothes" from James Fraser and showed it to Edward Irving, whose opinion of the draft, along with his own, John reports.

John A. Carlyle to Carlyle, 12 February 1831

He *'perfectly agreed with you in what you had said about religion & the state of society,'* & wished much it were in his power to talk largely with you of these matters. You had shown great power, & copiousness & 'learning.' The MS might be altered & expanded into a book likely to produce a great & salutary impression at the present time. The character of Teufelsdreck,—the meaning of which name, by the way, he seemed to have no conception of—he thought was very graphically & 'humourously' drawn. He submitted, at the same time; that there was perhaps too little action in proportion to the machinery employed; that the preliminary matter of the first chapter was too long; that you seemed to have poured out the rich flood of your own thoughts, without caring whether the reader might feel it possible to keep pace with you, or bear the load of ideas you were heaping upon him. All these deficiencies were attributable to your having written for the Magazine. More subdivisions, more resting points, might make the work more acceptable & effectual. . . . Irving thinks one cannot make any thing by honest writing of books, but only by writing for Reviews &c; and he speaks from experience. I do not believe it would be possible to find any book-seller to undertake the publication of a first volume; but if the whole were finished I do not think it would be difficult to find one on advantageous terms, —indeed I sh*d* engage to find one myself.—You must come hither yourself this very spring if possible & see what is going on. . . . You would soon collect a number of young people who are striving after better things & without any guidance. I know some such myself & they are almost my only associates.

—The Collected Letters of Thomas and Jane Welsh Carlyle, v. 5, pp. 233–234

* * *

Carlyle reports on one of many visits to publisher John Murray in this excerpt.

Carlyle to Jane Welsh Carlyle, 17 August 1831

This morning I returned to Albemarle Street; the Bookseller was first denied to me, then showed his broad one-eyed face, and with fair speeches signified that his family were all ill, and he had been called into the country; and my Manuscript—lay still unopened! I reminded him, not without emphasis, of the engagement made, and how I had nothing else to do here, but see that matter brought to an end: to all which he pleaded hard in extenuation, and for "two or three days" a further allowance. I made him *name* a new day: "Saturday first"; then I am to return and hear how the matter stands. I begin to fear this Blockhead will spin me out into still longer delays: it is already becoming a question with me, how far I should let him run without taking delay for final rejection. He is said to be noted for procrastination; but also for honourableness, even munificence. My prospects apart from him are not brilliant: however, loss of time is the worst of all losses; he shall not keep me dancing round him very long, go how it may.

> *—The Collected Letters of Thomas and Jane Welsh Carlyle,*
> v. 5, p. 341

* * *

Carlyle to Murray, 19 August 1831

DEAR SIR,

As I am naturally very anxious to have this little business that lies between us off my hands—and, perhaps, a few minutes' conversation would suffice to settle it all—I will again request, in case I should be so unlucky as to miss you in Albemarle Street, that you would have the goodness to appoint me a short meeting at any, the earliest, hour that suits your convenience.

> I remain, dear Sir, yours truly,
> THOMAS CARLYLE.
> *—Samuel Smiles, A Publisher and His Friends. Memoir and Correspondence of the Late John Murray,* p. 351

* * *

Carlyle's study at Craigenputtoch, in which he composed Sartor Resartus *(photograph by J. Patrick; from Joan M. Sloan,* The Carlyle Country, *Special Collections, Thomas Cooper Library, University of South Carolina)*

Carlyle reports on his further dealings with publishers in this excerpt.

Carlyle to Jane Welsh Carlyle, 22 August 1831

On Saturday morning I set out for Albemarle Street; taking up your Seal by the way; which Seal I reckoned well done (for 10 shillings), and hope the Leddy herself will be of the same mind. Murray as usual was not in; but an answer lay for me: my poor Teufelsdreck wrapped in new paper, with a Letter stuck under the pack thread! I took it with a silent fury, and walked off. The Letter said, he regretted exceedingly &c that—all his Literary friends were out of town, he himself occupied with a sick family in the country; that he had conceived the finest hopes &c; in short that Teufelsdreck had never been looked into; but that if I would let him keep it for a month, he would *then* be able to say a word, and by God's blessing a favourable one. I walked on thro' Regent-Street, and looked in upon James Fraser the Bookseller, and sat down in his backshop to rest me. First of all it became apparent here that Fraser had not and could not have any proposal to make about his Magazine worth listening to for half a minute; but that the whole concern was damnable and well nigh damned. Secondly we got to talk about Teufelsdreck: when after much hithering and thithering about the black state of trade &c., it turned out that honest James would publish the Book for me, on this principle: If I would give *him* a sum not exceeding £150 sterling! "I think you had better wait a little," said an Edinburgh Advocate to me since, when he heard of this proposal: "Yes," I answered, "it is my purpose to wait to the end of Eternity first."—"But the Public will not buy Books"—"The Public has done the wisest thing it could; and ought never more to buy what they call Books."

Spurning at Destiny, yet in the mildest terms taking leave of Fraser, I strode thro' these streets, carrying Teuf*k* openly in my hand, *not* like a gentleman. I took a pipe and glass of water, and counsel with myself. I was bilious and sad, and thought of my dear Jeannie, for whom also were these struggles, with an inexpressible tenderness. Having rested a little, I set out again to the Longmans to hear what they had to say. The German Lit. Hist. having soon been despatched I describe Teufelsdreck; bargain that they are to look at it themselves; and send it back again in two days; that is tomorrow. They are honest, rugged, punctual-looking people, and will keep their word; but their chance of *declining* seems to me a hundred to one. Meanwhile I keep looking out on all hands, for another issue. Perhaps I shall have to march thro' the whole squad of scoundrels, and try them all. *A la bonne heure!* [Well and good!] I have a problem which *is* possible: either to get Dreck printed, or to ascertain that I *cannot* and so tie him up and come home with him. So fear nothing, Love. I care not a doit for the worst; and thou too hast the heart of a heroine, art worthy of me were I the highest of heroes. Nay, my persuasion that Teuf*k* is in his place and his time here grows stronger the more I see of London and its philosophy: the Doctrine of the *Phoenix,* of *Nat. Supernaturalism* and the whole Clothes Philosophy (be it but well stated) is exactly what all intelligent men are wanting.

. . . .

. . . Jeffrey asked to see my *Ms.* when the Longmans had done with it: he would look thro' it, and see what he could *talk* to Murray concerning it. I gladly consented: and thus for the while the matter rests. Murray is clearly the man, if he *will*: only I have *lost* ten days by him already; for he might have told me what he did finally tell in one day.

–The Collected Letters of Thomas
and Jane Welsh Carlyle,
v. 5, pp. 353–355

* * *

In this excerpt Jane uses one of Carlyle's nicknames for his Sartor Resartus *manuscript.*

Jane Welsh Carlyle to Carlyle, 1 September 1831

. . . My beloved *Dreck!* my jewel of great price! The builders despise thee; but thou wilt yet be *brought out with shouting,* and I shall live to see thee in thy place. All these discouragements do but increase my confidence, as a candle burns brighter for being snuffed; for *Dreck* is imperishable, indestructible as the substance of the four elements; and all Booksellerdom, all Devildom cannot prevail against him!

–"More New Letters of Jane Welsh Carlyle," edited by Alexander Carlyle, in *Nineteenth Century and After,* 76 (July–December 1914): 344

* * *

After receiving an unfavorable report from his reader whom he described as "a Gentleman in the highest class of men of Letters" and "an accomplished German Scholar," Murray returned the manuscript to Carlyle on 6 October. Carlyle kept and included the response of Murray's reader in the "Testimonies of Authors" that prefaced the first English trade edition of his work.

Reader's Report on *Sartor Resartus*

Taster to Bookseller.–"The Author of *Teufelsdröckh* is a person of talent; his work displays here and there some felicity of thought and expression, considerable fancy and knowledge: but whether or not it would take with the public seems doubtful. For a *jeu d'esprit* of that kind it is too long; it would have suited better as an essay or article than as a volume. The Author has no great tact; his wit is frequently heavy; and reminds one of the German Baron who took to leaping on tables, and answered that he was learning to be lively. *Is* the work a translation?"

Sartor Resartus, p. v

* * *

Carlyle related the end of his experience with Murray in this excerpt.

Carlyle to John A. Carlyle, 21 October 1831

As to *Teufelsdreck,* I may conclude this first section of his history in few words. Murray, on my renewed demand some days after your departure, forwarded me the Manuscript with a polite enough note, and a "Criticism" from some altogether immortal "master of German Literature," to me quite unknown; which Criticism (a miserable, Dandiacal *quodlibet,* in the usual vein) did *not* authorise the Publication in these times. Whereupon, inspecting the Paper to ascertain that it was all there, we (my good Lady and I) wrapped all up, and laid it by under lock and key, to wait patiently for better times, or if so were ordered, to the *end* of times: and then despatching a very cordial-looking note to Murray, wound up the whole matter, not without composure of soul. Now that the Reform Bill is all to begin again, it may for aught I know be months before the Trade experience any revival; thus *Dreck* may perhaps be considered as postponed *sine die:* with which result also I am perfectly contented. What I have written I have written: the reading of it is another party's concern.

–Letters of Thomas Carlyle, 1826–1836,
pp. 262–263

* * *

Letter from Murray to Carlyle, 14 September 1831, in which the publisher alludes to the circumstance that Carlyle had let Longman, Rees, & Co. see his manuscript (The Trustees of the National Library of Scotland MS 1796)

In this excerpt Carlyle proposes the serialization of his book, which he retitled Sartor Resartus *in September. "O.Y." refers to the pseudonym of William Maginn, editor of* Fraser's.

Carlyle to James Fraser, 27 May 1833

Most probably you recollect the Manuscript *Book* I had with me in London; and how during that Reform hurly-burly, which unluckily still continues and is like to continue, I failed to make any bargain about it. The Manuscript still lies in my drawer; and now after long deliberation I have determined to slit it up into strips, and send it forth in the Periodical way; for which in any case it was perhaps better adapted. The pains I took with the composition of it, truly, were greater than even I might have thought necessary, had this been foreseen: but what then? Care of that sort is never altogether thrown away; far better too much than too little. I reckon that it will be easy for the Magazine Printer to save me some thirty or forty complete copies, as he prints it; these can then be bound up and distributed among my Friends likely to profit thereby; and in the end of all we can *re*print it into a Book proper, if that seem good. Your Magazine is the first I think of for this object; and I must have got a distinct negative from you before I go any farther. Listen to me, then, and judge.

The Book is at present named "Thoughts on Clothes; or Life and Opinions of Herr D. Teufels-drockh, D. U. J."; but perhaps we might see right to alter the title a little; for the rest, some brief Introduction could fit it handsomely enough into its new destination: it is already divided into three "Books," and farther into very short "Chapters," capable in all ways of subdivision. Nay some tell me, what perhaps is true, that taking a few chapters at a time is really the profitablest way of reading it. There may be in all some Eight sheets of *Fraser*. It is put together in the fashion of a kind of Didactic Novel; but indeed properly *like* nothing yet extant: I used to characterise it briefly as a kind of "Satirical Extravaganza on Things in General"; it contains more of my opinions on Art, Politics, Religion, Heaven, Earth and Air, than all the things I have yet written. The Creed promulgated on all these things, as you may judge, is *mine,* and firmly *believed:* for the rest, the main Actor in the business ("Editor of these Sheets," as he often calls himself) assumes a kind of Conservative (though Anti-quack) character; and would suit *Fraser* perhaps better than any other Magazine. The ultimate result, however, I need hardly premise, is a deep religious speculative-radicalism (so I call it for want of a better name), with which you are already well enough acquainted in me.

There are only five persons that have yet read this Manuscript: of whom two have expressed themselves (I mean convinced me that they *are*) considerably interested and gratified; two quite *struck,* "overwhelmed with astonishment and new hope" (this is the result I aimed at for souls worthy of hope); and one in secret discontented and displeased. William Fraser is a sixth reader, or rather half-reader; for I think he had only got half-way or so; and I never learned his opinion. With him, if you like, at this stage of the business you can consult freely about it. My own conjecture is that *Teufelsdrockh,* whenever published, will astonish most that read it, be wholly understood by very few; but to the astonishment of some will add touches of (almost the deepest) spiritual interest, with others quite the opposite feeling. I think I can practically prophesy that for some six or eight months (for it must be published

without interruption), it would be apt at least to *keep the eyes* of the Public on you.

Such is all the description I can give you, in these limits: now what say you to it? Let me hear as soon as you can; for the time seems come to set these little bits of Doctrine forth; and, as I said, till your finale arrive, I can do nothing. Would you like to see the Manuscript yourself? It can come, and return, by Coach for a few shillings, if you think of that: it will of course want the Introduction, and various other "O. Y.'s" that will perhaps be useful. I need not remind you that about showing it to any third party (as I have learned by experience) there is a certain delicacy to be observed: I shall like to hear from you first. Write to me, therefore, with the same openness as I have done to you; we shall then soon see how it lies between us.

–*Letters of Thomas Carlyle, 1826–1836,*
pp. 364–367

* * *

This excerpt is from an undated letter.

John A. Carlyle to Carlyle, circa 1833

I have read 'Sartor' twice over faithfully, and noted all the passages that pleased me especially. There are touches in it that go deeper I think than any thing I have seen of our times, streams of true light through that Serbonian bog lighting up the abysses of Despair. The first time I took it up my head had well nigh been split before I got through the first and second parts. The second time it was more instructive, and I was better able to separate *[sic]* the ore from the dross, to see the mystic significance beneath that perplexed jargon of half German half English which it has pleased. 'The universal professor' to clothe most of his ideas with; and to enjoy and appropriate the fragments of clear and deep Truth that here and there shines forth from amidst it. I think there are the seeds of higher things in that small book than I have found in any work of our times; yet I cannot much regret that it is published so. It is a document lying ready for use, as you observe, and cannot be annihilated. If it be God's will to spare you, you will speak out the truths it contains in a worthier fashion. They will grow in your heart, and in the hearts of those that love and know you. Teufelsdrech *[sic]* has borne the toughest part of the battle with his earthload, and there is stuff enough in him yet to gain a complete victory, and come forth in triumph, and tell the world the foes he has had and the weapons with which he has overcome them all! There is light on his path, he has escaped from those sulphurious regions of the nether abyss! Poor Teufelsdrech! his 'Time-case' and Earthly Tabernacle has been sadly buffetted, and scathed, but the Light burns only the more purely and fervently within it! I shed hot tears when I think what thou hast come through in that internecine warfare with the Powers of Darkness! Be of good cheer the time of triumph & freedom [is] not distant but at hand!

—*The Collected Letters of Thomas and Jane Welsh Carlyle,* v. 7, p. 354

* * *

This excerpt is from the thirty-seventh portrait in a "Gallery of Literary Characters" series appearing in Frazer's Magazine. *In a 25 June 1833 letter to his mother Carlyle describes the article, saying it "will edify you very little; in fact it is hardly intelligible (not at all so except to persons of the craft), but complimentary enough, and for so foolish a business may be considered as better than a wiser thing. The writer is one Dr Maginn, a mad rattling Irishman; of whom perhaps you have heard me speak. He wishes me well in his way; which indeed is very far from mine. So let us be thankful for all mercies"* (The Collected Letters of Thomas and Jane Welsh Carlyle, *v. 6, p. 406).*

Thomas Carlyle, Esq.
William Maginn

Here hast thou, O Reader! the-from stone-printed effigies of Thomas Carlyle, the thunderwor-doversetter of Herr Johann Wolfgang von Goethe. These fingers, now in listless occupation supporting his head, or clutching that outward integument which with the head holds so singular a relation, that those who philosophically examine, and with a fire-glance penetrate into the contents of the great majority of the orb-shaped knobs which form the upper extremity of man, know not with assured critic-craft to decide whether the hat was made to cover the head, or the head erected as a peg to hang the hat upon;—yea, these fingers have transferred some of the most harmonious and mystic passages,—to the initiated, mild-shining, inaudible-light instinct—and to the uninitiated, dark and untransparent as the shadows of Eleusis—of those forty volumes of musical wisdom which are commonly known by the title of *Goethe's Worke,* from the Fatherlandish dialect of High-Dutch to the Allgemeine-Mid-Lothianish of Auld Reekie. Over-set Goethe hath Carlyle not in the ordinary manner of language-turners, who content themselves with giving, according to the capacity of knowingness or honesty within them, the meaning or the idea (if any there be) of the original book-fashioner, on whom their secondhand-pen-mongery is employed; but with reverential thought,

word-worshipping even the articulable clothing wherein the clear and ethereal harmony of Goethe is invested, Carlyle hath bestowed upon us the *Wilhelm Meister,* and other works, so Teutonical in raiment, in the structure of sentence, the modulation of phrase, and the round-about, hubble-bubble, rumfustianish (*hübble-bübblen, rümfüstianischen*), roly-poly growlery of style, so Germanically set forth, that it is with difficulty we can recognize them to be translations at all.

Come, come, some reader will impatiently exclaim,—quite enough of this! A whole page of imitative Carlylese would be as bad as the influenza. . . .

. . . .

He is an honourable and worthy man, and talks the most unquestionable High Fifeshire. Of our German scholars, he is clearly the first; and it is generally suspected that he has an idea that he understands the meaning of the books which he is continually reading . . . .

—*Fraser's Magazine,* 7 (June 1833): 706

* * *

In this excerpt Mill refers to Carlyle's "Count Cagliostro: in Two Flights," which appeared in Fraser's *in July and August 1833.*

Mill to Carlyle, 5 September 1833

About that Cagliostro and that Teufelsdreck, by the way, it has frequently occurred to me of late to ask of myself and also of you, whether that mode of writing between sarcasm or irony and earnest, be really deserving of so much honour as you give to it by making use of it so frequently. I do not say that it is not good: all modes of writing, in the hands of a sincere man, are good, provided they are intelligible. But are there many things, worth saying, and capable of being said in that manner which cannot be as well or better said in a more direct way? The same doubt has occasionally occurred to me respecting much of your phraseology, which fails to bring home your meaning to the comprehension of most readers so well as would perhaps be done by commoner and more familiar phrases: however this last I say with the most perfect submission, because I am sure that every one speaks and writes best in his own mother tongue, the language in which he thinks.

—*The Earlier Letters of John Stuart Mill,* v. 1, p. 176

To Jane W. Carlyle

This little Book, little Milestone in a desolate, confused, yet not (as we hope) unblessed Pilgrimage we make in common, is with heart's gratitude inscribed by her affectionate

T. C.

London, 2ᵈ March, 1836.

Carlyle's inscription to his wife on the flyleaf of a copy of Sartor Resartus *bound from the sheets of its publication in* Fraser's Magazine
(University of Pennsylvania Library)

"Clotted Nonsense"
The First Review of *Sartor Resartus*

As a periodical publication, Sartor Resartus *was generally not reviewed. However, one anonymous review of the magazine publication caught Carlyle's eye. Carlyle included this excerpt from the 1 April 1834 issue of the* Sun *newspaper among the prefatory "Testimonies of Authors" section in the 1838 English trade edition of* Sartor Resartus.

Sartor Resartus is what old Dennis used to call 'a heap of clotted nonsense,' mixed however, here and there, with passages marked by thought and striking poetic vigour. But what does the writer mean by 'Baphometic fire-baptism?' Why cannot he lay aside his pedantry, and write so as to make himself generally intelligible? We quote by way of curiosity a sentence from the *Sartor Resartus;* which may be read either backwards or forwards, for it is equally intelligible either way. Indeed, by beginning at the tail, and so working up to the head, we think the reader will stand the fairest chance of getting at its meaning. . . .

—Sartor Resartus, pp. v–vi

Book Publication of *Sartor Resartus*

Although the serialized version of Sartor Resartus *was largely overlooked by British readers, it was enthusiastically received in New England, where the private copies of Carlyle's book that he sent Emerson were circulated. Emerson privately remonstrated with Carlyle over his eccentric style, but he worked to advance his friend's career. In 1836 Emerson orchestrated an American edition of the work and wrote a preface for the volume. Although some reviewers, such as Alexander Everett, were confused by Carlyle's pose in the work as German editor Diogenes Teufelsdröckh, most critics appreciated the satire.*

This excerpt is from Emerson's initial letter to Carlyle, written some nine months after the American visited Craigenputtock. Emerson's close—"If any word in my letter should provoke you to a reply I shall rejoice in my sauciness"—was taken up in Carlyle's letter of 12 August 1834.

Emerson to Carlyle, 14 May 1834

In Liverpool I wrote to Mr Fraser to send me his Magazine, and I have now received four numbers of the *Sartor Resartus,* for whose light, thanks evermore. I am glad that one living scholar is self-centred, and will be true to himself though none

The beginning of Emerson's first letter to Carlyle (The Trustees of the National Library of Scotland MS 2882)

ever were before; who, as Montaigne says, "puts his ear close by himself, and holds his breath and listens." And none can be offended with the self-subsistency of one so catholic and jocund. And 't is good to have a new eye inspect our mouldy social forms, our politics, and schools, and religion. I say *our,* for it cannot have escaped you that a lecture upon these topics written for England may be read to America. Evermore thanks for the brave stand you have made for Spiritualism in these writings. But has literature any parallel in the oddity of the vehicle chosen to convey this treasure? I delight in the contents; the form, which my defective apprehension for a joke makes me not appreciate, I leave to your merry discretion. And yet did ever wise and philanthropic author use so defying a diction? As if society were not sufficiently shy of truth without providing it beforehand with an objection to the form. Can it be that this humor proceeds from a despair of finding a contemporary audience, and so the Prophet feels at liberty to utter his message in droll sounds. Did you not tell me, Mr. Thomas Carlyle, sitting upon one of your broad hills, that it was Jesus Christ built Dunscore Kirk yonder? If you love such sequences, then admit, as you will, that no poet is sent into the world before his time; that all the departed thinkers and actors have paved your way; that (at least when you surrender yourself) nations and ages do guide your pen, yes, and common goose-quills as well as your diamond graver. Believe then that harp and ear are formed by one revolution of the wheel; that men are waiting to hear your epical song; and so be pleased to skip those excursive involved glees, and give us the simple air, without the volley of variations. At least in some of your prefaces you should give us the theory of your rhetoric. I comprehend not why you should lavish in that spendthrift style of yours celestial truths. Bacon and Plato have something too solid to say than that they can afford to be humorists. You are dispensing that which is rarest, namely, the simplest truths,—truths which lie next to consciousness, and which only the Platos and Goethes perceive. I look for the hour with impatience when the vehicle will be worthy of the spirit,—when the word will be as simple, and so as resistless, as the thought,—and, in short, when your words will be one with things. I have no hope that you will find suddenly a large audience.

– The Correspondence of Thomas Carlyle and Ralph Waldo Emerson, 1834–1872, v. 1, pp. 13–15

* * *

In this excerpt Carlyle evinces relief that the periodical publication of his book at least meant that his manuscript had escaped accidental destruction. Less than a year later the manuscript of his work on the French Revolution was mistakenly burned.

Carlyle to Emerson, 12 August 1834

You thank me for *Teufelsdröckh:* how much more ought I to thank you for your hearty, genuine though extravagant acknowledgement of it! Blessed is the voice that amid dispiritment, stupidity and contradiction pro-

claims to us: *Euge!* Nothing ever was more ungenial than the soil this poor Teufelsdröckhish seedcorn has been thrown on here; none cries, Good speed to it; the sorriest nettle or hemlock seed, one would think, had been more welcome. For indeed our British periodical critics, and especially the public of *Fraser's Magazine* (which I believe I have now done with), exceed all speech; require not even contempt, only oblivion. Poor Teufelsdröckh!–Creature of mischance, miscalculation, and thousand-fold obstruction! Here nevertheless he is, as you see; has struggled across the Stygian marshes, and now, as a stitched Pamphlet "for Friends," cannot be *burnt,* or lost before his time. I send you one copy for your own behoof; three others you yourself can perhaps find fit readers for: as you spoke in the plural number, I thought there might be three; more would rather surprise me. . . . With regard to style and so forth, what you call your "saucy" objections are not only most intelligible to me, but welcome and instructive. You say well that I take up that attitude because I have no known public, am *alone* under the Heavens, speaking into friendly or unfriendly space; add only, that I will not defend such attitude, that I call it questionable, tentative, and only the best that I, in these mad times, could conveniently hit upon.

– The Correspondence of Thomas Carlyle and Ralph Waldo Emerson, v. 1, pp. 20–22

* * *

This excerpt is from a letter in which Emerson reported the death of his brother and wrote of the consolation he found in Carlyle's achievement and his friendly letter: "It, for the moment, realizes the hope to which I have clung with both hands, through each disappointment, that I might converse with a man whose ear of faith was not stopped, and whose argument I could not predict."

Emerson to Carlyle, 20 November 1834

I feel like congratulating you upon the cold welcome which, you say, Teufelsdröckh has met. As it is not earthly happy, it is marked of a high sacred sort. I like it a great deal better than ever, and before it was all published, I had eaten nearly all my words of objection. But do not think it shall lack a present popularity. That it should not be known seems possible, for if a memoir of Laplace had been thrown into that muck-heap of Fraser's Magazine, who would be the wiser? But this has too much wit and imagination not to strike a class who would not care for it as a faithful mirror of this very Hour. But you know the proverb, "To be fortunate, be not too wise." The great men of the day are on a plane so low as to be thoroughly intelligible to the vulgar.

Nevertheless, as God maketh the world forevermore, whatever the devils may seem to do, so the thoughts of the best minds always become the last opinion of Society. Truth is ever born in a manger, but is compensated by living till it has all souls for its kingdom. Far, far better seems to me the unpopularity of this Philosophical Poem (shall I call it?) than the adulation that followed your eminent friend Goethe.

– The Correspondence of Thomas Carlyle and Ralph Waldo Emerson, v.1, p. 29

* * *

This excerpt is from a letter in which Emerson wrote that he knew of "some thirty or more intelligent persons" who "understand and highly appreciate the Sartor.*"*

Emerson to Carlyle, 12 March 1835

. . . Some friends here are very desirous that Mr. Fraser should send out to the bookseller here fifty or a hundred copies of the *Sartor.* So many we want very much; they would be sold at once. If we knew that two or three hundred would be taken up, we should reprint it now. But we think it better to satisfy the known inquirers for the book first, and when they have extended the demand for it, then to reproduce it, a naturalized Yankee. The lovers of Teufelsdröckh here are sufficiently enthusiastic. I am an icicle to them. They think England must be blind and deaf if the Professor makes no more impression there than yet appears. I, with the most affectionate wishes for Thomas Carlyle's fame, am mainly bent on securing the medicinal virtues of his book for my young neighbors. The good people think he overpraises Goethe. There I give him up to their wrath. But I bid them mark his unsleeping moral sentiment; that every other moralist occasionally nods, becomes complaisant and traditional; but this man is without interval on the side of equity and humanity!

– The Correspondence of Thomas Carlyle and Ralph Waldo Emerson, v. 1, pp. 48–49

* * *

This excerpt is from a letter in which Emerson urged Carlyle to give a lecture series in America. The "new work" that Emerson mentions is The French Revolution.

Emerson to Carlyle, 30 April 1835

I wish you to know that we do not depend for your *éclat* on your being already known to rich men here. You are not. Nothing has ever been published here designating you by name. But Dr. Channing reads and respects you. That is a fact of importance to our project. Several clergymen, Messrs. Frothingham, Ripley, Francis, all of them scholars and Spiritualists, (some of them, unluckily, called Unitarian,) love you dearly, and will work heartily in your behalf. Mr. Frothingham, a worthy and accomplished man, more like Erasmus than Luther, said to me on parting, the other day, "You cannot express in terms too extravagant my desire that he should come." George Ripley, having heard, through your letter to me, that nobody in England had responded to the *Sartor,* had secretly written you a most reverential letter, which, by dint of coaxing, he read to me, though he said there was but one step from the sublime to the ridiculous. I prayed him, though I thought the letter did him no justice, save to his heart, to send you it or another; and he says he will. He is a very able young man, even if his letter should not show it. He said he could, and would, bring many persons to hear you, and you should be sure of his utmost aid. Dr. Bradford, a medical man, is of good courage. Mr. Loring, a lawyer, said, "Invite Mr. and Mrs. Carlyle to spend a couple of months at my house," (I assured him I was too selfish for that,) "and if our people," he said, "cannot find out his worth, I will subscribe, with others, to make him whole of any expense he shall incur in coming."

. . . .

On the other hand, I make no doubt you shall be sure of some opposition. Andrews Norton, one of our best heads, once a theological professor, and a destroying critic, lives upon a rich estate at Cambridge, and frigidly excludes the Diderot paper from a *Select Journal* edited by him, with the remark, "Another paper of the Teufelsdröckh School." The University perhaps, and much that is conservative in literature and religion, I apprehend, will give you its cordial opposition, and what eccentricity can be collected from the Obituary Notice on Goethe, or from the *Sartor,* shall be mustered to demolish you. Nor yet do I feel quite certain of this. If we get a good tide with us, we shall sweep away the whole inertia, which is the whole force of these gentlemen, except Norton. That you do not like the Unitarians will never hurt you at all, if possibly you do like the Calvinists. If you have any friendly relations to your native Church, fail not to bring a letter from a Scottish Calvinist to a Calvinist here, and your fortune is made. But that were too good to happen.

Since things are so, can you not, my dear sir, finish your new work and cross the great water in September or October, and try the experiment of a winter in America? I cannot but think that if we do not make out a case strong enough to make you build your house, at least you should pitch your tent among us. The country is, as you say, worth visiting, and to give much pleasure to a few persons will be some inducement to you. I am afraid to press this matter. To me, as you can divine, it would be an unspeakable comfort; and the more, that I hope before that time so far to settle my own affairs as to have a wife and a house to receive you. Tell Mrs. Carlyle, with my affectionate regards, that some friends whom she does not yet know do hope with me to have her company for the next winter at our house, and shall not cease to hope it until you come.

– The Correspondence of Thomas Carlyle and Ralph Waldo Emerson, v. 1 pp. 59–62

* * *

These excerpts are from one of the most detailed and grati-fying responses Carlyle received on Sartor Resartus. *Sterling's allusion to "Jean Paul" as a model for Carlyle's hero is a refer-ence to the German writer Jean Paul Richter. Carlyle included an edited version of this letter in his* Life of John Sterling.

John Sterling to Carlyle, 29 May 1835

My dear Carlyle,–I have now read twice, with care, the wondrous account of Teufelsdröckh and his Opinions; and I need not say that it has given me much to think of. It falls in with the feelings and tastes which were, for years, the ruling ones of my life; but which you will not be angry with me when I say that I am infi-nitely and hourly thankful for having escaped from. Not that I think of this state of mind as one with which I have no longer any concern. The sense of oneness of life and power in all existence; and of a boundless exu-berance of beauty around us, to which most men are well-nigh dead, is a possession which no one that has ever enjoyed it would wish to lose. When to this we add the deep feeling of the difference between the actual and the ideal in Nature, and still more in Man; and bring in, to explain this, the principle of duty, as that which con-nects us with a possible Higher State, and sets us in progress towards it,–we have a cycle of thoughts which was the whole spiritual empire of the wisest Pagans, and which might well supply food for the wide specula-tions and richly creative fancy of Teufelsdröckh, or his prototype Jean Paul.

How then comes it, we cannot but ask, that these ideas, displayed assuredly with no want of eloquence, vivacity of earnestness, have found, unless I am much mistaken, so little acceptance among the best and most energetic minds in this country? In a country where millions read the Bible, and thousands Shakespeare; where Wordsworth circulates through book-clubs and drawing-rooms; where there are innumerable admirers of your favourite Burns; and where Coleridge, by send-ing from his solitude the voice of earnest spiritual

instruction, came to be beloved, studied and mourned for, by no small or careless school of disciples?–To answer this question would, of course, require more thought and knowledge than I can pretend to bring to it. But there are some points on which I will venture to say a few words.

In the first place, as to the form of composition,–which may be called, I think, the Rhapsodico-Reflective. In this the *Sartor Resartus* resembles some of the master-works of human invention, which have been acknowledged as such by many genera-tions; and especially the works of Rabelais, Mon-taigne, Sterne and Swift.

. . . .

. . . comparing the Teufelsdröckh Epopee only with those other modern works,–it is noticeable that Rabelais, Montaigne and Sterne have trusted for the currency of their writings, in a great degree, the use of obscene and sensual stimulants. Rabelais, besides, was full of contemporary and personal satire; and seems to have been a champion in the great cause of his time,–as was Montaigne also,–that of the right of thought in all competent minds, unrestrained by any outward author-ity. Montaigne, moreover, contains more pleasant and lively gossip, and more distinct good-humoured paint-ing of his own character and daily habits than any other writer I know. Sterne is never obscure, and never moral; and the costume of his subjects is drawn from the familiar experiences of his own time and country: and Swift, again, has the same merit of the clearest per-spicuity, joined to that of the most homely, unaffected, forcible English. These points of difference seem to me the chief ones which bear against the success of the *Sar-tor*. On the other hand, there is in Teufelsdröckh a depth and fervour of feeling, and a power of serious elo-quence, far beyond that of any of these four writers; and to which indeed there is nothing at all comparable in any of them, except perhaps now and then, and very imperfectly, in Montaigne.

Of the other points of comparison there are two which I would chiefly dwell on: and first as to the lan-guage. A good deal of this is positively barbarous. "Environment," "vestural," "stertorous," "visualised," "complected," and others to be found I think in the first twenty pages,–are words, so far as I know, without any authority; some of them contrary to analogy; and none repaying by their value the disadvantage of novelty. To these must be added new and erroneous locutions: "whole other tissues" for *all the other,* and similar uses of the word *whole;* "orients" for *pearls;* "lucid" and "lucent" employed as if they were different in meaning; "hulls" perpetually for *coverings,* it being a word hardly used, and then only for the husk of a nut; "to insure a man of misapprehension;" "talented," a mere newspaper and hustings word, invented, I believe, by O'Connell.

I must also mention the constant recurrence of some words in a quaint and queer connection, which gives a grotesque and somewhat repulsive mannerism to many sentences. Of these the commonest offender is "quite;" which appears in almost every page, and gives at first a droll kind of emphasis; but soon becomes wearisome. "Nay," "manifold," "cunning enough significance," "faculty" (meaning a man's rational or moral *power*), "special," "not without," haunt the reader as if in some uneasy dream which does not rise to the dignity of nightmare. Some of these strange mannerisms fall under the general head of a singularity peculiar, so far as I know, to Teufelsdröckh. For instance, that of the incessant use of a sort of odd superfluous qualification of his assertions; which seems to give the character of deliberateness and caution to the style, but in time sounds like mere trick or involuntary habit. "Almost" does more than yeoman's, *almost* slave's service in this way. Something similar may be remarked of the use of the double negative by way of affirmation.

Under this head, of language, may be mentioned, though not with strict grammatical accuracy, two standing characteristics of the Professor's style,—at least as rendered into English: *First,* the composition of words, such as "snow-and-rosebloom maiden:" an attractive damsel doubtless in Germany; but, with all her charms, somewhat uncouth here. "Life-vision" is another example; and many more might be found. To say nothing of the innumerable cases in which the words are only intelligible as a compound term, though not distinguished by hyphens. Of course the composition of words is sometimes allowable even in English: but the habit of dealing with German seems to have produced, in the pages before us, a prodigious superabundance of this form of expression; which gives harshness and strangeness, where the matter would at all events have been surprising enough. *Secondly,* I object, with the same qualification, to the frequent use of *inversion;* which generally appears as a transposition of the two members of a clause, in a way, which would not have been practised in conversation. It certainly gives emphasis and force, and often serves to point the meaning. But a style may be fatiguing and faulty precisely by being too emphatic, forcible and pointed; and so straining the attention to find its meaning, or the admiration to appreciate its beauty.

Another class of considerations connects itself with the heightened and plethoric fulness of the style; its accumulation and contrast of imagery; its occasional jerking and almost spasmodic violence;—and above all, the painful subjective excitement, which seems the element and groundwork even of every description of

Nature; often taking the shape of sarcasm or broad jest, but never subsiding into calm. There is also a point which I should think worth attending to, were I planning a similar book: I mean the importance, in a work of imagination, of not too much disturbing in the reader's mind the balance of the New and Old. The former addresses itself to his active, the latter to his passive faculty; and these are mutually dependent, and must co-exist in certain proportion, if you wish to combine his sympathy and progressive exertion with willingness and ease of attention. This should be taken into account in forming a style; for of course it cannot be consciously thought of in composing each sentence.

. . . .

All this, of course, appears to me true and relevant; but I cannot help feeling that it is, after all, but a poor piece of quackery to comment on a multitude of phenomena without adverting to the principle which lies at the root, and gives the true meaning to them all. Now this principle I seem to myself to find in the state of mind which is attributed to Teufelsdröckh; in his state of mind, I say, not in his opinions, though these are, in him as in all men, most important,—being one of the best indices to his state of mind. Now what distinguishes him, not merely from the greatest and best men who have been on earth for eighteen hundred years, but from the whole body of those who have been working forwards towards the good, and have been the salt and light of the world, is this: That he does not believe in a God. Do not be indignant, I am blaming no one;— but if I write my thoughts, I must write them honestly.

Teufelsdrockh does not belong to the herd of sensual and thoughtless men; because he does perceive in all Existence a unity of power; because he does believe that this is a real power external to him and dominant to a certain extent over him, and does not think that he is himself a shadow in a world of shadows. He has a deep feeling of the beautiful, the good and the true; and a faith in their final victory.

At the same time, how evident is the strong inward unrest, the Titanic heaving of mountain on mountain; the storm-like rushing over land and sea in search of peace. He writhes and roars under his consciousness of the difference in himself between the possible and the actual, the hoped-for and the existent. He feels that duty is the highest law of his own being; and knowing how it bids the waves be stilled into an icy fixedness and grandeur, he trusts (but with a boundless inward misgiving) that there is a principle of order which will reduce all confusion to shape and clearness. But wanting peace himself, his fierce dissatisfaction fixes on all that is weak, corrupt and imperfect around him; and instead of a calm and steady co-operation with all those who are endeavouring to apply the highest ideas as remedies for the worst evils, he holds himself aloof in savage isolation; and cherishes (though he dare not own) a stern joy at the prospect of that Catastrophe which is to turn loose again the elements of man's social life, and give for a time the victory to evil;–in hopes that each new convulsion of the world must bring us nearer to the ultimate restoration of all things; fancying that each may be the last. Wanting the calm and cheerful reliance, which would be the spring of active exertion, he flatters his own distemper by persuading himself that his own age and generation are peculiarly feeble and decayed. . . .

Something of this state of mind I may say that I understand; for I have myself experienced it. And the root of the matter appears to me: A want of sympathy with the great body of those who are now endeavouring to guide and help onward their fellow men. And in what is this alienation grounded? It is, as I believe, simply in the difference on that point: viz. the clear, deep, habitual recognition of a one Living *Personal* God, essentially good, wise, true and holy, the Author of all that exists; and a reunion with whom is the only end of all rational beings. This belief * * * *[There follow now several pages on 'Personal God,' and other abstruse or indeed properly unspeakable matters; these, and a general Postscript of qualifying purport, I will suppress. . . .]*

–*The Life of John Sterling*, pp. 143–154

* * *

This excerpt is from a long letter George Ripley wrote after seeing one of Carlyle's letters to Emerson, which he said convinced him that Carlyle was "an actual Incarnation, and not merely a Presence and a Force." Ripley was a Unitarian minister and the editor of the Christian Examiner.

George Ripley to Carlyle, 1 June 1835

I am impelled by a yearning sympathy, to raise my voice to your ear across the wide waste of waters over which the music of your soul-melody has sounded to this distant spot. I cannot address you as a stranger for the revelations of your mind have long been to me a source of the highest inspiration and joy. I have communed with your spirit in the utterance of its deep wisdom, and when I have felt the significance of your mystic sayings, my heart has leaped up with the response, "This unknown Being is my Brother." The sentiment of reverence and awe has filled my soul when Idea after Idea from the Primal Fountain of Truth has flashed upon me from your kindling page, and I have felt that I would traverse forests and cross the ocean to

express my gratitude to such a gifted Teacher of Humanity.

Allow me, Sir, with the plainness of our plain-spoken land to relate to you the successive steps of my acquaintance-ship with your mind. Several years since with only a prophetic sense of the untold treasures of German thought, I read your article on German Literature in the Edinburgh. I was then a babe in this kind of knowledge, but felt at once the strongest sympathy with your views. The cares of life, and its urgent duties, prevented me at that time, from studying in this department with due diligence, but every voice of encomium on what I considered my morning-star, was like words of encouragement from a mother's lips. I read, times without number, your defense of a nation and a literature, which a narrow prejudice had proscribed, but which I saw as "through a glass darkly" was instinct with a holy and a living spirit. The magnificent article on Burns came next. I cannot tell the joy with which I hailed it as the rising of a new light in our dark time. Then came Schiller's Life. By a happy accident I was the first to discover it in a neglected corner of a Bookseller's shop. I did not know the Author's name, nor that the Reviewer and the Biographer were the same person. That pure, monumental structure of whitest marble to the memory of Schiller, filled me with Reverence and Love towards the Poet, and his biographer. The casual English copy which had come into my hands, was soon diffused through a wide circle of friends, and read and extolled with most disinterested but enthusiastic admiration. Since that time, you may perhaps be aware, a beautiful Edition has been published here and ranks among our most popular works. I have no space to tell you of the effect of your different Reviews, which after some time, I learned to ascribe to their true author.–Let me pass them over and come at once to Teufelsdrock–dear, genial, misinterpreted, much abused, long-suffering Teufelsdrock. My studies had led me in a different direction, & it is only within a few months, that I have read "Sartor Resartus." I regard it as the most significant indication of the present Age. It stands there, alone, a huge, mysterious, magnificent Symbol of the Time upon which we have fallen. It is the cry of the Heart & the Flesh for the Living God. England, my Brother! fellow Spirit of the Eternal,–has for more than one century, been hemmed in with the Finite, girt around with the brazen walls of Custom, she has had no sense & no soul for the voice of the Infinite, which is sounding forth from this vocal Universe. Your ear has tuned itself to catch the Echoes, which come from beyond the shores of Time. The Ocean-melody from its mysterious depths has been poured into your Soul, and you are seeking fit utterance therefor. God speed thee,– Brother–God, of whom you are an inspired Prophet, a true Shekinah. I see the Urim and Thummin written on thy brow. Go on in the strength of that Spirit, whose Son you are, keep thyself pure, be not afraid of their faces, and declare the whole counsel of God whether men will hear or whether they will forbear.

–The Collected Letters of Thomas and Jane Welsh Carlyle, v. 8, pp. 185–186

* * *

Carlyle discussed Sterling's criticism in this excerpted letter. He disparages religious poet Robert Montgomery's Satan *(1830) in passing and is likely referring to letters from America he had received when he writes that Sterling should not "suppose the poor Book has* not *been responded to."*

Carlyle to Sterling, 4 June 1835

I said to Mill the other day that your Name was HOPEFUL; of which truth surely this copious refreshing shower of really kind and genial criticism you have bestowed on the hardened, kiln-burnt, altogether contradictory Professor Teufelsdröckh, is new proof. Greater faith I have not found in Israel! Neither here shall faith and hope wholly fail: know, my Friend, that your shower does not fall as on mere barren bricks, like water spilt on the ground; that I take it hopefully in, with great desire (knowing what spirit it is of) to *assimilate* such portion of it as the nature of things will allow. So much, on this sheet, I must announce to you, were it at full gallop, and in the most imperfect words.

Your objections as to phraseology and style have good grounds to stand on; many of them indeed are considerations to which I myself was not blind; which there (unluckily) were no means of doing more than nodding to as one passed. A man has but a certain strength; imperfections cling to him, which if he wait till he have brushed off entirely, he will spin forever on his axis, advancing nowhither. Know thy thought, *believe* it; front Heaven and Earth with it,–in whatsoever *words* Nature and Art have made readiest for thee! If one has thoughts not hitherto uttered in English Books, I see nothing for it but that you must use words not found there, must *make* words,–with moderation and discretion, of course. That I have not always done it *so*, proves only that I was not strong enough; an accusation to which I for one will never plead not guilty. For the rest, pray that I may have more and more strength! Surely too, as I said, all these *coal-marks* of yours shall be duly considered, for the first and even for the second

time, and help me on my way. With unspeakable cheerfulness I give up *"Talented":* indeed, but for the plain statement you make, I could have sworn such word had never, except for parodistic ironical purposes, risen from my inkhorn, or passed my lips. Too much evil can hardly be said of it: while speech of it at all is necessary.–But finally, do you reckon this really a time for Purism of Style; or that Style (mere dictionary Style) has much to do with the worth or unworth of a Book? I do not: with whole ragged battalions of Scott's-Novel Scotch, with Irish, German, French, and even Newspaper Cockney (when "Literature" is little other than a Newspaper) storming in on us, and the whole structure of our Johnsonian English breaking up from its foundations,–revolution *there* as visible as anywhere else!

You ask, How it comes that none of the "leading minds" of this country (if one knew where to find them) have given the "Clothes-Philosophy" any response? Why, my good friend, not one of them has had the happiness of seeing it! It issued thro' one of the main *cloacas* of Periodical Literature, where no leading mind, I fancy, looks, if he can help it: the poor Book cannot be destroyed by fire or other violence now, but solely by the *general* law of Destiny; and *I* have nothing more to do with it henceforth. How it chanced that no Bookseller would print it (in an epoch when Satan Montgomery runs, or seems to run, thro' thirteen editions), and the morning Papers (on its issuing thro' the *cloaca*) sang together over such a creation: this truly is a question, but a different one. Meanwhile, do not suppose the poor Book has *not* been responded to: for the historical fact is, I could show very curious response to it here; not ungratifying, and fully three times as much as I count on, as the wretched farrago itself deserved.

You say finally, as the key to the whole mystery that Teufelsdröckh does not believe in a "personal God." It is frankly said, with a friendly honesty for which I love you. A grave charge nevertheless, an *awful* charge: to which, if I mistake not, the Professor, laying his hand on his heart, will reply with some gesture expressing the solemnest *denial*. In gesture, rather than in speech; for "the Highest *cannot* be spoken of in words." "Personal," "impersonal," One, Three, *what* meaning can any mortal (after all) attach to them in reference to such an object? *Wer darf ihn NENNEN?* I dare not, and do not. That you dare and do (to some greater extent) is a matter I am far from taking offence at: nay, with all sincerity, I can rejoice that you have a creed of that kind, which gives you happy thoughts, nerves you for good actions, brings you into readier communion with many good men; my true wish is that such creed may long hold compactly together in you, and be "a covert from the heat, a shelter from the storm, as the shadow of a great rock in a weary land." Well is it if we have a printed Litany to pray from; and yet not ill if we *can* pray even in *silence*, for silence too is audible *there*. Finally, assure yourself I am neither Pagan nor Turk, nor circumcised Jew, but an unfortunate Christian individual resident at Chelsea in *this* year of Grace; neither Pantheist nor Pottheist, nor any Theist or *ist* whatsoever; having the most decided contempt for all manner of Systembuilders and Sectfounders—so far as contempt may be compatible with so mild a nature; feeling well beforehand (taught by experience) that all such are and even must be *wrong*. By God's blessing, one has got two eyes to look with; and also a mind capable of knowing, of believing: that is all the creed I will at this time insist on. And now may I beg one thing: that whenever in my thought or your own you fall on any dogma that tends to estrange you from me, pray believe *that* to be *false;*—false as Beelzebub till you get clearer evidence.

—Letters of Thomas Carlyle to John Stuart Mill, John Sterling, and Robert Browning, pp. 191–194

* * *

Carlyle alluded to Ripley's letter in this excerpt.

Carlyle to John A. Carlyle, 10 August 1835

I had a Letter from Boston in America, with the signature "George Ripley"; full of the most enthusiastic estimation; really a good feeling ill-expressed, struggling for expression: *Teufelsdröckh* he calls "a crying out of the heart and the flesh for the living God"; one of the chief Signs of the Era, etc. etc.; and withal bids me by the name of Brother, go on in God's name, and falter for no man. Ripley seems to be a Clergyman of some Church (I think Emerson mentioned him to me): his Letter gave me no comfort at the time, it seemed so overdone; but it does now occasionally some, when I think of it.

—Letters of Thomas Carlyle, 1826–1836, pp. 542–543

* * *

These excerpts are from a twenty-eight-page review article titled "Thomas Carlyle" that was based on one of the fifty-eight copies of Sartor Resartus, *"Reprinted for friends, from Fraser's Magazine." After reading this article by the editor of the* North American Review, *Carlyle wrote his mother on 24 December 1835 that the reviewer was "good-natured" but "rather stupid" and that he would take him up on his offer of a welcome in America only as a last resort, though the "Yankees" seemed a "very good sort of people" (The Collected Letters of Thomas and Jane Welsh Carlyle, v. 8, p. 278). Carlyle included this*

review among the "Testimonies of Authors" in the 1838 English edition of Sartor Resartus.

"Deep Thought, Sound Principle, and Fine Writing" Review of *Sartor Resartus*
Alexander Everett

. . . We have said that the volume came before the public under rather suspicious circumstances, and, after a careful survey of the whole ground, our belief is, that no such persons as Professor Teufelsdroeckh or Counsellor Heuschrecke ever existed; that the six paper bags, with their China-ink inscriptions and multifarious contents, are a mere figment of the brain; that the "present editor" is the only person who has ever written upon the Philosophy of Clothes; and that the *Sartor Resartus* is the only treatise that has yet appeared upon that subject;—in short, that the whole account of the origin of the work before us, which the supposed editor relates with so much gravity, and of which we have given a brief abstract, is in plain English, a *hum*.

Without troubling our readers at any great length with our reasons for entertaining these suspicions, we may remark, that the absence of all other information on the subject, excepting what is contained in the work, is itself a fact of a most significant character. The whole German press, as well as the particular one where the work purports to have been printed, seems to be under the control of *Stillschweigen und Co.*—Silence and Company. If the Clothes-Philosophy and its author are making so great a sensation throughout Germany as is pretended, how happens it that the only notice we have of the fact is contained in a few numbers of a monthly magazine, published at London? How happens it that no intelligence about the matter has come out directly to this country? We pique ourselves, here in New England, upon knowing at least as much of what is going on in the literary way in the old Dutch motherland, as our brethren of the fast-anchored isle; but thus far we have no tidings whatever of the "extensive, close-printed, close-meditated volume," which forms the subject of this pretended commentary. Again, we would respectfully inquire of the "present editor," upon what part of the map of Germany we are to look for the city of Weissnichtwo,—"Know-not-where," at which place the work is supposed to have been printed and the author to have resided. It has been our fortune to visit several portions of the German territory, and to examine pretty carefully, at different times and for various purposes, maps of the whole, but we have no recollection of any such place.

. . . .

Now, without intending to adopt a too rigid standard of morals, we own that we doubt a little the propriety of offering to the public a treatise on Things in General, under the name and in the form of an Essay on Dress. For ourselves, advanced as we unfortunately are in the journey of life, far beyond the period when dress is practically a matter of interest, we have no hesitation in saying that the real subject of the work is to us more attractive than the ostensible one. But this is probably not the case with the mass of readers. To the younger portion of the community, which constitutes every where the very great majority, the subject of dress is one of intense and paramount importance. An author who treats it appeals, like the poet, to the young men and maidens,—*virginibus puerisque*,—and calls upon them by all the motives which habitually operate most strongly upon their feelings, to buy this book. When, after opening their purses for this purpose, they have carried home the work in triumph, expecting to find in it some particular instruction in regard to the tying of their neckcloths, or the cut of their corsets, and meet with nothing better than a dissertation on Things in General, they will,—to use the mildest terms,—not be in very good humor. If the last improvements in legislation, which we have made in this country, should have found their way to England, the author, we think, would stand some chance of being *Lynched*.

. . . .

We must here close our extracts from this little volume, which as our readers, we trust, are by this time aware, contains under a quaint and singular form, a great deal of deep thought, sound principle, and fine writing. It is, we believe, no secret in England or here, that it is the work of a person to whom the public is indebted for a number of articles in the late British Reviews, which have attracted great attention by the singularity of their style, and the richness and depth of their matter. Among these may be mentioned particularly those on *Characteristics* and the *Life of Burns* in the Edinburgh Review, and on *Goethe* in the Foreign Quarterly. We have been partly led to take this notice of the work before us by the wish, which the author expresses, that a knowledge of his labors might penetrate into the Far West. We take pleasure in introducing to the American public a writer, whose name is yet in a great measure unknown among us, but who is destined, we think, to occupy a large space in the literary world. We have herd it intimated, that Mr. Carlyle had it in contemplation to visit this country, and we can venture to assure him, that, should he carry this inten-

tion into effect, he will meet with a cordial welcome. If his conversation should prove as agreeable as his writings, and he should feel a disposition to take up his abode in the "Far West," we have little doubt that he may find in some one of the hundred universities of our country, a *Weissnichtwo*, at which he may profess his favorite science of Things-in-General with even more satisfaction and advantage, than in the Edinburgh Review or Fraser's Magazine.

—*The North American Review,* 41 (October 1835): 455–459, 481–482

* * *

The American edition of Sartus Resartus *was set from "the ephemeral pamphlets" of* Fraser's Magazine *and published on 9 April 1836. Emerson's brief introduction, titled "Preface of the American Editors," was unsigned.*

Preface for the American Edition of *Sartor Resartus*
Ralph Waldo Emerson

The Editors have been induced, by the expressed desire of many persons, to collect the following sheets out of the ephemeral pamphlets in which they first appeared, under the conviction that they contain in themselves the assurance of a longer date.

The Editors have no expectation that this little work will have a sudden and general popularity. They will not undertake, as there is no need, to justify the gay costume in which the Author delights to dress his thoughts, or the German idioms with which he has sportively sprinkled his pages. It is his humor to advance the gravest speculations upon the gravest topics in a quaint and burlesque style. If his masquerade offend any of his audience, to that degree that they will not hear what he has to say, it may chance to draw others to listen to his wisdom; and what work of imagination can hope to please all? But we will venture to remark that the distaste excited by these peculiarities, in some readers, is greatest at first, and is soon forgotten; and that the foreign dress and aspect of the work are quite superficial, and cover a genuine Saxon heart. We believe, no book has been published for many years, written in a more sincere style of idiomatic English, or which discovers an equal mastery over all the riches of the language. The author makes ample amends for the occasional eccentricity of his genius, not only by frequent bursts of pure splendor, but by the wit and sense which never fail him.

But what will chiefly commend the book to the discerning reader is the manifest design of the work,

SARTOR RESARTUS.

IN THREE BOOKS.

Mein Vermächtniß, wie herrlich weit und breit!
Die Zeit ist mein Vermächtniß, mein Acker ist die Zeit.

BOSTON:

JAMES MUNROE AND COMPANY.

M DCCC XXXVI.

Title page for the first American edition, for which Emerson wrote a preface (Special Collections, Thomas Cooper Library, University of South Carolina)

which is, a Criticism upon the Spirit of the Age,–we had almost said, of the hour, in which we live; exhibiting, in the most just and novel light, the present aspects of Religion, Politics, Literature, Arts, and Social Life. Under all his gaiety, the writer has an earnest meaning, and discovers an insight into the manifold wants and tendencies of human nature, which is very rare among our popular authors. The philanthropy and the purity of moral sentiment, which inspire the work, will find their way to the heart of every lover of virtue.

–Sartor Resartus, pp. iii–v

* * *

In this excerpted Carlyle writes after having received a copy of Emerson's book Nature *(1836) and the American edition of* Sartor Resartus.

Carlyle to Emerson, 13 February 1837

Your little Book and the Copy of *Teufelsdröckh* came safely; soon after I had written. . . . George Ripley tells me you are printing another edition; much good may it do you! There is now also a kind of whisper and whimper rising *here* about printing one. I said to myself once, when Bookseller Fraser shrieked so loud at a certain message you sent him: "Perhaps after all they *will* print this poor rag of a thing into a Book, after I am dead it may be,–if so seem good to them. *Either* way!"– As it is, we leave the poor orphan to its destiny, all the more cheerfully. . . . It [the review of *Sartor Resartus* in *The North American*] was not at all an unfriendly review; but had an opacity of matter-of-fact in it that filled one with amazement. Since the Irish Bishop who said there were some things in *Gulliver* on which he for one would keep his belief *suspended,* nothing equal to it, on that side, has come athwart me. However, he *has* made out that Teufelsdröckh is, in all human probability, a fictitious character; which is always something, for an Inquirer into Truth.

–The Correspondence of Thomas Carlyle and Ralph Waldo Emerson, pp. 110–112

* * *

These excerpts are from a ten-page review written by a prominent Unitarian minister. In a letter to John Carlyle on 21 March 1837, Carlyle says of the review, "It pleased me very much, tho' it would have been very vain to believe it all. It was here and there a kind of idealized image of me however, and had more true perception and appreciation than all the other critiques, laudations and vituperations I had seen of myself" (New Letters, p. 65).

"An Earnest and Full Spirit"
Review of *Sartor Resartus*
Nathaniel Frothingham

In giving our readers some account of this singular production, we will begin by reversing the usual method of our vocation, and instead of a review utter a prophesy. Indeed the book is so very odd, that some departure from the common course seems the most appropriate to any notice of it. We predict, then, that it will not be read through by a great many persons, nor be liked by all its readers. Some will pronounce it unintelligible, or boldly deny that it has any good sound meaning.

. . . .

. . . But then we plainly foresee that there will be others, who will make very different account of our Professor's lucubrations. They will admire his wildest extravagances, and discover in his most playful disportings a hidden wisdom; even as the worshippers of Goethe found, and find still, a perfect system of philosophy and a whole canon of Scripture in the wondrous *diablerie* of the *Faust*.

. . . .

For our own part, we shall not be much surprised either at the neglect and aversion that it will experience in some quarters, or the unqualified admiration that it will excite in others. We think that they may both be explained equally well, without impeaching the critical acuteness of either of the parties; though we by no means profess ourselves to

---

"All the Fame in England"

Harriet Martineau, a writer and advocate of women's rights who often visited the Carlyles at their London home, recorded this anecdote.

One day I was dining there alone. I had brought over from America twenty-five copies of his "Sartor Resartus," as reprinted there; and, having sold them at the English price, I had some money to put into his hand. I did put it into his hand the first time: but it made him uncomfortable, and he spent it in a pair of signet rings, for his wife and me, (her motto being "Point de faiblesse," and mine "Frisch zu!") This would never do; so, having imported and sold a second parcel, the difficulty was what to do with the money. My friend and I found that Carlyle was ordered weak brandy and water instead of wine; and we spent our few sovereigns in French brandy of the best quality, which we carried over one evening, when going to tea. Carlyle's amusement and delight at first, and all the evening after, whenever he turned his eyes towards the long-necked bottles, showed us that we had made a good choice. He declared that he had got a reward for his labours at last: and his wife asked me to dinner, all by myself, to taste the brandy. We three sat round the fire after dinner, and Carlyle mixed the toddy while Mrs. Carlyle and I discussed some literary matters, and speculated on fame and the love of it. Then Carlyle held out a glass of his mixture to me with, "Here,–take this. It is worth all the fame in England."

–Harriet Martineau's Autobiography,
v. 1, pp. 289–290

---

stand indifferent, or as a middle term, between them. We retain the lease of a small tenement in the *Wahngasse* [Whimsey Street] ourselves, and frankly own that this book has great charms for us. It is written with an earnest and full spirit, though under a freakish form. It is the work of a contemplative, fervent, accomplished mind. It abounds with just and original thoughts, mixed up with the most diverting fancies, and expressed in a style which, though rather grotesque, is of extraordinary copiousness, beauty, and power. The peculiarity, indeed, of the style is just that which will be most objected to and most relished, according to the tastes of different readers. We see nothing to forgive in it, though it is one of the last to be proposed for imitation. It certainly could not be changed without destroying the whole harmony of the performance. It is not only the appropriate dress, but a part of the very substance, of the work. If any will persist in calling it affected, we can only say that it seems to fall very naturally from the pen that employs it, and that such affectations are not often to be met with.

. . . .

It loves to bring together the low and the lofty, the learned and vulgar, the strange and familiar, the tragic and comic, into rather violent contrasts. We cannot say that it is always clear and sprightly. The words are often unusual, the digressions bewildering, the objects in view not very manifest. But it will seldom fail to repay a careful attention. The device of making a book by pretending to edit the papers of another person may appear to be rather a stale one, and has certainly been of late pressed quite unconscionably into the service. But in the present instance it was absolutely essential to the management of the author's plan, and has been so ingeniously availed of as quite to reconcile us to it.

. . . .

Such is a brief and extremely imperfect account of "Sartor Resartus," with its strange subject, and its still stranger method. Whether congenial or not with our tastes and intellectual habits, it is certainly one of the most extraordinary works of our day. It is wrought with great learning and ingenuity, though without the appearance of effort. It throws out the noblest conceptions as if at play, and its sparkling expressions seem kindled by the irrepressible fervor of a brilliant mind. It has imagination enough to give a poet renown; more sound religion and ethics than slumber in the folios of many a body of divinity; more periods than one would copy down in his note-book, to read and read again, than are to be found in all the writings together of many a one who has made himself famous everywhere for having written well. It is not equally sustained in every part; how should it be?—but we can scarcely look where we shall not find something of tenderness of sublimity or wit or wisdom;—something that makes us feel, and makes us reflect too, as deeply as some more pretending "Aids to Reflection."

What we chiefly prize in it is its philosophic, spiritual, humane cast of thought. It is in thorough opposition to the materialism and mechanisms of our grooved and iron-bound times. It resists the despotism of opinion seeking to rule by crowds and suffrages and machinists' devices. It soars away far beyond the theories of Utilitarian calculators. It spurns every thing shallow. It expands and lifts itself above every thing contracted. It places us at a free distance from the turmoil of vulgar and selfish life. It exposes many an abuse and illusion of the passing ages. It is spirit. Warm with kind affections, and almost wild with generous aspirations after the broadest truth and the highest good, it is elevating when it most amuses us. It even perplexes us to some wholesome intent. It rebukes the hard dogmatism of conceited disputers, till it makes it look as poor and as ridgy as it really is. Here are true "Materials for Thinking," while much that circulates with that label is but an insisting that men shall think perversely.

. . . .

We started with the acknowledgment that this book would be distasteful to many. But we fearlessly commend it to another many, who will find their hearts greatly in unison with it. It is not a work to be glanced at here and there. It should not be read through in a breath. It must be conned carefully, and not too much at a time. We do not say that it never put our very selves out of patience; but we declare in all sincerity, that we believe few books of its compass will reward the exercise of patience better.

—*Christian Examiner*, 21 (September 1836):
74–77, 79–80, 84

* * *

By 1838 British publishers Saunders and Otley were willing to produce an English edition of Sartor Resartus, *which was published without Carlyle's name and received mixed reviews. After Carlyle established himself with* The French Revolution, *publishers were more receptive to his work. Five English editions of* Sartor Resartus *were published during Carlyle's life.*

These excerpts are from an anonymous review that appeared in a magazine produced by the house that published Sartor Resartus.

"A Thoroughly British Heart"
Review of *Sartor Resartus*

In saying that Mr. Carlyle is one of the deepest thinking and most original minded writers of the present day, we merely repeat the confirmed opinion of the most intellectual and philosophical part of London and Edinburgh society—an opinion, too, which is now gaining ground rapidly even among those who, knowing him only by his writings, were at first deterred by the oddity of his manner and the German turn of his style and language. On the latter head, perhaps more objections have been raised by hasty and unthinking readers than the case justifies; and it would be difficult to prove on philological principles, that Mr. Carlyle's metaphysical terms, compound words, and compound figures, are *unenglish*. For ourselves we recognize the formal and unchangeable law in our plastic and elastic language—a rich mosaic made up of all idioms, but the grand substratum of which, together with its constitution and spirit is essentially Saxon. Sometimes, we confess, there is a sort of mistiness in Mr. Carlyle's sentences, but this never lasts long, and however much he may delight in wrapping himself in a German-looking mantle, he has English flesh and bones, thews and sinews, and a thoroughly British heart beneath it. His thoughts and feelings are national without prejudice or bigotry. Some heresies he has both in politics and poetry; but we let them pass. We admire his bold examining for himself, his total freedom from the thraldom of mere conventionalities we admire, even when it is at its roughest, his odd or crabbed style, in part because we are wearied to death with the trim and measured sentences of the mass of modern writers—sentences that look as if they had been turned on a turner's wheel, and that have, too often, no thought at all, or not more than a vague generality under their silky, sliding, shiny surface.

—*Metropolitan Magazine*, 23 (September 1838): 1

* * *

These excerpts are from an anonymous review that praises the "somewhat mysterious personage" of Professor Toufelsdröckh.

"Discursive, Light, Profound, Quaint, and Humorous"
Review of *Sartor Resartus*

By what fatality was it that the most *radically* Radical speculation upon men and things, which has appeared for many years, should have first come abroad in a violent

Tory periodical? This work, which was, but cannot always be, neglected in England, has been reprinted in America, in which land we have the authority of the late traveler Miss Martineau for saying, that the prophet has found the honour and acceptance not at first awarded in his own country. A collected edition of the papers, which went through several numbers of *Fraser's Magazine,* has, however, at length appeared in London; and we are further promised Mr Carlyle's Miscellaneous Works, which, we presume, must include his editorial labours also, or "The Life and opinions of Herr Teufelsdröckh," that true philosopher of the Radical school, and original expounder of *"the Philosophy of Clothes."*

. . . .

. . . We can, no more than the English translator, promise the Professor's discursive, light, profound, quaint, and humorous disquisitions, a permanent popularity in England; but this we promise: those who can *taste* him, will not easily forget his race.
– *Tait's Edinburgh Magazine,* 5 (September 1838): 611, 612

* * *

These excerpts are from a thirteen-page review article titled "Sartor Resartus," written twelve years after the publication of the American edition. While acknowledging the power of Carlyle's book, the critic argues that its influence on literature will not endure.

"Wild Unrest Everywhere Manifested"
Reflections on *Sartor Resartus*
Joseph H. Barrett

Sartor Resartus has pretty generally been spoken of as a succinct and free-spoken commentary upon whatever is most striking in modern society. The whole narrative is regarded as a fictitious framework, on which the satire is suspended; and the plot is supposed to have been so contrived as to come into collision, somewhere and somehow, in its development, with every topic the writer designs to animadvert upon. Teufelsdröckh, according to this view, is introduced solely for the purpose of turning up subjects for discourse–and the author leads him into all sorts of predicaments, in order to philosophize on the haps or mishaps which were beforehand determined on as texts, and which, by being aggregated about one person, come to possess a factitious unity. Readers so understanding the book, naturally enough, look upon the plan as rather an ill-devised and unwieldy one, and its execution as unnecessarily awkward and tedious. We are made to range through a great number of pages, whose sole office is to hold together a useless fable–to preserve its consistency, without in the least aiding the author's real design.

Poem by Carlyle about Sartor Resartus *(Beinecke Rare Book and Manuscript Library, Yale University)*

. . . .

. . . We willingly accept the exposition so generally received by Mr. Carlyle's admirers, that the book is "a sort of spiritual autobiography." With this key, the interpretation is comparatively easy—the peculiarities of thought and expression, and the wild unrest everywhere manifested, are with no great difficulty accounted for. The satire thus becomes, what satire invariably is, in greater or less degree, a kind of personal revenge—a retaliatory resistance against what, in actual life, has caused the writer uneasiness of mind, and left in his memory impressions permanently disagreeable, an offensive warfare of defence, carried on in behalf of one's pride.

. . . .

The writer of such a work as this is, must evidently be a man of large capacity, of quick sensibility, of restless imagination, and of impetuous and excitable temper. Whatever he undertakes in these pages, is sustained throughout, and exhibits no flagging of intellectual energy, however deficient it may be thought in coherence and taste. His strength, in a great measure ill-governed and unwieldy as it is, never deserts him. If he ever falls into a fit of imbecility, like those seasons Dr. Johnson records as part of his own experience, when mental energy was wanting even to count the strokes of the clock, we get no trace of his infirmity through a public exposure—his bow is always elastic and firm, his sharp-pointed arrows are ever ready, no matter how unwise or unskillful his aim. He has a reach of perception and sympathy that gathers in and domesticates among his own thoughts a vast multiplicity of objects—and we should much sooner charge that his views are too extended and limitless, than that they are one-sided or narrow.

. . . .

His temperament is of that excitable, ardent, and indefatigable kind that will take no rest, nor even suffer his spirit to be wearied out of its discontent. He cannot be satisfied with an approximate realization of his ideal, and his impatience at human dullness and imperfection is uncontrollable. Whatever seems to him to be true, is so vividly impressed on his mind—burns and glows with a light so clear and perfect—that he loses sight of the fact that everybody else has not just the same clearness of vision, does not take a similar point of view, or bring to the investigation a mind equally prepared—and with the same materials—as his own. Accordingly, he feels it is a condescension and a degradation, in which nobody has a right to require of him, to explain the process by which he arrives at a conclusion, or to reason a point which seems to him self-evident.

He speaks, for the most part, in the style of the oracle—certainly with all its authoritativeness, if not with a share of its ambiguity and obscurity. The Hebrew prophets were hardly more imperative—their language had little more of the tone of unreasoning and unaccommodating dictation. He rushes on with an almost resistless impetuosity, whither his convictions impel him, and, by mere sympathy and the strong current of his thoughts, carries with him his reader, unquestioning and unopposing, who has not a stout and resolute will of his own.

. . . .

The third and last Book develops the "Philosophy of Clothes," proper—and the biography here closes.

The *philosophy* of this volume has been a subject of considerable discussion—first, to ascertain what it really is, and secondly, to determine its true value. We should probably be thought to have evaded the chief and most weighty inquiry, were we to pass this matter by without due notice. But to attempt to make out a connected system from such unpromising materials, would of course be a very fruitless undertaking—and we deem it not uncharitable to question whether, in point of fact, at the time of putting Sartor Resartus to press, the author had himself any intelligible notions or doctrines of human life, or any well-digested "theory of the universe," aside from what was already included, by common consent, in the general belief of all civilized nations, and made the basis of their institutions, and of their practical wisdom.

. . . .

The extravagant and unnatural character of the figures employed by Mr. Carlyle to aid his expression, has often been noted and is not the least remarkable peculiarity of his writing. His metaphors and similes are of that exaggerated, impetuous, disproportionate kind, that evinces an imagination at once vigorous and undisciplined,—highly susceptible, yet deranged in its action. Fitness and adaptation are wanting. They make a momentary impression—vivid, like the full, dazzling blaze of the sun—as vague and as unabiding. They start up before the reader when little prepared for them, and where least of all he expected to see them. At first, they seem to be part of a concerted system to excite our continual wonder and amazement; afterwards they assume a more unaffected aspect, and serve to throw light far into the recess of the restless and turbulent spirit from which they issue. All his images—even those applied to the smallest and most trivial matters, are drawn from the vast and the violent in nature—storms, desert-winds, tornadoes, earthquakes, volcanoes, flames, the sea, and all objects of kindred qualities. He makes everything superlative; and whatever is huge or overpowering, needs only to partake of the solitude and disquiet of his own soul, to be forced into service, on the lightest occasion.

. . . .

The humor of Sartor Resartus is peculiar—sometimes covert and illusive; sometimes broad and hearty; sometimes affected; almost invariably cumbered with some awkwardness or downright folly. There are few efforts in this kind that we are involuntarily compelled to laugh at; and if an inward smile occasionally flashes across our mind, it is quite as often at the author's apparent self-gratulation and satisfaction in having made what he deems a palpable hit, as from any real enjoyment of the joke.

. . . .

The obscurity which is a standing objection, with many, against the writer of this volume, is chargeable mainly, perhaps, to the peculiarities of his style and expression, simply, but also in part to an inexcusable, if not, as would sometimes appear, an intentional ambiguity. It is sometimes hard to determine whether he really means to be taken in sober earnest, or ironically and in humor. Rather, we might say that, while the discriminating reader can, without much difficulty understand to which sense Mr. Carlyle really and at heart inclines, there is frequently an evident wish to avoid a direct and explicit committal to opinions which he fears may bring him into disrepute with his reader; and yet, covertly and by degrees, he aims to inculcate what he dare not avow. A book should be one thing or another—not an ambiguity. If an author means to profess a sincere "attachment to the institutions of our ancestors," and is really and in truth, "minded to defend these at all hazards," why should he qualify his avowal, by affirming his attachment to by *"true* though perhaps *feeble"*—and pretend to offer, "as no despicable pile" "to divert the current of innovation, such a volume as Teufelsdröckh's?" No one who knows the author will be likely to doubt that his real intent was anything rather than to sustain the institutions of which he speaks, just as they are; yet few will charge him with having designed, at the outset of his book, openly and honestly to declare his purpose to accelerate their overthrow. Why this disguise,—this shrinking behind the protection of an ambiguous humor?

. . . .

A serene tranquility broods over every creation of the highest genius. The spirit of the author shines out upon every part and feature of the work—placidly—as the calm moonlight rests upon every point of a varied landscape. Such a gentle and quiet composure is sought in vain throughout the "Life and Opinions of Herr Teufelsdröckh." The wild tumult and commotion of a midnight storm, sweeping across both land and sea—obscure, exciting, and powerful—flashes of lightning marking its footsteps and giving new awe to its ravages—seems a far more fitting image of the mood and temper in which this singular work had its conception. The very organism of the book—its style simply—while it clearly reveals the spirit which pervades it, could have originated in none other than a troubled, restless, and lawless, though most energetic mind. For the man who finds here any appearance of imbecility or dullness, or fails to recognize that—in spite of all the unfavorable indications that meet us at the outset, and the obstacles thrown in our way throughout—we are brought in communication with one whose thoughts take a wide range, and move with unusual rapidity and force, may charitably be supposed to have fallen short of a just comprehension of what the author is aiming to say. We cannot speak of Thomas Carlyle with contempt, or deny to Sartor Resartus a place among the writings that have given an impulse and a direction to the literature of the time. That impulse, however, is unnatural and transient, and the direction in a good measure, erroneous.

—American Whig Review,
9 (February 1849): 121–134

London and *The French Revolution*

On 10 June 1834 Carlyle and Jane moved from Craigenputtoch to Cheyne Row, Chelsea, in London. Carlyle was eager for the intellectual companions and connections available to him in London. In part because of his sensitive digestion, Carlyle seldom participated in the dinners frequently available to the London literati, but he and Jane regularly received visitors for tea at Cheyne Row in the afternoons.

During the 1830s the British working class agitated repeatedly for further extension of the franchise and other social and political reforms. The Reform Bill of 1832 did not satisfy this drive for democracy, and many British of the upper and middle classes feared that revolutionary sentiment would break out into violent rebellion. Before he had left Craigenputtoch, Carlyle had begun studying the French Revolution, and soon after settling into his new home, he committed himself to tracing the causes of the revolution, with an eye

Chronology that Carlyle created while writing "The Diamond Necklace," an essay on a jewelry swindling scheme in which Marie Antoinette was implicated but subsequently exonerated. Carlyle completed the essay, a prelude to his major work on the French Revolution, before he left Craigenputtoch, but it was not published until 1837 (Beinecke Rare Book and Manuscript Library, Yale University).

Looking for a London Home

In this excerpt from a 21 May 1834 letter to Jane in which he describes his house-hunting efforts in London, Carlyle reports stumbling upon the house that would be his home for the rest of his life. Earlier in the letter he commented: "Chelsea is unfashionable; it was once the resort of the Court and great, however; hence numerous old houses in it, at once cheap and excellent." He refers to the writer Leigh Hunt.

I proceed with a description of the Chelsea House. It is within a gunshot of Hunt's; but tho' tinkerish-nomadic, I find the Hunts are not intrusive; the sick old woman would perhaps of her own accord steer clear of us. The street makes a right-angle with Hunt's and runs down upon the River, which I suppose you might see, by stretching out your neck from our front windows, at a distance of 50 yards on the left. We are called "Cheyne Row" proper (pronounced, *Chainie Row*), and are a "genteel neighbourhood," two old Ladies on the one side, unknown character on the other but with "pianos" as Hunt said. The street is flag-pathed, sunk-storied, iron-railed, all old-fashioned and tightly done up; looks out on a rank of sturdy old *pollarded* (that is *beheaded*) Lime-trees, standing there like giants in *tawtie* [matted, shaggy] wigs (for the new boughs are still young) beyond this a high brick-wall, on the inside of which, from our upper stories, appear a garden surrounded with rather dim houses and questionable miscellanea, among other things, clothes drying. Backwards, a Garden (the size of our back one at Comely Bank) with trees &c, in bad culture; beyond this green hayfields and tree-avenues (once a Bishop's pleasure-grounds) an unpicturesque, yet rather cheerful outlook. The House itself is eminent, antique; wainscotted to the very ceiling, and has been all new-painted and repaired; broadish stair, with massive balustrade (in the old style) corniced and as thick as one's thigh; floors firm as a rock, wood of them here and there worm-eaten, yet capable of cleanness, and still with thrice the strength of a modern floor. And then as to room, Goody! There is room for a Mrs Dr Maxwell. Three stories besides the sunk story; in every one of them *three* apartments in depth (something like 40 feet in all; for it was 13 of my steps!): Thus there is a front dining room (marble chimney-piece &c); then a back

dining-room (or breakfast-room) a little narrower (by reason of the kitchen stair); then out from this, and narrower still (to allow a back-window, you consider), a china-room, or pantry, or I know not what, all shelved, and fit to hold crockery for the whole street. Such is the ground-area, which of course continues to the top, and furnishes *every* Bedroom with a dressing room, or even with a *second* bedroom. Red Bed will stand behind the drawing room; might have the shower-bath beyond it: the height of this story is 10 feet; of the ground floor 9 but some inches; of the topmost floor 8 feet 6; of the kitchen (where is a Pump and room forever) about the same. . . . No back-door (communicating with the street); bells in disorder but would be rectified; new locks, some of which threatened to act *à la Puttoch*, but seemed very oilless. On the whole a most massive, roomy, sufficient old house; with places, for example, to hang say three dozen hats or cloaks on; and as many crevices, and queer old presses, and shelved closets (all tight and new painted in their way) as would gratify the most covetous Goody. Rent *£35!* I confess I am strongly tempted; yet again incline rather towards the Brompton place (for what *use* have we for so much room?), and so go wavering between the two. Chelsea is a singular, heterogeneous kind of spot; very dirty and confused in some places, quite beautiful in others; abounding with antiquities and the traces of great men: Sir T. More, Steele, Smollett, &c &c. Our Row (which for the last three doors or so is a *street,* and none of the noblest) runs out upon a beautiful "Parade" (perhaps they call it) running along the shore of the River: shops &c, a broad highway, with huge shady trees; boats lying moored, and a smell of shipping and tar; Battersea Bridge (of wood) a few yards off; the broad River, with white-trowsered, white-shirted Cockneys dashing by like arrows in their long Canoes of Boats; beyond, the green beautiful knolls of Surr[e]y with their villages: on the whole a most artificial, green-painted, yet lively, fresh, almost opera-looking business, such as you can fancy.

—The Collected Letters of Thomas and Jane Welsh Carlyle, v. 7, pp. 172–173

to preventing such an event at home. In The French Revolution: A History, *the first work to be published under his own name, Carlyle strove to employ a more accessible style and to embody his philosophy that true history is epic poetry. As was his practice when approaching almost any subject, Carlyle emphasized the moral and spiritual dimensions of revolution.*

These excerpts are from the first letter Carlyle wrote from his new house, which he had promised to his mother. "It is not

only the first Letter I have written," he wrote, "but the first time I have put pen to paper."

Carlyle to Margaret A. Carlyle, 12 June 1834

With our renewed house-huntings, and how we dashed up and down for three or four days, in all manner of conveyances, where such were to be had cheap, and on our legs where not,—I need not detain you here. We saw various Houses; but the Chelsea House (tho' our Dame

Lease for the Cheyne Row house in which Carlyle lived for more than forty-six years (Carlyle's House Museum, London)

Mill and "the Paris *Histoire Parliamentaire*"

In his notes Carlyle records the help Mill offered in his research on the French Revolution. Forty volumes of Histoire Parlementaire de la Révolution française, ou Journal des Assemblées nationales depuis 1789 jusqu'en 1815 *were published in Paris, 1834–1838.*

From the first or nearly so, I had resolved upon the *French Revolutn*; and was reading, studying, ransacking the museum (to little purpose), with all my might. Country health was still ab*t* me; heart and strength still fearless of any toil. The weather was very hot; *defying* it (in hard almost brimless *hat*, wh*h* was *obligato* in that time of slavery) did sometimes throw me into colic; the museum collect*n* of *French Pamphts*, the completest of its sort in the world, did after six weeks of baffling wrestle, prove *in*accessible to me; and I had to leave them then,—so strong were *Chaos* and *Co* in that direct*n*. Happily John Mill had come to my aid, and the Paris *Histoire Parliamentaire* began to appear: Mill had himself great knowledge of the subject; he sent me down all his own Books on the subject (almost a cartload), and was generously profuse & unwearied in every kind of furtherance.

—The Collected Letters of Thomas and Jane Welsh Carlyle, v. 7, p. 289

did not think so at first, but thought and thinks *doubly* so afterwards) seemed nearly *twice* as good as any other we could get at the money: so, on Saturday afternoon we finally fixed; and moved hither, according to appointment, on Tuesday forenoon. Bessy Barnett had joined us from Birmingham the night before; and we came all down in a Hackney Coach, loaded with luggage, and *Chico* (the Canary-bird) singing on Bessy's knee. Jane says the little atom put great heart into her frequently thro' the journey: *he* sang aloud, wherever he might be; praising, in his way, the Maker that had given him Life and Food and fine weather. How much more should we!

About two hours after our arrival, one of Pickford's huge wagons came lumbering along, and half a dozen stout men began to haul in our Furniture. It had arrived the Saturday night before; they had sent it by canal from Liverpool, as some pounds the cheaper way, and also the safer. Their charge was something under seventeen pounds (porterage and all *etceteras* included); so that, on the whole, we have got the things brought all the way from Annan for at most £20; which is below the lowest I ever calculated on. As for the *damage*, it was not considerable; and had been done I rather conjecture mainly at Annan that night, when (as Waterbeck said) the sailors got

weary and impatient, and tumbled in the packages too much in the head-foremost style. But, indeed, there is *wonderfully little* ill done; the Canal people are exceedingly careful; the weather was wholly in our favour,—and did not begin raining till five minutes after everything was fairly within doors.

. . . .

. . . We lie safe down in a little bend of the river, away from all the great roads; have air and quiet hardly inferior to Craigenputtoch, an outlook from the back windows into mere leafy regions, with here and there a red high-peaked old roof looking thro'; and see nothing of London, except by day the summits of St Paul's Cathedral and Westminster Abbey, and by night the gleam of the great Babylon affronting the peaceful skies. Yet in *half an hour* (for it is under two miles to Piccadilly) we can be, with a pair of stout legs, in the most crowded part of the whole habitable Earth; and, even without legs, every quarter of an hour from sun to sun, a Coach will take you for six-pence from your own threshold, and set you down there again for another. We are southwest *from* the smoke; so during great part of the year we shall have no more to do with it than you. Nay even, in East winds, we are near *five* miles from the old, manufacturing part of London, and the smoke is all but gone before it reaches us.

—The Collected Letters of Thomas and Jane Welsh Carlyle, v. 7, pp. 206–207

* * *

This excerpt is from a letter to an old friend in Burnswark, just outside of Ecclefechan.

Carlyle to William Graham, 5 August 1834

. . . I have as good as bargained with a Bookseller to have a volume ready in Spring; I am to call it "French Revolution," and put my name to it. Pray that I may quit me like a true Scottish man, in this matter; for it is really important to me. I am already busy enough with it, for the labour is great. Such is my task; *all* else, as far as may be, I suffer to run by me, like the jingle of those chariot-wheels, which are to roll on without cooperation of mine; independent of me, or I of them.

—The Collected Letters of Thomas and Jane Welsh Carlyle, v. 7, pp. 254–255

* * *

Earlier in the letter from which this excerpt is taken, Carlyle wrote that it was his feeling that he should abandon the "whole despicable business" of writing for periodicals "and seek diligently out for some freer field to labour in."

Carlyle to Margaret A. Carlyle, 5 August 1834

. . . Meanwhile I employ all my days in getting ready for the new Book (on the French Revolution), and think, if I am spared with health, there is likelihood that it will be in print, with my name to it, early in spring. I will do my very best and truest; give me your prayers and hopes! This task of mine takes labour enough: I am up once or twice weekly at the British Museum for Books about it; these are almost my only occasions of visiting that fiercely tumultuous region of the city, which is at least four miles from me. I walk slowly up the shady side of the streets; and come slowly down again, about four o'clock, often smoking a cigar, and feeling more or less independent of all men.

–*The Collected Letters of Thomas and Jane Welsh Carlyle,* v. 7, p. 259

* * *

In this excerpt Carlyle uses the word sansculottism, *which derived from the custom that the democrats of the poorer classes in the French Revolution wore long trousers instead of knee-breeches (*sans *[without]* cullotte *[knee-breeches]).*

Carlyle to John A. Carlyle, 21 September 1834

. . . The best news is that I have actually *begun* that 'French Revolution,' and after two weeks of blotching and bloring [blurring] have produced–two clean pages! *Ach Gott!* But my hand is out; and I am altering my style too, and troubled about many things. Bilious, too, in these smothering, windless days. It shall be *such* a book: quite an epic poem of the Revolution: an apotheosis of Sansculottism! Seriously, when in good spirits I feel as if there were the matter of a very considerable work within me; but the task of shaping and uttering will be frightful. Here, as in so many other respects, I am alone, without models, without *limits* (this is a great want), and must–just do the best I can.

–James A. Froude, *Thomas Carlyle: A History of the First Forty Years of His Life,* v. 2, p. 456

* * *

Earlier in this letter to his mother from which this excerpt is taken, Carlyle reported that his work "went on with the more alacrity" after he had received news of her good health and that he had completed a "section of my task; the next section must very soon be begun; and a fierce struggle I expect with it."

Carlyle to Margaret A. Carlyle, 29 January 1835

My own work here gets forward as well as it can. I am very anxious to be perfectly accurate (which I find to have been exceedingly neglected by my forerunners); the consequence of that is great searching and trouble; yet the thing when one is doing it ought to *be done.* Hollow work always shows its hollowness one day or other: all men in all places at all times ought to *decline* working hollow. As to the reception I shall meet with, there is no calculating, nor indeed does it give me almost any anxiety whatever. The people that judge of Books and Men in these days are a wretched people, without wisdom, nay, without sincerity, which is the first chance for having wisdom; one is under the necessity of letting them babble out their foolish say, and heeding it no more than the cawing of rooks,–in whose sound, guidance is *not* for man or woman. If I write anything that has meaning [in] it such meaning *cannot* be lost. He that *gave* me the meaning will care fitly for it.

–*Letters of Thomas Carlyle, 1826–1836,* p. 485

Drawing room in Cheyne Row house during Carlyle's lifetime (photograph by C. Baly; from Carlyle Annual *[1991], Special Collections, Thomas Cooper Library, University of South Carolina)*

"The Miserablest Accident": Rewriting *The French Revolution*

In early March 1835, the only existing manuscript of volume one of The French Revolution *was burned beyond recovery. Mill, to whom Carlyle had entrusted the manuscript for commentary, arrived at Carlyle's door on the evening of March 6 to inform the author of the catastrophe. Carlyle's correspondence with his family and friends over the next few months reveals his dismay at the unfortunate event, but also the grace with which he handled it, the sympathy he received from family and friends, and the strategies he devised to meet the demands of rewriting.*

As Carlyle indicates in this letter to his publisher, his book had already been announced in the March issue of Fraser's Magazine: *"In 3 vols. small 8vo, / The French Revolution: / A History / In Three Books, / By Thomas Carlyle. / Book I. The Bastille. / Book II. The Constitution. / Book III. The Guillotine."*

Carlyle to James Fraser, 7 March 1835

My Dear Sir,

The miserablest accident (as we name such things) of my whole life has just befallen me; almost the only *accident* of any magnitude I had ever to complain of. I learned last night that my whole First Volume, by the silliest oversight and mistake (not on my part or my wife's), had *been destroyed,* except some three or four bits of leaves; and so the labour of five steadfast enough months had vanished irrecoverably; *worse* than if it had never been! I can be angry with no one; for they that were concerned in it have a far deeper sorrow than mine: it is purely the hand of Providence; and, by the blessing of Providence, I must struggle to take it as such,–in which case (as I trust you too understand) it would not be loss but gain.

That first volume (which pleased me better than anything I had ever done) *cannot* be written anew, for the spirit that animated it is past: but *another* first volume I will try, and shall make it, if not better or equal, *all* that I can. This only is clear to me: that I *can* write a Book on the French Revolution; and that, if I am spared long enough alive I will do it. Your Announcement (which several persons were just yesterday congratulating me on the hopeful look of) need not therefore be repeated for some months again? I *suppose* this; but it is *you* that are to judge and decide about that; with the knowledge that I, tooth and nail, am standing to the enterprise, and advancing daily, were it but at a snail's pace, as fast as is in me, to the fulfilment of it. I think the whole Book (if the Unseen Powers be propitious to me) may be ready against next publishing season; not the October time, but the one which succeeds that. It may, as I said and do believe, be for *good* yet to us all.

Under these circumstances will you put out your hand, and help me in some little things. In the first place, *do not mention* the mischance to any one: it would give great pain to some whom I love were it ever talked of; and could do no good. In the second place you must get me a *Biographie Universelle;* for like a bold gambler, having lost this throw, I am determined to *increase* the stakes, before throwing again. Let the *Biog. Universelle* therefore be bought, since I can get it no otherwise and have often felt the want of having it *close by:* you, by your knowledge of *second-hand* Booksellers &c will get it far cheaper than I can; let it be a bound copy or half-bound (easy to turn the leave of); I care not for any other property:–except indeed, which I think is not the case, there be more than one Edition; you would then of course ascertain which was best, and take that.–In the third place, pray try to get me more *paper* that were perfectly suitable: I was at one Hodge's (I think) in Drury Lane, where there was large choice and much cheaper but that too did not wholly answer. I inclose you a sheet the last of my old Dumfries stock (on which *Sartor* was written): both in size and texture (*ink*-taking &c) and every way, it is the best kind: if you could get it completely matched, I could take a *ream* or so. It were better however (indeed indispensably prudent) to send me a sheet first by way of specimen. *Do not* especially forget to return me the inclosed sheet; which you see has indication on it.–Finally the sooner these two things can be done for me, it will be the kinder.

Your Boy at this moment has entered with the pretty-looking Prospectuses! They make one sad to look upon them. Nevertheless, by God's blessing, they shall not be wholly useless one day, if not this day.

Now observe what I have spoken, and in what spirit towards you I speak it: the spirit of one who has faith in you not as a Tradesman only but as a man.

I hope to hear from you early in the week. Do not pity me; forward me rather as a runner that tho' *tripped* down, will not lie there, but rise and run again.

Always faithfully Yours, /

T. Carlyle.–

–The Collected Letters of Thomas and Jane Welsh Carlyle, v. 8, pp. 66–70

* * *

First page of Carlyle's letter to Fraser in which he informs the publisher of the destruction of his manuscript
(The Trustees of the National Library of Scotland Acc 6430)

Carlyle was struck by how distressed Mill was, as he later described in Reminiscences: *"How well do I still remember that night when he came to tell us, pale as Hector's ghost, that my unfortunate First Volume was burnt! It was like* half *sentence of death to us both; and we had to pretend to take it lightly, so dismal and ghastly was* his *horror at it, and try to talk of other matters." In his close, Carlyle refers to Mrs. Taylor, Mill's friend and future wife, who had accompanied Mill. Carlyle apparently never pressed Mill on the circumstances that led to the accident.*

Carlyle to Mill, 7 March 1835

MY DEAR MILL,

How are you? You left me last night with a look which I shall not soon forget. Is there anything that I could do or suffer or say to alleviate you? For I feel that your sorrow must be far sharper than mine; yours bound to be a *passive* one. How true is this of Richter: *"All* Evil is like a nightmare; the instant you begin to *stir* under it, it is *gone."*

I have ordered a *Biographie Universelle,* this morning;—and a better sort of paper. Thus, far from giving up the game, you see, I am risking another £10 on it. Courage, my Friend!

That I can never write *that* Volume again is indubitable: singular enough, the whole Earth could not get *it* back; but only a better or a worse one. There is the strangest dimness over it. A figure thrown into the melting-pot; but the metal (all that was golden or gold-like of that,—and *copper,* can be gathered) is there; the model also *is,* in my head. O my Friend, how easily might the bursting of some puny ligament or filament have abolished all light *there* too!

That I *can* write a Book on The French Revolution is (God be thanked for it) as clear to me as ever; also that if life be given me so long, I will. To it again, therefore! *Andar con Dios!*

I think you once said you could borrow me a *Campan?* Have you any more of *Lacretelle's* things; his 18me *Siecle?* (that is of almost no moment). The first vol. of *Genlis's Mem.?* &c. But I find *Campan* (if I get the *Biographie*) is the only one I shall really want much. Had I been a *trained* Compiler, I should not have wanted that. To make some search for it, I know, will be a kind of solace to you.

Thanks to Mrs. Taylor for her kind sympathies. May God guide, and bless you both! That is my true prayer.

Ever your affectionate Friend,
T. CARLYLE.
—Letters of Thomas Carlyle to John Stuart Mill, John Sterling, and Robert Browning, pp. 107–108

* * *

Mill to Carlyle, 7 March 1835

MY DEAR CARLYLE–I will endeavour as you advise, to think as little as I can of this misfortune, though I shall not be able to cease thinking of it until it is ascertained how far the loss is capable of being repaired–or rather reduced to a loss of time & labour only–There are hardly any means I would not joyfully take, if any existed by which I could myself be instrumental to remedying the mischief my carelessness has caused–That however depends not upon me. But there is one part of the evil–though I fear the least part–which I could repair–the loss to yourself of time & labour–that is of income. And I beg of you with an earnestness with which perhaps I may never again have need to ask anything as long as we live, that you will permit me to do this little as it is, towards remedying the consequences of my fault & lightening my self-reproach. It is what you would permit as a matter of course if I were a stranger to you–it is what is even *legally* due to you–and to have brought an evil upon a friend instead of a stranger is already a sufficient aggravation of one's regret, without the addition to it, of not being allowed to make even the poor amends one would make to a stranger.

If I could convince you what a relief this would be to me, & what an act of friendship–to say nothing of justice–it would be on your part I am sure you would not hesitate–Yours affectionately

J. S. MILL
–The Earlier Letters of John Stuart Mill, v. 1, pp. 252–253

* * *

Mill declined the offer Carlyle made in this letter to let him see his completed "Feast of Pikes" episode.

Carlyle to Mill, 9 March 1835

My Friend,

You shall do the thing you so earnestly entreat for: it is not unreasonable; *ungigmanic* it may either be or not be. How lucky, in this as in other instances, that neither of us has money for the lifting; that neither of us is wealthy, and one of us is poor! It has positively hereby become a case which money can remedy. For my own share I find that the thought of my having got day's wages for my labour will give a new face to the whole matter: what more do I ever expect (so often not finding it) but day's wages for my work? It is likely enough this may prove the only portion of the Book I may ever get so much for. I can attack the thing again, with unabated cheerfulness; and certainly, one may hope, do it better and not worse.

First pages of the letters Carlyle and Mill exchanged in the wake of the destruction of Carlyle's manuscript, 7 March 1835 (The Trustees of the National Library of Scotland MS 618.46)

India House
9th March
[1835]

My dear Carlyle — I will endeavour as you advise, to think as little as I can of this misfortune, though I shall not be able to cease thinking of it until it is ascertained how far the loss is capable of being repaired — or rather reduced to a loss of time & labour only — There are hardly any means I would not joyfully take, if any existed by which I could myself be instrumental to remedying the mischief my carelessness has caused — That however depends not upon me — But there is one part

For you again: the smart of having in so simple a way, forfeited so much money (which you also had to work for) may well burn out the other smart; and so, the precious feeling of a satisfied conscience succeeding to great pain, the whole business be healed, and even be made *wholer* than ever. Let us believe firmly that, to those who take them wisely, *all* things whatsoever are *good.*

I am to be out tonight, at tea with Allan Cunningham. The following nights we are at home: on Thursday night, I could even hope to give you the completed *Fête des Piques* (if I get on well),—provided you durst take it: with me it were no daring; for I think of all men living you are henceforth the least likely to commit such an oversight again. I mean also by the first good opportunity to let you see a little farther into my actual economic position here than you have yet done: these confusions, I feel, have thrown us still closer together than we were; and I hope in that sense too will be blessed.

One thing I forgot to mention on Saturday: That we will not *speak* of the misfortune, to any new unconcerned person; at least not till it is made good again, or made better. I had to impart it in general terms to the Bookseller Fraser, but only in general; as "an accident" chargeable on no one; and he has promised me to maintain perfect silence. My Brother John and my Mother must know of it; but no other has right to do so.

Among the Books needful one of the needfullest, as I now bethink me, is on your own shelves: Condorcet's *Life of Turgot.* Pray bring it in your pocket. I will also have de Stael's *Considerations;* but this I think I can procure perhaps more readily than you.—The thing must be made *better* than it was, or we shall never be able, not to forget it, but to laugh victorious in remembering it.

And so, now for the *Champ de Mars!* And with you be all good!

Your affectionate
T. CARLYLE
—*Letters of Thomas Carlyle to John Stuart Mill, John Sterling, and Robert Browning,* pp. 109–111

* * *

Carlyle did not write immediately to his brother or his mother about the burning of his manuscript. This excerpted letter was written in response to the first letter he had received from John after the incident.

Carlyle to John A. Carlyle, 23 March 1835

. . . Well, one night about three weeks ago, we sat at tea, and Mill's short rap was heard at the door: Jane rose to welcome him; but he stood there unresponsive, pale, the very picture of despair; said, half-articulately gasping, that she must go down and speak to "Mrs.

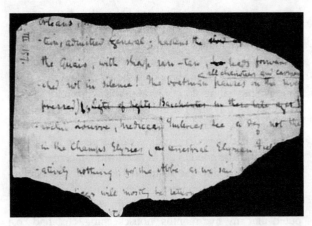

Scrap of the burnt manuscript of The French Revolution
(Carlyle's House Museum, London)

Taylor." . . . After some considerable additional gasping, I learned from Mill this fact: that my poor Manuscript, all except some four tattered leaves, was *annihilated!* He had left it out (too carelessly); it had been taken for waste-paper: and so five months of as tough labour as I could remember of, were as good as vanished, gone like a whiff of smoke.—There never in my life had come upon me any other *accident* of much moment; but this I could not but feel to be a sore one. The thing was *lost,* and perhaps worse; for I had not only forgotten all the structure of it, but the spirit it was written with was past; only the general impression seemed to remain, and the recollection that I was on the whole well satisfied with that, and could now hardly hope to equal it. Mill whom I had to comfort and speak peace to remained injudiciously enough till almost midnight, and my poor Dame and I had to sit talking of indifferent matters; and could not till then get our lament freely uttered. *She* was very good to me; and the thing did not beat us. I felt in general that I was as a little Schoolboy, who had laboriously written out his *Copy* as he could, and was showing it not without satisfaction to the Master: but lo! The Master had suddenly torn it, saying: "No, boy, thou must go and write it *better.*" What could I do but sorrowing go and try to obey. That night was a hard one; something from time to time tying me tight as it were all round the region of the heart, and strange dreams haunting me: however, I was not without good thoughts too that came like healing life into me; and I got it somewhat reasonably crushed down, not abolished, yet subjected to me with the resolution and prophecy of abolishing. . . . I got Bookshelves put up (for the whole House was *flowing* with Books), where the *Biographie* (not Fraser's, however, which was countermanded, but Mill's), with much else stands all ready, much readier than before: and so, having first finished out the Piece I was actually upon, I

began *again* at the beginning. Early the day after to-morrow (after a hard and quite novel kind of battle) I count on having the First Chapter on paper a second time, no worse than it was, though considerably different. The bitterness of the business is past therefore; and you must conceive me toiling along in that new way for many weeks to come. As for Mill I must yet tell you the best side of him. Next day after the accident he writes me a passionate Letter requesting with boundless earnestness to be allowed to make the loss good as far as *money* was concerned in it. I answered: Yes, since he so desired it; for in our circumstances it was not unreasonable: in about a week he accordingly transmits me a draft for £200; I had computed that my five months' housekeeping, etc., had cost me £100; which sum therefore and not two hundred was the one, I told him, I could take. He has been here since then; but has not sent the £100, though I suppose he will soon do it, and so the thing will end,—more handsomely than one could have expected. I ought to draw from it various practical "uses of improvement" (among others not to lend manuscripts again); and above all things try to do the work *better* than it was; in which case I shall never grudge the labour, but reckon it a goodhap.—It really seemed to me a Book of considerable significance; and not unlikely even to be of some interest at present: but that latter, and indeed all economical and other the like considerations had become profoundly indifferent to me; I felt that I was honestly writing down and delineating a World-Fact (which the Almighty had brought to pass in the world); that it was an *honest* work for me, and all men might do and say of it simply what seemed good to *them*.
—*Letters of Thomas Carlyle, 1826–1836,* pp. 498–501

* * *

Carlyle found the extraordinary task of writing anew what he had already written more difficult than he had anticipated, as is clear from this excerpt.

Carlyle to Margaret A. Carlyle, 12 May 1835

My Dear Mother—You will learn without regret that I am *idling,* or nearly so, for these last two days. My poor Work, the dreariest of its sort I ever undertook, was getting more and more untoward on me; I began to feel that toil and effort not only did not perceptibly advance it, but was even, by disheartening and disgusting me, retarding it. I gathered my papers together, therefore; sealed them up, and locked them in a drawer, with the determination not to touch *them* again for one week from that date. I flatter myself it was a very meritorious determination. A man must not only be able to work, but to give over working. I have many times stood doggedly to work; but this is the first time I ever deliberately laid it down without finishing

it. In fact, it is the strangest thing I ever tried that of re-writing my first Volume; one must vary his methods according to the task he has: take it gently, take it fiercely; you cannot tickle trouts in the way you spear whales. On the whole, it has given me very great trouble this poor Book, and Providence (in the shape of human Mismanagement) sent me the severest check of all: however, I still trust to get it written sufficiently: and if thou even *canst* not write it (as I have said to myself in late days), why then be content with that too: God's Creation will get along, exactly as it should do, *without* the writing of it.
—*Letters of Thomas Carlyle, 1826–1836,* pp. 522–524

* * *

This excerpt is from a letter in which he told his brother, as he had told his mother a month before, that he had put his work on the French Revolution away for a time and could face the possibility of not completing it.

Carlyle to John A. Carlyle, 15 June 1835

. . . I flung it by; saying, if I *never* write it, why it will never be written; not by Ink alone shall a man live or die. This is the first time in my life I ever did such a thing: neither do I doubt much but it was rather wise. It goes abreast with much that is coming to a crisis with me. You would feel astonished to see with what quietude I have laid down my head on its stone pillow in these circumstances, and said to Poverty, Dispiritment, Exclusion, Necessity and the Devil: Go *your* course, friends; behold, I lie here and rest! In fact, with all the despair that is round about me, there is not in myself I do think the least desperation: I feel rather, as if quite possibly I might be about *bursting* the accursed enchantment that has held me all my weary days in *nameless* thraldom; and actually beginning to be alive!
—*The Collected Letters of Thomas and Jane Welsh Carlyle,*
v. 8, p. 147

* * *

This excerpt is from a letter in which Carlyle wrote that he was returning to the "wretched burnt Manuscript" with "new vigour" after having been "altogether idle these five or six weeks; reading insignificant Books; talking to people; resting myself, till I saw what the days brought forth."

Carlyle to Margaret A. Carlyle, 1 July 1835

. . . That wretched burnt Manuscript must, if the "*gea* [vigour] of life" remain in me, be replaced: you cannot fancy how the whole business has got inexpressibly ugly to me, how I long to be done with it, and have my hands free again. "It shall be *done,* Sir," as the Cockneys say! After that,

Depiction of Carlyle watching his manuscript burn that appeared in an 1873 series of colored woodblock prints produced to introduce great names of the West to Japanese children (University of Tsukuba Library, Japan)

the whole world is before me, where to choose. I cannot say that I am, in the smallest degree "*tining* [losing] heart," in these perplexities: nay, I think in general, I have not been in as good heart, these ten years. London and its quackeries and follies and confusions does not daunt me; I look on all matters that pertain to it with a kind of silent defiance, confident to the last that the work my Maker meant me to do I shall verily do, let the Devil and *his* servants obstruct as they will. Have I not reason to thank God for all my sorrows too? They have burnt away much impurity that was in me; some things too they have called into life and vigour for me. At worst, I always feel that *here* is the place for me to make the struggle; distracted as the world is, it is still God's world, and here in the middle of it, not in solitude as at Puttoch, must I strike forth my capabilities, and work and do, while it is called Today. O Mother, if I can retain the precepts that you and the good men who have gone before us walked by, why should I fear aught under the stars?

              –*The Collected Letters of Thomas and Jane Welsh Carlyle*, v. 8, p. 164

* * *

In this excerpt, written six months to the day after he sent his brother a letter about the destruction of his manuscript, Carlyle was able to report that he was back to where he had been.

Carlyle to John A. Carlyle, 23 September 1835

First then, by the real blessing and favour of Heaven, I got *done* with that unutterable Manuscript, on Monday last. . . . The work does not seem to myself to be *very* much worse than it was; it is worse in the style of expression, but better compacted in the thought: as it goes through the Press I may help it somewhat. On the whole I feel like a man that had "nearly killed himself accomplishing *zero*." But zero or not zero, what a deliverance! I shall never without a kind of sacred shudder look back at the detestable state of enchantment I have worked in for these six months, and am now blessedly delivered from. The rest of the Book shall go on quite like child's play in comparison: also I do think it will be a *queer* Book; one of the *queerest* published in this cen-

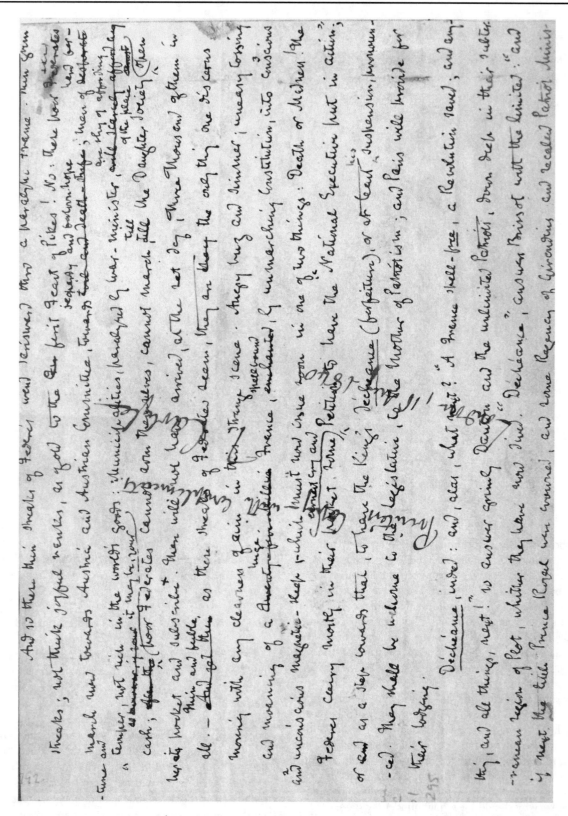

Two pages from the incomplete printer's copy for the second volume of The French Revolution
(Rodger L. Tall Collection, Thomas Cooper Library, University of South Carolina)

But to ever minds the *[illegible]* gate there mining phenomena, which left this the *[illegible]* in stead of Barberry's "In Heaven Marseillers Qui servait mes [illegible] who know how to see?"

Prompt to the request of Barberry, the Marseillers Municipality has got there men together; on the *[illegible]* morning of July the *[illegible]* reps, "Marchez, allez, le Tyran de Château (March, strike down the Ty- -rant of the *[illegible]*); and they will again appropriate marching," are marching, long journey, doubt- -ful errand; Enfants de la Patrie, may a good genius guide you! Their own wild head and what faith it has will guide them;—and is not that the mention of some genius, letter or verse? Five Hundred and seventeen able men, with Captains of fifty and tens; well armed all; musket or whatever went on this: so they drive three *[illegible]* of Cannon; for who knows what obstacles may *[illegible]*? Municipalities then are, *[illegible]* of *[illegible]*; Commandants with orders to *[illegible]* ever question volun- -teers: good, when armed arguments will not open a town-gate; if you have a betray'd to shun -or it! they have left their Phocean *[illegible]* many Phocean City and Sea-haven, with its hustle and its *[illegible]* *[illegible]* dockyards, alumni and olive gardens, orange-trees, the thronging Cours, with high-pennant Avenues, *[illegible]* *[illegible]* *[illegible]* *[illegible]* a never tops, and; while glittering besides that crown the hills, are all behind them, they wend their long wild way, from the extremity of French land, this' unknown cities, towards an unknown destiny; with a purpose that they know.

Much *[illegible]* this phenomena, and lodging in a *[illegible]* tall City or many houses-

tury, and *can*, though it cannot be popular, be better than that.

—Letters of Thomas Carlyle, 1826–1836, p. 548

* * *

With the rewriting of volume one behind him, Carlyle pushed on to complete the remainder of the work. By September 1836 he was working on volume three.

Carlyle to John A. Carlyle, 12 September 1836

. . . I have a great lesson to learn: that of *einmal fertig werden* [getting done once for all]. Much poring does but confuse, and reduce all to caudle. Get it done, and let there be an end! The bricklayer does not insist on all being smooth as *marble,* but only on all having a certain *degree* of smoothness and straightness; and so he gets a wall done. As to what you admonished about *style,* tho' you goodnaturedly fall away from it now, there was actually some profit in it, and some effect. It reminds me once more that there are always two parties to a good style: the contented Writer and the contented Reader. Many a little thing I propose to alter with an eye to greater clearness. But the grand point at present is to get done *briefly.* I find I have only eighty-eight pages in all, and infinite matters to cram into them. I purpose *investigating* almost no farther; but dashing in what I already have in some compendious, grandiose-massive way. There are some three Chapters yet: the first the *Girondins;* for Louis is now well guillotined. Forward!

—New Letters of Thomas Carlyle, v. 1, p. 33

* * *

Earlier in the letter from which this excerpt is taken, Carlyle assured Emerson as to his health: "be under no apprehension. I am always sick . . . it is weariness *merely; and now, by the bounty of Heaven, I am as it were within sight of land."*

Carlyle to Emerson, 5 November 1836

As to the Book, I do say seriously that it is a wild, savage, ruleless, very bad Book; which even you will not be able to like; much less any other man. Yet it contains strange things; sincerities drawn out of the heart of a man very strangely situated; reverent of nothing but what is reverable in all ages and places: so we will print it, and be done with it;—and try a new turn next time.

—The Correspondence of Thomas Carlyle and Ralph Waldo Emerson, 1834–1872 v. 1, pp. 102, 104

* * *

This excerpt is from a letter that Carlyle called "a pleasure to myself I have long looked forward to"—he had delayed responding to Sterling's last letter until he had finished his work on what he called "this malison of a Book."

Carlyle to Sterling, 17 January 1837

. . . it is over; five days ago I finished, about ten o'clock at night; and really was ready both to weep and to pray,—but did not do either, at least not visibly or audibly. The Bookseller has it, and the Printer has it; I expect the first sheet to-morrow: in not many weeks more, I can hope to wash my hands of it forever and a day. It is a thing disgusting to me by the faults of it; the merits of which, for it is not without merits, will not be seen for a long time. It is a wild savage Book, itself a kind of French Revolution;—which perhaps, if Providence have so ordered it, the world had better *not* accept when offered it? With all my heart! What I do know of it is that it has come hot out of my own soul; born in blackness, whirlwind and sorrow; that no man, for a long while, has stood speaking so completely alone under the Eternal Azure, in the character of man only; or is likely for a long while so to stand:—finally that it has come as near to choking the life out of me as any task I should like to under-take for some years to come; which also is an immense comfort, indeed the greatest of all.

—New Letters of Thomas Carlyle, v. 1, pp. 49, 50

* * *

This excerpt is from a letter written while Jane was suffering from the flu.

Jane Welsh Carlyle to Sterling, 1 February 1837

One great comfort, however, under all afflictions, is that 'The French Revolution' is happily concluded; at least, it will be a comfort when one is delivered from the tag-raggery of printers' devils, that at present drive one from post to pillar. *Quelle vie!* let no woman who values peace of soul ever dream of marrying an author! That is to say, if he is an honest one, who makes a conscience of doing the thing he pretends to do. But this I observe to you in confidence; should I state such a sentiment openly, I might happen to get myself torn in pieces by the host of my husband's lady admirers, who already, I suspect, think me too happy in not knowing my happiness.

—Letters and Memorials of Jane Welsh Carlyle, v. 1, p. 66

Lectures on German Literature

Lectures on a variety of topics, from literature to science, were popular entertainment in the nineteenth century, and Carlyle's friends pressed him to speak. While his nervous disposition made public speaking unattractive to him at first, he eventually decided to capitalize on the opportunity for profit without the intense labor of composition. He relied on friends to manage the logistics of the series, which, while not as profitable as he had hoped, was successful enough to encourage him to lecture again later in his career.

This excerpt is from a 10 April 1837 letter Carlyle wrote to John Stuart Mill.

Herewith I send you ten Prospectuses of that amazing Course of Lectures of mine. One will suffice for yourself; but according as you have opportunity, you may leave the other nine with such persons as you think them likely to concern. How the others, for they have 500 of them, are getting distributed I do not very specially know: but your section of the world, I think, must be nearly unvisited by them. If you can make use of more than ten, I suppose I can easily get you more. It is Miss Wilson and her Brother whom you once saw here; they, with Taylor chiefly, that are setting afoot this thing: one of the conditions of it is that I am not to hear a word of the business till the people are all met, we suppose three score or so, in Willis's Rooms.

—Letters of Thomas Carlyle to John Stuart Mill, John Sterling, and Robert Browning, pp. 151–152

This excerpt is from Carlyle's 30 May 1837 letter to John A. Carlyle.

As to the Lectures, I know not whether you saw in the Newspapers which I sent or which you might otherwise get hold of, what indications there were: but the truth is the thing went off not without effect; and I have great cause to be thankful that I am so handsomely quit of it. The audience, composed of mere quality and notabilities, was very humane to me; they seemed indeed to be not a little astonished at the wild Annandale voice, which occasionally got high and earnest; in these cases they sat as still under me as stones. I had, I think, 200 and odd. The pecuniary net-result is £135, the expenses being great, and the mismanagement of Booksellers &c coming in for something. But the ulterior issues of it may by possibility be less inconsiderable. It seems possible I may get into a kind of way of lecturing or otherwise speaking direct to my fellow-creatures; and so get delivered out of this awful quagmire of difficulties in which you have so long seen me struggle and wriggle. We will wait what the days bring. Heaven be thanked that it is *done,* for this time, so tolerably; and we here still alive! I hardly ever in my life had such a moment as that of the commencement when you were thinking of me at Rome. My Printers had only ceased the day before; I was wasted and fretted to a thread, my tongue let me drink as I would continued dry as charcoal: the people were there, I was obliged to stumble in, and start. *Ach Gott!*

—The Collected Letters of Thomas and Jane Welsh Carlyle, v. 9, pp. 214–215

The Response to *The French Revolution*

The French Revolution: A History was published in May 1837 and received a generally positive reception that established Carlyle as a major literary figure. The book raised important critical issues, including the place of interpretation and analysis in historical writing and the role of moral judgment of historical figures and events. Carlyle's power to bring individual people and incidents to life through vivid description was almost universally praised.

The French Revolution was also a success in the United States, and Emerson arranged for an American edition, which appeared on 25 December 1837. Over the following year Emerson forwarded to Carlyle £150 in profits, money which Carlyle waved in the face of his British publisher, from whom he had earned nothing for the domestic edition.

These excerpts are from an unsigned review that began with a discussion of originality and style: "Originality, without justness of thought, is but novelty of error; and originality of style, without sound taste and discretion, is sheer affectation." *Bibliographer Roger Tarr attributes this review to Lady Sydney Morgan, an Irish novelist and nationalist.*

"All-Pervading Absurdity"
Review of *The French Revolution*

. . . What need have we of a new History of the French Revolution? We have the contemporary history of that gigantic event in superabundance; and the time is not yet arrived for christening ourselves Posterity. We have looked carefully through these volumes; and, their peculiarity of style and the looseness of their reasoning apart, we have not found a fact in them that is not better told in Mignet, and twenty other unpretending historians. There is, moreover, in them the deadly *crambe repetita* of referring the faults and the failures of the Revolution to the speculative opinions, or "philosophism," as the author calls it, of the eighteenth century. "Faith," he

THE

FRENCH REVOLUTION:

A HISTORY.

IN THREE VOLUMES.

By THOMAS CARLYLE.

Μέγα ὁ ἀγὼν ἔστι, θεῖον γὰρ ἔργον· ὑπὲρ βασιλείας· ὑπὲρ ἐλευθερίας·
ὑπὲρ εὐροίας· ὑπὲρ ἀταραξίας.—ARRIANUS.
Δόγμα γὰρ αὐτῶν τίς μεταβάλλει; χωρὶς δὲ δογμάτων μεταβολῆς, τί
ἄλλο ἢ δουλεία στενόντων καὶ πείθεσθαι προσποιουμένων;—ANTONINUS.

VOL. I.—THE BASTILLE.

LONDON:

JAMES FRASER, 215 REGENT STREET.

M.DCCC.XXXVII.

Title page for The French Revolution *(Special Collections, Thomas Cooper Library, University of South Carolina)*

says, "is gone out; skepticism is come in. Evil abounds and accumulates; no one has faith to withstand it, to amend it, to begin by amending himself." Now, faith and skepticism had nothing directly to do with the affair; it was want, and misery, and oppression in the lower classes, utter corruption and incapacity in the higher, that made the revolt.

. . . .

The faults which we have been compelled thus to denounce, are the more provoking, as they are not unmingled with many finely conceived passages, and many just and vigorous reflections. The author's mind is so little accustomed to weigh carefully its own philosophy, and is so thoroughly inconsistent with itself, that the grossest absurdity in speculation does not prevent his perceiving and adopting truths in the closest relation of opposition to it. Thus, while he attributes evils innumerable to infidelity and philosophism, and openly

preaches passive obedience, religious and political, he does not the less wisely sum up the material causes of the revolt, and put forth many just views of men and things, and of the multiplied errors committed both "within and without the walls of Troy." So, too, as to style, amidst an all-pervading absurdity of mannerism, there are passages of great power, and occasionally of splendid, though impure eloquence.

—*Athenaeum*, no. 499 (20 May 1837): 353

* * *

These excerpts are from a thirty-six-page review Mill wrote in the hope of exerting an early, positive influence on the reception of his friend's book. In 1840 Mill claimed his review "greatly accelerated the success" of the work, which he believed was "strange & incomprehensible to the greater part of the public." He "got fair play" for the book because he "got the first word, blew the trumpet before it at its first coming out & by claiming for it the honours of highest genius frightened the small fry of critics from pronouncing a hasty condemnation" (The Earlier Letters of John Stuart Mill, v. 2, p. 427). Although he later wrote in his Autobiography *that "anybody, in a position to be read, who had expressed the same opinion at the precise time, and had made any tolerable statement of the just grounds for it, would have produced the same effect"(pp. 183–184), Mill was clearly proud of his initiative.*

"The Truest of Histories"
Review of *The French Revolution*
John Stuart Mill

This is not so much a history, as an epic poem; and notwithstanding, or even in consequence of this, the truest of histories. It is the history of the French Revolution, and the poetry of it, both in one; and on the whole no work of greater genius, either historical or poetical, has been produced in this country for many years.

. . . .

To any one who is perfectly satisfied with the best of the existing histories, it will be difficult to explain wherein the merit of Mr. Carlyle's book consists. If there be a person who, in reading the histories of Hume, Robertson, and Gibbon (works of extraordinary talent, and the works of great writers) has never felt that this, after all is not history—and that the lives and deeds of his fellow-creatures must be placed before him in quite another manner, if he is to know them, or feel them to be real beings, who once were alive, beings of his own flesh and blood, not mere shadows and dim abstractions; such a person, for whom plausible talk *about* a thing does as well as an image of the thing itself, feels no need of a book like Mr. Carlyle's; the want, which it is peculiarly fitted to supply, does not yet consciously exist in his mind. That such a want, however, is generally felt, may be inferred from the vast number of historical plays and historical romances, which have been written for no other purpose than to satisfy it. Mr Carlyle has been the first to shew that all which is done for history by the best historical play, by Schiller's Wallenstein, for example, or Vitet's admirable trilogy; may be done in a strictly true narrative, in which every incident rests on irrefragable authority; may be done, by means merely of an apt selection and judicious grouping of authentic facts.

It has been noted as a point which distinguishes Shakespeare from ordinary dramatists, that their characters are logical abstractions, his are human beings; that their kings are nothing but kings, their lovers nothing but lovers, their patriots, courtiers, villains, cowards, bullies, are each of them that, and that alone; while his are real men and women, who have these qualities, but have them in addition to their full share of all other qualities (not incompatible), which are incident to human nature. In Shakespeare, consequently, we feel we are in a world of realities; we are among such beings as really could exist, as do exist, or have existed, and as we can sympathise with; the faces we see around us are human faces, and not mere rudiments of such, or exaggerations of single features. This quality, so often pointed out as distinctive of Shakespeare's plays, distinguishes Mr. Carlyle's history. Never before did we take up a book calling itself by that name, a book treating of past times, and professing to be true, and find ourselves actually among human beings. We at once felt, that what had hitherto been to us mere abstractions, had become realities; the "forms of things unknown," which we fancied we knew, but knew their names merely, were, for the first time, with most startling effect, 'bodied forth' and "turned into shape."

. . . .

. . . the thing must be presented as it can exist only in the mind of a great poet: of one gifted with the two essential elements of the poetic character—creative imagination, which, from a chaos of scattered hints and confused testimonies, can summon up the Thing to appear before it as a completed whole: and that depth and breadth of feeling which makes all the images that are called up appear arrayed in whatever, of all that belongs to them, is naturally most affecting and impressive to the human soul.

We do not envy the person who can read Mr Carlyle's three volumes, and not recognize in him both these endowments in a most rare and remarkable degree. What is equally important to be said—he possesses in no less perfection that among the qualities necessary for his task, seemingly the most opposite to these, and in which the man of poetic imagination might be thought likeliest to be deficient; the quality of the historical day-drudge. A more pains-taking or accurate investigator of facts, and sifter of testimonies, never wielded the historical pen. We do not say this at random, but from a most extensive acquaintance with his materials, with his subject, and with the mode in which it has been treated by others.

. . . .

But it may be asked, what opinion has Mr. Carlyle formed of the French Revolution, as an event in universal history; and this question is entitled to an answer. It should be, however, premised, that in a history upon the plan of Mr. Carlyle's, the opinions of the writer are a matter of secondary importance. In reading an ordinary historian, we want to know his opinions, because it is mainly his *opinions* of things, and not the things themselves, that he sets before us; or if any features of the things themselves, those chiefly, which his *opinions* lead him to consider as of importance. Our readers have seen sufficient in the extracts we have made for them, to be satisfied that this is not Mr. Carlyle's method. Mr. Carlyle brings the thing before us in the *concrete*—clothed, not indeed in *all* its properties and circumstances, since these are infinite, but in as many of them as can be authentically ascertained and imaginatively realized: not prejudging that some of those properties and circumstances will prove instructive and others not, a prejudgment which is the fertile source of misrepresentation and one-sided historical delineation without end. Every one knows, who has attended (for instance) to the sifting of a complicated case by a court of justice, that as long as our image of the fact remains in the slightest degree vague and hazy and undefined, we cannot tell but that what we do *not* yet distinctly see may be precisely that on which all turns. Mr. Carlyle, therefore, brings us *acquainted* with persons, things, and events, before he suggests to us what to think of them: nay, we see that this is the very process by which he arrives at his own thoughts; he paints the thing to himself—he constructs a picture of it in his own mind, and does not, till afterwards, make any logical propositions about it at all. This done, his logical propositions concerning the thing may be true, or may be false; the thing is there, and any reader may find a totally different set of propositions in it if he can; as he might in the reality, if *that* had been before him.

. . . .

   . . . Nevertheless, we will not leave the subject without pointing out what appears to us to be the most prominent defect in our author's general mode of thinking. His own method being that of the artist, not of the man of science—working as he does by figuring things to himself as whole, not dissecting them into their parts—he appears, though perhaps it is but appearance, to entertain something like a contempt for the opposite method; and to go as much too far in his distrust of analysis and generalization, as others (the Constitutional party, for instance, in the French Revolution) went too far in their reliance upon it.

–London and Westminster Review, 27 (July 1837):
17, 18–19, 22, 43–44, 47

* * *

Carlyle responds to Mill's review of The French Revolution *in this excerpt.*

Carlyle to Mill, 18 July 1837

   No man, I think, need wish to be better reviewed. You have said openly of my poor Book what I durst not myself dream of it, but should have liked to dream had I dared. It is a courageous Article; carries its right to speak on the face of it; and speaks *so.* Innumerable dissonant small-deer of Newspaper columns must feel the wind struck out of them thereby, and keep silence or change their note. What good a Criticism can do to a Book may be considered as done. To a Book or to an Author: for I have literally not read any other Criticism at all, and even heard little of them; and consider myself well off indeed. . . . Half a dozen reviews like yours even would tend to do me incalculable mischief: I should have to say, as the Dumfries Weaver did when they made him Deacon of the Weavers, and drank his health, "Gentlemen, consider that I am still but a man."

*–The Collected Letters of Thomas and
Jane Welsh Carlyle,* v. 9, pp. 255–256

* * *

At the time of writing this review, ten years before the publication of his first major novel, Vanity Fair *(1847), William Makepeace Thackeray was becoming known in London for his contributions to periodicals. He was not the only reviewer to note that troubled England could profit from the tragic example of the French Revolution. Thackeray began his review by noting that Carlyle's work had "raised a strange storm of applause and discontent."*

"Extraordinary Powers"
Review of *The French Revolution*
William Makepeace Thackeray

   . . . To hear one party you would fancy the author was but a dull madman, indulging in wild vagaries of language and dispensing with common sense and reason, while according to another, his opinions are little short of inspiration, and his eloquence unbounded as his genius. We confess, that in reading the first few pages, we were not a little inclined to adopt the former opinion, and yet, after perusing the whole of this extraordinary work, we can allow, almost to the fullest extent, the high qualities with which Mr. Carlyle's idolators endow him.

. . . .

   . . . it is written in an eccentric prose, here and there disfigured by grotesque conceits and images; but, for all this, it betrays most extraordinary powers—learning, observation, and humour. Above all, it has no CANT. It teems with sound, hearty, philosophy (besides certain transcendentalisms which we do not pretend to understand), it possesses genius, if any book ever did. . . .

   We need scarcely recommend this book and its timely appearance, now that some of the questions solved in it seem almost likely to be battled over again. The hottest Radical in England may learn by it that there is something more necessary for him even than his mad liberty—the authority, namely, by which he retains his head on his shoulders and his money in his pocket, which privileges that by-word "liberty" is often unable to secure for him. It teaches (by as strong examples as ever taught any thing) to rulers and to ruled alike moderation, and yet there are many who would react the same dire tragedy, and repeat the experiment tried in France so fatally.

–The Times, 3 August 1837, p. 6

* * *

Separate Ways: The Friendship of Carlyle and Mill

From 1832 to 1835 Carlyle and Mill corresponded regularly on political, philosophical, and religious topics, but the friendship faded after the publication of The French Revolution *in 1837. Both men would later look back on their relationship.*

Carlyle made this note on the course of the friendship.

He had taken a great attach*t* to me (wh*h* lasted ab*t* 10 years, and then suddenly ended I never knew how): an altog*r* clear, logical, honest, amiable, affec*te* young man; and respected as such here, tho' sometimes felt to be rather *colourless,* even aqueous,—no *reli*g*n* in almost any form traceable in him. He was among our chief visitors & social elements at that time. Came to us in the ev*gs* once or twice a week; walked with me on Sundays &c; with a great deal of discourse not worthless to me in its kind.

– The Collected Letters of Thomas and Jane Welsh Carlyle, v. 7, p. 289

Mill reflected on Carlyle's power as a writer in his Autobiography.

I have already mentioned Carlyle's earlier writings as one of the channels through which I received the influences which enlarged my early narrow creed; but I do not think that those writings, by themselves, would ever have had any effect on my opinions. What truths they contained, though of the very kind which I was already receiving from other quarters, were presented in a form and vesture less suited than any other to give them access to a mind trained as mine had been. They seemed a haze of poetry and German metaphysics, in which almost the only clear thing was a strong animosity to most of the opinions which were the basis of my

mode of thought; religious skepticism, utilitarianism, the doctrine of circumstances, and the attaching any importance to democracy, logic, or political economy. Instead of my having been taught anything, in the first instance, by Carlyle, it was only in proportion as I came to see the same truths through media more suited to my mental constitution, that I recognised them in his writings. Then, indeed, the wonderful power with which he put them forth made a deep impression upon me, and I was during a long period one of his most fervent admirers; but the good his writings did me, was not as philosophy to instruct, but as poetry to animate. Even at the time when our acquaintance commenced, I was not sufficiently advanced in my new modes of thought, to appreciate him fully; a proof of which is, that on his showing me the manuscript of Sartor Resartus, his best and greatest work, which he had just then finished, I made little of it; though when it came out about two years afterwards in Fraser's Magazine I read it with enthusiastic admiration and the keenest delight. I did not seek and cultivate Carlyle less on account of the fundamental differences in our philosophy. He soon found out that I was not 'another mystic,' and when for the sake of my own integrity I wrote to him a distinct profession of all those of my opinions which I knew he most disliked, he replied that the chief difference between us was that I 'was as yet consciously nothing of a mystic.' I do not know at what period he gave up the expectation that I was destined to become one; but though both his and my opinions underwent in subsequent years considerable changes, we never approached much nearer to each other's modes of thought than we were in the first years of our acquaintance.

–John Stuart Mill, Autobiography, *pp. 148–149*

Emerson made these observations in August 1837.

"One of the World's Scholars" An Entry on Carlyle from Emerson's Journal

Carlyle: how the sight of his handwriting warms my heart at the little post window. How noble it seems to me that his words should run out of Nithsdale or London over land & sea, to Weimar, to Rome, to America, to Watertown, to Concord, to Louisville, that they should cheer & delight & invigorate me: A man seeking no reward, warping his genius, filing his mind to no dull public but content with the splendors of Nature & Art as he beholds them & resolute to announce them if his voice is orotund & shrill, in his own proper accents—please or displease the World, how noble that he should trust his eye & ear above all Lon-

don & know that in all England is no man that can see so far behind or forward; how good & just that amid the hootings of malignant men he should hear this & that whispered qualification of praise of Schiller, Burns, Diderot, &c the commended papers being more every year & the commendation louder. How noble that alone & unpraised he should still write for he knew not who, & find at last his readers in the valley of the Missisippi, and they should brood on the pictures he had painted & untwist the many colored meanings which he had spun & woven into so rich a web of sentences and domesticate in so many & remote heads the humor, the learning, and the philosophy which year by year in summer & in frost this lonely man had lived in the moors of Scotland. This man upholds & propels civilization. For every wooden post he knocks away he replaces one of stone. He cleanses and exalts men & leaves the world better. He knows & loves the heavenly stars and see fields below the trees & animals; he sees towered cities; royal houses; & poor men's chambers & reports the good he sees God thro' him telling this generation also that he has beholden his work & sees that it is good. He discharges his duty as one of the World's Scholars.

—Journals and Miscellaneous Notebooks of
Ralph Waldo Emerson, v. 5, pp. 358–359

* * *

Carlyle commented on the reception of The French Revolution *in this excerpt.*

Carlyle to John A. Carlyle, 12 August 1837

As to the success of the Book I *know* almost nothing, but suppose it to be considerably greater than I expected. Mill's Review was in a great style of eulogy, the best review a man could wish of himself. I understand there have been many reviews of very mixed character. I got one in the *Times* last week; thinking it might be worth more to you than the postage I sent it forward. The writer is one Thack[e]ray, a half-monstrous Cornish giant; kind of painter, Cambridge man, and Paris Newspaper Correspondent, who is now writing for life, in London: I have seen him at the Bullers' and at Sterling's; his article is rather like him, and I supposed calculated to do the Book good. I wish you had the Book itself.

—The Collected Letters of Thomas and Jane Welsh Carlyle,
v. 9, p. 288

* * *

Carlyle again referred to Thackeray's review in this excerpt.

Carlyle to Jane Welsh Carlyle, 18 August 1837

By the bye, this Article did us all some good here. It was a sunny Monday morning; Alick had been up here, Jamie and I were escorting him homewards. . . . Lo, on the top of the Potter Knowe (the height immediately behind Middlebie), Betty Smeal unfastening her luggage; presenting two Newspapers with their strokes in Goody's hand; one of which was this *Times!* They made me take place under the shade of the hedge and beech-trees, and read it all over to them, amid considerable laughter and applause. One is obliged to men in these circumstances, who say even with bluster and platitude greater than Thackeray's, Behold this man is not an ass.

—New Letters of Thomas Carlyle, v. 1, p. 83–84

* * *

Emerson wrote apologizing for not making a "speedier acknowledgment" of the gift of The French Revolution. *Later in his letter, from which this selection is drawn, Emerson predicted a "good reception" for* The French Revolution *in America and reported that 1,166 copies of* Sartor Resartus *had sold.*

Emerson to Carlyle, 13 September 1837

The *French Revolution* did not reach me until three weeks ago, having had at least two long pauses by the way, as I find, since landing. Between many visits received, and some literary haranguing done, I have read two volumes and half the third: and I think you a very good giant; disporting yourself with an original and vast ambition of fun; pleasure and peace not being strong enough for you, you choose to suck pain also, and teach fever and famine to dance and sing. I think you have written a wonderful book, which will last a very long time. I see that you have created a history, which the world will own to be such. You have recognized the existence of other persons than officers, and of other relations than civism. You have broken away from all books, and written a mind. It is a brave experiment, and the success is great. We have men in your story and not names merely; always men, though I may doubt sometimes whether I have the historic men. We have great facts—and selected facts—truly set down. We have always the co-presence of Humanity along with the imperfect damaged individuals. The soul's right of wonder is still left to us; and we have righteous praise and doom awarded, assuredly without cant. Yes, comfort yourself on that particular, O ungodliest divine man! thou cantest never. Finally, we have not–a dull word. Never was there a style so rapid as yours,–which no reader can outrun; and so it is for the most intelligent. I suppose nothing will astonish more than the audacious wit of cheerfulness which no tragedy and no magnitude of events can overpower or daunt. Henry VIII. loved a Man, and I see with joy my bard always equal to the crisis he represents. And so I thank you for your labor, and feel that your contemporaries ought to say, All hail, Brother! live forever: not only in the great Soul which thou largely inhalest, but also as a named person in this thy definite deed.

I will tell you more of the book when I have once got it at focal distance,–if that can ever be,–and muster my objections when I am sure of their ground. I insist, of course, that it might be more simple, less Gothically efflorescent. You will say no rules for the illumination of windows can apply to the Aurora Borealis. However, I find refreshment when every now and then a special fact slips into the narrative couched in sharp businesslike terms.

–*The Correspondence of Thomas Carlyle and Ralph Waldo Emerson*, v. 1, pp. 129–131

* * *

Carlyle developed a friendship in the late 1830s with John Forster, a reviewer and man of letters, who remained a staunch supporter of Carlyle throughout his life. This excerpt is the opening of Forster's review.

"Originality and Genius"
Review of *The French Revolution*
John Forster

This is one of the few books of our time that are likely to live for some generations beyond it, and we are, for that reason, not at all surprised at the equivocal reception it has had. Mr. Walter Savage Landor observes, in one of those masterly productions which we class in the same rank, that "he has been amused, in his earlier days, at watching the first appearance of such few books as he believed to be the production of some powerful intellect. He has seen people slowly rise up to them, like carp in a pond when food is thrown among them; some of which carp snatch suddenly at a morsel, and swallow it; others touch it gently with their barbe, pass deliberately by, and leave it; others wriggle and rub against it more disdainfully; others, in sober truth, know not what to make of it, swim round and round it, eye it on the sunny side, eye it on the shady; approach it, question it, shoulder it, flap it

John Forster, a photograph owned by the Carlyles (Columbia University Library, from Fred Kaplan, Thomas Carlyle: A Biography, *Thomas Cooper Library, University of South Carolina)*

with the tail, turn it over, look askance at it, take a pea-shell or a worm instead of it, and plunge again their contented heads into the comfortable mud: after some seasons the same food will suit their stomachs better." Among such carp as these the present volumes appear to have been thrown, and some years will pass before they begin to be generally relished–but relished they will be, and that thoroughly, sooner or later.

Mr. Carlyle has, in these volumes, written a book of unquestionable originality and genius. It is a book conceived in the Epic spirit, and written from the innermost heart of the writer. Everything in it is fresh and real, and it has all the fervour, exaltation, and impressiveness of poetry. Beyond comparison it is the finest book that has yet been published on that world-prodigy, the first French Revolution.

–*The Examiner* (17 September 1837): 596–598, 629–630

* * *

In this excerpt, from a letter to the son of his sister Jean Carlyle Aitken, Carlyle comments on the reception of The French Revolution.

Carlyle to James Aitken, 19 October 1837

. . . The *Book* goes off famously, with praise far higher than need be, compliments from right and left. As one new instance, the Manager of Covent Garden Theatre has sent me a free-ticket to his boxes for this season. He is one Macready; I almost think he was in Dumfries once; a very clever and altogether respectable man; who is making a struggle this year to redeem the Theatre from that stupidity and degradation the system of puffery and baseness of all sorts had brought it into; and for this reason wishes to rally round him all manner of intelligent persons,–the present writer among others! I went last night, it was really very good (and soon done, if you *leave* the Farce); I think of going once a week till I see better.

–*The Collected Letters of Thomas and Jane Welsh Carlyle*, v. 9, p. 335

* * *

Robert Southey had first written about the French Revolution in 1794, when he collaborated with Samuel Taylor Coleridge on the play The Fall of Robespierre. *Carlyle recalls meeting with Southey in the wake of the publication of his history. He recalls being in a depressed mood, which had not been lifted by the positive notices his work had received nor Jane's attempts to "irradiate" his darkness.*

Southey's Assent

Such being my posture and humour at that time, fancy my surprise at finding Southey full of sympathy, assent, and recognition of the amplest kind, for my poor new Book! We talked largely on the huge Event itself, which he had dwelt with openly or privately ever since his youth, and tended to interpret exactly as I,– the suicidal explosion of an old wicked world, too wicked, false and impious for living longer;–and seemed gratified, and as if grateful, that a strong voice had at last expressed that meaning. My poor *French Revolution* evidently appeared to him a Good Deed, a salutary bit of "scriptural" exposition for the public and for mankind; and this, I could perceive, was the soul of a great many minor approbations and admirations of detail, which he was too polite to speak of. As Southey was the only man of eminence that had ever taken such a view of me, and especially of this my first considerable Book, it seems strange that I should have felt so little real triumph in it as I did. For all other eminent men,

in regard to all my Books and Writings hitherto, and most of all in regard to this latest, had stood pointedly silent; dubitative, disapprobatory, many of them shaking their heads.

–*Reminiscences*, v. 2, p. 288

* * *

This review is of the first American edition of The French Revolution, *published by the Boston house of Charles C. Little on 25 December 1837. As Emerson explains in his 9 February 1838 letter to Carlyle, the review was heavily edited.*

"A Robust Flame Self-Kindled and Self-Fed"
Review of *The French Revolution*
Ralph Waldo Emerson

We welcome the appearance in this country of this extraordinary work. It is by far the largest, the most elaborate, and the best work which Mr. Carlyle has yet attempted, and although an accurate and extended history, not a whit less original and eccentric than any of his earlier productions. One thing has for some time been becoming plainer, and is now quite undeniable, that Mr. Carlyle's genius, whether benignant or baleful, is no transient meteor, and no expiring taper, but a robust flame self-kindled and self-fed, and more likely to light others into a conflagration, than to be speedily blown out. The work before us indicates an extent of resources, a power of labor, and powers of thought, seldom combined, and never without permanent effects.

It is a part of Mr. Carlyle's literary creed, "that all history is poetry, were it rightly told." The work before us is his own exemplification of his doctrine. The poetry consists in the historian's point of view. With the most accurate and lively delineation of the crowded actions of the revolution, there is the constant co-perception of the universal relations of each man. With a painter's eye for picturesque groups, and a boy's passion for exciting details, he combines a philosopher's habitual wonder as he stands before the insoluble mysteries of the Advent and Death of man. From this point of view, he is unable to part, and the noble and hopeful heart of the narrator breathes a music of humanity through every part of the tale. Always equal to his subject, he has first thought it through; and having seen in the sequence of events the illustration of high and beautiful laws which exist eternal in the reason of man, he beholds calmly like a god the fury of the action, secure in his own perception of the general harmony resulting from particular horror and pain. This elevation of the historian's point of view is not, however, procured at any expense of attention to details. Here is a chronicle as minute as Froissart, and a scrupulous weighing of historical evidence, which begets implicit trust. Above all, we have men in the story, and not names merely. The characters are so sharply drawn that they cannot be confounded or forgotten, though we may sometimes doubt whether the thrilling impersonation is in very deed the historic man whose name it bears.

We confess we feel much curiosity in regard to the immediate success of this bold and original experiment upon the public taste. It seems very certain that the chasm which existed in English literature, the want of a just history of the first French Revolution, is now filled in a manner to prevent all competition. But how far Mr. Carlyle's manifold innovations shall be reckoned worthy of adoption and of emulation, or what portion of them shall remain to himself incommunicable, as the anomalies of a genius too self-indulgent, time alone can show.

—*Christian Examiner*, 23 (January 1838): 386–387

* * *

"Unauthenticated by the Stamp of English Approval"

This excerpt is from an American article by James F. Clark titled "Thomas Carlyle: The German Scholar."

We have put together at the head of this article the name of a man, whose writings have for some years past been attracting the attention of the literary world. It is however a curious fact that he has received more attention and had more readers in this country, than in England, where they first appeared. This is curious, for the reason that they are of a profoundly meditative and reflective character; they deal with the highest and the gravest subjects of thought, and because the style is not that which he who runs can most easily read. It is noticeable therefore, that in this country, where almost everyone is running, where the stir of active life waxes most loud, where there are few professed scholars, and few who have leisure for the calm air of delicious studies, that we should have discovered the value of a man like this. All praise to the few, who are not in such a hurry but they can open an attentive ear to the good and valuable, though it comes unauthenticated by the stamp of English approval. And all praise to the many too, who are willing to follow the guidance of the zealous few, and incline a studious forehead over this Teutonic literature. . . .

—*Western Messenger*, 4 (February 1838): 417

In this excerpt Emerson reported on the American reception of The French Revolution.

Emerson to Carlyle, 9 February 1838

The book has the best success with the best. Young men say it is the only history they have ever read. The middle-aged and the old shake their heads, and cannot make anything of it. In short, it has the success of a book which, as people have not fashioned, has to fashion the people. It will take some time to win all, but it wins and will win. I sent a notice of it to the *Christian Examiner*, but the editor sent it all back to me except the first and last paragraphs; those he printed. And the editor of the *North American* declined giving a place to a paper from another friend of yours.
    —*The Correspondence of Thomas Carlyle and Ralph Waldo Emerson*, v. 1, p. 147–178

* * *

Carlyle reported to his mother that he had received a letter from his brother Jack, which was largely "occupied criticising our immortal French Revolution." *This excerpt refers only to the first volume of the work, which Carlyle said Jack had read in manuscript "with endless contradiction."*

John A. Carlyle to Carlyle, 18 February 1838

The book is like good substantial, natural food, here and there a little tough and homely it is true, but thoroughly done and such as a healthy stomach is pleased with and can turn to nourishment—no whipped painted froth that melts away to nothing in the mouth, and leaves you hungrier than before, if it does not give you permanent indigestion. One would think the 'pudding stomach of Old England' might make something of such a dish. She has been sadly reduced by spare diet of late, and a little training with such food *au naturel* would do her more good than all the quack remedies in the world—only the froth and spoon meat are so much more easily eaten.
    The Collected Letters of Thomas and Jane Welsh Carlyle, v. 10, p. 37

* * *

Emerson's Journal, early March 1838

I have read with astonishment & unabated curiosity & pleasure Carlyle's Revolution again half through the second volume. I cannot help feeling that he squanders his genius. Why should an imagination such as never rejoiced before the face of God since Shakspear be content to play? Why should he trifle & joke? I cannot see; I cannot praise. It seems to me, he should have writ in such deep earnest that he should have trembled to his fingers' ends with the terror & the beauty of his visions. Is it not true that with all his majestic toleration[,] his infinite superiority as a man to the flocks of clean & unclean creatures he describes, that yet he takes a point of view somewhat higher than his insight or any human insight can profitably use & maintain, that there is therefore some inequality between his power of painting which is matchless & his power of explaining which satisfies not. Somewhere you must let out all the length of all the reins. There is somewhat real; there is God.

—Journals and Miscellaneous Notebooks of Ralph Waldo Emerson, v. 5, p. 459

* * *

These excerpts are from a seventeen-page review "mingling praise and blame."

"Considerable Imperfections"
Review of *The French Revolution*
C. A. Bartol

. . . It has become common to accompany a book with drawings illustrative of its scenes; as in Goethe's Faust. "The History of the French Revolution" does not need them! For we know not what gallery of pictures could equal these word-paintings in truth and effect.

. . . .

But it is time we should come to some general judgment of the work before us. . . . In these respects [originality and genius] it is the most remarkable production of the day. But referred to an Ideal model, it shows, as everything finite and actual must, considerable imperfections. The question in this view is, What is the object of a History? And what are the faculties and means of the true Historian? A perfect History is the revival of the past in its events, its spirit, its causes and results, and its character. The faculties needful then are plainly, first, exact learning that the facts may be possessed: next, imaginative and sympathetic discernment that the *meaning* facts may be selected from the rest, and those workings of the soul beheld which produce all other agitations; then, profound reflection, to investigate the sources of human action and analyze the principles developed from age to age; and lastly, moral judgment to perceive the religious quality of actions, men, and nations.

We see, then, no work requires greater combination of powers than the true History, nor can we expect often to find them existing in perfect balance. The first

two, knowledge and insight, Mr. Carlyle surely has in a very remarkable degree. For deep reflection and just judgment he does not seem to us so distinguished. He begins in the midst and leaves off in the midst, careless of cause and effect. He does indeed, as he proceeds, cast quite significant occasional glances at the origin of the horrors he depicts, and the light of some noble idea is ever upon his page; but he never sets himself to that serious consideration, which this topic demands. In his other writings he makes some striking allusions. In his article upon Diderot, in the Foreign Quarterly Review for April, 1833, he says—"French Philosophy resided in the persons of the French philosophers; and, as a mighty deep-struggling Force was at work there. Deep-struggling, irrepressible; the subterranean fire which long heaved unquietly, and shook all things with an ominous motion, was here, we can say, forming itself a decided spiracle, which, by and by, as French Revolution, became that volcano-crater, world-famous, world-appalling, world-maddening, as yet very far from closed!" But the only thought apparent on the point in question consists in allusions and intuitions. There is no coherent and digested view. Mr. Carlyle indeed takes no pains to conceal his contempt of the logic-faculty in man, "the hand-lamp of what I call attorney-logic." And for barren syllogisms, not touching and drawing life from Reality, or attempting to embrace what is incomprehensible and infinite, we may have as much scorn as he. But there is a power, not simply of seeing, which he so much lauds, but of *seeing things in connexion:* not of inferring one thing from another, but beholding their essential coherence; and this power unfolds cause and effect, as well as actual scenes in the historical progress of man. And this, so far from being a vulgar power, is the most exalted faculty of the human intellect. We have read articles upon the Revolution, in which it was more strikingly displayed than in these volumes. The highest style of thought, expressed in writing or speech, is not a succession of brilliant particulars volatile as quicksilver, one clause leaving the mind as another enters, and the whole fading in air like a strain of music at last, but that where all the parts are held in union by the strictest method, where the view, opened more and more widely, becomes more and more intensely interesting, the force of all that precedes being gathered upon each sentence, and accumulated with overwhelming power at the close. This is the style of the highest mind, philosophic as well as poetic, but is not yet attained by Mr. Carlyle.

—Christian Examiner, 24 (July 1838): 347, 356–357

* * *

A Book to Muse Over

Then I am slowly reading Carlyle's "French Revolution," which should be called rhapsodies—not a history. Some one said, a history in flashes of lightning. And provided I take only small doses, and not too frequently, it is not merely agreeable, but fascinating. It is just the book one should buy, to muse over and spell, rather than read through.

—Diary, Reminiscences, and Correspondence of
Henry Crabb Robinson, v. 3, p. 171

These excerpts are from a review by a New England Transcendentalist and social activist.

"The English Poet of Our Epoch?"
Review of *The French Revolution*
William Ellery Channing

Carlyle, we feel sure, has dropped all conventional spectacles, and opened his eyes to the true characteristic of our times,—which is, that the "better sort" are being elbowed more and more for room by the "poorer sort," as they step forward to gather a share of the manna on life's wilderness. Perhaps he thinks it high time, that they are who are clad in decencies and good manners should busy themselves in teaching their brother "sans-culottes" to wear suitable garments. We believe then that our author was led to a study and history of the French Revolution, because he saw it illustrating in such characters of fire the irrepressible instinct of all men to assert and exercise their natural rights;—and the absolute necessity which there is, therefore, that man's essential equality with man should be recognized.

. . . .

And now what has he produced? A history? Thiers, Mignet, Guizot forbid! We for ourselves call this French Revolution an Epic Poem; or, rather say the root, trunk, and branches of such a poem, not yet full clothed with rhythm and melody indeed, but still hanging out its tassels and budding on the sprays. And here, by the way, may it not be asked whether Carlyle is not emphatically the English poet of our epoch? Is he not Shelley and Wordsworth combined, and greater than either? Thus far indeed we have seen this luminary in a critical phase chiefly. But it is not because he has read, in the life of the men he has apotheosized, true poems, incarnations of that ideal he worshipped? It seems to us an accident, that prose and criticism, not odes and posi-

tive life, have been his vein. Had he but form and tune what a poet was there! This book we say is a poem, the most remarkable of our time. It is not like a written book; it is rather like the running soliloquy of some wonderfully living and life-giving mind, as it reads a "good formula" of history; —a sort of resurrection of the dry bones of fact at the word of the prophet. Marvelous indeed!

. . . .

The *point of view,* from which Carlyle has written his history, is one which few men strive to gain, and which fewer still are competent to reach. He has looked upon the French Revolution, not as a man of one nation surveys the public deeds of another; nor as a man of one age reviews the vicissitudes of a time gone by. Still less has he viewed it, as a religionist from the cold heights, where he awaits his hour of translation, throws pitying regards on the bustling vanities of earth; or as a philosophist, from his inflated theory of life, spies out, while he soars, the battle of ideas. And it is not either in the passionless and pure and patient watching, with which a spirit, whose faith has passed into knowledge, awaits the harmonious unfoldings of Heaven's purposes, that he has sent his gaze upon that social movement. But it is as a *human spirit,* that Carlyle has endeavored to enter into the conscious purposes, the unconscious strivings of *human spirits;* with wonder and awe at the mighty forces which work so peacefully, yet burst out so madly in one and all at times. He has set him down before this terrible display of human energy, as at a mighty chasm which revealed the inner deeps of man, where gigantic passions heave and stir under

Carlyle's reading chair at his Cheyne Row home (photograph by
C. Baly; from Carlyle Annual *[1991], Special Collections,*
Thomas Cooper Library, University of South Carolina)

mountains of custom; while Free-will, attracted to move around the centre of holiness, binds their elements of discord into a habitable world. As a *man* Carlyle would study *man*.

. . . .

. . . He is kind, and pitiful, and tolerant of weakness, if it only does not affect to seem what it is not, and paint the livid cheek with mock hues of health. This leads us to say a word of his irony and humor, and he is full of both, though chiefly of the latter. No man has a keener eye for incongruities. It is not the feebleness of men, or the smallness of their achievements, which excites his mirth;—for where there is humbleness in the aspiration, he is of all most ready to see the Psyche in the crawling worm. But what appears to him so droll is the complacence and boastfulness, with which crowds build their Babel to climb to heaven, and the shouts of "glory" with which they put on the cap-stone, when their tower is after all so very far beneath the clouds. He loves so truly what is good in man, that he can

afford to laugh at his meannesses. His respect for the essential and genuine grows with his success in exposing the artificial. Under the quaint puffings and paddings of "vanity fair" he does really see living men. He joins in the carnival. He looks upon it as a masquerade, and it is with real frolic that he snatches off the false nose or the reverend beard, and shows the real features of the dolt who would pass for a Solomon.

           —*Boston Quarterly Review*, 1 (October 1838): 409–410,
                               411–412, 413

* * *

Later critics, both friends and adversaries, often echoed Mill's early complaint that Carlyle reported events without providing adequate analysis to identify their meaning and relevance. These excerpts are from a thirteen-page review by the Italian revolutionary Giuseppe Mazzini, who was a great admirer of Jane Carlyle.

"Deemed Harmless"
Review of the Second English Edition
of *The French Revolution*
Giuseppe Mazzini

     When the book appeared, if we recollect right, the praise was almost unanimous. The organs of opinions diametrically opposed fraternized in admiration. Soft and sympathetic phrases arose together from the two hostile camps which, here as elsewhere, divide society between them. In a concord so unusual, as regarding notable men treating of notable subjects, there was an indication at once of the good and the bad of the performance. It was a homage paid to the incontestably eminent and dazzling talent of the author—an unfeigned admiration imperiously called forth by an artistical fervour and a vigour of execution that have no rivals amongst us at the present day; but to those who know how thoroughly inflexible is the logic of party, it was a proof that the work was deemed harmless, and that men might applaud it without being thence led on to serious concessions. But can it be such, and be complete—useful—equal to the wants of the epoch? No; it cannot.

. . . .

     . . . Every historian of our times . . . must embrace his subject in all its spiritual unity, from a lofty point of sight, indicated by intelligence and approved by conscience; he must then place it in relation with universal history in order to assign it a rank,—a function,—a degree on the scale of social development; and this more or less attained, he must thence deduce the character and bearing of each act,—the appreciation of the morality of each agent. Without ever losing sight of this

---

"A Hundred Gold Sovereigns!"

This excerpt from Carlyle's 8 February 1839 letter to Emerson was written after he had received a bank note for the American publication of The French Revolution.

     Your welcome little Letter, with the astonishing inclosure, arrived safe four days ago; right welcome, as all your Letters are, and bringing as these usually do the best news I get here. The miraculous draught of Paper I have just sent to a sure hand in Liverpool, there to lie till in due time it have ripened into a crop of a hundred gold sovereigns! On this subject, which gives room for so many thoughts, there is little that can be said, that were not an impertinence more or less. The matter grows serious to me, enjoins me to be silent and reflect. I will say, at any rate, there never came money into my hands I was so proud of; the promise of a blessing looks from the face of it; nay, it *will be twice* blessed. So I will ejaculate, with the Arabs, *Allah akbar!* and walk silent by the shore of the many-sounding Babel-tumult, meditating on much. Thanks to the mysterious all-bounteous Guide of men, and to you my true Brother, far over the sea!—For the rest, I showed Fraser this Nehemiah document, and said I hoped he would blush very deep; —which indeed the poor creature did, till I was absolutely sorry for him.

          —*The Correspondence of Thomas Carlyle
          and Ralph Waldo Emerson, 1834–1872*,
                 v. 1, pp. 211–212

engraven on the souls of men; it has fixed in the bosom of the French people a conscience of the inviolability of French nationality, in the *bosom* of every people a conscience of their strength, of the triumph reserved for every strong, active, and collective will. Politically, it summed up and ended one epoch of humanity, and placed us all on the threshold of another. And all this is indestructible. Neither protocols, nor constitutional treaties, nor the ukases of absolute powers, shall avail to efface it.

  This is what, if he desired to do a useful work, Mr. Carlyle should have told us in his own powerful language; but this is what he has not even attempted to set himself on the search after. Led astray by the false method he has adopted, or erring, perhaps, from the absence of a philosophical method, he has done no more than give us *tableaux,* wonderful in their execution, but nothing in conception, without connection, without a bearing. His book is the French Revolution *illustrated*–illustrated by the hand of a master we know, but one from whom we expected a different labour.

. . . .

Giuseppe Mazzini, a photograph owned by the Carlyles. Mazzini was a frequent visitor at Cheyne Row (Columbia University Library, from Fred Kaplan, Thomas Carlyle: A Biography, *Thomas Cooper Library, University of South Carolina).*

guiding clue, he must reproduce the material facts with exactness and impartiality, but in such a manner that, endowed to the eye of the reader with transparency, as it were, they may afford a passage to the ideas that gave them birth, and of which they are but the symbolic manifestation; and in this last section it is that the powers of the artist, his talents as a painter and colourist, his personal feelings, will find a field wide enough, and will link our sympathies with his; but we are convinced, that for all this, he must possess a conception of humanity, and Mr. Carlyle has none, and seeks none.

  This is the capital crime of the work, and if we are urgent upon it, it is because, though it be the only one which it would not be beneath such a work or such a man to examine into, no one that we know of has yet done it.

. . . .

  . . . The French Revolution has left the feeling of right, that of liberty, and that of equality, ineffaceably

Jane Carlyle's visiting card (Carlyle's House Museum, London)

. . . By rejecting the general meaning of his subject in relation to the history of the world, the historian has also lost the meaning of each successive fact in regard to the subject itself. By foregoing the determination of the humanitarian purpose of the French Revolution, he has lost the only directing index that could guide him in the choice of facts. By foregoing the knowledge of a providential law placed as a link, a scale of approach between God and man through humanity, he has lost the sentiment of human grandeur, he has found himself placed between the infinite and the *individual,* catching at every instant from this contrast a kind of terror of the former, and of pity, nothing more than pity, for the latter.

. . . .

. . . The unity of the event is divided into two parts, the soul and the body as it were; and the soul is hidden from his eyes, and whatever may be the power of the galvanism that the author brings to bear on the body our eyes witness in motion, we all of us feel that it is not the less a corpse.

—*Monthly Chronicle,* 5 (January 1840): 71, 74, 75, 81, 88

"So Majestic a Piece of *Blague*": Carlyle and the Sinking of the *Vengeur*

In The French Revolution *Carlyle reported the accepted version of the sinking of the French ship* Vengeur, *which held that the revolutionary sailors went down firing on their attackers and shouting "Vive la République!" In "On the Sinking of the* Vengeur*" in the July 1839 issue of* Fraser's Magazine, *Carlyle describes how he came to question what he had written and his determination to correct the record.*

Carlyle first explains how he was led to repeat what he has come to regard as a fabrication.

Very many years ago, in some worthless English History of the French Revolution, the first that had come in my way, I read this incident; coldly recorded, without controversy, without favour or feud; and, naturally enough, it *burnt* itself indelibly into the boyish imagination; and indeed is, with the murder of the Princess de Lamballe, all that I now remember of that same worthless English History. Coming afterwards to write of the French Revolution myself; finding this story so solemnly authenticated, and not knowing that, in its intrinsic character, it had ever been so much as questioned, I wrote it down nothing doubting; as other English writers had done; the fruit of which, happily now got to maturity so far as I am concerned, you are here to see ripen itself, by the following stages.

Carlyle then discusses the eyewitness account of Rear-Admiral A. J. Griffiths, who at the time of the incident was a fourth lieutenant aboard a British ship involved in the action. This excerpt is from Griffiths's letter that first appeared in the Sun *newspaper and was reprinted in other papers in November 1838.*

MR. EDITOR,– Since the period of Lord Howe's victory, on 1st June 1794, the story of the *Vengeur* French 74-gun ship going down with colours flying, and her crew crying *Vive le République, Vive la Liberté,* etc., and the farther absurdity that they continued firing the maindeck guns after her lower deck was immersed, has been declared, and has recently been reasserted by a French author. It originated, no doubt, on the part of the French, in political and exciting motives,–precisely as Bonaparte caused his victory at Trafalgar to be promulgated through France. While these reports and confident assertions were confined to our neighbours, it seemed little worth the while to contradict it. But now, when two English authors of celebrity, Mr. Alison, in his *History of Europe during the French Revolution,* and Mr. Carlyle, in his similar work, give it the confirmation of English authority, I consider it right thus to declare that the whole story is a ridiculous piece of nonsense.

Finding no corroboration for the "official" French version of the event and concluding that Griffiths's account of the orderly surrender of the French before their ship sunk was reliable, Carlyle professes his admiration for the "unparalleled courage" of the original chronicler.

. . . That a son of Adam should venture on constructing so majestic a piece of *blague,* and hang it out dextrously, like the Earth itself, on *Nothing,* to be believed and venerated by twenty-five million sons of Adam for such a length of time, the basis of it all the while being simply Zero and Nonentity: there is in this a greatness, nay, a kind of sublimity that strikes us silent,– as if 'the Infinite disclosed itself,' and we had a glimpse of the ancient Reign of Chaos and Nox!

For his own part, Carlyle thanks Rear Admiral Griffiths for correcting the record and speaks to his own responsibility as a writer.

. . . I, having once been led to assert the fable, hold myself bound, on all fit occasions, to *un*assert it with equal emphasis. Till it please to disappear altogether from the world, as it ought to do, let it lie, as a copper shilling, nailed to the counter, and seen by all customers to be copper.

Heroes Past and Present: 1838–1849

After the appearance of The French Revolution *in 1837, Carlyle was a public figure whose writings, activities, and personality prompted commentary on both sides of the Atlantic. In the next dozen years Carlyle enlarged his reputation as a social critic, biographer, and historian through a steady stream of work, including* On Heroes, Hero Worship & the Heroic in History *(1841),* Past and Present *(1843), and* Oliver Cromwell's Letters and Speeches *(1845). Critics attempted to come to terms with his ideas as a coherent philosophy and assess his influence on literature and culture. Fellow writers—Elizabeth Barrett Browning, Ralph Waldo Emerson, Edgar Allan Poe, Henry David Thoreau, and Margaret Fuller—also registered their opinions.*

A Second Lecture Series

Building on the success of his lectures on German literature in 1837, Carlyle from April to July 1838 presented another series, "On the History of Literature." The six lectures were reviewed by William Makepeace Thackeray in the Times *and Leigh Hunt in the* Examiner.

"First Lecture on the History of Literature"
William Makepeace Thackeray

Mr. Carlyle's first lecture on the history of literature appears to us both in its defects and its merits a very remarkable exhibition of a description of mind not common in our age and country, and which a period of busy and luminous refinement is not perhaps the most likely to produce. That which would most catch the eye of a chance visitant to the lecture-room was doubtless the cultivated and intelligent aspect of the audience, of whom an unusually large proportion appeared to be of a high order, both as to station and education, and in whom there was consequently a great number of pleasing and expressive countenances; but that in the lecturer himself which first attracted attention was the look of strong and ardent individual character, such as fashion and outward advantages never can form, and sometimes tend to stifle. And in harmony with this was the whole discourse which he delivered—often rough, broken, wavering, and sometimes almost weak and

Thomas Carlyle, 1839 (sketch by Count D'Orsay, from David Alec Wilson, Life of Carlyle, *Thomas Cooper Library, University of South Carolina)*

abortive; but full throughout of earnest purpose, abundant knowledge, and a half suppressed struggling fire of zeal and conviction, which gave a flash of headlong impulse to faltering sentences, and lighted up and clothed in dignity, meanings half obscure, and undeveloped images. But it is worth considering whether we cannot much more easily obtain and may not purchase at a lower price the most dexterous and ready exhibition of popular and modish talents and acquirements, than the utterances half colloquial, half lyrical, of a man who has evidently not inherited his views, or caught them by contagion, but has been urged by an insatiable thirst for truth, and has won it for himself, and his own

A Friendship with Robert Browning

One of Carlyle's friendships during the 1840s was with poet Robert Browning, whom he first met at a party at Leigh Hunt's in early 1836. In this excerpt William Allingham, an Irish poet who was a devoted admirer of Carlyle, recalls a conversation with Browning about Carlyle.

Browning.–'Then you could not know him. His personality was most attaching. I shall never get over it.

'He first made my acquaintance, not I his. I first saw him at Leigh Hunt's, and very properly sat silent for my part all the time. When he lectured, I subscribed and went, and coming out one day he spoke to me, "How do you do, Mr. Browning?" I said I had hardly thought he could recollect me. "O yes, I recollect you very well–will you come and see me? I live down in Chelsea."

'I did call, and he told me afterwards that he had on that occasion conceived an unfavourable opinion of me, because I wore (what was usual then) a green riding-coat of cut-away shape. If he had seen me no more I might have figured in his diary as a kind of sporting-man in aspect. He was always thoroughly kind to me.'

–William Allingham's Diary, pp. 310–311

* * *

This 21 June 1841 letter from Carlyle to Browning shows the personal interest he took in the younger writer.

My dear Sir,

Many months ago you were kind enough to send me your *Sordello;* and now this day I have been looking into your *Pippa passes,* for which also I am your debtor. If I have made no answer hitherto, it was surely not for want of interest in you, for want of estimation of you: both Pieces have given rise to many reflexions in me, not without friendly hopes and anxieties in due measure. Alas, it is so seldom that any word one can speak is not worse than a word still unspoken;–seldom that one man, by *his* speaking or his silence, can, in great vital interests, help one another at all!–

Unless I very greatly mistake, judging from these two works, you seem to possess a rare spiritual gift, practical, pictorial, intellectual, by whatever name we may prefer calling it; to unfold which into articulate cleverness is naturally the problem of all problems for you. This noble endowment, it seems to me farther, you are *not* at present on the best way for unfolding;–and if the world had loudly called itself content with these two Poems, my surmise is, the world could have rendered you no fataller disservice than that same! Believe me I speak with sincerity; and if I had not loved you well, I would not have spoken at all.

A long battle, I could guess, lies before you, full of toil and pain, and all sorts of real *fighting:* a man attains to nothing here below without that. Is it not verily the highest prize you fight for? Fight on; that is to say, follow truly, with steadfast singleness of purpose, with valiant humbleness and openness of heart, what best light you can attain to; following truly so, better and ever better light will rise on you. The light we ourselves gain, by our very errors if not otherwise, is the only precious light. Victory, what I call victory, if well fought for, is sure to you.

If your own choice happened to point that way, I for one should hail it as a good omen that your next work were written in prose! Not that I deny your poetic faculty; far, very far from that. But unless poetic faculty mean a higher-power of common understanding, I know not what it means. One must first make a *true* intellectual representation of a thing, before any poetic interest that is true will supervene. All *cartoons* are geometrical withal; and cannot be made till we have fully learnt to make mere *diagrams* well. It is this that I mean by prose;–which hint of mine, most probably inapplicable as present, may perhaps at some future day come usefully to mind.

But enough of this: why have I written all this? Because I esteem yours no common case; and think such a man is not to be treated in the common way.

And so persist in God's name, as you best see and can; and understand always that my true prayer for you is, Good speed in the name of God!

I would have called for you last year when I had a horse, and some twice rode thro' your suburb; but stupidly I had forgotten your address;–and you, you never came again hither!

Believe me, Yours most truly,

T. Carlyle

–The Collected Letters of Thomas and Jane Welsh Carlyle, v. 13, pp. 155–156

inmost cravings, by hard contentions and the perilous labours of mental mining. When the result of
such efforts has been not merely the attainment of a
devout faith in reason and conscience, and of a large
and pure humanity, but also of a comprehensive and
guiding knowledge as to the whole progress and all
the achievements of man's nature, the utterances of
his affectionate wisdom in the midst of London, in
point of wealth, and combined labour the metropolis
of the world's history, becomes at once curious to all,
and to the better minds we will add precious, nay,
pathetic. Such was the impression made on us by the
lecture of yesterday; and as the lecturer obviously felt
incumbered by the difficulties of opening such a subject, and will in each discourse march on towards
more and more delightful and fertile matter, we antic-
ipate from his future lectures an amount of pleasure
and profit such as those perhaps only will perfectly
conceive who are already familiar with his generous,
imaginative, and soul-fraught writings.

> –*Times,* 1 May 1938, p. 5

***

*Carlyle had read Thackeray's review of his first lecture
when he wrote the letter to his sister from which this excerpt is
drawn.*

Carlyle to Jean Carlyle Aitken, 1 May 1838

. . . After much *trembling* and preparation, yesterday our first Lecture was actually got delivered. The
Times I spoke of above contains a very kind notice of it
(written I understand by the man that reviewed my Book
there): I fancy my Mother will send it forward to some of
you and that you will all see it. I wish it could be kept for
me; it and the rest that may follow; they will be worth
looking at 10 years hence: but on the whole that is no
matter.–Our entrance into the enterprise was, as usual,
performed under *mixed* auspices. My health, or rather I
should say my nerves and heart were not good: tremble,
tremble, like an ague fever, now hot with hope, oftenest
cold with fear, and on the whole extremely sour many
times that I was bound to *be* so shivered and quivered
when all I prayed for was a life of quietness, of silence!
To worsen the matter, poor Jane caught this Influenza
that is going here, and after escaping all winter and
spring much better than we could have hoped, fell ill and
very ill just three days before the grand Business was to
begin! Thank Heaven, she got as suddenly round again,
and even got herself smuggled away yesterday, and in a
private manner heard me preach. It was not so bad as
last year; nor perhaps so good. I was very quiet; kept my
tremblings down; and in the sick state I was in my mind

*Jane Welsh Carlyle (drawing by Samuel Lawrence, from David Alec
Wilson,* Life of Carlyle, *Thomas Cooper Library,
University of South Carolina)*

felt half lame,–like a spavined horse which I did *not* whip
into heat. We shall be in many moods yet, before the "six
weeks" end. But I suppose the thing *will* be got over in
some tolerable way; and that is all I request of Heaven
about it.–One thing is to be regretted in it, that the
arrangements, and announcements and the rest of that,
do not seem to be considered as what they ought to have
been. I left it all to two idle friends of mine, a Mr Wilson
and a Mr Darwin; and I believe they did what they
could, but "Easter-week" and small circumstances which
you would not understand were against them:
whereby the thing is not fairly tried after all, and the
money-produce of it may be somewhat less than it
would otherwise have been. I expected vaguely perhaps
£300 for it, but shall now be well content with 2. These
as you may guess are *family-secrets;* no one else has any
business to know about them. Perhaps the audience may
increase a little as the thing goes on; perhaps not: they
seemed already (I am told) to be some 140; but the
expenses of the business are huge in proportion. And
now enough of all that. Nothing could be friendlier than

my reception; I have kind friends there, whom I ought never to forget. Hope with me that it will all end handsomely, and I be at liberty once more to "get out of this." If I had health and impudence, great things lie before me here; but I have neither the one nor the other; and on the whole do not want great things–O Heaven, peace, peace, that is all I want!

–*The Collected Letters of Thomas Carlyle and Jane Welsh Carlyle,* v. 10, pp. 70–72

* * *

These excerpts are from Carlyle's letter to his mother written after his lectures on literature had ended.

Carlyle to Margaret A. Carlyle, 12 June 1838

Without a moment's delay I am bound to put you *out of pain,* and say that these Lectures are over and all is right with me here. We finished yesterday; I write today, and hope to get you a frank of any extent tomorrow. So let us be thankful; for, as I tell you, it is all right.

. . . The Lectures, tho' at first ill arranged, went on better and better, and grew at last, or threatened to grow, quite a flaming affair. I had people "greeting" [weeping] yesterday &c! I was quite as well pleased that we *ended* there, and did not make any farther racket about it: I have too good evidence (in poor Edward Irving's case) what a *racket* comes to at last; and want, for my share, to have nothing at all to do with such things. What the money amount will be I do not yet know for a day or two: but I ought to tell *you* that the success of the thing, taking all sides of it together, seems to have been very considerable; far greater than I at all expected: and so are we not well thro' it? My audience was supposed to be "the best, for rank, beauty and intelligence, ever collected in London"! I had bonny braw [finely dressed] Dames, Ladies this and Ladies that,–tho' I durst not look at them, lest they should put me out. I had old men of four score; men middle-aged with fine steel-grey heads; young men of the Universities, of the Law professions: all sitting quite mum there, and the Annandale voice *gollying* [roaring] at them; very strange to consider. Again and again I say we should be thankful;–and, above all things, shut our lips together again, and try to be quiet a little. They proposed giving me "a dinner," some of them; but I declined it: "Literary Institutions" more than one express desire that I would lecture for *them;* but this also (their wages being small and their Lecturers generally despicable) I decline. This morning I have

---

A "Cheerful Welcome" in America

This excerpt is from an article titled "Thomas Carlyle" by Isaac Jewett.

It may not, perhaps, be known to all the readers of this Magazine, that the most remarkable thinker of the present century, and the most voluminous English writer for the past ten years, is the gentleman whose name stands at the head of this article. In his own land, we believe that he enjoys but a sort of prophet's fame; and we can well recall the half-respectful and half-sneering tone in which, by a book-seller of Regent street, he was, one year ago, pronounced the "*mad* Carlyle." We dare not say of him, as most devoutly we do believe, of their greatest dramatic poet, the English of this age are unworthy; but we will express the thought that they have thus far failed to properly appreciate one of the most original minds, that has yet developed itself into the nineteenth century.

In this country, Mr. Carlyle has met with some success: most of his works have been republished; and, in that city of the East which is pre-eminently distinguished as the intellectual emporium of the Union, his name has already become a household word. Throughout our land his works are daily following his name; and we note it down, as one extraordinary type of the time, that, in so many parts of this matter-developing, matter-moulding, and matter-enjoying nation, so spiritual a man has found such cheerful welcome.

–*Hesperian,* 2 (November 1838): 5

---

written off a handsome refusal to the "City of London Literary Institution," leaving the door open however, should it at any time become *necessity* with me to enter. And so *this* matter is over: good luck to it!

As to my health it did not suffer so much as I had reason to dread: I was awaking at 3 in the morning &c when the thing began; but afterwards I got to sleep till 7 and even 8, and did not suffer nearly so much. I am no doubt shaken and stirred up considerably into a kind of "raised [inflamed]" state, which I like very ill; but in few days I shall get still enough, and probably even too still. One must work; either with long moderate pain, or else with short great pain: the short way is best according to my notion.

–*The Collected Letters of Thomas Carlyle and Jane Welsh Carlyle,* v. 10, pp. 93–95

Critical and Miscellaneous Essays: A "Joint-Stock American Plan"

Because the American edition of The French Revolution *was much more profitable for Carlyle than was the English edition, he decided to have* Critical and Miscellaneous Essays *published in America before it appeared in England. Carlyle's English publisher, James Fraser, agreed to having it printed in America from the type already set for the American edition by James Munroe in 1838. Unexpected tariffs led all involved to conclude that the experiment was not worth repeating. Fraser's English edition appeared in September 1839. The work met mixed reviews, as critics grappled with issues of morality and style.*

Writer Harriet Martineau, no stranger to publishing economics, provided this anecdote on Carlyle's work on Critical and Miscellaneous Essays.

"As If It Had Burned His Fingers" Carlyle's Method of Revising Proofs
Harriet Martineau

In 1837, he came to me to ask how he should manage, if he accepted a proposal from Fraser to publish his pieces as a collection of "Miscellanies." After discussing the money part of the business, I begged him to let me undertake the proof-correcting,—supposing of course that the pieces were to be simply reprinted. He nearly agreed to let me do this, but afterwards changed his mind. The reason for my offer was that the sight of his proofs had more than once really alarmed me,—so irresolute, as well as fastidious, did he seem to be as to the expression of his plainest thoughts. Almost every other word was altered; and revise followed upon revise. I saw at once that this way of proceeding must be very harassing to him; and also that profit must be cut off to a most serious degree by this absurdly expensive method of printing. I told him that it would turn out just so if he would not allow his "Miscellanies" to be reprinted just as they stood, in the form in which people had admired, and now desired to possess them. As might be expected, the printing went on very slowly, and there seemed every probability that this simple reprint would stand over to another season. One day, while in my study, I heard a prodigious sound of laughter on the stairs; and in came Carlyle, laughing loud. He had been laughing in that manner all the way from the printing-office in Charing Cross. As soon as he could, he told me what it was about. He had been to the office to urge on the printer: and the man said "Why, Sir you really are so very hard upon us with your corrections! They take so much time, you see!" After some remonstrance, Carlyle observed that he had been accustomed to this sort of thing,—that he had got works printed in Scotland, and . . . "Yes, indeed, Sir," interrupted the printer. "We are aware of that. We have a man

A Day in the Life of Carlyle

Francis Espinasse, the son of a French immigrant to Edinburgh, was a journalist and man of letters who as a young man was encouraged by Carlyle and became a frequent visitor at Cheyne Row. He recorded his impressions of the Carlyles in his literary memoir.

Carlyle's daily life, especially if he were writing a book, was, when I first knew him, simplicity, not to say monotony, itself. He worked till three in the afternoon, with intermissions, occasional in the case of visitors, either familiar friends, or strangers who came properly introduced–frequent when he felt, which was often, the want of a pipe. At three, weather permitting, he sallied forth to walk (if he did not ride) till five, well pleased if he had a more or less intelligent companion of his pedestrianism to talk to, after what had generally been for him a long spell of silence. Then, Mrs. Carlyle presiding, he took his seat at the tea-table, where there seldom failed to be a guest or two. In summer there was usually, after tea, an adjournment of Carlyle and any smokers to the fireless kitchen, where was an abundant supply of churchwarden pipes and York River tobacco, with tumblers and a jug of fair water, though for dinner-guests (who were not very frequent) there was provided a bottle of excellent port (from Leith), with a post-prandial glass of brandy and water. The feast of reason and the flow of soul finished at ten, when Carlyle started for another walk, to 'purchase a sleep,' as he phrased it. He stepped out swiftly in those years, following the King's Road, and then turning up that 'long, unlovely' Sloan Street, at the top of which any companion he may have had was bidden Good-night, Carlyle retracing his steps to home, and, I believe, a supper of porridge, made of the best oat-meal, sent specially for him from Scotland. It was when accompanying him occasionally on these nocturnal walks that I found him readiest to afford glimpses of his innermost being. During one of them he spoke of his feeling towards his fellow-men as 'abhorrence mingled with pity.' Such a declaration from one's guide, philosopher, and friend was not of a kind to induce a disciple to take genial views of mankind.

—Francis Espinasse, *Literary Recollections and Sketches*, pp. 264–265

here from Edinburgh; and when he took up a bit of your copy, he dropped it as if it had burnt his fingers, and cried out 'Lord have mercy! have you got that man to print for? Lord knows when we shall get done,—with all his corrections!'" Carlyle could not reply for laughing, and he came to tell me that I was not singular in my opinion about his method of revising.

—*Harriet Martineau's Autobiography*, v. 1, pp. 290–291

* * *

In these excerpts Carlyle discusses the first two volumes of Critical and Miscellaneous Essays *produced by the American publisher.*

Carlyle to Ralph Waldo Emerson, 2 December 1838

Fraser is charmed with the look of your two volumes; declares them unsurpassable by art of his; and wishes (what is the main part of this message) that you would send his cargo in the *bound* state, bound and lettered as these are, with the sole difference that the leaves be *not* cut, or shaved on the sides, our English fashion being to have them *rough.* He is impatient that the Book were here; desires further that it be sent to the Port of London rather than another Port, and that it be packed in *boxes* "to keep the covers of the volumes safe,"—all which I doubt not the Packers and the Shippers of New England have dexterity enough to manage for the best, without desire of his. If you have printed off nothing yet, I will desire for my own behoof that Two hundred and *sixty* be the number sent; I find I shall need some ten to give away: if your first sheet is printed off, let the number stand as it was. It would be an improvement if you could print our title-pages on paper a little stronger; that would stand *ink,* I mean: the fly leaves in the same, if you have such paper convenient; if not, not. Farther as to the matter of the title-page, it seems to me your Printer might give a bolder and a broader type to the words "Critical and Miscellaneous," and add after "Essays" with a colon (:), the line "Collected and Republished," with a colon also; then the "By," &c. "In Four Volumes, Vol. I.," &c. I mean that we want, in general, a little more ink and decisiveness: show your man the title-page of the English *French Revolution,* or look at it yourself, and you will know. R. W. E.'s "Advertisement," friendly and good, as all his dealings are to me ward, will of course be suppressed in the English copies. I see not that with propriety I can say anything by way of substitute: silence and the New England *imprint* will tell the story as eloquently as there is need.

. . . .

Fraser is to sell the Four Volumes at Two Guineas here. On studying accurately your program of the American mercantile method, I stood amazed to contrast it with our English one. The Bookseller here admits that he could, by diligent bargaining, get up such a book for something like the same cost or a *little* more; but the "laws of the trade" deduct from the very front of the selling price—how much think you?—*forty per cent* and odd, when your man has only

fifteen; for the mere act of vending! To cover all, they charge that enormous price. (A man, while I stood consulting with Fraser, came in and asked for Carlyle's *Revolution;* they showed it him, he asked the price; and exclaimed, "Guinea and a half! I can get it from America for nine shillings!" and indignantly went his way; not without reason.) There are "laws of the trade" which ought to be *repealed;* which I will take the liberty of contravening to all lengths by all opportunities—if I had but the power! But if this joint-stock American plan prosper, it will answer rarely.

—*The Correspondence of Thomas Carlyle and Ralph Waldo Emerson, 1834–1872,* v. 1, pp. 201–202, 204

* * *

In this excerpt "poor James" is publisher James Fraser.

Carlyle to Emerson, 24 June 1839

. . . What has shocked poor James much more is a circumstance which your Boston Booksellers have no power to avoid: the "enormousness" of the charges in our Port here! He sends me the account of them last Saturday, with eyes—such as drew Priam's curtains: £31 and odd silver, whereof £28 as duty on Books at £5 per cwt. is charged by the rapacious Custom-house alone! What help, O James? I answer: we cannot bombard the British Custom-house, and sack it, and explode it; we must yield, and pay it the money; thankful for what is still left.—On the whole, one has to learn by trying. This notable finance-expedient, of printing in the one country what is to be sold in the other, did not take Vandalic custom-houses into view, which nevertheless do seem to exist. We must persist in it for the present reciprocal pair of times, having started in it for these: but on future occasions always, we can ask the past; and *see* whether it be not better to let each side of the water stand on its own basis.

As for your "accounts," my Friend, I find them clear as day, verifiable to the uttermost farthing. You are a good man to conquer your horror of arithmetic; and, like hydrophobic Peter of Russia making himself a sailor, become an Accountant for my sake. But now will you forgive me if I never do verify this same account, or look at it more in this world except as a memento of affection, its arithmetical ciphers so many hierograms, really *sacred* to me! A reflection I cannot but make is that at bottom this money was all yours; not a penny of it belonged to me by any law except that of helpful Friendship. I feel as if I could not examine it without a kind of crime. For the rest, you may rejoice to think that, thanks to you and the Books, and to Heaven over

A Petition on the Copyright Bill

Carlyle wrote this petition in support of a bill before Parliament to extend the protection of copyright to sixty years from the date of publication. Thomas Tegg, bookseller and publisher of cheap reprints of popular works, published three pamphlets against the proposal. A compromise bill extending the period of copyright to include the author's life plus seven years, or forty-two years from publication, whichever was longer, passed on 1 July 1842 and remained in force until 1911.

To the Honourable the Commons of England in Parliament assembled, the Petition of Thomas Carlyle, a Writer of Books,

Humbly showeth,

That your petitioner has written certain books, being incited thereto by various innocent or laudable considerations, chiefly by the thought that said books might in the end be found to be worth something.

That your petitioner had not the happiness to receive from Mr. Thomas Tegg, or any Publisher, Republisher, Printer, Bookseller, Bookbuyer, or other the like man or body of men, any encouragement or countenance in the writing of said books, or to discern any chance of receiving such; but wrote them of effort of his own and the favour of Heaven.

That all useful labour is worthy of recompense; that all honest labour is worthy of the chance of recompense; that the giving and assuring to each man what recompense his labour has actually merited, may be said to be the business of all Legislation, Polity, Government and Social Arrangement whatsoever among men;—a business indispensable to attempt, impossible to accomplish accurately, difficult to accomplish without inaccuracies that become enormous, insupportable, and the parent of Social Confusions which never altogether end.

That your petitioner does not undertake to say what recompense in money this labour of his may deserve; whether it deserves any recompense in money, or whether money in any quantity could hire him to do the like.

That this his labour has found hitherto, in money or money's worth, small recompense or none; that he is by no means sure of its ever finding recompense, but thinks that, if so, it will be at a distant time, when he, the labourer, will probably no longer be in need of money, and those dear to him will still be in need of it.

That the law does at least protect all persons in selling the production of their labour at what they can get for it, in all market-places, to all lengths of time. Much more than this the law does to many, but so much it does to all, and less than this to none.

That your petitioner cannot discover himself to have done unlawfully in this his said labour of writing books, or to have become criminal, or have forfeited the law's protection thereby. Contrariwise your petitioner believes firmly that he is innocent in said labour; that if he be found in the long-run to have written a genuine enduring book, his merit therein, and desert towards England and English and other men, will be considerable, not easily estimable in money; that on the other hand, if his book proves false and ephemeral, he and it will be abolished and forgotten, and no harm done.

That, in this manner, your petitioner plays no unfair game against the world; his stake being life itself, so to speak (for the penalty is death by starvation), and the world's stake nothing till once it see the dice thrown; so that in any case the world cannot lose.

That in the happy and long-doubtful event of the game's going in his favour, your petitioner submits that the small winnings thereof do belong to him or his, and that no other mortal has justly either part or lot in them at all, now, henceforth or forever.

May it therefore please your Honourable House to protect him in said happy and long-doubtful event; and (by passing your Copyright Bill) forbid all Thomas Teggs and other extraneous persons, entirely unconcerned in this adventure of his, to steal from him his small winnings, for a space of sixty years at the shortest. After sixty years, unless your Honourable House provide otherwise, they may begin to steal.

And your petitioner will ever pray.

Thomas Carlyle

– The Examiner, 7 April 1839

all, I am for the present no longer poor; but have a reasonable prospect of existing, which, as I calculate, is literally the *most* that money can do for a man. Not for these twelve years, never since I had a house to maintain with money, have I had as much money in my possession as even now. *Allah kerim!*

– The Correspondence of Thomas Carlyle and Ralph Waldo Emerson, 1834–1872, v. 1, pp. 257–259

* * *

These excerpts are from a sixty-eight-page article ostensibly treating Critical and Miscellaneous Essays *and* Sartor Resartus. *At the end of the article John Stuart Mill, the editor of* The London and Westminster Review, *called it an "attempt by one of our most valued contributors (we believe the first attempt yet made) at a calm and comprehensive estimate of a man, for whom our admiration has already been unreservedly expressed, and whose genius and worth have shed some rays of their brightness on our own pages."*

"A Genuine Coherent View of Life"
An Assessment of Carlyle's Writings
John Sterling

Knowledge without belief, and belief without knowledge, divide in the main the English world between them. The apparent exceptions are generally cases of compromise, when men are content to half-believe one thing, and half-say another; for a whole belief would demand its own complete expression. . . . Semi-sincere persuasions, semi-candid declarations, make up our limbo of public opinion. There is often, perhaps most often, heart in the words; but often too—how often who dare ask? within the heart a lie.

. . . .

Is it not then strange that in such a world, in such a country, and among those light-hearted Edinburgh Reviewers, a man should rise and proclaim a creed; not a new and more ingenious form of words, but a truth to be embraced with the whole heart, and in which the heart shall find as his has found, strength for all combats, and consolation, though stern not festal, under all sorrows? Amid the masses of English printing sent forth every day, part designed for the most trivial entertainment, part black with the narrowest and most lifeless sectarian dogmatism, part, and perhaps the best, exhibiting only facts and theories in physical science, and part filled with the vulgarest economical projects and details, which would turn all life into a process of cookery, culinary, political, or sentimental—how few writings are there that contain like these a distinct doctrine as to the position and calling of man, capable of affording nourishment to the heart and support to the will, and in harmony at the same time with the social state of the world, and with the most enlarged and brightened insight which human wisdom has yet attained to?

We have been so little prepared to look for such an appearance that it is difficult for us to realize the conception of a genuine coherent view of life thus presented to us in a book of our day, which shall be neither a slight compendium of a few moral truisms, flavoured with a few immoral refinements and paradoxes, such as constitute the floating ethics and religion of the time; nor a fierce and gloomy distortion of some eternal idea torn from its pure sphere of celestial light to be raved about by the ignorant whom it has half-enlightened, and half made frantic. But here, in our judgment—that is, in the judgment of one man who speaks considerately what he fixedly believes—we have the thought of a

---

wide, and above all, of a deep soul, which has expressed, in fitting words, the fruits of patient reflection, of piercing observation, of knowledge many-sided and conscientious, of devoutest awe, and faithfullest love. To expound his faith in our language will seem not unpresumptuous, while his own is at hand and may be read by all. But as a hint and foretaste of what is written in his works, it may be said that Mr. Carlyle thus teaches:

1.

The Universe, including Man as its Chief Object, is all a region of Wonder and mysterious Truth, demanding, before all other feelings, Reverence, as the Condition of Insight.

2.

For he who rejects from his Thoughts all that he cannot perfectly analyze and comprehend, all that claims veneration, never will meditate on the primary fact of Existence. Yet what is so necessary to the Being of a Thing, so certainly the deepest secret in it, as Being itself? All else is an object—all qualities and properties viewed without reverence to this, which is their root and life, cannot, rightly speaking, be understood, though they may be counted, measured, and handled.

3.

Religion therefore is the highest bond between Man and the Universe. The world rises out of unknown sacred depths before the soul, which it ever draws into contemplation of it. It repels the man into entire ignorance only when he fails to acknowledge the unfathomable Depth which he and it belong to.

4.

But at best we are immensely ignorant. Around us is a fullness of life, now vocal in a tone, now visible in a gleam, but of which we never can measure the whole compass, or number and explore the endless forces.

5.

Yet, to him who looks aright, the divine substance of all is to be seen kindling at moments in the smallest, no less than in the grandest thing that is—for Existence is itself divine, and awakens in him who contemplates, a sense of divinity such as men of old were fain to call prophetic.

6.

This sense of the Divine, penetrating and brightening a man's whole nature, attuning his utterance, and unfolding into images that blaze out of the darkness of custom and practice, and shape themselves into a completeness of their own—this is Poetry—the highest Form of the God-like in Man's being, the freest recognition of the God-like in All.

7.

As there is a poetic Light dormant in all Things, to which the Music of our Feelings gives the signal of awakening—so especially is this true of man, in whom dwells the Knowledge of Existence as well as the Fact.

8.

Thus the seer finds in his brethren, of every age and land, the most perplexing, indeed, startling, woeful, but also the highest, fairest, amplest, all-suggestive figures of his life-long vision.

9.

But to know and understand even Man is not for man the foremost task. We are made, by the craft of Nature—of Him whom Nature clothes, veils, and manifests—chiefly to be ourselves makers. To work, to do, is our calling—that for which we were called forth to be.

10.

Knowledge and Strength in their highest and most harmonious energy, are the reward only of the noblest effort. But all who toil in any work, when the work is not a mere winnowing of chaff, are doing humanly, worthily.

11.

Therefore, to trace men and their ways through the dusky mazes of the Past, and among all the confusions of our own time,—to see what they are doing, and how, and why—is itself a work fit for a thoughtful and affectionate mind, and will not be without fruit either for them or him.

12.

But in this survey of all things round us, and in the experience of ourselves, which we shall certainly gain if we attempt such devout and sympathetic observation, Evil, Grief, Horror, Shame, Follies, Errors, Frailties of all kinds, will needs press upon the eye and heart. And thus the habitual temper of the best will rather be strenuous and severe than light and joyous.

13.

A cutting sorrow, a weary indignation, will not be far from him who duly weighs the world. But in unswerving labour for high ends, in valour, and simplicity in truth with himself and with all men, there shall still be a sustaining power. So shall he have faith in a good ever present, but bleeding and in mourners' garments, among the sons of men. And by perseverance to the end, life may be completed bravely and worthily, though with no bacchanalian triumph.

We are far from wishing any one to pin his faith on these propositions, either as absolutely, still less as completely true—or as adequate statements of Mr. Carlyle's views.

. . . .

The clearness of the eye to see whatever is permanent and substantial, and the fervour and strength of heart to love it as the sole good of life, are thus, in our view, Mr. Carlyle's pre-eminent characteristics, as those of every man entitled to the fame of the most generous order of greatness. Not to paint the good which he sees and loves, or see it painted, and enjoy the sight; not to understand it, and exult in the knowledge of it; but to take his position upon it, and for it alone to breathe, to move, to fight, to mourn, and die–this is the destination which he has chosen for himself. His avowal of it and exhortation to do the like is the object of all his writings. And, reasonably considered, it is no mean service to which he is thus bound.

. . . .

It has more than once happened, in the course of this essay, that the name of Luther has come in contact with that of Mr. Carlyle, and on the whole, startling as the assertion must at first sight seem, and extreme as the outward differences undoubtedly are, there is no one known in literary history whom the British writer so nearly resembles in the essentials of his character. . . . We find in both the same sincerity, largeness, and fervour, similar sudden and robust eloquence, and broad and unshackled views of all things; a flowing cordiality based on a deep and severe, often almost dismal and sepulchral conscientiousness; an equal liability to fierce and scornful prejudice, and indulgence of the ultimate possibilities, almost impossibilities, of exaggeration, yet with an entire superiority to merely frivolous and ingenious paradox. In each, one sees in everything the man says, and not merely in the great and premeditated proclamations, the same individual physiognomic stamp; the royal broad arrow not only on the anchor and the cannon, but on the gimlet and the tenpenny nail. Their fundamental unity of conception lives in a religious awe of the Divine, as revealed in the universe, and in the inspired hearts, and heart-kindled acts and utterance of men. The true knowledge of this, pouring itself out at great epochs in poetic deeds and words, has always been subsequently analyzed into dogma, and stifled and petrified in authoritative, not intuitive symbols. Now, of both these men it is the great labour to restore the old free animation of this truth, and to lead men to find in the enjoyment of it the only, but all-sufficient, liberation from selfishness and death.

–*London and Westminster Review*,
33 (October 1839): 1, 3–5, 11, 64

* * *

These excerpts are from an anonymous reviewer. Literary Examiner and Western Monthly Review *was a short-lived literary magazine published in Pittsburgh.*

"Earnest Intellectuality"
Review of *Critical and Miscellaneous Essays*

These volumes are made up of Reviews and Dissertations originally published, through a series of years, in some of the leading British Quarterlies and Monthlies. They are however of a far less fugitive character, than the productions which even these repositories are found ordinarily to contain. . . . They are of a kind to be read always with interest, and not without profit. Every article abounds with *thought,* set forth in clear, striking and impressive forms and capable of being extensively applied, far beyond the particular occasions and themes by which it is brought into view. Carlyle is certainly one of the most original writers of the time, whatever judgement we may be pleased to entertain of the manner or the spirit of his writings.

Objections have been made to his style; and we are disposed to allow, not without reason. A very considerable change indeed has passed upon him in this respect, since he commenced his career as a writer.–He was at one time as smooth and regular, as any critic of good taste could desire. Gradually however he has contrived to clothe himself with a costume, which is anything *but* smooth, which may be said rather to set at defiance all established literary proprieties. . . . His style certainly professes a peculiarly graphic and dramatic force; especially after you have become somewhat accustomed to it, and get hold fairly of the spirit with which it is animated.–It may be characterised as clear, compact and forcible, for its own particular ends and purposes; "full of originality, picturesqueness, and merry vigor," to use an expression of his own in relation to another virtue, though often "distracted into tortuosities, dislocations, starting out into crotchets, cramp turns, quaintness, and hidden satire." Strange words in abundance occur, strange phrases, strange images, and strange constructions; such as no common writer could by any possibility get hold of, or manage with any sort of effect; and yet here all fall in wondrously with the requisitions of the subject, and seem to carry along with them a light and power which could not for the most part be obtained so well from any other quarter. The author succeeds, far beyond what is common, in making his views transparent, and clothing his subject, whatever it may be, with the lights and shadows that play upon it in his own mind. He gives you not dull prosing descriptions; but sets you down in a sort of felt contact with what he asks you to look at, and allows you to examine it with a living interest, as though it were at the time under your own eyes. So far his style, we think, is deserving of all commendation; far more interesting to read, and of far richer fruit for the understanding, than the rotund periods of Gibbon, or the free-and-easy elegance even of Sir Walter Scott. But all this in Carlyle is injured plainly by a measure of affectation, which often turns him aside from the clear, full simplicity of which he is otherwise so capable, and which he is professedly concerned to realize. The very exuberance of his imagination, and the astonishing command he seems to have of words, become a temptation to him frequently to play the mountebank in his own way, at the expense of all good taste, and not at all to the edification of the reader before whom he thus condescends to perform. His tricks at such times are indeed such as no one but himself could well accomplish; but still they *are* tricks, and as such disfigure the page on which they appear. At other times also, where there is not exactly this departure from dignity, the same inward copiousness on the part of the writer betrays him into the fault of saying too much, dwelling too long on the same thought variously drawn out and embellished. In this way accordingly his style grows tedious on occasions, even when it continues to be full of vivacity, variety and force.

. . . .

Thomas Carlyle, whatever be his faults, may well be recommended to all who have a disposition and capacity for thinking, as a writer who cannot be read without profit on the score to which our attention has now been turned. Whatever subject he handles, his mind seems to move always in an ambient atmosphere of earnest intellectuality, which moulds and shapes all his reflections, and communicates a peculiar force to his words. He deals continually with what may be called the *under-sense,* (untersinn), of existence, always diving beneath that surface, and laboring to expose the inward spiritual economy of his theme; always aiming to bring out its universal meaning and true spiritual bearings, as they may be considered important for the world generally. Independently altogether of the direct information such a writer may impart, the influence he exerts on the reader's mind, if he be susceptible of thought, exciting it and putting it into motion, is something which we can hardly value too highly.

. . . .

In grasping and unfolding character, Carlyle is often peculiarly felicitous. To understand a man, especially if he have any sort of originality, and life of his own, within him, it is necessary that we should be able to enter into the very structure of his being, morally considered, so as to look at the world from the same point of view, and in full sympathy for the time with his feelings. Seldom, indeed, however is this done; and our best descriptions of character are generally taken from the surface of life only, while the deep workings of the spirit, the true inward economy of the man's history, is not understood or explained at all. Carlyle always takes his survey from within; and his portraits are generally of the most striking sort. Such life-sketches we have in the volumes before us of *Edward Irving, Byron, Walter Scott, Johnson, Boswell, Goethe, Mirabeau, Diderot,* and others.

. . . .

We have spoken of faults in Carlyle's style; it is necessary however that we should notice a more serious defect in his writings, which appears in their *spirit.* . . . Affectation and theatricality, more or less, characterize all Carlyle's writings.–Then again there is a vein of cynical sharpness in his spirit, which is by no means pleasant. With all his professed liberality of feeling, and world-philanthropy, you cannot well avoid the impression that a great deal of cold bitter selfishness is still lodged in his spiritual temperament.–There is a flippancy frequently in his manner of touching on the subject of human misery; a disposition to throw the ludicrous and the sad into wild incongruous juxtaposition; a reckless humor of mocking and illustrating at times, one may say, over the woes and sorrows, vices and follies, of mankind; which, take it altogether, makes you uncomfortable, and inspires you with no special reverence for the personal character of the Author himself. This fault enters very seriously into his 'History of the French Revolution.'

Once more; the *religious* tone of Carlyle's writings cannot be considered sound or good. What may be his private creed exactly with regard to religion, has not it seems been fully made known. . . . It is no uncommon thing indeed for literary men to be thus unevangelical, (as though Literature and Religion are totally distinct provinces of thought), carefully shunning all reference to strictly religious ideas; but the difficulty in the present case is, that the writer claims to be more than a Man of Letters simple, in the common acceptation of the term. He comes before us as a Moral Teacher, and with very considerable effect reads us lessons on our own spiritual constitution, its resources and requisitions; in a way that cannot fail, so far as we are induced to yield him our spirits, to modify and control materially our ideas of religion itself. In such circumstances especially error, if it be radical, becomes a serious matter, and we have need to consider where we are, and to put ourselves fully on our guard. Such error, we think, insidiously clothed in garments of light, runs through the whole of Carlyle's theory of religion, so far as it is made to appear in his written works. We hear full enough from him of the degradation and misery of mankind (especially in this nineteenth century, for which he seems to entertain the most sovereign contempt); but after all the ideas of *guilt,* and moral *depravity,* as they meet us on every page of the bible, are very much thrown into the shade; and one might imagine, as he treats the subject, that sin was a fatal physical condition of our life in the world, a sort of foreign accident merely to our being, rather than a constituent of our true spiritual character; our *calamity* more than our *crime.* Our redemption accordingly, and restoration to holiness, is not to flow exclusively and directly from the cross of Christ; but must be the result rather of a right education, and a vigorous inward battling on our own part, till we shall be enabled to sit as it were 'serene upon the floods,' and sway at will the elements of our destiny.

–*Literary Examiner and Western Monthly Review,*
1 (December 1839): 459–460, 463–464

* * *

This review appeared in a magazine published in Charleston, South Carolina, edited by the Southern novelist William Gilmore Simms, an admirer of Carlyle. The reviewer begins by describing what he calls "Carlyle's Miscellanies" and arguing that Carlyle's reputation had been harmed by admirers and imitators.

"A High Intellect and a Sound Heart"
Review of *Critical and Miscellaneous Essays*
E. DeLeon

. . . What we complain of here, is, that injustice has been done to our author, because his censors have not gone up to fountain head, but have judged him by the productions of his imitators, his own not being read; he is not even allowed a hearing before judges, but the moment his name is mentioned, an outcry is raised, of "German Mysticism!" "Transcendentalism!" "want of common sense!" and his unhappy advocate is lucky, should the company conclude, that he himself is not entirely bewildered and deranged, but only suffering under a partial eclipse of reason, which attendance on a few political meetings and public elections, will dispel and cure. For our own part, we have attentively read all the writings of Carlyle, by him recognized as genuine; at first, with labor and difficulty, but finally, with ever increasing pleasure and profit; for after penetrating through the outer hull of a difficult and distorted style, no one can fail to observe a power and grasp of mind, a strength and originality of conception, visi-

---

"Just Published in America"

William Makepeace Thackeray praised Carlyle's work in this excerpt from an early December 1839 letter to his mother.

I wish you could get Carlyle's Miscellaneous Criticisms, now just published in America. I have read a little in the book, a nobler one does not live in our language I am sure, and one that will have such an effect on our ways of thought and prejudices. Criticism has been a party matter with us till now, and literature a poor political lackey–please God we shall begin ere long to love art for art's sake. It is Carlyle who has worked more than any other to give it it's independence.

–*The Letters and Private Papers of William Makepeace Thackeray,* v. 1, p. 396

ble in the works of but few writers of the present day, and many readers who have commenced his works, for the purpose of hostile criticism, have shared the fate of the prophet of old, who "came to curse but remained to bless." In these earlier writings, too, can be traced the growth and progress of an individual mind; the doubts and difficulties through which it must wade before attaining truth; the gleams of sunshine unexpectedly breaking in upon dark places; and the final adoption of much, which first excited censure and dislike; for as surely as "the hand of the dyer becomes tinged with the colors in which he works," as certainly does the mind of the scholar, become imbued with the spirit of those authors with whom he holds most frequent commune. And thus, Carlyle, who commences his career with sharp and bitter censure of the obscurity and affectation of the German style, ends by himself adopting them, in his elaborate works of a later day. We are not sure however, whether in strict justice, the term "affectation" ought to be applied to him, since very different causes often produce the same effects; with his imitators there can be no doubt; they are quaint and fantastical by rule and measure, straining violently after oddity; perplexing and mystifying their unhappy readers with a "set design and of malice aforethought." and should therefore suffer the just punishment for "such cases made and provided;" but with their master it is different; the earnest truth-seeking nature of the man, forbids the supposition of such paltry trickery to gain applause; against "shams and formulas" of all kinds, he has most resolutely set his face; all his writings bear the impress of a deep sincerity which cannot be feigned; and if his style is strange and peculiar, we can hardly think, that it is intentionally vicious; but that his mode of thinking being peculiar and his mind thoroughly imbued with German Literature, his style may have been unconsciously colored by these circumstances, and has now become habitual to him; nay, in his own sketch of the character and writings of Jean Paul Richter, we think we can trace no few points of similarity with our author himself.

. . . .

. . . After reading his essays, you seem to have passed some hours in the presence of the great ones of the earth; for he carries you with him, not only into the *study* of a Goethe and a Schiller, but lifts the curtain of their domestic life, exhibits them in the situation of husband, son and father, shows how the sunshine of domestic happiness casts its reflection on the written page; and thus enforce the lesson, taught by all experience, that a high intellect and a sound heart, usually accompany each other. Our author possesses, in addition to his other qualifications, that enlarged and liberal spirit which recognises merit wherever it exists unshackled by any sectional bigotry; and thus the High-Church Johnson, the Catholic Schlegel, the Jewish Mendlesohn, and the scoffing Voltaire, all receive their full measure of recognition at his hands, which in itself is a proof, that truth is to him more lovely than the bitter championship of established articles of faith; the Procrustean bed of piety, much in use in these later days.

. . . .

. . . To turn from the writings to the man. We can readily trace his leading characteristics, by what he has accomplished, he is evidently no hidebound pedant, whose whole life has been a fruitless chase after some stubborn "Greek particle;" nor like some hapless professors, has he consumed his days in desperate efforts to climb the intellectual tread-mill of metaphysics, where with apparent progression there is no actual advance; but with clear vision and native power, has sought to "look through Nature up to Nature's God." He seems to have regarded literature, not as an *end,* but as a means whereby to solve the great problems of the universe; not as a world independent of the external, but as the written record of the thoughts and hopes of the highest of our species; the great utility of which, is to teach us the universal wants of mankind, and how those wants can be best supplied.

–*Magnolia; Or, Southern Appalachian* (February 1843): 96–97, 98, 99

Chartism: A Paper "about that 'Working-Class' Business"

In 1838 a group of political activists presented a People's Charter to Parliament calling for six governmental reforms, including universal suffrage. In Chartism *as well as in* Past and Present, *Carlyle argues that spiritual renewal, not tinkering with the political system, is the answer to the problems facing England in the nineteenth century. Critics on both sides of the Atlantic criticized Carlyle for failing to offer realistic solutions to England's political crisis.*

This excerpt is from a letter to his brother written from Templand, when Carlyle was just beginning Chartism.

Carlyle to John A. Carlyle, 2 August 1838

I have endeavoured to be busy here ever since Tuesday morning; but cannot say I get on well in any sense. I awake every morning at some unreasonable hour, 7, 5 or even 3; and no breakfast is going till half past 9. I will try it a day or two longer; if with no better issue, I will over to Scotsbrig, taking my *desk* with me; there at least one can have breakfast a little earlier! It is as of old the chosen region of *clatter* this; Jane wrote to me she was "nearly dead of clatter." I am always moderately well in solitude, utterly alone; and oftenest contrive to be that way. You will still have time, I think, for another frank to me *here:* if I should even be off, the frank can follow me without difficulty.

I daily splash down something on paper about that "working-class" business; but I am not yet got at all into the heart of it, I have not found the *back-bone* of it at all; and can hardly yet venture to say that I have in any sort got into *motion* decisively. I must and will persist. There seems no use in *living* to me, if it be not writing, or preparing to write. My faculties these two years have lain dormant; I feel impatient to get repossession of them.

–*The Collected Letters of Thomas Carlyle and Jane Welsh Carlyle,* v. 11, p. 163

* * *

Chartism, *which Carlyle reports finishing in this excerpt from a letter to his friend Sterling, was published as a small book by James Fraser in December 1839.*

Carlyle to John Sterling, 25 November 1839

. . . Only last week I finished an astonishing piece of work, a long Review Article, thick pamphlet or little volume, entitled *"Chartism."* Lockhart has it, for it was partly promised to him at least the refusal of it was: and that I conjecture, will be all he will enjoy of it. Such an Article, equally astonishing to Girondin Radicals, Donothing Aristocrat Conservatives, and Unbelieving Dilettante Whigs, can hope for no harbour in any review. Lockhart refusing it, I mean to print it at my own expense; so in any case you will see it, and have the pleasure of crying Shame over it. The thing has lain in my head and heart these ten, some of it twenty years; one is right glad to be delivered of such a thing on any terms.

—New Letters of Thomas Carlyle, v. 1,
pp. 173–174

* * *

This excerpt is from an anonymous review in a London periodical.

"Above all Politics"
Review of *Chartism*

EDUCATION and EMIGRATION: these are the two great and vital panacea recommended by Mr. Carlyle in his own peculiar and extraordinary manner, as remedies for the social evils which seem to beset us on all hands. Far above all politics and political party are the considerations which this high-thoughted and deep-hearted writer brings to bear on the nominal subject of his eloquent pamphlet–"Chartism;" and especially worthy are they of the attention of *all* parties, on that very account.

—New Monthly Magazine, 58 (1840): 293

* * *

This excerpt is from an unattributed review written by Lady Sydney Morgan, who had reviewed Carlyle's The French Revolution *negatively.*

"Advice Given to Children"
Review of *Chartism*

We have not space to follow the author step by step through his argument. We shall, therefore, come at once to the main link, which has been dropped, in the chain of his reasoning. He teaches that the one thing needful is, that the aristocracy of the land (meaning, we suppose, its true aristocracy, that of virtue and of intelligence) should combine to guide and govern the working classes, who are incapable of guiding and governing themselves; and he appears to consider all debates on franchises, and the machinery of government, as little

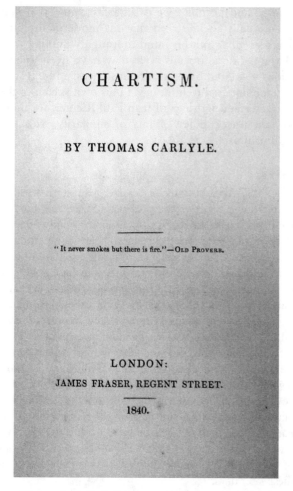

CHARTISM.

BY THOMAS CARLYLE.

" It never smokes but there is fire."—OLD PROVERB.

LONDON:
JAMES FRASER, REGENT STREET.

1840.

Title page for the book Carlyle wrote in response to a charter for government reform presented to Parliament in 1838 (Special Collections, Thomas Cooper Library, University of South Carolina)

better than lost labour. The aristocracy are required to educate and to feed the masses, and to provide for the expatriation of supernumeraries. Is this not tantamount to the advice given to children to catch the birds by putting salt on their tails? Mr. Carlyle, who complains that the lessons of the French Revolution are neglected by Englishmen, must be aware that the object of all its long suite of changes and violences was precisely to determine how this aristocracy can be got together. He certainly does not intend that the knights of this Eglintoun Tournament and the *chevaliers* of Crockford's are the parties to be trusted. But the whole experience of the world unites in proving that exclusive aristocracies will always govern for exclusive interests; and that they who have no necessity for thinking to earn their livelihood, will rarely take the trouble to think on other points. If the uneducated are for ever to be excluded from voting for members of parliament, we are in a vicious circle, from which no escape has hitherto been discovered. The educated are the few, and the few will take care to exclude the many in perpetuity. The masses must have a share in the government, even in order that their intellectual necessities may be provided for. Vicarious government has been tried for six thousand years, and found wanting. The theory of self-government is not therefore to be fillipped off with a sarcasm or a sneer.

–*Athenaeum*, no. 637 (11 January 1840): 29

* * *

This excerpt is from an anonymous review.

"Mere Expediency"
Review of *Chartism*

. . . Surely all this turbulence and uneasiness, this rick-burning and cattle-houghing, these trades' unions and half-armed confederacies, must have been produced by a pre-existing necessity of some sort, and must finally lead to some tangible, incontrovertible consequences. But what does Mr. Carlyle's book tell us about all these things? Simply that they are, and that they ought not to be; and then goes on to give us a prescription for the malaria, leaving the corrupt atmosphere and fetid marshes that caused it, and that will cause it again and again after its immediate effects shall have been vanquished, just as he found them. This is not the philosophy of Chartism; it is not the philosophy of anything: it is not philosophy at all; it is mere expediency, getting rid of an existing pressure, and consigning to another generation the higher, more difficult, and nobler labour of investigating and removing the primal source of the evil.

–*Monthly Chronicle*, 5 (February 1840): 97–107

* * *

This excerpt is from a letter in which Emerson reported that Chartism *was to be published in America by Little and Brown in Boston: "The book to sell for fifty cents: the Bookseller's commission twenty per cent on the Retail price. The author's profit fifteen cents per copy."*

Emerson to Carlyle, 21 April 1840

Chartism arrived at Concord by mail not until one of the last days of March though dated by you, I think, 21st of December. I returned home on the 3rd of April, and found it waiting. All that is therein said, is well & strongly said, and as the words are barbed and feathered the memory of men cannot choose but carry them whithersoever men go. And yet I thought the book

itself instructed me to look for more. We seemed to have a right to an answer less concise to a question so grave and humane, and put with energy and eloquence. I mean that whatever probabilities or possibilities of solution occurred should have been opened to us in some detail. But now it stands as a preliminary word, and you will one day, when the fact itself is riper, write the Second Lesson; or those whom you have instructed will.

–*The Correspondence of Thomas Carlyle and Ralph Waldo Emerson, 1834–1872*, v. 1, pp. 281–282

* * *

This excerpt is from a review of the American edition of Chartism. *Orestes Brownson, the editor of the* Boston Quarterly Review, *was an influential political essayist and religious philosopher. He began his review with praise of Carlyle's achievement: "His works are characterized by freshness and power, as well as by strangeness and singularity, and must be read with interest, even when they cannot be with approbation."*

"No Sense a Constructive Genius"
Review of *Chartism*
Orestes Brownson

The little work, named at the head of this article, is a fair sample of his peculiar excellences, and also of his peculiar defects. As a work intended to excite attention and lead the mind to an investigation of a great subject, it possesses no ordinary value; but as a work intended to throw light on a difficult question, and to afford some positive directions to the statesman and the philanthropist, it is not worth much. Carlyle, like his imitators in this country, though he declaims against the destructives, possesses in no sense a constructive genius. He is good as a demolisher, but pitiable enough as a builder. No man sees more clearly that the present is defective and unworthy to be retained; he is a brave and successful warrior against it, whether reference be had to its literature, its politics, its philosophy, or its religion; but when the question comes up concerning what ought to be, what should take the place of what is, we regret to say, he affords us no essential aid, scarcely a useful hint. He has fine spiritual instincts, has outgrown materialism, loathes skepticism, sees clearly the absolute necessity of faith in both God and man, and insists upon it with due sincerity and earnestness; but with feelings very nearly akin to despair. He does not appear to have found as yet a faith for himself, and his writings have almost invariably a skeptical tendency. He has doubtless a sort of faith in God, or an overwhelming Necessity, but we cannot perceive that he has any faith in man or in man's efforts. Society is wrong, but he mocks at our sincerest and best directed efforts to right it. It cannot subsist as it is; that is clear: but what shall be done to make it what it ought to be, that he saith not. Of all writers we are acquainted with, he is the least satisfactory. He is dissatisfied with everything himself, and he leaves his readers dissatisfied with everything. Hopeless himself, he makes them also hopeless, especially if they have strong social tendencies, and are hungering and thirsting to work out the regeneration of their race.

. . . .

Mr. Carlyle, contrary to his wont, in the pamphlet we have named, commends two projects for the relief of the workingman, which he finds others have suggested,—universal education, and general emigration. Universal education we shall not be thought likely to depreciate; but we confess that we are unable to see it in that sovereign remedy for the evils of the social state as it is, which some of our friends do, or say they do. We have little faith in the power of education to elevate a people compelled to labor from twelve to sixteen hours a day, and to experience for no mean portion of the time a paucity of even the necessaries of life, let alone its comforts. . . .

General emigration can at best afford only a temporary relief, for the colony will soon become an empire, and reproduce all the injustices and wretchedness of the mother country. Nor is general emigration necessary. England, if she would be just, could support a larger population than she now numbers. The evil is not from over population, but from the unequal repartition of the fruits of industry.

—*Boston Quarterly Review*, 3 (July 1840):
358–359, 364–365

* * *

This excerpt is from a five-page anonymous review article of the American edition.

"Swollen Vanity"
Review of *Chartism*

Many things in Mr. Carlyle's former writings would lead us to think that, while too often carried away by the love of making a sensation, he was yet in the main a man of sincerity, bent on some good end. But Chartism staggers our faith. . . . Imagine it

placed by a bookseller on its first appearance, in the hands of a minister of the Home Department, of a member of Parliament, of a philanthropist like Wilberforce, anxious for new light from any quarter on the hard questions it professes to discuss, and which might then be agitating the public mind, nay, shaking a kingdom to its centre; and with what indignation, as he puzzled himself over the swollen vanity, would he squir it from his window into the kennel, or consign it to the flames. Let Mr. Carlyle, the Romance writer, when he evolves his Sartors and Diamond Necklaces, be wayward as he will, let him dress up his ideas in literary swaddling clothes of every imaginable hue, let him don his party-colored coat, mount his cap and bells, and with every variety of grimace amuse, astonish, or befool such as may try to read, and we should be tempted to let the show proceed without a word of remonstrance; nay, as in the case of Professor Teufelsdröckh, we might heartily applaud the successful harlequin. But when this ludicrous exhibition is brought upon what may justly be regarded as holier ground, when it thrusts itself in where the great rights of humanity are discussed, diverting the attention from the gravest themes by the most offensive displays of personal vanity, we think that common people, those not by nature transcendentally strung, may be pardoned if they raise an objection. We do object accordingly. We took up his book for information, but found little else than a fresh theatrical parading of the author.

—*Christian Examiner*, 29 (September 1840):
119–120

* * *

These excerpts are from a fifty-seven-page review article that treated Critical and Miscellaneous Essays, The French Revolution, Sartor Resartus, *and* Chartism. *In a 3 October 1840 letter to his brother John, Carlyle referred to William Sewell, an Anglican minister, as a "well-disposed, not stupid man."*

"Something Hollow and Unsound"
An Assessment of Carlyle's Writings
William Sewell

These remarkable volumes contain many grave errors: they exhibit vagueness, and misconception, and apparently total ignorance in points of the utmost importance. They profess to be on subjects of ethics, philosophy, and religion, and yet, notwithstanding a plausible phraseology scattered here and there, they make no profession of a definite Christianity; and if it were fair to put hints and general sentiments together, and to charge the writer with the conclusions to which they probably will bring his readers, we should be compelled to describe them as a new profession of Pantheism. Yet there is so much truth in them, and so many evidences, not only of an inquiring and deep-thinking mind, but of a humble, trustful, and affectionate heart, that we have not the slightest inclination to speak of them otherwise than kindly. We are very willing to believe that what is false and bad belongs to the evil circumstances of the day—what is good and true to the author himself; and to hope that more light and knowledge will bring him right at last, since already he has advanced so far in defiance of the difficulties around him.

. . . .

Faith, therefore, must be restored; but how? And here it is that we begin to discern that, with all the truth and warm-heartedness, and sound practical observations, which appear in so many parts of Mr. Carlyle's speculations, there is somewhere or another something hollow and unsound, which cannot be trusted. He is a specimen of a naturally good and gifted man, thrown up from the bottom of a corrupted society, almost by a caprice of nature, and struggling by his own efforts to support himself, but struggling in vain. He requires, as all good and wise men must require, the spirit of *faith;* of a child-like, obedient, affectionate, docile reverence to man, as to the minister of God. He requires it both for himself and for Society. He is searching around in the world for objects on which this feeling may fasten. He has never heard, or never listened to the only voice which can give him what he wants; to those nobler strains of Christian wisdom which once were the common voice of Christendom, and in England, even during the worst of times, were never wholly silenced.

. . . .

. . . Mr. Carlyle will be the first to acknowledge that the whole universe around us, physical, intellectual, and moral, is the creation of one Creator. He goes still farther: he calls it the 'form,' 'the symbol,' 'the vestment,' 'the outward exhibition,' to fleshly eyes, of that invisible Spirit; and he is right: and without forms and outward vestments that Spirit cannot be made known to us. And those forms are in themselves valueless; they are 'shams and lies,' except so far as they represent faithfully the internal attributes of Him from whom all creation flowed, and to whom it must return. And the question between the Pantheist and the Christian, setting aside the fact of a revelation, is simply this: *how* are we to read the knowledge of God; *how* are we to learn his real nature, his true will, from which creation proceeded, according to which it was shaped, and to which we must conform our thoughts, and words, and works, and actions, if we would attain truth, and goodness, and happiness?—It must be, says the Pantheist, from outward forms—from the volume of Nature:—

'And truly a volume of Nature it is, whose author and writer is God. To read it! Dost thou, does man, so much as well know the alphabet thereof? With its words, sentences, and grand descriptive pages, poetical and philosophical, spread out through solar systems, and thousands of years, we shall not try thee. It is a volume written in celestial hieroglyphics, in the true sacred writing, of which even prophets are happy that they can read here a line and there a line. As for your institutes and academies of science, they strive bravely, and from amid the thick-crowded, inextricably intertwisted hieroglyphic writings, pick out, by dexterous combination, some letters in the vulgar character, and therefrom put together this, and the other economic recipes of high avail in practice.'—*Sartor Resartus,* p, 267.

Mr. Carlyle is right. The book of nature *is* a volume of 'thick-crowded, inextricably intertwisted hieroglyphic writing;' and all the efforts of science *have* done, and *can* do, little more than pick out a few of its commonest and most obvious meanings. But, if these are the only forms supplied us by the Creator of the world, through which to learn His nature—that nature, without a knowledge of which there can be no truth and no goodness—what is to become of man? It is not so with that human spirit, of which directly we see as little as we see of God himself, the knowledge of which is as essential to our moral duties and affections as the knowledge of God is to our religion, and the nature of which we alike learn through forms and symbols. Man's spirit has not only the form of vestment of a body, through which to make itself visible—as the material creation renders visible to us the Deity—but it has also recorded acts, writings and deeds; and the acts of a man are a still clearer intimation of his character than his physiognomy. But more than this: it has words; and words not only orally delivered, but preserved, and fixed, and capable of transmission in

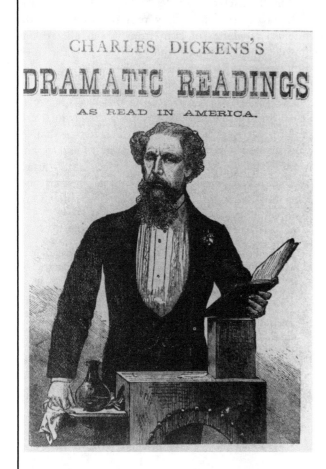

CHARLES DICKENS'S
DRAMATIC READINGS
AS READ IN AMERICA.

Drawing from the cover of the 1876 American edition of "Doctor Marigold" (Dickens House Museum)

"Thou Shalt *Not* in Anywise Steal at All!"

Carlyle first met Charles Dickens in March 1840 when the young novelist was in the early years of his immensely popular career. Although Carlyle had little use for novels, he admired Dickens's optimism and energy. Carlyle's experiences with American pirates prompted his support of Dickens's agitation for an international copyright law. However, no such effective copyright law was enacted in their lifetimes.

This excerpt is from a 26 March 1842 letter that Carlyle wrote to Dickens, who was on tour in America. Carlyle's putting the word "Nation" in quotation marks is in some measure explained by his assertion earlier in the letter that Britain and the United States "properly, are not Two Nations, but one—indivisible by Parliament, Congress, or any kind of Human Law or Diplomacy; being already united by Heaven's Act of Parliament, and the Everlasting Law of Nature and Fact."

. . . In an ancient book, reverenced I should hope on both sides of the Ocean, it was thousands of years ago written down in the most decisive and explicit manner, "Thou *shalt not* steal." That thou belongest to a different "Nation," and canst steal without being certainly hanged for it, gives thee no permission to steal! Thou shalt *not* in anywise steal at all! So it is written down, for Nations and for Men, in the Law-Book of the Maker of this Universe. Nay, poor Jeremy Bentham and others step in here, and will demonstrate that it is actually our true convenience and expediency not to steal; which I for my share, on the great scale and on the small, and in all conceivable scales and shapes, do also firmly believe it to be.

–John Forster, *The Life of Charles Dickens,*
pp. 235–236

---

writing; and it is from these mainly that we derive the knowledge of the minds of our fellow-men; from their words more than from their works, and from their works more than from their features. What should we say to a man who should persist in interpreting character by phrenology or physiognomy, without reference to a long course of authenticated actions, and express verbal declarations of sentiment and will? What should we think if our Creator had condemned us to such a mode of ascertaining the movements of the mind in our fellow-creatures? What ought to be our judgment of those who would think it sufficient, and would reject the help of any other information, even though promised and held out? And yet such is the proceeding of the Pantheist

in relation to God. He sees nature, the physiognomy of God, spread before him in its beautiful and glorious garb. He is told also of a history of God's dealings, preserved to him in the Bible by the same kind of testimony which he admits and subscribes to in all other histories; and he hears also a boast (let us suppose that it is only a boast) that certain persons are in possession of words spoken by God himself, and declaring His nature and attributes; yet both the last he sets aside, and refuses to consult them, as if they did not exist.

–*Quarterly Review,* 66 (September 1840):
446, 471, 489–491

Dickens's letter written in response to Carlyle's praise of American Notes for General Circulation *(1842). Dickens had sent Carlyle an inscribed copy of his work on 19 October (New York Public Library).*

Founding the London Library

Carlyle's frustration with attempting to do research for The French Revolution *in the public reading rooms of the British Library and conflicts with the library's staff led him to spearhead a movement to establish the London Library, a lending library from which scholars could borrow resources for study at home. Founded in 1841, the library is now the largest independent lending library in the world, with more than a million books and periodical volumes.*

Carlyle's friend Richard Monckton Milnes was a poet, biographer, and member of Parliament.

Carlyle to Richard Monckton Milnes, 26 May 1840

Dear Milnes,

Your Note arrives at the moment when I was about writing to you, or coming to speak with you (had it not been for this rain), concerning our great Library Scheme;–which you, treasonably, deserted last Saturday; but must in no wise desert on Wednesday (tomorrow) at the same place and hour!

Come, and come with some program in your hand of what *a Public Meeting* ought to be, and can be, in the present state of matters as to this business. All able men are wanted; some able man is indispensable. We had got 150 names, 50 of them within the last week; scattered indications of all sorts were beginning to show themselves above ground in an altogether hopeful manner: it seemed manifest that the thing was extensively taking root; that if we could *heat* it by one good burst of sun-splendour, or artificial furnace *flash*-splendour, it would germinate straightway, and soon fill all Cockneydom with its boughs and leaves! Come, I say; and get up the natural-artificial *caloric* in a workmanlike manner!

Spedding was to speak to Lord Clarendon for President; failing whom you were to speak to Lord Northampton: some in the fervour of desperate zeal even proposed Lord Brougham. I went to Pusey yesterday; found him hopefully disposed; got his promise to attend on Wednesday, if some mysterious accident did not prevent. Forster's is No 58, Lincoln's Inn Fields; the hour is half past two. You are actually bound to come;–and also to bring Fitzgerald and others; him above all. Is not his invisibility there, in the Carlton Ida, these two weeks, wellnigh inexcusable? Let him descend, with thunder in his right hand,–in the Devil's name!

As to Thursday,–I will tell you on Wednesday. I have got cold, I cannot sleep, I have to dine out tonight; I am fast becoming one of the wretchedest of men. Have you any pity? Not you.

Yours ever truly (unpitied)
T. Carlyle.

Cannot you bring Lord Eliot with you on Wednesday? Pusey says, he is strong for us.

–The Collected Letters of Thomas Carlyle and Jane Welsh Carlyle, v. 12, pp. 153–154

* * *

Carlyle made this speech on 24 June 1840 at a London Library meeting at the Freemasons' Tavern.

"A Crying Want in this Great London"
Seconding the Need for a Library
Thomas Carlyle

It does not become us, who are as yet only struggling for existence, who are merely nascent, and have nothing but hopes and a good purpose, to commence by casting any censure on the British Museum. Accordingly we mean no censure by this resolution. We will leave the British Museum standing on its own basis, and be very thankful that such a Library exists in this country. But supposing it to be managed with the most perfect skill and success, even according to the ideal of such an Institution, still I will assert that this other Library of ours is requisite also. In the first place by the very nature of the thing, a great quantity of people are excluded altogether from the British Museum as a reading room. Every man engaged in business is occupied during the hours it is kept open; and innumerable classes of persons find it extremely inconvenient to attend the British Museum Library at all. But granting that they all could go there, I would ask any literary man, any reader of books, any man intimately acquainted with the reading of books, whether he can read them to any purpose in the British Museum? (Cheers.) A book is a kind of thing that requires a man to be self-collected. He must be alone with it. (Cheers.) A good book is the purest essence of a human soul. How could a man take it into a crowd, with bustle of all sorts going on around him? The good of a book is not the facts that can be got out of it, but the kind of resonance that it awakens in our own minds. (Cheers.) A book may strike out of us a thousand things, may make us know a thousand things which it does not know itself. For this purpose I decidedly say, that no man can read a book well, with the bustle of three or four hundred people about him. Even for getting the mere facts which a book contains, a man can do more with it in his own apartment, in the solitude of one night, than in a week in such a place as the British Museum. Neither with regard to circulating Libraries are we bound to utter any kind of censure; Circulating Libraries are what they *can be* in the circumstances. I believe that if a man had the heroism to collect a body of great books, to get together the cream of the knowledge that exists in the world, and let it be gradually known that he had such a Library, he would find his advantage in it in the long run; but it would be only in the long run; he must wait ten or twenty years, perhaps a lifetime; he must be a kind of martyr. You could not expect a purveyor of Circulating Literature to be that! (Cheers and laughter.) The question for such a person to ask is not: "Are you wanting to read a wise book?" but "Have you got sixpence in your pocket to pay for the reading of *any* book?" (Laughter.) Consequently he must have an eye to the prurient appetite of the great million, and furnish them with any kind of garbage they will have. The result is melancholy—making bad worse;—for every bad book begets an appetite for reading a worse one. (Cheers.) Thus we come to the age of pinchbeck in Literature, and to falsehoods of all kinds. So, leaving all other institutions, the British Museum, and the Circulating Libraries, to stand, I

say that a decidedly good Library of good books is a crying want in this great London. How can I be called upon to demonstrate a thing that is as clear as the sun? London has more men and intellect waiting to be developed than any place in the world ever had assembled. Yet there is no place on the civilised earth so ill supplied with materials for reading for those who are not rich. (Cheers.) I have read an account of a Public Library in Iceland, which the King of Denmark founded there. There is not a peasant in Iceland, that cannot bring home books to his hut, better than men can in London. Positively it is a kind of disgrace to us, which we ought to assemble and put an end to with all convenient despatch. The founding of a Library is one of the greatest things we can do with regard to results. It is one of the quietest of things; there is nothing that I know of at bottom more important. Everyone able to read a good book becomes a wiser man. He becomes a similar centre of light and order, and just insight into the things around him. A collection of good books contains all the nobleness and wisdom of the world before us. Every heroic and victorious soul has left his stamp upon it. A collection of books is the best of all Universities; for the University only teaches us how to read the book: you must go to the book itself for what it is. I call it a Church also—which every devout soul may enter—a Church but with no quarrelling no Church-rates—

"The remainder of the sentence," says the reporter, "was drowned in cheers and laughter, in the midst of which Mr. Carlyle sat down."

—*The Examiner*, 28 June 1840, p. 408

Title page for the prospectus for the London Library (The Trustees of the National Library of Scotland MS 3.408)

* * *

This solicitation letter was printed as a circular. William Dougal Christie became secretary for the London Library committee in June 1840. He was a barrister and M.P. for Weymouth, 1842–1847.

Carlyle and William D. Christie to members of the London Library, 14 December 1840

SIR,

WE are instructed by the Committee of the LONDON LIBRARY to inform you that at a Meeting held by them on Saturday, the 28th of November, it was resolved,—

That the Library shall be opened, and books issued on the first of May, 1841.

That the entrance-money, £5, be now declared due, and the subscribers requested to pay the same to Messrs. Bouverie and Co., 11 Haymarket.

That the first annual subscription of £2 be declared due on the first of May, 1841.

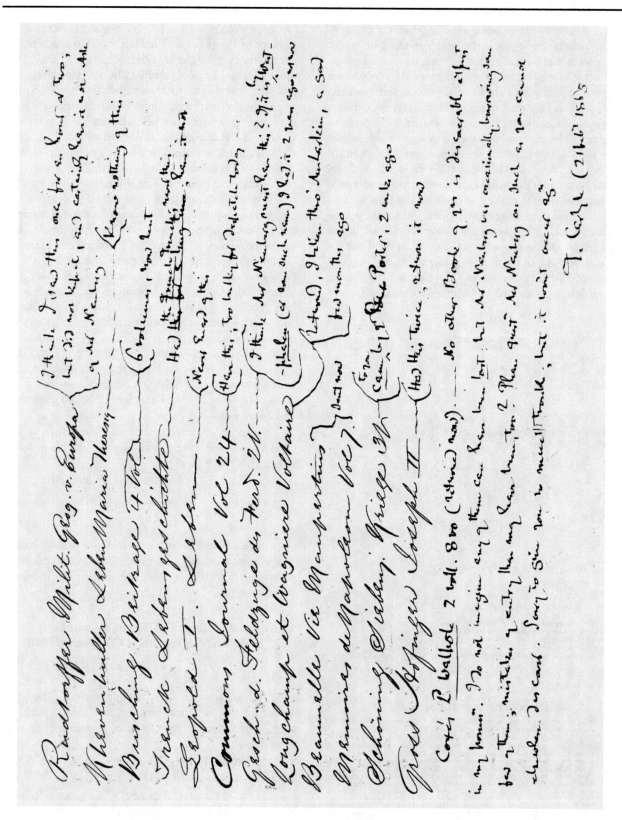

List of books from the London Library charged to Carlyle, annotated by Carlyle on 2 February 1865
(Beinecke Rare Book and Manuscript Library, Yale University)

We have therefore to request, unless it should have already been done, the early payment of your entrance-money.

The Committee are now of necessity actively engaged in the collection of books for the Library. In collecting books for a Library which is to embrace every department of literature and philosophy, they must of course proceed both systematically, and with that fair degree of attention to all subjects, which will for a long time preclude the possibility of completeness in any one. The Committee are anxious, however, to combine, so far as is possible, an adherence to system with the satisfaction of the wants of subscribers; and with this view we are instructed to invite you to send in to the Committee a *list of the books which you are likely to apply for from the library*. The Committee wish it to be understood that they do not bind themselves to the purchase of the books named, but that they will be happy to be guided by your wishes, so far as is compatible with the system of their proceeding.

We are also instructed to state, that the Committee will be glad to receive any donations which you may be kindly disposed to make to an institution having very large objects in view, and requiring very large means for their adequate realization; and that they will feel obliged by any exertions which you may have it in your power to make in the way of promising additional subscribers.

We have the honour to be, / Sir, /

Your faithful and obedient servants,

T. CARLYLE } Honorary

W.D. CHRISTIE } Secretaries.

—*The Collected Letters of Thomas Carlyle and Jane Welsh Carlyle*, v. 12, pp. 362–363

* * *

This excerpted letter concerns the appointment of John George Cochrane, who became the first librarian for the institution and prepared the Catalogue of the London Library, *which was first published in 1842. Carlyle refers to Sir George Cornewall Lewis, a member of Parliament.*

Carlyle to Christie, 31 December 1840

What I have known or got to believe of Cochrane is that he possesses sense, energy, discretion, enterprise; that his whole life has been a qualifying of himself for the management of such a business, and that now he would undertake it, sharing the risks along with us, in such a spirit as promises, were reasonable field granted him, the best results for us.

. . . .

Lewis says, we must feel our way, save our £50, get a subordinate man, and *then* when we have

Bust of Carlyle in the entrance hall of the London Library (from Carlyle and the London Library, *Special Collections, Thomas Cooper Library, University of South Carolina)*

succeeded, appoint some Cochrane over him! It is like sending out a military expedition for conquest in foreign countries under a *serjeant,* with strict proviso that when he has made conquests, we will send a General! Alas, too clearly, there will never be any General needed.

. . . .

My notion of the Librarian's function does not imply that he shall be king over us; nay that he shall ever quit the address and manner of a *servant* to the Library; but he will be as a *wise* servant, watchful, diligent, discerning what is what, incessantly endeavouring, *rough-hewing* all things for us; and, under the guise of a wise servant, *ruling* actually while he serves. Like a Nobleman's Steward: that is in some sort the definition of him. We may make more or not so much approximation to getting such a man. But I am deeply sensible that with no such man we are still hovering among the shallows, a cargo to win or to lose. No enterprise in this world ever prospered without some one man standing to it not *par amours,* but heart and soul as a business.

—*Carlyle and the London Library*, 25–32

On Heroes, Hero-Worship, & the Heroic in History: A Last Lecture Series

By early April 1840 Carlyle was making plans for a new series of lectures, which proved to be the last such series he gave. Carlyle lectured primarily to earn income. Although anxious about public speaking, he refused to read prepared texts, instead relying on notes to speak. A stenographer recorded the lectures as they were given, and Carlyle used these transcripts in revising the lectures for publication. The lectures were published as a book by James Fraser in June 1841. Critics explored the style and morality of the work, especially its compatibility with Christianity.

Thomas Wilson and his sister Jane had been part of the group that had arranged Carlyle's earlier lecture series on literature. Carlyle's series ended with "The Hero as King," and he treated Robert Burns in an earlier lecture, "The Hero as a Man of Letters."

Carlyle to Thomas Wilson, 3 April 1840

Dear Mr. Wilson,

I have again some thoughts of inflicting a Course of Lectures on you; the title to be "On Heroes, Hero-worship and the Heroic in Human History," or some such thing,–beginning with Odin the Norse God, ending (say) with Robert Burns the Scotch Poet! Pray ask Miss Wilson, what she thinks of *that?*

As it will be necessary in a few days now, I suppose, to decide either for Yes or No, might I not ask of you to look in, some time soon, at the old Lecture-shop in Portman Square, and see how matters stand there, to compute for me the time and seasons; to &c &c, in your old helpful way! The Lectures would be Six in Number; the *Book*-keeper would be Bookseller *Fraser,* this year.

I am riding daily, and cannot, without losing a ride, see any one but those good souls that will come here to see *me,*–before 2 o'clock, or after 5. Yet I will meet you any day, as I ought and must.–For the rest, I am the more loath to lose a ride, as I feel deeply, from the nature of this course if it do take effect, that the Lectures will depend more on my horse than me,–on the state of my health and spirits, that is to say: literally so!

Believe me, / Yours always

T. Carlyle

–*The Collected Letters of Thomas Carlyle and Jane Welsh Carlyle,* v. 12, pp. 95–96

* * *

This excerpt is from a letter in which Carlyle told his mother that he thought his lecture prospectuses were probably printed "and lying at Fraser's."

Carlyle and Jane Welsh Carlyle to Margaret A. Carlyle, 14 April 1840

. . . For the last two days, I have taken, as a kind of relief, to splashing down upon paper, at great length, and quite off-hand, as fast as the pen will go, whatsoever thing I *might* speak in the course of these same Lectures: it will help me at least to speak *some*thing when I come to the place! I still mean to *speak,* however, and in no wise to *read;* I have found out by trial that I *cannot* read, that I have not p[l]ayactor enough in me for that. I must *give* the people what *is in me* at the time, be it good or bad.

You would probably see the advertisement in last *Examiner,*–or rather you *will* probably, tomorrow. You shall get a Prospectus too by and by. Nay who knows but you may see the Lectures themselves, this time! There is a kind of speculation about having them taken in shorthand, and printed as a volume with corrections. A certain Review Editor (the *new* Editor of the *Westminster*–for Mill has given it up) came to me the other day, with a proposal to have a short-hand reporter of his own, and print the result in his review, and give me– £50. It was £80 in all, he said; for the reporter (if first-rate) would cost about £30! I *rejected* this proposal totally, without hesitation;–the said *new* Editor's being a decided *Dud* was reason enough for that, had there been no other. Yet we shall see what comes of it, on some other side. The Reporter will hardly get £30 from me, I think; one would rather try to report it oneself.

–*The Collected Letters of Thomas Carlyle and Jane Welsh Carlyle,* v. 12, pp. 110–111

* * *

This excerpt is from Carlyle's letter to Thomas Erskine, laird of Linlathen, a Scottish theologian and author of Remarks on the Internal Evidence for the Truth of Revealed Religion *(1820) and* The Doctrine of Election, and its connection with the General Tenor of Christianity *(1837).*

Carlyle to Thomas Erskine, April 1840

Let all that love me keep far away on occasions of that kind. I am in no case so sorry for myself as when standing up there bewildered, distracted, nine-tenths of my poor faculty lost in terror and wretchedness, a spectacle to men. It is my most ardent hope that this exhibition may be my last of such; that Necessity, with her

Carlyle's list of recipients of complimentary tickets to his lecture series, "On Heroes, Hero-Worship, and the Heroic in Human History"
(Beinecke Rare Book and Manuscript Library, Yale University)

ON

HEROES, HERO-WORSHIP,

AND

THE HEROIC IN HUMAN HISTORY.

LECTURE I.
THE HERO AS DIVINITY. Odin. Paganism; Scandinavian Mythology.

LECTURE II.
THE HERO AS PROPHET. Mahomet: Islam.

LECTURE III.
THE HERO AS POET. Dante; Shakspeare.

LECTURE IV.
THE HERO AS PRIEST. Luther, Knox: English Puritanism.

LECTURE V.
THE HERO AS MAN OF LETTERS. Johnson, Rousseau, Burns.

LECTURE VI.
THE HERO AS KING. Cromwell; Napoleon: Modern Revolutionism.

SUBSCRIPTION TO THE COURSE, ONE GUINEA.

To commence on Tuesday, the 5th of May, at Three o'clock precisely, at the Lecture-Room,
17 Edward Street, Portman Square;
And to be continued on the succeeding Tuesdays and Fridays.

Syllabuses and Tickets to be had at Mr. FRASER'S, 215 Regent Street, and at the Lecture-Room.

Schedule for the lectures Carlyle gave in 1840 (Beinecke Rare Book and Manuscript Library, Yale University)

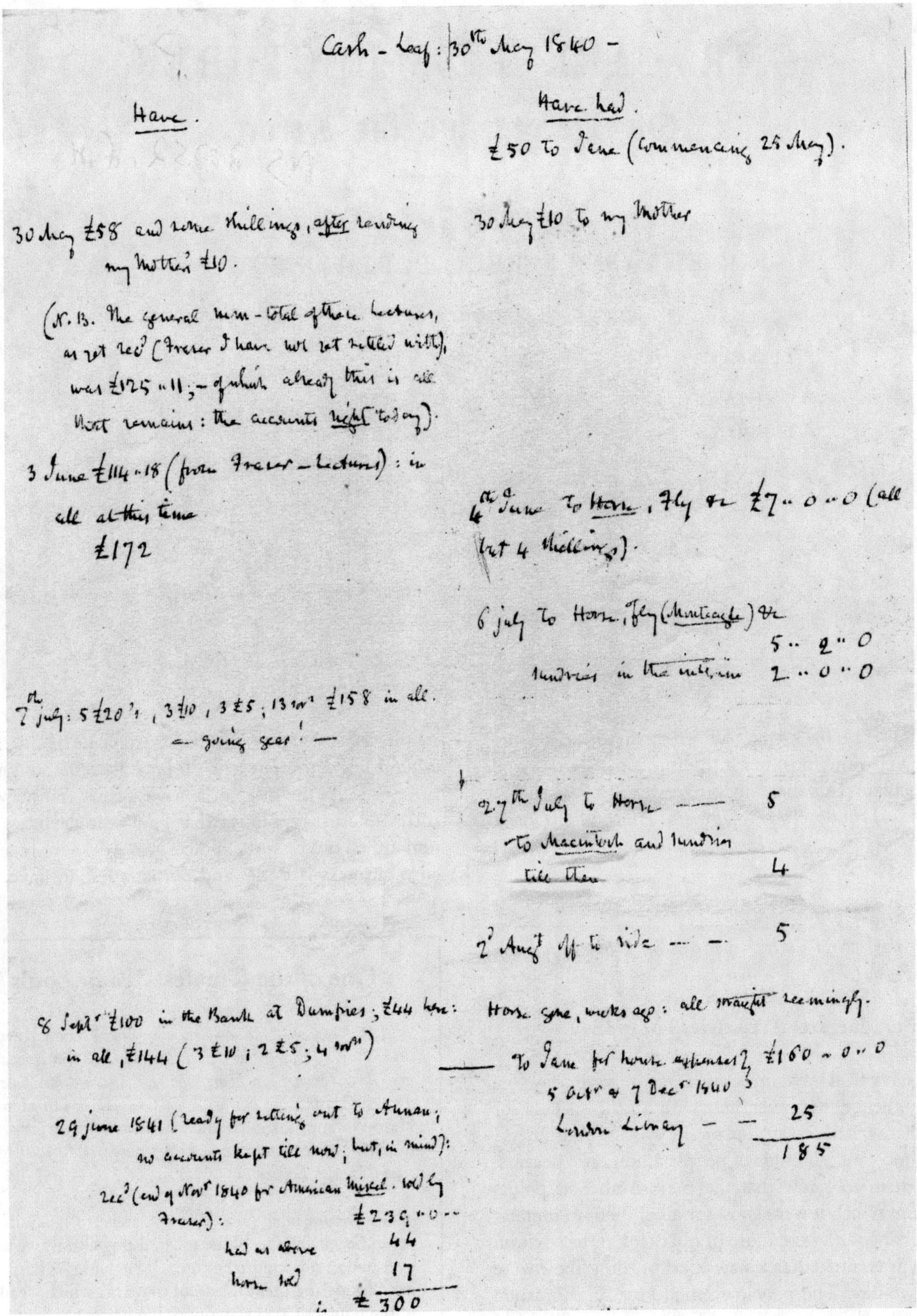

[Handwritten manuscript page — Carlyle's financial accounts, beginning "Cash – Leaf: 30th May 1840". Two columns headed "Have." and "Have had." with entries and figures including £58, £10, £172, £158, £144, £185, £300.]

A portion of Carlyle's accounting of his finances for his lecture series (The Trustees of the National Library of Scotland MS 20752)

MR. CARLYLE'S LECTURES
On Heroes and the Heroic.

LECTURE-ROOM,
17 EDWARDS STREET, PORTMAN SQUARE.

TUESDAY . . . . . May 5	FRIDAY . . . . . . May 15
FRIDAY . . . . . . — 8	TUESDAY . . . . . — 19
TUESDAY . . . . . — 12	FRIDAY . . . . . — 22

Each Lecture to commence at Three o'clock precisely.

265   T. Carlyle

Admission ticket to Carlyle's lectures on heroes, with Carlyle's signature (Special Collections, Thomas Cooper Library, University of South Carolina)

bayonet at my back, may never again drive me up thither, a creature most fit for uttering himself in a flood of inarticulate tears than any other way.
–James A. Froude, *Thomas Carlyle: A History of His Life in London, 1834–1881*, v. 1, p. 184

* * *

In this excerpt Carlyle reports on his lecture titled "The Hero as Prophet."

Carlyle to Margaret A. Carlyle, 9 May 1840

May 9.–I gave my second lecture yesterday to a larger audience than ever, and with all the success, or more, that was necessary for me. It was on Mahomet. I had bishops and all kinds of people among my hearers. I gave them to know that the poor Arab had points about him which it were good for all of them to imitate; that probably *they* were more of quacks than he; that, in short, it was altogether a new kind of thing they were hearing to-day. The people seemed greatly astonished and greatly pleased. I vomited forth on them like wild Annandale grapeshot. They laughed, applauded, &c. In short, it was all right, and I suppose it was by much the best lecture I shall have the luck to give this time; for really it all depends on what we call luck. I cannot say

in the least whether my lecture will be good or bad when I begin to deliver it. So far it is well enough. And now, alas! As the price of a good lecture my nerves are thrown into such a flurry that I got little sleep last night, and am all out of sorts to-day. Two weeks more and the sore business is done, and perhaps I shall never try it

"One of the Greatest Tragic Souls"

From soon after the completion of The French Revolution, *Carlyle began reading about English Civil War revolutionary Oliver Cromwell, a figure who had interested him since the 1820s. Carlyle spoke and wrote on Cromwell in* On Heroes, Hero-Worship & the Heroic in History, *but his fascination continued, as he confided in a 15 September 1840 letter to his friend Thomas Erskine.*

I have got lately, not till very lately, to fancy that I see in Cromwell one of the greatest tragic souls we have ever had in this kindred of ours. The matter is Past; but it is among the great things of the Past, which, seen or unseen, never fade away out of the Present.
–James A. Froude, *Thomas Carlyle: A History of His Life in London 1834–1881*, v. 1, p. 197

another time. My audience is between two and three hundred, and grew a great deal larger after the first lecture. I expect to clear 200*l.* out of it. That is the result, and next year I hope I may be able to dispense with that aid, since it must be purchased with *such a tirrivee,* which I like so ill.

–James A. Froude, *Thomas Carlyle: A History of His Life in London, 1834–1881,* v. 1, pp. 181–182

***

This excerpt is from a letter Carlyle wrote while he was revising his lectures for publication.

Carlyle to Emerson, 2 July 1840

My Lectures were in May, about *Great Men.* The misery of it was hardly equal to that of former years, yet still was very hateful. I had got to a certain feeling of superiority over my audience; as if I had something to tell them, and would tell it them. At times I felt as if I could, in the end, learn to speak. The beautiful people listened with boundless tolerance, eager attention. I meant to tell them, among other things, that man was still alive, Nature not dead or like to die; that all true men continued true to this hour,–Odin himself true, and the Grand Lama of Thibet himself not wholly a lie. The Lecture on Mahomet ("the Hero as Prophet") astonished my worthy friends beyond measure. It seems then this Mahomet was not a quack? Not a bit of him! That he is a better Christian, with his "bastard Christianity," than the most of us shovel-hatted? I guess than almost any of you!–Not so much as Oliver Cromwell ("the Hero as King") would I allow to have been a Quack. All quacks I asserted to be and to have been Nothing, *chaff* that would not grow: my poor Mahomet "was *wheat* with barn sweepings"; Nature had tolerantly hidden the barn sweepings; and as to the *wheat,* behold she had said Yes to it, and it was growing!–On the whole, I fear I did little but confuse my esteemed audience: I was amazed, after all their reading of me, to be understood so ill;–gratified nevertheless to see how the rudest *speech* of a man's heart goes into men's hearts, and is the welcomest thing there. Withal I regretted that I had not six months of preaching, whereby to learn to preach, and explain things fully! In the fire of the moment I had all but decided on setting out for America this autumn, and preaching far and wide like a very lion there. Quit your paper formulas, my brethren,–equivalent to old wooden idols, *un*devine as they: in the name of God, understand that you are alive, and that God is alive! Did the Upholsterer make this Universe? Were you created by the Tailor? I tell you, and conjure

you to believe me literally, No, a thousand times No! Thus did I mean to preach, on "Heroes, Hero-worship, and the Heroic"; in America too. Alas! The fire of determination died away again: all that I did resolve upon was to write these Lectures down, and in *some* way promulgate them farther. Two of them accordingly are actually written; the Third to be begun on Monday: it is my chief work here, ever since the end of May. Whether I go to preach them a second time extempore in America rests once more with the Destinies. It is a shame to talk so much about a thing, and have it still hang *in nubibus:* but I was, and perhaps am, really nearer doing it than I had ever before been.

–*The Correspondence of Thomas Carlyle and Ralph Waldo Emerson, 1834–1872,* v. 1, pp. 319–321

***

These excerpts are from an appreciative American reviewer who yet asserts that Carlyle's new work is "full of his faults of endless repetition; hammering on a thought till every sense of the reader aches, and an arrogant bitterness of tone which seems growing upon him."

"A Man in Convulsions"
Review of *On Heroes, Hero-Worship, & the Heroic in History*
Margaret Fuller

Although the name of Thomas Carlyle is rarely mentioned in the critical journals of this country, there is no living writer who is more sure of immediate attention from a large circle of readers, or who exercises a greater influence than he in these United States. Since the publication of his article on the characteristics of our time in the Edinburgh Review, and afterwards of the Sartor, this influence has been deepening and extending year by year, till now thousands turn an eager ear to the most distant note of his clarion.

. . . .

This book is somewhat less objectionable than the French Revolution to those not absolutely unjust critics, who said they would sooner "dine for a week on pepper, than read through the two volumes." Yet it is too highly seasoned, tediously emphatic, and the mind as well as the style is obviously in want of the verdure of repose. An acute observer said that the best criticism on his works would be his own remark, that a man in convulsions is not proved to be strong because six healthy men cannot hold him. We are not consoled by his brilliancy and the room he has obtained for an infinity of quips and cranks and witty turns for the corruption of his style, and the more important loss of chasteness, temperance, and harmony in his mind observable since he first was made known to the public.

Yet let thanks, manifold thanks, close this and all chapters that begin with his name.

                                        –*The Dial*, 2 (July 1841): 131, 133

* * *

These excerpts are from a two-part examination of Carlyle's work in an organ for the Oxford Movement published in London.

"A False Direction"
Review of *On Heroes, Hero-Worship, & the Heroic in History*
William Thomson

We must now, however, betake ourselves to Mr. Carlyle's last work, which has given occasion to these remarks, and in which all his faults have, we think, come to a head. What we have yet to say upon them will therefore be best done mainly with reference to it. Indeed he could hardly have chosen a subject more indicative of himself than that which has inspired it. *Hero-worship* seems to us the predominant principle of his character. His whole search in history is for great men. Great men, according to him, regulate the world's destinies, and he all but says, such can do no wrong. Let us consider for awhile this same principle of hero-worship so dominant in the mind of Mr. Carlyle, and so congenial, we venture to say, in spite of his opinion to the contrary, to the temper of the age in which we live.

Is it a good or a bad principle? Whichever it be, we confess we should not much like a person–above all, a young person–who had no tendency to it. A mind destitute of a sense of greatness must be destitute of "imagination, honourable aims, free commune with the choir that cannot die." And of all sublunary greatness none certainly is so mysterious, so captivating, at times so overwhelming, as that which resides in our fellow-man. It is surely a generous and purifying feeling that we have towards the names of Dante, Shakspeare, Bacon, Newton, and Burke–the feeling which every young Englishman of the present day, who is worth anything, has towards the names of Wordsworth and Coleridge–the feeling which all Englishmen whatever have towards that of Wellington. God did not create such excellent works as those great men without meaning them to be contemplated and admired. The thought of a fellow-mortal, alike us in so many things, being at the same time so different in others,–having powers not only in another degree, but quite another kind from our own,–the perception in him of that indefinable but most real gift of genius, whereby he is not merely abler than his fellows, but placed beyond the reach of comparison, whereby he is not so properly styled *able* as *creative,*–seeing by intuition more than others can by any process of observation or induction,–capable at her thrilling moment of uttering the thrilling word, and daring the one unlooked for and decisive deed; this, as we have said, is the most fascinating and ennobling of earthly thoughts. We should have no objection to as much of it being expressed as is felt by Mr. Carlyle, provided he would take pains to guard it from taking a false direction.

But, unfortunately, he takes no such pains. The sense of greatness, unless the mind's homage be carefully given where alone it is fully due, is too sure to become the worship of greatness. In such a result Mr. Carlyle apparently sees nothing wrong, nothing to be dreaded. His only fear is lest great men be not exalted enough. Idolatry would seem in his eyes to be no sin. The gift of greatness, according to him, can hardly be considered too much bound up with the man in whom we find it residing. Now, we cannot but think that, like every other leading sentiment of our nature, this enthusiasm for great men requires to be exercised with continual self-mistrust. We must always remember that the greatness we are contemplating is God's work, and only great for that reason–that the true use of it, therefore, must be to lead our thoughts to Him, instead of permit-

---

"He Ran about like a School Boy"

Harriet Martineau was an invalid when Carlyle visited her at Newcastle-on-Tyne in 1841 en route to Scotland for a summer vacation. This excerpt is from an 8 August 1841 letter she wrote to Ralph Waldo Emerson.

Carlyle was here the other day, & is about to come again, with his wife (who grows upon me continually.) . . . He was, the other day, like a transformed man. Every feature was changed & every action. He has always before been the most miserable person I have ever known,–pricked & pierced with suffering,–suffering of which no one knows the cause, for which no sufficient cause is apparent. The tenderest & most patient sympathy can hardly endure his complaints, so unintermitting as they are.–so habitual have his groans become. But the other day, he was *gay*. His laugh was loosened,–his countenance relaxed, & he ran about like a school boy. And he was as tender as if I was dying. It was one of the happiest days I ever passed.

                                –*The Correspondence of Emerson and Carlyle*,
                                p. 309

ting them to repose on anything short of Him; that the whole ought to be viewed as His gift, continually bestowed by his good pleasure, and liable, at the same good pleasure, to be withdrawn. With this primary limitation, our *Hero-worship,* if we are to designate our reverence for greatness by that name, will be preserved from its chief danger–that of becoming idolatry.

–*Christian Remembrancer,* 3 (March 1842): 348–349

Hero-worship (to adopt Mr. Carlyle's nomenclature) is not, however, forbidden to the Christian. He, as well as Mr. Carlyle, looks with fond admiration on his "hero as prophet;" "hero as priest;" "hero as poet;" "hero as man of letters," "hero as king." But with how mighty a difference! His love and honour for them is bounded by their love and honour for their common Head, and Example, even the Son of God; and then he does but honour Christ in their persons. He admires their fidelity to the true faith: that is his mark of a hero. How did they serve our heavenly king, and push the confines of this kingdom upon earth to places before shut out from it? This is what he wishes to know.

. . . .

. . . It is unfair to wind men up by eloquence to the action-point, without then telling them what to do. All this fine talk, and nothing to come of it! They are drawn on to admire characters they had before contemned, or at best not admired; and this on no ground of reason, but in faith of Mr. Carlyle's infallible insight; they find beauties where was barrenness–greatness, where all seemed small. But what next? They are not told what a hero is; nor how to know one if they meet him; nor how they are to become heroes; nor how to admire the heroic in others. In short, they have heard much eloquent eulogy of certain men, mostly of doubtful reputation, tending to no practical result, at variance with all they have been accustomed to hold, and settling nothing of what it has unsettled. Are they better?

. . . .

But let us now attempt to pierce deeper into the philosophy of the work under notice–to ascertain Mr. Carlyle's esoteric conception of a hero. From what has been brought forward, it appears that of each class he has produced, for the most part, either irrelevant instance, or not the best. What, then, is the inner principle on which the selection has been made? We have been able to discover one mark only, common to all the examples adduced, which we beg permission to name, but not disrespectfully, *radical pugnacity.*

. . . .

. . . It is at least a curious coincidence, that his heroes all offend against magistrate, priest, or law; and agree in no other respect. Is not, as we said, a degree of radical pugnacity the leading feature in his conception of heroism? He seems never sure of his man till he sees him fighting, and the kind of battle he prefers is that waged against things having an *à priori* claim to be held sacred.

–*Christian Remembrancer,* 6 (August 1843): 125, 126, 136, 137

* * *

These excerpts are from a long letter written in response to William Thompson's review of On Heroes, Hero-Worship & the Heroic in History. *Frederick D. Maurice was a minister and influential Christian Socialist. Carlyle commented on the review in his journal on 10 October: "A word from F. Maurice, in defence of me from some Church-of-England reviewer, is also gratifying. One knows not whether even such things are a benefit, are not a new peril and bewilderment" (*The Collected Letters of Thomas and Jane Welsh Carlyle, *v. 17, pp. 191–193).*

"A Delight in What Is Living and True"
A Reply to a Christian Reviewer
Frederick D. Maurice

Your reviewer's remarks on Mr. Carlyle generally are derived from his book on Hero-worship. . . . A writer who speaks of Mahomet, Cromwell, and Rousseau, as heroes, seems, *prima facie,* guilty of a rude insult to the feelings and judgment of his readers. Your reviewer thinks that the evidence of his guilt is increased, not diminished, by the fact that he has joined with these other names, such as that of Dante, with which it is proper and catholic to have sympathy; for he argues, that the quality in the good men which calls forth Mr. Carlyle's admiration must be one which they have in common with the evil men–must be, therefore, itself evil, something which detracts from the worth and completeness of their characters: and by an ingenious and analytical process, he arrives at the conclusion, that the essentially-heroical element, according to Mr. Carlyle, is a radical contempt and defiance of authority. How very satisfactory this conclusion will appear to those who read the review, and who do not read the book reviewed, I can well understand. What can be so satisfactory as an elaborate analysis, leading to a definite, tangible, and, what is still more delightful, a documentary result? Those who do read the book will be tempted to ask themselves whether the reviewer's determination as to what Mr. Carlyle's opinion of the heroical must be, or his own declaration of what it is, has most claim to attention and belief; for it so happens that the two statements entirely disagree. Mr. Carlyle says that, in his judgment, (I quote from memory, not having the book at hand,) a hero is one who *looks*

Alfred Tennyson (Mansell Collection: from Simon Heffer, Moral Desperado: A Life of Thomas Carlyle, *Thomas Cooper Library, University of South Carolina)*

straight into the face of things, is not content with second-hand reports of them, and does not submit to receive semblance for realities. This quality, not radical defiance of authority, he discovers, in different measure, in all the men of whom he speaks; to this he attributes the power which they exercised and the reverence which they commanded.

. . . .

As far as my own experience has gone, the warmest admirers of Mr. Carlyle are to be found among very simple people, women especially, who love their Bible above all other books, and would hate any which did not lead them to love it more. Such persons, with that faculty of love which so far excels the merely judicial faculty in subtlety and discrimination, have detected something at the heart of his writings which reached into their deepest faith and convictions, and have thrown aside, as wholly extraneous, or at all events as unintelligible, what seemed to contradict them. You may tell such readers that they have been all wrong–that you know better; but you will not easily convince them. Not pride, not self-will, but genuine humility, self-distrust, affectionate charity to that which

has imparted wisdom, are enlisted against you. Your arguments, and criticisms, and sneers, will not seem to them the least in accordance with the spirit of the Bible or the Church; they will still obstinately declare that Mr. Carlyle has done more to give them a delight in what is living and true, and therefore, into the Bible and the Church, than you have.

–*Christian Remembrancer,* 6 (October 1843):
455–456, 460–461

* * *

This excerpt from a long review titled "Carlyle's Heroes" treats Carlyle's style.

"Considerable Progress"
Review of *On Heroes, Hero-Worship*
  & the Heroic in History
Joseph H. Barrett

Between the date of Sartor Resartus and that of the six lectures "On Heroes, Hero-Worship, and the Heroic in History"–a period of about ten years–it is

A Friendship with Alfred Tennyson

Carlyle began a lasting friendship with the poet Alfred Tennyson in the 1840s. Smoking, riding, and walking were Carlyle's favorite recreations, and in Tennyson, Carlyle found a favorite smoking partner.

This excerpt is from a letter Jane Welsh Carlyle wrote to a friend, dated 31 January 1845.

Carlyle went to dine at Mr. Chadwick's the other day and I not being yet equal to a dinner altho I was asked to "come in a blanket and stay all night!" had made up my mind for a nice long quiet evening of *looking into the fire,* when I heard a carriage drive up, and men's voices asking questions, and then the carriage was *sent away!* And the men proved to be Alfred Tennyson of all people and his friend Mr. Moxon– Alfred lives in the country and only comes to London rarely and for a few days so that I was overwhelmed with the sense of Carlyle's misfortune in having missed the man he likes best, for stupid Chadwicks, especially as he had gone against his will at *my* earnest persuasion. Alfred is dreadfully embarrassed with women alone–for he entertains at one and the same moment a feeling of almost adoration for them and an ineffable contempt! Adoration I suppose for what they *might be*–contempt for what they *are!* The only chance of my getting any right good of him was to make him forget my *womanness*–so I did just as Carlyle would have done had he been there; got out *pipes* and TOBACCO–and *brandy and water*–with a deluge of *tea* over and above.–The effect of these accessories was miraculous–he *professed* to be *ashamed* of polluting my room "felt" he said "as if he were stealing cups and sacred vessels in the Temple" but he smoked on all the same–for *three* mortal hours!– talking like an angel–only exactly as if he were talking with a clever *man*–which–being a thing I am not used to–men always *adapting* their conversation to

what they *take to be a* woman's taste–strained me to a terrible pitch of intellectuality–When Carlyle came home at Twelve and found me all *alone* in an atmosphere of tobacco so thick that you might have cut it with a knife his astonishment was considerable!

–The Collected Letters of Thomas and Jane Welsh Carlyle, v. 19, pp. 16–17

William Allingham related this anecdote about Carlyle and Tennyson's smoking.

He learned smoking as a schoolboy. It is the only 'creature comfort' that has given him any satisfaction. After working for some hours he always has 'an interlude of tobacco.' He smokes long clay pipes, made at Paisley, whence he gets them by the box. 'No pipes good for anything can be got in England.' He likes best a new pipe, and used, when first I knew him, to smoke a new pipe every day, its predecessor being put out at night on the door-step for who would to carry away.

I have more than once heard Carlyle talk about Tennyson's smoking, and also T. of Carlyle's. Each thought the other smoked too much–or at all events too strong tobacco. T. carefully dries his tobacco before putting it into the pipe, which, he says, lessens the strength, while C. asserts that this process makes it stronger. T. has a wooden frame for his pipes, holding, I think, fourteen, which hangs over the chimney-piece of his study, and he smokes No. 1 to-day, No. 2 to-morrow, and so on, coming round in a fortnight to No. 1 again.

–William Allingham's Diary, pp. 237–238

manifest that a considerable progress had been made by the author of these works, both in respect to worldly experience and spiritual culture. Whatever change there is in the style of expression, indeed, might naturally be supposed to have arisen, in some measure, from the peculiarity of his position as a lecturer, conscious of the presence of real, human auditors, to whom he must make himself clearly and readily understood, on the spot, or else fail entirely of his purpose. The influence of this single circumstance is so plainly discernible and so salutary, that we almost wish all his writings to have been subject to the same conditions, and composed under the same consciousness of what is evidently required of every man who assumes a stand as an interpreter between ideas and the living world. To

most writers, probably, such a restraint would be anything but advantageous, and so far from compelling his thoughts to take a proper outward shape would be likely to check their genial flow, and give their expression an air of confusion. In this instance, the effect is to lop off extravagances, to restrain our unbecoming violence of feeling and lawlessness of imagination, and to curb an egotistical defiance of the taste and opinions of his contemporaries, which the actual presence of an audience would render, in point of fact, as in some of his works it is in substance, a breach of propriety and true politeness.

–American Whig Review, 9 (April 1849): 339

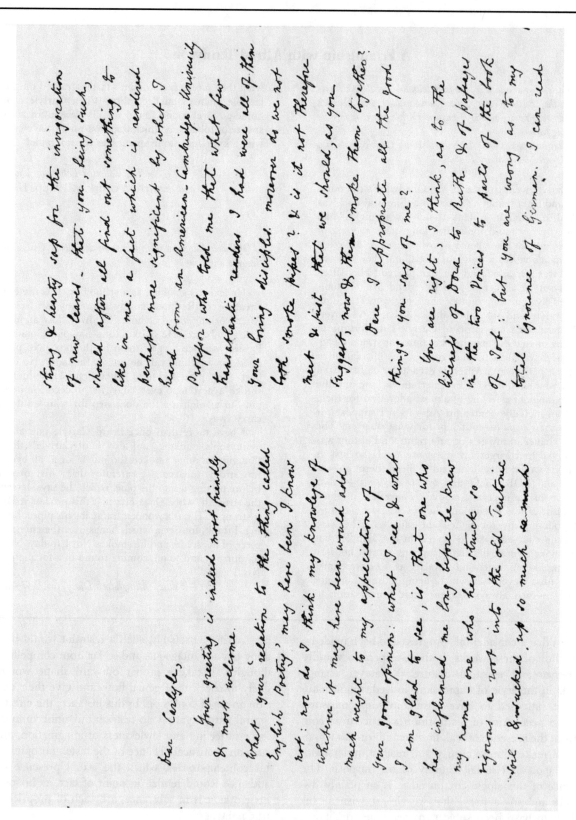

The first letter from Alfred Tennyson to Carlyle, 9 December 1842, in which he agrees to Carlyle's suggestion that they smoke their pipes together (Beinecke Rare Book and Manuscript Library, Yale University)

... it a little: whether I could when summer it was written some years ago. I do not now recollect: most probably not as my German is a rather late accomplishment & I have no remembrance of having been whispered to by the fair Müllerin.

With Jean Paul I have long ago had some acquaintance through your translation of Quintal Fixlein – a model of translation. Jean Paul talking English. It is not singular that you should find something in me that reminds you of him; for he is both a man after my own heart, & one who embraced the feelings & humours & fancies of many men, writing like one that lived on a planet among worlds – but only Western – Oriental but septentrional – Austral to boot.

Altogether your letter is the most grateful thing that has happened to me for a long time. This year, in consequence of overtrust, I have got far in

among the Hand & trembles of this world; & am now wretched to some purpose: your letter is it a voice hailing me to come out into a Harlech place & where the birds off my coat as soon as I may.

I am seldom in London & very seldom make any stay: I expect however to be there presently & if I do anything but just this I will come & see you

Ever yours
A Tennyson

Dec. 9.

Past and Present:
An "Iliad of English Woes"

While he was continuing research on Oliver Cromwell through seventeenth-century sources, Carlyle remained interested in the contemporary problems his country faced, including its struggle with poverty, prostitution, alcoholism, unsanitary living conditions, and a growing demand among the working classes for representation in government. From December 1841 till February 1842, Carlyle put his work on Cromwell aside to write Past and Present, *which draws lessons for nineteenth-century England from a medieval monastery and its exceptional Abbot Samson.*

Reviewers generally responded to Past and Present—*published by Chapman and Hall in April 1843—according to what they hoped it would be. Those who expected practical solutions were disappointed, as they had been by* Chartism, *while those who looked for a sermon on the spiritual sources of the nation's problems, preached by a perceptive prophet, were gratified. Criticism of Carlyle's style persisted among both those who opposed and those who supported his ideas. Some reviewers began sounding the note, often repeated in later years, that Carlyle focused only on the negative, exaggerating society's problems.*

This excerpt is from a letter Carlyle wrote a few months before he began work on Past and Present. *He was responding to Emerson's 15 August 1842 letter, which has been lost, so the substance of Emerson's "bibliopolic advice" is unknown.*

Carlyle to Emerson, 29 August 1842

Your bibliopolic advice about Cromwell or my next Book shall be carefully attended, if I live ever to write another Book! But I have again got down into primeval Night; and live alone and mute with the *Manes,* as you say; uncertain whether I shall ever more see day. I am partly ashamed of myself; but cannot help it. One of my grand difficulties I suspect to be that I cannot write *two Books at once;* cannot be in the seventeenth century and in the nineteenth at one and the same moment; a feat which excels even that of the Irishman's *bird:* "Nobody but a bird can be in two places at once!" For my heart is sick and sore in behalf of my own poor generation; nay, I feel withal as if the one hope of help for it consisted in the possibility of new Cromwells and new Puritans: thus do the two centuries stand related to me, the seventeenth *worthless* except precisely in so far as it can be made the *nineteenth;* and yet let anybody try that enterprise! Heaven help me.–I believe at least that I ought *to hold my tongue;* more especially at present.

—*The Correspondence of Thomas Carlyle and Ralph Waldo Emerson, 1834–1872,* v. 2, pp. 10–11

* * *

This excerpt indicates that Carlyle had temporarily turned away from Oliver Cromwell as a subject.

Jane Welsh Carlyle to Jeannie Welsh, 8 January 1843

Dear I will tell you a secret but see that you keep it to yourself–Carlyle is no more writing about *Oliver Cromwell* than you and I are! I have known this for a good while–you will wonder that I should not have known it all along–the fact is his papers were a good time more resembling hieroglyphics than finished manuscript. I could not be at the trouble of making them out–then when I came to find, on days when I chanced to look, pages about *the present fashion of men's coats*–about the rage of novelties–puffing everything or anything except *"Cromwell Oliver"*–I had no misgivings–I know he has such a way of tacking on extraneous discussions to his subject–but when I found at last a long biography of that *Abbot Samson!* Then indeed–I asked what on earth *has* all this to do with Cromwell–and learned that Cromwell was not begun–that probably half a dozen other volumes will be published before that. Nevertheless for I know not what reason he lets everybody go on questioning him of his Cromwell and answers so as to leave them in the persuasion he is very busy with that and nothing else.

—*Jane Welsh Carlyle: Letters to Her Family, 1839–1863,* p. 79

* * *

Carlyle made rapid progress on Past and Present. *This excerpt is from a letter written when his work was nearing completion.*

Carlyle to Margaret A. Carlyle, 20 January 1843

. . . I hope it will be a rather useful kind of book. It goes rather in a fiery strain about the present condition of men in general, and the strange pass they are coming to; and I calculate it may awaken here and there a slumbering blockhead to rub his eyes and consider what he is about in God's creation–a thing highly desirable at present. I found I could not go on with Cromwell, or with anything else, till I had disburdened my heart somewhat in regard to all that. The look of the world is really quite oppressive to me. Eleven thousand souls in Paisley alone living on three-halfpence a day, and the governors of the land all busy shooting partridges and passing corn-laws the while! It is a thing no man with a speaking tongue in his head is entitled to be silent about. My only difficulty is that I have far *too much* to say, and require great address in deciding how to say it.

–James A. Froude, *Thomas Carlyle: A History of His Life in London, 1834–1881*, v. 1, p. 285

* * *

This excerpt is from a letter in which Emerson acknowledges receiving Past and Present. *In the same letter Emerson wrote that he found it "only too popular"; he went on to discuss how "the cheap press" was changing the American book market: "Every English book of any name or credit is instantly converted into a newspaper or coarse pamphlet."*

Emerson to Carlyle, 29 April 1843

. . . It is true contemporary history, which other books are not, and you have fairly set solid London city afloat in bright mirage in the air. I quarrel only with the popular assumption, which is perhaps a condition of the Humour itself, that the state of society is a new state, and was not the same thing in the days of Rabelais, & of Aristophanes, as of Carlyle. . . . But this Book, with all its affluence of wit, of insight, & of daring hints, is born for a longevity which I will not now compute.–In one respect, as I hinted above, it is only too good, so sure of success, I mean, that you are no longer secure of any respect to your property in our freebooting America.

–*The Correspondence of Thomas Carlyle and Ralph Waldo Emerson, 1834–1872*, v. 2, p. 29–30

* * *

One of the earliest reviews was by John Forster, who had positively reviewed The French Revolution *for* The Examiner. *Earlier in the review from which this excerpt is taken, Forster claims that there is little in the new work "to startle those who have read and understood the former writing of Mr. Carlyle. There is much in it all, we think, not only to startle but do good to those who have admired without understanding them."*

"Broad Unshackled Views"
Review of *Past and Present*
John Forster

. . . In estimates of *great* and *small,* we find ourselves often opposed to Mr Carlyle; his perpetual settings forth of class against class, and not a few of his doctrines of property, and yearnings for a new feudal system, we strongly condemn; and if, as some hints would have us suppose, his ideal of a modern governor can get no farther than the Oliver Cromwell of two cen-

---

"Always Either Speaking or Writing"

Never surely was there an eminent man of letters–not Macaulay himself, for even he had his brilliant flashes of silence–to whom, as to this Apostle of Silence, it seemed in so great a degree a necessity of his nature to be always either speaking or writing. If Carlyle read, it was pencil in hand, to indite comments, grave or gay, and often pregnant, on the margin of the book. The volumes which he borrowed from the London Library might alone furnish a diligent and admiring student and collector with a mass of interesting marginalia. After a day spent in writing or in talking, in either or in both, he would often, before going to bed, seize his pen and soliloquize in his Journal. If you came upon him, when he was taking his walks abroad, you saw his lips moving, and knew he was muttering to himself. Sometimes at home, when he thought the company dull or unsympathetic, he would, rather than be silent, recite, in impressive monotone, a favourite passage of an English poet, notably Milton's touching and noble lines on his blindness in the third book of 'Paradise Lost.' Once at the beginning of his acquaintance with me, when he had exhausted the monitions which he thought suited to my youthful mind, he entertained and instructed me with an account of the evolution of Arabic numerals 2, 3, etc., up to 9, by the additions of strokes and curves to the perpendicular straight line which denotes the primitive numeral 1.

–Francis Espinasse, *Literary Recollections and Sketches*, p. 205

---

turies back, we would rather take our place among the Dead Sea Apes, where Mr Carlyle would in that case infallibly place us, than in the file of such and Abbot Samson's worshippers. But all deductions and drawbacks made, we repeat that this is a most remarkable book, and imperatively claims the attention of all thinking people. It is the book of a sincere man, of a man terribly in earnest. It is no indifferent sign of the times, no unmeaning type of the matter they are laden with, that such a book should be deliberately published for the class among whom Mr Carlyle's readers are found. Full as they may think it of anomalies and discords, disfigured by hyperbolical and exaggerated phrase, weakened by its oracular tone of vehemence and self-reliance–there is not one of them that will fail to discover something of the rare and pure truth that is in it, the broad unshackled views, the freedom of mind and heart, the genuine faith and enthusiasm. No listener can be wholly indifferent when a man of genius speaks.

This is no place for discussion of the infinite weighty questions involved in *Past and Present.* The reader is referred to the book, which, whatever other effect it produces, will without doubt set him actively and zealously thinking on the all important heads of its discourse. It is about the greatest merit a book can have.

—*The Examiner*, 29 April 1843, p. 260

* * *

These excerpts are from a review that was published in two parts. Lady Sydney Morgan negatively reviewed The French Revolution *and* Chartism *for this influential London periodical.*

"Book Is a Failure"
Review of *Past and Present*
Lady Sydney Morgan

. . . Mr. Carlyle seems to be, by instinct, a poet more than a philosopher—more a metaphysician than an observer; and the haste with which he gallops through a string of musty images, to an inference half formed, and of unfruitful generality, is in all likelihood the result of a temperament readily excitable beyond the control of patient judgment. But hopeless as we may be of turning talents of no mean and ordinary power into more useful channels, and of persuading Mr. Carlyle to subordinate his glowing though disorderly rhetoric to the service of pure reason, we cannot, must not, disguise the truth, that his book is a failure,—and is so, precisely from those very causes which he considers as his distinctive excellencies and beauties.

—*Athenaeum*, no. 811 (13 May 1843): 453

* * *

In this excerpt, the reviewer refers to Armida, an enchantress in Torquato Tasso's Jerusalem Delivered. *Armida's enchanted palace, a reference to the place in which she bewitched Rinaldo, signifies a pleasant but purely imaginary domain.*

The notion of comparing the past to the disadvantage of the present, is a poet's notion: an edifice raised in the realms of pure fancy: an Armida's enchanted palace or an Armida's person. Any schoolboy would muster fact enough to show the infinite superiority of modern times in every particular, both moral and physical. If our ancestors had not our evils to contend with, neither had they a tithe of our benefits. Taking even to the uttermost Mr. Carlyle's discouraging views of the condition of the working classes, is that condition comparable with the unbroken series of plague, war, and famine, which, in the boasted twelfth century, desolated the isle, and made life one continued suffering? But, again, is the present stagnation of trade really a necessary ingredient in our civilization, or an

accident? Are we really more destitute of will and resources for arriving at a happier condition than our ancestors? Above all, in making the attempt, are we not to deal with men as they are, to work with the materials that are before us? Is it philosophy to idly invoke an irrevocable past, and to imagine that effects can be received in the absence of their causes? No: Mr. Carlyle's admirers would perhaps admit that such is not the truth, and they would tell us it is—poetry; we say it is childishness and absurdity.

—*Athenaeum*, no. 812 (20 May 1843): 481

* * *

This excerpt is from a letter thanking Carlyle for an inscribed copy of Past and Present. *The followers of Edward Pusey, a professor of Hebrew at Christ Church, Oxford, were derogatorily called Puseyites. Pusey was a leader in the Oxford Movement, which sought to restore liturgy and ceremony to the Anglican Church and opposed liberal theology. John Henry Newman was also a leader in the movement.*

Thomas Spedding to Carlyle, 26 May 1843

It is time for me to render you thanks for "Past and Present" . . . and the main thing is that I have read the book with great appetite, and as much digestion as my dividend of gastric power is equal to. The prize qualification in a recipient, to wit sympathy, is not wanting in me—for a dim dumb consciousness that our life philosophy was resting upon a false basis had been fretting my inwards from my youth up. . . . I believe it to be the same with multitudes of

Page from the manuscript of Past and Present *for his "Morrison's Pill" chapter. In his third paragraph, Carlyle alludes to the quack remedy that provides his title: "How it is to be cured? Brothers, I am sorry I have got no Morrison's Pill for curing the maladies of Society"*
(Beinecke Rare Book and Manuscript Library, Yale University).

my cast and calibre, and that there is latent in our time honesty enough to overturn Mammon if it could only get itself into harness; and what would be more to the purpose still, get itself emancipated from those dead forms and ghosts of spiritualism which oppress us more than our stomach philosophy itself—

Stomach philosophy is a down-right plain-spoken institution, and has much to say for itself, but J. Bull's notions and utterances of and concerning the ideal and invisible are as you say unexampled in this world. They will stand in your way as a prophet even more than his Mammonism. No sect will take you by the hand, unless it be the Puseyites (for I understand that Newman has introduced you into Oxford and that he alone could have saved you from the common hangman there). The only way to promulgate yourself rapidly would be to proclaim a "secession"—take a Proprietary Chapel with handsome pew-rents—and pour forth Carlylese in black or white tailorage from the pulpit. In this case in a few months I would ensure you an auditory pressed down, shaken together, and running over: but whether they would do more than listen, and afterwards set up opposition chapels with adverse eloquence? The letters of the alphabet are your surest tools in the end; and will bear you triumphant.

–K. J. Fielding, "Carlyle and the Speddings: New Letters," *Carlyle Newsletter,* 7 (Spring 1986): 14–15

* * *

"Irritating Reading"

Harriet Martineau included this private assessment in a spring 1843 letter to her cousin Fanny Wedgwood. "Emily" is Emily Taylor, who evidently assumed that Carlyle continued writing for money. Her hope was that the 1842 copyright law, which assured authors of royalties, would allow writers such as Carlyle to stop writing before their work began to repeat itself.

"Past and Present," *very* bad, insolent, bitter, one-sided, and full of weary repetitions. I found it weary and irritating reading, except abbot Samson and some few passages. His injustice to the aristocracy is shameful,—and his conceit. And how weary one is of Burns and the Champion &c! Why does he not get new types?—Emily says of it (but in this view I don't agree) that it will be the best part of the copyright Bill if it enables people to stop in time. C. will not stop, but say the same things over and over (till he dies,) once a year.

–*Harriet Martineau's Letters to Fanny Wedgwood,* p. 56

These excerpts are from an anonymous review originally titled "Thomas Carlyle's Past and Present." It appeared in Tait's Edinburgh Magazine, a reformist periodical founded by William Tait that provided an alternative to the Tory Blackwood's Edinburgh Magazine.

"A Preacher Out of the Pulpit"
Review of *Past and Present*

Thomas Carlyle, in the common use of the English language, is not a poet. Much less does he look like a philosopher—as philosophers, calm, cool, and reasoning, are wont to be; a critic, though he has criticized a great deal, you cannot call him in the common sense at all; to science he has no pretence, one of the most unscientific men of decided grasp perhaps that breathes; political economy and statistics he hates; law he declares to be a mere sham; at legislation certainly he aims, and that on a great scale; but legislation, he says expressly, is not his business, and he has no business to intermeddle with it. What, then, shall we make of him? He is a preacher, a preacher out of the pulpit,—a prophet perhaps: for in these respectable days, when no man can preach or prophesy in the regular pulpits who cannot squeeze his thoughts into the orthodox dialect of the Thirty-nine Articles, or The Confession of Faith,—a thinker of power and originality, a soul burdened with a moral message to its fellow-souls—a heart from the fiery centre of Nature shot direct, as some one phrases it, literally "raging with humanity." Such an one, though meant by nature for occupying a pulpit, finding the entrance into the churches as they now are, guarded by grim comminatory clauses, and barricaded by thorny formulas, which he cannot swallow, necessarily becomes a wandering prophet, a preacher of the wilderness, whose house is where he can find shelter, and whose dinner must often be brought to him by ravens: what, since the invention of printing, we call a prophet no longer, but only a writer of books, a literary man of a very strange and eccentric character. Such a preacher, such a prophet is Thomas Carlyle; and if you do not take up "Past and Present" in this serious acceptation, you had better throw it down. The book is not written for you.

. . . .

Adam Smiths, and Ricardos, and M'Cullochs, we have enough in every shop: they are prophets, too, after their fashion; and whoso denounces them is not wise. But there is an older and a more venerable gospel than that of political economy, of which Mr. Carlyle is one of the most notable modern missionaries; and among other definitions of wealth in these mercantile times,—in this mechanical age,—in this money-making country,—there was need of a strong and an earnest voice to call out loudly in every street this one also—

"Not Loving, Nor Large"

In her 1 June 1843 letter to Emerson, Margaret Fuller assessed Past and Present.

Carlyle's book I have, in some sense, read. It is witty, full of pictures, as usual. I would have gone through with it, if only for the sketch of Samson, and two or three bits of fun which happen to please me. No doubt it may be of use to rouse the unthinking to a sense of those great dangers and sorrows. But how open is he to his own assault. He rails himself out of breath at the short-sighted, yet sees scarce a step before him. There is no valuable doctrine in his book, except the Goethean, *Do to-day the nearest duty.* Many are ready for that, could they but find the way. This he does not show. His proposed measures say nothing. Educate the people. That cannot be done by books, or voluntary effort, under these paralyzing cir-cumstances. Emigration! According to his own esti-mate of the increases of population, relief that way can have very slight effect. He ends as he began; as he did in Chartism. Everything is very bad. You are fools and hypocrites, or you would make it better. I cannot but sympathize with him about hero-worship; for I, too, have had my fits of rage at the stupid irrev-erence of little minds, which also is made a parade of by the pedantic and the worldly. Yet it is a good sign. Democracy is the way to the new aristocracy, as irre-ligion to religion. By and by, if there are great men, they will not be brilliant exceptions, redeemer, but favorable samples of their kind.

Mr. C's tone is no better than before. He is not lov-ing, nor large; but he seems more healthy and gay.

—The Letters of Margaret Fuller, v. 3, p. 128

"THE WEALTH OF A MAN IS THE NUMBER OF THINGS WHICH HE LOVES AND BLESSES, WHICH HE IS LOVED AND BLESSED BY." There was need of a prophet to preach the old gospel of Christ, "The kingdom of Heaven is within you," some-where out of the pulpit,—a gospel altogether contrary to that now preached in the pulpit by the Puseyites.

—Tait's Edinburgh Magazine,
10 (June 1843): 341, 344

* * *

This excerpt is from a review originally titled "Past and Present, by Carlyle." Blackwood's Edinburgh Magazine *was a conservative periodical founded by publisher William Blackwood.*

"Every Age but His Own"
Review of *Past and Present*
William H. Smith

Past and Present, if it does not enhance, ought not, we think, to diminish from the reputation of its author; but as a *mannerism* becomes increasingly disagreeable by repetition, we suspect that, without having less merit, this work will have less popularity than its predecessors.

. . . .

Mr Carlyle censures our poor century for its lack of faith; yet the kind of faith it possesses, which has grown up in it, which is *here* at this present, he has no respect for, treats with no manner of tenderness. What *other* would he have? He deals out to it no measure of philosophical justice. He accepts the faith of every age but his own. He will accept, as the best thing possible, the trustful and hopeful spirit of dark and superstitious periods; but if the more enlightened piety of his own age be at variance even with the most subtle and diffi-cult tenets of his own philosophy, he will make no com-promise with it, he casts it away for contemptuous infidelity to trample on as it pleases. When visiting the past, how indulgent, kind, and considerate he is! . . . But when he turns from the past to the present, all this charity and indulgence are at an end.

—Blackwood's Edinburgh Magazine,
54 (July 1843): 129, 130–131

* * *

This excerpt is from a review originally titled "The Present State of Society." Brownson also reviewed Chartism.

"Intolerant Only to Sham"
Review of *Past and Present*
Orestes Brownson

The book before us is a remarkable, but a mel-ancholy production; it is the wail of a true manly heart, over the misery and wretchedness he sees everywhere around, and from which he himself is not exempt. No man sees more clearly the comic, or feels more keenly the tragic, there is in our age, especially our English and American portion of it; yet no one views with a truer or more loving spirit the universal wrongs and sufferings of our Saxon

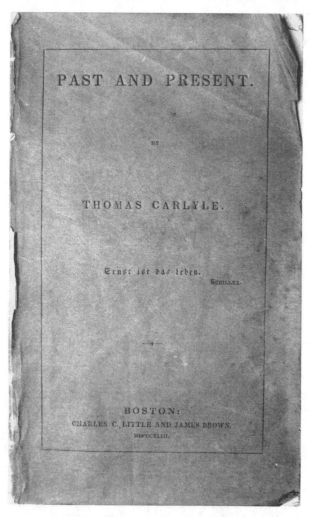

Paper cover for the American edition of the book in which Carlyle promoted his vision of an ordered society ruled by a virtuous leader (Carlyle's House Museum, London)

race. He is sadly, nay, at times terribly in earnest; but his voice loses never its melody in becoming indignant; his heart is grieved, and his soul is sick, and his whole being laments over the miseries, the meannesses, the cants, the emptiness, the quackeries, of the evil times on which we have fallen; but he laments in sorrow not in wrath,—in anguish of spirit, but not altogether without hope. In his very severity, in his most scorching rebukes, he is mild, tolerant, loving to all that *is;* intolerant only to sham, more make-believe, vacuity, Nothing pretending to be Something. We like his earnestness, and also the cheerfulness, so to speak, which he maintains even in his profoundest sorrow.

—*Democratic Review,* 13 (July 1843): 18

* * *

These excerpts are from a review of the American edition of Past and Present, *published by Little and Brown.*

"A Brave and Just Book"
Review of *Past and Present*
Ralph Waldo Emerson

Here is Carlyle's new poem, his Iliad of English woes, to follow his poem on France, entitled the History of the French Revolution. In its first aspect, it is a political tract, and since Burke, since Milton, we have had nothing to compare with it. It grapples honestly with the facts lying before all men, groups and disposes them with a master's mind—and with a heart full of manly tenderness, offers his best counsel to his brothers. . . . It is a brave and just book and not a semblance. "No new truth," say the critics on all sides. Is it so? truth is very old: but the merit of seers is not to invent, but to dispose objects in their right places, and he is the commander who is always in the mount, whose eye not only sees details, but throws crowds of details into their right arrangement and a larger and juster totality than any other. The book makes great approaches to true contemporary history, a very rare success, and firmly holds up to daylight the absurdities still tolerated in the English and European system. It is such an appeal to the conscience and honor of England as cannot be forgotten, or be feigned to be forgotten. It has the merit which belongs to every honest book, that it was self-examining before it was eloquent, and so hits all other men, and, as the country people say of good preaching, "comes bounce down into every pew." Every reader shall carry away something. The scholar shall read and write, the farmer and mechanic shall toil with new resolution, nor forget the book when they resume their labor.

. . . .

"A Success of an Unusual and Very Desirable Kind"

This excerpt concerning Past and Present *is from Jane Welsh Carlyle's 27 August 1843 letter to her husband. She refers to Joseph Henry Garnier, a German journalist.*

Garnier also told me that the book had a success of an unusual and very desirable kind; it was not so much that people spoke about it, as that they spoke out of it; in these mysterious conventions of his, your phrases, he said, were become a part of the general dialect.

—*Letters and Memorials of Jane Welsh Carlyle,* v. 1, p. 249–250

It requires great courage in a man of letters to handle the contemporary practical questions; not because he then has all men for his rivals, but because of the infinite entanglements of the problem, and the waste of strength in gathering unripe fruits. The task is superhuman; and the poet knows well, that a little time will do more than the most puissant genius. Time stills the loud noise of opinions, sinks the small, raises the great, so that the true emerges without effort and in perfect harmony to all eyes; but the truth of the present hour, except in particulars and single relations, is unattainable. . . .

But when the political aspects are so calamitous, that the sympathies of the man overpower the habits of the poet, a higher than literary inspiration may succor him. It is a costly proof of character, that the most renowned scholar of England should take his reputation in his hand, and should descend into the ring, and he has added to his love whatever honor his opinions may forfeit. To atone for this departure from the vows of the scholar and his eternal duties, to this secular charity, we have at least this gain, that here is a message which those to whom it was addressed cannot choose but hear. Though they die, they must listen. It is plain that whether by hope or by fear, or were it only by delight in the panorama of brilliant images, all the great classes of English society must read, even those whose existence it proscribes. Poor Queen Victoria,–poor Sir Robert Peel,–poor Primate and Bishops,–poor Dukes and Lords! there is no help in place or pride or in looking another way; a grain of wit is more penetrating than the lightning of the night-storm, which no curtains or shutters will keep out. Here is a book which will be read, no thanks to anybody but itself. What pains, what hopes, what vows, shall come of the reading! Here is a book as full of treason as an egg is full of meat, and every lordship and worship and high form and ceremony of English conservatism tossed like a football into the air, and kept in the air with merciless kicks and rebounds, and yet not a word is punishable by statute. The wit has eluded all official zeal; and yet these dire jokes, these cunning thrusts, this flaming sword of Cherubim waved high in air illuminates the whole horizon, and shows to the eyes of the universe every wound it inflicts. Worst of all for the party attacked, it bereaves them beforehand of all sympathy, by anticipating the plea of poetic and humane conservation, and impressing the reader with the conviction, that the satirist himself has the truest love for everything old and excellent in English land and institutions, and a genuine respect for the basis of truth in those whom he exposes.

We are at some loss how to state what strikes us as the fault of this remarkable book, for the variety and excellence of the talent displayed in it is pretty sure to leave all special criticism in the wrong. And we may easily fail in expressing the general objection which we feel. It appears to us as a certain disproportion in the picture, caused by the obtrusion of the whims of the painter. In this work, as in his former labors, Mr. Carlyle reminds us of a sick giant. His humors, are expressed with so much force of constitution, that his fancies are more attractive and more credible than the sanity of duller men. But the habitual exaggeration of the tone wearies whilst it stimulates. It is felt to be so much deduction from the universality of the picture. It is not serene sunshine, but everything is seen in lurid stormlights. Every object attitudinizes, to the very mountains and stars almost, under the refractions of this wonderful humorist, and instead of the common earth and sky, we have a Martin's Creation or Judgment Day. A crisis has always arrived which requires a *deus ex machina*. One can hardly credit, whilst under the spell of this magician, that the world always had the same bankrupt look, to foregoing ages as to us,–as of a failed world just recollecting its old withered forces to begin again and try to do a little business.

. . . .

And yet the gravity of the times, the manifold and increasing dangers of the English state, may easily excuse some over-coloring of the picture, and we at this distance are not so far removed from any of the specific evils, and are deeply participant in too many, not to share the gloom, and thank the love and the courage of the counsellor. This book is full of humanity, and nothing is more excellent in this, as in all Mr. Carlyle's works, than the attitude of the writer. He has the dignity of a man of letters who knows what belongs to him, and never deviates from his sphere; a continuer of the great line of scholars, and sustains their office in the highest credit and honor. If the good heaven have any word to impart to this unworthy generation, here is one scribe qualified and clothed for its occasion. One excellence he has in an age of Mammon and of criticism, that he never suffers the eye of his wonder to close. Let who will be the dupe of trifles, he cannot keep his eye off from that gracious Infinite which embosoms us. As a literary artist, he has great merits, beginning with the main one, that he never wrote one dull line. How well read, how adroit, what thousand arts in his one art of writing; with his expedient for expressing those unproven opinions which he entertains but will not endorse, by summoning one of his men of straw from the cell, and the respectable Sauerteig, or Teufelsdrock,

"The Celestial Mirror
of a Friend's Heart"

In this exerpt from his 31 October 1843 letter to Emerson, Carlyle responds to Emerson's reveiw of Past and Present *that that he saw in* The Dial, *which had been "voted in" at the London Library.*

In this last Number of the *Dial,* which by the bye your Bookseller never forwarded to me, I found one little Essay, a criticism on myself,—which, if it should do me mischief, may the gods forgive you for! It is considerably the most dangerous thing I have read for some years. A decided likeness of myself recognisable in it, as in the celestial mirror of a friend's heart; but so enlarged, exaggerated, all *transfigured,*—the most delicious, the most dangerous thing! Well, I suppose I must try to assimilate it also, to turn it also to good if I be able. Eulogies, dyslogies, in which one finds no features of one's own natural face, are easily dealt with; easily left unread, as stuff for lighting fires, such is the insipidity, the wearisome *nonentity* of pabulum like that: but here is another sort of matter! "The beautifullest piece of criticism I have read for many a day," says every one that speaks of it. May the gods forgive you.—I have purchased a copy for three shillings, and sent it to my Mother: one of the *indubitable* benefits I could think of in regard to it.

—The Collected Letters of Thomas Carlyle and Jane Welsh Carlyle, v. 17, pp.163–164

cence. Plato is the purple ancient, and Bacon and Milton the moderns of the richest strains. Burke sometimes reaches to that exuberant fulness, though deficient in depth. Carlyle in his strange half mad way, has entered the Field of the Cloth of Gold, and shown a vigor and wealth of resource, which has no rival in the tourney play of these times;—the indubitable champion of England. Carlyle is the first domestication of the modern system with its infinity of details into style. We have been civilizing very fast, building London and Paris, and now planting New England and India, New Holland and Oregon,—and it has not appeared in literature,—there has been no analogous expansion and recomposition in books. Carlyle's style is the first emergence of all this wealth and labor, with which the world has gone with child so long. London and Europe tunnelled, graded, corn-lawed, with trade-nobility, and east and west Indies for dependencies, and America, with the Rocky Hills in the horizon, have never before been conquered in literature. This is the first invasion and conquest. How like an air-balloon or bird of Jove does he seem to float over the continent, and stooping here and there pounce on a fact as a symbol which was never a symbol before. This is the first experiment; and something of rudeness and haste must be pardoned to so great an achievement. It will be done again and again, sharper, simpler, but fortunate is he who did it first, though never so giant-like and fabulous. This grandiose character pervades his wit and his imagination. We have never had anything in literature so like earthquakes, as the laughter of Carlyle. He "shakes with his mountain mirth." It is like the laughter of the Genii in the horizon. These jokes shake down Parliament-house and Windsor Castle, Temple, and Tower, and the future shall echo the dangerous peals. The other particular of magnificence is in his rhymes. Carlyle is a poet who is altogether too burly in his frame and habit to submit to the limits of metre. Yet he is full of rhythm not only in the perpetual melody of his periods, but in the burdens, refrains, and grand returns of his sense and music. Whatever thought or motto has once appeared to him fraught with meaning, becomes an omen to him henceforward and is sure to return with deeper tones and weightier import, now as promise, now as threat, now as confirmation, in gigantic reverberation, as if the hills, the horizon, and the next ages returned the sound.

—The Dial, 4 (July 1843): 96, 98–102

* * *

or Dryasdust, or Picturesque Traveller says what is put into his mouth and disappears. That morbid temperament has given his rhetoric a somewhat bloated character, a luxury to many imaginative and learned persons, like a showery south wind with its sunbursts and rapid chasing of lights and glooms over the landscape, and yet its offensiveness to multitudes of reluctant lovers makes us often wish some concession were possible on the part of the humorist. Yet it must not be forgotten that in all his fun of castanets, or playing of tunes with a whiplash like some renowned charioteers,—in all this glad and needful venting of his redundant spirits,—he does yet ever and anon, as if catching the glance of one wise man in the crowd, quit his tempestuous key, and lance at him in clear level tone the very word, and then with new glee returns to his game. He is like a lover or an outlaw who wraps up his message in a serenade, which is nonsense to the sentinel, but salvation to the ear for which it is meant. He does not dodge the question, but gives sincerity where it is due.

One word more respecting this remarkable style. We have in literature few specimens of magnifi-

These excerpts are from a thirty-one-page article that was evidently largely written in 1841, when the author, Joseph (Giuseppe) Mazzini, showed it to Jane Carlyle. Although it was published as a review article of On Heroes, Hero-Worship & the Heroic in History, Sartor Resartus *and* Past and Present, *Mazzini begins by saying his focus is Carlyle, not any particular work: "We gladly take the opportunity offered by the publication of a new work by Mr. Carlyle, to express our opinion of this remarkable writer." Mazzini had earlier reviewed* The French Revolution.

"Life and Nothingness"
An Assessment of Carlyle
Joseph Mazzini

There are differences between Mr. Carlyle's manner of viewing things and ours, which we have to premise; but we will not do this without first avowing his incontestable merits,—merits which at the present day are as important as they are rare, which in him are so elevated as to command the respect and admiration even of those who rank under another standard, and the sympathy and gratitude of those who, like ourselves, are in the main upon the same side, and who differ only respecting the choice of means and the road to pursue.

Above all, we would note the sincerity of the writer. What he writes, he not only thinks, but feels. He may deceive himself,—he cannot deceive us; for what he says, even when it is not the truth, is yet *true*,—*his* individuality, *his* errors, *his* incomplete views of things,—realities, and not nonentities,—the truth limited, we might say, for error springing from sincerity in a high intellect is no other than such. He seeks good with conscientious zeal, not from a love of fame, not even from the gratification of the discovery; his motive is the love of his fellow-men, a deep and active feeling of duty, for he believes this to be the mission of man upon earth. He writes a book, as he would do a good action. . . . There is generally so much calmness and impartiality in his attacks, so much conviction in his thoughts, so entire an absence of egotism, that we are compelled to listen to what, if uttered by any other man with anger or contempt, would excite a storm of opposition. There is never anger in the language of Mr. Carlyle; disdain he has, but without bitterness, and when it gleams across his pages, it speedily disappears under a smile of sorrow and of pity, the rainbow after a storm. He condemns, because there are things which neither heaven nor earth can justify; but his reader always feels that it is a painful duty he fulfils. . . .

Carlyle, fourth from left, at a reading of Dickens's work, 1844 (drawing by Daniel Maclise, from David Alec Wilson, Life of Carlyle, *Thomas Cooper Library, University of South Carolina)*

Drawings of the Carlyles
by Elizabeth Paulet

Elizabeth Paulet and her husband, Etienne, were friends of the Carlyles. Elizabeth took part in a writing group with Geraldine Jewsbury and Jane Carlyle. The drawing to the right suggests the high regard in which her friends held Jane Carlyle. The drawing at the bottom of the page is more obscure. In her article "Elizabeth Paulet and the Carlyles," published in the Spring 1987 issue of the Carlyle Newsletter, *Bettina Lehmbeck provides an explanation: "What seems to have occurred is that a pair of Carlyle's trousers was mended while he 'enjoyed his smoke' (as seen through the window). In the caricature we apparently see the footman with the trousers, a tailor, and the even dimmer figure of Etienne Paulet looking through his eyeglass."*

An 1844 sketch of Jane Welsh Carlyle by Elizabeth Paulet (Columbia University Library; from Rosemary Ashton, Thomas and Jane Carlyle: Portrait of a Marriage, *Collection of Frances Frame)*

A sketch by Elizabeth Paulet, August 1843 (The Trustees of the National Library of Scotland MS 603)

We place in the second rank his tendencies toward the ideal,–that which we shall call, for want of a better word, his spiritualism. He is the most ardent and powerful combatant of our day in that re-action, which is slowly working against the strong materialism that for a century and a half has maintained a progressive usurpation, one while in the writings of Locke, Bolingbroke or Pope, at another in those of Smith and Bentham, and has tended, by the doctrines of self-interest and material well-being, to the enthronement of selfishness in men's hearts. . . .

We place in the third rank our author's cosmopolitan tendencies–*humanitarian* we would say, if the word were in use; for cosmopolitism has at the present day come to indicate rather the indifference than the universality of sympathies. He well knows that there is a holy land, in which, under whatever latitude they may be born, men are brethren. He seeks among his equals in intelligence, not the English man, the Italian, the German, but *man:* he adores, not the god of one sect, of one period, or of one people, but God; and, as the reflex of God upon earth, the beautiful, the noble, the great, wherever he finds it: knowing well, that whencesoever it beams, it is, or will be, sooner or later for all.

. . . .

There is but one defect in Mr. Carlyle, in our opinion, but that one is vital: it influences all he does, it determines all his views; for logic and system rule the intellect even when the latter pretends to rise the most against them. We refer to his view of the *collective* intelligence of our times.

. . . .

Mr. Carlyle comprehends only the *individual:* the true sense of the unity of the human race escapes him. He sympathizes with all men, but it is with the life of each one, and not with their collective life. He readily looks at every man as the representative, the incarnation in a manner, of an idea; he does not believe in a "supreme idea," represented progressively by the development of mankind taken as a whole. He feels forcibly (rather indeed by the instinct of his heart, which revolts at actual evil, than by a clear conception of that which constitutes *life*) the want of a bond between the men who are around him: he does not feel sufficiently the existence of the bond between generations past, present and future. The great religious thought, *the continued development of Humanity by a collective labour, according to an educational plan assigned by Providence,* fore-felt from age to

age by a few rare intellects, and proclaimed in the last fifty years by the greatest European thinkers, finds but a feeble echo, or rather no echo at all, in his soul. Progressive from an impulse of feeling, he shrinks back from the idea as soon as he sees it stated explicitly and systematically; and such expressions as "the progress of the species" and "perfectibility" never drop from his pen unaccompanied by a taint of irony, which we confess is to us inexplicable. He seems to regard the human race rather as an aggregate of similar individuals, distinct powers in juxtaposition, than as an association of labourers, distributed in groups, and impelled on different paths toward one single object. . . .

We protest, in the name of the democratic spirit of the age, against such ideas. History is not the biography of great men; the history of mankind is the history of the progressive religion of mankind, and of the translation by symbols, or external actions, of that religion. The great men of the earth are but the marking-stones on the road of humanity: they are the priests of its religion.

. . . .

. . . There is a deep discouragement, a very despair, at the bottom of all that bold fervour of belief which characterizes many of Mr. Carlyle's pages. To us he seems to seek God rather as a refuge, than as the source of right and of power: from his lips, at times so daring, we seem to hear every instant the cry of the Breton mariner–"My God, protect me! my bark is so small and thy ocean so vast!"

Now all this is partly true, and nevertheless it is all partly false: true, inasmuch as it is the legitimate consequence from Mr. Carlyle's starting-point; false, in a higher and more comprehensive point of view. . . . For it matters little that *our* individual powers be of the smallest amount in relation to the object to be attained; it matters little that the result of *our* action be lost in a distance which is beyond our calculation; we know that the powers of millions of men, our brethren, will succeed to the work after us, in the same track,–we know that the object attained, be it when it may, will be the result of *all* our efforts combined.

The object–an object to be pursued collectively, an ideal to be realized as far as possible here below, by the association of all our faculties and all our powers . . . this alone gives value and method to the life and acts of the individual. Mr. Carlyle seems to us almost always to forget this. Being thus without a sound criterion whereby to estimate individual acts, he is compelled to value them rather by the power which has been expended upon them, by the energy and perseverance which they betray, than by the nature of the object toward which they are directed, and their relation to that object. Hence arises that kind of indifference which makes him, we will not say esteem, but love, equally men whose whole life has been spent in pursuing contrary objects,–Johnson and Cromwell, for example. Hence proceeds that spirit of fatalism (to call things by their right names) which remotely pervades his work on the French Revolution; which makes him sympathize so much with bold deeds, admire ability, under whatever form displayed, and so often hail, at the risk of becoming an advocate of despotism, might as the token of right.

. . . .

. . . A perpetual antagonism prevails throughout all that he does; his instincts drive him to action, his theory to contemplation. Faith and discouragement alternate in his works, as they must in his soul. He weaves and unweaves his web, like Penelope: he preaches by turns life and nothingness: he destroys the powers of his readers, by continually carrying them from heaven to hell, from hell to heaven. Ardent, and almost menacing, upon the ground of idea, he becomes timid and sceptical as soon as he is engaged on that of its application. . . . Have patience, he says, to those who complain; all will come to pass, but not in your way: God will provide the means. By whom then will God provide means upon earth unless by us? are we not his agents here below?

. . . .

. . . The rule which he adopts is that laid down by Goethe,–"Do the duty which lies nearest thee." And this rule is good, inasfar as it is, like all other moral rules, susceptible of a wide interpretation,– bad, so far as, taken literally, and falling into the hands of men whose tendencies to self-sacrifice are feeble, it may lead to the revival of selfishness, and cause that which at bottom should only be regarded as the wages of duty to be mistaken for duty itself. . . . There are at the present day but too many who imagine they have perfectly done their duty, because they are kind toward their friends, affectionate in their families, inoffensive toward the rest of the world. The maxim of Goethe and of Mr. Carlyle will always suit and serve such men, by transforming into duties the

individual, domestic or other affections,–in other words, the consolations of life. Mr. Carlyle probably does not carry out his maxim in practice; but his principle leads to this result, and cannot theoretically have any other.

–*British and Foreign Review,* 16 (1844): 265–266, 269, 271, 274–275, 277–279, 284–285, 289

* * *

"Wanting the *Sentiment Collectif*"

This excerpt is from Jane Welsh Carlyle's 6 July 1841 letter to Carlyle in which she reacts to Mazzini's article. She refers to John Mitchell Kemble of the British and Foreign Review.

Mazzini has written a long and eloquent article on you which he brought to me to be read the other day before offering it to Kemble "as a guarantee he said" for its giving you no offence, for tho he had said the same things to you a hundred times in speech, you might think them less friendly in print– and if *I* said imprimatur he would feel secure on that head–The first part is the most glowing transcendant praise–Every good quality and every great faculty under Heaven are abundantly allowed but then he says, "our task becomes less pleasant" and he points out your grand want–a *vital* one vitiating all the good and beautiful rest–very want of the "*sentiment collectif* [collective feeling]" and then away he goes full sail into *progres humanitarianism* and "all that sort of thing"–I told him–that I was certain you would care "the least in the world for being publicly taxed with wanting the *sentiment collectif* that you did not I was sure consider it a thing worth any ones while to have, so long as you were so praised for your *profundity* your *sincerity* your sympathy (of the *individu* [individual]) &c &c–and so the article was to be offered at least I hope they will print it for it is admirable *from his point of view*–By the way he remarks that Monsieur Carlyle in inculcating the necessi[ty] of *retener la langue* [holding the tongue] means it only for those who do not hold *his* views– that the talent of *silence* in fact however much he may commend it is not *his*–that such a spirit cannot be compressed into silence, cannot *love* silence otherwise than "*platoniquement comme on peut dire* [platonically, as one may say]"–very good!–

–The Collected Letters of Thomas Carlyle and Jane Welsh Carlyle, v. 13, pp. 171–172

These excerpts are from an essay on Carlyle that Elizabeth Barrett wrote in 1844.

"A Gifted Poet"
An Assessment of Carlyle
Elizabeth Barrett

According to the view of the *microcosmus,* what is said of the world itself, may be said of every individual in it; and what is said of the individual, may be predicated of the world. Now, the individual mind has been compared to a prisoner in a dark room, or in a room which would be dark but for the windows of the same, meaning the senses in a figure,—nothing being in the mind without the mediation of the senses, as Locke held,—"except" . . . as Leibnitz acutely added in modification, . . . "the mind itself." Thus is it with the individual, and thus with the general humanity. . . . And to return to our first figure,—what the senses are to the individual mind, men of genius are to the general mind. Scantily assigned by Providence for necessary ends, one original thinker strikes a window out here, and another there; wielding the mallet sharply, and leaving it to others to fashion grooves and frames, and complete advantage into convenience.

That Mr. Carlyle is one of the men of genius thus referred to, and that he has knocked out his window from the blind wall of his century, we may add without any fear of contradiction. We may say too that it is a window to the east,—and that some men complain of a certain bleakness in the wind which enters at it, when they should rather congratulate themselves and him on the aspect of the new sun beheld through it,—the orient hope of which, he has so discovered to their eyes. And let us take occasion to observe here, and to bear in memory through every subsequent remark we may be called upon to make,—that it has not been his object to discover to us any specific prospect—not the mountain to the right, nor the oak-wood to the left, nor the river which runs down between,—but the SUN, which renders visible all these.

When "the most thinking people" had, at the sound of all sorts of steam-engines, sufficiently worshipped that idol of utilitarianism which Jeremy Bentham the king had set up,—the voice of the prophet was heard praying three times a day, with magnanimous re-iteration, towards Jerusalem,—towards old Jerusalem, be it observed,—and also towards the place of sun-rising for ultimate generations.

Carlyle as painted in 1844 by John Linnell (National Portrait Gallery, Edinburgh; from Letters of Thomas Carlyle to John Stuart Mill, John Sterling, and Robert Browning, *Special Collections, Thomas Cooper Library, University of South Carolina)*

. . . .

We have named Carlyle in connection with Bentham, and we believe that you will find in "your philosophy," no better antithesis for one, than is the other. There is as much resemblance between them as is necessary for antithetic unlikeness. Each headed a great movement among thinking men; and each made a language for himself to speak with; and neither of them originated what they taught. Bentham's work was done by systematizing; and Carlyle's, by reviving and reiterating. And as from the beginning of the world, the two great principles of matter and spirit have combated,—whether in man's personality, between the flesh and the soul,—or in his speculativeness, between the practical and the ideal,—or in his mental expression, between science and poetry,—Bentham and Carlyle assumed the double van on opposite sides—Bentham gave an impulse to the material energies of his age, of the stuff of which he was himself made,—while Carlyle threw himself before the crushing chariots, not in sacrifice, but deprecation; . . . "Go aside—*there is a spirit even in the wheels!*"

Letter that Elizabeth Barrett sent to Carlyle with her 1844 collection, Poems. *As the wife of Robert Browning, Elizabeth Barrett Browning came to know the Carlyles personally (Beinecke Rare Book and Manuscript Library, Yale University).*

. . . .

. . . Mr. Carlyle is not an originator, but a renewer, although his medium is highly original; and it remains to us to recognise that he is none the less important teacher on that account, and that there was none the less necessity for his teaching. "The great fire-heart," as he calls it, of human nature may burn too long without stirring,—burn inwardly, cake outwardly, and sink deeply into its own ashes: and to emancipate the flame clear and bright, it is necessary to stir it up strongly from the lowest bar. To do this, is the aim and end of all poetry of a high order,—this,—to resume human nature from its beginning, and return to first principles of thought and first elements of feeling; this,—to dissolve from eye and ear the film of habit and convention, and to let Beauty and Truth run gushing upon unencrusted perceptive faculties; for as Religion makes a man a child again innocently,—so should poetry make a man a child again perceptively. This is what a poet [must] try for; and in this aim, Carlyle is, as he has been called, a poet, and a great one—only what the poet does for the individual reader and the actual instincts, Carlyle would do for Society collectively. . . . He is reproached with not being practical—Mr. Carlyle is not practical. But he is practical for many intents of the inner life, and teaches well the Doing of Being.

. . . .

. . . He is a poet also, by his insight into the activity of moral causes working through the intellectual agencies of the mind. He is also a poet in the mode. He conducts his argument with none of your philosophical arrangements and marshalling of "for and against": his paragraphs come and go as they please. He proceeds, like a poet, rather by association than by uses of logic. His illustrations not only illustrate but bear a part in the reasoning,—the images standing out, like grand and beautiful Caryatides, to sustain the heights of the argument. Of his language we have spoken. Somewhat too slow and involved for eloquence, and too individual to be classical, it is yet the language of a gifted poet, the colour of whose soul eats itself into the words.

—Literary Anecdotes of the Nineteenth Century

A Singing Carlyle

Robert Browning commenced a correspondence with Elizabeth Barrett after he read her Poems *(1844). They first met in 1845 and were married in 1847.*

This excerpt is from Browning's letter to Barrett of 26 February 1845.

I know Carlyle and love him—know him so well, that I would have told you he had shaken that grand head of his at "singing," so thoroughly does he love and live by it. When I last saw him, a fortnight ago, he turned, from I don't know what other talk, quite abruptly on me with "Did you never try to write a *Song?* Of all things in the world, *that* I should be proudest to do." Then came his definition of a song—then, with an appealing look to Mrs. C.,—"I always say that some day *"in spite of nature and my stars"* I shall burst into a song" (he is not mechanically "musical," he meant,—and the music is the poetry, he holds, and should enwrap the thought as Donne says "an amber-drop enwraps a bee") and then he began to recite an old Scotch song, stopping at the first rude couplet—"The beginning words are merely to set the tune, they tell me"—and then again at the couplet about—or, to the effect that—"give me" (but in broad Scotch—) "give me but my lass, I care not for my cogie." *"He says,"* quoth Carlyle magisterially,—"that if you allow him the love of his lass, you may take away all else,—even his cogie, his cup or can, and he cares not"—just as a professor expounds Lycophron. And just before I left England, six months ago, did not I hear him croon, if not certainly, sing "Charlie is my darling"—("my *darling*" with an adoring emphasis—) and then he stood back, as it were, from the song, to look at it better, and said "How must that notion of ideal wondorous perfection have impressed itself in this old Jacobite's "young Cavalier" . . ("They go to save their land—and the *young Cavalier!*"—) when I who cared nothing about such a rag of a man, cannot but feel as he felt, in speaking his words after him"! After saying which, he would be sure to counsel everybody to get their heads clear of all singing!

This excerpt is from Barrett's letter to Browning sent in response the following day.

I am delighted to hear all you say to me of . . . the great teacher of the age, Carlyle, who is also yours & mine. He fills the office of a poet—does he not? . . by analyzing humanity back into its elements, to the destruction of the conventions of the hour. That is—strictly speaking . . the office of the poet,—is it not?—and he discharges it fully—& with a wider intelligibility perhaps as far as the contemporary period is concerned, than if he did forthwith 'burst into a song.'

—The Brownings' Correspondence, v. 10, pp. 98–99, 101

Oliver Cromwell's Letters and Speeches: "A Series of Fixed *Rock*-Summits"

Oliver Cromwell's intense energy, religious conviction, and ability to act attracted Carlyle. Long interested in the reformer, Carlyle spoke about Cromwell in 1840 in his lecture on the hero as king. Carlyle found much of the historical materials dealing with Cromwell biased. To gather information and to improve his motivation to write, he visited Cromwell's home as well as revolutionary battlefields. Carlyle struggled until December 1843 to decide upon the form his work should take, electing finally to edit Cromwell's papers instead of writing a biography. Chapman and Hall published Oliver Cromwell's Letters and Speeches *on 27 November 1845.*

Carlyle's portrait of Cromwell as driven reformer who sincerely desired to do God's work clashed with the accepted British understanding of the man as a power-hungry hypocrite. While reviewers generally praised Carlyle's painstaking editing, they debated the accuracy of his depiction of Cromwell; his presentation of Charles I, the king whom Cromwell executed; and continued to discuss the morality of Carlyle's conception of heroism. Although some Irish reviewers lauded the book, many were outraged at Carlyle's treatment of Cromwell's crushing of the Irish Rebellion.

These excerpts are from a letter Carlyle wrote from Ely, Cambridgeshire, while he was "on a pilgrimage to Cromwell-land."

Carlyle to John Sterling, 6 September 1842

. . . I believe this Ely Cathedral is one of the "finest," as they call it, in all England, and from me also few masses of architecture could win more admiration; but I recoil everywhere from treating these things as a *dilettantism* at all; the impressions they give are too deep and sad to have anything to do with the shape of stones. To-night, as the heaving bellows blew, and the yellow sunshine streamed in thro' those high windows, and my footfalls and the poor country lad's were the only sounds from below, I looked aloft, and my eyes filled with very tears to look at all this, and remember beside it (wedded to it now, and *reconciled* with it for me) Oliver Cromwell's, "Cease your fooling, and come out, Sir!" In these two antagonisms lie what volumes of meaning!–

But to quit the sentimental and vague (in spite of Bagmen), know, dear Sterling, that I have clearly discovered the very House where my Friend Oliver dwelt and boiled his kettle some two hundred and two years ago; nay half an hour ago I actually sat and smoked a pipe upon *his* Horse-block, the very stone, which still lies at the entrance to the stables, split in two and shoved a little aside to make room for a piece of pavement, but left lying as too unmanageable still for removal, in a place so stagnant as Ely! I think there are few better pilgrimages left possible for a

man at present. Oliver's House stands close by St. Mary's Church-yard; a mean shrunk-looking aged house, with "the biggest *tithe-barn* except one in all England": the Mr. Page who occupied it in Noble's time died only two years ago; a new arrangement has been made about Cathedral tithes, and the Oliver House now stands vacant, not like ever to be occupied again, and will soon probably vanish from the Earth. Could you persuade no Cambridge acquaintance who sketches to go up and take a portrait of it while there is yet time? Really it were well worth while. Soon, soon, or else never!

—*New Letters of Thomas Carlyle*, v. 1, p. 268–269

* * *

"A Hero and a Blackguard"

Carlyle's interest in Oliver Cromwell as a subject began early. This excerpt is from a 27 April 1822 letter to his brother Alexander.

My purpose (but this only among yourselves!) is to come out with a kind of Essay on the Civil Wars, the Commonwealth of England–not to write a history of them–but to exhibit if I can some features of the national character as it was then displayed, supporting my remarks by mental portraits, drawn with my best ability, of Cromwell, Laud, Geo: Fox, Milton, Hyde &c the most distinguished of the actors in this great scene. I may of course intersperse the work of delineation with all the ideas, which I can gather from any point of the Universe. If I live with even moderate health, I purpose to do this; and if I can but finish it according to my own conception of what it should be, I shall feel much happier than if I had inherited much gold & silver. The Critics too may say of it either nothing or any thing, according to their own good pleasure; if it once please my own mighty self, I do not value them or their opinion a single rush. Long habit has inured me to live with a very limited & therefore a dearer circle of approvers: all I aim at is to convince my own conscience that I have not taken their approbation without some just claims to it.

—*The Collected Letters of Thomas and Jane Welsh Carlyle*, v. 2, p. 94

This excerpt is dated December 1826 in Carlyle's notebook.

What a fine thing a *Life of Cromwell*, like the *Vie de Charles XII* would be! The wily fanatic himself, in his own most singular features, at once a hero and a blackguard pettifogging scrub; and the wild image of his Times reflected from his accompaniment! I would travel ten miles on foot to see his *soul* represented as I once saw his body in the Castle of Warwick.–

—*Two Note Books of Thomas Carlyle*, p. 93

A portion of Carlyle's notes on members of the Long Parliament, dated 30 June 1842 (Beinecke Rare Book and Manuscript Library, Yale University)

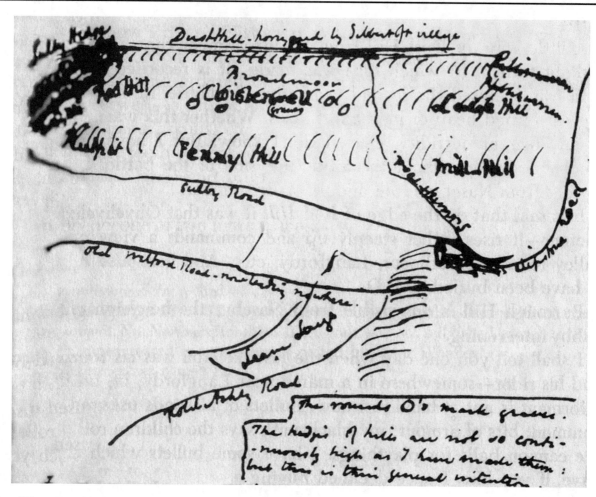

Map of Naseby Battlefield that Edward FitzGerald included in his 23 September 1842 letter to Carlyle (from The Letters of Edward FitzGerald, *Thomas Cooper Library, University of South Carolina)*

Carlyle employed the assistance of willing friends, such as Edward FitzGerald, during his research. In this excerpt he describes his visit to Naseby Battlefield, site of a major Parliamentarian victory on 14 June 1645, during the English Civil War. Sir Thomas Fairfax commanded the army, with Cromwell as lieutenant-general of cavalry, and second-in-command.

Edward FitzGerald to Carlyle, 23 September 1842

I took a walk over the Field with my Blacksmith yesterday, and wished you had been with us: you would then have seen every thing very clearly. All the questions in your letter I cannot yet answer: but some I can and will, so that you may apply to your map with perhaps some clearer light. But I cannot help saying again I wish you would come here: Laurence talks of coming here on Saturday. Besides the country itself, I have found a great map of the *Lord*ship at the Vicar's: this map drawn in 1800—before the enclosure—with *all* the old names, *some*

positions of the army, of the graves of the dead, etcc. If I come to town I will bring it with me: but I cannot send it. All the old names of the localities are in present use—and none other. What you write "*Lantford* hedges" is "*Langfordy* hedges"—that is, the long hedge that runs all the way from near to *Rutpit* Hill to Broadmoor, and divides the Lordship of Sulby from that of Naseby. The hedge itself is generally called "Sulby Hedge": but the land on our side of it, is called always "*Langfordy*." "Fanny" or "Famny Hill" is "*Fenny* Hill" which rises out of *Rutpit* Hill, and runs eastward toward the village. "Lean Leaf" is "Lean Leys" . . . is a slightly rising pasture that reaches *to* the hill on which the village is built toward the west: which hill (wonderful to say) has no name in particular, and so may be called Lean Leys Hill.

–The Letters of Edward FitzGerald,
v. 1, pp. 352–353

* * *

should be left as prisoners to the mercy of the Lieut.-General. Which articles were performed, and the enemy marched forth accordingly. No sooner were the enemy marched away, but upon Monday the renowned *Lieut.-Gen. Cromwell* advanced with 4000 horse and 3000 foot towards *Deniston Castle*, which being taken in, the passage into the west will be free and open.—*Merc. Civ. Sept.* 18 *to* 25.

Lieut.-Gen. Cromwell, hath taken in the *Devizes*, 5 pieces of ordnance, besides some lesser pieces, and 300 arms, besides good store of powder, bullet, match, and other ammunition, and no want of provisions; the enemy marched to *Worcester*, a party of *Cromwell's* horse are gone to *Denington*, and the foot follow to block them up. *Lacock* is besieged, and *Col. Welden's* brigade is gone to join with *Major-Gen. Massey.*—*Perf. Occ. Sept.* 19 *to* 26.

This day, we understood, that *Lieut.-Gen. Cromwell* came before *Winchester* the 27 past; the enemy disputed, the city being fortified as well as the castle, but the gate being fired, our men entered. The *Lieut.-Gen. Cromwell* is battering the castle with 2 great guns, there are about 300 and odd in it, he will (it is believed) be master of it in a few days.—*True Inf. Oct.* 4.

We this day received intelligence, that *Lieut.-Gen. Cromwell* was come before *Winchester*, with a resolution not to depart from it until he had reduced both town and castle to the obedience of the Parliament. The city made some opposition contrary to his expectation, but having fired the bridge, he quickly found a means to enter the city and subdue it. We hear that he did send unto the *Bishop of Winchester*, and offered him a guard to secure his person, but the Bishop flying into the castle, refused the courtesy. Afterwards the castle being begun to be battered by 2 pieces of ordnance, he sent to the Lieut.-Gen. giving him thanks for the great favour offered to him, and being now more sensible what it was, he desired the enjoyment of it; to whom the wise Lieut.-Gen. replied, that since he made not use of the courtesy, but wilfully did run away from it, he must partake of the same condition as the others who are with him in the castle, and if he were taken, he must expect to be used as a prisoner of war.—*Diary or ex. Jour. Oct.* 2 *to* 9.

Lieut.-Gen. Cromwell's letter on the surrender of *Winchester.*

" Sir,

"I came to *Winchester* on the Lord's day, the 28 of September, with *Col. Pickering*, commanding his own, *Col. Montague's*, and *Sir Hardress Waller's* regiments; after some dispute with the governor, we entered the towne, I summoned the castle, was denyed, whereupon we fell to prepare batteries, which we could not perfect (some of our guns being out of order) untill Friday following, our batterie was six gunnes, which being finished, after one fireing round, I sent him a second summons for a treaty, which they refused, whereupon we went on with our work, and made a breach in the wall neare the Black Tower; which after about 200 shot we thought stormable, and purposed on Monday morning to attempt it. On Sunday night, about ten of the clock, the governour beate a parley, desiring to treat, I agreed unto it, and sent *Col. Hammond* and *Major Harrison* in to him, who agreed upon these enclosed articles. Sir, this is the addition of another mercy, you see God is not weary in doing you good; I confesse, Sir, his favour to you is as visible, when he comes by his power upon the hearts of your enemies, making them quit places of strength to you, as when he gives courage to your souldiers to attempt hard things, his goodnesse in this is much to be acknowledged; for the castle was well manned with 680 horse and foot, there being neare 200 gentlemen, officers, and their servants; well victualled with 15000 wait of cheese, very great store of wheat and beer, neer 20 barrels of powder, 7 peeces of cannon; the workes were exceeding good and strong. It is very likely it would have cost much blood to have gained it by storme; we have not lost 12 men: this is repeated to you, that God may have all the praise, for it is all his due.

" Sir, I rest your most humble servant,

" *Oliver Cromwell.*"

The articles of the surrender were these:—1. That the *Lord Ogle* shall deliver up the castle of *Winchester*, with all the arms, ordnance, ammunition, provision, and all function of war whatsoever therein, without any embezzlement, waste, or spoil, unto that officer or officers as shall be

A page from Carlyle's copy of Machell Stace's 1810 book Cromwelliana. A Chronological Detail of Events in which Oliver Cromwell was Engaged; from the year 1642 to his Death, 1658, *with Carlyle's annotation (Houghton Library, Harvard University)*

"*Oliver* Is an *Impossibility*"
Carlyle's Journal, 25 October 1842

For many months there has been no writing here. Alas! what was there to write? About myself, nothing; or less if that was possible. I have not got one word to stand upon paper in regard to Oliver. The beginnings of work are even more formidable than the executing of it. I seem to myself at present, and for a long while past, to be sunk deep, fifty miles deep, below the region of articulation, and, if I ever rise to speak again, must raise whole continents with me. Some hundreds of times I have felt, and scores of times I have said and written, that *Oliver* is an *impossibility;* yet I am still found at it, without any visible results at all. Remorse, too, for my sinful, disgraceful sloth accompanies me, as it well may. I am, as it were, without a language. Tons of dull books have I read on this matter, and it is still only looming as through thick mists on my eye. There looming, or flaming visible–did it ever flame, which it has never yet been made to do–in what terms am I to set it forth? I wish often I could write rhyme. A new form from centre to surface, unlike what I find anywhere in myself or others, would alone be appropriate for the indescribable chiaroscuro and waste bewilderment of this subject.

–James A. Froude, *Thomas Carlyle: A History of His Life in London, 1834–1881,* v. 1, pp. 279–280

* * *

Amalie Bölte was a German novelist and translator who worked in England as a governess from 1839 to 1851. She met the Carlyles in 1841, and in 1843 Jane helped Bölte find a position in the home of Charles and Isabella Buller. This excerpt is from a letter written in the midst of a London winter marked by "dark dismal fog which we open our eyes upon every morning."

Jane Welsh Carlyle to Amalie Bölte, 23 December 1843

. . . To keep one's soul and body together seems to be quite as much as one is *up to under* the circumstances. I attempt nothing more. As there is nothing which I so much detest as *failure* where I have *willed,* so I take precious care never to will anything as to which I have a presentiment of failing. My husband is more imprudent, he goes on still *willing* to write this *Life of Cromwell* under the most desperate apprehension that it will "never come to anything"–and as if people had the use of their faculties in all states of the atmosphere! And so he does himself a deal of harm and nobody any good. He came into this room the other morning when I was sitting peaceably darning his stockings, and laid a great bundle of papers on my fire, enough to have kindled the chimney, if it had not been, provi-

dentially, swept quite lately–the kindling of a chimney (as you in your German ignorance may perhaps not be aware) subjecting one here in London to the awful visitation of three fire-engines! besides a fine of five pounds! I fancied it the contents of his waste-paper-basket that he was ridding himself of by this summary process. But happening to look up at his face, I saw in its grim concentrated self-complacency the astounding truth, that it was all his labour since he returned from Scotland that had been there sent up the vent, in smoke! "He had discovered over night" he said "that he must take up *the damnable thing* on quite a new tact!" Oh a very *damnable thing* indeed! I tell you in secret, I begin to be seriously afraid that his *Life of Cromwell* is going to have the same strange fate as the child of a certain, French marchioness that I once read of, which never could *get* itself *born,* tho' carried about in her for twenty years till she died! A wit is said to have once asked this poor woman if "Madame was not thinking of swallowing a tutor for her son?" So one might ask Carlyle if he is not thinking of swallowing a publisher for his book? Only that he is too miserable poor fellow without the addition of being laughed at. In lamenting his slow progress, or rather non-progress he said to me one day with a naivete altogether touching, "Well! They may *twaddle* as they like about the miseries of a bad conscience: but I should like to know whether Judas Iscariot was *more* miserable than Thomas Carlyle who never did anything *criminal, so far as he remembers!*" Ah my dear, this is all very amusing to *write* about, but to *transact?* God help us well thro' it!

–*The Last Words of Thomas Carlyle,* pp. 369–371

* * *

These excerpts are from a letter written in response to FitzGerald's letter of 3 January. Carlyle uses the epithet "Dryasdust," borrowed from Sir Walter Scott, to refer to antiquarians and historians without imagination.

Carlyle to Edward FitzGerald, 9 January 1844

Your Letter comes to me in a "good hour,"–makes for me what the French call a *bonheur!* I am sunk in inexpressible confusions; and any kind voice of encouragement is right welcome. Surely if ever I do get this *Book on Cromwell* finished, we will smoke a pipe of triumph over it, and rejoice to remember difficulties undergone! Alas, for the present, I cannot so much as get it begun. . . . It is really something like the *sixth* time, that I have *burnt* considerable masses of written attempts at commencing the unwriteable; and to this hour it remains properly uncommenced. And it must be commenced, and (if God please) finished;–I shall have but a poor time of it otherwise! Let

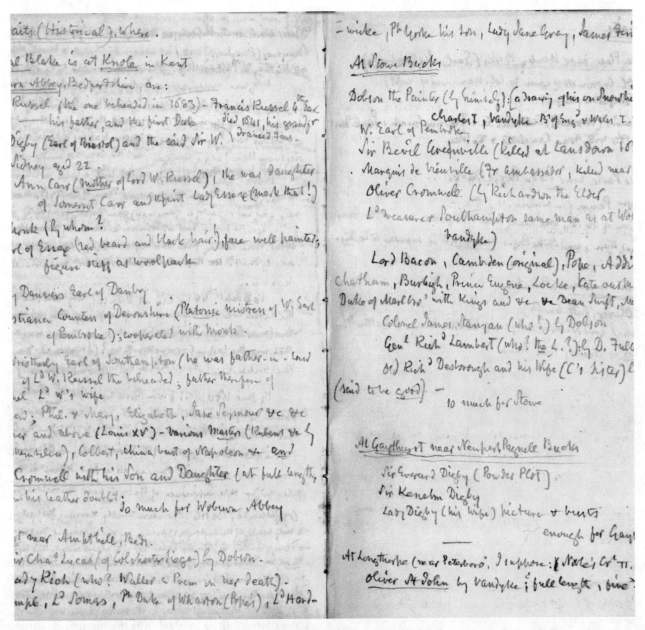

Pages from a notebook Carlyle used in his work on Oliver Cromwell's Letters and Speeches *(Beinecke Rare Book and Manuscript Library, Yale University)*

me be silent; let my next Note to you say: I *am* launched; by the blessing of Heaven, I hope to sail, to arrive! Surely there was no such business as the writing of a Life of Oliver Cromwell for the present race of Englishmen, in the present distracted darkness of the whole subject, ever before laid upon a human sinner?–

One of the things I have at length got to discern as doable is the gathering of all Oliver's Letters and Speeches, and stringing them together according to the order of time: a series of fixed *rock*-summits, in the infinite ocean of froth, confusion, lies and stu-

pidity, which hitherto constitutes the "History" of Cromwell, as Dryasdust has printed it and read it. This I am at present doing;–tho' this is not what I have the real difficulty in doing. I have made considerable progress; Time has eaten up most of Oliver's utterances; but a fraction still remains: these I can and will see printed, set in some kind of order.

–*The Collected Letters of Thomas Carlyle and Jane Welsh Carlyle,* v. 17, p. 233–234

***

Carlyle also enlisted Robert Browning to help him in his research.

Robert Browning to Henry William Field, 14 June 1844

My dear Sir,

Mr Carlyle has commissioned me to say, that he fears he has not succeeded in making you acquainted with his precise object in regard to the *Autograph Letter of Cromwell,* on the subject of which you so kindly communicated with him a few weeks ago: he apprehends you may suppose that his business is with all of the interesting documents, illustrative drawings, &c. which you mention—whereas his only concern is with the letter itself, of which a copy will greatly oblige him; a preeminent feature in the work on which he is engaged, being the number of similar inedited manuscript papers of the Protector, contributed by some of the most distinguished personages in the Country.

He desires me, therefore, to beg on his part that you will have the goodness either to furnish him with an accurate copy of the Letter, or to allow me to call on you, at any time you may appoint, and make one—Mr Carlyle's engagements unfortunately precluding the possibility of his visiting you in person. He will however be happy to see you any morning after 2. p.m.

Pray believe me,
My dear Sir,
Your obedient servant,
Robert Browning.
–The Brownings' Correspondence, v. 9, p. 16

* * *

This excerpt is from a letter written as Carlyle was nearing the end of his work editing Cromwell's papers. The two-volume work was published in November 1845.

Carlyle to Edward FitzGerald, 18 August 1845

Cromwell's own things are now all out of my hands,–the last this very day: but there is a conclusion to do, an Index &c &c: there is still certainly a fortnight's work in the business. You will get the Book to try your hand upon in October (so the Booksellers arrange):–a very tough job of reading; but if you read well, I hope it will shew you more of Cromwell than you have fallen in with hitherto. I reckon it to be like the letting of the Brook upon the Augean Stables; it is meant to tell the whole world what Cromwell is, and move their attention and exertions towards him:–there will be mountains of *dung* swum away in this manner by

and by, and the real face of Oliver's History will at length become apparent to them.

–The Collected Letters of Thomas Carlyle and Jane Welsh Carlyle, v. 19, p. 153

* * *

This excerpt is from an anonymous review.

"An Appeal against the Verdict of History" Review of *Oliver Cromwell's Letters and Speeches*

. . . As to its form, it consists of such Letters and Speeches of Oliver Cromwell as Mr. Carlyle has been able anywhere and anyhow to find–carefully printed and edited with unexampled pains, the whole of them being re-punctuated, re-spelled, re-arranged in sentences and paragraphs, interpolated and illustrated so as to make it next to impossible for the reader to misunderstand their purport, or remain in ignorance of their general relations to historical events. The result is obtained in such perfection as clearly to demonstrate that the labour of obtaining it was indeed a labour of love. It is, moreover, valuable from the consideration that the whole mass of matter, but for this extraordinary manipulation of it, would have been unreadable, since not a single line of it was ever designed for literary publication, much less polite reading; but all is, when properly characterized, dry, hard and technical, as befits records that relate to business and business only, aiming rather at clearness of style than ornament, and hastily expressing itself in the readiest, not the choicest, phrases. The want of attraction in such papers naturally leads to an oblivion of their contents–has led to it in this instance; nor would Mr. Carlyle's merely reprinting them in a correct form have induced their perusal; it is the manner in which he has set them that now makes them lustrous with meaning, so as not only to be available for reference, but actually to be popularly readable as dramatic presentations of a character able and worthy to sway the destinies of an empire.

This is high praise, but it is deserved: there is, however, one drawback to it—one which stands in the way of its dramatic truth—a want of antagonism. We see Cromwell in these pages; but we do not see Charles, save as a mere shadow hovering in the background of events—nay, we scarcely see anybody else. We have the documents about Cromwell at full—more than at full, "with elucidations;" but the other persons of the scene are cut down to mere shreds; even worse—exhibited as shreds in grotesque

"The Whole Matter Simmering in the *Living* Mind"

In this excerpt from a 5 December 1845 letter to his friend Alexander Scott, Carlyle reflected on his approach to writing about Oliver Cromwell.

. . . It has been a work of infinite disgust and hopeless toil; on the whole really a kind of *pious* work,–more like a work of piety than any other I have done. So far as this *is* the case it already has its reward: and for the rest, if the practical English mind do gradually come to understand, and believe as a very fact, that it once had a Hero and Heroism in this man and his work, my poor dry bones of a Compilation may prove to be a better "Poem" than many that go by that name! We will leave it with the Destinies; right glad that we, not entirely disgracefully, have got done with it,–ungainly as it is in these bad days.

You ask me how I proceed in taking Notes on such occasions. I would very gladly tell you all my methods if I had any; but really I have as it were none. I go into the business with all the intelligence, patience, silence and other gifts and virtues that I have; find that ten times or a hundred times as many could be profitably expended there, and still prove insufficient: and as for plan, I find that every new business requires as it were a new scheme of operations, which amid infinite bungling and plunging unfolds itself at intervals (very scantily, after all) as I get along. The great thing is, Not to stop and break down; to know that *virtue* is very indispensable, that one must not stop because new and ever new drafts upon one's virtue must be honoured!–But as to the special point of taking Excerpts, I think I universally, from

habit or otherwise, rather avoid *writing* beyond the very minimum; mark in pencil the very smallest indication that will direct me to the thing again; and on the whole try to keep the whole matter simmering in the *living* mind and memory rather than laid up in paper bundles or otherwise laid up in the inert way. For this certainly turns out to be a truth: Only what you at last *have living* in your own memory and heart is worth putting down to be printed; this alone has much chance to get into the living heart and memory of other men. And here indeed, I believe, is the essence of all the rules I have ever been able to devise for myself. I have tried various schemes of arrangement and artificial helps to remembrance; paper-bags with labels, little paper-books, paper-bundles, etc., etc.: but the use of such things, I take it, depends on the habits and humours of the individual; what can be recommended universally seems to me mainly the above. My paper-bags (filled with little scraps all in pencil) have often enough come to little for me; and indeed in general when writing, I am surrounded with a rubbish of papers that have come to little:–this only will come to much for all of us, To keep the thing you are elaborating as much as possible actually *in* your own living mind; in order that this same mind, as much awake as possible, may have a chance to make something of it!–And so I will shut up my lumber-shop again; and wish you right good speed in yours.

–New Letters of Thomas Carlyle, v. 2, pp. 10–12

---

attitudes, on occasions when, in reality, they made a dignified appearance.

. . . .

Mr. Carlyle speaks with scorn of all (save one) preceding biographers of Cromwell, designating them by names of obloquy. . . . Properly speaking, therefore, Mr. Carlyle's book is an Appeal against the verdict of History; and readers must accordingly form themselves not merely into a grand jury, but into a high court of appeal for hearing it. To do this properly they must consider it in combination with such verdict and its bases. For our own parts, we had, more than a quarter of a century since, and after a careful examination, come to the conclusion that the verdict was pronounced in the absence of evidence which might and should have been produced; and that it must be reversed.

–Athenaeum, no. 945 (6 December 1845): 1165–1167

* * *

These excerpts are from a review by a critic who had previously praised The French Revolution *and* Past and Present.

"Mr Carlyle's Full-Length Figure of Oliver Cromwell"
Review of *Oliver Cromwell's Letters and Speeches*
John Forster

Thinking this book a most important contribution to the history of the greatest event that was ever transacted in England, we hope the earnest study of all thinking men will be given to it. We cannot hope that it will not be very variously judged. We think there are not a few opinions in it which the "Elucidator" himself would not make any obstinate fight for, in a wider battle-field. But we believe it to be without precedent or example as a book of patient, honest, dignified research; as a book of unwearied diligence and labour; and as a manly and high-voiced appeal from the shows and shadows of ignorance and imperfect judgement, to the eternal substance of Truth and History.

. . . .

At what cost of labour this task has been discharged, we suspect few will believe . . . . The plan was, to re-punctuate and re-spell both letters and speeches; to divide them into paragraphs in the modern manner; to add or rectify a word (always indicated by single commas) where the struggling sense required it; in no respect to alter, either the sense or the smallest features in the physiognomy of the original; and in every instance to show, by prefatory illustrative matter, or by dramatic interpolations, the precise relation of the letter or speech to the general history, or its special effect on the immediate and particular occasion, of the time. And with most marvellous minuteness, with most unwearied care and vigilance, with extraordinary spirit and a most life-like effect, this is done with every letter and with every speech. We can imagine no man sustained in such a task but by the strongest sense of duty. To talk of a labour of love in such a case, is absurd. No man could love such labour. We may depend upon it that where the fruits of any particular labour are the most loveable, the labour itself has been the least so.

And much to be admired and loved, we think, in all its main features and proportions, is the Great Figure thus educed for us from the mists and shadows of the Past. Brought back for us with all that could commend him to our human brotherhood. Shown to us in his habit as he lived; with the reality of his human life around him; with his great, robust, massive mind, with his honest, stout, English heart; talking to us, in words often for the first time here articulate and intelligible; becoming again for us the dutiful gentle son, the quiet county gentleman, the tender and sportive husband, the fond father, the active soldier, the daring political leader, the powerful sovereign; still steady and unmoved to the transient outward appearances of This world, still wrestling and trampling forward to the great thought of Another; and passing through every instant of his term of life as through a Marston Moor, a Worcester, or Dunbar. Such is Mr Carlyle's full-length Figure of Oliver Cromwell. No longer with face confused, distorted, or enigmatical; its rough and coarser edges not abated, but softened in the light of sympathy and grateful love; its features dark with the inevitable sadness that besets the greatest deeds that are done in this world, yet lustrous with the manly tenderness which waits upon the doers of such deeds; and the whole of it set forth here, not to amuse an indolent languid hour, but, by its high and noble lessons, to reprove, to teach, and edify us all.

– The Examiner, no. 1976 (13 December 1845): 787–789

* * *

"Full of Sense"

This letter was written by Jane Welsh Carlyle in response to the review that was published in the 13 December 1845 issue of The Examiner.

My dear Mr. Forster,—A woman is constantly getting warned against following 'the impulses of her heart!' Why, I never could imagine! for all the grand blunders I am conscious of having committed in life have resulted from neglecting or gainsaying the impulses of my heart, to follow the insights of my understanding, or, still worse, of other understandings. And so I am now arrived at this with it, that I have flung my understanding to the dogs; and think, do, say, and feel just exactly as nature prompts me. Well, having just finished the reading of your article on 'Cromwell,' nature prompts me to take pen and paper, and tell you that I think it devilishly well done, and quite as meritorious as the book itself; only that there is not so much bulk of it! Now, do not fancy it is my wife-nature that is so excited. I am a bad wife in so far as regards care about what is said of my husband's books in newspapers or elsewhere. I am always so thankful to have them done, and out of the house, that the praise or blame they meet with afterwards is of the utmost insignificance to me. It is not, then, because your article covers him with generous praise that I am so delighted with it; but because it is full of sense, and highmindedness of its own; and most eloquently written. As Mrs. Norton would way, 'I love you for writing it;' only nobody will impute to me a fraudulent use of that word!

My pen—all pens here—refuse to write intelligibly. We are to come home in a fortnight hence, and I hope to see you then.

Ever yours affectionately,
J.C.
Love to the Macreadys.

—Letters and Memorials of Jane Welsh Carlyle, pp. 359–360

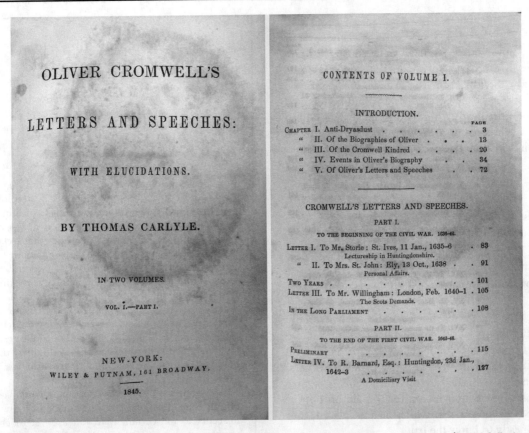

Title page and first page of the table of contents for the first American edition of Carlyle's work on Cromwell (Special Collections, Thomas Cooper Library, University of South Carolina)

These excerpts are from an early American review. "Old Noll" is an epithet applied to Cromwell by his enemies.

"The Sauls from the Davids"
Review of *Oliver Cromwell's Letters and Speeches*

In short we have not time to say all we think, but we stick to the received notions of Old Noll, with his great red nose, hard heart, long head and crafty ambiguities. Nobody ever doubted his great abilities and force of will, neither doubt we that he was made an "Instrument" just as he professeth. But as to looking on him through Mr. Carlyle's glasses we shall not be sneered or stormed into it, unless he has other proof to offer than is shown yet. And we resent the violence he offers both to our prejudices and our perceptions. If he has become interested in Oliver or any other pet hyena, by studying his habits, is that any reason we should admit him to our Pantheon? No! our imbecility shall keep fast the door against any thing, short of proofs that in the Hyena a God is incarnated. Mr. Carlyle declares that he sees it, but we really cannot. The Hyena is surely not out of the kingdom of God, but as to being the finest emblem of what is divine—no! no!

"Counsel for All Men"

This excerpt is from a January 1846 letter written by the American educator Bronson Alcott, who had met Carlyle in England in 1842.

What a noble Book this last of Carlyles for the study of a modern man. I know not if a more commanding word has been spoken by Mortal since Cromwell's time. It is counsel for all men. All my past reading seems languid and pale beside these strenuous and flashing thoughts of Carlyle. It comes quite opportunely too. Cromwell and his Time are admirable studies for us, fierce Republicans as we are; and may help us to see the vast difference between Royal Self-Rule and a Government of Brutes and Clown. His time is a Glass of ours. Our Country is no less charged with Revolt, no less luxuriant the crop of Unbelief. Sorcery and Confusions dire, shooting forth in the Social Hotbed. Our fortunes too seem fearfully forecast in those of the English Commonwealth. What Luther, Cromwell, and the N. England Puritans won for us, has been surrendered already, and there remains for us, (what is even now apparent to all wise men) but to fall asunder. With the recovery and rise of these Principles in Majestic Souls, we may predict the fall of our social Evils....

–The Letters of A. Bronson Alcott, p. 125

· · · · · · · · · ·

We know you do with all your soul love kings and heroes, Mr. Carlyle, but we are not sure you would always know the Sauls from the Davids. We fear, if you had the disposal of the holy oil, you would be tempted to pour it on the head of him who is taller by the head than all his bretheren, without sufficient care as to purity of inward testimony.

–*New York Tribune,* 19 December 1845, p. 1

* * *

These excerpts are from an anonymous Irish review originally titled "Carlyle's Cromwell."

"Edited with Extreme Care"
Review of *Oliver Cromwell's Letters and Speeches*

. . . One great good, however, the book assuredly will do,–the theory of Cromwell's hypocrisy must, we think, be for ever discarded. Self-deception, as with all men, is busy with him–with him less than with others, as we think it established by the documents now produced by his new commentator, that he did his best to understand the position in which he was placed, and sought honestly to know the truth.

· · · · · · · · · ·

But whatever view may be taken of the Civil Wars of England–and the contest will, of course, be still viewed with the party biasses of each person who examines the subject–it will be from henceforth impossible to disregard the letters and speeches of Cromwell himself. Let us differ, or let us agree with him, here are his own letters and speeches–every one letter a business-letter–every one speech a business-speech–most of them being not after-written statements of facts, but letters and speeches, themselves constituting very material parts of the transactions on which they throw light. Hitherto these have been, for the most part, disregarded, the feeling of Cromwell's hypocrisy having been so engrafted on the minds of the historians who have written of his times, that these, the most important records of a period of perhaps unexampled interest, have been neglected.

This never again can be their fate. Of modern writers, Mr. Forster alone seems to have at all approached to an appreciation of their true value. They are now edited with extreme care. All authentic information calculated to illustrate them, that diligent study could glean from existing memoirs of the time, is supplied; and it appears to us certain, that where they are inconsistent with received views, such views must be

Ireland and "the *Truth* about Oliver Cromwell"

In this excerpt from his 19 February 1848 letter to his friend Charles Gavin Duffy, Carlyle responds to a review that he mistakenly believed Duffy had written. John Mitchel, the actual author of the review, was an Irish nationalist who admired Carlyle but was critical of his understanding of Ireland.

We read your review of *Cromwell* in the *Nation* last week; and could not but pronounce it heroic! The pain you were to get by these remarks of mine was very present to me while I wrote; but it was not to be avoided. I do deliberately consider that Ireland is actually called upon to know the *truth* about Oliver Cromwell; that it for the present does not at all know the truth about him, and about the meaning of him,–and ought, the sooner the better, to know it. That you, across such a mahlstrom of Irish indignation, have nevertheless discerned for yourself that the man was a Hero, full of Manhood, Earnestness, and Valour,–this, I think, is the creditablest thing I have yet known of you, and to me also is a very great satisfaction. Depend upon it, such a man, wherever he goes in God's Creation, means *good* and not ill! Alas, Alas, that is a long crabbed chapter: but it seems to me certain that you are yet to change your views in regard to many matters in that province and what depends on it. For example, how would you like if, after all these denunciations by such witnesses as Clarendon, Carte &c who had no kind of chance to know about the matter, it should turn out to be the actual God's Fact that Cromwell did not in any respect depart from the established rules of War while in Ireland; did not as he himself says (in a Paper I have lately got within reach of) "sanction or order the death of any one not found in arms?" I believe you would like very ill to be found defending what *is not,* even with all Ireland, England, and Scotland joining chorus with you!

My surmise is, that this will yet turn out to be the acknowledged fact: evidence to the contrary I must say I have yet found none that seems at all conclusive;–and if you will give me a list of the witnesses to the fact, I will actually go again to the Museum and do my best to sift the truth out of them. But alas there is no fact at all about the History of Cromwell that I have been able to satisfy myself about but I had first of all to bid an insane shrieking whirlwind of exasperated and astonished witnessers, "Be silent you, till we see!"–I have taken down your Authorities from the *Nation;* pray give more if you have them.

–The Collected Letters of Thomas Carlyle and Jane Welsh Carlyle, v. 20, pp. 103–106

modified, not alone with reference to the facts contained or implied in these letters and speeches, but that henceforth Cromwell must be regarded as a plain-spoken, strait-forward man—in his habitual feelings, and affections kindly—and who, in peaceful times, in which the relations of society were not disturbed, would have been a man singularly happy, as in every existing record of his domestic life, he seems to have taken a sensible view of all that related to others as well as to himself. To have removed from his portrait, much that disfigured and marred its true expression, was a task well worth undertaking; and, on the whole, we regard Mr. Carlyle as very successful in his generous enterprise.

–*Dublin University Magazine,*
27 (February 1846): 228–245

* * *

These excerpts are from a long review in which the critic asserts that the view which Carlyle's book "presents of the character of Cromwell is, we think, on the whole, the most satisfactory in our language." But he does not regard such an estimate to be high praise, going on to claim that the "faults of the work before us are as material as its excellences." Robert Vaughn was a Congregationalist minister and author who founded the British Quarterly Review *and served as its editor from February 1845 to October 1865.*

"Too Much the Art of Speechmaking"
Review of *Oliver Cromwell's Letters and Speeches*
Robert Vaughn

. . . History has not another subject making so large a demand on the capacity of the historian to distinguish between rumor and fact—between lies and the truth. Mr. Carlyle gives little credence to the royalist authors who sent forth their lucubrations after the blessed year 1660; nor does he confide in everything said at an earlier period by parties who claim to be honoured as persons governed by strict religious principle, or by a stern Roman virtue. We think he is quite right in being so far suspicious of these people. He has considered their means of knowledge, and their temptations to falsehood, and he has judged of them accordingly.

It is a defect, however, that we have not been informed more distinctly of the grounds of his decision in some cases. But the cause of this deficiency is the cause of defects in this form, and in many more, in all Mr. Carlyle's later productions. We have spoken of him as a gentleman who would fain float on over the sea of literature in the sullen majesty of a Dreadnought. But there is one fear with which this author is beset more

than almost any man in the world of letters—the fear of being dull. . . . Hence, in history, the labours of our Author have been always a piecemeal business. He has rarely given you anything beyond outline; even that being often left incomplete. Your detention longer in one direction, it is thought, might be fatal to your patience; and your want of information is a small matter, compared with your want of wakefulness. With all his independence, Mr. Carlyle has shown, in this respect, a most praiseworthy consideration of the weakness of our degenerate times. The mischief is, that from this cause, his histories always need to be read along with other histories. They are generally obscure, sometimes wholly unmeaning, if taken alone. What man who has not read the history of the French Revolution elsewhere, could possible understand the book which Mr. Carlyle has published under that name, and further described as a 'History?' Who among us could tell what to receive and what to reject in the history of modern Europe, if that history had been always written with the contempt of authorities and of completeness observable in that work? In history we want vivacity, but we also want fullness—the whole truth. We want vigour, but we cannot dispense with proofs. The French historians have known how to unite these advantages. But to this object the genius of Mr. Carlyle appears to have been unequal. He has had to make his choice, and, as the result, history in his hands has become too much the art of speechmaking. Men of intelligence read such productions, not with the expectation of being safely instructed on the subject to which they relate, but for the sake of the things which a capricious but clever man may be expected to bring to such a topic.

. . . .

In nearly all respects, the estimate of the character of Cromwell published twenty years since by Mr. Macaulay, is fully as independent, honourable, and just, as this now published by Mr. Carlyle. But in one respect we give the precedence greatly to Mr. Carlyle's portraiture. He does justice to the religion of Cromwell. His philosophy, if not always based on the clearest and the most comprehensive logic, is, in this instance, pregnant with candour, and with sound feeling. We may question his maxim—that a truly great man can be neither hypocrite nor liar. But we fully participate in his manly scorn of those narrow-headed and narrow-hearted persons, who can see nothing better than cant, fanaticism, and 'besotted superstition,' in the apparent piety of this great captain. Here the most well-meaning of Cromwell's judges have commonly broken down. They have been able to explain many things which needed explanation; but to suppose that the language in which he expressed himself in respect to his faith and feeling as a Christian, was that of a sincere truth-speaking man, has been their great difficulty. This perplexity, however, will not be greatly felt by men who have hearts as well as heads. Men who have known what that puritanism really is, of which Cromwell was the high-souled embodiment, can believe him to the last, when he tells them of his trust in God as nerving his arm in the day of battle, and of his hope, in respect to a future world as being his master hope, even while striving so mightily to give a better adjustment to the affairs of the present. Mr. Carlyle has knowledge enough of the man Cromwell, and of the thing Puritanism, and of the susceptibilities of his own lofty and earnest spirit, to give his hero full credit of integrity in his professed religious feeling. It is this feature of the work before us which is to us its great charm.

–British Quarterly Review, 3 (1 February 1846): 52–53, 60–61

* * *

In this thirty-nine-page article, from which this excerpt is drawn, the reviewer observes that for Carlyle Cromwell is "his man of men—his hero: and every other character comes in for a share of censure and disparagement, as it diverges from that exclusive standard."

"Two Remarkable Minds"
Review of *Oliver Cromwell's Letters and Speeches*
John J. Taylor

. . . Intermingled with the historical illustration, are reflections by the Elucidator—deeply impregnated with his own strong individuality, often original, and almost always worth the trouble of thoughtful consideration. One of the most interesting features of the work, is this juxtaposition, as it were, of two remarkable minds—one, after the interval of two centuries, and in a very different moral atmosphere, interpreting the other—the recluse and meditative student of the 19th century, wide-read in literature, and nursed in the high speculations of German philosophy, looking out from his 'high lonely tower' with warm enthusiasm on the ancient battlefield of England, to explain and justify the movements of the man of action, who once reduced it under him by the might of his arm and the terror of his name.—What we least like in the Editor's execution of his task, is the constant interpolation of his own sentiments in the course of Cromwell's speeches—violently breaking off the natural connection of ideas, forestalling the reader's judgment, and—as if he were afraid of the result—not allowing the speech to produce its own impression. We acknowledge with admiration Mr. Carlyle's genius; but he uses largely the chartered license of his order.

We must, however, notice one capital excellence in his book—the scrupulous fidelity with which he has discharged the duties of editor and historian. No consciousness of genius has exempted him from the responsibilities of laborious research and minute accuracy. Where truth was concerned—where a fact had to be established—he has not deemed the fixing of a single date beneath his care. Nothing indeed is more remarkable in these volumes, than the union of hard, dry, scholarlike industry—such as Strype or Birch need not have been ashamed of—with a keen observant eye for all that is curious and striking in actual life, and a rich exuberance of poetical feeling, which—perhaps after some discussion of authorities or collation of dates, implying infinitely more toil than is displayed—flows over unexpectedly in a strain of impassioned, enthusiasm or deep spiritual earnestness worthy of Novalis or Jean Paul.

–Prospective Review, 2 (February 1846): 126–127

* * *

These excerpts are from a seventy-two-page review in which James B. Mozley criticizes Carlyle's conception of the hero: "Mr. Carlyle's idea of the hero is a simple one. He lays down, as essential, one great characteristic, and one only. That characteristic is power." A member of the Oxford Movement, Mozley served as an editor of the Christian Remembrancer from 1844 until 1855.

"Cromwell's Dog"
Review of *Oliver Cromwell's Letters and Speeches*
James B. Mozley

. . . The Puritans are under no obligation to Mr. Carlyle, for his portrait. He makes them majestic. But they were not majestic. They were not majestic, and they cannot be made so either by Mr. Carlyle or by anyone else. They were fierce, courageous, enthusiastic, rigid men; very awkward, longwinded, and pompous; with a grimness and solemnity of an absurd cast. They affected sublimity, obtruded religion, made free with Scripture, and spoke through their noses. They were tremendous on the field of battle, ridiculous out of it. As some poets are only striking when they horrify, the Puritans were only awful when they were charging. They depended on the drawn swords, the black moving columns, and all the terrible iron features of a field of battle, for what greatness they had. So long as they speak, or move, or look, only as soldiers, their stern courage befriends them, and they allow a hard and insipid greatness; but take their character out of its iron case, and it shows its weakness; it cannot express itself upon open ground, without exposing itself; and it runs into contortions, nodosities, and grimaces. Such is the image of Puritanism which authentic accounts have handed down. The party have managed, as a matter of fact, to get themselves permanently laughed at. They have allowed an absurd portrait to come down to us. National tradition has settled their character; and the author of Hudibras and Sir Walter Scott are felt to speak with authority.

The Puritans therefore do not wear their grandeur to much purpose in Mr. Carlyle's pages. Their sublimity sits awkwardly upon them. He is obviously putting a dress on them, and dramatizing them. He is obviously vapouring and spouting. A bombastic struggle with fact pervades his descriptions; and he has to resist throughout, the uniform tradition of two centuries. He is aware of his difficulty: and he complains and remonstrates. An old established joke annoys him at every turn. He wages a perpetual war with 'derisive epithets'. He has perpetually to be saying—you must not laugh at my heroes.

. . . .

Mr. Carlyle has a very simple answer to the question, whether Cromwell was a hypocrite or not; one much more simple, in our opinion, than acute. He has the most unbounded, impetuous, jubilant confidence in him; he enjoys the undisturbed luxury of infantine security and primaeval faith, with respect to his biographical subject matter. Whatever Cromwell does is great, pure, splendid; if Cromwell does it that is enough: it springs from the depths and the eternities: not a breath must be heard, not a look endured, against it. Whatever Cromwell has done, is doing, or may be about to do, must all be submissively swallowed; and the reader must have a positive belief in him, as if he were some divine principle out of which nothing but what was admirable could proceed. Whatever shape it assumes, the divine reality is the same; and all the issues of the ever involving problem simply present themselves to be admitted, upon a law of mathematical necessity. The biographer attends obsequiously on his hero, and changes as he changes. When Cromwell thought a thing, it was right; when he ceases to think it, it is not right. Mr. Carlyle has an unqualified contempt for ceremonial so long as Cromwell is a plain republican; but when Cromwell has state coaches, lifeguards, lacqueys, and pages, Mr. Carlyle has then a word to say for 'due ceremonial and decent observance.' A dirty shirt was heroic when Cromwell wore one: a gold hatband and velvet are not unheroic when Cromwell becomes a neat dresser. . . . He does not explain these variations; the one fact of Cromwell explains all. With an overbearing and somewhat childish exultation he brandishes his fact; he thrusts his idol on our captured worship; he glories in a bravo demonstration of force, and rides triumphantly in the wake of the great man to

whom he has appended himself. He attaches himself to his hero like an affectionate but unreasoning animal. And Cromwell's dog, if the Lord Protector kept such a companion, never looked in his face more wistfully or licked his hand more confidingly, gambolled about him more exuberantly, than his biographer, in mind, does. He will hear no inferences, believe no facts against his hero: he will not say, why he will not hear, and why he will not believe. He has no reason. He is contented, he rejoices, he is delighted at having none. He is proud of being unreasonable; and having the O.C. instinct pure and unalloyed within him. Such is Mr. Carlyle's treatment of the question of Cromwell's character.

—*Christian Remembrancer,* 11 (April 1846): 244, 258–259, 302–303

* * *

One American who was not pleased by Carlyle's work was the poet and short-story writer Edgar Allan Poe. He wrote this note on the author in his "Marginalia" column.

"Rant and Cant"
An Assessment of Carlyle
Edgar Allan Poe

I have not the slightest faith in Carlyle. In ten years—possibly in five—he will be remembered only as a butt for sarcasm. His linguistic Euphuisms might very well have been taken as *prima facie* evidence of his philosophic ones; they were the froth which indicated, first, the shallowness, and secondly, the confusion of the waters. I would blame no man of sense for leaving the works of Carlyle unread, merely on account of these Euphuisms; for it might be shown *à priori,* that no man capable of producing a definite impression upon his age or race, could or would commit himself to such inanities and insanities. The hook about "Hero-Worship"—is it possible that it ever excited a feeling beyond contempt? *No* hero-worshipper can possess anything within himself. That man is no man, who stands in awe of his fellowman. Genius regards genius with respect—with even enthusiastic admiration—but there is nothing of worship in the admiration, for it springs from a thorough cognizance of the one admired—from a perfect *sympathy,* the result of this cognizance; and it is needless to say, that sympathy and worship are antagonistic. Your hero-worshippers—your Shakspeare worshippers, for example—what do they know about Shakspeare? They worship him—rant about him—lecture about him—about *him, him,* and nothing else—for no other reason than that he is utterly beyond their comprehension. They have arrived at the idea of his greatness from the pertinacity with which men have called him great. As for their own opinion about him—they really have none at all. In general, the very smallest of mankind are the class of men-worshippers. *Not one* out of this class has ever accomplished anything beyond a very contemptible mediocrity.

Carlyle, however, has rendered an important service (to posterity, at least) in pushing rant and cant to that degree of excess which inevitably induces reaction. Had he not appeared, we might have gone on for yet another century, Emerson-izing in prose, Wordsworth-izing in poetry, and Fourier-izing in philosophy, Wilson-izing in criticism–Hudson-izing and Tom O'Bedlam-izing in everything. The author of the "Sartor Resartus," however, has overthrown the various arguments of his own order, by a personal *reductio ad absurdum.* Yet an Olympiad, perhaps, and the whole horde will be swept bodily from the memory of man–or be remembered only when we have occasion to talk of such fantastic tricks as erewhile, were performed by the Abderites.

–*Democratic Review,* 18 (April 1846): 271

* * *

This excerpt is from a sixty-six-page anonymous Irish review originally titled "The Great Irish Insurrection."

"The Cromwelliad"
Review of *Oliver Cromwell's Letters and Speeches*

Mr. Carlyle admits that his is "one other dull book added to the thousand, dull every one of them which have been issued on this subject, and that the very sound of Puritanism has become tedious as a tale of past stupidities." He may have merely uttered this in the excess of his modesty, but we can assure him that it is a sober truth, at least as far as his own book is concerned. That he has been able to strip the most eventful period of our history of all interest, is a wonderful and original triumph of the genius of Carlylism. His two great volumes are in fact an interminable sermon, written in the most approved cant of methodism, and addressed–nay, stare not gentle reader, for we use Mr. Carlyle's own words–addressed, we say, to *serious readers.* Take the following as a very favourable specimen of the style, manner, and matter of the book.

> "These authentic utterances of the *man* Oliver himself, I have gathered *them* far and near; fished them up from the foul Lethean quagmire where they lay buried; I have washed or endeavoured to wash them clean from foreign stupidities, (such a job of brick-washing as I do not long to repeat,) and the world shall now see them in their own shape. Working for long years in these *unspeakable* historic provinces of which the *reader has already had account,* it becomes more apparent to one that *this man* Oliver Cromwell was, as the popular fancy represents him, the soul of

the Puritanic Revolt, without whom it had never been a revolt transcendently memorable, and an epoch in the world's History; that, in fact, he, more than is common in such cases, does deserve to give his name to the period in question, and have the Puritan revolt considered as a *Cromwelliad,* which issue is very visible for it. . . . . May it prosper with a *few serious readers.*"

We have had heretofore the Luciad, the Henriad, and the Dunciad, and now, to draw up the rear of all the ads, we have got the Cromwelliad. It is not written like the other "ads" in heroics, but in plain though by no means unassuming prose, and is indeed as prosy a book as ever was penned even by Mr. Carlyle. . . . There is scarcely a page in the book in which he does not tax his reader's faith to believe some absurd paradox, which, according to Mr. Carlyle, constitutes *a part of the eternal soul of things.* We get no more information from him about this very untangible commodity, the eternal soul of things, than that the ranters, persecutors, murderers and hypocrites of the seventeenth century, formed part of it. He talks of God-worship which, saving your presence, is Puritanism, and of Devil-worship which is the gentle name he gives to the faith of all the rest of the world in the seventeenth century, and of all the world at present without any exceptions whatever. If you reply that you see in this people nothing but bigotry, hypocrisy, fanaticism, and cruelty, he pities you because you do not understand the *eternal harmonies* and the *eternal laws* which governed the Puritans. When a man gets into his gas balloon, and talks to us from the clouds about eternal laws and everlasting harmonies, we wait quietly until he descends, and then we ask him what he thinks of the practice of cutting throats and picking pockets. Carlyle's style is, in fact, in literature, what Puritanism was in religion–a madness, an imposture, or at best a senseless fanaticism; and hence it is scarcely wonderful that he should commit the extravagance of making the Roundheads heroes, and idolatry of worshipping Cromwell. He laments most pathetically that all heroism has left the earth; but if the Covenanters and Puritans were heroes, the "want of a hero is certainly a most uncommon want." He could surely supply himself with a real live hero in the Rotundo or Exeter Hall. What would he think of a new prose epic called the M'Nelliad or Plumtreiad? They have all the essential characteristics of his heroes; they are bigoted, intolerant, and quote the Old Testament instead of the Gospel. . . . Heroes of this kind have unfortunately been very common in the world; there are vast numbers of them still to be found amongst the eveangelical swaddlers, methodists, and convenanters, and Mr. Carlyle need not fear that the species shall become extinct so long as hatred of truth, hypocrisy, and avarice, reign in the hearts of men. Our chief complaint is, not that he applauds the miserable and detestable cant of the Puritans, that he idolizes Cromwell, who, if he be a hypocrite–and what rea-

Margaret Fuller's Impressions of Carlyle

Margaret Fuller visited the Carlyles in November and December of 1846. These descriptions, written for Ralph Waldo Emerson, were included in her posthumously published memoirs.

Of the people I saw in London, you will wish me to speak first of the Carlyles. Mr. C. came to see me at once, and appointed an evening to be passed at their house. That first time, I was delighted with him. He was in a very sweet humor,–full of wit and pathos, without being overbearing or oppressive. I was quite carried away with the rich flow of his discourse; and the hearty, noble earnestness of his personal being brought back the charm which once was upon his writing, before I wearied of it. I admired his Scotch, his way of singing his great full sentences, so that each one was like the stanza of a narrative ballad. He let me talk, now and then, enough to free my lungs and change my position, so that I did not get tired. That evening, he talked of the present state of things in England, giving light, witty sketches of the men of the day, fanatics and others, and some sweet, homely stories he told of things he had known of the Scotch peasantry. Of you he spoke with hearty kindness; and he told, with beautiful feeling, a story of some poor farmer, or artisan, in the country, who on Sunday lays aside that cark and care of that dirty English world, and sits reading the Essays, and looking upon the sea.

I left him that night, intending to go out very often to their house. I assure you there never was anything so witty as Carlyle's description of — —. It was enough to kill one with laughing. I, on my side, contributed a story to his fund of anecdote on this subject, and it was fully appreciated. Carlyle is worth a thousand of you for that;–he is not ashamed to laugh, when he is amused, but goes on in a cordial human fashion.

Fuller later writes of attending a dinner party at the Carlyles' home.

For a couple of hours, he was talking about poetry, and the whole harangue was one eloquent proclamation of the defects in his own mind. Tennyson wrote in verse because the schoolmasters had taught him that it was great to do so, and had thus, unfortunately, been turned from the true path for a man. Burns had, in like manner, been turned from his vocation. Shakspeare had not the good sense to see that it would have been better to write straight on in prose;–and such nonsense, which, though amusing enough at first, he ran to death after a while.

The most amusing part is always when he comes back to some refrain, as in the French Revolution of the sea-green. In this instance, it was Petrarch and *Laura,* the last word pronounced with his ineffable sarcasm of drawl. Although he said this over fifty times, I could not ever help laughing when *Laura* would come,–Carlyle running his chin out, when he spoke it, and his eyes glancing till they looked like the eyes and beak of a bird of prey. Poor Laura! Lucky for her that her poet had already got her safely canonized beyond the reach of this Teufelsdrockh vulture.

. . . .

I had, afterward, some talk with Mrs. C., whom hitherto I had only seen, for who can speak while her husband is there? I like her very much;–she is full of grace, sweetness, and talent. Her eyes are sad and charming.

. . . .

Paris, Dec., 1846.–Carlyle allows no one a chance, but bears down all opposition, not only by his wit and onset of words, resistless in their sharpness as so many bayonets, but by actual physical superiority,–raising his voice, and rushing on his opponent with a torrent of sound. This is not in the least from unwillingness to allow freedom to others. On the contrary, no man would more enjoy a manly resistance to his thought. But it is the habit of a mind accustomed to follow out its own impulse, as the hawk its prey, and which knows not how to stop in the chase. Carlyle, indeed, is arrogant and overbearing; but in his arrogance there is no littleness,–no self-love. It is the heroic arrogance of some old Scandinavian conqueror;–it is his nature, and the untamable energy that had given him power to crush the dragons. You do not love him, perhaps, not revere; and perhaps, also, he would only laugh at you if you did; but you like him heartily, and like to see him the powerful smith, the Siegfried, melting all the old iron in his furnace till it glows to a sunset red, and burns you, if you senselessly go too near. He seems, to me, quite isolated,–lovely as the desert,–yet never was a man more fitted to prize a man, could he find one to match his mood. He finds them, but only in the past.

–Memoirs of Margaret Fuller Ossoli,
v. 2, pp. 184–189

sonable man can doubt it–must have been the most detestable of mankind, and if he were sincere must have been possessed by the devil; it is not that he praises the convenanters so long as they assist Oliver, but when perceiving his designs of usurpation they oppose him, he can afford them no better names than *red-nosed presbyterians full of brandy and presbyterian texts of scripture;* but that he sighs for

the return of those times whose faith was the most abominable hypocrisy and the most diabolical bigotry, and whose works were the wholesale robbery, plunder, and murder of their neighbours.

–Dublin Review, 21 (September 1846): 66–69

* * *

These excerpts are from a two-part article published in March and April 1847 on Carlyle and his Works *by Henry David Thoreau, who had yet to publish his first book.*

"Bread of Life"
An Assessment of Carlyle's Writings
Henry David Thoreau

He is, in fact, the best tempered, and not the least impartial of reviewers. He goes out of his way to do justice to profligates and quacks. There is somewhat even Christian, in the rarest and most peculiar sense, in his universal brotherliness, his simple, child-like endurance, and earnest, honest endeavor, with sympathy for the like. And this fact is not insignificant, that he is almost the only writer of biography, of the lives of men in modern times. So kind and generous a tribute to the genius of Burns cannot be expected again, and is not needed. We honor him for his noble reverence for Luther, and his patient, almost reverent study of Goethe's genius, anxious that no shadow of his author's meaning escape him for want of trustful attention. . . .

Carlyle, to adopt his own classification, is himself the hero, as literary man. There is no more notable working-man in England, in Manchester or Birmingham, or the mines round about. We know not how many hours a-day he toils, nor for what wages, exactly, we only know the results for us. We hear through the London fog and smoke the steady systole, diastole, and vibratory hum, from "Somebody's Works" there; the "Print Works" say some; the "Chemicals," say others; where something at any rate, is manufactured which we remember to have seen in the market. This is the place, then. Literature has come to mean, to the ears of laboring men, something idle, something cunning and pretty merely, because the nine hundred and ninety-nine really write for fame or for amusement. But as the laborer works, and soberly by the sweat of his brow earns bread for his body, so this man *works* anxiously and *sadly,* to get bread of life, and dispense it.

. . . .

Not withstanding the very genuine, admirable, and loyal tributes to Burns, Schiller, Goethe, and others, Carlyle is not a critic of poetry. In the book of heroes, Shakspeare, the hero as poet, comes off rather slimly. His sympathy, as we said, is with the man of endeavor, not using the life got, but still bravely getting their life. "In fact," as he says of Cromwell, "every where we have to notice the decisive, practical *eye* of this man; how he drives toward the practical and practicable: has a genuine insight into what *is* fact." You must have very stout legs to get noticed at all by him. . . .

What he says of poetry is rapidly uttered and suggestive of a thought, rather than the deliberate development of any. He answers your question, What is poetry? By writing a special poem, as that Norse one, for instance, in the Book of Heroes, altogether wild and original;—answers your question, What is light? By kindling a blaze which dazzles you, and pales sun and moon, and not as a peasant might, by opening a shutter. And, certainly you would say that this question never could be answered but by the grandest of poems; yet he has not dull breath and stupidity enough, perhaps, to give the most deliberate and universal answer, such as the fates wring from illiterate and unthinking men. He answers like Thor, with a stroke of his hammer, whose dint makes a valley in the earth's surface.

Carlyle is not a *seer,* but a brave looker-on and reviewer; not the most free and catholic observer of men and events, for they are likely to find him preoccupied, but unexpectedly free and catholic when they fall within the focus of his lens. He does not live in the present hour, and read men and books as they occur for his theme, but having chosen this, he directs his studies to this end.

. . . .

Carlyle speaks of Nature with a certain unconscious pathos for the most part. She is to him a receded but ever memorable splendor, casting still a reflected light over all his scenery. As we read his books here in New England, where there are potatoes enough, and every man can get his living peacefully and sportively as the birds and bees, and need think no more of that, it seems to us as if by the world he often meant London, at the head of the tide upon the Thames, the sorest place on the face of the

---

"More Character than Intellect"

This observation is from Emerson's journal in 1847.

In Carlyle as in Byron, one is more struck with the rhetoric than with the matter. He has manly superiority rather than intellectuality, & so makes good hard hits all the time. There is more character than intellect in every sentence. Herein strongly resembling Samuel Johnson.

—Journals and Miscellaneous Notebooks of Ralph Waldo Emerson, v. 10, p. 78

Robert and Elizabeth Barrett Browning, 1861, photographs owned by the Carlyles (Columbia University Rare Book and Manuscript Library)

earth, the very citadel of conservatism. Possibly a South African village might have furnished a more hopeful and more exacting audience, or in the silence of the wilderness and the desert, he might have addressed himself more entirely to his true audience posterity.

In his writings, we should say that he as conspicuously as any, though with little enough expressed or even conscious sympathy, represents the Reformer class, and all the better for not being the acknowledged leader of any. In him the universal plaint is most settled, unappeasable and serious. Until a thousand named and nameless grievances are righted, there will be no repose for him in the lap of nature, or the seclusion of science and literature. By foreseeing it he hastens the crisis in the affairs of England, and is as good as many years added to her history.

—*Graham's Magazine*, 30 (April 1847): 238, 239, 240

Congratulations to the Brownings

This excerpt is from Carlyle's 23 June 1847 letter to Robert Browning.

Many thanks for your Italian Letter; which dropped in, by the Penny Post, with right good welcome, like a friendly neighbor, some week or two ago. I am right glad to hear of your welfare; your's and your fair Partner's. No marriage has taken place, within my circle, these many years, in which I could so heartily rejoice. You I had known, and judged of; her too, conclusively enough, if less directly; and certainly if ever there was a union indicated by the finger of Heaven itself, and sanctioned and prescribed by the Eternal Laws under which poor transitory Sons of Adam live, it seemed to me, from all I could hear or know of it, to be this! Courage, therefore; follow piously the Heavenly Omens, and fear not.

—*The Collected Letters of Thomas and Jane Welsh Carlyle*, v. 14, pp. 239

The Squire Papers Controversy: "The First Most Flagrant Dupe"

While Carlyle was preparing the third edition of Oliver Cromwell's Letters and Speeches *in 1847, he was contacted by William Squire, who claimed descent from a man who served under Cromwell. Squire purported to possess a journal that included letters by Cromwell. Carlyle received a favorable report on Squire from Edward FitzGerald, whom he had asked to investigate the claim. When Carlyle facilitated the publication of the letters in* Fraser's Magazine *in December 1847, questions about their authenticity immediately arose. Carlyle affirmed the legitimacy of the letters—which many years later were proven to be forgeries—and included them in the third edition of his work, published in 1850.*

This excerpt is from a long letter in which FitzGerald reported his impressions of Squire.

Edward FitzGerald to Carlyle, 29 June 1847

Last week I went over to Yarmouth and saw Squire. I was prepared, and I think you were, to find a quaint old gentleman of the last century. Alas for guesses at History! I found a wholesome, well-grown, florid, clear-eyed, open-browed, man of about my own age! There was no difficulty at all in coming to the subject at once, and tackling it. Squire is, I think, a straightforward, choleric, ingenious fellow—a little mad—cracks away at his family affairs. "One brother is a rascal—and another a spend-thrift—his father was of amazing size—a prodigious eater, etc.—the family all gone to *smithers*," etc. I liked Squire well: and told him he must go to you; I am sure you will like him better than the London penny-a-liners. He is rather a study: and besides he can tell you bits of his Ancestor's journal; which will indeed make you tear your hair for what is burned—Between two and three hundred folio pages of MSS. by a fellow who served under Oliver; been sent on secret service by him; dreaded him: but could not help serving him. Squire told me a few circumstances which he had picked up in running over the Journal before he burnt it; and which you ought to hear from himself before long.
— *The Letters of Edward FitzGerald,* v. 1, pp. 563–565

* * *

These excerpts are from an article commenting on the newly discovered letters—"Thirty-five Unpublished Letters of Oliver Cromwell. Communicated by Thomas Car-lyle to Fraser's Magazine*"—which appeared six weeks after the letters were first published. Although the authorship of the article was unacknowledged, it is known that it was written by Carlyle and John Forster. The authors early on maintain that Carlyle himself "is neither forger, nor abettor of forgery. He is the first most flagrant dupe, if any imposition has been practised." William Squire, not identified, is described as "a worthy and honourable gentleman, whom we shall call A. B.," who inherited certain "family peculiarities."*

"The Question of Authenticity"

. . . Then came into light those dreary dark old papers of which mention has been made.

They proved to be a journal, interspersed with letters of Cromwell and others, but mostly written by one Samuel Squire, a subaltern in the famed Regiment of Ironsides, who belonged to the "Stilton Troup," and had served with Oliver from the first mount of that indomitable corps, as cornet, and then as auditor. . . .

Here was a discovery indeed! Yet was it natural that A. B., being as we have described him, should straightway hand it over without condition or questioning to the collector of Cromwell's letters? We think not. We find what he really did to be in no respect surprising. He broke ground by sending a fact obtained from the journal, of which Mr. Carlyle had proclaimed himself much in need; and then "in simple, rugged, and trustworthy, though rather peculiar dialect" (a "little astonished to find that Oliver Cromwell was actually not a miscreant, hypocrite, &c., as heretofore represented") related what he was in possession of. For the correspondence that followed, the reader must go to Mr Carlyle's statement. It is all very credible to us, very natural, and very lamentable; but extremely difficult to tell. Given the earnest, eager, passionate Cromwell worshipper and champion, on the one hand,—and the conscientious, honest, single-hearted, but strangely shadow-hunted A. B., with what Mr Carlyle would call his fatuous mysteries, fatuous vandalisms, and general half-mad procedure, on the other,—nor can we well see how the affair was to issue in any better result. This result was what we may call, on A. B.'s part, an honourable capitulation or compromise. Unable wholly to reject what had been for centuries a family religion, as little able utterly to reject Mr Carlyle's claim to a sort of property in what remained of Cromwell, he resolved scrupulously to copy whatever letters written by the latter he could find in his ancestor's journal, whatever brief notes by his ancestor were needed to explain them, and then destroy journal, letters, and all. The over-tremulous are often, for that reason,

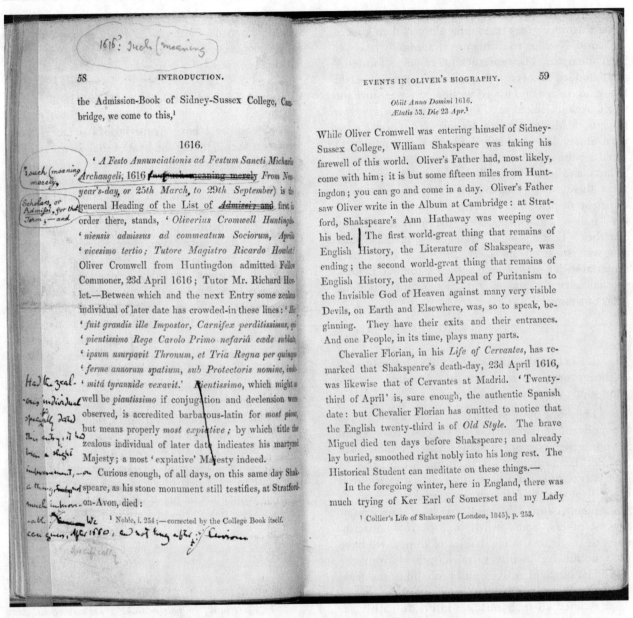

Pages from Carlyle's copy of the third English edition of Oliver Cromwell's Letters and Speeches, *which he was annotating to prepare for a subsequent edition (Beinecke Rare Book and Manuscript Library, Yale University)*

also the over-resolute; and A. B. carried out his terrible "sacrificial" resolve. The letters, invaluable as mere autograph; the journal of which they were a part, perhaps the most precious fragment saved from the wreck of the greatest period of our English History; perished. Copies of thirty-five masterly and most life-like letters of Cromwell were sent to Mr Carlyle in one packet, with accompanying intimation that the originals were reduced to ashes. Vain was all passionate clamour for them. They were gone.

. . . .

Now to the question of authenticity. We will preface what we have to offer with the remark, that if, instead of receiving these letters with the warrant of Mr. Carlyle's belief in them, we had picked them up in the street, it would not have occurred to us to doubt them. We take the internal evidence in their favour to be decisive. They prove themselves, we think; to any man of unclouded apprehension, and competent acquaintance with the time and man of which they treat. Our own acquaintance with both, we beg to add, is not of recent date, nor obtained without careful and conscientious study.

In the first place, then, let us say that if these letters are a forgery, they stand quite alone of their kind in the world. Nothing so daring or extraordinary has ever been attempted. They are stuck full of points for detection; studded all over with liabilities or possibilities of that kind, such as no forged writing ever was since the world began. Look at any *Eikon Basilike, Ossian, Epistles of Phalaris,* or Modern French *Mémoires de la Convention,* or what not; and in nothing is the forgery so careful as to avoid anything in the shape of narrative, of statements of facts, and such like. It fills its pages with mere sentiment; there is not a date to be got out of it, not a name of person or place that can help being given; its sound is all hollow and vacant, as of "damp wind in empty churches." That a "forger," trying his apprentice-hand, and with so small an object, should or could have achieved such a master-piece as these Cromwell Letters, we shall esteem, as soon as it is made out, to be nothing short of a miracle!

. . . .

. . . Let us add that what we have hitherto seen of the grounds set forth for the suspected forgery seem to us altogether worthless.

They rest upon surmises that particular words are modern, and so forth. One suggests that "stand no nonsense" is modern slang. Another that *"Miss Andrews"* is an obvious anachronism. A third that "a new cravat" was an article of dress first introduced at the Restoration. A fourth that *Keziah* is a woman's not a man's name. We could ourselves, if necessary, suggest others. Some words, one or two subscriptions to the letters, a few names of things, we have little doubt are incorrect transcriptions from the originals; but that A. B., in all probability the least learned man in England in such matters, should have avoided all such mistakes in his difficult task, would in our opinion have tended far more than any other circumstance, to *suggest* a forgery. The truth is that we attach no importance to this "word-grubbing" in any such inquiry. It is a kind of criticism which may tend much to perplex the minds of the ignorant, and to increase doubt–that very questionable commodity; but which cannot, by the nature of it, in almost any case, issue in certainty–the alone desirable result. No man knows the exact date at which a given word was used for the first time in human speech or writing. How can he, or ever could he–the dustiest Dryasdust of them all?

–*The Examiner* (15 January 1848): 35–37

* * *

Later in the letter from which this excerpt is taken, Carlyle maintains that Squire's letters are not historically significant: "Let every man believe as he lists; there is properly not a pennyworth of historical value attached to belief or to disbelief!"

Carlyle to Edward FitzGerald, 1 March 1848

Of Squire I have heard little; his face I have never yet seen. During the heat of that distracted jargon about the Letters (more distracted jargon never came my way before), I sent, one day, three clippings of Newspapers which I had got somewhere, openly calling in question the authenticity of the Squire story and documents: these three clippings I enclosed in an empty cover, merely writing "compliments" in the inside, and despatched them to Yarmouth. Answer, next day, arrived; written as if by a wild lion, or *body* of lions, several writing at once;–really an affecting Letter, for poor Squire was ill of influenza, and his whole soul was stirred up into astonishment, contempt, and rage literally beyond speech. I saw it would have been easy to bring him up to any *negative* Editor in London, with a tremendous oak stick in his hand, and a kind of "logic" that would have much surprised the negative Editor! But in fact I was afraid of Bedlam itself for poor Squire, and was filled with respect and pity for him; wrote accordingly a soothing letter, advising him not to mind a whit all that barking of street dogs, but to sit quiet, to grow well, and come and see me,–which last he promised to do, but has never yet done; nor have I heard a whisper of him since.

–*The Collected Letters of Thomas Carlyle and Jane Welsh Carlyle,* v. 22, p. 258

* * *

This excerpt is from notes, dated 25 January 1849, that Carlyle took upon his first meeting with William Squire.

"Radically Honest"
Carlyle's Impression of William Squire

The day before yesterday, about one o'clock, there was suddenly ushered in upon me here–"Mr. Squire!"–the mysterious far-famed proprietor and annihilator of the *Squire MS.*, whom I had often longed to see, whom in these very days, being busy with preparation for a Third Edition, I had felt that I must go to Yarmouth to see, if he did not keep his promise to come to me. Here he was at last; and right welcome.

A man of round rosy face; large grey eyes, full of innocence yet of unquiet vehemence, and slightly *crow-*

A Friendship with Harriet Baring, Lady Ashburton

The wife of Bingham Baring, Lord Ashburton, Harriet Baring associated with the greatest intellects and talents of her time. Carlyle was drawn to Lady Ashburton's charm and confidence and joined her circle of admirers in the 1840s and 1850s. Jane soon came to resent Carlyle's attentiveness to Lady Ashburton, which starkly contrasted to his focus on work while at home with her.

In this excerpt from a 30 December 1845 letter to her friend Mary Russell, Jane Carlyle records her first impression of Lady Ashburton after a long visit.

We are just returned from our Hampshire visit—and I can answer for one of us being so worn out with *"strenuous idleness"* as I do not remember ever to have been before! Six weeks have I been doing absolutely nothing but playing at battledoor and shuttlecock—chess—talking nonsense—and getting rid of a certain fraction of this mortal life as *cleverly* and uselessly as possible—nothing could exceed the sumptuosity and elegance of the whole thing—nor its *uselessness!* O dear me! I wonder why so many people wish for high position and great wealth when it is such an "open secret" what all *that* amounts to in these days—merely to emancipating people from all those practical difficulties which might teach them the *fact* of things, and sympathy with their fellowcreatures. This Lady Harriet Baring whom we have just been staying with is the very cleverest woman—out of sight—that I ever saw in my life—(and I have seen all our "distinguished Authoresses") moreover she is full of energy and sincerity—and has I am quite sure an excellent heart—yet so perverted has she been by the training and life long humouring incident to her high position that I question if in her *whole life* she have done as much for her fellowcreatures as *my mother* in *one year*—or whether she will ever break thro' the cobwebs she is entangled in so as to be any thing other than the *most amusing* and most *graceful* woman of her time. The sight of such a woman should make one very content with one's own trials even when they feel to be rather hard!

—The Collected Letters of Thomas and Jane Welsh Carlyle,
v. 20, p. 85

This excerpt is from a 28 July 1846 letter from Carlyle to Lady Ashburton.

A thousand salutations go from me daily towards Stanhope Street; not one of which you get to hear of! On the whole, what poorer are you? Last Wednesday this week, late, past midnight, while you were at Lansdown House, all radiant to me and beautiful there, I, very ugly at Chelsea, amid my packages and lonesome wrecks, wrote you a Note: but that also you never heard of; I put it straightway in the fire, and went to sleep in silence.—O Daughter of Adam most beautiful: O Son of Adam, in several respects, most *un*beautiful!—

But the essential thing is to tell you that my Wife is considerably better, and still in the way of improving; that she means to continue here for certain weeks yet, and then proceed to East Lothian (Haddington) before she return. We have talked of you: do not suppose that she does other, or ever did other, than respect and even love you,—tho' with some degree of terror. Baseless, I do believe.

As for me I go to Ireland; uncertain yet on what day or for how many days: certain only that I mean to be in Annandale fairly to wait to intercept you in that region. About the 10th or 12th of August you cross the Border: at Carlisle I am only 20 miles from you, at Langholm only 14;—twice as far would I walk on foot at any time for "one blink of your bonny face," as the Scotch songs very justly call it. You will duly warn me, will you not? You are full of charity to me;—for which the Supreme Destinies will certainly reward you. I, if I could ever reward you, Oh, would I not! But it is a vain hope that. Adieu dear Lady mine,—*mine* yes, and yet forever no!

—The Collected Letters of Thomas and Jane Welsh Carlyle,
v. 20, pp. 261–262

This excerpt is from a letter Carlyle wrote to his wife, 14 August 1846, as he was traveling to visit the Barings.

No word from you yet; not the scrape of a pen this morning either. It is not right, my poor dear Jeannie! it is not just nor according to *fact;* and it deeply distresses and disturbs me who had no need of disturbance or distress otherwise, if all were well known to thee. . . .

Silence is better than most speech in the case. This, however, I will say and repeat: 'The annals of insanity contain nothing madder than "jealousy" directed against such a journey as I have before me to-day.' Believed or not, that is verily a fact. To the deepest bottom of my heart that I can sound, I find far other feelings, far other humours and thoughts at present than belong to 'jealousy' on your part. Alas! alas! I must, on the whole, allow the infernal deities to go *their* full swing: but madness shall not conquer, if all my saints can hinder it. Oh, my Jeannie! my own true Jeannie! bravest little life-companion, hitherto, into what courses are we tending? God assist us both, and keep us free of frightful Niagaras and temptations of Satan. I am, indeed, very miserable. My mother asks: 'No word from Jane yet?' And, in spite of her astonishment, I am obliged to answer: '*None.*'

—James A. Froude, *Thomas Carlyle: A History of His Life in London, 1834–1881,* v. 1, pp. 391–392

footed, as beseemed an age of forty otherwise apparent. Head big, roundish, and not ill shaped; figure rather slighter than I had expected; 5 feet 10, and that of a man active and rapid, rather than robust or heavy. Dress by no means exquisite; bottle-green frock or top-coat somewhat gone about the button holes, as I gradually noticed, linen not splendidly clean; nevertheless nothing mean or unpleasant about the air of the man; free-and-easy aspect as of the kind of man called gentleman in the country towns, and one of the sort that was above dress.

Something radically honest, even brave and benevolent, was in the man's look, nay something *blowsy* and almost jolly yet with a singular dash of exasperation, often quiet *vehemency,* such as the eyes had at the first glance told me of.

–William Wright, "The Squire Papers," *English Historical Review,* 1 (April 1886): 311–348

Lady Harriet Ashburton (Carlyle's House Museum, London, from Fred Kaplan, Thomas Carlyle: A Biography, *Thomas Cooper Library, University of South Carolina)*

Carlyle at the End of the 1840s

Carlyle turned his attention in 1848 to relations between England and Ireland, writing several newspaper articles. In July and August 1849, Carlyle toured Ireland with Charles Gavin Duffy, a young Irish political activist and reformer, to assess the situation in person. He recorded his findings in "Reminiscences of my Irish Journey in 1849," which was published as a book in 1882. Carlyle's reactionary rhetoric was beginning to alienate intellectuals and former supporters, which became evident after the publication of his "An Occasional Discourse on the Negro Question"–a racist analysis of problems between the British colonial government and native populations of the West Indies–in Fraser's Magazine *in the last month of the decade.*

These excerpts are from Mill's 13 May 1848 letter to the editor of The Examiner. *The journal had published Carlyle's "Repeal of the Union" on 29 April 1848.*

Pipe case and associated items given to Carlyle by Harriet Ashburton (Carlyle's House Museum, London)

"The Divine Messiahship of England"
A Response to Carlyle's "Repeal of the Union"
John Stuart Mill

The doctrine of your correspondent is (to quote his own words) that 'the Destinies have laid upon England a heavier, terribler job of labour than any people has been saddled with in these generations'–no other than that of 'conquering Anarchy:' that this, which is 'England's work, appointed her by the so-called Destinies and Divine Providence,' cannot go on unless Ireland is either English, or in English hands; and that consequently the repeal of the Union is 'flatly forbidden by the laws of the universe.'

This is a new phasis of the Hebrew prophet of these later days, the Ezekiel of England. The spirit of his prophesying is quite changed. Instead of telling of the sins and errors of England, and warning her of 'wrath to come,' as he has been wont to do, he preaches the divine Messiahship of England, proclaims her the prime minister of Omnipotence on this earth, commissioned to reduce it all (or as much of it as is convenient to herself) into order and harmony, or at all events, under that pretext, into submission, even into 'slavery,' under her own power–will it or will it not.

When an assumption of this sort is coolly made, and the already ample self-conceit of John Bull encouraged to invest itself with the imaginary dignity of an appointed minister of 'the laws of the universe,' the proper answer would seem to be simply to deny the premises. Where is the evidence that England has received any such mandate from the supreme powers? Where are her credentials? By what signs has she shown that the 'conquering of anarchy' is the work specially appointed to her from above?

If the test is to be (and one cannot imagine your correspondent appealing to any other), her having given proof of the *capacity* to do it, it so happens that England is precisely the one country among all others, which has had the opportunity of showing, and has conclusively shown, that she has *not* that capacity. For five centuries, to speak within bounds, has this very corner of earth in question, this Ireland, been given over to her by the 'destinies and divine providences,' as a test of what capacity she has for reducing chaos into order. For five centuries has she had Ireland under her absolute, resistless power, to show what she could do in the way of 'conquering anarchy'–and the result is the most total, disastrous, ignominious failure yet known to history. No other nation ever had such an opportunity for so prolonged a period, and made such a use of it.

. . . .

"On our Journey towards Sligo . . . "

Charles Gavin Duffy recorded this incident of their Irish trip in his memoir of Carlyle.

On our journey towards Sligo an incident occurred so unexpected and characteristic that it deserves to be mentioned. We were inside passengers by a mail coach, and before it started a young bride and bridegroom on their honeymoon joined us. The bride was charming, and Carlyle courteously talked to her about sight-seeing and the pleasures of travelling, mounting at times to higher themes, like a man who never had a care. He got out of the coach for a moment at a roadside station, and the bride, whom I happened to have known at Belfast, from whence she came, immediately exclaimed, "Who is that twaddling old Scotchman who allows no one to utter a word but himself?" I was so tickled by this illustration of the folly of scattering pearls in unsuitable places, that I burst into a guffaw of laughter, which was not easily extinguished. In the evening Carlyle asked me what I had been laughing at so boisterously. I told him, expecting him to be as much amused as I was. But philosophers, I suppose, don't like to be laughed at by young brides, for he was as much disconcerted by the incident as a beau of four-and-twenty. The absurdity of her judgment he refused to see, and was disposed to insist that she was a charming embodiment of the *vox populi*, for undoubtedly he was an old Scotchman, and probably twaddled a good deal to no purpose.

–*Conversations with Carlyle*, pp. 112–113

"Gurlyle"

This excerpt is from William Makepeace Thackeray's letter to Edward FitzGerald, dated March–May 1848.

Gurlyle is immensely grand and savage now. He has a Cromwellian letter against the Irish in this weeks Examiner I declare it seems like insanity almost his contempt for all mankind, and the way in w. he shirks from the argument when called upon to préciser his own remedies for the state of things.

–*The Letters and Private Papers of William Makepeace Thackeray*, v. 2, p. 366

No, sir: rely on it, that England has no mission, just now, to keep other nations out of anarchy; but on the contrary, will have to learn, from the experience which other nations are now in a way of acquiring, the means by which alone it can henceforth be averted from herself.

–*The Examiner,* no. 2102 (13 May 1848): 307–308

* * *

This article, which was published as a tribute to Carlyle after his death, was compiled from Emerson's letters from England in 1848.

Impressions of Thomas Carlyle in 1848
Ralph Waldo Emerson

THOMAS CARLYLE is an immense talker, as extraordinary in his conversation as in his writing,–I think even more so.

He is not mainly a scholar, like the most of my acquaintances, but a practical Scotchman, such as you would find in any sadler's or iron-dealer's shop, and then only accidentally, and by a surprising addition, the admirable scholar and writer he is. If you would know precisely how he talks, just suppose Hugh Whelan (the gardener) had found leisure enough in addition to all his daily work to read Plato and Shakespeare, Augustine and Calvin, and, remaining Hugh Whelan all the time, should talk scornfully of all this nonsense of books that he had bothered with, and you shall have just the tone and talk and laughter of Carlyle.

I called him a trip-hammer with "an Æolian attachment." He has, too, the strong religious tinge you sometimes find in burly people. That, and all his qualities, have a certain virulence, coupled though it be in his case with the utmost impatience of Christendom and Jewdom and all existing presentments of the good old story. He talks like a very unhappy man,–profoundly solitary, displeased and hindered by all men and things about him, and, biding his time, meditating how to undermine and explode the whole world of nonsense which torments him. He is obviously greatly respected by all sorts of people,–understands his own value quite as well as Webster, of whom his behavior sometimes reminds me,–and can see society on his own terms.

And, though no mortal in America could pretend to talk with Carlyle, who is also as remarkable in England as the Tower of London, yet neither would he in any manner satisfy us (Americans) or begin to answer the questions which we ask. He is a very national figure, and would by no means bear transplantation. They keep Carlyle as a sort of portable

Carlyle in 1848 (photograph by Mcnab; from Jane Welsh Carlyle: Letters to Her Family, 1839–1863, *Special Collections, Thomas Cooper Library, University of South Carolina)*

cathedral-bell, which they like to produce in companies where he is unknown, and set a-swinging, to the surprise and consternation of all persons, bishops, courtiers, scholars, writers, and, as in companies here (in England) no man is named or introduced, great is the effect and great the inquiry. Forster of Rawdon described to me a dinner at the *table d'hôte* of some provincial hotel where he carried Carlyle, and where an Irish canon had uttered something; Carlyle began to talk, first to the waiters and then to the walls, and then, lastly, unmistakably to the priest, in a manner that frighted the whole company.

Young men, especially those holding liberal opinions, press to see him, but it strikes me like being hot to see the mathematical or Greek professor before they have got their lesson. It needs something more than a clean shirt and reading German to visit him. He treats them with contempt; they profess freedom, and he stands for slavery; they praise republics, and he likes the Russian Czar; they admire Cobden and free trade, and he is a protectionist in political economy; they will eat vegetables, and drink water, and he is a Scotchman who thinks English national character has a pure enthu-

A Continuing Relationship

Carlyle's friendship with Emerson continued in the 1840s, and Emerson lodged at Cheyne Row when he came to England to lecture in 1848. This excerpt is from Emerson's journal.

I found at Liverpool, after a couple of days, a letter which had been seeking me, from Carlyle, addressed to "R.W.E.–on the instant when he lands in England," conveying the heartiest welcome & urgent invitation to house & hearth. And finding that I should not be wanted for a week in the Lecture-rooms I came down to London, on Monday, &, at 10 at night, the door was opened to me by Jane Carlyle, and the man himself was behind her with a lamp in the hall. They were very little changed from their old selves of fourteen years ago (in August) when I left them at Craigenputtock. "Well," said Carlyle, "here we are shoveled together again!" The floodgates of his talk are quickly opened, & the river is a plentiful stream. We had a wide talk that night, until nearly 1 o'clock, & at breakfast next morning, again. At noon or later we walked forth to Hyde Park, & the palaces, about two miles from here to the National Gallery, & to the Strand, Carlyle melting all Westminster & London into his talk & laughter, as he goes. Here, in his house, we breakfast about 9, & Carlyle is very prone, his wife says to sleep till 10 or 11, if he has no company. An immense talker, and, altogether as extraordinary in that, as in his writing; I think, even more so. You will never discover his real vigor & range, or how much more he might do, than he has ever done, without seeing him. My few hours' discourse with him, long ago, in Scotland, gave me not enough knowledge of him; & I have now, at last, been taken by surprise, by him.

– Journals and Miscellaneous Notebooks of Ralph Waldo Emerson, v. 10, pp. 540–541

This excerpt is from Carlyle's 19 April 1849 letter responding to a gift from Emerson.

Still more interesting is the barrel of genuine Corn ears,–Indian Cobs of edible grain, from the Barn of Emerson himself! It came all safe and right, according to your charitable program; without cost or trouble to us of any kind; not without curious interest and satisfaction! The recipes contained in the precedent letter, duly weighed by the competent jury of housewives (at least by my own Wife and Lady Ashburton), were judged to be of decided promise, reasonable-looking every one of them; and now that the stuff itself is come, I am happy to assure you that it forms a new epoch for us all in the Maize department: we find the grain *sweet,* among the sweetest, with a touch even of the taste of *nuts* in it, and profess with contrition that properly we have never tasted Indian Corn before. Millers of due faculty (with millstones of *iron*) being scarce in the Cockney region, and even cooks liable to err, the Ashburtons have on their resources undertaken the brunt of the problem: one of their own Surrey or Hampshire millers is to grind the stuff, and their own cook, a Frenchman commander of a whole squadron, is to undertake the dressing according to the rules: Yesterday the Barrel went off to their country place in Surrey,–a small Bag of select ears being retained here, for our own private experimenting;–and so by and by we shall see what comes of it.–I on my side have already drawn up a fit proclamation of the excellences of this invaluable corn, and admonitions as to the benighted state of English eaters in regard to it;–to appear in *Fraser's Magazine,* or I know not where, very soon. It is really a small contribution towards World-History, this small act of yours and ours: there is no doubt to me, now that I taste the real grain, but all Europe will henceforth have to rely more and more upon your Western Valleys and this article. How beautiful to think of lean tough Yankee settlers, tough as gutta-percha, with most *occult* unsubduable fire in their belly, steering over the Western Mountains, to annihilate the jungle, and bring bacon and corn out of it for the Posterity of Adam!

– The Correspondence of Thomas Carlyle and Ralph Waldo Emerson, 1834–1872, v. 2, pp. 205–207

---

siasm for beef and mutton, describes with gusto the crowds of people who gaze at the sirloins in the dealer's shop-window, and even likes the Scotch night-cap; they praise moral suasion; he goes for murder, money, capital punishment, and other pretty abominations of English law. They wish freedom of the press, and he thinks the first thing he would do, if he got into Parliament, would be to turn out the reporters, and stop all manner of mischievous speaking to Buncombe and wind-bags. "In the Long Parliament," he says, "the only great Parliament,–they sat secret and silent, grave as an ecumenical council, and I know not what they would have done to anybody that had got in there, and attempted to tell out-of-doors what they did." They go for free institutions, for letting things alone, and only giving opportunity and motive to every man; he for a stringent government that shows people what they must do, and makes them do it. "Here," he says, "the Parliament gathers up six millions of pounds every year, to give to the poor, and yet the people starve. I think if they would give it to me, to provide the poor with labor, and with authority to make them work, or shoot them,–and I to be hanged if I did not do it,–I could find them in plenty of Indian meal."

He throws himself readily on the other side. If you urge free trade, he remembers that every laborer is a monopolist. The navigation laws of England made its commerce. "St. John was insulted by the Dutch; he came home, got the law passed that foreign vessels should pay high fees, and it cut the throat of the Dutch, and made the English trade." If you boast of the growth of the country, and show him the wonderful results of the census, he finds nothing so depressing as the sight of a great mob. He saw once, as he told me, three or four miles of human beings, and fancied that "the airth was some great cheese, and these were mites." If a Tory takes heart at his hatred of stump-oratory and model republics, he replies: "Yes, the idea of a pig-headed soldier who will obey orders, and fire on his own father at the command of his officer, is a great comfort to the aristocratic mind." It is not so much that Carlyle cares for this or that dogma, as that he likes genuineness (the source of all strength) in his companions.

If a scholar goes into a camp of lumbermen or a gang of riggers, those men will quickly detect any fault of character. Nothing will pass with them but what is real and sound. So this man is a hammer that crushes mediocrity and pretension. He detects weakness on the instant, and touches it. He has a vivacious, aggressive temperament, and unimpressionable. The literary, the fashionable, the political man, each fresh from triumphs in his own sphere, comes eagerly to see this man, whose fun they have heartily enjoyed, sure of a welcome, and are struck with despair at the first onset. His firm, victorious, scoffing vituperation strikes them with chill and hesitation. His talk often reminds you of what was said of Johnson: "If his pistol missed fire he would knock you down with the butt-end."

Mere intellectual partisanship wearies him; he detects in an instant if a man stands for any cause to which he is not born and organically committed. A natural defender of anything, a lover who will live and die for that which he speaks for, and who does not care for him, or for anything but his own business,–he respects: and the nobler this object, of course, the better. He hates a literary trifler, and if, after Guizot had been a tool of Louis Philippe for years, he is now to come and write essays on the character of Washington, on "The Beautiful," and on "Philosophy of History," he thinks that nothing.

Great is his reverence for realities,–for all such traits as spring from the intrinsic nature of the actor. He humors this into the idolatry of strength. A strong nature has a charm for him, previous, it would seem, to all inquiry whether the force be divine or diabolic. He preaches, as by cannonade, the doctrine that every noble nature was made by God, and contains, if savage passions, also fit checks and grand impulses, and, however extravagant, will keep its orbit and return from far.

Nor can that decorum which is the idol of the Englishman, and in attaining which the Englishman exceeds all nations, win from him any obeisance. He is eaten up with indignation against such as desire to make a fair show in the flesh.

Combined with this warfare on respectabilities, and, indeed, pointing all his satire, is the severity of his moral sentiment. In proportion to the peals of laughter amid which he strips the plumes of a pretender and shows the lean hypocrisy to every vantage of ridicule, does he worship whatever enthusiasm, fortitude, love, or other sign of a good nature is in a man.

There is nothing deeper in his constitution than his humor, than the considerate, condescending good-nature with which he looks at every object in existence, as a man might look at a mouse. He feels that the perfection of health is sportiveness, and will not look grave even at dullness or tragedy.

His guiding genius is his moral sense, his perception of the sole importance of truth and justice; but that is a truth of character, not of catechisms.

He says, "There is properly no religion in England. These idle nobles at Tattersall's,–there is no work or word of serious purpose in them; they have this great lying church; and life is a humbug." He prefers Cambridge to Oxford, but he thinks Oxford and Cambridge education indurates the young men, as the Styx hardened Achilles, so that when they come forth of them, they say, "Now we are proof: we have gone through all the degrees, and are case-hardened against the veracities of the Universe; nor man nor God can penetrate us."

Wellington he respects as real and honest, and as having made up his mind, once for all, that he will not have to do with any kind of a lie.

Edwin Chadwick is one of his heroes,–who proposes to provide every house in London with pure water, sixty gallons to every head, at a penny a week; and in the decay and downfall of all religions, Carlyle thinks that the only religious act which a man nowadays can securely perform is to wash himself well.

Of course the new French Revolution of 1848 was the best thing he had seen, and the teaching this great swindler, Louis Philippe, that there is a God's justice in the Universe, after all, was a great satisfaction. Czar Nicholas was his hero: for, in the ignominy of Europe, when all thrones fell like card-houses, and no man was found with conscience enough to fire a gun for his crown, but every one ran away in a *coucou*, with his head shaved, through the Barrière de Passy, one man remained who believed he was put there by God

Almighty to govern his empire, and, by the help of God, had resolved to stand there.

He was very serious about the bad times; he had seen this evil coming, but thought it would not come in his time. But now 'tis coming, and the only good he sees in it is the visible appearance of the gods. He thinks it the only question for wise men, instead of art, and fine fancies, and poetry, and such things,—to address themselves to the problem of society. This confusion is the inevitable end of such falsehood and nonsense as they have been embroiled with.

Carlyle has, best of all men in England, kept the manly attitude in his time. He has stood for scholars, asking no scholar what he should say. Holding an honored place in the best society, he has stood for the people, for the Chartist, for the pauper, intrepidly and scornfully teaching the nobles their peremptory duties.

His errors of opinion are as nothing in comparison with this merit, in my judgment. This *aplomb* cannot be mimicked; it is the speaking to the heart of the thing. And in England, where the morgue of aristocracy has very slowly admitted scholars into society,—a very few houses only in the high circles being ever opened to them,—he has carried himself erect, made himself a power confessed by all men, and taught scholars their lofty duty. He never feared the face of man.

—*Scribner's Monthly Magazine,* 22 (May 1881): 89–92

* * *

This letter, evidently written to an aspiring author, reveals how Carlyle conceived his profession at midcentury.

Carlyle to an unidentified correspondent, 19 June 1849

Sir,

You must in no wise dream of quitting your present situation till you have found footing on another. No man, by many interviews, could possibly judge of your fitness for any form of Authorship; and if I or anybody did ever know that you were fit, and could certify the same with never such assurance, it would still be far from surmounting the difficulty,—your distance from actual employment would still be far, very far! In no province of human industry is there hungrier competition, and more dark stolidity awarding the decision, than in that same.

A man prepares himself for Authorship by silently amassing knowledge for a long time, above all by silently amassing *wisdom,* patience, perseverance and human virtues; he gradually tries (in Peri-

odicals, Newspapers &c) whether he *can* write with acceptance, taking with loyal patience such answer as he *gets;*—and after that, looks out for some feasible engagement; very seldom, I believe, finding one that is not *un*wholesome and wellnigh intolerable to him.

Your experience much misleads you, furthermore, as to the kind of associates, and form of companionship you might help to fall into as Subeditor or Author in general. Not here, any more than in your present place, will a wise and honourable soul feel himself in the least at home. To such a one the world is not anywhere a "school of virtue"; it is rather, at present especially, as an abominable kennel of mad dogs that a good man will have to view his co-mates in most professions,—with pity, not with rage, in *silence* generally, yet with a determined resolution to keep apart from *their* downward course, and (with Heaven's help) by no means to do as they do.—Authorship, I am sorry to say, offers no exception to this sad rule, but is rather one of the more flagrant instances of it.

Among the respectablest and *enviablest* men I have ever known in this world have been three or four instances of handicraftsmen, mechanical labourers. With courageous patience, thrift, prudence, and piety of heart (very rare virtues at present) I know no situation in life more safe and wholesome. If you have superior gifts and strength, it is natural you should struggle upwards, but I would by no means recommend Authorship or any merely speculative and *talking* trade, as the course.

Yours in haste, T. Carlyle
—*The Collected Letters of Thomas Carlyle and Jane Welsh Carlyle,* v. 24, p. 74

"By No Means a Safe Author"

In his forty-five-page essay on Carlyle, George Henry Lewes argued that the knowledge conveyed by Carlyle's writings, when "viewed in reference to instruction, . . . does not often rise above the level of Half-truths."

On the whole . . . he is by no means a safe author to put into the hands of young men who do not bring some power of independent thinking to what they read. His half-truths, and his truths exaggerated so as to become untruths, are thrust upon you so capriciously, that the uninitiated, and such as consult him only by snatches, are in danger of carrying away some new crudity at every new reading.

—*British Quarterly Review,* 10 (1 August 1849): 28, 34

Quiet Within and Storm Without: 1850–1865

The fifteen years from 1850 to 1865 were Carlyle's last productive period as a writer. Latter-Day Pamphlets *(1850) alienated many liberals with what were regarded as his reactionary opinions, particularly on the question of race and slavery. Carlyle's argument about black workers in the West Indies was more sophisticated than many of his critics allowed. Fred Kaplan in* Thomas Carlyle: A Biography *(1983) states flatly that Carlyle did not favor slavery: "In fact, he accused Abolitionists and liberals of attempting to impose, for their own narrow and selfish purposes, conditions of independence on blacks who were unprepared for them and who could not possibly function effectively either in their own interests or in the interests of the community. What was deemed emancipation was in reality desertion" (p. 489). Nevertheless, Carlyle's reputation suffered as a result. His subsequent major works,* The Life of John Sterling *(1851) and his six-volume* History of Friedrich II. of Prussia, *called Frederick the Great (1858–1865), were often reviewed by critics who were predisposed against his work.*

"Occasional Discourse on the Negro Question" and *Latter-Day Pamphlets*

Thomas Carlyle in the 1850s (Special Collections, Thomas Cooper Library, University of South Carolina)

In the last half of the 1840s, while he was still involved in preparing revised editions of Oliver Cromwell's Letters and Speeches *(1845), Carlyle was also writing essays on contemporary issues. He examined the problems facing the British colonial government in the West Indies in the controversial essay "An Occasional Discourse on the Negro Question" (Fraser's Magazine, December 1849) and criticized British institutions in a series of eight essays collected as* Latter-Day Pamphlets *(1850).*

The hostility that greeted "An Occasional Discourse on the Negro Question"—which was republished as An Occasional Discourse on the Nigger Question *(1853)—set the tone for the reception of Carlyle's pamphlets—"The Present Time," "Model Prisons," "Downing Street," "New Downing Street," "Stump-Orator," "Parliaments," "Hudson's Statue," and "Jesuitism"—which were initially published individually from February to August 1850.*

As they had in earlier responses to Carlyle's social criticism, reviewers faulted him for not providing practical suggestions to solve the problems he identified. Some reviewers disparaged him for emphasizing power over goodness and viewed the pamphlets as indications of Carlyle's overall moral decline.

These excerpts are from a six-page letter "To the Editor of Fraser's Magazine" that was published under the title "The Negro Question" and signed as by "D." The author was John Stuart Mill, who in 1848 had written a letter to the editor responding to Carlyle's views on Ireland.

"A Professed Moral Reformer"
A Response to Carlyle's "Occasional Discourse on the Negro Question"
John Stuart Mill

Sir,

Your last month's Number contains a speech against the 'rights of Negros,' the doctrines and spirit of which ought not to pass without remonstrance. The author issues his opinions, or rather ordinances, under imposing auspices; no less than those of the 'immortal gods.' 'The Powers,' 'the Destinies,' announce through him, not only what *will* be, but what *shall* be done; what they 'have decided upon, passed their eternal act of parliament for.' This is speaking 'as one having authority'; but authority from whom? If by the quality of the message we may judge of those who sent it, *not* from any powers to whom just or good men acknowledge allegiance. This so-called 'eternal Act of Parliament' is no new law, but the old law of the strongest,—a law against which the great teachers of mankind have in all ages protested:—it is the law of force and cunning; the law that whoever is more powerful than another, is 'born lord' of that other, the other being born his 'servant,' who must be 'compelled to work' for him by 'beneficent whip,' if 'other methods avail not.'

. . . .

. . . That negroes should exist, and enjoy existence, on so little work, is a scandal in his eyes, worse than their former slavery. It must be put a stop to at any price. He does not 'wish to see' them slaves again 'if it can be avoided;' but 'decidedly' they 'will have to be servants,' 'servants to the whites,' 'compelled to labour;' and 'not to go idle another minute.' 'Black Quashee,' 'up to the ears in pumpkins,' and 'working about half an hour a day,' is to him the abominations of abominations. I have so serious a quarrel with him about principles, that I have no time to spare for his facts: but let me remark, how easily he takes for granted those which fit his case. Because he reads in some blue-book of a strike for wages in Demerara, such as he may read of any day in Manchester, he draws a picture of negro inactivity, copied from the wildest prophesies of the slavery party before emancipation. If the negroes worked no more than 'half an hour a day,' would the sugar crops, in all except notoriously bad seasons, be as considerable, so little diminished from what they were in the time of slavery, as is proved by the Customhouse return? But it is not the fact of the question, so much as the moralities of it, that I care to dispute your contributor.

A black man working no more than your contributor affirms that they work, is, he says, 'an eye-sorrow,' a 'blister on the skin of the state,' and many other things

equally disagreeable; to *work* being the grand duty of man. 'To do competent work, to labour honestly according to the ability given them; for that, and for no other purpose, was each one of us sent into this world.' Whoever prevents him from this his 'sacred appointment to labour while he lives on earth' is 'his deadliest enemy.' If it be 'his own indolence' that prevents him, 'the first *right* he has' is that all wiser and more industrious persons shall, 'by some wise means, compel him to do the work he is fit for.' Why not at once say that, 'by some wise means,' every thing should be made right in the world? . . .

This pet theory of your contributor about work, we all know well enough, though some persons might not be prepared for so bold an application of it. Let me say a few words on this 'gospel of work'—which, to my mind, as justly deserves the name of a cant as any of those which he has opposed, while the truth it contains is immeasurably farther from being the whole truth than that contained in the words Benevolence, Fraternity, or any other of his catalogue of contemptibilities. . . .

Work, I imagine, is not a good in itself. There is nothing laudable in work for work's sake. To work voluntarily for a worthy object is laudable; but what constitutes a worthy object? On this matter, the oracle of which your contributor is the prophet has never yet been prevailed on to declare itself. He revolves in an eternal circle round the idea of work, as if turning up the earth, or driving a shuttle or a quill, were ends of themselves, and the ends of human existence. . . .

In the present case, it seems, a noble object means 'spices.' 'The gods wish, besides pumpkins, that spices and valuable products be grown in their West Indies'— the 'noble elements of cinnamon, sugar, coffee, pepper black and grey,' 'things far nobler than pumpkins.' Why so? Is what supports life, inferior in dignity to what merely gratifies the sense of taste? Is it the verdict of the 'immortal gods' that pepper is noble, freedom (even freedom from the lash) contemptible? But spices lead 'towards commerces, arts, politics, and social developments.' Perhaps so; but of what sort? When they must be produced by slaves, the 'politics and social developments' they lead to are such as the world, I hope, will not choose to be cursed with much longer.

. . . .

But the great ethical doctrine of the Discourse, than which a doctrine more damnable, I should think, never was propounded by a professed moral reformer, is, that one kind of human beings are born servants to another kind. . . . By 'born wiser,' I will suppose him to mean, born more capable of wisdom: a proposition which, he says, no mortal can doubt, but which I will make bold to say, that a full moiety of all thinking persons, who have attended to the subject, either doubt or positively deny. . . . But I again renounce all advantage from facts; were the whites born ever so superior in intelligence to the blacks, and competent by nature to instruct and advise them, it would not be the less monstrous to assert that they had therefore a right either to subdue them by force, or circumvent them by superior skill; to throw upon them the toils and hardships of life, reserving for themselves, under the misapplied name of work, its agreeable excitements.

—Fraser's Magazine, 41 (January 1850): 25–30

* * *

In this excerpt from a letter to his brother, Carlyle is evidently unaware that Mill was the "hide-bound dunce" who had criticized his "Occasional Discourse on the Negro Question."

Carlyle to John A. Carlyle, 9 January 1850

To-day I send two Books; one of which is *Emerson's Lectures,* a Book of yours, which may perhaps amuse you in a dark evening: it came here, with a copy for myself, two nights ago. The other is *Fraser* for my Mother; some better reading in it than usual. An attack on my *Negro Question* is of very slender structure,–I do not in the least know by whom. By some "man of rank," Forster says the Newspapers say; by some poor hide-bound dunce, I have no hesitation in replying.– Alas, this is but the first *sough* of the storm I shall have to raise among that class of cattle, when I do fairly open my pack, and make known to them what my mind is;– as really now must soon be done!

—New Letters of Thomas Carlyle, v. 2, pp. 84–85

* * *

This excerpt is from a letter Carlyle sent to his sister.

Carlyle to Jean Carlyle Aitken, 26 January 1850

After long tumbling and wrestling about with a mass of confused written-stuff here, which has been oppressing me for months and years past,–I have decided at last to give vent to myself in a Series of Pamphlets; "Latter-day Pamphlets" is the name I have given them, as significant of the ruinous overwhelmed and almost dying condition in which the world paints itself to me. The First, about what they call the "New Era," is to come out at the beginning of February now instant: it is quite gone from *me;* they are printing the *Second* even (which is for March); and I have begun this day to turn the *Third* over in my mind. A questionable enterprise; but I could not help it! I think there will be perhaps a

dozen Pamphlets in all,–two volumes when completed;–and it is to be expected they will occasion loud astonishment, condemnation, and a universal barking of "Whaf-thaf? Bow-wow!" from all the dogs of the Parish.–A Paper I published in *Fraser* about *Niggers* has raised no end of clamour; poor scraggy critics, of the "benevolent" school, giving vent to their amazement, and uttering their "Whaf-thaf? Bow-wow!" in a great variety of dialects up and down all the country, as I am informed. That will be neither chaff nor sand to what they will hear in these "Latter-day" Discourses, poor souls! All the twaddling *sects* of the country, from Swedenborgians to Jesuits, have for the last ten years been laying claim to "T. Carlyle," each for itself; and now they will all find that the said "T." belongs to a sect of his own, which is worthy of instant damnation. All which is precisely as it must be, and as it should be. Nay, we have a considerable amusement over it here; being, I do suppose, about as well situated for speaking what is our own mind on occasion as perhaps any "free king" of these parts, or these times! A much more questionable consideration is that of one's *bodily health* holding out thro' the job:–but that too we must risk; trying to take all precautions as we go.

—New Letters of Thomas Carlyle, v. 2, pp. 86–87

* * *

John Greenleaf Whittier was a noted American poet and abolitionist. These excerpts are from his essay "Thomas Carlyle on the Slave Question."

"Unspeakably Wicked"
Response to "Occasional Discourse on the Negro Question"
John Greenleaf Whittier

A late number of Fraser's Magazine contains an article bearing the unmistakable impress of the Anglo-German peculiarities of Thomas Carlyle, entitled "An Occasional Discourse on the Negro Question," which would be interesting as a literary curiosity were it not in spirit and tendency so unspeakably wicked as to excite in every rightminded reader a feeling of amazement and disgust. With a hard, brutal audacity, a blasphemous irreverence, and a sneering mockery which would do honor to the devil of Faust, it takes issue with the moral sense of mankind and the precepts of Christianity. . . . Whatever is hollow and hypocritical in politics, morals, or religion comes very properly within the scope of his mockery, and we bid him God speed in applying his satirical lash upon it. Impostures and frauds of all kinds deserve nothing better than detection

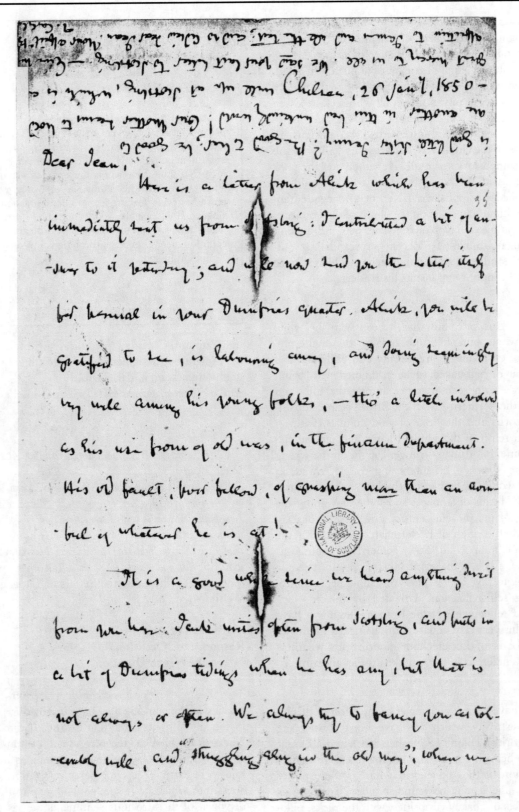

First page of Carlyle's 26 January 1850 letter to Jean Carlyle Aitken in which he later confides his plan "to give vent to myself in a Series of Pamphlets"
(The Trustees of the National Library of Scotland MS 513)

and exposure. Let him blow them up to his heart's content, as Daniel did the image of Bell and the Dragon.

But our author, in this matter of negro slavery, has undertaken to apply his explosive pitch and rosin, not to the affectation of humanity, but to humanity itself. He mocks at pity, scoffs at all who seek to lessen the amount of pain and suffering, sneers at and denies the most sacred rights, and mercilessly consigns an entire class of the children of his heavenly Father to the doom of compulsory servitude. He vituperates the poor black man with a course brutality which would do credit to a Mississippi slave driver, or a renegade Yankee dealer in human cattle on the banks of the Potomac. His rhetoric has a flavor of the slave pen and auction block—vulgar, unmanly, indecent––a scandalous outrage upon good taste and refined feeling—which at once degrades the author and insults his readers.

. . . .

. . . And pray how has it been with the white race, for whom our philosopher claims the divine prerogative of enslaving? Some twenty and odd centuries ago, a pair of half-naked savages, daubed with paint, might have been seen roaming among the hills and woods of the northern part of the British island, subsisting on acorns and the flesh of wild animals, with an occasional relish of the smoked hams and pickled fingers of some unfortunate stranger caught on the wrong side of the Tweed. This interesting couple reared, as they best could, a family of children, who, in turn, became the heads of families; and some time about the beginning of the present century one of their descendants in the borough of Ecclefechan rejoiced over the birth of a man child now somewhat famous as "Thomas Carlyle, a maker of books." Does it become such a one to rave against the West India negro's incapacity for self-civilization? Unaided by the arts, sciences, and refinements of the Romans, he might have been, at this very day, squatted on his naked haunches in the woods of Ecclefechan, painting his weather-hardened epidermis in the sun like his Pict ancestors.

. . . .

We have no fears whatever of the effect of this literary monstrosity which we have been considering upon the British colonies. Quashee, black and ignorant as he may be, will not "get himself made a slave again." The mission of the "beneficent whip" is there pretty well over; and it may now find its place in museums and cabinets of ghastly curiosities, with the racks, pillories, thumbscrews, and branding irons of old days. What we have feared, however, is, that the advocates and defenders of slaveholding in this country might find in this Discourse matter of encouragement, and

---

Carlyle's Capitals

This excerpt is from an article titled "Writing and Opinion of Thomas Carlyle" by the American critic Henry William Field.

Another thing quite remarkable in Carlyle is *intenseness of expression*, whatever be the subject. Even in his wit and ridicule he is as earnest as in his open and vehement denunciations. His desire to be emphatic appears in such a little thing as his unexampled use of capital letters with which he commences not only every sentence but every leading word. The impression is quite singular at the first glance over one of his pages. Capital letters are as plentiful with him as ordinary type with common men; as giants in Brobdignag were as thick as pigmies in Lilliput.

—New Englander, 8 (February 1850): 55

---

that our anti-Christian prejudices against the colored man might be strengthened and confirmed by its malignant vituperation and sarcasm.

—Literary Recreations and Miscellanies, pp. 34–35, 39–40, 44

* * *

This brief excerpt, which appeared in an American abolitionist newspaper, is "from a letter lately received from an esteemed English correspondent." Writing to Margaret A. Carlyle on 24 April 1850, Carlyle responded: "But here is a Yankee Newspaper that came yesterday, with a dud of a criticism in it; which rather than burn it in the fire, I may as well send you to read and then to light your pipe with. This is getting a very unruly world; and people speak in a loud irreverent voice now everywhere!" (The Collected Letters of Thomas and Jane Welsh Carlyle, v. 25, p. 69).

"Atrocious Sentiments"
Response to "Occasional Discourse on the Negro Question"

I suppose your slaveholders are now probably exalting in the new ally they have obtained in the liberty-loving, equal rights-defending *Chartist,* Thomas Carlyle. The article which has recently issued from his pen must stamp his memory with infamy, so long as his name is known in earth, except, he perceives in time the moral abyss into which he has fallen, and give to the world a disvowal of the atrocious sentiments he has uttered in the pages of Fraser's Magazine. The article has been severely commented on by several papers, and I am not without hope that he will be replied to by one well qualified to do it, on this side of the Atlantic. It would be

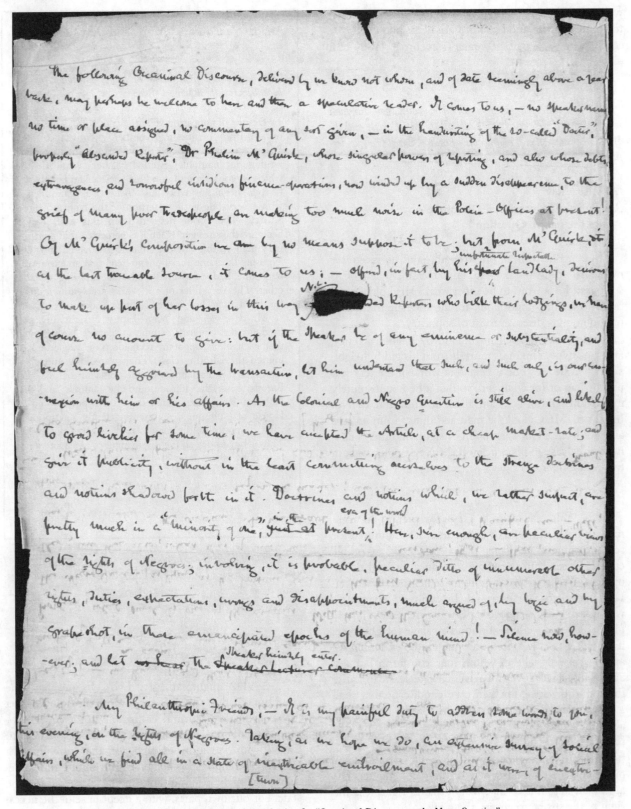

Page from Carlyle's revised introduction for "Occasional Discourse on the Negro Question"
(Beinecke Rare Book and Manuscript Library, Yale University)

well to let him feel that he has won for himself the contempt of the wise and good of both hemispheres.

—*Boston Liberator* (15 February 1850): 26

* * *

These excerpts are from an anonymous New England response to Carlyle's essay, originally titled "Mr. Carlyle and the W. I. Negro Question," that begins by calling Carlyle "a wonderful man," "a queer man," and "a genius."

"A False View"
Response to "Occasional Discourse on the Negro Question"

. . . But with all his strength,—and he is a *strong* man also,—he is weak; and, unlike Paul, when he is strongest, he is wont to be most weak. His boldest and most powerful compositions are those where the Christian mind may discover most of sophistry.

He raises himself in mid-air, by balloon agency, and looks down upon us mortals from his giddy height, and when he sees one *is earnest*—at work—it matters *little* upon what, or for what end, so that it be not absolutely infernal in sight of gods and men, he dubs him a Hero. In a word, Mr. C. looks at man and things from *his own*, and not from a Christian point of sight; and this is eminently the case in his article on the Negro Question, in the last number of Fraser's Magazine.

. . . .

. . . He may point to Hayti for ever, as an argument in favor of his theory, that the black is unfitted for self-government; i.e., when placed under like favorable circumstances with the white for education and development. We would ask him to remember that even Hayti produced a Henri and Toussaint L'Ouverture—which last, wise, self-governing white men most basely murdered; that we have a quondam slave (or Quashee, if he will,)—to name no more—one Frederick Douglass, amongst us, the like of whom may rise up in Jamaica and Antigua, to govern Englishmen; at least, to cause the soil to produce, for their own good, cane that shall *not* rot; 'celestial spices,' too, which—and the English are able—they may purchase of Quashee, he, meanwhile, scorning and repudiating 'most beneficent whip.'

In our estimation, Mr. Carlyle—as we said at the outset—has taken a false view of the whole matter. His argument amounts to this: Might makes right; it is the right of the strong to govern the weak.

—*Boston Liberator* (22 February 1850): 31

* * *

An "Extraordinary" Man's Support for Slavery

This excerpt is from George Fitzhugh's introduction for his book defending the institution of slavery.

Despite of appearing vain and egotistical, we cannot refrain from mentioning another circumstance that encourages us to write. At the very time when we were writing our pamphlet entitled "Slavery Justified," in which we took ground that Free Society had failed, Mr. Carlyle began to write his "*Latter Day* Pamphlets," whose very title is the assertion of the failure of Free Society. The proof derived from this coincidence becomes the stronger, when it is perceived that an ordinary man on this side the Atlantic discovered and was exposing the same social phenomena that an extraordinary one had discovered and was exposing on the other. The very titles of our works are synonymous—for the "Latter Day" is the "Failure of Society."

Mr. Carlyle, and Miss Fanny Wright (in her England the Civilizer) vindicate Slavery by shewing that each of its apparent relaxations in England has injured the laboring class. They were fully and ably represented in Parliament by their ancient masters, the Barons. Since the Throne, and the Church, and the Nobility, have been stripped of their power, and a House of Commons, representing lands and money, rules despotically, the masses have become outlawed. They labor under all the disadvantages of slavery, and have none of the rights of slaves.

—*Cannibals All! Or, Slaves without Masters*,
pp. xx–xxi

These excerpts are from an anonymous American review of the first of Carlyle's Latter-Day Pamphlets. *The review, originally titled "Carlyle's Pamphlet," was published in* The Literary World, *a New York weekly magazine.*

"Screech-Owl"
Review of "The Present Time"

A VERY nightmare of a book. Its problem, the condition of the world question and the solution, set down in the key, but undecipherable in the processes—the Millennium. A weary, heavy-laden journey to travel, with vexation enough for the individual, a heavier care and responsibility for the family, and something well-nigh insupportable in the aggregate of the state. For our own parts, with a deep sense of the necessities of the way, we would choose a different guide and monitor than the screech-owl Thomas Carlyle. Not by such howlings as in these pamphlet utterances was society built up when men segregated from beasts, but with

A "LATTER-DAY" NIGHTMARE, BROUGHT ON BY READING THOMAS CARLYLE HIS PAMPHLETS.

Cartoon appearing in the April 1850 issue of Punch *(from Rodger L. Tarr, Research Files for the Thomas Carlyle Bibliography, Special Collections, Thomas Cooper Library, University of South Carolina)*

the heavenly music of the poet's lyre. Cassandra might assist at the overthrow of Troy, but the walls of Thebes rose before Amphion. Would it not be well for our galvanized pamphleteer to consider this and relax a little his clattering of skeletons, the novel instrument he has introduced into the harmonies of literature!

. . . .

America, somehow or other, is a special target for our pamphleteer's good-nature. . . . One of the numerous Mrs. Harrises whom Carlyle employs as his familiars, must be brought in for another bit of dirty work. "What have the American cousins done?" growls Smelfungus, "they have doubled their population every twenty years. They have begotten, with a rapidity beyond recorded example, Eighteen Millions of the greatest *bores* ever seen in this world before: that, hitherto, is their feat for history!" 18,000,000 of bores is a great number, and their united force undoubtedly tremendous; but if Mr. Carlyle and his rival American five cent per copy publishers go on at the rate of Latter Day Pamphlets No. I, he will be even with them yet. It would be a safe bet to take the odds in his favor.

                    –*Literary World*, 6 (16 March 1850): 275–276

* * *

This anonymous review is from an American periodical.

"Sage Spasms of Ulterior Humanity"
Review of "The Present Time"

Nothing of the Mormon here!–no Joe Smith utterances, and "Latter-day Saint" vaticinations from Deseret. These be, rather, sybilline leaves torn from the heart-tablets of the mightiest of hero-men,–the flashing, the coruscating, the exploding Thomas Carlyle,–man of mouth-mystery, lip-lingo, voice-verbiage,–with ideas marching in grim and grotesque procession, on stilts, on their heads, on all-fours, on broomsticks, on donkeys mincing out of pure contrariness tail foremost, railing on rails, rolling on swollen bladders inflated with pseudo-German gas,–shouting, spouting, growling, and grumbling;

"So have we heard ten cats in stormy weather,
   Squeak, squeal, squall, squabble, screech, and scream together."

Pamphlet "Number One," is on "the Present Time;"–not the *past*,–that goblin ghost of defunct inanity, gibbering among broken tomb-stones, and eating from coffin-plates on mouldy boards;–not the *future*,–

that non-entity, which when it comes out of the womb of nothingness, is no more itself, or any self;–but the *present,* aye, the present, the glorious, phantasmagoric, aguish, double-jointed, volcano-brooding, thunder-belching, earthquake-gendering, blatant and flatulent present! This is the magic theme of Carlylianistic ponderings and sage spasms of ulterior humanity, big with the bursting bombs of intellectuality, revelling in floods of fool-goosery and muds of disguised and bedizened duncery.

With what illuminated 'cuteness doth he paint the social state of American boredom, as "Anarchy *plus* a street-constable!" and democracy as demonocracy in a demon-strative devel-opement. But even this is Miltonically grand and Satanically noble, as compared with the crazy monarchies and cracky aristocracies of poor old tumble-down Europe. Hear the oracle himself! "If the thing called Government merely drift to and fro, no whither, on the popular vortexes, like some carcass of a drowned ass, constitutionally put 'at the top of affairs,' popular indignation will infallibly accumulate upon it: one day, the popular lightning, descending forked and horrible from the black air, will annihilate said supreme carcass, and smite *it* home to its native ooze again!" Page 37. Hah! sayst thou me, Nuncle Tommy! "Annihilate said supreme carcass," and "smite it home" after it is annihilated! Say, shall it verify the prayer of the confessant at the camp-meeting, who would fain have been "annihilated into a toad?" And in what Dutch college, beery and tobacconalian, didst thou learn that "carcasses of drowned asses" are "natives" of the "ooze" which is their "home"? Lucid politician! Lurid legislator! And what is thy patent remedy for the ragged misery of England's millions of paupers and "Captainless vagrants"? Wouldst thou enslave them for their good? Wouldst thou in very deed say to each of them: "Here is work for you!–Refuse to strike into it; shirk the heavy labor; disobey the rules–I will admonish and endeavor to incite you; if in vain, I will flog you; if still in vain, I will at last shoot you, and make God's Earth, and the forlorn hope in God's Battle, free of you"? Page 45. Somewhat atrocious philanthropy this! yea, rather truculent, thou dark-souled pepper-pot, thou ascetic vinegar-cruet, on the dinner-table of modern literature! Out upon thee! We have done with thee. We have caulked thy hull with thine own oakum. We have paid it with thine own pitch-mop. And now we push thy craft adrift. Avaunt! Scull! Paddle! Claw off! Get thee out of arrow-shot from thine own bow! Drift out of sight, and leave not a wake behind!

–*Christian Observatory,* 4 (April 1850): 189–191

* * *

The pervasive negative reaction to Carlyle's pamphlets is indicated by this article, originally titled "Punch's Police," which was published in the American magazine The Literary World. *The anonymous author imagines Carlyle brought before the comic figure Mr. Punch as judge.*

"Reckless and Alarming Conduct"
Response to *Latter-Day Pamphlets*

Yesterday a gentleman of the name of Thomas Carlyle was brought before Mr. Punch, charged with being unable to take care of his own literary reputation–a very first-rate reputation until a few months past–but now, in consequence of the reckless and alarming conduct of the accused, in a most dangerous condition; indeed, in the opinion of very competent authorities, fast sinking.

The office was crowded by many distinguished persons, all of them manifesting the most tender anxiety towards the accused; who, however, did not seem to feel the seriousness of his situation but, on the contrary, with folded arms and determined expression of visage, called the worthy magistrate (Mr. Punch) a "windbag," a "serf of flunkeydom," and "an ape of the Dead Sea."

John Nokes, a policeman with a literary turn, proved that he had long known the doings of the accused. Witness first became acquainted with him through his "Life of Schiller," a work done in the very best and decentest manner, in which no offence whatever was committed against the people's English; for he, John Nokes, had no idea that English should be called either "king's" or "queen's" but emphatically "the people's English." Had since known the accused through *"Sartor Resartus,"* "The French Revolution," "Past and Present," and "Oliver Cromwell." From time to time, as he went on, witness had marked with considerable anxiety, an increasing wildness, a daring eccentricity, of manner in the doings of the accused, frequently observing that he delighted to crack and dislocate the joints of language and to melt down and alloy sterling English into nothing better than German silver. Nevertheless, witness did not believe the reputation of the accused in any positive danger, until some three or four months back, when he detected him running wildly up and down the pages of "Fraser's Magazine," pelting all sorts of gibberish at the heads of Jamaica niggers–fantastically reproaching them for being "up to the ears, content in pumpkins, when they should work for sugar and spices" for their white masters–threatening them with the whip, and, in a word, dealing in language only dear to the heart–witness meant pockets–of Yankee slave-owners and Brazilian planters. Since then, witness had named his suspicions to several most

James Anthony Froude and John Ruskin, photographs owned by the Carlyles. Both men became good friends of the Carlyles in the 1850s. Carlyle named Froude as one of his literary executors (Rare Book and Manuscript Library, Columbia University, from Thomas Carlyle: A Biography, *Thomas Cooper Library, University of South Carolina).*

respectable publishers, warning them to have an eye upon the offender.

Peter Williams, teacher at the Lamb-and-Flag Ragged School, deposed that he had purchased two numbers of a work by the accused, called "Latter-day Pamphlets." The first number appeared to him (witness) to develop rabid symptoms,—but in the second, in Model Prisons, there was nothing in it but barking and froth. (Here several passages were read that fully bore out the opinion of the witness; passages which created a melancholy sensation in court, many persons sighing deeply, and in more than one instance dropping "some natural tears.")—Witness did not believe it consistent with public safety that, in his present temper, the accused should be trusted with pen-and-ink. If permitted the use of such dangerous weapons he would—until recovered from his present indisposition—inevitably inflict upon his reputation a mischief from which it could not recover. As it was, witness considered it far from safe.

Mr. Punch asked the accused if he had anything to say; whereupon accused, with a withering smile replied:

"Preternatural Eternal Oceans"—"Inhuman Humanitarians"—"Eiderdown Philanthropy"—"Wide-reverberating Cant"—"Work Sans Holiday"—"Three Cheers more, and Eternal, Inimitable, and Antipodean Fraternity"—

"Pumpkingdom, Flunkeydom, Foolscapdom, and Pen-and-Inkdom!"

Mr. Punch observed, this was a melancholy case. He could not release the accused unless upon good and sufficient surety. Whereupon two gentlemen—publishers of the first respectability—declared themselves willing to be bound, that the accused should not, until in a more healthful frame of mind, be allowed the use of paper and goose-quills.

It is believed that if accused again offend, the whole body of publishers will insist upon his compulsory silence. Let us, however, hope better things.

        –*The Literary World,* 6 (20 April 1850): 402–403

* * *

Carlyle was negotiating terms with his publisher in the midst of his ongoing pamphlet series and the controversy it inspired.

Carlyle to Edward Chapman, 29 April 1850

There is no question of "advances" in this matter: what payment I get out of the Pamphlets, and whether I get it tomorrow, or this time twelve month, or this time ten years, is happily not a vital point with me at all. The one indispensable thing is, that I have a fair, and above all a *clear* bargain as to the matter; that so my imagination be no longer annoyed and confused by the prospect of an ugly pecuniary evil to unravel, at the end of all this hard work of another kind. Such a bargain, which we ought to have made before ever starting at all, will now require to be made before going farther.

. . . .

Pray let me know therefore, in some definite shape, what you can do that there be no doubt, or bother about it whatever, in time coming. Long ago at Forster's, I remember, you spoke about £20 per Pamphlet if the sale reached 2,000; this is precisely the sum I now fix on, now when the sale extends into the *fours* or towards them. What is *fair* put into a *clear* shape, is the thing I want;—and this, so far as I can see into such matters, seems to me to be it.

If upon consideration you find that you have still nothing but "half profit" to offer me, or some lower sum than this I mention,—the question will arise whether our Enterprise, in its current shape, ought not immediately to terminate? At the end of No 6, then might a dart be drawn across the page, and some kind of conclusion, whether as pause or finale, be attained: what remains for me to say, I could manage to be said in other ways, perhaps less laborious to me, and certainly definite in their pecuniary issues at least.

The money you have "lost" by me I take as a piece of sad news,— all the sadder as I am not the least conscious of its having come my way in the shape of "gain." The fact is, I cannot understand it at all. Nor would I advise or wish that such a process on your part or any person's part should continue on my behalf!— But I conclude you are only bantering me, and do not mean much by those doleful tidings.

— The Collected Letters of Thomas and Jane Welsh Carlyle, v. 25, pp. 75–76

* * *

This excerpt is from an unsigned review written by a Scottish lawyer and satirist. Earlier in this essay, the reviewer listed Carlyle's previous works and asked, "Can any living man point to a single practical passage in any of these volumes? If not, what is the real value of Mr. Carlyle's writings?"

"A New Crotchet"
Review of *Latter-Day Pamphlets*
William Edmonstoune Aytoun

One peculiarity there is about the *Latter-day Pamphlets*, as contra-distinguished from their author's previous incubations, which has amused us not a little. Mr.

Carlyle has hitherto been understood to favour the cause of self-styled Liberalism. His mania, or rather his maunderings, on the subject of the Protector gained him the applause of many who are little less than theoretical republicans, and who regard as a glorious deed the regicide of the unfortunate Charles. Moreover, certain passages in his *History of the French Revolution* tended to strengthen this idea; he had a kindly side for Danton, and saw evident marks of heroism in the loathsome miscreant whom, in his usual absurd jargon, he styles 'the pale sea-green Incorruptible,' Robespierre. On this ground his works were received with approbation by a section of the public press; and we used to hear him lauded and commended as a writer of the profoundest stamp, as a deep original thinker, a thorough-paced philanthropist, the champion of genuine greatness, and the unflinching enemy of delusions. Now, however, things are altered. Mr. Carlyle has got a new crotchet into his head, and to the utter discomfiture of his former admirers, he manifests a truculent and ultra-tyrannical spirit, abuses the political economists, wants to have a strong coercive government, indicates a decided leaning to the whip and the musket as effectual modes of reasoning, and, in short, abjures democracy! The sensation caused by this extraordinary change of sentiment has been as great as if Joe Hume had declared himself a spendthrift.

—Blackwood's Edinburgh Magazine, 67 (June 1850): 645

* * *

This excerpt is from an article by Carlyle's friend John Forster, who in his unsigned essay maintains that "In his Latter-day Pamphlets, *Mr Carlyle is simply expressing the same views, and in the same manner, that he has for many years. The only difference is, that instead of pouring out the vials of his humour (we use the word in Ben Jonson's sense) on the French of the first French revolution, or on the contemporaries of Cromwell or on Jocelyn de Brakelonde, he is now pouring them out upon our own."*

"Stern Truthfulness and Intense Kindness"
Review of *Latter-Day Pamphlets*

. . . The most characteristic feature of Mr. Carlyle's mind—the very essence, we may say, of his being— is his intense and all-pervading honesty of purpose and truthfulness. He seeks for truth, for absolute certain truth, with the impassioned earnestness of a zealot, a bigot, an adorer. Often we are to seek and find, in the very impatience of his impetuous nature at the bare suspicion that some lurking fallacy or delusion may still have hold of him, the explanation of his fiercest denunciations. For next in the scale of preponderance to his love of truth, is his general and all-embracing spirit of tolerance and love. There is no writer of this, or any age, who has more perseveringly or more successfully laboured to detect those elements of goodness which lurk even in the minds of the most depraved. These two qualities, stern truthfulness and intense kindness, the principle of Duty and the principle of Affection, admirably check and balance each other, in all the operations of his mind; and have guided him to the discovery of profound general truths. Here, too, we have to add, that the very abstraction from active affairs of life which renders him vague and uninstructive on special measures, by compelling him to look on the busy world from a different point of view and through a different medium to that of its more active members, enables him frequently to throw a light upon its affairs in which it is most wholesome and beneficial to contemplate them.

Now all these qualities are to be found in the *Latter-Day Pamphlets*–abundantly to be found–though neighboured with other qualities less desirable, and which we freely give up to their objectors. We want only what is good in them to be recognised; as, soon or late, it assuredly must be. The critics who object that they contain no tangible measures for adoption are quite right. . . . We concede, too, that a man who is perpetually crying out for real government ought to have much clearer and less vague notions of what government ought to do. This over-exacting spirit renders Mr Carlyle unjust in his attacks upon many philanthropists and liberals. . . . But these are mere errors of detail; attributable, all of them, to his want of practical conversance with the field of observation into which he has entered. The general truths which he enumerates we find to be, on the contrary, for the most part worthy of all acceptance.

–*Examiner*, no. 2213 (29 June 1850): 404, 405

* * *

This excerpt is from a letter Carlyle wrote as he was working on his last pamphlet, "Jesuitism."

Carlyle to John Forster, 5 July 1850

Many thanks for your call and your Note, and all your goodness to me! The *Examiner* is excellent; nothing can be kinder, or shew a more friendly meaning towards me;– and, you may believe me, this is all the good, or nearly all, the brotherliest critic could do me in these sorrowful operations of mine! If indeed any critic or person can do me any good or even any real ill in them at all? Alas, there *is* no help for a poor devil in such cases; he must try if he can welter thro', and get done with it; that will help him, that will be a kind of refuge for him!

On the whole, the people greedily read and buy these Pamphlets, and violently abuse them, I believe: this means that the people take their physic, and that it is physic to them: what other response could be expected or desired by me?

–*The Collected Letters of Thomas and Jane Welsh Carlyle*, v. 5, pp. 113–114

* * *

This unsigned review of Carlyle's pamphlets appeared in a pro-slavery periodical published in Charleston, South Carolina. The first sentence refers to the American editions of Latter-Day Pamphlets *published in New York by Harper and in Boston by Phillips, Sampson.*

"Superior to Cant and False Philanthropy"
Review of *Latter-Day Pamphlets*

Here are two very neat editions of Carlyle's Latter Day Pamphlets, one of those publications which cannot be dismissed in a single paragraph. We reserve it for a future moment of greater space and leisure. Carlyle has offended the people of the North, since he has come out, sensibly, philosophically, and like a man, superior to cant and false philanthropy, in favour of negro slavery. They now discover that he is a fool, a twattler, and, like Father Mathew, has lived just a year too long. We perceive but little falling off, in these pamphlets, from the stern, old, prophetic Carlyle whom we have known before. "He repeats himself!" cry aloud the donkeys of literature; as if they did not repeat themselves, day after day, to the eternal sickening of all good men's stomachs–as if Isaiah, and all the prophets had not need, hourly, to repeat themselves, since the wretched communities to which they addressed entreaty and imprecation, in vain, were also repeating themselves, with increasing vice and venom, with neither remorse nor understanding. But the wonder is, to see so many of our Southern persons–not having read these pamphlets–actually repeating the clamours of their Yankee file-leaders–actually denouncing, in their abominable blindness, one of their best friends and champions. What if Carlyle does sneer at the American people as a race of bores: we need not be solicitous in the defense of the Yankee part of the nation. And, it is this part which has been boring him, and all other English writers, by visit and letter, until the best tempered person in the would might well be angry.

–*Southern Quarterly Review*, 17 (July 1850): 509

* * *

This excerpt is from an unsigned column in an American periodical.

"A Sick Giant"
Review of "Hudson's Statue"

The seventh number of *Carlyle's Latter-Day Pamphlets*, issued by Harper and Brothers, is a mere seven-fold repetition of the ancient discontent of the author, whose mirth is changed into a permanent wail, and for whom the "brave o-erhanging firmament has become only a foul and pestilential congregation of vapors." The subject of this number is the "Statue of Hudson," the great deposed Railway King. It says much more of statues in general, than of this particular one of Hudson's. Like all the recent productions of Carlyle, it reminds us of the strugglings of a sick giant, whom his friends in mercy should compel to take to his bed and turn his face to the wall.

–*Harper's Magazine*, 1 (August 1850): 430, 571

* * *

"False Analogies"
An Example from "The Present Time"

The anonymous reviewer of Latter-Day Pamphlets *for* Eclectic Review *argued that "the present series of pamphlets exhibits most of the excellences, with more than an ordinary share of the faults, of the author." He cites the employment of false analogies as "anything but a venial fault in one who professes so profound a hatred of shams and falsehoods."*

. . . The following may serve as another example in point:–

'Certainly Emancipation proceeds with rapid strides among us, this pood while; and has got to such a length as might give rise to reflections in men of a serious turn. West Indian Blacks are emancipated, and, it appears, refuse to work: Irish Whites have long been entirely emancipated, and nobody asks them to work, or, on condition of finding them potatoes (which, of course, is indispensable), permits them to work. Among speculative person, a question has sometimes risen: In the progress of Emancipation, are we to look for a time than all the horses also are to be emancipated, and brought toe the supply-and-demand principle?. . . .

–*The Present Time*, pp. 30–32

It is true, we admit–true even to a truism–that it will not do to 'emancipate the horses;' but it is not quite so true that to emancipate Blacks and Whites is an equally pernicious and utterly foolish thing. The very illustration is degrading, and unworthy of Mr. Carlyle's insight. He who can see so much in the constitution of horses, might, we should have thought, see more in the constitution of man, however obscured.

–*Eclectic Review*, 102 (October 1850): 389–391

This poem by Erastus W. Ellsworth was published in an American periodical.

To Mr. Carlyle

SAGE cynic Carlyle, "cut and come again."
Be bold, we dwell in flesh, put on the lash;
But pray excuse us, till we feel the pain,
From roaring Oh! To warn thee thou art rash.
Tough Jonathan no woman is, nor swoons,
Till Hurt bites through his boots and pantaloons.
Thou great self-twisted, crabbed, gnarled and bent,
What dost thou mean by telling us our shores
Are populous with "eighteen million bores!"
Or do we spell amiss thy true intent,
Which might have been an awkward compliment!
For, since Time was, our earth did never ken
Such bores–such borers, as our Yankee men.
Sir, we are "nothing else," and proud to say
That we are penetrative every way.
Through deserts, forests, mountains, we have sent
Ploughs, rifles, picks, across a continent.
Of distant ports, unpierced, are few or none:
Even El Dorado we have dug upon.
We bore, for love or gala, the antipodes–
Even now, for thy lost Star, the Arctic man.
All tools we use, that time and chance allot,
From patent schemes, to patent guns and shot:
But always boring never augering ill,
Unless the bore run out against our will–
Thou hast us there–But thou dost ask us, too,
What "Fact" we have developed, great and new.
Oh! hard propounder!–admirable Sphinx!–
Stone-headed Image, that so deeply thinks!–
Eyes, that no wave the mirrored heavens could show,
Profoundly sat upon the sands below!
Our eyes can only answer with a stare,
That ache to see an old thing any where.
One *fact*, indeed, we have not yet educed:
A wit approved that England has abused.
England we love, whose venerable stones
Are kept and cherished o'er our fathers bones;
And shot at, though we be, from that gray Isle,
At "Paper bullets of the brain" we smile–
At least, we scarce, again, shall dodge Carlyle.

–*Sartain's Union Magazine*,
7 (November 1850): 267

* * *

These excerpts are from a forty-eight-page pamphlet, Perforations in the "Latter-Day Pamphlets," *said to be "edited" by abolitionist Elizur Wright. The American author identified himself only as one of the "Eighteen Millions of Bores."*

"Towering Contempt for Abolitionism"
Response to *Latter-Day Pamphlets*
Elizur Wright

In his veneration of the chattel slavery of the Africans, and his towering contempt for abolitionism, Mr. Carlyle outdoes the late lamented John C. Calhoun. Somehow or other, in his closet there in Cheyne Row, Chelsea, hard by the Thames, he has imbibed a contempt for the negro or ebony-cut man, so intense and transcendental that it would be considered a little extravagant in the patriarchal kingdom of South Carolina. Somehow or other he has got it into his wise and almost prophetic head that whereas the slave overseer is a successful and thrifty captain of labor, and his negro slave a genuine and effective toiler, the free negro is necessarily the very incarnation of idleness. He sinks the whole sable style of humanity under this condemnation, without exception or qualification. Meeting a dingy Douglass or a pitchy Ward, who has worked his way from chattlehood up to the side of the ablest of white Sanhedrim Doctors and Senators, hero-worshiper as he is reported to be, he is ready to address the runaway in the following contemptuous and profane words. (See Model Prisons, page 25.) "And you Quashee, my pumpkin,—(not a bad fellow either, this poor Quashee, when tolerably guided!)—idle Quashee, I say you must get the Devil *sent away* from your elbow, my poor dark friend! In this world there will be no existence for you otherwise. No, not as the brother of your folly will I live beside you. Please to with draw out of my way if I am not to contradict your folly, and amend it, and put it in the stocks if it will not amend. By the Eternal Maker, it is on that footing alone that you and I can live together!"

Now I think that if Thomas Carlyle were to undertake the task of *tolerably guiding,* by means of the stocks and such like, either Douglass or Ward or some others I wot of, he would indeed find them "some pumpkins." If he did not, he would succeed better than one Thomas Auld and others. But the simple hearted and verdant man has been utterly imposed upon as to facts, by some West Indian overseer or bankrupt slave proprietor, who has taken advantage of his intense antipathy to cant and prejudice against the Exeter Hall platform. Idleness! good God! that is on the other side. Idleness in its most unmitigated form has carried the whip and instilled its own image into the negro at the point of it. This is an education to laziness which the African must have time to recover from. Carlyle is yet to be disabused of a legion of lies, which lazy vagabonds, too lazy to brush their own coats, have poured into his unsophisticated ears. Does Carlyle dare to accuse George Stephen, as true a man as ever opened his eyes to a British sky, of cant and twaddle? Let him read George Stephen's volumes *delineating* the law and practice of West Indian Slavery, and see what it was that emancipation has ruined. He will there see that slavery was to the planter nothing but bankruptcy and ruin, revolving in short cycles, while to the slave, to say the least, it was a monstrously awkward mode of producing industry.

. . . .

Carlyle deems that slaves are made in heaven. Their collars are marked and padlocked there, and it is presumption for Parliament, Congress or any human legislation to undo the padlock or file off the mark. Indeed he affirms that it is impossible. But then he tells us that these Heaven-labelled-and-padlocked slaves are everywhere, and even where we least suspect. They invade and pollute the ballot-box, and may now be, for aught we know, in Congress, or they may have just returned from the Nashville Convention. Again, *vice versa,* some, whom Heaven has labelled FREE, may be hoeing cotton on a peck of corn a week, with hope of salt fish at Christmas. So this discovery of Carlyle, is, after all, not very practical, or consolatory to the slaveholders. *They* are only troubled to keep in slavery those whom Heaven has manifestly *not* padlocked. It is for these they deny the alphabet and the Arabic figures, and want a Supreme Court of 17,000 judges and an innumerable legion of bloodhounds, biped and quadruped, wants which Heaven will never supply whatever Congress may do.

. . . .

. . . Our amiable and wise friend Carlyle, wrapped in the deep piety of his fear-worship—truly in the "latter days" of that religion—longing to see stronger sceptres of iron and longer whips of leather, may rail at us as a no-government people, and attribute our "roast goose and apple sauce" to a little "respect for the street constable," and a great deal of "fertile waste land." The truth we claim to be, that we are beginning to have sense enough to dispense with kings and born rulers, and do our own governing in a quiet and inexpensive way, and with this faculty we will take in good part the broad hint to make our calls shorter and less frequent at Cheyne Row, and console ourselves as well as we can for the absence among our progeny of any such wise, noble and admirable souls, as he who compliments negro slavery from that snug domicil.

—*Perforations in the "Latter-Day Pamphlets,"*
pp. 34–36, 41–42, 48

* * *

In this excerpt Carlyle relates a specific instance in which he believes he was affected by Wright's Perforations *in the "Latter-Day Pamphlets."* Emerson, *who was writing a memoir of Margaret Fuller Ossoli, had given letters requesting information on the author to his friend Samuel Gray Ward, who had agreed to try to find the correspondents. Ward, however, apparently heeding Wright's call to shun Carlyle, had decided not to visit him at Cheyne Row.*

Carlyle to Emerson, 14 November 1850

You are often enough present to my thoughts; but yesterday there came a little incident which has brought you rather vividly upon the scene for me. A certain Mr "S. E. Ward" from Boston sends us, yesterday morning by post, a Note of yours addressed to Mazzini, whom he cannot find; and indicates that he retains a similar one addressed to myself, and (in the most courteous, kindly, and dignified manner, if Mercy prevent not) is about carrying it off with him again to America! To give Mercy a chance, I by the first opportunity get under way for Morley's Hôtel, the Address of Mr Ward; find there that Mr Ward, since morning, *has been* on the road towards Liverpool and America, and that the function of Mercy is quite extinct in this instance! My reflections as I wandered home again were none of the pleasantest. Of this Mr Ward I had heard some tradition, as of an intelligent, accomplished, and superior man; such a man's acquaintance, of whatever complexion he be, is and was always a precious thing to me, well worth acquiring where possible; not to say that any friend of yours, whatever his qualities otherwise, carries with him an imperative key to all bolts and locks of mine, real or imaginary. In fact I felt punished;– and who knows, if the case were seen into, whether I deserve it? What "business" it was that deprived me of a call from Mr Ward, or of the possibility of calling on him, I know very well,– and Elizur Wright, the little dog, and others know! But the fact in that matter is very far different indeed from the superficial semblance; and I appeal to all the *gentlemen* that are in America for a candid interpretation of the same. "Eighteen million bores." good Heavens don't I know how many of that species we also have; and how with us, as with you, the difference between *them* and the Eighteen thousand noble-men and *non*-bores is immeasurable and inconceivable; and how, with us as with you, the *latter* small company, sons of the Empyrean, will have to fling the former huge one, sons of Mammon and Mud, into some kind of chains again, reduce them to some kind of silence again,– unless the old Mud-Demons are to rise and devour us all? Truly it is so I construe it: and if Elizur Wright and the Eighteen millions are well justified in their anger at me, E. S. Ward and the Eighteen thou-

sand owe me thanks and new love. That is my decided opinion, in spite of you all! And so, along with Ward, probably in the same ship with him, there shall go my protest against the conduct of Ward; and the declaration that to the last I will protest! Which will wind up the matter (without any word of yours on it) at this time,– –For the rest, tho' Elizur sent me his Pamphlet, it is a fact I have not read a word of it, nor shall ever read. My Wife read it; but I was away, with far other things in my head; and it was "lent to various persons" till it died!– Enough and ten times more than enough of all that.

. . . .

. . . Let us well remember it; and yet remember too that it is *not* good always, or ever, to be "at ease in Zion"; good often to be in fierce rage in Zion; and that the vile Pythons of this Mud-World do verily require to have sun-arrows shot into them, and red-hot pokers struck thro' them, according to occasion: woe to the man that carries either of these weapons, and does not use it in their presence!

–*The Correspondence of Thomas Carlyle and Ralph Waldo Emerson, 1834–1872,* pp. 220–223

* * *

These excerpts are from a forty-page article that Carlyle mentioned in his 6 November 1850 letter to Jean Carlyle Aitken: "A good many 'reviews' seem still to be going on about me: one in the North British Review *(the writer guessable to me) I read yesterday; friendly, but reporting hostilities without end or measure, which I never knew of, much less cared for!"* (The Collected Letters of Thomas and Jane Welsh Carlyle, *v. 25, p. 276*).

A friend and supporter of Carlyle, David Masson was a Scot who visited Cheyne Row in the 1840s. Carlyle assisted Masson in finding a publisher for his book on Shakespeare's sonnets in July 1848. Masson went on to have a successful career as a writer, editor, and professor whose books included Carlyle Personally and in his Writings: Two Lectures *(1885).*

"Unpopular Reception"
Response to *Latter-Day Pamphlets*
David Masson

. . . For some years, it may have been observed, a reaction has been in process against Mr. Carlyle and his doctrine—a reaction, the elements of which were in existence before, but have only recently come together and assumed something like a declared organization. It is nearly half a generation since Mr. Carlyle became an intellectual power in this country; and certainly rarely, if ever, in the history of literature, has such a phenomenon been witnessed as that of his influence. Throughout the whole atmosphere of this island his spirit has diffused itself, so that there is probably not an educated man under forty years of age, from Caithness to Cornwall, that can honestly say he has not been more or less affected by it. Even in the department of action his existence has been felt. Persons acquainted with the circumstances, and capable of tracing the affiliation, discern evidences of his effects equally in the Irish Rebellion and in the English Catholic movement. And in literature the extent to which he has operated upon society is still more apparent. Not to speak of his express imitators, one can hardly take up a book or a periodical without finding in every page some expression or some mode of thinking that bears the mintmark of his genius. "Hero-worship," "The Condition-of-England question," "Flunkeyism,"—these, and hundreds of other phrases, either first coined by him, or first laid hold of and naturalized by him, are now gladly used by many that upon the whole have no great liking for him, or even hold him in aversion. We have even observed that many of his critics abuse him in language which, when analyzed, is found to consist of a detritus of his own ideas.

But, though his influence has been thus extensive and profound, there have never been wanting men openly antipathetic to it.

. . . .

The publication of the *Latter-Day Pamphlets* has brought the controversy to a crisis. Never before, probably, was there a publication so provocative of rage, hatred, and personal malevolence. Whatever amount of antipathy to Mr. Carlyle previously existed throughout the reading community, has been by this concentrated and brought out into explicit manifestation. Simultaneously over the whole kingdom the scattered elements of dislike have mustered themselves; so that nearly the whole force of the critical demonstration that has been made *apropos* of the author's reappearance in the field of literature, has been on the part of the reaction. In all circles, and on the most various occasions, there have been outbreaks of a spirit of resistance to him amounting almost to malignity. Lord John Russell in the House of Commons takes a highly elaborated revenge for certain impolite allusions to him in the *Pamphlets,* by incidentally referring to their author as "a clever but whimsical writer." With a similar affectation of condescending unconcern to cover what is in reality the most intense bitterness of feeling, some critics write as if they would have it believed they thought of the author only as a poor driveller that all persons of sense had long ceased to listen to. Others, again, more honestly, assail and vituperate him with the whole force of their undis-

guised abhorrence. The correspondent of one American newspaper coolly accounts to the Transatlantic public for the "insane" tone of the *Pamphlets* by the information that "Thomas is believed to have recently taken to whiskey." We have ourselves heard him cursed by name in open society; and were it possible to accumulate in some distinct and visible shape all the imprecations and other expressions of rage and ill-will that the pamphlets have elicited, we fancy the display would be something fearful. In short, at the present moment, Mr. Carlyle is unpopular with at least one half of the kingdom.

. . . .

But there are deeper reasons for the formidable display of animosity with which the *Pamphlets* have been greeted. The *Pamphlets* contain in themselves matter more irritating and blistering than any of the author's previous writings. They come more directly into conflict with prevailing sentiments, parties, and interests; and are, in fact, a more explicit assertion than the author had before made, that he detaches himself from the devotees of pure and pleasurable literature, and regards himself as a social agent or recognised force in the country, charged with a special commission and special responsibilities. He has here, as it were, completed his career of respect for his fellow-men; parted with the last shred of his care for their approbation; reached the pulpit, where it is the condemnation of his own soul if he does not speak out, even if they stone him; and determined with himself that whatever may have been his method hitherto, now it his function most emphatically to "make a row about things." And certainly he has done so. . . .

In considering this extremely unpopular reception which the *Latter-Day Pamphlets* have met with, not in all, certainly, but in many quarters, one thing surely seems pretty clear; to wit—that nobody knew better that the outburst was coming than the author did himself. Whatever unpopularity has been or may yet be the consequence of these Pamphlets, the author has knowingly, resolutely, and deliberately braved it. . . . We should not imagine, for example, that, as he wrote the tract on *Model Prisons,* he expected it would bring him in a great deal of praise; nor, accordingly should we suppose that he was much disappointed at not getting it. Or, to speak more plainly, there is not, we should infer from all the evidence we can get, a single man connected with the literature of this country, more thoroughly insensible than Mr. Carlyle to the mere titillation of critical opinion. In this respect, we are disposed to believe, he reaches an absolutely heroic standard, the contemplation of which might shame many of us.

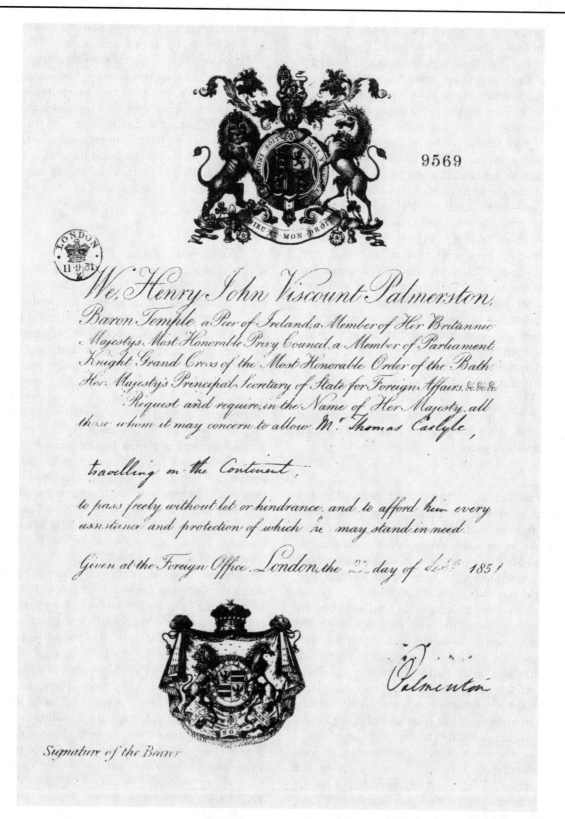

A passport that was issued to Carlyle for a journey to Paris he took with Robert and Elizabeth Barrett Browning in September 1851
(The Trustees of the National Library of Scotland CH 889)

....

. . . A thing may be intellectually a commonplace, long before it is morally familiar; and as boys used to be taught to remember facts of parochial consequence by receiving beatings contemporaneously with them, so one is none the worse for being belaboured with an important truth through many more sentences, and in much more ponderous language, than might suffice for its mere intellectual conveyance. If, when you have changed your lodging, the postman makes a mistake in the delivery of your letters, it may not be sufficient simply to tell him once more the alteration you wish him to remember; but if you detain him in the street, hold him for ten minutes by the button, and punish him for his mistake by monotonously talking about the matter over and over again, till he actually perspires under your redundancy, you will have sufficient security in the poor fellow's sensations against any similar blundering in the future. And so sometimes with Mr. Carlyle. His pamphlets are, in fact, in many passages, exactly such street lectures to the postman. The reader would fain be off; like the postman he has his letters to deliver along the street, and his other business to do; and he protests that he perfectly understands what Mr. Carlyle has been good enough to tell him, and that he will not forget it; but all in vain; again and again the information is repeated; the phrases "justice," "the immensities," "the eternal fact of things," are tumbled upon him with a frequency unexampled except in the Koran; and, when at last he is released, it is with a ringing in the ears, a universal sense of stupor, and knees absolutely knocking against each other for faintness.

–*North British Review* (November 1850): 3–4, 6–11

* * *

Carlyle discussed the response to Latter-Day Pamphlets *in this excerpt from a letter to his brother.*

Carlyle to Alexander Carlyle, 15 November 1850

I was utterly done before, in the end of July last, I could get those wild *Pamphlets* off my hand; the last two in particular did try all the obstinacy I was master of; and really, to my own mind, had something of worth in them in that respect, if in no other. They have done little for me hitherto, these *Pamphlets,* in any outward respect; the money of them (which however I could happily do independently of) has been mostly pocketed by the Bookseller; so negligent was I in bargaining about them; and as to their reception from mankind, you never in your life heard such a screaming and squealing,–a universal "*screigh* as of stuck pigs," stuck to

the heart, all running about with gillies in their sides, and bleeding to death by the hand of a *friend!* Really it was something like that; but there were other better sounds also perceptible in a low key; and as I kept far away from the universal "screigh," and would not read a word of the balderdash that was written upon me, and was zealously abetted by my Wife in that obstinate course too,– it was in truth rather entertaining to hear the said universal "screigh" from the distance, and served as a sign that at least the medicine had been *swallowed,* and that probably (as old Keble used to say) "it had took an effect upon them."–In late weeks, now that the thing is all over, I find the tone perceptibly altering, and have no doubt it will alter to the right pitch, or even beyond it,– like the Irishman's jamb, "plumb *and more.*" They had much need of a dose like that, the stupid blockheads of this generation.

–*New Letters of Thomas Carlyle,*
v. 2, pp. 101–102

* * *

These excerpts are from a twenty-page unsigned article.

"The Sufficency of the Human Mind"
Review of *Latter-Day Pamphlets*

. . . His habits of thought and his love of paradox would make it difficult for him to agree long with any set of men; we shall presently see that to what are now commonly called liberal opinions he has the most irreconcilable repugnance. As long as the oracle uttered mere vague rumblings, all was well; it condemned what existed, and the liberals could not conceive that any remedy could even be imagined except the ballot-box. But the oracle has lately begun to speak articulately; and, to the great consternation of the liberals, it has very plainly pronounced an utter and total condemnation of their whole theory. The confusion has accordingly been great. They deplore over him as a backsliding brother. Punch thinks that his prophet is mad. The delusion seems to have been altogether self-created. It requires no very diligent study of Mr. Carlyle to see that his whole theory of life and morals is so widely different from that of the ordinary run of the modern liberal school, that they may be almost said to be absolutely opposed to each other. In one word, he is a Stoic, and they are Epicureans.

....

We have said that he is a Stoic; by which we mean that the leading tendency of his philosophy is to assert the sufficiency of the human mind for itself and its own happiness under all possible circumstances. Its ancient professors refused to admit that any thing external could interfere with the happiness of their ideal wise man; and Mr. Carlyle would certainly rather teach us to endure pain than persuade us to shun it. He has very plainly said, that in schemes for the extirpation of pain he, at least, will have no part. In that strange book, "Sartor Resartus," which, in spite of its grotesque humour, no doubt contains the confession of the genuine faith of the writer, he is most explicit upon this point: "Say to happiness *of every kind,* 'I can do without thee.'" "With self-renunciation life begins."

. . . .

It may perhaps be worth while to consider for a little while the tendencies and the prospects of this new Stoicism. It seems on the whole to be far better and nobler than the prevalent Epicureanism, against which it protests. Its tendency is to fortify the mental and moral energies. It inculcates the sense of duty, the contempt of pleasure and pain. As a mere protest against popular errors, it is useful, as tending even in its extravagancies, to redress and set right the balance. Nor are its faults few or trifling. It tends to substitute the worship of power for that of goodness. Its professor is valued less for his willingness to do the will of God, than for his energy in working out his own. The old Stoics were consistently fatalists. It has another, and what will probably be a much more frequent danger. He who trusts to the strength of his own heart, will surely find some day that it is in truth very weak; human nature cannot be made strong by resolving that it will be so; and it will be well for the Stoical philosopher if he does not find, in the hour of his weakness, that the reed on which he leant is gone into his hand and pierced it, if the reaction from his too high opinion of his own virtue, does not drive him into despair and disregard of any.

–*English Review,* 16 (January 1852): 335, 338, 340

* * *

In this excerpt Carlyle refers to the publication of his essay on the "Negro Question" that he had revised for publication as a pamphlet. In addition to changing his title to Occasional Discourse on the Nigger Question, *he added thirty-two paragraphs.*

Carlyle to John A. Carlyle, 1 July 1853

I sent the *Nigger* Pamphlet &c in a Parcel to you the other day: the man paid me £20 for 4,000; and they have nothing that I do not well believe. I did not send a Copy to my Mother; meaning *you* to

judge if it w*d* not afflict *her* to read it,–and to warn me, and take measures accordingly. Nobody but Jean at Dumfries has got a Copy; *item* my own Jane,–who, if you think right to warn her, will keep it quite out of my Mother's sight at Scotsbrig. But perhaps it may not be so offensive there now?

–*The Collected Letters of Thomas Carlyle and Jane Welsh Carlyle,* v. 28, p. 182

* * *

This excerpt is from a letter in which Emerson apologized for not keeping up with his end of the correspondence: "For you,– I have too much constitutional regard and ––, not to feel remorse for my short-comings and slow-comings, and I remember the maxim which the French stole from our Indians,–and it was worth stealing,–'Let not the grass grow on the path of friendship.'"

Emerson to Carlyle, 11 March 1854

. . . I lately looked into *Jesuitism,* a Latter-Day Pamphlet, and found why you like those papers so well. I think you have cleared your skirts; it is a pretty good minority of one; enunciating with brilliant malice what shall be the universal opinion of the next edition of mankind. And the sanity was so manifest, that I felt that the over-gods had cleared their skirts also to this generation, in not leaving themselves without witness, though without this single voice perhaps I should not acquit them. Also I pardon the world that reads the book as though it read it not, when I see your inveterated humours. It required courage and required conditions that feuilletonists are not the persons to name or qualify, this writing Rabelais in 1850. And to do this alone.–You must even pitch your tune to suit yourself. We must let Arctic navigators and deep-sea divers wear what astonishing coats, and eat what meats–wheat or whale–they like, without criticism.

I read further, sidewise and backwards, in these pamphlets, without exhausting them. I have not ceased to think of the great warm heart that sends them forth, and which I, with others, sometimes tax with satire, and with not being warm enough–for this poor world;–I too,– though I know its meltings to-me-ward.

–*The Correspondence of Thomas Carlyle and Ralph Waldo Emerson, 1834–1872,* v. 2, pp. 231–232

A Life of "Poor" John Sterling

John Stuart Mill had introduced Carlyle to John Sterling in February 1835. Sterling had originally studied for the church but had changed course and pursued a writing career, during which he at times appealed to Carlyle for criticism. His literary works include the novel Arthur Coningsby (1833) and Poems (1839). When the thirty-eight-year-old Sterling died of consumption in 1844, leaving his papers in the hands of Carlyle and Sterling's Cambridge tutor, Archbishop Julius Hare, Carlyle was still involved in work on Oliver Cromwell's Letters and Speeches (1845) and left to his co-executor the task of publishing Sterling's writings.

Carlyle, however, was critical of the biographical sketch the archbishop produced for the two-volume collection of Sterling's Essays and Tales (1848). He believed that the portrayal of Sterling as a devout Anglican was completely inaccurate. With the completion of Latter-Day Pamphlets, Carlyle decided to answer Hare's book with his own biography of Sterling, which was published in London by Chapman and Hall on 10 October 1851.

Most reviewers of The Life of John Sterling praised Carlyle's sincere and lucid style in the book, but many also took issue with his portrayal of Sterling's religious struggle and with Carlyle's motivations for writing the biography.

This excerpt from a letter to his mother indicates Carlyle's immediate dissatisfaction with Hare's work.

Carlyle to Margaret A. Carlyle, 12 February 1848

A book consisting of my poor friend John Sterling's scattered writings has just come out, edited by one Julius Hare, an Archdeacon, soon to be a Bishop, they say; a good man, but rather a weak one, with a Life of Sterling which by no means contents me altogether. Probably one of my first tasks will be something in reference to this work of poor Sterling's; for he left it in charge to me too, and I surrendered my share of the task to the Archdeacon, being so busy with 'Cromwell' at the time. But I am bound by very sacred considerations to keep a sharp eye over it, and will consider what can now be done. Sterling was a noble creature, but had too little patience, and indeed too thin and sick a constitution of body, to turn his fine gifts to the best account.

–James A. Froude, *Thomas Carlyle: A History of His Life in London*, v. 1, pp. 418–419

* * *

Emerson and Sterling were friends and correspondents.

Emerson's Journal, September or October 1851

In reading Carlyle's "Life of Sterling," I still feel, as of old, that the best service C. has rendered is to Rhetoric, or the Art of Writing. Now here is a book in which the vicious conventions of writing are all dropped; you have no board interposed between you & the writer's mind, but he talks flexibly, now high, now low, in loud hard emphasis, then in undertones, then laughs outright, then calmly narrates, then hints or raises an eyebrow, & all this living narration is daguerreotyped for you in his page. He has gone nigher to the wind than any other craft. No book can any longer be tolerable in the old husky Neal-on-the-Puritans model. But he does not, for all that, very much uncover his secret mind.

– *Journals and Miscellaneous Notebooks of Ralph Waldo Emerson*, v. 11, pp. 448–449

John Sterling, circa 1840 (from Life of Friedrich Schiller [1825]; Life of John Sterling [1851]: Two Biographies, Special Collections, Thomas Cooper Library, University of South Carolina)

* * *

LIFE OF THE AUTHOR.   ix

he held when he first went to College, he told
me that, while a boy, he read through the
whole Edinburgh Review from its beginning;
a diet than which hardly any could yield less
wholesome food for a young mind, and which
could scarcely fail to puff it up with the wind of
self-conceit.

In the autumn of 1824 he went to Trinity
College, Cambridge, where he became one of the
pupils at my classical lectures.   Here I was soon
attracted by the marks of his genial intellect and
spirit.   A good scholar indeed, in the common
sense of that phrase, he never was: few Englishmen become so, without going through a
regular course of scholastic instruction.   But he
was something better, inasmuch as he soon
shewed that he could relish and delight in the
beauty of Greek poetry, and the practical and
speculative wisdom of Greek history and philosophy.   Thus began an acquaintance, which
subsequently ripened into one of the most precious friendships vouchsafed to me during my
life.

Here let me mention an instance of the self-
forgetting energy and impetuosity which distinguished him even from his childhood.   One
day, while we were at lecture, we were alarmed

a 3

A page from Carlyle's annotated copy of Julius Hare's biographical sketch of Sterling in Essays and Tales *(1848)*
(Houghton Library, Harvard University)

Letters from John Sterling to his parents, with Carlyle's editing and annotations: left, an 8 October 1838 letter to his mother; right, a 12 March 1842 letter to his father (Beinecke Rare Book and Manuscript Library, Yale University)

(To his father) — Import.
12 March 1842.

× × × × × × × × × × × × ×

Important to me as these matters are I feel as if there were something unfeeling, in writing, of them, under the pressure of such news as ours from India. If the Caboot Troops have perished, England has not received such a blow from an enemy, nor anything approaching it, since Buckingham's expedition to the Isle of Rhé. Walcheren destroyed us by climate; Corunna with all its loss had much of glory. But here we are dismally injured by mere barbarians, in a war on our part shamefully unjust as well as foolish: a combination of disgrace & calamity that would have shocked Augustus even more than the defeat of Varus. One of the 4 Officers with Macnaghten, was George Lawrence, a brother-in-law of Nat Barton, a distinguished man, & the father of 5 totally unprovided children — He is a prisoner, if not since murdered. Macnaghten I do not pity, he was the prime author of the whole mad war. But Burnes, & the women; our regiments to India however, I feel sure, is safe.

So roll the months as Faith, such

is the tickering of the great wheel — theology as heard them by a good ear. I willingly

J. S.

Thus far, July 22

Chap. — Naples —

In the bleak weather of this Spring 1842, he was again abroad for a little while;

These excerpts are from an unsigned eight-page review.

"Noble Indeed"
Review of *The Life of John Sterling*

. . . Any man reading his book, and knowing that, whatever may be the author's faults, not Calumny herself can call him hypocrite, will be struck with the tender almost womanly affection he bears to the departed Sterling.

. . . .

. . . A man who gives his life for another is indeed a very meritorious man; making this abatement from his merit, that in all probability such an one doesn't know distinctly what better to do with his life—has not got an infant family certainly; and that death on such conditions is the easiest way for a vain and weak man, having the opportunity, to obtain a great reputation. But for him who (not by simple dying, which thousands have voluntarily undertaken for very trivial things, but) by an earnest unquailing, sleepless labour in behalf of Heaven and humanity, has reaped golden opinions from more than one nation—for such a man to gather together these well-earned trophies and risk them all in behalf of the *reputation* of a dead man, who cannot thank him—at least not yet—is noble indeed.

. . . .

Here we must conclude these remarks conscious that we have not done justice to our readers, Carlyle, or ourselves. But let it be understood that we have said so much in behalf of the present author because we are convinced that he is vastly misunderstood; because we believe, from a careful study of almost all he has written, and in full consciousness of many faults, that Carlyle is, in fact, *an eminently religious man*. This, indeed, is the great secret of his success; it is this that has given him that influence on the public mind which, *like* his Christianity, is a hundredfold greater than is generally surmised.

–*Tait's Edinburgh Magazine,*
18 (November 1851):
701–703

* * *

This excerpt is from Thackeray's two-page review of a biography he finds particularly interesting for providing "glimpses of the biographer." Thackeray mentions a hostile review by Samuel Phillips that appeared in the Times *on 1 November 1851.*

"Against the Make-Believe which Reigns"
Review of *The Life of John Sterling*
William Makepeace Thackeray

Turning to other considerations, let us not forget to note the plain and emphatic language in which at last he speaks out his deep-rooted antagonism to all Established Churches. Much abuse, much hatred, this will probably draw down. Is not the *Times* article an alarum? To all orthodox minds Carlyle must now unhesitatingly stand confessed as *not* of them. Hitherto he has written on religious subjects, as if he hated Cant and Shams; but somehow, by the very ambiguity of his language, he has always seemed *to have a Bishop in tow*. Now he has fairly cut cables, and leaves the Bishop to tow himself as he best may. Our readers are too much interested in the cause of free *utterance,* not to welcome such accession. Not that Carlyle has passed over to our camp. We cannot accurately determine *what* his religious opinions are; but we do not suppose they are such as we hold. In the greater cause, however, in that which transcends all forms and formulas, and gives to *every* creed its rights of utterance and organization, Carlyle is working by his powerful denunciations against the *make-believe* which reigns at the present day. For it is in the want of due recognition of free thought that so much hypocrisy lives; men pretend to believe what they do not believe, because that belief is called respectable.

–*Leader,* 2 (8 November 1851): 1067

* * *

These excerpts are from an unsigned four-page review by the woman who as George Eliot became one of the most popular novelists of the Victorian age. At the time of this review, written some seven years before she made her reputation with the novel Adam Bede *(1859), she was an assistant editor at the* Westminster Review.

"A Labour of Love"
Review of *The Life of John Sterling*

. . . The public, then, since it is content to do without biographies of much more remarkable men, cannot be supposed to have felt any pressing demand even for a single life of Sterling; still less, it might be thought, when so distinguished a writer as Archdeacon Hare had furnished this, could there be any need for another. But, in opposition to the majority of Mr. Carlyle's critics, we agree with him that the first life is properly the justification of the second. Even among the readers personally unacquainted with Sterling, those who sympathised with his ultimate alienation from the

Poor Sterling, he was by nature appointed for a
Poet, then,—a Poet after his sort, or recogniser and
delineator of the Beautiful; and not for a Priest at all?
Striving towards the sunny heights out of such a level
and through such an element as ours in these days is,
he had strange aberrations appointed him, and painful
wanderings amid the miserable gas-lights, bog-fires,
dancing meteors and putrid phosphorescences which
form the guidance of a young human soul at present!
Not till after trying all manner of sublimely illuminated
places, and finding that the basis of them was putridity,
artificial gas and quaking bog, did he, when his strength
was all done, discover his true sacred hill, and passionately climb thither while life was fast ebbing!—
A tragic history, as all histories are, yet a gallant, brave
and noble one as not many are. It is what to a radiant
son of the Muses, and bright messenger of the harmonious Wisdoms, this poor world, if he have not strength
enough, and *inertia* enough, and amid his harmonious
eloquences silence enough, has provided at present.
Many a high-striving, too-hasty soul, seeking guidance
towards eternal excellence from the official Blackartists
and successful Professors of political, ecclesiastical, philosophical, commercial, general and particular legerde-
main, will recognise his own history in this image of a
fellow pilgrim's.

Over-haste was his continual fault; over-haste, and
want of the due strength,—alas, mere want of the due
inertia chiefly; which is so common a gift for most part;
and proves so inexorably needful withal! He was good
and generous and true; joyful where there was joy, patient and silent where endurance was required of him;
shook innumerable sorrows, and thick-crowding forms
of pain, gallantly away from him; fared frankly forward, and with scrupulous care to tread on no one's
toes. True, above all, one may call him; a man of
perfect veracity in thought, word and deed. Integrity
towards all men, integrity had ripened with him into
chivalrous generosity; there was no guile nor baseness
anywhere found in him. Transparent as crystal; he
could not hide anything sinister, if such had been
him. A more perfectly transparent soul I have never
known. It was beautiful, to read all those interior
movements; the little shades of affectations, ostenta-
tions; transient spurts of anger which never grew to
the length of settled spleen: all so naive, so childlike,
the very faults grew beautiful to you. And so he played
his part among us, and has now ended it: in this first
half of the Nineteenth Century, such was the shape of
human destinies the world and he made out between
them.

A portion of a galley proof for The Life of John Sterling *with Carlyle's emendations (Edinburgh University Library, Special Collections)*

Church, rather than with his transient conformity, were likely to be dissatisfied with the entirely apologetic tone of Hare's life, which, indeed, is confessedly an incomplete presentation of Sterling's mental course after his opinions diverged from those of his clerical biographer; while those attached friends (and Sterling possessed the happy magic that secures many such) who knew him best during this latter part of his career, would naturally be pained to have it represented, though only by implication, as a sort of deepening declension ending in a virtual retraction. Of such friends Carlyle was the most eminent, and perhaps the most highly valued, and, as co-trustee with Archdeacon Hare of Sterling's literary character and writings, he felt a kind of responsibility that no mistaken idea of his departed friend should remain before the world without correction. Evidently, however, his "Life of Sterling" was not so much the conscientious discharge of a trust as a labour of love, and to this is owing its strong charm. Carlyle here shows us his "sunny side." We no longer see him breathing out threatenings and slaughter as in the Latter-Day Pamphlets, but moving among the charities and amenities of life, loving and beloved—a Teufelsdröckh still, but humanized by a Blumine worthy of him. We have often wished that genius would incline itself more frequently to the task of the biographer,—that when some great or good personage dies, instead of the dreary three or five volumed compilations of letter, and diary, and detail, little to the purpose, which two-thirds of the reading public have not the chance, nor the other third the inclination, to read, we could have a real "laife," setting forth briefly and vividly the man's inward and outward struggles, aims, and achievements, so as to make clear the meaning which his experience has for his fellows. A few such lives (chiefly, indeed, autobiographies) the world possesses, and they have, perhaps, been more influential on the formation of character than any other kind of reading. But the conditions required for the perfection of life writing,—personal intimacy, a loving and poetic nature which sees the beauty and the depth of familiar things, and the artistic power which seizes characteristic points and renders them with life-like effect,—are seldom found in combination. "The Life of Sterling," is an instance of this rare conjunction. Its comparatively tame scenes and incidents gather picturesqueness and interest under the rich lights of Carlyle's mind. We are told neither too little nor too much; the facts noted, the letters selected, are all such as serve to give the liveliest conception of what Sterling was and what he did; and though the book speaks much of other persons, this collateral matter is all a kind of scene-painting, and is accessory to the main purpose.

. . . .

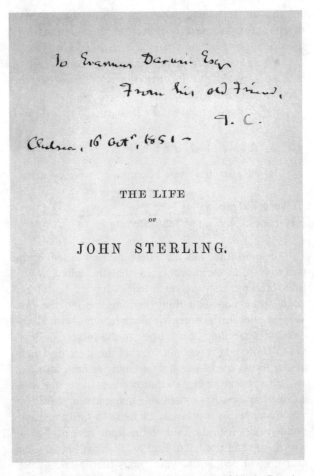

Title page with Carlyle's inscription to the brother of Charles Darwin (Special Collections, Thomas Cooper Library, University of South Carolina)

From the period when Carlyle's own acquaintance with Sterling commenced, the Life has a double interest, from the glimpses it gives us of the writer, as well as of his hero. We are made present at their first introduction to each other; we get a lively idea of their colloquies and walks together, and in this easy way, without any heavy disquisition or narrative, we obtain a clear insight into Sterling's character and mental progress. Above all, we are gladdened with a perception of the affinity that exists between noble souls, in spite of diversity in ideas—in what Carlyle calls "the logical outcome" of the faculties. This "Life of Sterling" is a touching monument of the capability human nature possesses of the highest love, the love of the good and beautiful in character, which is, after all, the essence of piety. The style of the work, too, is for the most part at once pure and rich; there are passages of deep pathos which come upon the reader like a strain of solemn music, and others which show that aptness of epithet, that masterly power of close delineation, in which, perhaps, no writer has excelled Carlyle.

We have said that we think this second "Life of Sterling" justified by the first; but were it not so, the book would justify itself.

—*Westminster Review*, 57 (January 1852): 248-251

* * *

These excerpts are from a thirteen-page unsigned review.

"A Very Vulgar Failing"
Review of *The Life of John Sterling*

Some simple folk have been pleased to see, in the narrative of Archdeacon Hare, that the gifted youth, John Sterling, may be regarded as having had some good—some Christian thing in him even to the last. Whereupon, forth comes Mr. Carlyle, who, with all the dexterous handling he can bring to the subject, endeavors to show that it was not so; that the seeming Christianity of his friend was only seeming at best, and that at the last every vestige of that obsolete affair had vanished from him. As our amiable manipulator makes his way towards this conclusion, he looks toward the disappointed ones with the kind of glee upon his muscles for which we shall not try to find an adjective—saying, 'So much, good people, for your pious John Sterling; you see what *I* did for him in that way!' In the whole history of infidel literature, we know of nothing to exceed this. Yet this is the man whom some Christian ministers can be vain to reckon among their friends and familiar acquaintance; and this is the book, too, which some of the said ministers can recommend to the youth under their influence! We wish we could believe in the extinction of the race called wolves in sheep's clothing—we wish we could regard phenomena of this complexion as unknown even among professed evangelical nonconformists.

But a closer investigation of Archdeacon Hare's 'Life of Sterling' will serve to explain *the* reason which induced Mr. Carlyle to follow with his supplement. Pantheism, or Carlyleism, or Nihilism, or whatever we may call the creed which consists in believing that no creed is possible, and 'that none of the many things we are in doubt about, and need to have demonstrated and rendered probable, can by any alchemy be made a religion for us,' is no sure preservation against a very vulgar failing, the failing of vanity. Now, it does so happen that the name of Carlyle is only twice mentioned by Archdeacon Hare in the whole of his book, so far as we can discover, and in the few instances in which it occurs in

quotations from Sterling's letters and papers given in the 'Life,'—eight we think in all,—four at least are accompanied by very questionable annotations:— 'Inadequacy of Carlyle's views;' his 'Chartism,' full of inconsistencies and fallacies;' his 'Heroes,' 'on the whole more free from delusive paradox than his other works;' Thirlwall's 'History,' superior to all in English for depth and compass, 'unless—*prepare to laugh*—Carlyle's.'

—*British Quarterly Review*, 15 (3 April 1852): 245-246

* * *

These excerpts are from a fourteen-page unsigned review.

"The Power of Evil"
Review of *The Life of John Sterling*

It is with feelings of unmitigated disgust that we turn to Mr. Carlyle's remarks on this epoch in Sterling's life. We will not pain our readers by transcribing them. A gloom was now to overshadow the rest of poor Sterling's life; he was to be brought within the reach of Mr. Carlyle's personal influence. That Satan has agents striving continuously to draw away those of whom it might be hoped that they were beginning to tread the paths of life, can hardly be doubted by those who read that gentleman's own account of his intercourse with Sterling. Our own opinion of Mr. Carlyle was never a very exalted one, but it has been materially modified by the memoir we are now considering. That Mr. Carlyle is possessed of considerable powers, is undoubted; that his clear-sightedness is garbed in most intolerable affectation, is obvious to all; and that his powers are deliberately consecrated to the power of evil is, alas! too plainly manifest to the Christian Observer. . . .

We will not sicken our readers by narrating the successive gladiatorial thrusts with which Mr. Carlyle endeavoured to destroy Sterling's weakened religious faith, nor the exultant triumph with which he commemorates each well-planted hit.

. . . .

. . . The object of this work has in it something almost awfully painful. It is written confessedly to show that what almost every rational man—though Mr. Carlyle does not—will regard as deep errors of opinion and faults of character in the subject of his memoir, had not been brought to light by Mr. Hare as they ought to be. Sterling, according to the present writer, only deviated occasionally into better things, but was in the main a proud despiser of all established opinion, and a thorough-grained infidel. We are afraid that the biographer has in a measure

"A Complicated Aggravation"
Carlyle and Lady Ashburton in the 1850s

Carlyle's attentions to Harriet Baring, Lady Ashburton, continued to provoke Jane Welsh Carlyle in the 1850s, as this excerpt from her 15 October 1851 letter to her sister Jean indicates.

I suppose I ought to feel by this time quite resigned to such annoyances–or rather I ought to feel and to have always felt quite superior to them–but I am angry and sorrowful all the same–It is not of course any caprice *she* can show to me that annoys me–I have long given up the generous attempt at loving her–But it is to see *him* always starting up to defend everything she does and says and no matter whether it be capricious behaviour towards his *wife*–so long as she flatters himself with delicate attentions–. . . With your letter came a note from Lady A to *Mr* C which turned out to be an invitation to *him* for this evening at 9 and after that another note came begging he would come at 8–and he is now off there again–I will not write any more tonight being in rather a bitter mood and the best in such moments is if possible to consume one's own smoke–since one cannot help *smoking*–

–The Collected Letters of Thomas and Jane Welsh Carlyle,
v. 26, pp. 205–206

Carlyle's fascination with Lady Ashburton lasted until her death in May 1857–an event that did not solve the problems that had evolved in the Carlyles' marriage. In an 11 November 1876 letter to Carlyle's future biographer James A. Froude, Geraldine Jewsbury provided her insight into the troubled couple.

With her habit of pushing every thing to the extreme–and of *expecting* to find the most *logical* consecutiveness in what people said did or professed–I don't know wh[o] fared the *worst* the people or herself.–Mr C–once said to me of her that she had the *deepest* & tenderest feelings–but *narrow* Any other wife wd have laughed at Mr C's *bewitchment* with L*y* A*n* but to *her* there was a complicated *aggravation* wh. made it *very* hard to endure–L*y* A. was admired for sayings & doings for w*h* she was–*snubbed. She* saw thro' L*y* A's little ways & *grande dame* manners & knew *what they were worth.* she contrasted them with the daily hourly endeavors she was making that *his* life shd. be as free from hindrances as possible–he put *her* aside for his WORK–but lingered in the "Primrose path of dalliance" for the sake of a great lady who liked to have a philosopher in chair–L*y* A. was excessively capricious towards her. & made her feel she cared more about *him* than about *her*–w*h* was always *lèse majesté* with *her.*–she was *never* allowed to visit any where but at the G– & the mortifications & vexations she *felt* tho' they were often & often *self made* were none the less intolerable to her. At *first* she was charmed with L*y* A.–but soon found she had *no real hold* on *her.* nor ever c*d* or w*d* have. The sufferings were *real* intense & at times *too grievous to be borne.*–C–did *not* understand all this & only felt her to be *unreasonable* Mrs C–was *proud*–& proud of her Pride. it was indeed enormous. but a quality she admired *in herself & in others.*

–The Collected Letters of Thomas and Jane Welsh Carlyle,
v. 30, pp. 263–266

succeeded in thus lowering the character of Sterling: and that though there was much in him which was calculated to awaken pity, and possibly regard, it is too obvious that there was much also, very much, to lament and condemn.

–Christian Observer, 52 (April 1852): 271, 275

* * *

These excerpts are from an unsigned four-page review.

"What Carlyle Is"
Review of *The Life of John Sterling*

During the fall of the past year this beautiful tribute to the memory of his deceased friend was published by one of the greatest men in the country. Because he is one of the greatest men in the country,

and because the book has been much abused as well as much praised, the general public are curious to know what manner of man was his friend on whom he has bestowed a Biography, and thus the first edition is already exhausted. Probably the abuse, more than the praise, has furthered the sale of the book, and in this way it has been a public benefit. For much as we desire to get foolish and bad books out of the way, still more do we desire to see good books–books stamped with true genius, lying in everyone's way. The new "Life of Sterling" is full of genius from beginning to end, though written in "a very swift and immediate" style, as the author says. In addition to that, it is one of the best biographies ever written–the very flower and model of biographical writing.

. . . .

Geraldine Jewsbury, a friend of the Carlyles who became a confidant of Jane Welsh Carlyle. This 1855 photograph was owned by the Carlyles (Rare Book and Manuscript Library, Columbia University; from Thomas Carlyle: A Biography, *Thomas Cooper Library, University of South Carolina).*

All those persons who are in the habit of regarding Carlyle as a strong, violent man, without gentle impulses and soft warm sympathies, should read this Life of Sterling. He makes no moan for the loss of his friend; but this book is a sort of "In Memoriam" in accordance with his nature, as that of Tennyson is with his.

. . . .

If the world did not need a Life of *Sterling,*–if it could well do without knowing exactly what *he was,* it could not do so well without knowing what Carlyle is. Nothing that he has yet published shows the gentle side of his nature so well–not even "The Sartor."

–Sharpe's London Magazine, 15 (1852): 52–55

A Quiet Place to Work

From his youth Carlyle required solitude and silence to write. At Cheyne Row he was annoyed by various disruptions, including piano playing by the daughters of neighboring tenants. In 1853 he became exasperated with noisy birds owned by the tenant of No. 6 Cheyne Row, and, after unsuccessful attempts to resolve the situation, he elected to construct a "soundproof" study at the top of his house. Although Jane negotiated peace with the owner of the offending fowls in December 1853, construction of the room proceeded. The garret turned out to be somewhat less than soundproof, but Carlyle still used it as a retreat for his work.

This excerpt is from a letter to Carlyle's sister.

Carlyle to Jean Carlyle Aitken, 11 August 1853

All summer I have been more or less annoyed with *noises,* even accidental ones, which get free access thro' my open windows; all the tinkering and "repairing" has done me no good in that respect. A very despicable, very intolerable sort of sufferings,–as poor Aird and others, can testify! At length, after deep deliberation, I have fairly decided to have a top story put upon the House, one big apart*t* 20 feet square, with thin *double* walls, light from the top &c, and artfully ventilated,– into which no sound *can* come; and all the cocks in Nature may crow round it, without my hearing a whisper of them! My notion is, it really will answer. John Chorley, a practical Liverpool *railway* man who is very loyal to me, went to Cubitts the Chief Builders here, told them my sad case, "a Literary man" &c &c; and they agreed to send a *right man,* with estimates, with &c &c: and here accordingly he is this very day mounting his scaffolds and ladders from the street,– to work *altogether from the outside;* and to have done "*within* six weeks"! I did not think of building again so soon: but Jane too encouraged and urged me; and indeed I have a feeling that this may prove one of the usefullest things I ever built. Our next neighbour's poultry (and even his poor *self,* a coarse and poor but not a *bad* one), I perceive, will before long be got quite rid of: but henceforth I hope to be independent of all men and all dogs, cocks and household or street noises,– which are waxing every year in this Chelsea with the furious building &c that now goes on in the once quiet suburb!–As everything is rigorously *estimated,* and Chorley is to be Clerk of the works, I design not to interfere in the business at all; but sit at my work within doors. If it grow too bad, we can run to Addiscombe, only 10 miles off, and beautiful enough for the Queen & Albert (or a still better pair): and the very thought of that renders one more patient from day to day.

–The Collected Letters of Thomas and Jane Welsh Carlyle, v. 28, p. 245

* * *

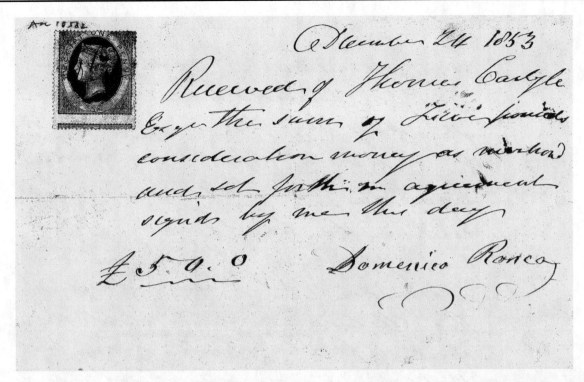

Receipt and agreement that Jane negotiated with neighbors for removal of what she described as "Demon-birds" in her Christmas Day letter to Charles Redwood (The Trustees of the National Library of Scotland Acc 10582)

This excerpt is from a letter to a friend. Carlyle had lodged with Redwood, a Welsh lawyer and an admirer, during a long vacation in Wales, summer 1843.

Jane Welsh Carlyle to Charles Redwood, 25 December 1853

Mr Carlyle and I were on a visit at Lord Ashburtons which commenced on the 4*th* of December and was to have lasted till about newyears day. But last Monday I was despatched to London about certain– *Cocks!* and a *Macaw!* which you have perhaps heard of– "the great first Cause least understood" of that "Silent apartment" which Mr C built this summer at an outlay of some 200£ The Silent Apartment having proved a complete failure having proved in fact *the* apartment most accessible to sound in the whole house (no wonder! having 14 air-holes in frank and free communication with the before and behind!) it became imperative, that unless we were both to be landed in Bedlam *he* thro' these Demon-birds and I thro their effects on *him*– some thing else should be done of real efficacy– *Poisoning* them was his fixed idea; but *that* I held him back from all I could–especially at this time of the year when the newspapers have no *debates* to fill their pages,– such

a recourse would have been questionable. It was finally settled we should try to *take* the house *no* 6 ourselves for three years and eject the present occupants– –*if we could*–and to achieve *this* I was sent to Chelsea "quite promiscuously"–To be in time for the Xmas term, the utmost despatch was needed–The fine people at the Grange, were greatly *amused* as well as astonished to see a Wife sent off from the midst of Xmas festivities to consult with house agents and house owners–But Mr C was quite right in insisting "She can do it better than I"–Decidedly he had neither the temper nor the dexterity(!) to bring this romantic undertaking to the happy issue *I* have brought it to–For I not only *got* the house but got rid of it when gotten, and by the potency of a notice to quit got rid of the whole lot of birds in consideration of a present of 5£– and have my neighbour *legally* bound at this moment "not to keep or allow to be kept on these premises any birds *or other nuisance* under penalty of 10£ and a notice to quit"–I will *tell* you someday how I managed it –

–*The Collected Letters of Thomas and Jane Welsh Carlyle*, v. 28, pp. 350–351

* * *

In consideration of the sum
of Five pounds paid to me
this day by Thomas Carlyle
Esq.r I hereby promise and
agree that I will immediately
remove the fowls and other
birds from my house and
premises N.o 6 Great Cheyne
Row Chelsea and undertake
that no fowls *or other nuisance* shall ever be
kept by me or any other persons
upon the said premises N.o 6
Great Cheyne Row Chelsea or any
part thereof *during my tenancy* under a penalty of
Ten pounds to be forfeited to
the said Thomas Carlyle Esq.
to be recoverable in her Majesty's
court of Law. Witness my hand
this 21.st day of December 1853

Domino Romer

Witness Tho.s Leighton

This excerpt is the closing of Dickens's letter.

Charles Dickens to Jane Welsh Carlyle, 9 March 1854

I send Carlyle herewith, my love, a large Newfoundland dog, a blood-hound whose bay is very fine, three Cochin China cocks and thirteen hens, and a Cockatoo. When you want the Cockatoo to scream louder then he always does, please aggravate him with a red handkerchief; but I hope you will find his natural noise sufficient—particularly as he is always pleased when the dogs fight, and they generally fight all day. They only howl at night.

Dear Mrs. Carlyle | Very Faithfully Yours
Charles Dickens
           —*The Letters of Charles Dickens*, v. 7, pp. 287–288

* * *

Carlyle appraised his new study in this excerpt.

Carlyle to Jean Carlyle Aitken, 16 May 1854

This is the first day of my getting up into my celebrated New Room; I write to you at present under a magnificent sky-light, and shut out by double doors from all concern (so far as possible) with the external world!. . . .

The room considered as a *soundless* apartment may be safely pronounced an evident *failure:* I do hear all manner of sharp noises,– much reduced in intensity, but still perfectly audible; it is only the *dull* noises that are quite annihilated: for the rest, it *can* be defined as an eminently *quiet* room, far *less* noise in it than in any other; it is roomy too, all my own (to stick *maps* on the wall &c &c), and perfectly isolated from the rest of the house; the *light* too, as I have said, is beyond praise. No doubt had I once got the steam up, and succeeded in falling to work with any complete heartiness, I shall find the place a real improvement: & Jane meanwhile is very proud of the fine new drawingroom she has realized for herself. I am to be out of that till the time of fires come again; and she has it, or will soon have it, in a very bright state indeed, now that I am out of it.

           —*The Collected Letters of Thomas and Jane Welsh Carlyle*, v. 29, pp. 100–101

The Dedication of *Hard Times*

This excerpt is from Charles Dickens's 13 July 1854 letter to Carlyle.

I am going, next month, to publish in One Volume a story now coming out in Household Words, called Hard Times. I have constructed it patiently, with a view to its publication altogether in a compact cheap form. It contains what I do devoutly hope will shake some people in a terrible mistake of these days, when so presented. I know it contains nothing in which you do not think with me, for no man knows your books better than I. I want to put in the first page of it, that is inscribed to Thomas Carlyle. May I?

           —*The Letters of Charles Dickens*, v. 7, p. 367

Carlyle accepted the honor; and the dedication reads: "Inscribed / To / THOMAS CARLYLE."

A Biography of Friedrich II of Prussia

In the early 1850s Carlyle searched for the subject for what he was sure would be his last great project, settling at last on writing a biography of Friedrich II. of Prussia, better known as Frederick the Great. Through the 1850s and the first half of the 1860s, Carlyle worked diligently on his massive biography, and Jane was frequently ill. Their income remained modest, and Jane ran the house with strict economy on an allowance allotted to her by Carlyle.

Writing a biography of Frederick the Great had occurred to Carlyle as early as 1830, and he read widely about the man long before beginning what became a six-volume work. Almost from the outset, however, Carlyle expressed doubts about Frederick's true moral greatness—questions echoed later by readers and critics—but he knew of no other suitable subject and so pressed on. In September 1852, he journeyed to Germany with Joseph Neuberg, an admirer and volunteer research assistant, to obtain books and portraits of Frederick and to visit key battlefields.

In 1856 Carlyle began writing his Frederick the Great biography, despite continuing doubts about the project. He felt the work had chosen him, not vice versa. A mountain of material on the German leader, even more massive than what was available on Oliver Cromwell, threatened to bury him. He benefited from the devoted assistance of several younger admirers, including Neuberg and Henry Larkin, who created summaries, indexes, and maps for the work. Carlyle composed Frederick the Great in his new, soundproof study, isolated from Jane even more than before. Although he complained fre-

The Acorns of an Oak
George Eliot on the Influence of Thomas Carlyle

This excerpt is the beginning of George Eliot's unsigned review of Passages Selected from the Writing of Thomas Carlyle *(1855), a work compiled by Thomas Ballantyne.*

It has been well said that the highest aim in education is analogous to the highest aim in mathematics, namely, to obtain not *results* but *powers,* not particular solutions, but the means by which endless solutions may be wrought. He is the most effective educator who aims less at perfecting specific requirements than at producing that mental condition which renders acquirements easy, and leads to their useful application; who does not seek to make his pupils moral by enjoining particular courses of action, but by bringing into activity the feelings and sympathies that must issue in noble action. On the same ground it may be said that the most effective writer is not he who announces a particular discovery, who convinces men of a particular conclusion, who demonstrates that this measure is right and that measure wrong; but he who rouses in others the activities that must issue in discovery, who awakes men from their indifference to the right and the wrong, who nerves their energies to seek for the truth and live up to it at whatever cost.

The influence of such a writer is dynamic. He does not teach men how to use sword and musket, but he inspires their souls with courage and sends a strong will into their muscles. He does not, perhaps, enrich your stock of data, but he clears away the film from your eyes that you may search for data to some purpose. He does not, perhaps, convince you, but he strikes you, undeceives you, animates you. You are not directly fed by his books, but you are braced as by a walk up to an alpine summit, and yet subdued to calm and reverence as by the sublime things to be seen from that summit.

Such a writer is Thomas Carlyle. It is an idle question to ask whether his books will be read a century hence: if they were all burnt as the grandest of Suttees on his funeral pile, it would be only like cutting down an oak after its acorns have a sown a forest. For there is hardly a superior or active mind of this generation that has not been modified by Carlyle's writings; there has hardly been an English book written for the last ten or twelve years that would not have been different if Carlyle had not lived. The character of his influence is best seen in the fact that many of the men who have the least agreement with his opinions are those to whom the reading of *Sartor Resartus* was an epoch in the history of their minds. The extent of his influence may be best seen in the fact that ideas which were startling novelties when he first wrote them are now become common-places. And we think few men will be found to say that this influence on the whole has not been for good. There are plenty who question the justice of Carlyle's estimates of past men and past times, plenty who quarrel with the exaggerations of the *Latter-Day Pamphlets,* and who are as far as possible from looking for an amendment of things from a Carlylian theocracy with the "greatest man," as a Joshua who is to smite the wicked (and the stupid) till the going down of the sun. But for any large nature, those points of difference are quite incidental. It is not as a theorist, but as a great and beautiful human nature, that Carlyle influences us. . . . When he is saying the very opposite of what we think, he says it so finely, with such hearty conviction—he makes the object about which we differ stand out in such grand relief under the clear light of his strong and honest intellect—he appeals so constantly to our sense of the manly and the truthful—that we are obliged to say "Hear! hear!" to the writer before we can give the decorous "Oh! oh!" to his opinions.

Much twaddling criticism has been spent on Carlyle's style. Unquestionably there are some genuine minds, not at all given to twaddle, to whom his style is antipathetic, who find it as unendurable as an English lady finds peppermint. Against antipathies there is no arguing; they are misfortunes. But instinctive repulsion apart, surely there is no one who can read and relish Carlyle without feeling that they could no more wish him to have written in another style than they could wish Gothic architecture not to be Gothic, or Raffaelle not to be Raffaellesque. It is the fashion to speak of Carlyle almost exclusively as a philosopher; but, to our thinking, he is yet more of an artist than a philosopher. He glances deep down into human nature, and shows the causes of human actions; he seizes grand generalisations, and traces them in the particular with wonderful acumen; and in all this he is a philosopher. But, perhaps, his greatest power lies in concrete presentation. No novelist has made his creations live for us more thoroughly than Carlyle has made Mirabeau and the men of the French Revolution, Cromwell and the Puritans. What humour in his pictures! Yet what depth of appreciation, what reverence for the great and godlike under every sort of earthly mummery!

—Leader, 6 (27 October 1855): 1034–1035

A Quarter-Century of Contemplation:
Carlyle's Enduring Interest in Frederick the Great

In this excerpt from his 21 May 1830 letter to G. R. Gleig, Carlyle writes of his interest in Frederick the Great. Gleig had "urged Carlyle to contribute a 'Popular History of Germany' to The Library of General Knowledge (The Collected Letters of Thomas and Jane Welsh Carlyle, *v. 5, p. 102).*

Meanwhile to show you how ready I were, could any good be done, I make the following proposal:

Frederick the Great, as an Author, Soldier, King and Man, well deserves to have his History written; better perhaps than Charles XII, whose Biography by Voltaire has always seemed to me one of the most delightful Books. Let your Publishers offer me Three hundred pounds, and time to heat the historico-biographical crucible and fill it and fuse it properly, and I will give them the best single Volume I can on the brave Fritz: I think it might be ready before this time twelvemonth; and very probably I might go to Germany in winter to inquire into it better.

This is the most eligible enterprise I can think of at present: if you can arrange your side of it on these terms, I shall be very happy to hear so, as soon as possible, and proceed forthwith to take measures for performing mine. I do believe, a rather good Book might be written on the subject; at all events, I am willing to try.

– The Collected Letters of Thomas and Jane Welsh Carlyle, v. 5, p. 102

Fifteen years later Carlyle continued to contemplate the importance of the Prussian leader, as is shown by this excerpt from his 22 October 1845 letter to his friend Karl August Varnhagen von Ense.

In my Scotch seclusion I read Preuss's two Books on *Friedrich*, which you sent me a long time ago. The liveliest curiosity awoke in me to know more and ever more about that king. Certainly if there is a Hero for an Epic in these ages– and why should there not in these ages as well as others?– then this is he! But he remains still very dark to me; and Preuss, though full of minute knowledge and seemingly very authentic, is not exactly my man for all purposes! In fact I should like to know much more about this king; and if of your own knowledge, or with Herr Preuss's help, you could at any time send me a few names of likely Books on the subject, they would not be lost upon me.

–Richard Preuss, "Letters of Carlyle to Varnhagen von Ense," New Review, 6 (April 1892): 429

More than six years later Carlyle was preparing for a project to which he had not yet committed himself, as is evident from this excerpt from his 16 February 1852 letter to Harriet Ashburton. He was still some four years away from beginning the writing of his biography.

I continue reading about *Frederic*, ordering Maps, running after books, &c., to see what I am to order. The thing seems to myself very idle: what have I, here where I am, to say about the "lean drill-serjeant of the World"? I do not even grow to love him better: a really mediocre intellect, a hard withered Soul; great only in his invincible courage, in his constant unconscious loyalty to truth and fact: the last and only *King* I know of in Europe since Cromwell:–should we, or should we not, leave him to Mahon and Company? On the whole, I will lay out a few pounds upon him; and read a little further, so long as it continues amusing to me.

–David Alec Wilson, Life of Carlyle, v. 5, p. 25

quently about the project, it served to distract him from two potentially deleterious emotions: his grief over his mother's death on 25 December 1853 and consternation over Jane's health and her unhappiness over his relationship with Lady Ashburton.

This excerpt is the first portion of the budget, dated 12 February 1855, that Jane Carlyle prepared for her husband. A "Femme incomprise" may be translated as a "misunderstood" or an "unappreciated woman," the French adjective having both English meanings. Carlyle labeled the document "Jane's Missive on the Budget" and added a note: "The enclosed was read with great laughter; had been found lying on my table as I returned out of the frosty garden from smoking. Debt is already paid off. Quarterly income to be 58l. henceforth, and all is settled to poor Goody's heart's content. The piece is so clever that I cannot just yet find in my heart to burn it, as perhaps I ought to do."

Budget of a Femme Incomprise
Jane Welsh Carlyle

I don't choose to *speak* again on the *money question!* The 'replies' from the Noble Lord are unfair and unkind, and little to the purpose. When you tell me 'I pester your life out about money,' that 'your soul is sick with hearing about it,' that 'I had better make the money I have serve,' 'at all rates, hang it, let you alone of it'–all that I call perfectly unfair, the reverse of kind, and tending to nothing but disagreement. If I were greedy or extravagant or a bad manager, you would be justified in 'staving me off' with loud words; but you cannot say *that* of me (whatever else)–cannot *think* it of me. At least, I am sure that I never 'asked for more' from you or anyone, not even from my own mother, in all my life, and that through six and twenty years I have

Two views of the soundproof garret study at the top of the Carlyles' Cheyne Row house (top, photograph by A. Long, from Carlyle Annual *[1991],*
Thomas Cooper Library, University of South Carolina; bottom, from Reginald Blunt, The Carlyle's Chelsea Home, *Special Collections,*
Thomas Cooper Library, University of South Carolina)

kept house for you at more or less cost according to given circumstances, but always on less than it costs the generality of people living in the same style. What I should have expected you to say rather would have been: 'My dear, you *must* be dreadfully hampered in your finances, and dreadfully anxious and unhappy about it, and quite desperate of *making it do,* since *you* are "asking for more." Make me understand the case, then. I can and will help you out of that *sordid* suffering at least, either by giving you more, if that be found prudent to do, or by reducing our wants to within the present means.' That is the sort of thing you would have said had you been a perfect man; so I suppose you are not a perfect man. Then, instead of crying in my bed half the night after, I would have explained my budget to you in peace and confidence. But now I am driven to explain it on paper 'in a state of mind;' *driven,* for I cannot, it is not in my nature to live 'entangled in the details,' *and I will not.* I would sooner hang myself, though 'pestering you about money' is also more repugnant to me than you dream of.

You don't understand why the allowance which sufficed in former years no longer suffices. That is what I would explain to the Noble Lord if he would but– what shall I say?–*keep his temper.*

The beginning of my embarrassments, it will not surprise the Noble Lord to learn, since it has also been 'the beginning of' almost every human ill to himself, was *the repairing of the house.* There was a destruction, an *irregularity,* an *incessant recurrence of small incidental expenses,* during all that period, or *two* periods, through which I found myself in September gone a year, *ten* pounds behind, instead of having some pounds saved up towards the winter's coals. I could have worked round 'out of that,' however, in course of time, if habits of *unpinched* housekeeping had not been long taken to by *you* as well as myself, and if new unavoidable or not to be avoided *current* expenses had not followed close on those incidental ones. I will show the Noble Lord, with his permission, what the new current expenses *are,* and to what they amount per annum. (Hear, hear! and cries of 'Be brief!')

1. We have a servant of 'higher grade' than we ever ventured on before; more expensive in money. Anne's wages are 16 pounds a year; Fanny's were 13. Most of the others had 12; and Anne never dreams of being other than *well fed.* The others *scrambled* for their living out of ours. Her regular meat dinner at one o'clock, regular allowance of butter, &c., adds at least three pounds a year to the *year's* bills. But she plagues us with no fits of illness nor of *drunkenness,* no *warnings* nor complainings. She does perfectly what she is *paid* and *fed* to do. I see houses not so well kept with 'cook,' 'housemaid,' and 'manservant'

(Question!). Anne is the last item I should vote for retrenching in. I may set her down, however, at six additional pounds.

2. We have now gas and water 'laid on,' both producing admirable results. But betwixt 'water laid on' at one pound sixteen shillings per annum, with *shilling* to turncock, and water carried at fourpence a week there is a yearly difference of 19 shillings and four pence; and betwixt *gas* all the year round and a few sixpenny boxes of lights in the winter the difference may be computed at *fifteen shillings.* These two excellent innovations, then, increase the yearly expenditure by one pound fourteen shillings and four pence–a trifle to speak of; but you, my Lord, born and bred in thrifty Scotland, must know well the proverb, 'Every little mak's a mickle.'

3. We are higher *taxed.* Within the last eighteen months there has been added to the Lighting, Pavement, and Improvement Rate ten shillings yearly, to the Poor Rate one pound, to the sewer rate ten shillings; and now the doubled Income Tax makes a difference of 5*l.* 16*s.* 8*d.* yearly, which sums, added together, amount to a difference of 7*l.* 16*s.* 8*d.* yearly, on taxes which already amounted to 17*l.* 12*s.* 8*d.* There need be no reflections for want of taxes.

4. Provisions of all sorts are higher priced than in former years. Four shillings a week for bread, instead of two shillings and sixpence, makes at the year's end a difference of 3*l.*18*s.* Butter has kept all the year round 2*d.* a pound dearer than I ever knew it. On the quantity we use–two pounds and a half per week 'quite reg'lar'–there is a difference of 21*s.* 8*d.* by the year. Butcher's meat is a penny a pound dearer. At the rate of a pound and a half a day, *bones* included–no exorbitant allowance for three people– the difference on that at the year's end would be 2*l.* 5*s.* 6*d.* Coals, which had been for some years at 21*s.* per ton, cost this year 26*s.*, last year 29*s.*, bought judiciously, too. If I had had to pay 50*s.* a ton for them, as some housewives had to, God knows what would have become of me. (Passionate cries of 'Question! question!') We burn, or used to burn–I am afraid they are going faster this winter–twelve tons, one year with another. Candles are *riz:* composites a shilling a pound, instead of 10*d.;* dips 8 pence, instead of 5*d.* or 6*d.* Of the former we burn three pounds in nine days–the greater part of the year you sit so late–and of dips two pounds a fortnight on the average of the whole year. Bacon is 2*d.* a pound dearer; soap ditto; potatoes, at the cheapest, a penny a pound, instead of three pounds for 2*d.* We use three pounds of potatoes in two day's meals. Who could imagine that at the year's end that makes a difference of 15*s.* 2*d.* on one's mere potatoes? Compute

all this, and you will find that the difference on *provisions* cannot be under twelve pounds in the year.

5. What I should blush to state if I were not *at bay,* so to speak: ever since we have been in London *you* have, in the handsomest manner, paid the winter's butter with *your own money,* though it was not in the bond. And this gentlemanlike proceeding on your part, till the butter became uneatable, was a good two pounds saved me.

Add up these differences:–

	£	s.	d.
1. Rise on servant	6	0	0
2. Rise on light and water	1	14	0
3. On taxes	7	16	8
4. On provisions	12	0	0
5. Cessation of butter	2	0	0
You will find a total of	£29	10	8

My calculation will be found quite correct, though I am not strong in arithmetic. I have *thochtered* all this well in my head, and *indignation* makes a sort of arithmetic, as well as verses. Do you finally understand why the allowance which sufficed formerly no longer suffices, and pity my difficulties instead of being angry at them?

–Thomas Carlyle: A History of His Life in London,
v. 2, pp. 162–170

* * *

This excerpt is from a letter that Carlyle began by thanking Emerson for writing to him: "You know not in the least, I perceive, nor can be made to understand at all, how indispensable your Letters are to me. How you are and have for a long time been, the one of all the sons of Adam who, I felt, completely understood what I was saying; and answered with a truly human voice,–inexpressibly consolatory to a poor man, in his lonesome pilgrimage, towards the evening of the day!"

Carlyle to Emerson, 13 May 1855

. . . Well, whether you write to me or not, I reserve to myself the privilege of writing to you, so long as we both continue in this world! As the beneficent Presences vanish from me, one after the other, those that remain are the more precious, and I will not part with them, not with chief of them, beyond all.

This last year has been a grimmer lonelier one with me than any I can recollect for a long time. I did not go the Country at all in summer or winter; refused even my Christmas at The Grange with the Ashburtons,–it was too sad an anniversary for me;–I have sat here in my garret, wriggling and wrestling on the worst

Sketch of Carlyle, circa 1855 (sketch by Richard Doyle, from New Letters, *Special Collections, Thomas Cooper Library, University of South Carolina)*

"Well Enough out of Egypt"
James Martineau on Carlyle's Religious Influence

James Martineau, the brother of Harriet Martineau, believed that Christ was human, not divine. He named Carlyle as one of the significant religious influences of the age, as he discussed in his article "Personal Influences on Our Present Theology: Newman–Coleridge–Carlyle." As is clear from this excerpt, Martineau believed that Carlyle's importance was limited to his early writing.

. . . So long as Mr. Carlyle spoke with any hope to the inward reverence of men, and in giving voice to their spiritual discontents made them feel that they were emerging from mean scepticisms into nobler inspirations, he was a deliverer to captives out of number. But the early voice of hope has become fainter and fainter, first passing into an infinite pathos, and then lost in humorous mocking or immeasurable scorn: and men cannot be permanently held by their antipathies and distrusts, and cease to look for any thing from a rebellion that never ends in peace. He gets us well enough out of Egypt and all its filthy idolatries; but, alas! his Red Sea will not divide, and the promised land is far as ever, and the question presses, whether "we are to die in the wilderness?" For a just estimate of Mr. Carlyle as an historian and man of letters the time is not yet come. But his specific action on the *religion* of the age (of which alone we speak) already belongs in a great measure to the past, and is little likely to offer new elements for appreciation.

–National Review, 3 (October 1856): 449–494

Joseph Neuberg, who assisted Carlyle in his research, photograph owned by the Carlyles (from Life of Carlyle, *Special Collections, Thomas Cooper Library, University of South Carolina)*

terms with a Task that I cannot do, that generally seems to me not worth doing, and yet *must* be *done.* These are truly the terms. I never had such a business in my life before. Frederick himself is a pretty little man to me, veracious, courageous, invincible in his small sphere; but he does not rise into the empyrean regions, or kindle my heart round him at all; and his history, upon which there are wagon-loads of dull bad books, is the lost dislocated, unmanageably incoherent, altogether dusty, barren and beggarly production of the modern Muses as given hitherto. No man of *genius* ever saw him with eyes, except twice Mirabeau, for half an hour each time. And the wretched Books have no *indexes,* no precision of detail; and I am far away from Berlin and the seat of information;– and, in brief, shall be beaten miserably with this unwise enterprise in my old days; *and* (in fine) will consent to be so, and get through it if I can before I die. This of obstinacy is the one quality I still show; all my other qualities (hope, among them) often seem to have pretty much taken leave of me; but it is necessary to hold by this last. Pray for me; I will complain no more at present. General Washington gained the freedom of America–chiefly by this respectable

quality I talk of; nor can a history of Frederick be written, in Chelsea in the year 1855, except as *against* hope, and by planting yourself upon it in an extremely dogged manner.

–*The Correspondence of Thomas Carlyle and Ralph Waldo Emerson,* v. 2, pp. 277–279

* * *

Carlyle biographer David Alec Wilson suggests that Frederick Martin, whom Carlyle employed as a copyist, was stealing manuscripts from the author with hopes of profiting from them after Carlyle's death.

Carlyle to Joseph Neuberg, February 1857

Dear Neuberg, We are in utter despair here: "Book I" is lost (undiscoverable unless you happen to have it): in the name of all the saints, help us to find it again! *Lost* utterly it cannot at all be, without miracle; but it was laid by in a certain drawer here,– then given out to you, and I *think* brot. back by you:– and neither high nor low is there now sight to be got of it. An awful tempest in a teapot! If you know or can advise in any measure, do it by Note immediately.

For the rest, I want you to come on Wedy. evening (*Wednesday,* day after to-morrow) at 5 ½ p.m., and eat a mutton chop with Lewes and me,– Lewes having volunteered. It is to be hoped the MS. of Book I will have turned up in the interim!

–*Life of Carlyle,* v. 5, pp. 267–268

* * *

Henry Larkin began to work for Carlyle in December 1856, initially compiling indexes and summaries for a collected edition of the author's works. In summer 1857 he took on a new job.

"Maps and Battle-Plans"
Henry Larkin

But at the time of which I am now writing, while I was thus struggling with work which I wholly liked and appreciated, the ill-luck of weary and utterly incompatible labour, which has dogged my footsteps through life, was already barking at the door. One day I found Carlyle in great tribulation of spirit about maps and battle-plans, which had become necessary to illustrate the *Frederick,* then seething and spluttering on the anvil at the fiercest white heat; and which maps and plans he had found himself quite unable to arrange. He had tried his hand at them, and had at last thrown them from him in utter loathing and despair; and now wistfully appealed to me, to say 'whether amongst my many facilities of help, even map-making might not possibly be one.' I never

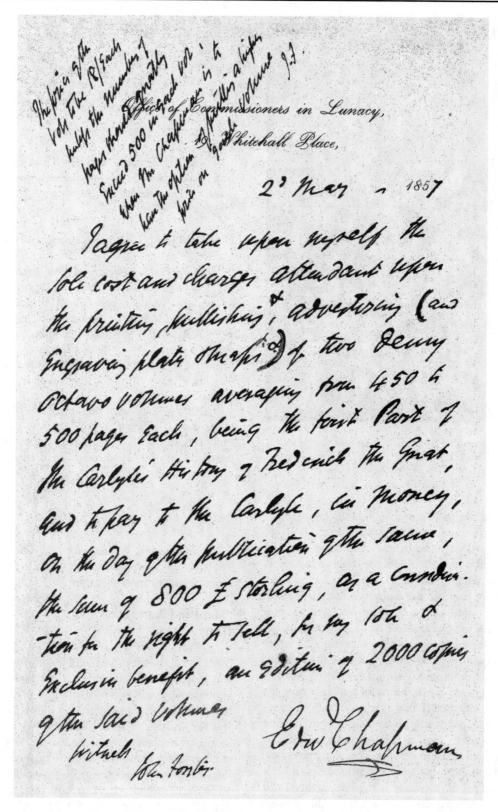

A letter to Carlyle from Edward Chapman, the publisher of History of Friedrich II. of Prussia
(The Trustees of the National Library of Scotland Acc 5074)

Carlyle at his desk in his garret and in the garden, July 1857 (top, Rare Book and Manuscript Library, from Fred Kaplan, Thomas Carlyle: A Biography, *Thomas Cooper Library, University of South Carolina; bottom, from Reginald Blunt,* The Carlyles' Chelsea Home, *Special Collections, Thomas Cooper Library, University of South Carolina)*

listened to any appeal with feelings of more real dismay than I listened then. I knew well that, do what I would, the whole thing would be as unconquerably intolerable to me, as it had already proved to himself. I had had long and very bitter experience, not of map-making and battle-plans, but of very kindred employment; and I knew with inward shuddering what it must mean for me. But what was I to do? Was I to refuse him, and throw him back upon his own despair, when he was so confidently and really so pathetically looking to me for deliverance? 'No,' I thought; 'I have put my hand to the work; and I will push through with it, come what may!'

I never saw Carlyle look so really grateful as when, with many misgivings, I promised to try what I could do.

–"Carlyle and Mrs. Carlyle: A Ten Years' Reminiscence, " *British Quarterly Review,* 74 (July 1881): 41

* * *

The critical response to Volumes I and II of Frederick the Great *was varied but tended to be more negative than positive. While some reviewers lauded Carlyle for thorough and painstaking research, others faulted him for relying on secondary sources. Even those who praised his power of description complained that he gave too much detail about minor figures. The two volumes traced Frederick's ancestry and concluded with his childhood, leading some critics to question Carlyle's sense of proportion and artistic structure. While some readers appreciated the author's humor, others found his presence in the work obtrusive, even exhibitionist. Complaints about insufficient analysis and interpretation of historical events, voiced previously with regard to* The French Revolution, *and the objection that Carlyle forgave brutality when it accompanied success, once raised against* On Heroes *and* Cromwell, *both resurfaced.*

This excerpt is the opening paragraph of an unsigned eight-page review.

"Conscientious Record
and Consummate Work of Art"
Review of *Frederick the Great,* volumes I and II

The portion of Mr. Carlyle's great work which is now published has equal claims to admiration as a faithful history and an exquisite masterpiece of art. As a history, it bears upon the face of it evidence of immense labour in sifting from immeasurable heaps of literary lumber the few scraps of precious truth which had lain buried in them— labour alike of patient delving and of painful judging amongst materials which his own Dryasdust himself, in spite of their affinity with his own nature, might have been expected to engage upon with dread. To have elicited by this toil a full, and clear, and quite original account, not

solely of the hero of the book as far as the narrative extends at present, but of all those events and persons also by whom the hero's character or state was influenced, is, strictly, the severe historian's triumph; whilst that of the artist manifests itself in the masterly arrangement of his vast mass of facts, in the life and strength and brilliancy with which his volumes are from the beginning to the end inspired, in the graphic force and beauty of occasional descriptions, and, most of all, in the wondrous skill with which these various qualities are made to co-operate with a startling humour and with strange wild images in giving unexampled condensation to his speech. But in both these respects, both as conscientious record and consummate work of art, Mr. Carlyle's present History differs rather in degree than kind from many of his earlier compositions. The homage which is paid to his genius now has been won with sore wrestling from an unwilling public, who disregarded writings by which it was only in a lesser measure merited more than thirty years ago. The eager welcome which this History of Frederick has received is undoubtedly a gratifying evidence of great progress in the reading world's intelligence and taste, but it is also an honourable and, we hope, an acceptable return to the author for the long career of manly, independent, and unflagging struggle through which it has at last been gained.

–*Gentleman's Magazine,* new series 5
(December 1858): 570

* * *

This excerpt is from an unsigned nineteen-page review.

"The Iliad of the Man of Action"
Review of *Frederick the Great,* volumes I and II

In the present half of his memoir Mr. Carlyle has taken for his hero an entirely different person from his special subject Frederick the Great; namely, his hero's father Friedrich Wilhelm the First, whose career to our thinking displays more of the ideal heroic than the son's. The volumes, when the work is completed, will thus divide themselves into two distinct memoirs; the Iliad of the man of action, to be followed by the Odyssey of the man of craft. This may be an error in the publication as a work of art; but the pleasant result to the reader is a dilogy where he only expected a drama. By a stroke of the author's pen, the reader wins a hundred per cent. The capital is doubled as the interest is divided, and biography gains all that the art of criticism loses. It is obvious too, we may urge this in apology of Carlyle's course of procedure, that in the early years of his hero, the treatment said hero received from his male parent counts for a considerable part in his training—the very rough riding-school in which he learned some of the

Portrait screen in Carlyle's Study (from Reginald Blunt, The Carlyles' Chelsea Home, *Special Collections, Thomas Cooper Library, University of South Carolina)*

Carlyle's Method:
"The Image of the Man Steadily in View"

Charles Gavin Duffy wrote of Carlyle's method of working in his memoir of his friend.

Speaking of his method of work, he said he had found the little wooden pegs, which washer-women employ to fasten cloths to a line, highly convenient for keeping together bits of notes and agenda on the same special point. It was his habit to paste on a screen in his workroom engraved portraits, when no better could be had, of the people he was then writing about. It kept the image of the man steadily in view, and one must have a clear image of him in the mind before it was in the least possible to make him be seen by the reader.

—Conversations with Carlyle, p. 92

most valuable lessons of his life. Wilhelm is thus a prominent figure for a lengthened period, but Carlyle makes him more than this, more interesting, more able, more admirable (with a thousand infirmities of temper it is true) than his successor, whose name gives a title to the memoir; and we must confess that with ourselves he is, and always has been, the greater favourite.

–*Dublin University Magazine,* 53 (January 1859): 16

* * *

These excerpts are from an unsigned fifty-three-page review.

"Out of All Proportion"
Review of *Frederick the Great,* volumes I and II

When a writer applies himself to produce the life of a man whose biography is already extant, with no fresh documents to throw new light on the subject of his memoir, he boldly challenges public attention on the ground of constructing novel theories out of old facts, or of his superior treatment of the subject to any of his predecessors. Mr. Carlyle candidly admits at the outset that he has no information in connexion with Frederic to impart, beyond that which the world is already in possession of. Indeed, he somewhat inconsistently avers that the time has not yet come when a faithful history of Frederic can be written, as important documents, most pertinent to the subject, are still kept back by this truth-loving Prussian Court, whose possessions are founded upon the adamant of justice. Mr. Carlyle has been to Berlin, and struggled with all the ardour of his nature to get a peep into its archives, but admittance was denied. It was surely ungracious for the magnates of that Court, when Mr. Carlyle knocked at the door for the requisite information, to refuse him a single glimpse. . . . Yet Mr. Carlyle, in hurrying into the field with no other authorities save the fulsome panegyrics of Förster, the well-known memoirs of Pöllnitz, and those of the Margravine of Bareith, with one or two other celebrities equally famous, which fall within the scope of his design, has laid himself open to be judged upon artistic grounds alone. As such we have not a moment's hesitation in pronouncing his history of Frederic a failure. Mr. Carlyle has got through one half of the work, and yet out of the fourteen hundred pages already written hardly forty refer to the hero of the memoir. The rest is entirely taken up either with a rambling account of contemporary events, or a lengthened narrative of Frederic William and the founders of the Prussian monarchy, after Dr. Preuss. What must be thought of a biographer who goes over the greater part of his space, and leaves his hero just breeched; or of the architect, who in con-

structing a building employs as foundations one half of the walls? These volumes can no more be called a history of Frederic, than the account of a man's ancestors and of the doings of their contemporaries can be said to be a history of himself. The fact is, Mr. Carlyle found himself in the condition of the painter with a canvas out of all proportion to his subject; and who, to fill up the background, was obliged to introduce events having no relation to his principal figure. His work reminds one of those mediæval pictures, in which Christ figures in the centre preaching in the Sanhedrim, while in one corner Paul is overthrown on his way to Tarsus, and in another the soldiers of Julian are expressing their astonishment at the descent of the miraculous shields from heaven.

To this utter violation of unity, we must add the absence of anything like correlation of distance, or subordination of parts. Mr. Carlyle has the unfortunate art of sketching all his subjects on the same level. . . . In history, there is the same relation to figures, in point of time, as in painting, with reference to space. The events which only incidentally affect the principal object, ought only to be briefly noticed,–to gloom, as it were, faintly on us in the distance. A bridge resting on the head of a man, or a horse feeding in a valley with the back of the animal in the clouds, is not half so grotesque as Mr. Carlyle's manner of bringing the least important figures in his work shoulder to shoulder with his principal personages, or hurriedly passing over the most important years of his hero's life, while he swells out some extraneous incident into colossal magnitude. . . .

The aim of Mr. Carlyle in so flagrantly violating historic unity has doubtless been to turn to account a great deal of matter lying profitless in his note-books, and not destined otherwise to see the light, as well as to beat up materials from all quarters of the universe for the amusement of his readers. The speculations of Voltaire on the Paris Bourse, and the amours of the philosopher with Madame du Chatelet, at Cirey, one would think have little to do with the subject; but these incidents had been previously collated by Mr. Carlyle, and will doubtless prove entertaining.

. . . .

. . . If this sort of thing is to continue, there is an end of cataloguing books. In opening a treatise on the Nicene Creed, we are not certain that we may not meet with an account of the Thirty Years' War . . . .

–*British Quarterly Review,* 29 (1 January 1859): 241–244

* * *

This excerpt is from a ten-page review. George Gilfillan was an author and minister of a Burgher Church at Dundee. Although he had written favorably about The French Revolution *for the* Dumfries Herald *in 1840 and later professed admiration for the author, he wrote in* Christianity and Our Era *(1857) that Carlyle's "discontent has darkened into something fiercer than misanthropy—into universal hatred."*

"Waxing Old"
Review of *Frederick the Great,* volumes I and II
George Gilfillan

But it is now time to turn to our author's latest work. It is by many thought his greatest, although we certainly do not coincide with this opinion. Were we to characterise it in a sentence, we might be tempted to call it Carlyle's own caricature of his 'History of the French Revolution.' This caricature is elaborate, and done, of course, by a friendly hand; but it is a caricature notwithstanding, and, as usual in such things, the faults are caught more closely than the beauties. The endless repetitions, the flight of nicknames clouding every page, the gross and wilful grammatical freedoms, the glancing plusquam Gibbonic allusions to facts and incidents which the author deems the reader knows, but which are often revealed to him by these side-lights, imperfectly, and for the first time—the subacid stream of contempt and irony, the elaborate search for the picturesque, even in the most out of the way corners, and in defiance of all laws of unity and taste—the preference of bold and brilliant men to the obscurely good and the divinely weak—the exclamations and objurgations, the stifled oaths, half-crushed curses, and all the mad, miserable, yet laughing, rioting talk, as of the Titans in their prison-house of subterranean pain—are to be found in these two volumes of 1858, as well as in the three volumes of the 'French Revolution,' published in 1837, although not now producing such a strange and powerful effect. Carlyle is waxing old, (sixty-five, we believe,) and, hence, his original 'fury' no longer 'upholds him' to the full extent. Prometheus is now nodding occasionally on his rock of torment, although the chain be as thick, and the beak of the vulture as keen as ever. Yet the work is far from being unworthy of its author's genius. It discovers an amount of research perfectly marvellous, alike in its extent and its apparent accuracy. It shows in the most vivid, nay, glaring light the period of history to which it refers, and enables us to realize intensely the characters and incidents of the 18th century. The great objection, indeed, is that he casts a splendid lustre on a number of trifling circumstances, and imbecile or worthless characters. He turns his blazing torch on the haunts of unclean and doleful creatures—on the holes of scorpions, and the damp

grassy haunts of toads—as well as on the pastures where oxen fatten, and the lairs where lions repose. Hence, a great portion of both volumes is tedious, not from the defect of power in the writer, but from a want of interest in the subject. Who cares for these miserable 'double marriage' intrigues, or for those carousings of Frederick William with August the Strong? The author himself becomes conscious that he is trying the patience of his reader, and he seeks to arouse attention by doubling the dose of exclamations and minced oaths. He is like a man who, while reading a long tedious law-paper, should interrupt himself, ever and anon, by crying out to the unfortunate listener—'Hearken to this, won't you? Confound you, if you don't! By heavens! have you the impudence to nod at this sentence?' Carlyle tries another dodge still. He divides his dulness into minute portions, his chapters into *chapterlings,* and he spices each of these with a quaint and attractive title. Still, the general effect is weariness.

. . . .

On the whole, the work is an able and worthy contribution to the world's historic literature, although ponderous in size, excessive in price, negative and unsatisfactory in total result, and tediously prolix in many of its details. A clever redacteur might have condensed these two enormous volumes, containing somewhere about 1300 pages, into a moderate octave of 500. He could have done so on the easy plan of excluding all the oaths, one half of the exclamations, a third of the repetitions, and a fourth of the needless minutiæ, in fact. Were all the epithets and outcries, such as 'dilapidated strong,' 'tobacco parliaments,' 'respectable Debourgays,' 'August, the Strong Man of Sin,' &c. &c., to be curtailed, the merit and classical character of the book would doubtless be enhanced, but its personal identity would be destroyed.
—*Scottish Review,* 9 (January 1859): 40–41, 45–46

* * *

This excerpt is from a twenty-nine-page review by a barrister and translator of Dante's Divine Comedy.

"Deficient in Completion and Finish"
Review of *Frederick the Great,* volumes I and II
William F. Pollock

No history that was ever put together could, with few exceptions, be more chaotic and unintelligible than this work of Mr. Carlyle's. Without the help of the index at the end, it would be almost impossible to read the book through with profit, for want of continuous connexion between its parts, and the reader is sometimes tempted to indulge in a kind of Irish wish, that

Page from Carlyle's manuscript for History of Friedrich II. of Prussia
(Beinecke Rare Book and Manuscript Library, Yale University)

the index was in the body of the book. As a whole, the edifice which is now in course of erection by Mr. Carlyle is notably deficient in completion and finish. The scaffolding still remains standing round many portions of it; heaps of materials, in various stages of preparation for use in the structure, lie confusedly in all directions; and the wanderer through some of its dark and unfinished passages is always in risk of stumbling over a basket of the workman's tools. Here and there particular cantles of the work have been turned out in so workmanlike and perfect a manner as to make it the more to be lamented that the rest has been left in its present rude condition. The book is rather a collection of sketches, in different degrees forcible and accurate, for the composition of a picture, than a picture in which the rough contents of his portfolios have been brought under the complete mastery of the artist, and composed into a perfect and pleasing whole upon his canvas.

. . . .

There is a want of proportion, which can only be accounted for by the same erratic perversity which deforms so many of Mr. Carlyle's former writings, leading him to an apparently capricious omission of really important details on some places, while they are without mercy or evident reason accumulated in others. Even when an original document is set forth, it is so garbled by admixture with the editor's running comments, that it is not easy to separate the old text from the infiltration of the new gloss into all its crevices. There is certainly no intention to mislead, but this practice impairs the integrity of the writer's vouchers, communicates an air of romantic history to the whole, and so destroys the tone of reality which it is a special object to maintain. The new matter may be pertinent—it may be explanatory—it is often amusing—but the habit of appearing to give *verbatim* and *in extenso* that which, in fact, is coloured in almost every line by the peculiar tincture of the transcriber's mind, is unfavourable to historical accuracy, and cannot be recommended for imitation. . . .

One of Mr. Carlyle's peculiarities is, that he collects his materials in the view of his readers, and allows them to view him while engaged upon them. He may be seen as he moves about among them; sometimes venting his spleen upon them, but never wilfully attempting to make them appear something different from what they are, and rarely subduing them so as to make them fairly his own. In these respects his workmanship stands in remarkable contrast to that of another eminent living historian. Lord Macaulay's endeavour seems always to be to fuse his matter together to the utmost, and to exhibit only a finished performance of the highest polish. The covering is not withdrawn from it until it has received the last touches of the master, nor until every trace of the means

employed in its production has been removed from sight. He, as it were, absorbs his material, and makes it part of himself, to be afterwards reproduced, cast in his favourite mould, and thoroughly impressed with the fresh shape he desires it to assume and retain. The artist may enjoy for the time the triumph of having created masterpieces of composition, but they represent rather what he wishes to be accepted as the truth than the truth itself. Mr. Carlyle has the merit of making no statements which cannot be tested, and, if he is wrong in his deductions, he supplies the means for his own correction. . . . With all its faults, Mr. Carlyle's way of composing history is, of the two, the most faithful, and the most likely to be of use to his successors.

—The Quarterly Review, 105 (April 1859): 301–303

* * *

This excerpt is from a thirty-four-page article that treated Carlyle's biography and Œuvres de Frédéric le Grand (1846–1856) in twenty-four volumes. William Stigand was the author of The Life, Work, and Opinions of Heinrich Heine *(1875).*

"Little to Praise"
Review of *Frederick the Great,* volumes I and II
William Stigand

A publication which lays claim to the title of a history ought, in our opinion, to recommend itself to the reader by a perspicuous narrative, a vigorous and unaffected style, a just appreciation of truth and falsehood, a discriminating insight into character and the motives of human actions, an accurate survey of the sequence of events, and a conscientious regard for those who have previously laboured in the same vineyard. If it be too much to require that all these qualities be united in a historian, it is at least to be expected that they shall not all be wanting. But this is a test to which it is impossible to subject Mr. Carlyle's last production. By this rule his 'History of Frederic II.' would deserve to be remembered chiefly as a conspicuous example of all that a history ought not to be. . . .

Recognising, as we willingly do, the merits of some of Mr. Carlyle's earlier writings, the flashes of genius with which he has illuminated some important passages in history, the pathos and originality of many of his biographical and critical efforts, the generous audacity of his early career, and his simple and grand utterance of much that was good and much that was noble, we regret that he should have indulged his foibles and fostered his prejudices to such a degree, that we have little to praise and much to condemn in the volumes before us.

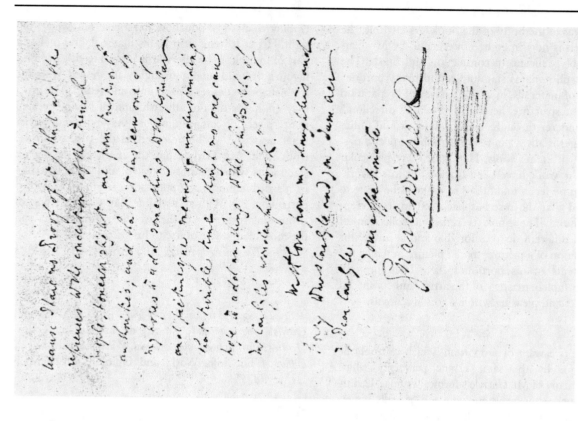

Letter from Charles Dickens to Carlyle, with which he enclosed the proofs for the last part of A Tale of Two Cities (1859). In the second paragraph Dickens writes that he refers to Carlyle's French Revolution in his preface: "it has been one of my hopes to add something to the popular and picturesque means of understanding that terrible time, though no one can hope to add anything to the philosophy of Mr. Carlyle's wonderful book" (Trustees of the National Library of Scotland MS 666).

. . . .

A more constant topic, however, than the ridicule of the nineteenth and eighteenth century, is the complaint of Mr. Carlyle in these volumes of the quantity of work he has had to do to write them. 'Carlylius in tormentis scripsit,' should be, in imitation of the epigraph in Frederic William's pictures, that of his work. The Prussian writers have evidently gone to work with malice prepense to write dull books for the torture of Mr. Carlyle. No abuse is sufficiently virulent for these honest labourers, who got together all the materials of which Mr. Carlyle has often made an insufficient use. Mr. Carlyle is not the first writer of history, nor consequently the first who has undertaken the labour of research; there are eminent writers still in existence who have consecrated as much research to one work as Mr. Carlyle has given to the whole of his writings. The late Mr. Prescott, suffering under an unexampled calamity, uttered no murmur at the slow toil which hard necessity inflicted upon him; nor has the most splendid historical genius the world has yet seen, permitted himself to use such contumelious language towards the darkest chronicler of the monkish ages as that with which Mr. Carlyle belabours the Prussian annalist.

–*Edinburgh Review,* 110 (October 1859): 376, 378

* * *

Henry Larkin was "a frequent vistor at Cheyne Row" for the decade he worked for Carlyle. In these excerpts he provides some insights on the couple.

"Their Two Lives"
Remembering Carlyle and Mrs. Carlyle
Henry Larkin

. . . I generally looked in in the forenoon, that time being usually most convenient to me. My practice was to go straight up to Carlyle in his sky-lighted study, and arrange whatever matter I had to consult him about; and then, as I passed down, have half-an-hour's chat with Mrs. Carlyle in the drawing-room. They were generally very pleasant half-hours. Sometimes there was some trifling commission to execute; sometimes a little difficulty, mechanical or other, she wanted to consult me about. . . .

It must have been about this time too that I gradually became alive to the intense dreariness of her own life. She had such a perfect mastery of herself, and such a stoical resolution to shut in her own misery from the eyes of the world, that I suppose not many even of her intimate frriends ever knew how much she was actually suffering. It was not merely the feeling of utter loneliness, arising from Calyle's moody absorption in his own work: All this, I

believe, she could have borne without flinching. Indeed she had such an unshaken faith in his genius, and such a queenly appreciation of her own prerogatives as his Wife, that I am convinced she would not, even at the worst, have exchanged her lowly position for the hightest in the land. I cannot for a moment suppose that their two lives were really blended into one. How, on such terms, could they be? . . . At the time I knew her, she possessed plenty of resources of her own, and friends and acquaintants in more than abundance; and she well knew how to hold her own in all wordy warfare, and give tit for tat all round with sparkling vivacity. She had also a mischievous delight in treading on the delicate toes of the conventional proprieties; and I have heard her say the most audacious things with a look of demure unconsciousness, which would have broken out into the pleasantest, or sharpest, mocking astonishment, if you were simple enough to profess being shocked. . . . I once took an opportunity of referring to what Sterling had said about her skill in writing; and ventured to wonder that she did not still try to find a little amusement in that way. But she shut me up very sharply by saying.–'Oh, Mr. Larkin, one writer is quite enough in a house.' And yet, I ought to say, I never once heard an angry word pass between themselves. . . .

I never knew a man more free from all personal vulgarities of any kind, or one whose presence carried with it such clear unassuming dignity of manhood; which I can only describe as a certain royal graciousness of manner, as different from a spirit of condescension as wisdom is different from personal pretentiousness. . . . Both Carlyle and Mrs. Carlyle had singularly expressive voices, and yet singularly different from each other, like the many tones of a powerful organ and the perfect modulations of a mellow flute. They both spoke heartily, with their genuine native accents, but with the easy grace of cultivated sincerity, and with no other rusticity of manner than daring to be true to the soil from which they sprang. They simply brought with them, into the midst of the French-polished upholstery of London conventional life, a vocal memory of the fresh breezes and living echoes of their own mountain streams, pine-trees, and thousand-tinted heather. But I should say that, even in his most genial moods, there was never anything we could call really 'playful' in Carlyle's thoughts or way of looking at things, as there so often was in his Wife's. I can hardly imagine that even in childhood he ever practically knew the meaning of happy 'play'–the pretty innocent skipping of kids and lambs, the simple bubbling-over of the cup of joy! I can only picture him as 'weary and heavy laden' from his birth. Laughter he had of many kinds; scornful, genial, triumphant; and even a strangely sympathetic laugh of reproving pity; but I should say, never the clear ring of overflowing heartfelt joy. Even his humour, richly abundant as it was, was never playful, like Shakespeare's, or like Thackeray's at his best; but always either grim or sadly pitiful, or else merely grotesquely admonitory. No sunny glances of childlike mirth and innocence ever sported within the sanctuary of his grimly earnest soul: more like a warning iridescence playing around purgatorial fires, half-revealing and half-concealing the incommunicable reality, was the grimly pathetic banter in which he so frequently shrouded the message his soul felt bound to deliver.

. . . .

With all this grim earnestness I do not suppose Mrs. Carlyle ever had any deep or real sympathy; and I sometimes think she may once have greatly over-estimated her own ability to rally him out of it. Perhaps she never altogether gave up the attempt. She was always very ready with playful surprises whenever a fair occasion served. One morning, after I had finished my business upstairs, I looked in at the drawing-room as usual, when she asked me whether Carlyle had mentioned 'that little paper he was to speak to me about.' I said, 'No; but that I supposed he had forgotten it, and that I would go back to inquire.' I went back: but Carlyle knew no more about it than I did. At last he got up from his table, where he was busily writing, and came down to ask her what it was. I followed him. She let us get close up to her table, where she was also writing; and then held up before us a slip of paper, upon which, while I was gone, she had written–'The 1st of April!' Carlyle and I looked at each other, laughing heartily at our mutual bewilderment; and then he strode off, and returned upstairs to his study. Whereupon she was highly triumphant at having, as she said, 'brought down *two* such philosophers with one shot!' 53–54

. . . She never hesitated about quizzing him, just as she did every one else; and I noticed that he always seemed to rather like it. Once he was giving me some little bit of copying or map-making to do, and was elaborately impressing on me the importance of dispatch, but at the same time, of there being no actual hurry about it; which was a way he had, like touching-up with the whip, and holding-in with the bridle at the same moment. I intimated my perfect understanding of his wishes; and quoted Goethe's well-known words, which had once made a deep impression on me, 'like a Star, unhasting and unresting.' 'Ah,' interposed Mrs. Carlyle, 'Carlyle is always hasting, and *never* resting;' which indeed was the saddest fact of both their lives. . . .

. . . .

Another significant little anecdote concerning Mrs. Carlyle which belongs to long afterwards, may as well be told now. She had a little pet lap-dog, named Nero, of which she was very fond. Carlyle used to take Nero out

Jane Welsh Carlyle with Nero, 31 July 1854 (Rare Book and Manuscript Library, Columbia University, from Thomas Carlyle: A Biography, *Thomas Cooper Library, University of South Carolina)*

with him for a run, every night when he went for his eleven o'clock walk; and I often noticed, when I have walked with him, how carefully he looked after his little charge; occasionally whistling to him (not exactly with his lips, but with a small pocket-whistle), lest he should run astray or otherwise come to grief. This little dog at last grew old and asthmatic, until it was a misery to look at his sufferings; until, in short, like many another little pet, he had to be kindly and painlessly put out of his little troubles. This was a great grief to Mrs. Carlyle, who never could quite reconcile herself to the clear necessity. She was telling her grief to a lady friend, who, I believe, had not been very long married, when her friend, trying to say something to comfort her, suggested, 'Why not have him stuffed?' 'Stuffed!' said Mrs. Carlyle, with a flash of indignation, 'would you stuff your Baby?' She was always very tender-hearted with her pets, and especially with her servants, whom she tried in every way to attach to her; sometimes, but not always, with perfect success.

–"Carlyle and Mrs. Carlyle: A Ten Years' Reminiscence," *British Quarterly Review,* 74 (July 1881): 48–55

A painting of the Carlyles at home (A Chelsea Interior, by William Tait; from David Alec Wilson, Life of Carlyle, *Special Collections, Thomas Cooper Library, University of South Carolina)*

Forward with *Frederick the Great*

With two volumes spent on Frederick's ancestry, Carlyle saw that he would have to write more than the four volumes he had initially projected in order to treat Frederick's life thoroughly. Further, by August 1858, with volumes I and II in press for publication in September, the unwilling traveler also realized that he needed to return to Germany in order to see the places he wanted to describe in the remaining volumes. He journeyed to Germany with Neuberg from late August until late September and, upon return, resumed work on the project, writing until mid-afternoon on most days and then riding out on Fritz, the horse he had named for Frederick.

Volume III of Frederick the Great *appeared in late April, 1862 and Volume IV in late January, 1864. Reaction resembled the response to volumes I and II. Some critics attempted to assess Carlyle's relation to his hero—the attraction Frederick held for Carlyle—while others tried to place the work in the context of Carlyle's evolving career. Carlyle's morality, his tone, and his choice of subject all came under fire.*

Late in September, 1863, Jane experienced a bad fall which left her bedridden for the next year, during which time she also suffered great pain in her womb. She moved out of the house to be nursed by various friends until mid September, 1864. Worried about his wife and exhausted himself, Carlyle struggled to complete his magnum opus, working in his upper room or, in May and June, 1864, in a rented house where Jane was staying near friends. His hand had begun to shake when he wrote, making composition difficult. With the continued help of Henry Larkin, however, he completed his thirteen-year ordeal in 1865.

Volumes V and VI appeared in March 1865. Critics almost universally agreed that Carlyle had chosen a subject ill suited to his personality and talent and regretted his attempts to hold Frederick up as a moral hero.

Carlyle wrote to Emerson on 9 April 1859, wondering if his friend had received "a Copy of Friedrich of Prussia, two big red volumes," that he had sent months before. Carlyle went on to complain about the work in which he was involved: "I never in my life was so near choked; swimming in this mother of Dead Dogs, and a long spell of it still ahead! I profoundly pity myself (if no one else does)." This excerpt is from Emerson's reply.

August 3. 36 O. Sq.ᵂ

Dear Carlyle

Perhaps this small present may be useful to you — It is the only steel pen with wᶜʰ I could ever write comfortably, and if it suits your hand as it does mine, why it will save you much pen-knife work and may make your life easier

Yours ever (Just on the point
of starting somewhither)

W M T.

It writes better the 2ᵈ day & following than the 1ˢᵗ. This I'm writing with in a week I shᵈ think in use. It's much best on a smooth paper. Note the number Gillott 303.

An 1859 letter from William Makepeace Thackeray to Carlyle that accompanied the gift of a pen (New York Public Library)

Emerson to Carlyle, 1 May 1859

I read without alarm your pathetical hints of your sad plight in the German labyrinth. I know too well what invitations & assurances brot you *in* there to fear any lack of guides to bring you out More presence of mind & easy change from the microscopic to the telescopic view, does not exist. I await peacefully your issue from your pretended afflictions.

—The Correspondence of Emerson and Carlyle, pp. 527–528

In the same letter, Emerson wrote that he had earlier read "our American reprint" of the biography and was enclosing "a leaf from my journal at the time, which I read the other night in one of my lectures at the 'Music Hall,' in Boston." This excerpt is from that journal entry.

. . . And meantime here has come into the country 3 months ago a book of *Carlyle,* History of Frederick, infinitely the wittiest book that ever was written, a book that one would think the English people would rise up in mass to thank him for, the donation by cordial acclamation & congratulate themselves that such a head existed among them, and much— sympathising & on its own account reading-America would make a new treaty extraordinary of joyful grateful delight with England, in acknowledgment of such a donation,—a book with so many memorable & heroic facts, working directly, too, to practice,—with new heroes, things unvoiced before, with a range of thought & wisdom, the largest & the most colloquially elastic, that ever was, not so much applying as inosculating to every need & sensibility of a man, so that I do not so much read a sterotype page, as I see the eyes of the writer looking into my eyes; all the way, chuckling with undertones & hums & winks & shrugs & long commanding glances, and stereoscoping every figure that passes & every hill, river, wood, hummock, & pebble in the long perspective, and withal a book that is a Judgment Day, too, for its moral verdict on the men & nations & manners of modern times.

With its wonderful new system of mnemonics, whereby great & insignificant men are ineffaceably ticketed & marked in the memory by what they were, had, & did.

And this book makes no noise: I have hardly seen a notice of it in any newspaper or journal, and you would think there was no such book; but the secret interior wits & hearts of men take note of it, not the less surely. They have said nothing lately in praise of the air, or of fire, or of the blessing of love, and yet, I suppose, they are sensible of these, & not less of this Book, which is like these.

—Journals and Miscellaneous Notebooks of Ralph Waldo Emerson, v. 14, pp. 273–274

* * *

In this excerpt from a letter written almost a year later, Carlyle refers to the journal entry in Emerson's letter of 1 May 1859.

Carlyle to Emerson, 30 April 1860

It is a special favour of Heaven to me that I hear of you again by this accident; and am made to answer a word *de Profundis.* It is constantly among the fairest of the few hopes that remain for me on the other side of this Stygian Abyss of a Frederich (should I ever get through it alive,) that I *shall then* begin writing to you again, who knows if not see you in the body before quite taking wing! For I feel always, what I have sometimes written, that there is (in a sense) but one completely human voice to me in this world, and that you are it, and have been,—thanks to you, whether you speak or not! Let me say also while I am at it, that the few words you sent me about those first Two Volumes are present with me in the far more frightful darknesses of these last Two; and indeed are often almost my one encouragement. That is a fact, and not exaggerated, though you think it is. I read some criticisms of my wretched Book, and hundreds of others I in the gross refused to read; they were in praise, they were in blame; but not one of them looked into the eyes of the object, and in genuine human fashion responded to its human strivings, and recognized it,— completely right, though with generous exaggeration! That was well done, and I can tell you: a human voice, far out in the waste deeps, among the inarticulate sea-krakens and obscene monsters, loud-roaring, inexpressibly ugly, dooming you as if to eternal solitude by way of wages,— "hath exceeding much refreshment in it," as my friend Oliver used to say.

—The Correspondence of Thomas Carlyle and Ralph Waldo Emerson, 1834–1872, v. 2, p. 272–274

* * *

This is a letter from Carlyle's printer. The third volume of History of Friedrich II. of Prussia, *called* Frederick the Great *was not published until April or May 1862.*

Charles Robson to Carlyle, 14 March 1861

Dear Sir,

I send you the slips completing the chapter, but I have not been able to make out a great deal of it, though I have spent far more time over it than I can spare; and the poor Compositors are at their wits' end. In fact, the whole of this part ought to be copied out. I never saw such imperfect copy before. Much of it is mere abbreviation, and referring backwards and for-

Carlyle and his horse, Fritz, 2 August 1861 (Carlyle's House Museum, London)

wards. I am quite out of heart with it; and fear, if there be any more like this, I shall be obliged to send it to you as it comes from the hands of the Compositors, as I cannot find time, among my many calls upon it, for deciphering such copy. I am sorry to write this, and have deferred till I can no longer get on.

Your obedient servant,
Charles Robson.

–David Alec Wilson, *Life of Carlyle,* v. 5, p. 426

* * *

This excerpt is from a twenty-four-page review by a frequent contributor to the Dublin Review. *Abraham's essays were collected in* Essays, Historical, Critical and Political *(1868).*

"His Idol's Doings"
Review of *Frederick the Great,* **volume III**
G. W. Abraham

Frederick II. has commonly been regarded as great in the art of war, a subtle politician, and withal not as careless of the real interests of his subjects as were many of the kings of his time. While such were the political qualities of Frederick, the whole world is of one mind to regard his moral qualities as amongst the least creditable which could belong to king or subject; and much of what is commendable in his policy, may be traced, as is generally belived, to the defects of character in question. The career of Frederick everywhere gives evidence of coldheartedness, insincerity, and irreligion. . . . Such, in a few words, is the estimate which posterity has formed, with scarcely any dissent so far, of the character of Frederick II.; and to do Mr. Carlyle justice, he has not sought to vary this estimate in the least, nor is it his habit to do so in his biographies. He leaves that department to other men. Mr. Froude is at liberty to reinstate our Henry VIII. in character, and to set him up as a model of kingly virtue and wise policy. Miss Strickland may take in hand the character of Mary Stuart, or of Queen Mary of England, and do the best she can with them to clear up doubts and to clear away misapprehension. Those who seek to re-establish character, follow a uniform plan. They set up in their own minds a standard of morality, not necessarily the ten commandments; they may take it from Plato or Confucius as well; but to this acknowledged standard they will endeavour to make it appear, by the best means at their disposal, that the character of their favourite conforms.

Mr. Carlyle adopts a more honest course; he assumes his hero, whoever that may be, to be the standard of perfection, and that being so, it were a hard case if the standard should not be made to conform to itself. Perhaps we are wrong in saying that Mr. Carlyle has no standard of abstract perfection apart from the character of any one of his heroes. It must be admitted that all the objects of his worship have one feature in common, which may, therefore, be assumed as the abstract of perfection, and that is the attainment of power over their fellows by whatever means. That mastery once attained, Mr. Carlyle adopts all the acts of his hero, concerning himself not in the least about what men are usually agreed to consider the morality of those acts. We never find an express apology rendered by Mr. Carlyle for anything done, permitted, or omitted, by his hero. Nor, on the other hand, does the historian of Frederick indulge in any of that laboured and lavish praise with which party writers, Lord Macaulay, for instance, and Lord Russell, venerate their demigods. Mr. Carlyle identifies himself too completely and too rejoicingly with Frederick to spend vulgar praise upon him. His admiration betrays itself in every line by the unreserved adoption of all his idol's doings, and by a total absence of censure, or even of what might be called criticism. In short, he allows it to be seen throughout, that Frederick, or whatever powerful and cunning man is for the time being the object of his affections, has exclusive possession of his heart and understanding. In reading Mr. Carlyle's work, however, you feel that you learn a great deal, and that a great many facts, strangely coloured, it is true, and sometimes distorted, are brought under observation. Let what will come of it, you have in his volumes, the result of curious learning, active industry, and rich, though wayward fancy. If not very enthusiastic and shallow yourself, you can correct the false colouring, reduce the facts to something like their natural size, and read with very considerable information and profit.

              –*Dublin Review*, 51 (May 1862): 406–407

* * *

These excerpts are from an unsigned review written in the midst of the Civil War.

"Frederick Against All Comers"
Review of *Frederick the Great,* volume III

Carlyle has at last finished the third volume of his history of *Frederick the Great* and the Harpers pub-

lish it for the benefit of American readers. Frederick obtained the name of a mighty warrior, in his time and hence is designated the *Great,* as Alexander was. The present day is excessively warlike. Every man in the United States is either a soldier, or becoming one, or criticising the actions of those who are in the field learning the game that Frederick played at. The publication of this third volume of Frederick the Great's history by Carlyle is, therefore, very opportune, for it presents to us the first four years of warfare by the Prussian King when he was an apprentice at the business.

. . . .

Let Carlyle write; it is his necessity. He cannot stop if he would. But the reader can cut short his acquaintance with the products of his pen when he pleases. And so, we encourage all who have an inclination to military hero-worship to take hold fearlessly of the third volume of the history of Frederick the Great. We shall not tell the student what he will find, for that might blunt his curiosity. But this we will say, that whatever of savage sympathy, of gigantic exaggeration, of monstrous morality, and atrocious apotheosis can be thrown into the characterization of a hero by an author whose faith is pagan, and whose practice is that of devil-worshipers, will be found in Carlyle's history of Frederick the Great.

Carlyle is condemned by most critics as being neither a gentleman nor a Christian, but his writings are read and admired by millions who claim to be both. They believe him to be diabolical, but yet they never think of consigning him to the pit. They regard his genius as genuine and essentially human, but yet it revels chiefly with ghosts and ghouls. The whole amount of it is, the public do not understand Carlyle. He is simply a modern pagan, inheriting the spirit of the Roman without its personality.

As a class of modern philosophers believe the monkey to be the connecting link between man and beast, so Carlyle believes a Hero (Frederick for instance,) to be the intermediary between men and gods.

Carlyle's Heroes in human shape answer to the Jupiters, the Venuses, the Bachuses and Mercuries of the Romans. The latter, in Roman estimation, were as good deities as Heaven had; and yet they were patrons of courtezans, drunkards and thieves. The feasts of the gods on Olympus were counterparts of earthly carouses, and the Hebes that served the nectar were the "pretty waiter girls" of the day in which Carlyle lives. If a Roman, believing or pretending to believe in such stupendous stuff, at all events using the machinery of the system in his literary works, could yet be pungent and satirical as Horace, sweetly pastoral as Virgil, ornate and eloquent as Cicero, . . . why should not Carlyle, adhering to the same enormous and degrading system of brutalities and bestialities, write books as vigorous, as instructive and powerful as Roman ever wrote? Critic, pray tell us.

Perhaps Carlyle has no right to be a pagan, living as he does in this age of light. That raises a new question, belonging to ethics and having nothing to do with the wars of Frederick. Carlyle *is* a pagan—he believes in . . . the men who *win,* and who are *therefore* heroes and demi-gods, between whose huge legs he orders all mankind to creep. The world to him is a grand allegory, full of giants of the Apollyon order. Carlyle has a contempt for the poor "Christian" who would fight the giant, but with the zest of a buffer would pit giant against giant, so as to enjoy the fray. He is now backing the giant Frederick against all comers.

—*The New York Times,* 29 September 1862, p. 2

* * *

Lord Ashburton, with whom Carlyle maintained a friendship even after the death of Lady Ashburton (from New Letters and Memorials of Jane Welsh Carlyle, *Special Collections, Thomas Cooper Library, University of South Carolina)*

"A Beautiful Bit of Friendly Munificence"

In this letter of 2 November 1862 Carlyle, who was then at work on the fourth volume of his biography, replies to Lord Ashburton's offer of a horse to replace the author's horse Fritz.

Dear Lord Ashburton,

On at last fairly considering the Horse question, "Fritz" (my own poor old quadruped) *versus* your noble Grey (whh. might be mine), I have to admit.—

1st. That poor old Fritz is adequate apparently to carry me thro his Namesake's sad business (*more* adequate, at least, than I am to be carried).

2nd. That *he* is my old friend (almost the one friend I am to have in these dark winter months); whom it were a sin, and a remorse, to desert in his decay.

3rd. That *change* of any kind will be attended with trouble, with uncertainty, better to be avoided in this my nearly extinct conditn.

And, in fine, that I am not permitted to accept your flattering offer; but only to regard it (whh. I always will and must) as a beautiful bit of friendly munificence,—and in that way, retain the *Soul* of it, as a lasting possession. This is the real truth of the affair. . . .

I mean to call again *quam primum* (as soon as possible).

My Proofsheets, my &c. in the muddy dark weather, drive me delirious.

Yours ever faithfully,

T. Carlyle

—David Alec Wilson, *Life of Carlyle,* v. 5, p. 478

These excerpts are from a two-page review in an influential American magazine.

"The Saddest and the Merriest Story"
Review of *Frederick the Great,* volume III

. . . To do this was an appalling labor, for the skeleton thereof was scattered through the crypts of many kingdoms; yet, by the commanding genius of Mr. Carlyle, bone hath not only come to his bone, but they have been clothed with flesh and blood, so that the captains of the age, and, moreover, the masses, as they appeared in their blind tusslings, are restored to sight with the freshness and fulness of Nature. Although this historical review is strictly literature, it is altogether incomparable for vividness and originality of presentation. The treatment of official personages is startlingly new. All ceremony toward them gives place to a fearful familiarity, as of one who not only sees through and through them, but oversees. Grave Emptiness and strutting Vanity, found in high places, are mocked with immortal mimicry. Indeed, those of the "wind-bag" species generally, wherever they appear in important affairs, are so admirably exposed, that we see how they inevitably lead States to disaster and leave them ruins, while their pompous and feeble methods of doing it are so put as to call forth the contemptuous smiles, yea, the derisive laughter, of all coming generations. In fine, the alternate light and shade, which so change the aspect and make the mood of human nature, were never so touched in before; and therefore it is the saddest and the merriest story ever told.

. . . It is not only one of the greatest of histories and of biographies, but nothing in literature, from any other pen, bears any likeness to it. It is truly a solitary work,–the effort of a vast and lonely nature to find a meet companion among the departed.

–*Atlantic Monthly*, 10 (November 1862): 642–643

* * *

This excerpt is from a letter in which Emerson acknowledged that he had long ago received "the third volume of Friedrich, with your autograph inscription, and read it with joy." Carlyle's inscription read "To Ralph Waldo Emerson Esq/ with many regards: T Carlyle/ Chelsea, 17 May 1862."

Emerson to Carlyle, 8 December 1862

. . . The book was heartily grateful, and square to the author's imperial scale. You have lighted the glooms, and engineered away the pits, whereof you poetically pleased yourself with complaining, in your sometime letter to me, clean out of it, according to the high Italian rule, and have let sunshine and pure air enfold the scene. First, I read it honestly through for the history; then I pause and speculate on the Muse that inspires, and the friend that reports it. 'Tis sovereignly written, above all literature, dictating to all mortals what they shall accept as fated and final for their salvation. It is mankind's Bill of Rights and Duties, the royal proclamation of Intellect ascending the throne, announcing its good pleasure, that, hereafter, *as heretofore,* and now once for all, the World shall be governed by Commonsense and law of Morals, or shall go to ruin.

But the manner of it!–the author sitting as Demiurgus, trotting out his manikins, coaxing and bantering them, amused with their good performance, patting them on the back, and rating the naughty dolls when they misbehave; and communicating his mind ever in measure, just as much as the young public can understand; hinting the future,

when it would be useful; recalling now and then illustrative antecedents of the actor, impressing the reader that he is in possession of the entire history centrally seen, that his investigation has been exhaustive, and that he descends too on the petty plot of Prussia from higher and cosmical surveys. Better I like the sound sense and the absolute independence of the tone, which may put kings in fear. And, as the reader shares, according to his intelligence, the haughty *coup d' oeil* of this genius, and shares it with delight, I recommend to all governors, English, French, Austrian, and other, to double their guards, and look carefully to the censorship of the press. I find, as ever in your books, that one man has deserved well of mankind for restoring the Scholar's profession to its highest use and dignity. I find also that you are very wilful, and have made a covenant with your eyes that they shall not see anything you do not wish they should. But I was heartily glad to read somewhere that your book was nearly finished in the manuscript, for I could wish you to sit and taste your fame, if that were not contrary to the law of Olympus. My joints ache to think of your rugged labor. Now that you have conquered to yourself such a huge kingdom among men, can you not give yourself breath, and chat a little, an Emeritus in the eternal university, and write a gossiping letter to an old American friend or so? Also, I own that I have no right to say this last–I who write never.

–*The Correspondence of Thomas Carlyle and Ralph Waldo Emerson, 1834–1872,* v. 2, pp. 278–280

* * *

"Something Cosmic and True"

This excerpt is from Carlyle's 4 December 1862 letter to his brother John.

This day is my sixty-seventh birthday. Time, Death, Eternity: what an element this is that all of us have! . . . If I were only done with my book! But really now it is getting to be high time. My weariness of it, occasionally, no tongue can tell; at other times I am rather pleased to feel myself shaping, according to ability, so long as I live, something cosmic and true out of the chaotic, mendacious and unknown. Oh that I had done with it, *done!*

–David Alec Wilson, *Life of Carlyle,*
v. 5, pp. 487–488

No. 3.

No. 6.   No. 7.

Page from a brochure about a Frederick the Great monument, with Carlyle's notes (Beinecke Rare Book and Manuscript Library, Yale University)

"A Terrible Piece of Work"

Moncure Daniel Conway, an American who was introduced through Emerson, first met the Carlyles in summer 1863, as Carlyle's work on his biography of Frederick the Great was drawing to a close.

In a modest old house, apart from the great whirl of fashion, resided Carlyle, the man to whose wonderful genius more than to any other is to be attributed the intellectual and spiritual activity of his generation. The building he inhabited was significant to him. "Look at these bricks," he said; "not one of them is a lie. Let a brick be once honestly burnt, and the cement good, and your wall will stand till the trump of Doom blows it down! These bricks are as sharp as the day they were put up, and the mortar is now limestone. The houses all around us crumble, the bricks in them were made to crumble after sixty years—that being the extent of most of the leases. They are of a piece with the general rottenness and falsehood of the time."

A strange thrill passed over me when I first stood face to face with these grand features. Emerson had introduced me (the letter is printed in their Correspondence), and he met me, pipe in mouth, cordially. For a few moments I was left with Mrs. Carlyle, who was too thin and pale to preserve traces of beauty, but had a look of refinement and dignity. Among the solemn portraits on the wall were two modern miniatures of beautiful ladies nude to the waist. "You may be surprised," she said, "at seeing such portraits in a grave house like this. They were found in the tent of a Russian officer during the Crimean war, and presented to Carlyle." Cheerful, kindly, witty, and frank, she conversed pleasantly of the habits and labours of Carlyle. She thought of the Life of Frederick a terrible piece of work, and wished that Frederick had died when a baby. "The book is like one of those plants that grow up smoothly and then forms a knot, smoothly again and then forms another knot, and so on; what Carlyle is when one of those knots is being passed must be left to the imagination." Carlyle was a picture of meekness when his wife said this.

—*Autobiography, Memories and Experiences of Moncure Daniel Conway*, v. 1, pp. 351–352

This excerpt is from a seventeen-page review.

"Extraordinarily Clear"
Review of *Frederick the Great*, volume IV
James F. Stephen

Notwithstanding his constant ridicule of picturesque tourists, his skill in verbal ichnography, if not in the representation of landscape, is almost unequalled in literature. No historian makes battles equally intelligible as far as he undertakes to describe them, although he instinctively avoids the technical details of Napier and Thiers. He appears to have examined all Frederick's battle-fields with the minutest care, and what he saw his readers may see almost as distinctly. . . . It is true that history is not generally written in similar detail, but the description of the country renders the subsequent account of the battle extraordinarily clear, and it fixes the event in the memory by associating it with external objects.

—*Fraser's Magazine*, 69 (May 1864): 539–556

* * *

These excerpts are from a twenty-five-page article. James Freeman Clarke had written an admiring letter to Carlyle in 1836. A temperance, antislavery, and women's suffrage advocate, Clarke was a professor of the Harvard Divinity School (1867–1871).

The Two Carlyles, Or Carlyle Past and Carlyle Present
Review of *Frederick the Great*, volume IV
James F. Clarke

We have here a fourth volume, in five hundred pages, of Carlyle's Frederick the Great, by which the story is brought down to 1757, and to the end of the first campaign in the Seven Years' War. At the rate at which the work has hitherto proceeded, it will take four more volumes to complete it. We should not much object to this prolixity, if the biography was written in the earlier manner of its author, as in those wonderful pictures of the French Revolution. But, alas! the present Thomas Carlyle is not *that* Carlyle. As we plod on, with determined effort, through these tangles, this swamp, where no path is to be seen, we say, Can this be really the work of that child of genius, whose words once shone with auroral light, who could look a subject out of confusion into order, whose every sentence we prized, whose lightest phrase had a precious worth?

. . . .

Carlyle's "Frederick the Great" seems to us a badly written book. Let us confine ourselves to the present volume, containing the fifteenth, sixteenth, and seventeenth chapters. Nothing in these chapters is brought out clearly. When we have finished the volume, the mind is filled with a confusion of vague images. We know that Mr. Carlyle is not bound to "provide us with brains" as well as with a history, but neither was he so bound in other days. Yet no such con-

First page of a Carlyle letter to James Anthony Froude in which he confides his concerns about his wife's health (Edinburgh University Library, Special Collections AAF [Carlyle 27])

fusion was left after reading the "French Revolution." How brilliantly distinct was every leading event, every influential person, every pathetic or poetic episode, in that charmed narrative. Who can forget Carlyle's account of the "Menads," the King's "Flight to Varennes," the Constitutions that "would not march," the "September Massacres," "Charlotte Corday,"— every chief tragic movement, every grotesque episode, moving forward, distinct and clear, to the final issue, "a whiff of grapeshot"? Is there anything like that in this confused "Frederick"?

. . . .

. . . Reports of eyewitnesses are, no doubt, picturesque and valuable; but only so, on condition of being properly arranged, and tending, in their use, toward some positive result. Then the tone of banter, of irony, almost of *persiflage,* is very discouraging. If the whole story of Friedrich is so unintelligible, uninteresting, or incommunicable, why take the trouble to write it? The *poco-curante* air with which he narrates, as though it were of no great consequence whether he told his story or not, contrasts wonderfully with his early earnestness. Carlyle writes this history like a man thoroughly *blasé*. Impossible for him to take any interest in it himself,—how then does he expect to interest us? Has he not himself told us, in his former writings, that the man who proposes to teach others anything must be good enough to believe it first himself?

Here, then, is the problem we have to solve. How came this change from the Carlyle of the Past to the Carlyle of the Present,—from Carlyle the universal believer to Carlyle the universal sceptic,—from him to whom the world was full of wonder and beauty, to him who can see in it nothing but Force on the one side and Shams on the other? What changed that tender, loving, brave soul into this hard cynic? And how was it, as Faith and Love faded out of him, that the life passed from his thought, the glory from his pen,—and the page, once alive with flashing ideas, turned into this confused heap of rubbish, in which silver spoons, old shoes, gold sovereigns, and copper pennies are pitched out promiscuously, for the patient reader to sift and pick over as he can? In reading the Carlyle of thirty years ago, we were like California miners,—come upon a rich *placer*, never before opened, where we could all become rich in a day. Now the reader of Carlyle is a *chiffonier*, raking in a heap of street-dust for whatever precious matters may turn up.

. . . .

How is it that this great change should have taken place? Men change,—but not often in this way. The ardent reformer often hardens into the stiff conservative. The radical in religion is very likely to join the Catholic Church. If a Catholic changes his religion, he goes over to atheism. To swing from one extreme to another, is a common experience. But it is a new thing to see calmness in youth, violence in age,—to find the young man wise and all-sided, the old man bigoted and narrow. But such has been the course with Carlyle.

We think the explanation to be this.

Thomas Carlyle from the beginning has not shown the least appreciation of the essential thing in Christianity. Brought up in Scotland, inheriting from Calvinism a sense of truth, a love of justice, and a reverence for the Jewish Bible, he has never passed out of Judaism into Christianity. To him, Oliver Cromwell is the best type of true religion. Inflexible justice is the best attribute of God or man. He is a worshipper of Jehovah, not of the God and Father of the Lord Jesus Christ. He sees in God truth and justice; he does not see in him love.

Thomas Carlyle, 30 September 1864 (Edinburgh University Library, Special Collections AAF [Carlyle 24])

. . . .

. . . But believe only in justice and truth,—omit the doctrine of forgiveness, redemption, salvation,—and faith in Providence becomes sooner or later a dark desparing fatalism. The dark problem of evil remains insoluble without the doctrine of redemption.

So it was that Carlyle, seeing at first the chief duty of man to be the worship of reality, the love of truth,—next made that virtue to consist in sincerity, or being in earnest. Truth was being true to one's self. In this lay the essence of heroism. So that Burns, being sincere and earnest, was a hero,—Mohammed was a hero,—Cromwell was a hero,—Mirabeau and Danton were heroes,—and Frederick the Great was a hero. That which was first the love of truth, and caused him to reverence the calm intellectual force of Schiller and Goethe, soon became earnestness and sincerity, and then became power. For the proof of earnestness is power. So from power, by eliminating all love, all tenderness, as being only rose-water philanthropy, he at last became a worshipper of mere will, of force in its grossest form.

. . . .

The first Carlyle was an enthusiast, the last Carlyle is a cynic. From enthusiasm to cynicism, from the spirit of reverence to the spirit of contempt, the way seems long, but the condition of arriving is simple. Discard LOVE, and the whole road is passed over. Divorce love from truth, and truth ceases to be open and receptive,—ceases to be a positive function, turns into acrid criticism, bitter disdain, cruel and hollow laughter, empty of all inward peace. Such is the road which Carlyle has passed over, from his earnest, hopeful youth to his bitter old age. His only use to us now is in this moral which we have attempted to draw from his career.

—*Christian Examiner,* 77 (September 1864): 206–210, 226–226, 231

* * *

James Russell Lowell was a poet, abolitionist, and editor of the North American Review.

"Vivid Pictures"
Review of *Frederick the Great,* volume IV
James Russell Lowell

With the gift of song, Carlyle would have been the greatest of epic poets since Homer. Without it, to modulate and harmonize and bring parts into their proper relation, he is the most amorphous of humorists, the most shining avatar of whim the world has ever seen. Beginning with a hearty contempt for shams, he has come at length to believe in brute force as the only reality, and has as little sense of justice as Thackeray allowed to women. But with all deductions, he remains the profoundest critic and the most dramatic imagination of modern times. Never was there a more striking example of that *ingenium perfervidum* long ago said to be characteristic of his countrymen. His is one of the natures, rare in these latter centuries, capable of rising to a white heat; but once fairly kindled, he is like a three-decker on fire, and his shotted guns go off, as the glow reaches them, alike dangerous to friend or foe. Though he seems more and more to confound material with moral success, yet there is always something wholesome in his unswerving loyalty to reality, as he understands it. History, in the true sense, he does not and cannot write, for he looks on mankind as a herd

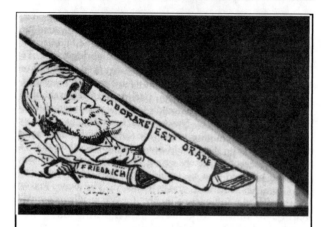

A cartoon that was published during Carlyle's struggles with his biography of Frederick the Great (Columbia University Library; from Fred Kaplan, Thomas Carlyle: A Biography, *Thomas Cooper Library, University of South Carolina)*

"Laborare Est Orare"

In a letter to Joseph Ormond, Carlyle wrote of a proverb that in large measure defined his life.

. . . Properly there is but one man, as I often say, who is worthy of respect in this world: he that can work at something. The old Monks had a proverb, "Laborare est orare, To work is to pray"; the meaning of which goes far deeper than they perhaps were aware of. He that works well and nobly, not as a slave for mere money-hire, but as a man withal and in the spirit of a man, he, if any, is in real communication with his Unseen Author, making a perpetual pious appeal to the Invisible Powers of this Universe,—which respond to him, if he is faithful"

—*The Collected Letters of Thomas and Jane Welsh Carlyle,* v. 15, p. 121

without volition, and without moral force; but such vivid pictures of events, such living conceptions of character, we find nowhere else in prose. The figures of most historians seem like dolls stuffed with bran, whose whole substance runs out through any hole that criticism may tear in them, but Carlyle's are so real, that, if you prick them, they bleed. He seems a little wearied, here and there, in this Friedrich, with the multiplicity of detail, and does his filling-in rather shabbily; but he still remains in his own way, like his hero, the Only, and such episodes as that of Voltaire in the present volume would make the fortune of any other writer.

—*North American Review,* 99 (October 1864): 628

. . . .

Anecdote (rather *false*) of Friedrich having had a
Te-Deum done on the organ at Charlottenburg for his
own private behoof. Saxons, in the last Russian inroad
upon Berlin, had got into Charlottenburg, and smashed
everything to ruin, in a savagely revengeful mood.
Friedrich, coming home, took a silent view of the havoc
there; ordered the organ to be hastily repaired, the
organ-people to be there on a certain day: he himself
sat waiting at the time fixed; and, wrapt in a cloud
of reflexions Olympian, Abysmal, had the Ambrosian
Song executed for him there, as the preliminary step,
True or not, I do not know; but few Sons of Adam
had more reason for a piously-thankful feeling towards
the Past, a piously-valiant towards the Future. What
man had been delivered from such devouring combina-
tions? And the ruin worked by them lay monstrous
and appalling all round. Friedrich himself is broken
with years; his kingdom lies in haggard slashed condition, worn to skin and bone: How is the King, re-
sourceless, to remedy it? That is now the seemingly
impossible problem. Begin it,—thereby alone will it
ever cease to be impossible. Friedrich begins, we may
say, on the first morrow morning; labours, as in the
march to Leuthen; finds it to become more possible,
day after day, month after month, the farther he strives
with it. "Why not leave it to Nature?" Well; that
was the easiest plan, but it was not Friedrich's. His
remaining moneys, alloyed with copper, he distributes
to the most necessitous: 'all his artillery horses' are
parted into plough-teams, and given to those who can
otherwise get none: think what a fine figure of rye and
barley, instead of mere windlestraws, beggary and deso-
lation, was realised by that act alone. Nature is ready
to do much; will of herself cover, with some veil of
grass and lichen, the nakedness of ruin; but her victorious act, when she can accomplish it, is that of getting
you to go with her handsomely, and change disaster
itself into new wealth, new wisdom and valour, which
are wealth in all kinds; California mere zero to them,
zero or less, a frightful *minus* quantity! Friedrich's
procedures in this matter I believe to be little less

A portion of Carlyle's revised galley proof for book 21 of the final volume of History of Friedrich II
(Beinecke Rare Book and Manuscript Library, Yale University)

didactic than those other, which are so celebrated in war: but no Dryasdust, not even a Dryasdust of the Dismal Science, has gone into them, rendered men familiar with them in their details and results. His Silesian Bank was of itself [Can I explain that?]. Friedrich, many sometimes tell us, was as great in Peace as in War: and truly, in the economic and material promises, my own impressions, gathered painfully in darkness and contradiction of the Dismal-Science Doctors, is much to that effect. A first-rate Husbandman (as his Father had been), who not only defended his Nation, but made it rich beyond what seemed possible, and diligently sowed annuals into it, and perennials, which flourish aloft at this day. / Mirabeau's *Monarchie Prussienne*, 8 voll. (?), composed, or hastily cobbled together, some Twenty years after this period, contains the best tabular view one anywhere gets of Friedrich's economics, military and other practical methods and resources (solid exact Tables, and intelligent intelligible descriptions, done by Mauvillon Fils), and so far as Mirabeau is concerned, of a certain small Essay done in big type, shoved into the belly of each volume, and eloquently recommending, with respectful censures and regrets over Friedrich, the Gospel of Free Trade, dear to Papa Mirabeau. The Son is himself a convert; far above lying even to please Papa; but one can see, the thought of Papa gives him new fire of expression. They are eloquent ruggedly strong Essays, those of Mirabeau upon Free Trade;—they contain, in condensed shape, everything we were privileged to hear, seventy years later, from all organs, jews-harps and scrannel-pipes, on the same sublime subject: "God is great, and Plugson is his Prophet. Thus saith the Lord, Buy in the cheapest market, sell in the dearest!" To which the afflicted human mind listens what it can; —and after seventy years, mournfully asks itself and Mirabeau, " M. le Comte, would there have been in Prussia, for example, any Trade at all, any Nation at all, had it always been left Free? There had been mere sand and quagmire, and a community of wolves, M. le Comte. Have the goodness to terminate that Litany, and take up another!

This excerpt is from a two-page article by a reviewer who had given a positive notice to the fourth volume of the biography for a different publication.

"A Representative Man"
Review of *Frederick the Great,* volumes V and VI
James F. Stephen

THE concluding volumes of Mr. Carlyle's *Frederick the Great* have appeared, and a premature death cannot now intervene to add one more melancholy example to the long list of great historical works left half finished. Now that we can look on the work as a whole, we can see how large a scope it permitted to Mr. Carlyle's peculiar powers, how apt a subject it afforded for the application of his peculiar theories, but also how far it has failed to let Mr. Carlyle do justice to himself. Mr. Carlyle has a knowledge of Europe in the eighteenth century which is wholly unrivalled, and the history of Frederick involves the history of Germany, France, and England, and of a large portion of French and German literature. Mr. Carlyle has a marvellous power of condensing the result of his researches and reflections into pregnant, epigrammatic, half-ludicrous sentences or

Carlyle's pen and inkwell (Carlyle's House Museum, London)

expressions; and the various persons who floated to the top of European society in the middle of the last century were exactly suited to be described in this way, having a certain limited interest for the modern world, and being neither too wise nor too good to be dashed off with a humorous epithet or two. Further, Mr. Carlyle has a passion for accuracy of detail. He loves to take the utmost pains to make his geography and his chronology right. He is not satisfied with knowing that Frederick and his army crossed a brook; he wants also to know whether this brook had a gravelly or a muddy bottom. He is not satisfied with knowing that the brook was crossed on such a day of such a month, but he wants also to know what was the hour and the minute. Frederick's history offers an ample field for this sort of labour, for Frederick was continually, for near thirty years, crossing brooks, and the glory and delight of finding out these brooks is much increased by the dismal character of the country where they are to be discovered. A man who sets himself to describe very accurately and minutely the bogs of Bohemia may have the satisfaction of thinking that, if he can carry his readers successfully through this amount of topography, he can carry them through anything. Frederick, too, presents many of the qualities which Mr. Carlyle has spent his life in trying to make the world admire. He was very hard-working, very despotic, with a stern purpose to which he succeeded in making other men bend, and full of a bulldog courage. Undoubtedly he was a captain of men and a captain of industry, and made many millions of men fight, or dig, or die, as he pleased. But the life of Frederick totally fails to give Mr. Carlyle scope for his power of seizing that which is pious, noble, and good in the characters of pious, noble, and good men. He feels this, and shows that he feels it. He is obliged to be constantly patronizing Frederick, making the best of him, exclaiming and protesting that, although he was a heathenish old brute, he still fought and wrought so well that anything may be forgiven him. It may, therefore, seem as if the choice of Frederick were to be regretted, and that Mr. Carlyle might have devoted to a better purpose the maturest years of his intellectual power, We do not think so. . . . To do things moderately good, with a perfect indifference to the feelings of everyone, is the ideal of human life which Mr. Carlyle, amid some waverings, has set himself to preach up for the last thirty years; and Frederick the Great approaches this ideal sufficiently to warrant Mr. Carlyle in choosing him as a representative man.

–The Saturday Review, 19 (22 April 1865): 476–478

* * *

This excerpt is from a letter in which Emerson remarked on reading the volumes completing Carlyle's biography of Frederick the Great after the American Civil War had ended: "I read these in the bright days of our new peace, which added a lustre to every genial work. Now first we had a right to read, for the very bookworms were driven out of doors whilst the war lasted."

Emerson to Carlyle, 7 January 1866

. . . I found in the book no trace of age, which your letter so impressively claimed. In the book, the hand does not shake, the mind is ubiquitous. The treatment is so spontaneous, self-respecting, defiant,– liberties with your hero, as if he were your client, or your son, and you were proud of him, and yet can check and chide him, and even put him in the corner when he is not a good boy,– freedoms with kings, and reputations, and nations, yes, and with principles too–that each reader, I suppose, feels complimented by the confidences with which he is honored by this free-tongued masterful Hermes. . . . This humor of telling the story in a gale,–bantering, scoffing, at the hero, at the enemy, at the learned reporters,– is a perpetual flattery to the admiring student,–the author abusing the whole world as mad dunces,– all but you and I, reader! Ellery Channing borrowed my Volumes V. and VI., worked slowly through them,–midway came to me for Volumes I. II., III. IV,. which he had long already read, and at last returned all with this word, "If you write to Mr Carlyle, you may say to him, that I have read these books, and they have made it impossible for me to read any other books but his."
— *The Correspondence of Thomas Carlyle and Ralph Waldo Emerson, 1834–1872, v. 2, pp. 294–295*

***

This is an excerpt from a twenty-six-page article. Lowell had given a brief positive notice of the fourth volume of the biography.

"An Artist He Is Not"
Review of *Frederick the Great*, volumes V and VI
James Russell Lowell

. . . Mr. Carlyle has no artistic sense of form or rhythm, scarcely of proportion. . . . With a conceptive imagination vigorous beyond any in his generation, with a mastery of language equalled only by the greatest poets, he wants altogether the plastic imagination, the shaping faculty, which would have made him a poet in the highest sense. He is a preacher and a prophet,–anything you will,–but an artist he is not, and never can be. It is always the knots and gnarls of the oak that he admires, never the perfect and balanced tree.

It is certainly more agreeable to be grateful for what we owe an author, than to blame him for what he cannot give us. But it is the business of a critic to trace faults of style and of thought to their root in character and temperament,–to show their necessary relation to, and dependence on, each other,–and to find some more trustworthy explanation than mere wantonness of will for the moral obliquities of a man so largely moulded and gifted as Mr. Carlyle. . . . Comparative criticism teaches us that moral and æsthetic defects are more nearly related than is commonly supposed. Had Mr. Carlyle been fitted out completely by nature as an artist, he would have had an ideal in his work which would have lifted his mind away from the muddier part of him, and trained him to the habit of seeking and seeing the harmony rather than the discord and contradiction of things.

. . . .

. . . Perhaps something of Mr. Carlyle's irritability is to be laid to the account of his early schoolmastership at Ecclefechan. This great booby World is such a dull boy, and will not learn the lesson we have taken such pains in expounding for the fiftieth time. Well, then, if eloquence, if example, if the awful warning of other little boys who neglected their accidence and came to the gallows, if none of these avail, the birch at least is left, and we will try that.

. . . .

. . . Mr. Carlyle seems to be in the condition of a man who uses stimulants, and must increase his dose from day to day as the senses become dulled under the spur. He began by admiring strength of character and purpose, and the manly self-denial which makes a humble fortune great by steadfast loyalty to duty. He has gone on till mere strength has become such washy weakness that there is no longer any titillation in it; and nothing short of downright violence will rouse his nerves now to the needed excitement. . . . Meanwhile the world's wheels have got fairly stalled in mire and other matter of every vilest consistency and most disgustful smell. What are we to do? Mr. Carlyle will not let us make a lever with a rail from the next fence, or call in the neighbors. That would be too commonplace and cowardly, too anarchical. No; he would have us sit down beside him in the slough, and shout lustily for Hercules. If that indispensable demigod will not or cannot come, we can find a useful and instructive solace, during the intervals of shouting, in a hearty abuse of human nature which, at the long last, is always to blame.

—North American Review, 102 (April 1866): 428–432

* * *

These excerpts are from an essay by an admirer who visited Carlyle during the period in which he was working on his biography of Frederick the Great. Lewis Pelly entered the East India Company service in 1840. He later served as a conservative member of Parliament.

Glimpses of Carlyle
Lewis Pelly

Many among us feel that our lives have been largely influenced by some one man or book that we chanced to become acquainted with in early youth.

I was lying idle on the deck of a P. and O. steamer, wondering whether life was worth living, when my hand happened to light on a tattered volume of Carlyle's *Miscellanies,* in which I found his essay on Burns and his second essay on Goethe. These papers read to me almost like a new revelation of life, and seemed to show that when earnestly regarded, the future, even of a lieutenant in the East India Company's service, was susceptible of development. On reaching England I fell in with *Sartor Resartus* and *Past and Present,* works which yet further attracted me to their author.

. . . .

Shortly afterwards Mr. Carlyle asked me to tea, and, with Mrs. Carlyle, received me in his simply furnished drawing-room. He soon worried me into an argument and upset everything I ventured to advance. Tea over, he went to the mantelpiece and filled his pipe which he smoked often, and which I suspect affected his digestion, for he complained more than once of dyspepsia, and I ventured to suggest that his smoking might perhaps injure and depress him. "Yes," he said, "and the doctors told me the same thing. I left off smoking and was very meeserable; so I took to it again, and was very meeserable still; but I thought it better to smoke and be meeserable than to go without." His pipe being filled he descended, as was his wont, to the small garden in rear of the house to commune with the Eternal Silences. But just as he was closing the door Mrs. Carlyle called out, "Why, when Mazzini was here the other night, you took the side of the argument that Mr. Pelly did this evening." Carlyle, putting his head round the door, merely said, "And what's the use of a man if he cannot take two sides of an argument?"

. . . .

Eventually I returned to the East, and was ordered to ride from the capital of Persia to the Indian Frontier, in view to reporting on the political condition of the intervening territories. I was at Herat in 1860, when the Persian army, beaten by the Turcomans, was retreating along the line of the Moorgab; and when on this, and other public accounts, affairs were somewhat disturbed, and one's head at times felt a little loose on one's shoulders. I was lying one evening outside the walls of the Herat Fort, under the starlight and near the singularly beautiful mausoleum of the Timur family, when it occurred to me that I was unaccountably calm and happy for an ordinary man who found himself a thousand miles away from any other European, and surrounded by excitable Asiatics, some of whom had old blood feuds with the Indian Government. On reflection, however, I attributed my mental condition to the influence of Carlyle, and I remember repeating to myself the lines which he had translated from Goethe, and which in that, as in many other crises, have shot strength and solace into my heart:—

> "The future hides in it
> Gladness and sorrow:
> We press still thorow,
> Naught that abides in it
> Daunting us—onward.
>
> "And solemn before us
> Veiled the dark Portal,
> Goal of all Mortal.
> Stars silent rest o'er us,
> Graves under us silent.
>
> "Whilst earnest thou gazest
> Comes boding of terror,
> Comes phantasm and error:
> Perplexing the bravest
> With doubt and misgiving.
>
> "But heard are the voices—
> Heard are the sages,
> The World's and the Ages:
> 'Choose well, your choice is
> Brief and yet endless.
>
> "'Here eyes do regard you
> In Eternity's stillness;
> Here is all fulness,
> Ye brave, to reward you;
> Work and despair not.'"

The next morning I went into the bazaar and selected a finely-woven camel's-hair robe, and a small Persian prayer-carpet of exquisite colour and texture, and resolved to carry both of them with me through Afghanistan and Beloochistan for transmis-

Living with the Carlyles
Recollections of Jessie Hiddlestone

These excerpts are from the account of a maid who served the Carlyles during the last year of their life together. With the cook, Mrs. Warren, Jessie Hiddlestone "slept in the big attic where Fre-derick the Great had been written. . . . Master was easy to get on with, was just like clockwork—anyone could serve him, and he was never exacting. I was there from July, 1865, to August, 1866, and never heard him raise his voice but once, and that was to his brother John."

After tea he sat and read. If she went out, he sat in the little room off the dining-room, with his elbows on the table, his two hands at each side of his head, fingers generally on the temples to shade his eyes from the light of the candle. He sat steadily reading on and on, without moving. But if she was in, they both remained in the dining-room, she at one end of a little oblong table and he at the other, and two candles on it.

'The slightest noise disturbed them. None of the clocks in the house was ever allowed to strike.

'After several hours of reading, he was ready for sup-per, which was often porridge. Then after ten o'clock, he took the key to let himself in by, and went out for his final walk and smoke. While he was out, I examined the candles. If any of them was less than half finished, I replaced it with one that was half finished or more. This was to make sure he would not sit late when he came in and took up a book, as he used to do. He was likely to sit up many hours if the candles went on burning.

'If he did not sleep on retiring, he rose and walked about inside the house or in the back garden. He may have gone out occasionally. It was because I was punc-tual I pleased him. Clean shirts, socks and so on were supplied at fixed hours, which never changed. I attended to all that, and never a word was said or needed. But I would not have stayed many months with Mrs. Carlyle alone, although I liked her. She was very affectionate, but as changeable as a child. Another differ-ence was this. He never said nasty things about people behind their backs. He said anything of that sort face to face.

. . . .

'What surprised me most of all was when she said once, "We are poor, you know." I could see the house was run very economically. The furniture was old-fashioned. She received many presents, too. Twice a week, ham-pers came from Lord Ashburton's farm with the freshest of butter, four or five new eggs, a little cream, and so on. There were several others eager to send her anything she would take; and she had to be wary in speaking of dresses. If she praised anything in the hearing of any of several wealthy ladies, they would be anxious to con-trive how to get her to accept a present of a new dress or something of that sort. Mrs. Carlyle said to me once, "If I did not receive so much, I could not give away so much."

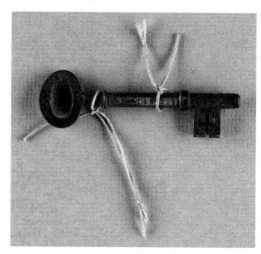

The key to Carlyle's soundproof study (Beinecke Rare Book and Manuscript Library, Yale University)

'Once she decided to make her husband a present of a sealskin vest, anonymously. She took an old one as a pattern to the tailor, taking it back when finished, to have it made exactly to her mind. Then she made a par-cel of it, wrote his address in a distinguished hand, and sent it to him by post on his birthday. In due course it was delivered and produced at the breakfast table. She affected ignorance to perfection. They talked of who sent it, guessing one and another. Carlyle examined the handwriting long and carefully. At length he said, "There's a 'T' I ought to know!" In the end he taxed her with it, and she confessed.

'One night I got a great fright—it was the time he used to go out, about eleven o'clock, and he was going up and down the stairs, saying nothing. Supposing something must be far wrong, I ran upstairs in alarm. Mrs. Carlyle was sitting in the drawing-room, and look-ing out through the open door to the staircase, laughing and laughing and counting master's progress as he went up and down.

'She told me, as well as she could for laughing, that he had wanted to go out, and she objected, as it was a very stormy night. He said he could not sleep without exercise. So she set him to go down to the dining-room and up to the top of the house and back again half a dozen times. She said that would tire him, and she would count. So there he was, going up and down, and she was counting, and he did not go out-of-doors that night, for once.

'They were simply devoted to each other,' was Jessie's conclusion.

—David Alec Wilson, *Life of Carlyle*, v. 6, pp. 33–39

sion to Cheyne Row. These articles, in fact, formed my only luggage, besides what was contained in my saddle-bags. The robe and rug reached Mr. Carlyle in due course, and many years afterwards my friend Miss F. told me that he had placed the little carpet under his writing-table in the upper chamber, and that the camel's-hair robe had been turned into a sort of dressing-gown, and used by him to the end of his life. She added, that it was this robe in which the late Sir Edgar Boehm had enveloped Carlyle's sitting figure, now placed in the Chelsea Gardens, and that the little carpet had been taken by Carlyle, in a fit of tenderness, to the dressing-table of his wife. . . .

. . . I asked him what he thought of Frederick's cavalry generals, Seidlitz and Ziethen. "Well," he said, "they were just famous gallopers." Now this was, perhaps, the only subject upon which my philosopher and guide could have roused me into contradiction. But fresh from my cavalry general, and imbued with all his lessons concerning the cavalry genius of Hannibal, Cromwell, Hyder Ali, and others, I rejoined somewhat sharply: "And do you not think, Mr. Carlyle, that as much genius can be shown in the handling of cavalry as in the writing of books?" "Well," he said, "there is something in that." So I went on to expound to him what General

Jacob had taught me about the fifteen campaigns of Hannibal, the battle of Dunbar, where the Lord delivered the enemy into the hand of Cromwell, and the letter of Hyder Ali to the English general. I concluded by referring to the battle of Rossbach, where Seidlitz, in command of the cavalry, repeatedly refused to obey the order of the king to charge until the right moment arrived, when he forthwith swept the foe from the field. Mr. Carlyle looked interested, but said nothing. When *The History of Frederick the Great* appeared, however, I was amused to find that Seidlitz and Ziethen had become great cavalry commanders, and that no mention was made of 'famous gallopers.' . . .

After many years I again returned from the East, and again met Carlyle, but he seemed to me an altered man. The enthusiasm was gone, and he appeared to take less interest in men and in affairs. The last time I saw him he was passing into the London Library. He looked aged, bent, and hopelessly sad; the wreck of a long and of a well-spent life. I lifted my hat to him, but he did not seem really to recognise me, and so he disappeared into the library, and not long after, through death, into eternity.

–Fortnightly Review, 57 (May 1892): 723–728

The Final Years: 1866–1881

Although Carlyle had completed his greatest works by 1865, he continued writing long after his seventieth birthday. He weathered Jane's death in 1866 and remained for the fifteen years that followed as important and controversial a figure as he had been for the previous three decades.

April 1866: A Rectorship and Jane's Death

In November 1865 the students of the University of Edinburgh honored Carlyle by electing him to the largely ceremonial position of rector by a margin of more than two to one over Benjamin Disraeli. Although Carlyle was anxious about a return to public speaking, his inaugural address on 2 April 1866 was a great success. While he was still away from home, he received the news that Jane, his wife of nearly forty years, had suddenly died.

John Tyndall, a younger man who was a longtime admirer of Carlyle and had known him for years, traveled with the author to Edinburgh. An established scientist, Tyndall received an honorary degree at the same ceremony at which Carlyle spoke.

"A Perfect Triumph"
On Carlyle's Edinburgh Addresss
John Tyndall

The eventful day came, and we assembled in the anteroom of the hall in which the address was to be delivered—Carlyle in his rector's robe, Huxley, Ramsay, Erskine, and myself in more sober gowns. We were all four to be doctored. The great man of the occasion had declined the honour, pleading humorously that in heaven there might be some confusion between him and his brother John, if they both bore the title of doctor. I went up to Carlyle, and earnestly scanning his face, asked: 'How do you feel?' He returned my gaze, curved his lip, shook his head, and answered not a word. 'Now,' I said, 'you have to practice what you have been preaching all your life, and prove yourself a hero.' He again shook his head, but said nothing. A procession was formed, and we moved, amid the plaudits of the students, towards the platform. Carlyle took his place in the rector's chair, and the ceremony of conferring

Thomas Carlyle in 1867 (photograph by Julia Margaret Cameron; The Metropolitan Museum of Art, The Alfred Stieglitz Collection; from Fred Kaplan, Thomas Carlyle: A Biography, *Thomas Cooper Library, University of South Carolina)*

degrees began. Looking at the sea of faces below me—young, eager, expectant, waiting to be lifted up by the words of the prophet they had chosen—I forgot all about the degrees. Suddenly I found an elbow among my ribs—'Tyndall, they are calling for you.' I promptly stood at ''tention' and underwent the process of baptism. The degrees conferred, a fine tall young fellow rose and proclaimed with ringing voice from the platform the honour that had been conferred on 'the foremost of living Scotchmen.' The cheers were loud and long.

Carlyle stood up, threw off his robe, like an ancient David declining the unproved armour of

VOAT FOR A. WARD, THE KONSERVITIF KANDID8!

Voat for A. Ward, the yung Stoodint's Frend and Preseptir!!

VOAT FOR A. WARD,

The Keepir of the grate Wacks Work Show!!! Admission, only 6d.

(I HEV to thank the Konservitif Committy for hevin' put out a Flag to draw atenshun to my Grate Show, which will be xhibited in thare rumes after Saterday ; Admishun 6d.)

Mr Disrelly is now almoast sertin to withdra from the kontist, and I wil then be soal Konservitif Kandid8. My clames to the offiss are unqueshtined. I hev testimoanyels from Profesir Holoway, President Johnson, Mr Smith, and other publik karikters.

No wun wil voat for Mr Karlile when they hev perewsed the followin' dispashunate staitmint : In the interists of trewth, moralitey, and the Konservatifs, I hearbi bring forwurd the foloin' chargis agenst Mr Karlile's Religush, Litterery, and Politikel Karikter. (*N.B.*— My reedirs wil observ that I hev alredy lerned a filusofik methud of arangemint at the Yewniversetty.)

I.—Objecshuns to Mr K.'s Religush and Moril Karikter.

1. He hes never cleerly statid his convicshun that all the Aposils belongd to the Presbiterean Church, xceptin' Jewdas who wos a Romun Kathilik.

2. Thare is no sattisFactry evidence that he wares a white Chokir on Sundis.

3. Mr K.'s wurks air in the opinyun of me and the Konservatif Committy, so subversif of moralitey and religun that we hev never red them.

4. He hes never ritten to Mesirs Kaster and Polucks, the leedirs of the Conservitif party, to congratilait them upon thare Talonts and elokens, and upon thare sukces as rejeneriters of the yewnivers generully. (This is a fatil objecshun.)

5. He hes never patrinised Pershunily or otherYs my grate moril Wacks Wurk Xhibishun —Admishun, 6d.

II.—Objecshuns to Mr K.'s Litterery Karikter.

1. In his buke cald " Heerow Wurship," he hes twise put a Komah whare I think thare should be a Semmy Koalin.

2. In his fulish wurk, "Sarter Resartis," he hes yewsed the wurd "tailor," which I, like all Conservitifs and other edikated peepil, spel "taler." We Conservitifs air kritikel about spelin'.

3. The prise of his bukes is tew hi ; Mr D.'s and mine kan be bowt for wun shilin', and wil sune be redewsd to 6pens (*En. Bee.*—Notiss to the publik.)

III.—Objecshuns to Mr K.'s politikel karikter.

1. He hes never changd sids like Mr D. and me.

2. It is not sertin that he subskribes to the Edenberry evenin' CowRant.

3. HE IS NOT A KONSERVITIF NOR A POLITIKEL ADVENTUR LIKE MR D. AND ME.

This last objecshun setils the matir. T. K. hes now no Chans. My elekshun is sertin. VOAT FOR WARD.

Sins ritin the abuve, wun of my Konservitif frens has sugestid another grate objecshun to Mr K. as rekter of a set of Gentele yung men like the Konservitif Club, vis.: that he dusnt Ware kid gluvs like us, and frekqyents Mekanik's Institoots and sich Lo plases.

(The publik wil notiss that we Konservitifs hev been calin' Mr K.'s Comitty "hornets." They hev sertinly stung us A few.)

My laiter thowts air as foloos :—In my first wurk upon the Elekshun I find I hev so Smashd up the Konservitifs, that I kant Mend them Agen, so I begin to think of changin' sids and adoptin' the sensibil Tikket wuns more. If no further notiss is ishewed, stoodints may giv me thare voats howevir ; and in all kases the Grate Wacks Wurk Show wil be open as yewsuil, Admishun, 6d.

An election poster for the rectorship in which Edinburgh students imitate the American humorist Artemus Ward in comparing Carlyle to his rival Benjamin Disraeli (Edinburgh University Library, Special Collections Da12)

WISDOM AND WIND-BAG.

Illustration from the 14 April 1866 issue of Punch *contrasting Carlyle with the more typical orators of the day (from Rodger L. Tarr, Research Files for the Thomas Carlyle Bibliography, Special Collections, Thomas Cooper Library, University of South Carolina)*

"Words That Teach the Nations"

This excerpt from a notice of Carlyle's speech at the University of Edinburgh was titled "Lord Rector."

While able and unable talkers, and others of the spouting sort, are going round the shallow political puddles, and lashing them into one knows not what mud splash and dirty water storms there riseth, brethren, in the very midst, as a silver fountain, one calm voice of a wise man. The Ages shall call him a great man, when much botching-tailor and Snob nomenclature shall be revised and infinitely corrected. From Caledonian pulpit speaking unto rough raw lads, that philosopher is worthy of your ears, even if for some moments you sustain an appreciable loss of CHANCELLOR SILVERTONGUES'S rhetoric, or more tolerable privation of QUAKER BOUNCE'S blare. For, regard him how you may, this THOMAS of Chelsea hath the root of the matter in him, while others do but wave branches, not altogether, it would seem, of olive. He goes for the Truth, when for the most part men are content to mumble truism, and not a few run jocundly away with lies. Uncomely may be the garb or outside form of his teaching, to those who love the trim gardens, but the Truth is with him, the *magna veritas*. Small effort maketh he to paint you a rosy-coloured picture, nor is he at all mindful to light it up with pantomime-ending fires, bringing down the curtain with frantic plaudit of the

unwise. The best he has for you is Work—and Hope. You who will not be content with this, friends, away with you, and at the first corner you shall hear what not of your greatness and goodness and grandeur, and seven-league-bootedness in the onward course of perfectibility and all that sort of thing.

. . . .

One would fancy some able draughtsman presenting Wind-bag in full blast, and our calm THOMAS demanding what kind of hideous object is he who speaketh fluently but untruly. There is room for such picture, and it shall be remembered when Wind-bag hath altogether burst. Yet for those rough Caledonian lads THOMAS had his words of manly cheer, showing that if Life be mostly a struggle, there come sun-bursts for those who have the gift to raise their eyes, not so common a gift as is supposed. To be earnest, to be wary, to be hopeful, such were his noways dim and inarticulate teachings. Brave old man, wise old man. Amid the cacklings cometh his human voice, and all unspoiled hearts ring answer and thanks. You, young Caledonians, be proud that it was to you he said the words that teach the nations. Honour to you from all of us, from all good men, THOMAS CARLYLE! *Diceant Immo quibus placet hæc sententia.*

–Punch, 50 (14 April 1866): 154–155

Saul, and in his carefully-brushed brown morning-coat came forward to the table. With nervous fingers he grasped the leaf, and stooping over it looked earnestly down upon the audience. 'They tell me,' he said, 'that I ought to have written this address, and out of deference to the counsel I tried to do so, once, twice, thrice. But what I wrote was only fit for the fire, and to the fire it was compendiously committed. You must therefore listen to and accept what I say to you as coming straight from the heart.' He began, and the world already knows what he said. I attended more to the aspect of the audience than to the speech of the orator, which contained nothing new to me. I could, however, mark its influence on the palpitating crowd below. They were stirred as if by subterranean fire. For an hour and a half he held them spellbound, and when he ended the emotion previously pent up burst forth in a roar of acclamation. With a joyful heart and clear conscience I could redeem my promise to Mrs. Carlyle. From the nearest telegraph-office I sent her a despatch of three words: 'A perfect triumph,' and returned towards the hall. Noticing a commotion in the street, I came up with the crowd. It was no street brawl; it was not the settlement of a quarrel, but a consensus of acclamation, cheers and 'bravos,' and a general shying of caps into the air! Looking ahead I saw two venerable old men walking slowly arm-in-arm in advance of the crowd. They were Carlyle and Erskine. The rector's audience had turned out to do honour to their hero. Nothing in the whole ceremony affected Carlyle so deeply as this display of fervour in the open air.

—*New Fragments,* pp. 362–364

***

Moncure Daniel Conway, a American Southerner and friend of the Carlyles who had traveled to hear Carlyle speak in Edinburgh, remembers being greeted by John Tyndall: "Taking my hand, he said, 'This is the real kind of tie between America and England. Carlyle belongs equally to both.'" This account is from Conway's 1904 memoir.

"A Transparency of His Thought and Feeling" On Carlyle's Edinburgh Address
Moncure Daniel Conway

No reader in the twentieth century can realise the impression made by Carlyle that day. There is no longer the clear historic background behind that figure—the weary trials, the poverty and want, the long, lonely studies, through which the little boy of fourteen climbed on to a youthful condition still more rugged, and finally, despite his alienation of pulpit and populace, gained this height. As Carlyle entered the university theatre there walked beside him the venerable Sir David Brewster, fourteen years his senior, who first recognised his ability and gave him literary employment. The one now Principal, the other Lord Rector, they moved forward in their gold-laced robes, while professors, students, ladies, stood up cheering, waving hats, handkerchiefs, programmes, in ecstasy. Near me sat Huxley, and not far away Tyndall, in whose eyes I saw tears unless my own dim eyes deceived me. Carlyle sat there during the preliminaries, scanning the faces before him, among which were a score that would bring to him memories of this or that quiet retreat in Scotland known in youth or boyhood.

Before he began his address, Carlyle shook himself free of the gold lace gown and laid it on the back of a chair. This movement excited audible mirth in the audience, and the face of the old Principal beamed. For myself I saw in the act the biographer of Cromwell saying, "Take away that bauble!" No stage actor could with more art have indicated that the conventionalities were about to be laid aside. I had, as I thought, seen and heard Carlyle in every mood and expression, but now discovered what immeasurable resources lay in this man; the grand sincerity, the drolleries, the auroral flashes of mystical intimation, the lightnings of scorn for things low and base—all of these severally taking on physiognomical expression in word, tone, movement of the head, colour of the face, brought before us a being whose physical form was a transparency of his thought and feeling.

When Carlyle sat down there was an audible motion, as of breath long held, by all present; then a cry from the students, an exultation; they rose up, all arose, waving their arms excitedly; some pressed forward, as if wishing to embrace him, or to clasp his knees; others were weeping: what had been heard that day was more than could be reported; it was the ineffable spirit that went forth from the deeps of a great heart and from the ages stored up in it, and deep answered unto deep.

—*Autobiography, Memories and Experiences of Moncure Daniel Conway,* v. 2, pp. 86–87

***

A Last Leave-Taking

The months leading up to Carlyle's speech at Edinburgh were difficult for the Carlyles because of his growing anxiety. John Tyndall describes the couple's last moments together.

It was arranged that he should go first to Freystone, in Yorkshire, and pay a short visit to Lord Houghton. On the morning of March 29, 1866, I drove to Cheyne Row, and found him punctually ready at the appointed hour. Order was Carlyle's first law, and punctuality was one of the chief factors of order. He was therefore punctual. On a table in a small back parlour below-stairs stood a 'siphon,' protected by wickerwork. Carlyle was conservative in habit, and in his old age he held on to the brown brandy which was in vogue in his younger days. Into a tumbler Mrs. Carlyle poured a moderate quantity of this brandy, and filled it up with the foaming water from the siphon. He drank it off, and they kissed each other—for the last time. At the door she suddenly said to me, 'For God's sake send me one line by telegraph when all is over.' This said, and the promise given, we drove away.

—New Fragments, p. 358

On 21 April 1866 Jane Welsh Carlyle went out for her afternoon carriage ride, which included a turn through Hyde Park. At the park she stopped to let a small dog, which she was keeping for a friend, out to run. The dog was struck by another carriage but not seriously hurt. Jane fetched the dog and reentered the carriage. She was discovered soon thereafter dead, leaning back with her eyes closed. Carlyle was immediately summoned back from Edinburgh, where he had traveled to be inaugurated as rector of the university. In accordance with her wish, Jane's body was returned to Haddington, and she was buried next to her father on April 27. In the months immediately after Jane's death, Carlyle wrote a memoir of her and of their relationship and collected and arranged Jane's letters.

"His Wife Lay Silent"
John Tyndall

I drove forthwith to Chelsea. The door was opened by Carlyle's old servant, Mrs. Warren, who informed me that her master was in the garden. I joined him there, and we immediately went upstairs together. It would be idle, perhaps sacrilegious on my part, to attempt any repetition of his language. In words, the flow of which might be compared to a molten torrent, he referred to the early days of his wife and himself—to their struggles against poverty and obstruction; to her valiant encouragement in hours of depression; to their life on the moors, in Edinburgh, and in London—how lovingly and loyally she had made of herself a soft cushion to protect him from the rude collisions of the world. . . . Three or four times during the narrative he utterly broke down. I could see the approach of the crisis, and prepare for it. After thus giving way, a few sympathetic words would cause him to rapidly pull himself together, and resume the flow of his discourse. . . . While he thus spoke to me, all that remained of his wife lay silent in an adjoining room.

—New Fragments, pp. 368–369

* * *

Carlyle's inscription to his friend, which he wrote the day before the death of Jane Welsh Carlyle (Special Collections, Thomas Cooper Library, University of South Carolina)

John Ruskin had begun visiting the Carlyles at their Chelsea home in the early 1850s and developed a close friendship with Carlyle. He learned of Jane Carlyle's death on the day that she died, as he happened to be bringing her flowers. Carlyle refers to Ruskin's letter of sympathy, which has been lost.

Carlyle to John Ruskin, 10 May 1866

Dear Ruskin,

Your kind words from Dijon were welcome to me: thanks. I did not doubt your sympathy in what has come; but it is better that I see it laid before me. You are yourself very unhappy, as I too well discern—heavy-laden, obstructed and dispirited; but you have a great work still ahead, and will gradually have to gird yourself up against the *heat of the day,* which is coming on for you,—as the Night too is coming. Think valiantly of these things.

I cannot write to you; I do not wish yet even to speak to anybody; find it more tolerable to gaze steadily in silence on the blackness of the abysses that have suddenly opened round me, and as it were swallowed up my poor little world. Day by day the stroke that has fallen, like a thunderbolt out of the skies all *blue* (as I often think), becomes more immeasurable to me; my life all hid in ruins, and the one light of it as if gone out. And yet there is an inexpressible beauty, and even an epic greatness (known only to God and me), in the Life of my victorious little Darling whom I shall see no more. Silence about all that; every word I speak or write of it seems to desecrate it,—so unworthy of the Fact now wrapt in the Eternities, as God has willed.

This day fortnight, about this hour (1 p.m.) we were lowering her dust to sleep with that of her Father, in the Abbey of Kirk of Haddington, as was our covenant for forty years back: since that day my life has been as *noiseless* as I could make it; and ought to continue so till I see farther. My Brother and Miss Welsh are still with me; everybody is and has been kind as Humanity could be; help me farther nobody can. If by slow degrees I *can* really do some useful work for the poor remainder of my days, it shall be well and fit; if otherwise, I already seem to see I shall soon follow whither she has gone. That is yet all.

Come and see me when you get home; come *oftener* and see me, and speak *more* frankly to me (for I am very true to your highest interests and you) while I still remain here.

You can do nothing for me in Italy; except come home improved. If you pass through or near Montey (in Valais, not far from Vevey, I think) you might call on (Dowager) Lady Ashburton, and bring me some report of her. Adieu, my friend, adieu.

                                        T. Carlyle
                    —*The Correspondence of Thomas Carlyle
                    and John Ruskin,* pp. 117–118

* * *

Ralph Waldo Emerson to Carlyle, 16 May 1866

My dear Carlyle,

I have just been shown a private letter from Moncure Conway to one of his friends here, giving some tidings of your sad return to an empty home. We had the first news last week. And so it is. The stroke long-threatened has fallen at last, in the mildest form to its victim, and relieved to you by long and repeated reprieves. I must think her fortunate also in this gentle departure, as she had been in her serene and honored career. We would not for ourselves count covetously the descending steps after we have passed the top of the mount, or grudge to spare some of the days of decay. And you will have the peace of knowing her safe, and no longer a victim. I have found myself recalling an old verse which one utters to the parting soul,—

> "For thou hast passed all change of human life,
> And not again to thee shall beauty die."

It is thirty-three years in July, I believe, since I first saw her, and her conversation and faultless manners gave assurance of a good and happy future. As I have not witnessed any decline, I can hardly believe in any, and still recall vividly the youthful wife and her blithe account of her letters and homages from Goethe, and the details she gave of her intended visit to Weimar, and its disappointment. Her goodness to me and to my friends was ever perfect, and all Americans have agreed in her praise. Elizabeth Hoar remembers her with entire sympathy and regard.

I could heartily wish to see you for an hour in these lonely days. Your friends, I know, will approach you as tenderly as friends can; and I can believe that labor—all whose precious secrets you know—will prove a consoler,—though it cannot quite avail,—for she was the rest that rewarded labor. It is good that you are strong, and built for endurance. Nor will you shun to consult the awful oracles which in these hours of tenderness are sometimes vouchsafed. If to any, to you.

I rejoice that she stayed to enjoy the knowledge of your good day at Edinburgh, which is a leaf we would not spare from your book of life. It was a right manly speech to be so made, and is a voucher of unbroken strength—and the surroundings, as I learn, were all the happiest,—with no hint of change.

I pray you bear in mind your own counsels. Long years you must still achieve, and, I hope, neither grief nor weariness will let you "join the dim choir of the bards that have been," until you have written the book I wish and wait for,—the sincerest confessions of your best hours.

My wife prays to be remembered to you with sympathy and affection.

Ever yours faithfully,

R. W. Emerson

—The Correspondence of Thomas Carlyle and Ralph Waldo Emerson, v. 2, pp. 298–300

* * *

In his Reminiscences, *written soon after his wife's death and edited and published after his own death, Carlyle remembered the "sufferings of my poor little woman" during his long struggle with his biography of Frederick the Great.*

"Beautiful and as Sunlight to Me"

. . . She was habitually in the feeblest health; often, for long whiles, grievously ill. Yet by an alchemy all her own, she had extracted grains as of gold out of every day, and seldom or never failed to have something bright and pleasant to tell me, when I reached home after my evening ride, the most foredone of men. In all, I rode, during that book, some 30,000 miles, much of it (all the winter part of it) under cloud of night, sun just setting when I mounted. All the rest of the day, I sat silent aloft; insisting upon work, and *such* work, *invitissimâ Minervâ* for that matter. Home between five and six, with mud mackintoshes off, and, the nightmares locked up for a while, I tried for an hour's sleep before my (solitary, *dietetic,* altogether simple, simple) bit of dinner; but first *always,* came up for half an hour to the drawing-room and Her; where a bright kindly fire was sure to be burning (candles hardly lit, all in trustful *chiaroscuro*), and a spoonful of brandy in water, with a pipe of tobacco (which I had learned to take sitting on the rug, with my back to the jamb,

and door never so little *open,* so that all the smoke, if I was careful, went up the chimney): this was the one bright portion of my black day. Oh those evening half-hours, how beautiful and blessed they were,—*not* awaiting me now on my home-coming, for the last ten weeks! She was oftenest reclining on the sofa; wearied enough, she too, with her day's doings and endurings. But her history, even of what was bad, had such grace and truth, and spontaneous tinkling melody of a naturally cheerful and loving heart, I never anywhere enjoyed the like. Her courage, patience, silent heroism, meanwhile, must often have been immense. Within the last two years or so she has told me about my talk to her of the Battle of Mollwitz on these occasions, while that was on the anvil. She was lying on the sofa; weak, but I knew little how weak, and patient, kind, quiet and good as ever. After tugging and wriggling through what inextricable labyrinth and Sloughs-of-despond, I still well remember, it appears I had at last *conquered* Mollwitz, saw it all clear ahead and round me, and took to telling her about it, in my poor bit of joy, night after night. I recollect she answered little, though kindly always. Privately, she at the time felt convinced she was dying:—dark winter, and such the weight of misery, and utter decay of strength;—and, night after night, my theme to her, *Mollwitz!* This she owned to me, within the last year or two;— which how could I listen to without shame and abasement? Never in my pretended-superior kind of life, have I done, for love of any creature, so supreme a kind of thing. It touches me at this moment with penitence and humiliation, yet with a kind of soft *religious* blessedness too.—She *read* the first two volumes of *Friedrich,* much of it in printer's sheets (while on visit to the aged Misses Donaldson at Haddington); her applause (should not I collect her fine Notekins and reposit them here?) was beautiful and as sunlight to me,— for I knew it was sincere withal, and unerringly straight upon the blot, however exaggerated by her great love of me. The other volumes (hardly even the third, I think) she never read,—I knew too well why; and submitted without murmur, save once or twice perhaps a little quiz on the subject, which did not afflict her, either. Too weak, too weak by far, for a dismal enterprise of that kind, as I knew too well!

—Reminiscences, v. 2, pp. 201–203

Jane Welsh Carlyle, 1865 (from Jane Welsh Carlyle Letters: Letters to Her Family, 1839–1863 *Special Collections, Thomas Cooper Library, University of South Carolina)*

After Jane

At Cheyne Row, Carlyle continued to receive visitors from England and abroad. Mary Aitken Carlyle, daughter of Carlyle's sister, Jean Carlyle Aitken, came in 1868 to take care of her uncle.

In these excerpts, an American visitor recalls meeting Carlyle on 28 August 1866.

"Carlyle in the Flesh"
George W. Smalley

A maid servant answered the bell, and I was shown into a room on the left of the narrow passage on the ground-floor. The room was dimly lighted. A lady came forward, whom I afterward knew as Mr. Carlyle's niece, Miss Aitken, and said in a whisper that her uncle was still asleep but that he expected me and I was to wait. On the left of the door, against the wall, was a sofa, and on the sofa was Mr. Carlyle. He soon woke and I introduced myself, Miss Aitken having vanished. Now I had heard before coming to England an awkward story or two of the great writer's odd way of receiving strangers. Americans, it was said, were less welcome than others; and though I knew very well that Mr. Emerson's introduction was the best I could have, I was not over-confident of a cordial greeting. But I found that in this, as in some other points, the Carlyle of common report and the actual Carlyle were two different persons. His hearty way of saying, "Eh! and so you are a friend of Mr. Emerson," and his outstretched hand, were quite enough to put a shy man at his ease. Not even in America had I ever seen anybody to whom ordinary social usages were more obviously indifferent. It was the hour when London dined, and in order to dine arrays itself in swallow-tail and white tie. Mr. Carlyle had dined early, and the tall figure that rose from the sofa was clad in a dressing-gown of a red pattern reaching his knees. He questioned me eagerly about

Mr. Emerson; about his health, and whether he meant to come to England again and how soon; and whether his fame at home grew, and his books sold. His manner as he spoke of his American friend was gentle and affectionate. It was the same afterward when he went back to that topic, as he often did.

As soon as he had satisfied the first keenness of his curiosity for the latest news about Mr. Emerson, he said he usually took a walk at this hour, and would I go with him? I remembered the pouring rain and wondered if he would go out in it, but the weather was a thing to which, as I found later, he gave no thought. By the time he had put on a coat and hat and seized his big stick, it rained no longer. It was quite dark, and it had long been his habit to walk after the sun had gone down. He did not seem to care for the river and the fresh currents of air which blew freely along its banks. His steps were bent toward the quieter corners of quiet old Chelsea. Almost the whole of that neighbourhood was at that time quite unknown to me, and I had no idea where we went. Nor did I care; it was enough for me that I was walking with Mr. Carlyle. It was a pleasure to note his firm, swift stride. His pace was such as few men of past seventy would have cared to set; and he maintained it to the end. The stream of talk ran not less swiftly. I have no notes of what was said, and should not use them if I had, but I remember clearly the subject and scope of his strange outpourings. Kindly and friendly as he was to me, out of the depth of his regard for the friend whose letter I had brought, he was then, and often afterward when I saw him, in a despairing and hostile mood with reference to the world in general. . . . It was past nine when we returned. The candles had been lighted. The fire—for though it was August a fire had been kindled—blazed cheerfully. The table was spread: the tea was made and keeping hot under its Scotch cosey; and by the time he had laid aside his wraps and reappeared in his ragged red dressing-gown, the stern, strong, sad face reflected the pleasant light which shone on it, and his mood changed with the changing circumstances.

. . . .

There was no detail of a life strange to him which had not some interest for him. He put all sort of questions as he sat behind his teapot and took huge sips from his cup and munched his bread and butter and plum-cake. He asked about the law in the United States, the schools of law, and the practice of it, and whether it much differed from English law, and how; and had I got here soon enough to visit the English courts and compare them with the American courts, and in which did I think a man had the better chance of getting justice done him—"supposing it was justice he

wanted"; and at which the loud, bitter laugh broke out again.

Answering as well as I could this volley of questions, I sat watching the old man and trying to make the Carlyle of my guesses and fancy match the Carlyle in the flesh, on whom I looked for the first time. There is little need to describe a face so well known as his; known by countless photographs and many prints of every degree of merit. It is so marked a face that I never saw a likeness of him which had not some unmistakable look of the man himself. No sign of decay was there about him. The eye was full, the glance swift, sure, penetrating. The hollowness of the socket, the deep shadow beneath the eye, were the traces, not of illness, except such as was chronic, but of lifelong vigil and study. "Writer of books," as he described himself in his famous petition, was stamped on every feature. A sad, stern face I called it just now, and I know not whether it was more sad or stern, nor whether the sadness of it was not deepest when he laughed. He had still a florid complexion, and the ruddy hue stood out strongly against the iron-gray hair which fell in shaggy clumps about his forehead, while the eyes, naturally deep-set, seemed lost beneath the thicket of eyebrow which overshadowed them. The moustache and beard he wore full; wrinkled and gnarled rather than curled. When he laughed, the grim squareness of the jaw showed itself. It was a portentous laugh; open-mouthed and deep-lunged, and prolonged; ending mostly in a shout of triumph, and seldom quite glad or kindly. The bony hands clutched the table meanwhile with a muscular grip, and the laugh was likely to be followed by a torrent of speech that bore down everything before it. Woe to the man who ventured to gainsay him when in that humour; as I more than once saw proof of afterward.

Tea and questions over, the strung fibres relaxed a little. He sat himself down by the fireside, on the floor, his back against the jamb of the chimney-piece, took a comb out of his pocket and combed down his tangled bushy hair till it hid his forehead altogether, and you could no longer see where the hair ended and the eyebrows began. This done, he filled and lighted his pipe; a long clay pipe quite new, known, I think, as a church-warden; quite two feet from bowl to mouthpiece. As the perfume of the tobacco filled the room and the clouds of smoke rolled about him, he began to talk again. It was no longer talk in the common sense of the word; there were no more questions, no pauses. It was a monologue, and no small part of it sounded strangely familiar, as if I had sat in that little parlour before and heard the same voice pouring out the same words and ideas. He had, in fact, by that time fallen into the habit of repeating orally what in days long gone he had written,—not consciously or purposely, but as if the same

Pages from Geraldine Jewsbury's memoir of Jane Welsh Carlyle with Carlyle's responses. Carlyle included some of Jewsbury's accounts in Reminiscences of Thomas Carlyle, *which was edited by James Anthony Froude and published after Carlyle's death in 1881 (The Trustees of the National Library of Scotland MS 532 and MS533).*

10   Thomas Carlyle.

mühen, auf allen Lebensgebieten jene Idee als das Wahre und Wesentliche gegen die Erscheinungen, als das Wechselnde und Unzulängliche geltend zu machen, — geltend zu machen mit der religiösen Ueberzeugung eines Priesters und der trauernden Resignation eines Propheten, liegt der Schlüssel zur Kenntniß seines Wesens und seiner geistigen Thätigkeit. Was man auch an den Schlußfolgerungen im einzelnen aussetzen möge, selten ist wol ein weltliches Evangelium mit so erschütterndem Ernst und so wunderbarer Beredsamkeit gepredigt worden, und vielleicht nie hat ein transscendentaler Denker mit dem kühnen Fluge der Speculation und der Phantasie eine so leidenschaftliche Hingabe an die Lösung der praktischen Probleme der gegenwärtigen Welt vereinigt als der Schriftsteller Thomas Carlyle.

Aber wenn so nach langem Schwanken der Würfel endlich gefallen war, so fehlte trotzdem noch viel, daß die aufgeregten Elemente zur Ruhe gekommen wären. Der Wille und die Begeisterung für eine bestimmte Arbeit waren da; doch das Feld war groß, die Wahl schwer, die Reihen der Mitarbeiter, unter denen es einen Platz zu finden galt, gedrängt voll. Trotzdem war es um so mehr von Bedeutung, einen Anfang zu machen, als das literarische Schaffen nicht blos die Ausführung eines innern Berufs erfüllen, sondern auch als Basis für eine unabhängige Existenz dienen sollte. Die nächste Möglichkeit, beide Zwecke zu vereinigen, bot die Journalistik dar und als Journalist fing Carlyle seine neue Laufbahn an. In Edinburgh herrschte damals ein angeregtes geistiges Leben. Der Genius Robert Burns' hatte den dichterischen Sinn des schottischen Volks in Bewegung gesetzt, Sir Walter Scott's Ruhm stand in voller Blüte; auch an wissenschaftlichen Notabilitäten war kein Mangel und die „Edinburgh Review" bildete das Centrum eines Kreises talentvoller Schriftsteller, deren Thätigkeit bereits über die Grenzen Englands hinaus Ansehen und Einfluß genoß. Andeutungen im „Sartor Resartus" deuten darauf hin, daß man schon vor der Zeit, von welcher wir reden, in den literarischen Cirkeln der Hauptstadt auf Carlyle als einen Mann von Geist und Originalität aufmerksam geworden war, und da er nun dorthin übersiedelte, um selbständig in die Reihen der literarischen Genossenschaft einzutreten, läßt sich denken, daß er den angeborenen Hang zur Einsamkeit bezwang und viel in jenen Kreisen verkehrte. Seine ersten bekannt gewordenen Arbeiten waren Artikel über Montesquieu, Montaigne, Nelson und die beiden Pitt's in Brewster's „Edinburgh Encyclopaedia", nebst einer im Laufe desselben Jahres (1823) veröffentlichten Uebersetzung von Legendre's Geometrie, mit einem hinzugefügten „Essay on Proportion" — einleitende Versuche, die er später der Aufnahme in seine gesammelten „Kleinern Schriften" („Miscellanies") nicht würdig achtete und deren einfache chronologische Erwähnung daher an dieser Stelle genügt. Der eigentliche Beginn einer bedeutungsvollen, genau abgegrenzten Epoche seiner literarischen Thätigkeit datirt erst von dem Jahre 1824, wo er seine Uebersetzung von Goethe's „Wilhelm Meister" herausgab. Um diese Zeit war er offenbar über seinen nächsten Studien- und Arbeitsplan zum Entschlusse gekommen. Seine Studien sollten vor allem die deutsche Literatur umfassen, und es sollte seine erste Arbeit sein, seinen Landsleuten die Resultate dieser Studien zu vermitteln. Wie er in der Vorrede zur Uebersetzung des „Wilhelm Meister" auseinandersetzte, war man bis dahin mit deutscher Literatur in England so gut wie unbekannt. Man hatte eine dunkle Vorstellung, daß Deutschland während der letzten hundert Jahre eine Anzahl von Dichtern hervorgebracht habe, die sich keinen unbedeutenden Ruf erworben; man nannte die Namen Klopstock, Wieland, Goethe und Schiller, und dieser und jener hatte eins oder das andere ihrer Werke in schlechten Uebersetzungen gelesen; aber die Begriffe von ihren Leistungen waren von der unbefriedigendsten Art und die vorherrschende Meinung ging dahin, daß Deutschland in wahrhafter Poesie und Bildung noch immer so weit hinter den andern Völkern

Page from Friedrich Althaus's 1866 German biography of Carlyle, with Carlyle's criticisms in the margin
(Trustees of the National Library of Scotland MS 1799)

"Along the Fringe of the Mediterranean"

This excerpt is from the memoir of John Tyndall, who accompanied Carlyle on a brief trip to the Mediterranean in December 1866.

. . . In the morning, at an early hour, I found him vigorously marching along the fringe of the Mediterranean. In the afternoon we had a long drive on the Corniche Road. The zenithal firmament, as we returned, was deep blue, the western sky a fiery crimson. Newton's suggestion–it could hardly be called a theory–as to the cause of the heavenly azure was mentioned. Carlyle had learned a good deal of natural philosophy from Leslie, of whom he preserved a grateful remembrance. From Leslie he had learnt Newton's view of the colour of the sky, and he now stood up for it. Leslie, he contended, was a high and trustworthy authority. 'An excellent man,' I admitted, 'in his own line, but not an authority on the point now under discussion.' Carlyle continued to press his point, while I continued to resist. He became

silent, and remained so for some time. A 'dépendance' of the Villa Madonna had been placed at his sole disposal, and in it his fire was blazing pleasantly when we returned from our drive. I helped him to put on his dressing-gown. Throwing himself into a chair, and pointing to another at the opposite side of the fire, he said: 'I didn't mean to contradict you. Sit down there and tell me all about it.' I sat down, and he listened with perfect patience to a lengthy dissertation on the undulatory theory, the laws of interference, and the colours of thin plates. As in all similar cases, his questions showed wonderful penetration. The power which made his pictures so vivid and so true enabled him to seize physical imagery with ease and accuracy. Discussions ending in this way were not unfrequent between us, and, in matters of science, I was always able, in the long run, to make prejudice yield to reason.

–New Fragments, pp. 374–375

Diploma presented to Carlyle by the Royal Society of Edinburgh on 3 December 1866 (Trustees of the National Library of Scotland CH 884)

trains of thought came back to him; and he was content to have a listener while he thought over the old problems that had vexed him, and once more offered his solution of them. Page after page of *Sartor* did he repeat, not *verbatim*, but in substance, and of that deep study called *Characteristics*, diverging then into *Past and Present*, and again into one or another of the *Latter Day Pamphlets*. I was fresh from reading most of these; all of them were at that time pretty well known to me, and I never had a stranger sensation than in thus hearing from the mouth of the philosopher the oral repetition of his written and printed wisdom. With intervals of silence or conversation of a more familiar kind, he went on thus for quite two hours. When it seemed to have come to an end I rose to take leave, and upon my telling him I was going to Berlin he asked me to come again on my return and bring him all the news of the Prussian capital.

—London Letters, pp. 250–252, 253–255

* * *

Carlyle again became involved in public debate when he contributed the essay "Shooting Niagara: and After?" to the August 1867 issue of Macmillan's Magazine. *He wrote the ferocious essay, which reiterated his opposition to democracy, in response to controversy surrounding Edward John Eyre, governor of the British colony of Jamaica, and the Reform Bill of 1867.*

In October 1865 Governor Eyre had brutally suppressed a violent native rebellion and imposed martial law. George William Gordon, the leader of the opposition to the British, was court-martialed and executed. Liberals in England protested the violation of civil rights, and a Jamaica Committee, headed by John Stuart Mill, was formed to investigate the incident. To oppose the prosecution of Eyre, whom he believed had acted courageously in a crisis, Carlyle chaired the "Eyre Defence Fund," which also enjoyed the support of Tennyson, Dickens, and Ruskin, and spoke out fiercely at meetings in September 1866. In April 1867, a grand jury refused to indict Eyre, and the controversy was ostensibly concluded. Carlyle, however, believed that the Reform Bill of 1867, which was then being hotly debated, represented an extension of rights to those who were unprepared to exercise them wisely—a circumstance similar to that which had resulted in anarchy and tragedy in Jamaica.

This unsigned response in an American periodical is an example of the public furor Carlyle's opinions continued to evoke.

Carlyle vs. the Human Race
A Response to "Shooting Niagra: And After?"

MR. CARLYLE is the twelfth juror railing at all the others. He is the lunatic glaring through the bars and laughing at the world for being mad. His essay "Shooting Niagara: and after?" is merely an ebullition of impotent cynicism. The whole world, he says, is madly rushing to

destruction; and for the English part of it the only hope is the British aristocracy, who must leave Parliament or reason, and save England by the drill-sergeant or brute force. As for us in America, we have ruined ourselves by an exquisitely silly sentimentality about freedom and emancipation of the "nigger," whereas the divine will is that the "nigger" shall be a slave; and men of about Mr. Thomas Carlyle's complexion are divinely appointed to drive them with whip and spur. Free labor is fol-de-rol. The best must govern. What kind of divine decision are you to get from a count of heads? Count of heads—when you can have such polite gentlemen to govern you as the English nobility, who have now nothing to do but to dispense hospitality with melancholy grace? Count of heads—when Providence and Mr. Thomas Carlyle have furnished such an example of Heaven appointed ruler as Frederick the Great, and especially his father? Count of heads—when you see what has come to pass in these later days in England, in America!

Nothing more pitiful can be imagined than this ferocious and inhuman onslaught upon human liberty and civilization. Here is a man who hates and despises an unfortunate race whom his countrymen and their descendants have indescribably abused and degraded, stealing them from their country and trampling them under foot. He constantly and carefully calls them "niggers." He snorts at human reason as an efficient influence and power in civilization; and Thomas Carlyle ends by roaring out, as the only gospel of social salvation, the feeble drivel of Lord John Manners, and the "Young England" of a quarter of a century ago:

"Let trade and commerce, art and learning die,
But spare, oh spare, our old nobility!"

It would be inconceivably comical if it were not unspeakably tragical. Let us cover the nakedness of our patriarch, and walk away with eyes hidden. His own imagination has not conceived, his own pen has not described a figure so mournful as his own. His cry is more than the "vanity, vanity" of the Preacher. It is not a lament; it is a shriek of scornful indignation. The world will not stop; April will bloom on to June; the seed will shoot and the blossom become fruit; the grain will turn from green to gold; the babe will grow into the boy, the boy into the man; "without haste, without rest," as his great Goethe sang; the law of nature and of man fulfills itself, and Thomas Carlyle sits shaking his fist, and spitting out imprecations because mankind will not accept a brutal old German tyrant as the ideal man, and a slave plantation as the fairest type of human society.

—Harper's Weekly, 11 (7 September 1867): 562

* * *

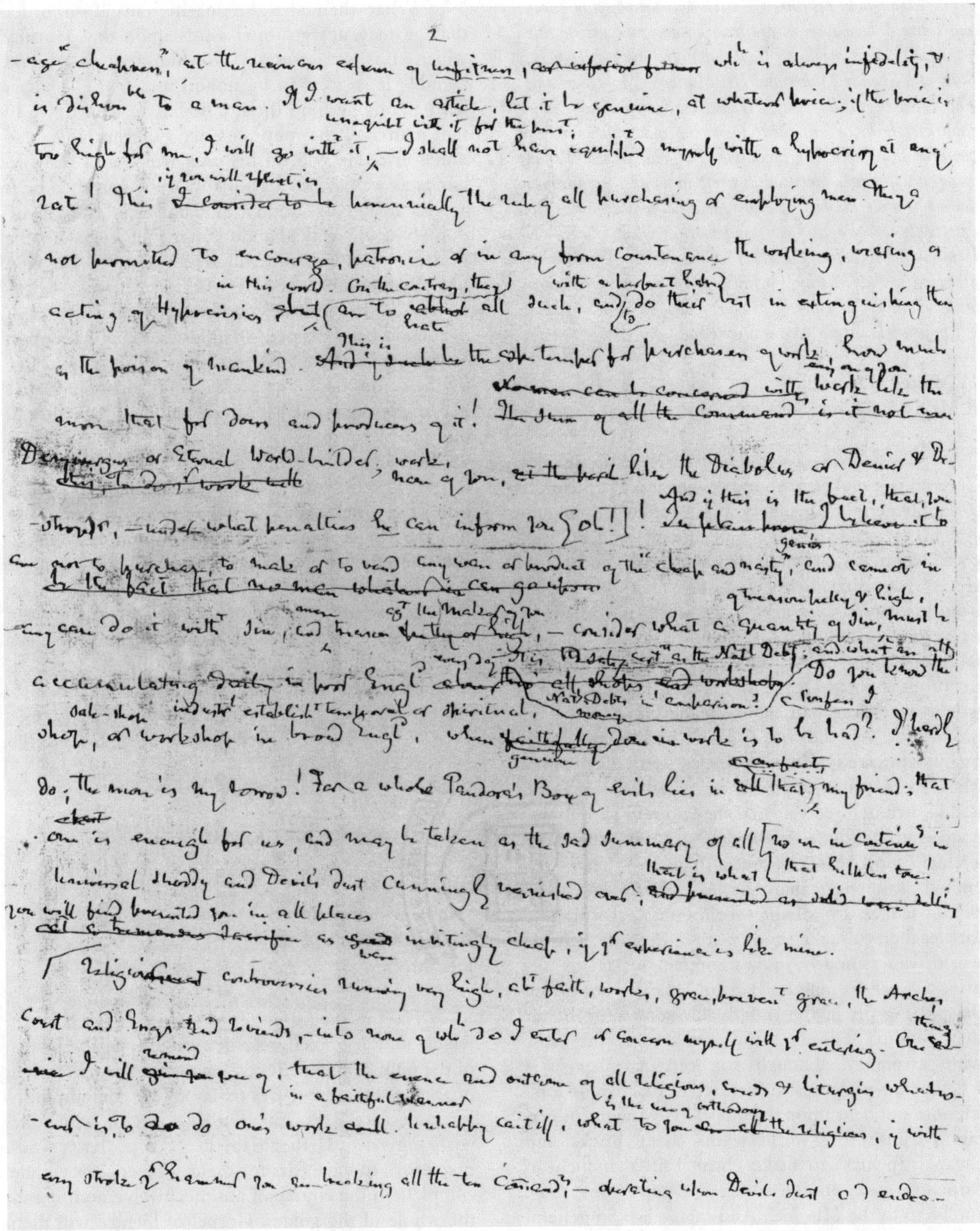

Page from the manuscript for Shooting Niagara: And After? *(Beinecke Rare Book and Manuscript Library, Yale University)*

Throughout his career, Carlyle was the object of parody and satire. These excerpts are from an unsigned article titled "An Essay on Carlylism: Containing the Very Melancholy Story of a Shoddy Maker and His Mutinous Maid-Servant." The writer begins his essay, "We are especially anxious in the remarks which we are about to make, and which we have ventured to connect with the name of a great man still living amongst us, to be understood as being in no degree desirous of detracting from the honour and reputation which he has most deservedly won by his honest and most excellent work." He then goes on to define Carlylism as the doctrine "that we are all going to the—Mischief!" And proceeds to examine, among other questions, whether "a maker of shoddy" can save himself in a world where "everything is bad."

"A Maker of Shoddy"
A Melancholy Story of Carlylism

. . . We will say that he himself [a student of Carlyle] is a maker of shoddy,—that it is his business to supply certain customers with a somewhat ephemeral article made of old woollen rags, and so concocted as to have some resemblance to good cloth. He is aware that in his way of business his profits from his capital are such as the world is content to allow as just,—ten per cent., shall we say, on his capital, or perhaps fifteen. He is aware at any rate that the profit is no greater to him making shoddy than it would have been had chance made him a maker of broadcloth. But the world wants shoddy, and some one must make it. He, nevertheless, according to his Master's teaching, is clearly in a perilous case. He had known before, well, that he who sells shoddy for good cloth, telling a lie about his shoddy,—that he is a thief. Since his childhood that had been well enough known to him, as it is known to, and acknowledged by all the world. But, according to this teacher, to make shoddy at all, even though the world wants shoddy, and is content to pay for it a price as such, is manifestly a sin. The sin lies not in the passing off of the shoddy for something better than shoddy. It is the same with bricks;—the same with carpentry. Though for certain purposes,—whether the purposes in themselves be wise or foolish does not bear upon the question,—though for certain purposes the world wants cheap bricks and cheap carpentry, to make cheap bricks and cheap carpentry is a sin for which the guilty one must surely go to the Mischief. And then, alas! So general is the demand for those articles in the present day that all manufacturers and all retail dealers must go to the Mischief because of them.

. . . .

What, then, shall he do,—he himself,—in order that he may not go downwards upon that journey which it is so necessary for him that he should avoid? "It is good to be honest and true." That at least stands by him, though he has broken down in that matter of the mutinous maid-servant and in so much else. He will do his own work with his own hands as well as he can possibly do it. But then he is a poor maker of shoddy, and must certainly abandon that. He will abandon it in obedience to the Master's teaching, and will take himself to the making of something else. He will make bricks,—bricks as well as they can be made, so that they shall last as the old bricks lasted, shall last for centuries upon centuries. But he cannot make such bricks, and live by the trade, except at a very long price. He makes his bricks, and not a builder among them all will buy them! No man wants such bricks. That it is the world that is wrong, and not he himself, in this matter, he is quite sure; for so his Master has taught him. The bricks could not have been better made had they been wanted for a new Solomon's temple. But there they are; and as no man will buy them, he must starve. It is the world that is wrong. The Master acknowledges that, too, very clearly. It is the world that is wrong, and he,—once shoddy-maker with a profit on which he could live, now brickmaker with no profit at all,—cannot put it right.

—*Saint Paul's Monthly Magazine,*
1 (December 1867): 297–298, 300

* * *

This excerpt is from a twenty-two-page article, titled "Carlyle," by the editor of The Fortnightly Review.

"Noble Monument"
An Assessment of Carlyle
John Morley

The new edition of Mr. Carlyle's works of which some eighteen volumes are now in the hands of the public, may be taken for the final presentation of all that the author has to say to his contemporaries, and to possess the settled form in which he wishes his words to go to those of posterity who may prove to have ears for them. The edition will be complete in the course of another twelvemonth, and the whole of the golden Gospel of Silence will then be effectively compressed in thirty fine volumes. After all has been said about self-indulgent mannerisms, moral perversities, phraseological outrages, and the rest, these volumes will remain the noble monument of the industry, originality, conscien-

Meeting the Queen

In March 1869 Carlyle met with Queen Victoria. Historian Charles Grote and his wife, scientist Charles Lyell and his wife, and Robert Browning were also present.

Carlyle provided this account in his 11 March letter to his sister Jean.

. . . "Interview" took place this day gone a week; nearly a week before that, the Dean and Dean*ess* (who is called Lady Augusta Stanley, once *Bruce,* an active hard and busy little woman) drove up here, and, in a solemnly mysterious, though half quizzical manner, invited me for Thursday, 4th, 5 P.M.:—Must come, a very "high or indeed highest person has long been desirous," etc., etc. I saw well enough it was the Queen incognita; and briefly agreed to come. "Half past 4 come *you!*" and then went their ways.

Walking up at the set time, I was there ushered into a long Drawingroom in their monastic edifice. I found no Stanley there; only at the farther end, a tall old *Gearpole* of a Mrs. Grote,—the most wooden woman I know in London or the world, who thinks herself very clever, etc.,—the sight of whom taught me to expect others; as accordingly, in a few minutes, fell out. Grote and Wife, Sir Chares Lyell and ditto, Browning and myself, these I saw were to be our party. "Better than bargain!" "There will take the edge of the thing, if edge it have!"—which it hadn't, nor threatened to have.

The Stanleys and we were all in a flow of talk, and some flunkies had done setting coffee-pots, tea-cups of sublime patterns, when Her Majesty, punctual to the minute, glided softly in, escorted by her Dame in waiting (a Dowager Duchess of Athol), and by the Princess Louise, decidedly a very pretty young lady, and *clever* too, as I found in speaking to her afterwards.

The Queen came softly forward, a kindly little smile on her face; gently shook hands with all three women, gently acknowledged with a nod the silent deep bow of us male monsters; and directly in her presence everybody was as if at ease again. She is a comely little lady, with a pair of kind clear and intelligent grey eyes; still looks plump and almost young (in spite of one broad wrinkle that shows in each cheek *occasionally*); has a fine soft low voice; soft indeed her whole manner is and melodiously perfect; it is impossible to imagine a *politer* little woman. Nothing the least imperious; all gentle, all *sincere*-looking, un-embarrassing, rather attractive even;—*makes* you feel too (if you have some sense in you) that she is Queen.

After a little word to each of us in succession as we stood,—to me it was, "Sorry you did not see my Daughter," Princess of Prussia (or "she sorry," perhaps?) which led us into Potsdam, Berlin, etc., for an instant or two; to Sir Charles Lydell I heard her say, "Gold in Sutherland," but quickly and delicately cut him *short* in responding; to Browning, "Are you writing anything?" (he has just been publishing the absurdist of things!); to Grote I did not hear what she said: but it was touch-and-go with everybody; Majesty visibly *without* interest or nearly so of her *own.* This done, Coffee (very black and muddy) was handed round; Queen and Three women taking seats (Queen in the corner of a sofa, Lady Deaness in opposite corner, Mrs. Grote in a chair *intrusively close* to Majesty, Lady Lyell modestly at the *diagonal* corner); we others obliged to stand, and hover within call. Coffee fairly done, Lady Augusta called me gently to "come and speak with Her Majesty." I obeyed, first asking, as an old infirmish man, Majesty's permission to *sit,* which was graciously conceded. Nothing of the least significance was said, nor *needed;* however my bit of dialogue went very well. "What part of Scotland I came from?" "Dumfriesshire (where Majesty might as well go some time); Carlisle, *i.e., "Caer-Lewel,* a place about the antiquity of King Solomon (according to Milton, whereat Majesty smiled); Border-Ballads (and even old Jamie Pool slightly alluded to,—not by name!); Glasgow, and even Grandfather's ride thither,—ending in mere *psalms* and streets *vacant* at half-past nine P.M.;—hard sound and genuine Presbyterian *root* of what has now shot up to be such a monstrously ugly Cabbage-tree and Hemlock-tree!" All which Her Majesty seemed to take rather well.

Whereupon Mrs. Grote rose, and good-naturedly brought forward her Husband to her own chair, *cheek by jowl* with Her Majesty, who evidently did not care a straw for him; but kindly asked, "Writing anything?" and one heard Aristotle, now that I have done with Plato," etc., etc.—but only for a minimum of time. Majesty herself (I think àpropos of some question of my *shaking hand*) said something about her own difficulty in writing by dictation, which brought forward Lady Lyell and Husband, mutually used to the operation. After which, talk becoming trivial, Majesty gracefully retired,—Lady Augusta with her,—and in ten minutes more, returned to receive our farewell bows; which, too, she did very prettily; and sailed out as if moving on skates, and bending her head towards us with a smile. By the Underground Railway I was home before seven, and out of the adventure, with only a headache of little moment.

Froude tells me there are foolish *myths* about the poor business; especially about my share of it; but this is the real truth;—*worth* to me, in strict speech all but nothing; the *myths* even less than nothing.

—*New Letters of Thomas Carlyle,* v. 2, pp. 252–255

First page of a publishing agreement for Carlyle's works, 29 April 1869 (The Trustees of the National Library of Scotland Acc 5074)

Publishing Carlyle's Collected Works

The first collection of Carlyle's works was a German translation, which ceased after six volumes, published from 1855 to 1856. Chapman and Hall were the first to offer a collected edition of Carlyle in English, with their Uniform Edition, published in sixteen volumes from 1857 to 1858. A Cheap Edition was printed in 1864 from the Uniform Edition and supplemented by an additional seven volumes for *Frederick the Great*, in 1869. From 1869 to 1871, Chapman and Hall published Carlyle's collected works in the thirty-volume Library Edition, and a thirty-seven-volume People's Edition by the same publisher followed in 1871–1874. The Cabinet Edition appeared in 1874, and the Copyright Edition in 1888. American versions of the Library, People's, Cabinet, and Copyright Editions were also published. Such a plenty of collected editions of his works attests to Carlyle's stature as an author and suggests a lasting influence.

tiousness, and genius of a noble character, and of an intellectual career that has exercised the profoundest sort of influence upon English feeling. Men who have long since moved far away from these spiritual latitudes, like those who still find an adequate shelter in them, can hardly help feeling as they turn over the pages of the now disused pieces which they once used to ponder daily, that whatever later teachers may have done in definitely shaping opinion, in giving specific form to sentiment, and in subjecting impulse to rational discipline, here was the friendly fire-bearer who first conveyed the Promethean spark, here the prophet who first smote the rock. That with this sense of obligation to the master, there mixes a less satisfactory reminiscence of youthful excess in imitative phrases, in unseasonably apostolic readiness towards exhortation and rebuke, in interest about the soul, a portion of which might more profitably have been converted into care for the head, is true in most cases. A hostile observer of bands of Carlylites at Oxford and elsewhere might have been justified in describing the imperative duty of work as the theme of many an hour of strenuous idleness, and the superiority of golden silence over silver speech as the text of endless bursts of jerky rapture, while a too constant invective against cant had its usual effect of developing cant with a difference. To the incorrigibly sentimental all this was sheer poison which continues tenaciously in the system. Others of robuster character no sooner came into contact with the world and its fortifying exigencies, than they at once began to assimilate the wholesome part of what they had taken in, while the rest falls gradually and silently out. When criticism has done its just work on the odious affectations of many of Mr. Carlyle's disciples, and about the nature of Mr. Carlyle's opinions and their worth as specific contributions, very few people will be found to deny that his influence in stimulating moral energy, in kindling enthusiasm for virtues worthy of enthusiasm, and in stirring a sense of the reality on the one hand and the unreality on the other of all that men can do or suffer, has not been surpassed by any teacher now living.

The degree of durability which this influence is likely to possess with the next and other generations is another and rather sterile question, which we are not now concerned to discuss. . . . Mr. Carlyle has been a most powerful solvent, but solvents are apt to become merely historic. The historian of the intellectual and moral movements of Great Britain during the present century, will fail ludicrously in his task if he omits to give a large and conspicu-

ous space to the author of *Sartor Resartus*. But it is one thing to study historically the ideas which have influenced our predecessors, and another thing to seek in them an influence fruitful to ourselves. It is to be hoped that one may doubt the permanent soundness of Mr. Carlyle's peculiar speculations, without either doubting or failing to share that warm affection and tender reverence which his personality has worthily inspired in many thousands of his readers.

—The Fortnightly Review, new series 8
(1 July 1870): 1–2

* * *

The "scarlet sins" Emerson refers to this excerpt are mainly Carlyle's comments in The Latter-Day Pamphlets.

Emerson to Carlyle, 15 October 1870

Your letter was most welcome, and most in that I thought I read, in what you say of not making the long promised visit hither, a little willingness to come. Think again, I pray you, of that Ocean Voyage, which is probably the best medicine and restorative which remains to us at your age and mine. Nine or ten days will bring you (and commonly with unexpected comfort and easements on the way,) to Boston. Every reading person in America holds you in exceptional regard, and will rejoice in your arrival. They have forgotten your scarlet sins before or during the war. I have long ceased to apologise for or explain your savage sayings about American or other republics or publics, and am willing that anointed men bearing with them authentic charters shall be laws to themselves as Plato willed. Genius is but a large infusion of Deity, and so brings a prerogative all its own. It has a right and duty to affront and amaze men by carrying out its perceptions defiantly, knowing well that time and fate will verify and explain what time and fate have through them said. We must not suggest to Michel Angelo, or Machiavel, or Rabelais, or Voltaire, or John Brown of Ossawottomie, (a great man,) or Carlyle, how they shall suppress their paradoxes and check their huge gait to keep accurate step with the procession on the street sidewalk. They are privileged persons, and may have their own swing for me.

—The Correspondence of Thomas Carlyle and Ralph Waldo Emerson, v. 2, pp. 336–337

* * *

VANITY FAIR. Oct. 22, 1870.

No. 103. MEN OF THE DAY No. 12.
"The Diogenes of the Modern Corinthians without his Tub."

Caricature of Carlyle by Carlo Pellegrini ("Ape") for the London magazine that was founded to expose contemporary vanities. The subcaption, "The Diogenes of the Modern Corinthians without his Tub," refers to the fourth-century Cynic philosopher who preached the virtue of the ascetic life and resided for a time in a tub (Rodger L. Tarr, Research Files for the Thomas Carlyle Bibliography, Special Collections, Thomas Cooper Library, University of South Carolina).

In this excerpt from his essay titled "Mr. John Morley's Essays" Robert Buchanan, a Scottish poet, novelist, and dramatist, responds to Morley's positive treatment of Carlyle.

"Vicious and False"
An Assessment of Carlyle
Robert Buchanan

. . . From the first hour of his career to the last, Carlyle has been perniciously preaching the Scotch identity–a type of moral force familiar to every Scotchman, a type which is separatist without being spiritual, and spacious without being benevolent–to a generation sadly in need of quite another sort of preacher. With a phrase perpetually in his mouth, which might just as well have been the Verbosities as the Eternities or the Verities, with a mind so self-conscious as to grant apotheosis to other minds only on the score of their affinity with itself, and with a heart so obtuse as never, in the long course of sixty years, to have felt one single pang for the distresses of man as a family and social being, with every vice of the typical Scotch character exaggerated into monstrosity by diligent culture and literary success, Mr. Carlyle can claim regard from this generation only on one score, that of his services as a duct to convey into our national life the best fruits of Teutonic genius and wisdom. His criticisms are as vicious and false as they are powerful. Had he been writing for a cultured people, who knew anything at all of the subjects under discussion, they would never have been listened to for a moment. He has, for example, mercilessly brutalised Burns in a pitiable attempt to apotheosise him from the separatist point of view; and he has popularized pictures of Richter and Novalis which fail to represent the subtle psychological truths these men lived to illustrate. For Voltaire as the master of *persiflage* he has perfect perception and savage condemnation, but of Voltaire as the apostle of humanity he has no knowledge whatever, simply because he has no heart whatever for humanity itself. He has written his own calendar of heroes, and has set therein the names of the monsters of the earth, from Fritz downwards,–always, be it remembered, aggrandizing these men on the monstrous side, and generally wronging them as successfully by this process as if his method were willfully destructive. Blind to the past, deaf to the present, dead to the future, he has cried aloud to a perverse generation till his very name has become the synonym for moral heartlessness and political obtusity. He has glorified the gallows and he has garlanded the rack. Heedless of the poor, unconscious of the suffering, diabolic to the erring, he has taught to functionaries the righteousness of a legal thirst for revenge, and has suggested to the fashioners of a new criminal code the eligibility of the old German system of destroying criminals by torture. He has never been on the side of the truth. He was for the lie in Jamaica, the lie in the South, the lie in Alsace and Lorraine. He could neither as a moralist see the sin of slavery, nor predict as a prophet the triumph of the abolitionists. He has been all heat and no light, a portentous and amazing futility. If he has done any good to any soul on the earth it has been by hardening that soul, and it is doubtful if Englishmen wanted any more hardening–by separating that soul's destiny from that of the race, as if the English character were not almost fatally separated already. He is not only, as Mr. Morley expresses it, "ostentatiously illogical and defiantly inconsistent;"–he pushes bad logic to the verge of conscious untruth, and in his inconsistency is wilfully criminal. He begins "with introspections and Eternities, and ends with blood and iron." He has impulses of generosity, but no abiding tenderness. He has a certain reverence of individual worth, especially if it be strong and assertive, but he has no pity for aggregate suffering, as if pain became any less when multiplied by twenty thousand. He is, in a word, the living illustration of the doom pronounced on him who, holding to God the mirror of a flawed nature, blasphemously bids all men be guided by the reflection dimly shadowed therein. Why should this man, like a sort of counsel for the prosecution, represent Providence? God *versus* Man, Mr. Carlyle prosecuting, and, alas! not one living soul competent or willing to say a word for the defence!

–*Contemporary Review,* 17 (June 1871): 328–329

* * *

These excerpts are from a twelve-page article titled "The Philosopher of Chelsea."

"A Very Great Influence"
An Assessment of Carlyle
T. L. C.

Great as has been the literary success achieved by "mad Carlyle," his works are destined to receive a far wider and more general welcome. I trust that, in the swift onward tendencies of this epoch towards mere material good, will come an intellectual reaction with which the spirituality of Carlyle may have much deep and grateful sympathy.

. . . .

That Thomas Carlyle–the poet, the philosopher, and the enlightened critic–will ever become a universal favourite; that he will be read by those "who daily read to daily forget" modern novels and newspapers–is what the most sanguine of his admirers would hardly venture to predicate. Such a fortune neither can he expect, nor would any sincere friend willingly promise for him. But I do certainly believe that, in this most serious, and his most meditative of modern nations, he is destined to exert a very great influence; that, over all our truly intellec-

---

"Life was Wholly Mystical"

John Tyndall records an occasion in the early 1870s when he described to Carlyle some biological experiments touching on the origins of life.

. . . He listened with profound attention to the explanation of the experiments. They were quite new to him; for *microbes, bacilli,* and *bacteria* were not then the household words which they are now. I could notice amazement in his eyes as we passed from putrefaction to antiseptic surgery, and from it to the germ theory of communicable disease. To Carlyle life was wholly mystical–incapable of explanation–and the conclusion to which the experiments pointed, that life was derived from antecedent life, and was not generated from dead matter, fell in with his notions of the fitness of things. Instead, therefore, of repelling him, the experiments gave him pleasure.

–*New Fragments,* p. 351

Carlyle as painted by J. McNeill Whistler in 1873 (from G. K. Chesterton and J. E. Hodder Williams, Thomas Carlyle, *Special Collections, Thomas Cooper Library, University of South Carolina)*

tual men and women, his cheerful and spiritual genius will extend its benignant sway; and that, one century hence, his progress through early indifference, and even opposition, up to final legitimate esteem, will be classed and recorded among many like extraordinary facts in intellectual history. Contemporaneous popularity and appreciation seldom crown a profoundly original man. The past abounds with instances illustrating this truth. It is not alone Shakespeare and Milton, but all the truly heaven-gifted men of all generations, who must, like Kepler, be content to wait for an audience, since God has waited so many thousand years for observers like themselves.

–*The Gentleman's Magazine*, 231 (July 1871): 159, 160

* * *

Coventry Patmore, a poet and novelist, remembers seeing Carlyle often in 1874–1875.

"More than Kind"
Coventry Patmore

During the year before we came to Hastings, when we lived in Campden Hill Road, I used constantly to see Carlyle. He was more than kind: his manners were affectionate to me, and I never left him without his begging me to come again soon. I was often his companion in his afternoon walks and drives, and spent many a long evening in his chimney-corner. I was a good listener, and never thought of contradicting him, any more than I should have thought of contradicting a locomotive at full speed. I was surprised to find how very few people he saw, though he appeared to be far from difficult of access. There was sel-

First page of Carlyle's reply to Harriet Mill, the sister of John Stuart Mill, who had written after her brother's death to ask Carlyle to deny that Mill had been responsible for the destruction of his manuscript of The French Revolution. Carlyle went on to write that he held no one to blame for the accident (Trustees of the National Library of Scotland MS 1778).

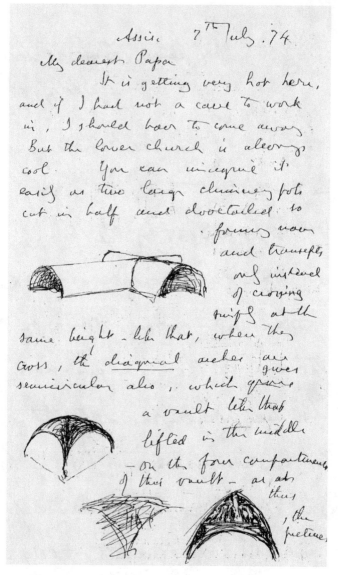

First page of a letter from John Ruskin to Carlyle (Trustees of the National Library of Scotland MS 556)

"The Heaven He Desired"

Carlyle remained close friends with John Ruskin, who visited his "Papa" regularly until Carlyle's death in 1881. In his diary for 24 April 1875, Ruskin recorded visiting Carlyle the day before: "Carlyle intensely interesting–pathetic infinitely. If only I could have written down every word."

He spoke of his own work with utter contempt–if it had any good in it, it was nothing but the dogged determination to carry it through so far as he could against all. (Alas, that I can't recollect the vigorous words expressing contemptible but overwhelming force of antagonism.) It needed 'the obstinacy of ten mules' to do *Frederick*. Of his own life, he spoke as a mere burden–

burden in the past 'only supportable by the help and affection of others and chiefly of that noble *one* whom I lost eleven years ago'–*nearly* literal this. No one could be more thankful than he would be, when the summons came, though of the future he knew nothing, except that if it *were* mere death, it was appointed by an entirely wise and righteous Creator (Still not half the power of his own beautiful words: I thought I couldn't have forgotten!) and, if there were any hope of being reunited to any soul one had loved, it was all the Heaven he desired, and could conceive of no Heaven without that.

– John Ruskin, *Diaries*, v. 3, p. 842

Carlyle with John A. Carlyle, Mary Carlyle Aitken, and Patrick Don Swan, provost of Kirkcaldy, who hosted Carlyle during his visit to the school in September 1874. Swan had been Carlyle's student when the latter taught at Kirkcaldy, 1816–1818 (photograph by J. Patrick, from Simon Heffer's Moral Desperado, Thomas Cooper Library, University of South Carolina).

dom anybody else with him when I spent my evenings at his house. I told him once that I had just finished reading his life of Frederick the Great, and I made one or two remarks showing my appreciation of it. I was quite astonished by the pathetic way in which he expressed himself pleased by what I said, and his humble complaint that he had heard so few sympathetic observations concerning his great work.

When I bade good-bye to him, Carlyle, with his hand on the open door, and without any conversation, said to me: 'Why don't you write a history of the Anglo-Saxons? You are the only man in England who could do it.' I have not the least idea what he meant, for I know little of history, and never professed to have any particular interest in the Anglo-Saxons.

–*Memoirs and Correspondence of Coventry Patmore* (London: George Bell and Sons, 1900), v. 1, p. 282

* * *

"The Early Kings of Norway" appeared in the January, February, and March issues of Fraser's Magazine *and was followed in April by "The Portraits of John Knox." In May 1875 the works were published together as* The Early Kings of Norway: also An Essay on the Portraits of John Knox–*the last new book Carlyle saw published. Reviewers questioned Carlyle's scholarship as well as his motives for writing about this period in Norwegian history.*

This excerpt is from a two-page review by the novelist Edmund Gosse.

"When the Many Were Ruled by One"
Review of *The Early Kings of Norway: also An Essay on the Portraits of John Knox*
Edmund Gosse

If it should be asked what it was that induced Mr. Carlyle to scrutinise with such loving care the more or less brutal deeds of hard-headed Norwegian monarchs of eight centuries ago, then an answer lies handy at our side in the pages of the eloquent historian himself. From the beginning of the book, where he lands the rough but salutary firmness of Halfdan the Black, down to the very epilogue, where he compares, greatly to the disadvantage of the later power, Olaf Tryggveson with a Parliament elected by universal suffrage, the charm of these early Norse chronicles is patent enough, namely, that they gave to the most determined opponent of modern liberalism a splendid opportunity of depicting a state of things when the many were ruled by one, and when brain and muscle combined in the person of a single man of men were enough to awe a rude population into order.

–*Athenaeum,* no. 2476 (10 April 1875): 481

* * *

An Honor Offered

On the suggestion of Lord Derby, Foreign Secretary, Prime Minister Benjamin Disraeli proposed to Queen Victoria that she honor Carlyle with the Grand Cross of Bath and a pension. The Queen agreed, and Disraeli wrote to Carlyle on 27 December 1874.

SIR,

A Government should recognise intellect. It elevates and sustains the tone of a nation. But it is an office which, adequately to fulfil, requires both courage and discrimination, as there is a chance of falling into favouritism and patronizing mediocrity, which, instead of elevating the national feeling, would eventually degrade and debase it.

In recommending Her Majesty to fit out an Arctic expedition, and in suggesting other measures of that class, her Government have shown their sympathy with science. I wish that the position of high letters should be equally acknowledged; but this is not so easy, because it is in the necessity of things that the test of merit cannot be so precise in literature as in science.

When I consider the literary world, I see only two living names which, I would fain believe, will be remembered; and they stand out in uncontested superiority. One is that of a poet; if not a great poet, a real one; and the other is your own.

I have advised the Queen to offer to confer a baronetcy on Mr. Tennyson, and the same distinction should be at your command, if you liked it. But I have remembered that, like myself, you are childless, and may not care for hereditary honors. I have therefore made up my mind, if agreeable to yourself, to recommend Her Majesty to confer on you the highest distinction for merit at her command, and which, I believe, has never yet been conferred by her except for direct services to the State. And that is the Grand Cross of the Bath.

I will speak with frankness on another point. It is not well that, in the sunset of life, you should be disturbed by common cares. I see no reason why a great author should not receive from the nation a pension as well as a lawyer and a statesman. Unfortunately the personal power of Her Majesty in this respect is limited; but still it is in the Queen's capacity to settle on an individual an amount equal to a good fellowship, and which was cheerfully accepted and enjoyed by the great spirit of Johnson, and the pure integrity of Southey.

'Have the goodness to let me know your feelings on these subjects.

Carlyle declined the proposal.

Yesterday, to my great surprise, I had the honour to receive your letter containing a magnificent proposal for my benefit, which will be memorable to me for the rest of my life. Allow me to say that the letter, both in purport and expression, is worthy to be called magnanimous and noble, that it is without example in my own poor history; and I think it is unexampled, too, in the history of governing persons towards men of letters at the present, as at any time; and that I will carefully preserve it as one of the things precious to memory and heart. A real treasure or benefit *it,* independent of all results from it.

This said to yourself and reposited with many feelings in my own grateful mind, I have only to add that your splendid and generous proposals for my practical behoof must not any of them take effect; that titles of honour are, in all degrees of them, out of keeping with the tenour of my own poor existence hitherto in this epoch of the world, and would be an encumbrance, not a furtherance to me; that as to money, it has, after long years of rigorous and frugal, but also (thank God, and those that are gone before me) not degrading poverty, become in this latter time amply abundant, even superabundant; more of it, too, now a hindrance, not a help to me; so that royal or other bounty would be more than thrown away in my case; and brief, that except the feeling of your fine and noble conduct on this occasion, which is a real and permanent possession, there cannot be anything to be done that would not now be a sorrow rather than a pleasure.

In a New Year's Day letter to his brother John, Carlyle wrote: "You would have been surprised, all of you, to have found unexpectedly your poor old Brother Tom converted into Sir Tom, Bart., but, alas, there was no danger at any moment of such a catastrophe. I do however truly admire the magnanimity of Dizzy in regard to me: he is the only man I almost never spoke of except with contempt, and if there is anything of scurrility anywhere chargeable against me, I am sorry to own he is the subject of it; and yet see, here he comes with a pan of hot coals for my guilty head!"

–David Alec Wilson, *Life of Carlyle,*
v. 6, pp. 343–345

This excerpt is from a two-page unsigned review titled "Carlyle's Early Kings of Norway."

"Singular Displays of Ignorance"
Review of *The Early Kings of Norway: also An Essay on the Portraits of John Knox*

. . . Mr. Carlyle gives us something for which it is not so easy to find a name. Perhaps we may best call it what Mr. Carlyle calls it himself—namely, "rough notes of the early Norway Kings hastily thrown together." But rough notes hastily thrown together, however great may be the reputation of the thrower, cannot serve our purpose, or indeed any purpose; or rather we might say that rough notes possibly might serve a purpose, but that what Mr. Carlyle gives us is not worthy even of the name of rough notes. The rough notes of a real scholar, the casual remarks which occur to him while going through a course of critical study, really might be of some use. They would most likely put us right on some point or other, and at all events they would set us thinking. But it is hard to conceive what object Mr. Carlyle can have set before himself, unless it be, as he does at the end, to point a moral in favour of wrong and violence and barbarism, and to show by the way his contempt for English history, and his ignorance of all modern research on the subject. Mr. Carlyle confesses that the rough notes which he has hastily thrown together are simply made out of Snorro, with some help from Dahlmann, and he ventures to add the following sentence:–

> In Histories of England (Rapin's excepted) next to nothing has been shown of the many and strong threads of connexion between English affairs and Norse.

To judge by the few references that Mr. Carlyle gives, one would think that he had read nothing later than Rapin. Perhaps he looked at Hume, and, finding nothing there to his purpose, thought there could not be anything anywhere else. It is perfectly plain that he knows nothing of modern writers of English history, whether in German or in English, who have done what they could under existing difficulties to trace the threads of connexion between English and Scandinavian affairs. It would seem that Mr. Carlyle, in the hasty throwing together of his rough notes, has not thought it worth while to look at any ancient records of English history, save an occasional glance at the Chronicles, or to look at any of their modern interpreters. If his manner of studying and writing had been a little less rough and hasty, if he had condescended to use those helps and lights which lie open to those who approach them in somewhat less of the Ber-

serker mood, he might have saved himself the singular displays of ignorance of English history which he makes throughout; he might have saved himself from leaving out some of the most striking and picturesque parts of his own story. Mr. Carlyle has a great name and has many admirers, but this does not make his rough and hasty notes on a subject which he has not really studied any better than the rough and hasty notes of any other man in the same case.

– *The Saturday Review,* 39 (12 June 1875): 758

* * *

This excerpt is from an unsigned twenty-five-page article titled "Mr. Carlyle." The critic regards Carlyle as a prime example of the contention that "wherever the illumination of Divine faith is wanting, delusions of which the baseness seems to us almost incredible easily co-exist with lofty genius and the keenest intellectual subtlety."

"Unaided Reason"
An Assessment of Carlyle

. . . Plato, like Carlyle, thought there were "more things in heaven and earth" than were dreamed of by his contemporaries. The Greek and the English seer differ chiefly in this, that the former perceived the inability of unaided reason to grasp the highest truth, and the latter does not. . . . Carlyle has no esteem even for the unanimous convictions of a race whom he considers "mostly fools." There is a high authority for that opinion, since Holy Scripture tells us that "the number of fools is infinite;" but who are the fools and who the wise is quite another question. Men of vast ability and learning have belonged to the first class, illiterate peasants and fishermen to the second. Mr. Carlyle remembers an instance, of which the late Lord Lytton, himself a man of rare attainments and versatile talent, truly said: "That which Plato and Zeno, Pythagoras and Socrates, could not do, was done by men whose ignorance would have been a by-word in the schools of the Greek. The gods of the vulgar were dethroned: the face of the world was changed!" This prodigy, often renewed on a smaller scale in later ages by apostolic missionaries—a Patrick, a Boniface, or a Francis Xavier—was accomplished by men whose human science did not extend beyond the navigation of a lake and the making of nets. But these truly "wise" men, whose disciples may be counted by millions at this hour, possessed a gift which fools have not, and which He who bestows it has called *"the precious gift of faith."* Of that gift Plato knew nothing, and Mr. Carlyle not much. The older philosopher would have joyfully accepted the *authority* which gives to faith its motive and determines its sphere, if he had known anything about it; the younger wastes his powerful intellect

An engraving of Carlyle by J. E. Boehm for a medallion that was presented to the author in celebration of his eightieth birthday (from G. K. Chesterton and J. E. Hodder Williams, Thomas Carlyle, *Special Collections, Thomas Cooper Library, University of South Carolina)*

Carlyle's Eightieth Birthday

Carlyle received a variety of honors on his eightieth birthday, 4 December 1875, including a letter of congratulation from Germany's chancellor, Otto von Bismarck, and a gold medallion by Boehm accompanied by a formal letter of congratulation signed by 119 of Carlyle's friends and leading British intellectuals and public figures.

Carlyle's reply to the 119 well-wishers was published in The New York Times *under the headline "Mr. Carlyle's Birthday."*

The following is the substance of a letter to one of the subscribers to the address to Mr. Carlyle:

This of the medal and formal address of friends was an altogether unexpected event, to be received as a conspicuous and peculiar honor, without example hitherto anywhere in my life. * * * To you * * * I address my thankful acknowledgments, which surely are deep and sincere, and will beg you to convey the same to all the kind friends so beautifully concerned in it. Let no one of you be other than assured that the beautiful transaction, in result, management, and intention, was altogether gratifying, welcome, and honorable to me, and that I cordially thank one and all of you for what you have been pleased to do. Your fine and noble gift shall remain among my precious possessions, and be the symbol to me of something still more golden than itself on the part of many dear and too generous friends, so long as I continue in this world. Your and theirs, from the heart, T. CARLYLE

—*The New York Times,* 5 January 1876, p. 2

in speculations which lead to nothing, and have no more substance or coherence than the morning dew or the evening breeze, because he rejects that authority as spurious, which Plato would not have done, and refuses to be guided by it. He prefers to follow the clue of his own unaided reason, and therefore is doomed to wander for ever in a maze from which there is no outlet. In rejecting this authority, for lack of which Plato doted and Aristotle dreamed, and possessing which millions of illiterate men have been deeper philosophers than either of them, Mr. Carlyle resembles the navigator or the student of astronomy who should break his compass, hide his chronometer, refuse to use the telescope, and throw the ephemerides into the fire, because it is beneath his dignity to derive assistance from anything which is not *himself.* The pagan sages made many mistakes, but not this. They felt the need of authority, and, as soon as it spoke, obeyed it. In the cities of Greece and the Imperial palaces of Rome, they bowed their necks under the sweet yoke of Christ and his Church. They wanted a guide, and knew their want. Clement, Justin Martyr, Augustine, and Ambrose used their reason *after* their conversion as they had used it before; but the Divine gift of faith by which it was now supplemented was to them, as to us, not only "the evidence of things not seen," but also an *intellectual power,* able to penetrate mysteries which had hitherto been veiled in darkness, and to resolve all the vague and formless *nebulæ* of religious thought into worlds of light, radiant with the splendour of truth. Yet it is in the name of reason that our modern pagans reject the very gift by which its weakness is compensated and its sphere indefinitely enlarged! Gross as were the delusions of the pagan mind, they hardly surpassed, if indeed they equalled, the amazing perversity of what is called "modern thought." Men who have learned to deny that reason itself is a gift of God, and prefer to consider it a product of molecular vibrations, or phosphoric combustion, or whatever the newest theory may be, naturally regard faith as the abdication of reason and the suppression of the will. It is, in fact, the sublimation of the one, and the direction of the other to its true object.

. . . .

The sum of the instruction which we derive from the writings of Mr. Carlyle, as far as they relate to questions of the soul, may be expressed as follows. There is, properly speaking, no such thing as permanent and indestructible truth. It may be one thing in one age, and a totally different thing in another. What was true of God and His revelation in the twelfth century "has become untrue" in the nineteenth; though God has not changed, nor His revelation either!

. . . .

Shades of Plato, Pythagoras, and Socrates, you are consoled! In the nineteenth century of the Christian era, with light all around them, there are men whose natural powers are only inferior to yours who use them worse than you did! They will neither accept the gift for which your souls yearned in vain, nor the authority which you invoked with vehement desire, and before which you would have bowed your mighty intellects in a transport of love and content. And therefore their philosophy is more grotesque than yours, their life a dream, their speech a raving, and their end confusion. Yet one hope remains. We will cherish it to the last. May St. Edmund and the Abbot Samson, and all holy and blessed souls of whom Mr. Carlyle has spoken with love and respect, obtain for him, in this final hour of a life which will soon be extinguished, reconciliation with that Holy Church of God which is for us men the only portal of Heaven, and the "obedience, pious reverence, and annihilation of self" which won for our fathers eternal life, but which *he* describes so well, and practises so ill.

–*Dublin Review,* 78 (January 1876):
97, 103–104, 120–122

* * *

In 1876 Britain seemed prepared to support the Ottoman Empire in a war against Russia, and Carlyle, outraged at the Turkish slaughter of twelve thousand Bulgarian peasants and convinced that Britain should ally with Russia, wrote a letter to the Times *condemning Disraeli's anti-Russian policy. In "The Ballad of the Bulgarie," poet Algernon Charles Swinburne, a former admirer of Carlyle, gently poked fun at the sage for this support. Swinburne's mild satire turned to fierce attack when he learned from a published interview with Emerson that Carlyle had said Swinburne "sits in a cesspool and adds to it."*

These excerpts are from an essay by Swinburne that was published as a book.

"No Small Surprise"
A Response to Carlyle on the "Eastern Question"
Algernon Charles Swinburne

Amid and above the many voices now jangling around what is called the Eastern Question, the sound of one voice like the blast of a trumpet has at length rung its message in all English ears after a sufficiently well-known fashion to a sufficiently unmistakable purport. A preacher who defends the gallows, an apostle who approves the lash, has lifted up his voice against oppression, and has cursed 'the unspeakable Turk' by all his gods: in the name of Francia and in the name of Mouravieff the champion of Eyre Pasha in Jamaica has uttered his sonorous note of protest against the misdeeds of Achmet Aga in Bulgaria. For all sincere and lifelong admirers of the greatest English writer now living among us in an old age more peaceful

though not more noble than was granted to the one Englishman we can remember yet greater in genius and in heart than he, it must be no small satisfaction, though it cannot but be no small surprise, to discover that there is actually some limit, however indefinable, to Mr. Carlyle's admiration of the strongest hand. But why the single exception which is to prove the else universal rule should be that particular instance which apparently it is, we may surely be permitted in all loyalty and humility to inquire. What is the peculiar sanctifying quality in the Bulgarian which is to exempt him at need from the good offices of 'beneficent whip' and 'portable gallows,' as from things insupportable and maleficent to him alone of human kind? What tie can it be which binds together such allies as Mr. Gladstone and Mr. Carlyle on a question of political philanthropy? Misery, we all know, makes strange bedfellows; but there would seem to be sympathies, religious or political, which bring stranger matches about than ever were made by misery. Is it a common love of liberty which links the veteran of letters to the veteran of politics? In this very epistle published by the Times of November 28 we see that the new champion of oppressed Christendom cannot resist the overwhelming temptation to turn aside and spit on the very name of liberty–'divine freedom, &c." His innate loathing of the mere word is too rabid and ungovernable an appetite to be suppressed or disguised for an instant. . . . It cannot be tyranny, it cannot be torture, it cannot be massacre to which Mr. Carlyle now objects. . . . He has always hated the very thought of liberty, abhorred the very notion of equality, abjured the very idea of fraternity, as he hates, abhors, and abjures them now. No man can doubt on which side or to what effect his potent voice would have been lifted at its utmost pitch before the throne of Herod or the judgment-seat of Pilate. No tetrarch or proconsul, no Mouravieff or Eyre of them all, would have been swifter to inflict or louder to invoke the sentence of beneficent whip, the doom of beneficent gallows, on the communist and stump-orator of Nazareth. Had there but lived and written under the shadow of the not as yet divine emperor Tiberius, doubtless as 'strictly honest and just a man' as any 'present Czar' or emperor of his kind, a pamphleteer as eloquent and as ardent an imperialist as these pitiful times of 'ballot-box, divine freedom, &c.' have brought forth even 'in this distracted country,' what a Latter-day Pamphlet on the Crucifixion, what an Occasional Discourse on the Nazarene Question, might we not now possess, whereby to lighten the darkness of history and adjust the balance of judgment! . . .

We may then presumably be permitted to dismiss without further discussion any possible theory of Christian sympathy with Christians on the part of a preacher to whom the spirit of every saying yet fathered on the Founder of Christianity should seem incomparably more hateful and contemptible than ever did the letter of any Diderot or Voltaire. . . . Is it then in the mere secular name of mercy or of chivalry, of decency or of manhood, that 'the unspeakable Turk should be immediately struck out of the question' to make room for the unspeakable Muscovite? Nay, for very shame, . . . it cannot be on any such plea as this that the sympathy or the indignation of any creature is now invoked by the patron of Eyre Pasha, the champion of Mouravieff Bey. Not all Englishmen have yet forgotten the horror and shame, the sickness of disgust, with which they learnt how the accomplices and the satellites of the former had devised and carried out such ultra-Bulgarian atrocities as the stripping and whipping of women by men in public with scourges of 'pianoforte wire.' It was the infliction of such tortures and such outrages as these . . . which evoked the vociferous acclamations and inflamed the tempestuous applause of Mr. Carlyle and his tail. . . . Really it grows more and more difficult for the sharpest eye of the most devout disciple to detect whereabouts in the prophetic mind of the North British evangelist he may discern the exact point at which tyranny or cruelty, torture or murder, violence or injustice, ceases to be something admirable and is transmuted as by witchcraft into something unspeakable. Cruelty in Ireland, cruelty in Jamaica, cruelty in the plantation, cruelty in the jail, each of these in turn has naturally provoked the stigmatic brand of his approbation, each in turn has deservedly incurred the indelible condemnation of his praise.

–Note of an English Republican on the Muscovite Crusade, pp. 3–10

* * *

In her 1877 memoir, writer Harriet Martineau reflected on her longtime friend.

The Influence of "This Singular Man"
Harriet Martineau

I have Carlyle's face under all aspects, from the deepest gloom to the most reckless or most genial mirth; and it seemed to me that each mood would make a totally different portrait. The sympathetic is by far the finest, in my eyes. His excess of sympathy has been, I believe, the master-pain of his life. He does not know what to do with it, and with its bitterness, seeing that human life is full of pain to those who look out for it: and the savageness which has come to be a main characteristic of this singular man is, in my opinion, a mere expression of his intolerable sympathy with the suffering. He cannot express his love and pity in natural acts, like other people; and it shows itself too often in unnatural speech. But to those who understand his eyes, his shy manner, his changing colour,

his sigh, and the constitutional *pudeur* which renders him silent about every thing that he feels the most deeply, his wild speech and abrupt manner are perfectly intelligible. I have felt to the depths of my heart what his sympathy was in my days of success and prosperity and apparent happiness without drawback; and again in sickness, pain, and hopelessness of being ever at ease again: I have observed the same strength of feeling towards all manner of sufferers; and I am confident that Carlyle's affections are too much for him, and the real cause of the "ferocity" with which he charges himself, and astonishes others. It must be such a strong love and honour as his friends feel for him that can compensate for the pain of witnessing his suffering life. When I knew him familiarly, he rarely slept, was wofully dyspeptic, and as variable as possible in mood. When my friend and I entered the little parlour at Cheyne Row, our host was usually miserable. Till he got his coffee, he asked a list of questions, without waiting for answers, and looked as if he was on the rack. After tea, he brightened and softened, and sent us home full of admiration and friendship, and sometimes with a hope that he would some day be happy.

. . . .

However much or little he may yet do, he certainly ought to be recognised as one of the chief influences of his time. Bad as is our political morality, and grievous as are our social short-comings, we are at least awakened to a sense of our sins: and I cannot but ascribe this awakening mainly to Carlyle. What Wordsworth did for poetry, in bringing us out of a conventional idea and method to a true and simple one, Carlyle has done for morality. He may be himself the most curious opposition to himself;—he may be the greatest mannerist of his age while denouncing conventionalism,—the greatest talker while eulogising silence,—the most woful complainer while glorifying fortitude,—the most uncertain and stormy in mood, while holding forth serenity as the greatest good within the reach of Man: but he has nevertheless infused into the mind of the English nation a sincerity, earnestness, healthfulness and courage which can be appreciated only by those who are old enough to tell what was our morbid state when Byron was the representative of our temper, the Clapham Church of our religion, and the rotten-borough system of our political morality. If I am warranted in believing that the society I am bidding farewell to is a vast improvement upon that which I was born into, I am confident that the blessed change is attributable to Carlyle more than to any single influence besides.

–Harriet Martineau's Autobiography, v. 1, pp. 287–288, 291–292

* * *

In these excerpts a longtime friend describes a last visit with Carlyle, then eighty-four.

"The Titan"
Charles Gavin Duffy

My final return to Europe took place in 1880. I arrived in London in the spring, and immediately visited Carlyle. It was deeply touching to see the Titan, who had never known languor or weakness, suffering from the dilapidations of old age. His right hand was nearly useless, and had to be supported by the left when he lifted it by a painful effort to his mouth. His talk was subdued in tone, but otherwise unaltered. It takes a long time to die, he said, with his old smile, and a gleam of humour in his eye. He was wrapped in a frieze dressing-gown, and for the first time wore a cap; but, though he was feeble, his face had not lost its character of power or authority. He was well enough, he declared, except from the effects of decay, which were rarely beautiful to see. His chief trouble was to be so inordinately long in departing. It was sad to have survived early friends, and the power of work. Up to seventy he had lost none of his faculties, but when his hand failed that loss entailed others. He could not dictate with satisfaction. He found, when he dictated, the words were about three times as many as he would employ *propria manu*. Composition was in fact a process which a man was accustomed to perform in private, and which could not be effectually performed in the presence of any person whatever. But he had written more than enough. If anybody wanted to know his opinions, they were not concealed. There were still subjects on which he had perhaps something to say, and could say it, for though he was suffering an euthanasia from the gradual decay of the machine, the mind was probably much as it used to be; but he was content to consider his work at an end. In looking back over his turbid and obstructed life, he saw only too well that he had scattered much seed by the wayside, which was as good as lost, leaving no visible issue behind. If it was sound vitalised seed it might perhaps spring up and blossom after many years; if not, in Heaven's name, let it rot. But much had been left altogether unspoken, because there was no fit audience discernible as yet, and a man's thoughts, though struggling for utterance, refused to utter themselves to the empty air. The discipline of delay and impediment, of which he had had considerable experience, was not, on the whole, a hostile element to labour in. In his later life he had some share of what men call prosperity; but, alas, it might well be doubted, if for him and for all men, trouble and trial were not a wholesomer condition than ease and prosperity.

. . . .

He walked no longer as of old, but he appointed an early day for me to share his customary drive from three o'clock to five. He was accompanied by his niece, whose care was now essential to his comfort. We drove to Streatham, through Clapham Common, and home by Battersea Park. Carlyle talked of things which the localities suggested. He spoke much as usual, except that his voice was feeble, and was so drowned by the noise of the road that I had to guess painfully at his meaning which used to be delivered with such clearness and vigour. I answered to what I was able to hear. He took occasional sips of brandy to keep up his strength, and solaced himself with a pipe.

I did not see him again before leaving London, and in the spring of the ensuing year the summons to his funeral, which followed me to the south of France, only reached me when the body was already on its way to Scotland. Time had brought to a close, not prematurely, but with many forewarnings, a friendship which nothing had disturbed, and which was one of the chief comforts of my life.

—Conversations with Carlyle, pp. 252–256

"The Vigour of His Puffs Astonished Me"

In this excerpt John Tyndall recalls the last time he saw Carlyle.

One other trivial item, almost the last, may be here set down. In his days of visible sinking, I took down to him a small supply of extremely old pale brandy from the stores of Justerini & Brooks, together with a few of the best cigars that I could find. On visiting him subsequently, I found that he had hardly touched either the one or the other. Thinking them worth a trial, I mixed some brandy and water in a tumbler, and placing a cigar between his fingers, gave him a light. The vigour of his puffs astonished me; his strength as a smoker seemed unimpaired. With the view of supporting him, I placed myself on the sofa behind him. After a time, putting aside the half-consumed cigar, he drank off the brandy-and-water, and with a smile gleaming in his eye, remarked 'That's well over.' Soon afterwards he fell asleep. Quietly relinquishing my position as pillow, I left him in slumber. This, to the best of my recollection, was the last time I saw Thomas Carlyle.

—New Fragments, pp. 389–390

The Death of Thomas Carlyle

After several months of decline, Carlyle died on 5 February 1881. His body was sent to Scotland, where he was buried at Ecclefechan on 10 February.

Although Carlyle refused burial at Westminster Abbey, the dean of the church preached a sermon there about Carlyle on 6 February 1881. These excerpts are from that sermon, which took as its beginning the thirteenth verse of the twenty-fourth chapter of Matthew: "The kingdom of heaven is likened unto a man which sowed good seed in his field."

Thomas Carlyle
Arthur Penrhyn Stanley

Early in his sermon Stanley asserted that "characters appear in the world which have a vivifying and regenerating effect, not so much for the sake of what they teach us, as for the sake of showing us how to think and how to act." He went on to cite such examples as Socrates, St. Paul, Martin Luther, and John Wesley before turning to Carlyle.

. . . Few will doubt that such a one was he who yesterday was taken from us. It may be that he will not be laid, as might have been expected, amongst the poets and scholars and sages whose dust rests within this Abbey; it may be that he was drawn by an irresistible longing towards the native hills of his own Dumfriesshire, and that there, beside the bones of his kindred, beside his father and his mother, and with the silent ministrations of the Church of Scotland, to which he still clung amidst all the vicissitudes of his long existence, will repose all that is earthly of Thomas Carlyle. But he belonged to a wider sphere than Scotland; for though by nationality a Scotchman, he yet was loved and honored wherever the British nation extends, wherever the English language is spoken. Suffer me, then, to say a few words on the good seed which he has sown in our hearts.

In his teaching, as in all things human, there were no doubt tares, or what some would account tares, which must be left to after times to adjust as best they can with the pure wheat which is gathered into the garner of God. There were imitations, parasitic exaggerations, of the genuine growth, which sometimes almost choked the original seed and disfigured its usefulness and its value; but of this we do not speak here. Gather them up into bundles and burn them. We speak only of him and of his best self. Nor would we now discourse at length on those brilliant gifts which gave such a charm to his writings and such an unexampled splendor to his conversation. All the world knows how the words and the deeds of former times became in his hands, as

Luther describes the Apostle's language, "not dead things, but living creatures with hands and feet." Every detail was presented before us, penetrated through and through with the fire of poetic imagination, which was the more powerful because it derived its warmth from facts gathered together by the most untiring industry.

. . . .

It was customary for those who honored him to speak of him as a "prophet." And if we take the word in its largest sense he truly deserved the name. He was a prophet, and felt himself to be a prophet, in the midst of an untoward generation; his prophet's mantle was his rough Scotch dialect, and his own peculiar diction, and his own secluded manner of life. He was a prophet most of all in the emphatic utterance of truths which no one else, or hardly any one else, ventured to deliver, and which he felt to be a message of good to a world sorely in need of them. He stood almost alone among the men of his time in opposing a stern, inflexible, resistance, to the whole drift and pressure of modern days towards exalting popular opinion and popular movements as oracles to be valued above the judgment of the few, above the judgment of the wise, the strong, and the good. . . . The whole framework and fabric of his mind was built up on the belief that there are not many wise, not many noble minds, not many destined by the Supreme Ruler of the universe to rule their fellows; that few are chosen, that "strait is the gate and narrow is the way, and few there be that find it." But when the few appear, when the great and good present themselves, it is the duty and the wisdom of the multitude to seek their guidance. A Luther, a Cromwell, a Goethe, were to him the born kings of men. This was his doctrine of the work of heroes; this, right or wrong, was the mission of his life. It is, all things considered, a fact much to be meditated upon; it is, all things considered, a seed which is worthy of our cultivation.

There is another feeling of the age to which he also stood resolutely opposed, or, rather, a feeling of the age which was resolutely opposed to him–the tendency to divide men into two hostile camps, parted from each other by watchwords and flags, and banners and tokens which we commonly designate by the name of party. He disparaged, perchance unduly, the usefulness, the necessity, of party organization or party spirit as a part of the secondary machinery by which the great affairs of the world are carried on; but he was a signal example of a man who not only could be measured by no party standard, but absolutely disregarded it. He never, during the whole course of his long life, took an active part–never, I believe, even voted–in those elections which, to most of us, are the very breath of our nostrils. For its own sake he cherished whatever was worth preserving; for its own sake he hailed whatever improvement was worth effecting. He cared not under what name or by what man the preservation or the improvement was achieved. This, too, is an ideal which few can attain, which still fewer attempt; but it is something to have had one man who was possessed by it as a vital and saving truth. And such a man was the Prophet of Chelsea. But there was that in him which, in spite of his own contemptuous description of the people, in spite of his scorn for the struggles of party, endeared him in no common degree even to those who most disagreed with him, even to the humblest classes of our great community. He was an eminent instance of how a man can trample on the most cherished idols of the market-place if yet he shows that he has in his heart of hearts the joys, the sorrows, the needs of his toiling, suffering fellow-creatures. In this way they insensibly felt drawn towards that tender, fervid nature which was weak when they were weak, which burned with indignation when they suffered wrong. They felt that if he despised them it was in love; if he refused to follow their bidding it was because he believed that their bidding was an illusion.

. . . The earnestness—the very word is almost his own—the earnestness, the seriousness with which he approached the great problems of all human life have made us feel them also. The tides of fashion have swept over the minds of many who once were swayed by his peculiar tones; but there must be many a young man whose first feelings of generosity and public spirit were roused within him by the cry as if from the very depths of the heart, "Where now are your Hengists and your Horsas? Where are those leaders who should be leading their people to useful employments, to distant countries—where are they? Preserving their game!" Before his withering indignation all false pretensions, all excuses for worthless idleness and selfish luxury fell away. The word which he invented to describe them has sunk perhaps into cant and hollowness; but it had a truth when first he uttered it. Those falsities were shams, and they who practiced them were guilty of the sin which the Bible, in scathing terms, calls hypocrisy.

And whence came this earnestness? Deep down in the bottom of his soul it sprang from his firm conviction that there was a higher, a better world than that visible to our outward senses. All who acted on this conviction—whether called saints in the middle ages, or Puritans in the seventeenth century, or what you like in our own day—he revered them, with all their eccentricities, as bright and burning examples of those who "sacrificed their lives to their higher natures, their worser to their better parts." In addressing the students at Edinburgh he bade them remember that the deep recognition of the eternal justice of heaven, and the unfailing punishment of crimes against the law of God, is at the origin and foundation of all the histories of nations. No nation which did not contemplate this wonderful universe with an awe-stricken and reverential belief that there was a great unknown, omnipotent, all-wise, and all-just Being superintending all men and all interests in it—no nation ever came to very much, nor did any man either, who forgot that. If a man forgot that, he forgot the most important part of his mission in the world. So he spoke, and the ground of his hope for Europe—of his hope, we may say, against hope—was that, after all, in any commonwealth where the Christian religion exists, nay, in any commonwealth where it has once existed, public and private virtue, the basis of all good, never can become extinct, but in every new age, and even after the deepest decline, there is a chance, and in the course of ages, the certainty, of renovation. The Divine depths of sorrow, the sanctity of sorrow, the life and death of the Divine man—these were to him Christianity. We stand, as it were, beside him whilst the grave has not yet closed over those flashing eyes, over those granite features, over that weird form on which we have so often looked, whilst the silence of death has fallen on that house which was once so frequented and so honored. We call up memories which occurred to ourselves. One such, in the far past, may perchance come with peculiar force to those whose work is appointed in this place. Many years ago, whilst I belonged to another cathedral, I met him in St. James's Park, and walked with him to his own house. It was during the Crimean war; and after hearing him denounce with his vigorous and perhaps exaggerated earnestness the chaos and confusion into which our Administration had fallen, and the doubt and distrust which pervaded all classes at the time, I ventured to ask him, "What, under the circumstances, is your advice to a Canon of an English Cathedral?" He grimly laughed at my question. He paused for a moment and then answered in homely and well-known words; but which were, as it happened, especially fitted to situations like that in which he was asked to give his counsel—"Whatsoever thy hand findeth to do, do it with all thy might." That is no doubt the lesson he leaves to each one of us in this place, and also to this weary world—the world of which he felt the weariness as age and infirmity grew upon him; the lesson which, in his more active days, he practiced to the very letter.

—Westminster Sermons: Sermons on Special Occasions Preached at Westminster Abbey, pp. 297, 298–305

* * *

Etching of Carlyle's funeral (Carlyle's House Museum, London)

In his memoir Tyndall writes that it was decided "to make the funeral as quiet and as simple as possible."

"One of the Glories of the World"
John Tyndall

Lecky, Froude, and myself formed a small delegation from London. We journeyed together northwards, halting at Carlisle for the night. Snow was on the ground next morning as we proceeded by rail to the station of Ecclefechan. Here we found the hearse powdered over by the frozen shower of the preceding night. Through the snow-slop we walked to Mainhill, the farmhouse where Carlyle, in 1824, completed the translation of 'Wilhelm Meister.' It may have been the state of the weather, but Mainhill seemed to me narrow, cold, humid, uncomfortable. We returned to Ecclefechan, I taking shelter for a time in the signalroom of the station. Here I conversed with the signalman, an intelligent fellow, who wished me to know that Mr. James Carlyle, who was still amongst them, was fit to take rank in point of intellect with his illustrious brother. At the appointed hour we joined the carriage procession to the churchyard. There, without funeral rite or prayer, we saw the coffin which contained the body of Carlyle lowered to its last resting-place. So passed away one of the glories of the world.

                                        —*New Fragments,* pp. 390–391

                        * * *

These excerpts are from a sixteen-page article by Henry James Sr., the father of William James, the psychologist, and Henry James, the novelist and critic. The elder James had been introduced to Carlyle by Emerson in the 1840s.

Some Personal Recollections of Carlyle
Henry James Sr.

Thomas Carlyle is incontestably dead at last, by the acknowledgment of all newspapers. I had, however, the pleasure of an intimate intercourse with him when he was an infinitely deader man than he is now, or ever will be again, I am persuaded, in the remotest *seculum seculorum.* I undoubtedly felt myself at the time every whit as dead (spiritually) as he was, and, to tell the truth, I never found him averse to admit my right of insight in regard to myself. But I could never bring him, much as he continually inspired me so to do, to face the philosophic possibility of this proposition in regard to himself. On the contrary, he invariably snorted at the bare presentation of the theme, and fled away from it, with his free, resentful heels high in air, like a spirited horse alarmed at the apparition of a wheelbarrow.

However, in spite of our fundamental difference about this burly life which now is, one insisting upon death as the properer name for it, the other bent upon maintaining every popular illusion concerning it, we had for long years what always appeared to me a very friendly intercourse, and I can never show myself sufficiently grateful to his kindly, hospitable *manes* for the many hours of unalloyed entertainment his ungrudging

To Members of General Council, Students, and others

CONNECTED WITH

EDINBURGH UNIVERSITY.

GENTLEMEN,

THOMAS CARLYLE, the foremost literary man, and Scotchman, of his generation, having just passed away, leaving behind him a name to which all ranks of his countrymen are combining to do homage, it has seemed to many that there are special reasons why the University of Edinburgh should be no less eager to pay some tribute to his memory. It was within her walls he was first stimulated into intellectual life; it was to her Students he came as their Rector to speak his words of cheer, and, as it chanced, farewell, when his literary career was ended; and it was to her custody, "from the love, favour, and affection which he bore to her," he bequeathed the legacy he left for "the advancement of education in his native Scotland."

In the sense of this obligation, and with a view to the discharge of the duty it imposes, a Meeting of Students, Members of General Council, and others interested, was held in the University on Friday, 25th March, at which it was resolved that steps should be immediately taken on the part of their *Alma Mater* and his, to express her sense of his worth, and his distinguished services, connected as these last were with those very interests for which she exists, and which must naturally be dear to her, and that the most appropriate form in which this could be expressed would be the institution of a Lectureship in History, to be known as "The Carlyle Lectureship," both because that was the department of study to which, as of the greatest spiritual importance, he devoted his life, and because the creation of such a lectureship would be a boon to the University.

To carry out this object, the meeting referred to appointed a Committee, representative of the General Council and of the various Faculties; and it now devolves upon them to appeal, in the furtherance of it, to you and all others interested, who, revering the name of Thomas Carlyle, would wish to see it associated in this way with the University. A considerable sum—about £2,500—will necessarily require to be raised, and the Committee, therefore, earnestly hope the contributions may both be liberal in themselves, and represent as many as possible of those who are in any way connected with her, or have her interest at heart.

By Order of the Committee,

C. W. CATHCART, *Chairman.*

UNIVERSITY OF EDINBURGH,
  31st March 1881.

Announcement of a Carlyle Memorial Fund at the University of Edinburgh (Edinburgh University Library, Special Collections DK.4.29)

fireside afforded me. I would like to reproduce from my notebook some of the recollections and observations with which those sunny hours impressed me, and so amuse, if I can, the readers of The Atlantic. These reminiscences were written many years ago, when the occurrences to which they relate were fresh in my memory; and they are exact, I need not say, almost to the letter. They will tend, I hope and am sure, to enhance the great personal prestige Carlyle enjoyed during life; for I cherish the most affectionate esteem for his memory, and could freely say or do nothing to wound that sentiment in any honest human breast. At the same time, I cannot doubt that the proper effect of much that I have to say will be to lower the estimation many persons have formed of Carlyle as a man of ideas. And this I should not be sorry for. Ideas are too divinely important to derive any consequence from the persons who maintain them. They are images or revelations, in intellectual form, of divine or infinite good, and therefore reflect upon men all the sanctity they possess, without receiving a particle from them. This estimate of Carlyle, *as a man of ideas,* always struck me as unfounded in point of fact. I think his admirers, at least his distant admirers, generally mistook the claim he made upon attention. They were apt to regard him as eminently a man of thought, whereas his intellect, as it seemed to me, except where his prejudices were involved, had not got beyond the stage of instinct. They insisted upon finding him a philosopher, but he was only and consummately a man of genius. They had the fatuity to deem him a great teacher, but he never avouched himself to be anything else than a great critic.

I intend no disparagement of Carlyle's moral qualities in saying that he was almost sure finally to disappoint one's admiration. I merely mean to say that he was without that breadth of humanitary sympathy which one likes to find in distinguished men; that he was deficient in spiritual as opposed to moral force. He was a man of great simplicity and sincerity in his personal manners and habits, and exhibited even an engaging sensibility to the claims of one's physical fellowship. But he was wholly impenetrable to the solicitations both of your heart and your understanding. I think he felt a helpless dread and distrust of you instantly that he found you had any positive hope in God or practical love to man. His own intellectual life consisted so much in bemoaning the vices of his race, or drew such inspiration from despair, that he could n't help regarding a man with contempt the instant he found him reconciled to the course of history. Pity is the highest style of intercourse he allowed himself with his kind. He compassionated all his friends in the measure of his affection for them. "Poor John Sterling, " he used always to say, "poor John Mill, poor Frederic Maurice, poor Neuberg, poor Arthur Helps, poor little Browning, poor little Lewes," and so on; as if the temple of his friendship were a hospital, and all its inmates scrofulous or paralytic.

. . . .

Carlyle had very much of the narrowness, intellectual and moral, which one might expect to find in a descendant of the old Covenanting stock, bred to believe in God as essentially inhuman, and in man, accordingly, as exposed to a great deal of divine treachery and vindictiveness, which were liable to come rattling about his devoted ears the moment his back was turned. I have no idea, of course, that this grim ancestral faith dwelt in Carlyle in any acute, but only in chronic, form. He did not actively acknowledge it, but it was latent in all his intellectual and moral personality, and made itself felt in that cynical, mocking humor and those bursts of tragic pathos which set off all his abstract views of life and destiny. But a genuine pity for man as sinner and sufferer underlay all his concrete judgments, and no thought of unkindness ever entered his bosom except for people who believed in God's undiminished presence and power in human affairs, and were therefore full of hope in our social future. A moral reformer like Louis Blane or Robert Dale Owen, a political reformer like Mr. Cobden or Mr. Bright; or a dietetic reformer like the late Mr. Greaves or our own Mr. Alcott, was sure to provoke his most acrid intellectual antipathy.

. . . .

Carlyle was, in truth, a hardened declaimer. He talked in a way vastly to tickle his auditors, and his enjoyment of their amusement was lively enough to sap his own intellectual integrity. Artist-like, he precipitated himself upon the picturesque in character and manners wherever he found it, and he did n't care a jot what incidental interest his precipitancy lacerated. He was used to harp so successfully on one string, the importance to men of *doing,* and the mere artistic effects he produced so infatuated him, that the whole thing tumbled off at last into a sheer insincerity, and he no longer saw any difference between *doing* and *doing* ill. He who best denounced a canting age became himself its most signal illustration, since even his denunciation of the vice succumbed to the prevalent usage, and announced itself at length a shameless cant.

. . . .

"He also spoke of a call he had just received from the new rector of the parish in which he lived. He had got some previous intimation of the rector's dutiful design, so that when he came Carlyle met him at the

The Carlyle Club.

—◆—

This Club has been formed for the purpose of affording to Disciples and Students of Carlyle, a means of meeting together, and of discussing the Religious, Political, and Social problems treated of in his writings. It is hoped that the intercourse of its Members will promote a feeling of mutual support among them, and enable the Club to exercise its influence in giving practical effect to his teaching.

The Club meets on the first Friday of every month, except August and September, when, after the transaction of business, a paper suggested by Carlyle's writings is read by a Member of the Club, and is followed by a discussion, in which visitors of all opinions are invited to take part.

A Special Meeting is held on the 4th December (being Carlyle's birthday), in place of the usual monthly meeting. Officers for the ensuing year will be elected on this occasion.

The conditions of Membership are, proposal by an existing Member, election by ballot, and assent to the following broad statement of the principles held by the Club :—

> " The Carlyle Club is composed of Disciples and Students of Carlyle,
> "who, being in hearty accord with him in the cardinal points of his
> "teaching, agree to do all they can to promote feelings of mutual
> "reliance and co-operation amongst themselves. Each individual
> "Member pledges himself to give his earnest thought to the con-
> "sideration of the doctrines propounded by Carlyle, and to aid to the
> "best of his power in giving practical effect to such of them as he can
> "conscientiously accept."

The subscription to the Club is Half-a-Guinea per annum, payable on the 1st January. Members joining in the latter half of the year are only asked to pay half the Annual Subscription.

Hon. Treasurer.—C. Oscar Gridley,
9, Duke Street, London Bridge, S.E.

Hon. Secretary.—Montgomery Carmichael,
38, Belsize Road, N.W., of whom any further information regarding the Club may be obtained.

CHARLES H. DOWNES,
President.

London, 1st March, 1881.

*Announcements for organization— first "Club," later "Society"—that was formed to honor Carlyle's literary legacy
(Trustees of the National Library of Scotland Acc. 10384)*

door, hat on head and cane in hand, ready for a walk. He apologized to the somewhat flustered visitor for not asking him in, but the fact was his health was so poor that a walk in the afternoon had become a necessity for him. Would the reverend gentleman be going towards the city, perhaps? Yes? Ah, then we can confer as we walk. Of course the reverend gentleman's animus in proffering the visit had been to feel his doughty parishioner's pulse, and ascertain once for all how it beat towards religion as by law established. And equally of course Carlyle had not the least intention of assisting at any such preposterous auscultation. The hopeful pair had no sooner begun their trudge, accordingly, than Carlyle proceeded to dismount his antagonist's dainty guns by a brisk discharge from his own ruder batteries. 'I have heard of your settlement in the parish,' he said, 'with great pleasure, and my friends give me great hope that you have a clear outlook at the very serious work that lies before you here. . . . But the main want of the world, as I gather, just now, and of this parish especially, which is that part of the world with which I am altogether best acquainted, is to discover some one who really knows God otherwise than by hearsay, and can tell us what divine work is actually to be done here and now in London streets, and not of a totally different work which behooved to be done two thousand years ago in old Judea. I have much hope that you are just the man we look for, and I give you my word that you will strike dissent dumb if such really be the case. What? Your road carries you now in another direction? Farewell, then! I am glad to find that we are capable of so good an understanding with each other.'

"Carlyle was full of glee in recounting this exploit, and his laugh like the roar of a mountain brook when the snow melts in spring. And it *is* funny, no doubt, to fancy how hopelessly asquint the rector's intellectual vision was bound to become as he pursued his solitary walk homeward. But, after all, there is nothing higher than fun in either of these experiences. It is capital fun, I admit, and I enjoyed Carlyle's enjoyment of it in this light, as much as anybody could. I only allow myself to characterize it thus strictly in order to show that Carlyle is not at all primarily the man of humanitary ideas and sympathies which many people fancy him to be. Of course he has a perfect right to be what he is, and no one has a keener appreciation of him in that real light than I have. I only insist that he has no manner of right to be reported to us in a false light, as we shall thereby lose to lesson which legitimately accrues to us from his immense personality.["]

. . . .

One more extract from my note-book, and I shall have done with it, for it is getting to be time to close my paper. I mentioned a while since the name of O'Connell, and apropos of this name I should like to cite a reminiscence which sets Carlyle in a touchingly amiable spiritual light.

"Sunday before last I found myself seated at Carlyle's with Mr. Woodman and an aid-de-camp of Lord Castlereagh, who had just returned from India, and was entertaining Mrs. Carlyle with any amount of anecdotes about the picturesque people he left behind him. To us enter Dr. John Carlyle and a certain Mr.—, a great burly Englishman, who has the faculty (according to an *aside* of Mrs. Carlyle, dexterously slipped in for my information) of always exciting Carlyle to frenzy by talk about O'Connell, of whom he is a thick-and-thin admirer. The weather topic and the health inquiry, on both sides, were soon quietly disposed of, but immediately after Mrs. Carlyle nudged my elbow, and whispered in a tone of dread, *'Now for the deluge!'* For she had heard the nasty din of politics commencing, and too well anticipated the fierce and merciless *mêlée* that was about to ensue. It speedily announced itself, hot and heavy, and for an hour poor breathless Mr. Woodman and myself, together with the awe-struck aid-de-camp, taking refuge under the skirts of outraged Mrs. Carlyle, assisted at a *lit de justice* such as we had none of us ever before imagined. At last tea was served, to our very great relief. But no! the conflict was quite unexhausted, apparently, and went on with ever new alacrity, under the inspiration of the grateful souchong. Mrs. Carlyle had placed me at her left hand, with belligerent or bellowing Mr. Bull next to me, and as her tea-table chanced to be inadequate to the number of her guests we were all constrained to sit in very close proximity. Soon after our amiable and estimable hostess had officiated at the tea-tray, I felt her foot crossing mine to reach the feet of my infuriated neighbor and implore peace! She successfully reached them, and succeeded fully, also, in bringing about her end, without any thanks to him, however. For the ruffian had no sooner felt the gentle, appealing pressure of her foot that he turned from Carlyle to meet her tender appeal with undisguised savagery. *'Why don't you,'* he fiercely screamed,– *'why don't you, Mrs. Carlyle, touch your husband's toe? I am sure he is greatly more to blame that I am!'* The whole company immediately broke forth in a burst of uncontrollable glee at this extraordinary specimen of manners, Carlyle himself taking the lead, and his amiable *convive*, seeing, I suppose, the mortifying spectacle he had made of himself, was content to 'sing small' for the remainder of the evening.["]

. . . .

It is quite time, then, in my opinion, that we should cease minding Carlyle's rococo airs and affectations; his antiquated strut and heroics, reminding us now of John Knox and now of Don Quixote; his owlish, obscene hootings at the endless divine day which is breaking over all the earth of our regenerate nature. We have no need that he or any other literary desperado should enlighten us as to the principles of God's administration, for we have a more sure word of prophecy in our own hearts,–a ray of the light which illumines every man who comes into the world, and is ample, if we follow it, to scatter every cloud that rests upon the course of history.

– *The Atlantic Monthly,* 47 (May 1881): 593–598, 604–605, 608

* * *

A Last Look
Algernon Charles Swinburne

Sick of self-love, Malvolio, like an owl
That hoots the sun rerisen where starlight sank,
With German garters crossed athwart thy frank
Stout Scottish legs, men watched thee snarl and scowl,
And boys responsive with reverberated howl
Shrilled, hearing how to thee the springtime stank
And as thine own soul all the world smelt rank
And as thine own thoughts Liberty seemed foul.
Now, for all ill thoughts nursed and ill words given
Not all condemned, not utterly forgiven,
Son of the storm and darkness, pass in peace.
Peace upon earth thou knewest not: now, being dead,
Rest, with nor curse nor blessing on thine head,
Where high-strung hate and strenuous envy cease.

– *The Complete Works of Algernon Charles Swinburne,* v. 5, p. 114

* * *

Walt Whitman wrote of Carlyle in The Literary World *on 12 February 1881, "We certainly have no one left like him. I doubt if any nation of the world has." These excerpts are from an essay on Carlyle that he included in his 1882 collection* Specimen Days & Collect.

Death of Thomas Carlyle
Walt Whitman

Feb. 10, '81–And so the flame of the lamp, after long wasting and flickering, has gone out entirely.

As a representative author, a literary figure, no man else will bequeath to the future more significant hints of our stormy era, its fierce paradoxes, its din, and its struggling parturition periods, than Carlyle. He belongs to our own branch of the stock, too: neither

Latin nor Greek, but altogether Gothic. Rugged, mountainous, volcanic, he was himself more a French Revolution than any of his volumes. In some respects, so far in the nineteenth century, the best-equipped, keenest mind, even from the college point of view, of all Britain; only he had an ailing body. Dyspepsia is to be traced in every page, and now and then fills the page. One may include among the lessons of his life–even though that life stretched to amazing length–how behind the tally of genius and morals stands the stomach, and gives a sort of casting vote.

Two conflicting agonistic elements seem to have contended in the man, sometimes pulling him different ways like wild horses. He was a cautious, conservative Scotchman, fully aware what a fetid gasbag much of modern radicalism is; but then his great heart demanded reform, demanded change–often terribly at odds, with his scornful brain. No author ever put so much wailing and despair into his books, sometimes palpable, oftener latent. He reminds me of that passage in Young's poems where as death presses closer and closer for his prey, the soul rushes hither and thither, appealing, shrieking, berating, to escape the general doom.

Of shortcomings, even positive blur-spots, from an American point of view, he has a serious share.

Not for his merely literary merit (though that was great)–not as "maker of books," but as launching into the self-complacent atmosphere of our days a rasping, questioning, dislocating agitation and shock, is Carlyle's final value. It is time the English-speaking peoples had some true idea about the vertebra of genius, namely power. As if they must always have it cut and biased to the fashion, like a lady's cloak! What a needed service he performs! How he shakes our comfortable reading circles with a touch of the old Hebraic anger and prophecy–and indeed it is just the same. Not Isaiah himself more scornful, more threatening: "The crown of pride, the drunkards of Ephraim, shall be trodden under feet: And the glorious beauty which is on the head of the fat valley shall be a fading flower." (The word prophecy is much misused; it is narrowed to prediction merely. That is not the main sense of the Hebrew word translated "prophet"; it means one whose mind bubbles up and pours forth as a fountain, from inner, divine spontaneities revealing God. Prediction is a very minor part of prophecy. The great matter is to reveal and outpour the Godlike suggestions pressing for birth in the soul. This is briefly the doctrine of the Friends or Quakers.)

Then the simplicity and amid ostensible frailty the towering strength of the man–a hardy oak knot, you could never wear out–an old farmer dressed in brown clothes, and not handsome–his very foibles fas-

Copy

The Mott - Salcombe - October 12/81

My dear Stephen
    I have read Bensons letter & this is my answer.

1. As to the Profits of the Reminiscences -
    a.   There was no agreement between Carlyle & myself
            He never mentioned the subject to me. The offer
            was purely voluntary on my part.
    b.   It was meant by me when first made, to extend
            only to the American profits, which were then
            expected to be considerable.   Mrs Carlyle took
            it to mean the whole profits & I allowed her interpretation.
    c   It did not imply that I was not to deduct something
            from the sum paid by the Publishers for my own labour
    d   It applied only to the profits of two thirds of the book
            which at the time the offer was made was not intended
            to include the account of Jane Welsh Carlyle - This is
            my own distinct property by Mrs Carlyle's will .

2 . As to the Biography -
            Mr Carlyle put his remaining papers in my hands
            in order that I should write it, with directions to burn.
            This I understood to imply that they were my own,
            and it was not till after several years that he desired
            me to return them to his niece when I had done with them
            I inferred from this that they were her eventual
            property & that I was no longer at liberty to burn .
    My offer to return them at once, was made in a moment
            of irritation at the unworthy treatment which I
            had received from Mrs Carlyle
            I conceived however at that time that the long
            labour which I had undergone over these papers

Letter from James Anthony Froude to James Fitzjames Stephen, in which Froude explains his conflict with Mary Aitken Carlyle, daughter of Carlyle's sister Jean and wife of Carlyle's nephew Alexander. Upon John A. Carlyle's death, control of many of Thomas Carlyle's manuscripts and papers had passed to Mary Aitken Carlyle. Stephen, along with John A. Carlyle and Froude, served as co-executors of Carlyle's estate (Trustees of the National Library of Scotland Acc. 5074).

would enable me to write the Biography without further use of them. Mrs Carlyle had disclaimed any wish to interfere with me in the use which I might make of the materials which I had already selected. and I was unwilling to remain in any relations whatever to Mrs Carlyle.

— _I withdraw that letter_ and that offer. _The greater part of the Biography is written_. the first part of it will be published in the spring. Mr Carlyle's family, his surviving brother & sister have earnestly protested against my abandoning the trust which Mr Carlyle himself committed to me. and I mean to fulfil it unless I am otherwise ordered by a Court of law.

— I myself individually, & also in my capacity as Executor am willing to carry out Mr Carlyle's wishes in giving over such of the papers as are properly to be eventually hers. but it must be first determined which of them are bequeathed to me as illustrative of the letters & memorials of the late Mr Carlyle

— If the whole collection be demanded immediately, I must first be satisfied that Mrs Carlyle has _now_ a right to be put in possession of them.

— I have offered to fulfil every claim which can be made upon me as a gentleman & a man of honour in the proposals which have been submitted to Mr Benson, subject only to my being able to carry out Mr Carlyle's personal instructions to me relating to his biography, but I find that I cannot do that duty adequately without retaining the papers until the book is finished.

— The question has become so complicated that I wish for myself that it should be properly sifted in a court. I can therefore make no further concessions; and I adhere to my resolution that unless the proposals are accepted before the end of this present month, they will be regarded as withdrawn —

Yours faithfully

J. A. Froude

cinating. Who cares that he wrote about Dr. Francia and "Shooting Niagara,"–and the "Nigger Question"–and didn't at all admire our United States? (I doubt if he ever thought or said half as bad words about us as we deserve.) . . .

The way to test how much has left his country were to consider, or try to consider, for a moment, the array of British thought, the resultant ensemble of the last fifty years, as existing to-day, *but with Carlyle left out.* It would be like an army with no artillery. The show were still a gay and rich one–Byron, Scott, Tennyson, and many more–horsemen and rapid infantry, and banners flying–but the last heavy roar so dear to the ear of the trained soldier, and that settles fate and victory, would be lacking.

For the last three years we in America have had transmitted glimpses of a thin-bodied, lonesome, wifeless, childless, very old man, lying on a sofa, kept out of bed by indomitable will, but of late, never well enough to take the open air. I have noted this news from time to time in brief descriptions in the papers. A week ago I read such an item just before I started out for my customary evening stroll between eight and nine. In the fine cold night, unusually clear (Feb. 5, '81), as I walked some open grounds adjacent, the condition of Carlyle, and his approaching–perhaps, even then actual–death, filled me with thoughts eluding statement, and curiously blending with the scene. The planet Venus, an hour high in the west, with all her volume and luster recovered (she has been shorn and languid for nearly a year), including an additional sentiment I never noticed before–not merely voluptuous, Paphian, steeping, fascinating–now with calm commanding seriousness and hauteur–the Milo Venus now. Upward to the zenith, Jupiter, Saturn, and the moon past her quarter, trailing in procession, with the Pleiades following, and the constellation Taurus, and red Aldebaran. Not a cloud in heaven. Orion strode through the southeast, with his glittering belt–and a trifle below hung the sun of the night, Sirius. Every star dilated, more vitreous, nearer than usual. Not as in some clear nights when the larger stars entirely outshine the rest. Every little star or cluster just as distinctly visible, and just as nigh. Berenice's Hair showing every gem, and new ones. To the northeast and north the Sickle, the Goat and Kids, Cassiopeia, Castor and Pollux, and the two Dippers. While through the whole of this silent indescribable show, inclosing and bathing my whole receptivity, ran the thought of Carlyle dying. (To soothe and spiritualize, and, as far as may be, solve the mysteries of death and genius, consider them under the stars at midnight.)

And now that he has gone hence, can it be that Thomas Carlyle, soon to chemically dissolve in ashes and by winds, remains an identity still? In ways perhaps eluding all the statements, lore, and speculations of ten thousand years–eluding all possible statements to mortal sense–does he yet exist, a definite, vital being, a spirit, an individual–perhaps now wafted in space among those stellar systems, which, suggestive and limitless as they are, merely edge more limitless, far more suggestive systems? I have no doubt of it. In silence, of a fine night, such questions are answered to the soul, the best answers that can be given. With me, too, when depressed by some specially sad event or tearing problem, I wait till I go out under the stars for the last voiceless satisfaction.

–*Specimen Days & Collect,* pp. 226–239

* * *

Carlyle appointed James Froude as the executor of his estate. The books Froude published–Carlyle's Reminiscences *(1881); a four-volume biography that included many of Carlyle's letters (1882, 1884); and two volumes of Jane Welsh Carlyle's letters (1883)–were controversial in their frank revelation of Carlyle's flaws. Charles Eliot Norton was so unhappy with Froude's edition of the* Reminiscences *that he published his own edition in 1887, and Alexander Carlyle was also displeased with Froude's biography of his uncle.*

These excerpts are from an American review written after the second two-volume set of Froude's biography of Carlyle had been published. Frederick Henry Hedge had written a positive review of Carlyle's Life of Schiller *in the July 1834 issue of* Christian Examiner.

"A Noble Nature Marred"
Review of Froude's Carlyle
Frederick Henry Hedge

In Mr. Froude's presentment of his hero, Carlyle is made to speak for himself through his journal and letters to kinsfolk and friends. The work is substantially an autobiography.

Here is one of the few men of letters who affect us more by their character than by their writings. I should rather say, whose writings affect us more through the character of the writer impressed upon them than through the subject-matter of their contents. A man of indisputable genius, who might have been a great poet, had not the moral interest, in men and things been so predominant in him as to make him the literary censor of his time. The seed of the Scottish Covenanters had found lodgement in a scholar's brain. For more than twenty-five centuries there has been no writer who approaches so nearly the old Hebrew prophets. A veritable Jeremiah in a nineteenth century Babylon!

. . . .

sleep are almost totally absent from the letters written from Craigenputtock. The simple, natural life, the wholesome air, the daily rides or drives, the pure food—milk, cream, eggs, oatmeal, the best of their kind—had restored completely the functions of a stomach never, perhaps, so far wrong as he had imagined. Carlyle had ceased to complain on this head, and in a person so extremely vocal when anything was amiss with him, silence is the best evidence that there was nothing to complain of. On the moors, as at Mainhill, at Edinburgh, or in London afterwards, he was always impatient, moody, irritable, violent. These humours were in his nature, and could no more be separated from them than his body could leap off its shadow. But, intolerable as he had found Craigenputtock in the later years of his residence there, he looked back to it afterwards as the happiest and wholesomest home that he had ever known. He could do fully twice as much work there, he said, as he could ever do afterwards in London; and many a time, when sick of fame and clatter and interruption, he longed to return to it.

To Mrs. Carlyle Craigenputtock had been a less salutary home. She might have borne the climate, and even benefited by it, if the other conditions had been less ungenial. But her life there, to begin with, had been a life of menial drudgery, unsolaced (for she could have endured and even enjoyed mere hardship) by more than an occasional word of encouragement or sympathy or compassion from her husband. To

Page from Froude's biography of Thomas Carlyle with the criticism of Alexander Carlyle in the margins (Trustees of the National Library of Scotland MS 751 & 752)

Cover for a booklet that includes an essay on Carlyle as a speaker. Such booklets were intended as reading matter for gentlemen's smoking rooms (Special Collections, Thomas Cooper Library, University of South Carolina).

Carlyle and the "Blast of Puffery"

What Carlyle's attitude would have been toward the use of his name and image to sell tobacco products is a matter for speculation. He was a smoker, but he had railed against the practice of advertising in a memorable passage written some thirty-eight years before his death.

Consider, for example, that great Hat seven-feet high, which now perambulates London Streets; which my Friend Sauerteig regarded justly as one of our English notabilities; "the topmost point as yet," said he, "would it were your culminating and returning point, to which English Puffery has been observed to reach!"—The Hatter in the Strand of London, instead of making better felt-hats than another, mounts a huge lath-and-plaster Hat seven feet high upon wheels; sends a man to drive it through the streets, hoping to be saved *thereby.* He has not attempted to *make* better hats, as he was appointed by the Universe to do, and as with this ingenuity of his he could very probably have done; but his whole industry is turned to *persuade* us that he has made such! He too knows that the Quack has become God. Laugh not at him, O reader; or do not laugh only. He has ceased to be comic; he is fast becoming tragic. To me, this all-deafening blast of Puffery, of poor Falsehood grown necessitous, of poor Heart-Atheism fallen now into Enchanted Workhouses, sounds too surely like a Doom's-blast! I have to say to myself in old dialect: "God's blessing is not written on all this; His curse is written on all this!" Unless perhaps the Universe *be* a chimera;—some old totally deranged eightday clock, dead as brass; which the Maker, if there ever was any Maker, has long ceased to meddle with?—To my Friend Sauerteig this poor seven-feet Hat-manufacturer, as the topstone of English Puffery, was very notable.

Alas, that we natives note him little, that we view him as a thing of course, is the very burden of the misery. We take it for granted, the most rigorous of us, that all men who have made anything are expected and entitled to make the loudest possible proclamation of it, and call on a discerning public to reward them for it. Every man his own trumpeter; that is, to a really alarming extent, the accepted rule. Make loudest proclamation of your Hat: true proclamation if that will do; if that will not do, then false proclamation,—to such extent of falsity as will serve your purpose; as will not seem too false to be credible!—I answer, once for all, that the fact is not so. Nature requires no man to make proclamation of his doings and hat-makings; Nature forbids all men to make such. There is not a man or hat-maker born into the world but feels, or has felt, that he is degrading himself if he speak of his excellencies and prowesses, and supremacy in his craft: his inmost heart says to him, "Leave thy friends to speak of these; if possible thy enemies to speak of these; but at all events, thy friends!" He feels that he is already a poor braggart; fast hastening to be a falsity and speaker of the Untruth.

—Past and Present (Berkeley, Los Angeles, London: University of California Press, 2005), pp. 143–144

A deeply religious man was Carlyle, the cherished friend of religious men, but without the intellectual beliefs which are commonly supposed to be essential to religion; a sincere Christian, for whom, however, historic Christianity was mostly mythical, and dogmatic Christianity a metaphysical juggle. He could not comprehend how men whom he otherwise respected and loved—Maurice, Thirlwal, above all, Sterling—could attach the importance they did to such conceits. He could not acquit them of a certain insincerity,—not conscious, but what might be called sincere insincerity, the most dangerous sort. His opinion of Maurice's vindication of the Thirty-nine Articles was expressed in doggerel rhymes, "which I virtuously spared Sterling the sight of." Ecclesiastical dilettanteism was an abomination to him. "That certain human souls living on this practical earth should think to save themselves and a ruined world by noisy, theoretic demonstrations of *the* Church instead of un-noisy, unconscious, but *practical,* total, heart-and-soul demon-

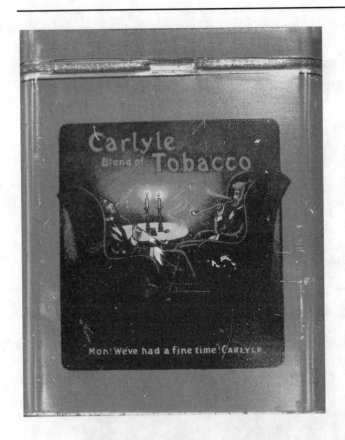

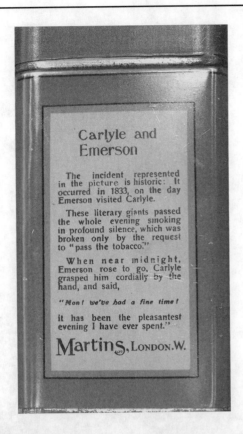

Carlyle and Emerson

The incident represented in the picture is historic: It occurred in 1833, on the day Emerson visited Carlyle.

These literary giants passed the whole evening smoking in profound silence, which was broken only by the request to "pass the tobacco."

When near midnight, Emerson rose to go, Carlyle grasped him cordially by the hand, and said,

"Mon! we've had a fine time!

it has been the pleasantest evening I have ever spent."

Martins, LONDON.W.

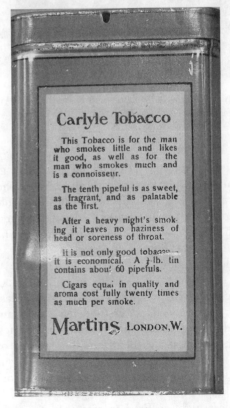

Carlyle Tobacco

This Tobacco is for the man who smokes little and likes it good, as well as for the man who smokes much and is a connoisseur.

The tenth pipeful is as sweet, as fragrant, and as palatable as the first.

After a heavy night's smoking it leaves no haziness of head or soreness of throat.

It is not only good tobacco it is economical. A ½-lb. tin contains about 60 pipefuls.

Cigars equal in quality and aroma cost fully twenty times as much per smoke.

Martins LONDON.W.

Four sides of a tin that uses Carlyle's fame to sell tobacco (Special Collections, Thomas Cooper Library, University of South Carolina)

Statue of Carlyle by J. E. Boehm at Chelsea (from Bertram Waldrom Matz, Thomas Carlyle: A Brief Account of His Life and Writings, *Special Collections, Thomas Cooper Library, University of South Carolina)*

stration of *a* Church: this in the circle of revolving ages, this also was a thing we were to see." Sterling had charged him with not believing in a personal God. He will not debate the matter. . . . He will not give names, but no man had ever a profounder conviction of the living God, the Eternal Reality, the dread Judge, who will judge the world in righteousness. Scarcely a letter to his own, scarcely an entry in his journal, but attests this overpowering God-consciousness. And is it not the foundation of all his political homilies?

The stern side of his character is the one best known to the world. It is therefore comforting to see revealed in these pages the tender, loving heart of the man as it utters itself in his letters to mother and wife. A most dutiful, affectionate son, he makes his poor old widowed mother at Scotsbrig the confidante of all his hopes, his doings and disappointments, and never fails,

in his deepest poverty, to send her some slight gift, such as narrow circumstances would allow. When she died at the age of eighty-four, he, being then fifty-eight, mourned her loss as a young husband might mourn the death of his new bride. There is nothing more beautiful, I think, in the history of literary men than Carlyle's love for his mother.

At home, he could make his poor wife wretched by his stormy petulance and endless *tracasseries;* but he well understood her worth and thoroughly appreciated her loving faithfulness. His letters addressed to her from the country overflow with the sweetest affection. Most piously he resolved, when absent, to be patient and forbearing and kind; but, once beneath his own roof again, a sleepless night sufficed to reawaken the old demon and rekindle the old fires. The spirit was willing, but, alas! the fleshly man was one boll of irritability from head to sole. . . .

How tragic it is that this loving pair, so fondly, devotedly attached the one to the other, should be nearest each other when separate; that, side by side, an unaccountable, fatal, mutually repellent atmosphere should operate to keep them asunder! The fault, though mainly, was not altogether on his side. In the matter of his fondness for the society of Lady Baring, she was certainly unreasonable. She knew in her heart that he prized his wife above all other women, but her independent spirit resented the great lady's patronage and her husband's willingness to be its subject. Moreover, she felt herself intellectually the equal of Lady Harriet, and could not bear to see herself eclipsed, as she fancied, in his estimation.

The depth of his affection for his wife and of his moral nature is abundantly shown in his inconsolable sorrow for her death, which lasted until his own.

. . . .

. . . When he spoke of the future and its uncertainties, he fell back invariably on the last words of his favorite hymn:–

"'Wir heissen euch hoffen' (We bid you hope)."

In that hope, he departed, leaving behind him the image of a noble nature marred in the conflict with a world which seemed to him hardened in shams and bristling with unveracities. Mentally, a man of colossal mould; heroic in doing, but not in bearing, voicing his antipathies with too impatient proclamation, infected with bitterness, given to much railing. A heavy discount this on his many and shining virtues! He could not, like his own Goethe, arrive to clearness, serene self-poise and reconciliation with the present through understanding of its import in relation to the future. He could prophesy of the "Everlasting yea," but did not attain thereto.

But what lofty independence of spirit, what proud humility! In early life, he was content to be poor, even

to the verge of pauperism, rather than cater by abuse of his talent to what he regarded as the false ideas of his time. He made court to no one, conceded nothing to wealth or rank. He refused a pension offered by government, and the offer of the Grand Order of Bath from the Queen; and though he accepted from the King of Prussia the Order of Merit, which would not require him to change his style from that of plain Thomas Carlyle, he wrote to his brother, "Had they sent me a quarter of a pound of good tobacco, the addition to my happiness would probably have been suitabler and greater." He cared not to be buried in Westminster Abbey, but chose rather that his bones should rest in the churchyard at Ecclefechan, among the lowly graves of his peasant kindred.

He would not seem, in view of his petulances, his wrath and bitterness, his inability to consume his own smoke, to have been altogether lovable. Yet was he dearly, devotedly loved by the choicest spirits of the land; more, I think, than any contemporary man of letters,–proof sufficient of noble qualities exceeding and compensating all his faults.

He was loved no less by the poor and mean. His latter years, when means were abundant, abounded in charities. A large *clientèle* of pensioners blessed the kind heart ever open to the cry of distress and the hand ever open to relieve. He chose to give with his own hand to the poor instead of dispensing his alms by proxy. These public organizations for relief of the destitute, he said, have a tendency to harden our hearts.

Carlyle is not, and never can be, popular. What genius was ever so, except it moved on the lines of popular amusement or uttered itself in song, with no aim beyond the entertainment of the hour? Not popular, but the sturdiest figure in the ranks of English literary men of this century, and the deepest soul that animated any.

The sacredness of duty, the dignity of labor, conscientious fidelity in performance, contempt of shams, uncompromising sincerity, fearless avowal of your convictions, non-conformity with uses you cannot approve,– these are the lessons he taught and–lived.

–*Unitarian Review,* 23 (February 1885), pp. 120–123, 133–134

Selected Secondary Works Cited

This listing of sources cited in the volume does not include nineteenth-century periodicals.

Raymond Clare Archibald, *Carlyle's First Love, Margaret Gordon Lady Bannerman; An Account of her Life, Ancestry and Homes, her Family and Friends* (London & New York: John Lane, 1910).

Rosemary Ashton, *Thomas and Jane Carlyle: Portrait of a Marriage* (London: Chatto & Windus, 2002).

Shirley Hoover Biggers, *British Author House Museums and Other Memorials: A Guide to Sites in England, Ireland, Scotland, and Wales* (Jefferson, N.C.: McFarland, 2002).

Reginald Blunt, *The Carlyles' Chelsea Home: Being some Account of No. 5, Cheyne Row* (London: Bell, 1895).

The Brownings' Correspondence, 15 volumes, edited by Philip Kelley and Ronald Hudson (Winfield, Kans.: Wedgestone Press, 1984–2005).

Jane Welsh Carlyle, "The *Simple Story* of My Own First Love," edited by K. J. Fielding, Ian Campbell, and Aileen Christianson (Edinburgh: The Carlyle Letters, Department of English, University of Edinburgh, 2001).

Carlyle and the London Library. Account of its Foundation: Together with Unpublished Letters of Thomas Carlyle to W. D. Christie, C.B., edited by Frederic Harrison, arranged by Mary Christie (London: Chapman & Hall, 1907).

Carlyle Annual (Flushing, N.Y.: Queens College Press, 1989–1993).

Carlyle's Birthplace: The Arched House, Ecclefechan, illustrated catalogue with a history of the house (London: The Carlyle's House Memorial Trust, 1911).

G. K. Chesterton and J. E. Hodder Williams, *Thomas Carlyle* (London: Hodder & Stoughton, 1902).

Moncure Daniel Conway, *Autobiography, Memories and Experiences of Moncure Daniel Conway,* 2 volumes (London: Cassell, 1904).

The Correspondence of Thomas Carlyle and John Ruskin, edited by George Allan Cate (Stanford: Stanford University Press, 1982).

Diary, Reminiscences, and Correspondence of Henry Crabb Robinson, edited by Thomas Sadler (London: Macmillan, 1869).

Elizabeth A. Drew, *Jane Welsh and Jane Carlyle* (London: Cape, 1928).

Andrew Landale Drummond, *Edward Irving and his Circle: Including some Consideration of the 'Tongues' Movement in the Light of Modern Psychology* (London: James Clarke, [1939?]).

Sir Charles Gavan Duffy, *Conversations with Carlyle* (London: Sampson Low, Marston, Searle & Rivington, 1892).

The Earlier Letters of John Stuart Mill, 1812–1848, 2 volumes, edited by Francis E. Mineka (London: Routledge & Kegan Paul, 1963).

Ralph Waldo Emerson, *English Traits* (Boston: Phillips, Sampson, 1856).

Francis Espinasse, *Literary Recollections and Sketches* (London: Hodder & Stoughton, 1893).

George Fitzhugh, *Cannibals All! Or, Slaves Without Masters* (Richmond, Va.: Morris, 1857).

John Forster, *The Life of Charles Dickens* (New York: Scribners, 1900).

James A. Froude, *Thomas Carlyle: A History of His Life in London, 1834–1881,* 2 volumes (London: Longmans, Green, 1884).

Froude, *Thomas Carlyle: A History of the First Forty Years of His Life, 1795–1835,* 2 volumes (London: Longmans, Green, 1882).

George M. Gould, *Biographic Clinics,* 6 volumes (Philadelphia: P. Blakiston's Son, 1903–1909).

Harriet Martineau's Autobiography, 2 volumes, edited by Maria Westman Chapman (Boston: Osgood, 1877).

Harriet Martineau's Letters to Fanny Wedgwood, edited by Elisabeth Sanders Arbuckle (Stanford, Cal.: Stanford University Press, 1983).

The Homes and Haunts of Thomas Carlyle (London: Westminster Gazette, 1895).

Jane Welsh Carlyle: Letters to Her Family, 1839–1863, edited by Leonard Huxley (London: Murray; New York: Doubleday, Page, 1924).

Journals and Miscellaneous Notebooks of Ralph Waldo Emerson, 16 volumes, edited by William H. Gillman (Cambridge: Belknap Press of Harvard University Press, 1960).

Fred Kaplan, *Thomas Carlyle: A Biography* (Ithaca, N.Y.: Cornell University Press, 1983).

The Letters and Memorials of Jane Welsh Carlyle, 3 volumes, edited by James Anthony Froude (London: Longmans, Green, 1883).

The Letters and Private Papers of William Makepeace Thackeray, 4 volumes, edited by Gordon N. Ray (Cambridge, Mass.: Harvard University Press, 1945–1946).

The Letters of A. Bronson Alcott, edited by Richard L. Herrnstadt (Ames: Iowa State University Press, 1969).

The Letters of Charles Dickens, 12 volumes, edited by Madeline House, Graham Story, and others (Oxford: Clarendon Press, 1965–2002).

The Letters of Edward FitzGerald, 4 volumes, edited by Alfred McKinley Terhune and Annabelle Burdick Terhune (Princeton: Princeton University Press, 1980).

The Letters of Margaret Fuller, 6 volumes, edited by Robert N. Hudspeth (Ithaca, N.Y.: Cornell University Press, 1983– [1984]).

The Letters of Ralph Waldo Emerson, 10 volumes, edited by Ralph L. Rusk (New York: Columbia University Press, 1995).

The Life, Letters, and Friendships of Richard Monckton Milnes, First Lord Houghton (London: Cassell, 1890).

Literary Anecdotes of the Nineteenth Century: Contributions towards a Literary History of the Period, 2 volumes, edited by W. Robertson Nicoll and Thomas J. Wise (London: Hodder & Staughton / New York: Dodd, Mead, 1895–1896).

Memoirs of Margaret Fuller Ossoli, 2 volumes (Boston: Phillips, Sampson, 1852).

Memoirs of the Life and Writings of Thomas Carlyle, with Personal Reminiscences and Selections from His Private Letters to Numerous Correspondents, 2 volumes, edited by Richard Herne Shepherd, assisted by Charles N. Williamson (London: W. H. Allen, 1881).

John Stuart Mill, *Autobiography,* edited by Harold J. Laski (London & New York: Oxford University Press, 1924).

Carlisle Moore, Rodger Tarr, and Chris Vanden Bossche, *Lectures on Carlyle & His Era, with a Supplement to the Catalogue of the Carlyle Holdings in the Norman and Charlotte Strouse Collection of Thomas Carlyle and the University Library,* edited and compiled by Jerry D. James and Charles S. Fineman (Santa Cruz: University Library, University of California, Santa Cruz, 1982).

John Ruskin, *Diaries,* 3 volumes, selected and edited by Joan Evans and John Howard Whitehouse (Oxford: Clarendon Press, 1956–1959).

Ruskin, *Praeterita: Outlines of Scenes and Thoughts Perhaps Worthy of Memory in My Past Life,* volume 35 in *The Works of John Ruskin,* Library Edition, 39 volumes, edited by E. T. Cook and Alexander Wedderburn (London: Longmans, Green, 1908).

John M. Sloan, *The Carlyle Country, with a Study of Carlyle's Life* (London: Chapman & Hall, 1904).

George W. Smalley, *London Letters and Some Others* (New York: Harper, 1891).

Samuel Smiles, *A Publisher and His Friends. Memoir and Correspondence of the Late John Murray, with an Account of the Origin and Progress of the House, 1768–1843* (London: Murray, 1891).

Arthur Penrhyn Stanley, "Thomas Carlyle," in *Westminster Sermons: Sermons on Special Occasions Preached at Westminster Abbey* (New York: Scribners, 1882), pp. 296–306.

The Story of a Flitting, a Hundred Years Ago. A Chelsea Centenary, 1834–June–1934 ([London]: Printed for The Chelsea Society by J. B. Shears and sold in aid of the Carlyle's House Endowment Fund, 1934).

Algernon Charles Swinburne, *Note of an English Republican on the Muscovite Crusade* (London: Chatto & Windus, 1876).

John Tyndall, *New Fragments* (New York: Appleton, 1896).

Walt Whitman, "Death of Thomas Carlyle," *Specimen Days & Collect* (Philadelphia: Rees Welsh, 1882), pp. 226–230.

John Greenleaf Whittier, "Thomas Carlyle on the Slave Question," in *Literary Recreations and Miscellanies* (Boston: Ticknor & Fields, 1854), pp. 34–46.

William Allingham's Diary, introduction by Geoffrey Grigson (Fontwell, Sx., U.K.: Centaur, 1967).

David Alec Wilson, *Life of Carlyle,* 6 volumes (London: Kegan Paul, Trench, Trübner; New York: Dutton, 1923–1934)—includes *Carlyle Till Marriage 1795–1826; Carlyle to the French Revolution 1826–1837; Carlyle on Cromwell and Others 1837–1848; Carlyle at His Zenith 1848–1853; Carlyle to Threescore and Ten 1853–1865;* and *Carlyle in Old Age 1865–1881* (completed by David Wilson MacArthur).

Elizur Wright, *Perforations in the "Latter-Day Pamphlets"* (Boston: Phillips, Sampson, 1850).

Cumulative Index

Dictionary of Literary Biography, Volumes 1-338
Dictionary of Literary Biography Yearbook, 1980-2002
Dictionary of Literary Biography Documentary Series, Volumes 1-19
Concise Dictionary of American Literary Biography, Volumes 1-7
Concise Dictionary of British Literary Biography, Volumes 1-8
Concise Dictionary of World Literary Biography, Volumes 1-4

Cumulative Index

DLB before number: *Dictionary of Literary Biography*, Volumes 1-338
Y before number: *Dictionary of Literary Biography Yearbook*, 1980-2002
DS before number: *Dictionary of Literary Biography Documentary Series*, Volumes 1-19
CDALB before number: *Concise Dictionary of American Literary Biography*, Volumes 1-7
CDBLB before number: *Concise Dictionary of British Literary Biography*, Volumes 1-8
CDWLB before number: *Concise Dictionary of World Literary Biography*, Volumes 1-4

M

P

ISBN-13: 978-0-7876-8156-2
ISBN-10: 0-7876-8156-3